THE CAMBRIDGE HISTORY OF

LATIN AMERICAN LAW IN GLOBAL PERSPECTIVE

Covering the precolonial period to the present, *The Cambridge History of Latin American Law in Global Perspective* provides a comprehensive overview of Latin American law, revealing the vast commonalities and differences within the continent as well as entanglements with countries around the world. Bringing together experts from across the Americas and Europe, this innovative treatment of Latin American law explains how law operated in different historical settings, introduces a wide variety of sources of legal knowledge, and focuses on law as a social practice. It sheds light on topics such as the history of indigenous peoples' laws, the significance of religion in law, Latin American independences, national constitutions and codifications, human rights, dictatorships, transitional justice and legal pluralism, and a broad panorama of key aspects of the history of statehood and law. This title is also available as Open Access on Cambridge Core.

Thomas Duve is a director at the Max Planck Institute for Legal History and Legal Theory and Professor of Comparative Legal History at Goethe University, Frankfurt. An expert in European and Latin American legal history, he specializes in the history of law and religion in a global perspective.

Tamar Herzog is Monroe Gutman Professor of Latin American Affairs at Harvard University and an affiliated faculty member at Harvard Law School. She is a legal historian of Spain, Portugal, and their overseas territories, having worked on colonial administration, penal justice, scribes, citizenship, land rights, and territorial conflicts.

THE CAMBRIDGE HISTORY OF
LATIN AMERICAN LAW IN GLOBAL PERSPECTIVE

*

Edited by
THOMAS DUVE
Max Planck Institute for Legal History and Legal Theory

TAMAR HERZOG
Harvard University

CAMBRIDGE
UNIVERSITY PRESS

CAMBRIDGE
UNIVERSITY PRESS

Shaftesbury Road, Cambridge CB2 8EA, United Kingdom

One Liberty Plaza, 20th Floor, New York, NY 10006, USA

477 Williamstown Road, Port Melbourne, VIC 3207, Australia

314–321, 3rd Floor, Plot 3, Splendor Forum, Jasola District Centre, New Delhi – 110025, India

103 Penang Road, #05–06/07, Visioncrest Commercial, Singapore 238467

Cambridge University Press is part of Cambridge University Press & Assessment, a department of the University of Cambridge.

We share the University's mission to contribute to society through the pursuit of education, learning, and research at the highest international levels of excellence.

www.cambridge.org
Information on this title: www.cambridge.org/9781316518045

DOI: 10.1017/9781009049450

First published 2024

A catalogue record for this publication is available from the British Library

A Cataloging-in-Publication data record for this book is available from the Library of Congress

ISBN 978-1-316-51804-5 Hardback

Contents

Contributors

Daniel Bonilla Maldonado is Professor of Law at the University of the Andes School of Law. Among his publications are *Legal Barbarians: Identity, Modern Comparative Law and the Global South* (2021) and, as editor, *Constitutionalism of the Global South* (2013).

Caroline Cunill teaches at the École des Hautes Études en Sciences Sociales in Paris. She is the author of *Los defensores de indios de Yucatán* (2012) and the editor of *Las lenguas indígenas en los tribunales de América Latina* (2019) and *Actores, redes y prácticas dialógicas en la construcción y uso de los archivos en América Latina* (2021).

Monica Dantas is a professor at the Brazilian Studies Institute and on the graduate program in social history at the University of São Paulo. Her research and publications focus on nineteenth-century Brazilian history, with an emphasis on social movements, political history, legal history, and the history of freemasonry.

Mariana Dias Paes is Research Group Leader of the 'Global Legal History on the Ground: Court Cases in African Archives' project at the Max Planck Institute for Legal History and Legal Theory in Frankfurt. Her most recent book is *Esclavos y tierras entre posesión y títulos: la construcción social del derecho de propiedad en Brasil* (2021).

Thomas Duve is a director at the Max Planck Institute for Legal History and Legal Theory and Professor of Comparative Legal History at Goethe University, Frankfurt. An expert in European and Latin American legal history, he specializes in the history of law and religion in a global perspective.

Tamar Herzog is Monroe Gutman Professor of Latin American Affairs at Harvard University and an affiliated faculty member at Harvard Law School. She is the author of 7 monographs, 4 edited volumes, and over 140 articles. Her latest book is *A Short History of European Law: The Last Two-and-a-Half Millennia* (2018).

José María Portillo is Professor of History at the University of the Basque Country. He has also taught in the United States, Mexico, and Colombia. His latest book is *Una historia atlántica de la nación y el Estado. España y las Españas en el siglo XIX* (2022).

Cristiano Paixão is Professor of Legal History and Constitutional Law at the University of Brasília Law School. He is a member of the Brazilian Amnesty Committee, a coordinator of the Anísio Teixeira Memory and Truth Commission, and Senior Labor Prosecutor in the Public Labor Prosecutor's Office.

Agustín Parise is Associate Professor of Law at Maastricht University and Secretary-General of the International Association of Legal Science (United Nations Educational, Scientific and Cultural Organization, France). He received his LLB and LLD from the University of Buenos Aires, his LLM from Louisiana State University, and his Ph.D. from Maastricht University.

Carlos Petit holds two Ph.D. degrees in law (University of Seville and University of Bologna) and a degree in history (University of Seville). Professor of Legal History at the Autonomous University of Barcelona, he currently works at the University of Huelva. His main field of research is the history of private law.

Roberto Saba earned his B.A. and M.A. from the University of São Paulo and his Ph.D. from the University of Pennsylvania. He is an Assistant Professor of American Studies at Wesleyan University. In 2021, he published *American Mirror: The United States and Brazil in the Age of Emancipation* (Princeton University Press).

Ruti Teitel is Ernst C. Stiefel Professor of Comparative Law at New York Law School. She is founding cochair of the American Society of International Law Interest Group on Transitional Justice and a member of the Council on Foreign Relations. Among her books are *Globalizing Transitional Justice* (2014), *Humanity's Law* (2011), and *Transitional Justice* (2000).

Valeria Vegh Weis is Professor of Law at Buenos Aires University and the National University of Quilmes. She is a research fellow at the University of Konstanz, a lecturer at the Free University of Berlin, and the winner of the 2021 Critical Criminology of the Year Award (Division of Critical Criminology and Social Justice of the American Society of Criminology).

Romina Zamora is Professor of Colonial History at the National University of Tucumán and a researcher at the National Scientific and Technical Research Council (Argentina). Her book *Casa Poblada y Buen Gobierno. Oeconomia católica y servicio personal en S. M. Tucumán, siglo XVIII* (2017) won the 2017 Argentine National Academy of History prize for the best published book.

Eduardo Zimmermann is Director of the graduate program in history at the University of San Andrés, Buenos Aires. Among his books are *Los liberales reformistas. La cuestión social en la Argentina, 1890–1916* (1995); *Judicial Institutions in Nineteenth-Century Latin America* (1999), as editor; and *Los saberes del Estado* (2012), *Las prácticas del Estado* (2012), *Construcción del Estado y fuerzas militares: América Latina, siglo XIX* (2012), as coeditor.

Introduction

THOMAS DUVE AND TAMAR HERZOG

This book is the result of a collective effort by a group of scholars from Latin America, Europe, and the USA, who together wished to write a legal history that would center on the common experiences of Latin American societies over a long time span, which began before Europeans invaded the continent and continues to date. The aim was to identify a narrative that would observe common trends, manifest the dramatic shifts that had occurred throughout this period, and insert these findings into a wider perspective. This would then reveal how various other regions of the globe were facing similar questions and that debates taking place in Latin America were often linked to discussions transpiring elsewhere, to which they both contributed and from which they received input and inspiration.

We feel deeply indebted to the scholars who have preceded us, and we recognize that the study of Latin American law has a long and important tradition. Beginning in the colonial period and throughout the nineteenth and twentieth centuries, detailed accounts described what constituted Latin American Law. Numerous scholars told us how, from the early 1500s onwards, European law was introduced and locally implemented by the various imperial powers. They surveyed the legal changes enacted by the new, independent Latin American states in the early nineteenth century and examined what had transpired since.

Their importance notwithstanding, traditionally these narratives tended to focus on a single empire (during the colonial period) or on a particular locality or state (thereafter). Often, the underlying concept of law they employed was state-centered and legalistic. It presumed that royal enactments (during the colonial period) and legislation (thereafter) were either the only source of law or at least the principal one. Many studies adopted a Eurocentric vision that highlighted the importation of European law while often characterizing this importation as a failure, either because European law was unfit for Latin American conditions or because individuals, groups, and authorities refused to obey it. In many narratives, precolonial, colonial, and postcolonial indigenous law was absent, as was the law practiced by Afro-Latin Americans. Existing legal histories of Latin America also tended to stress differences across the region while often ignoring common trajectories. Many studied the Latin American experience in isolation, assuming that – for better or for worse – it was radically distinct from all others or had evolved somewhat detached from developments elsewhere, as if colonialism, independence, the transition to new states, and the challenges states faced in the nineteenth and twentieth centuries were unique to this area.[1] Within this older bibliography, when relations with other parts of the globe were examined, it was mostly to affirm the hegemony of foreign ideas. The question how knowledge was translated into local realities, transformed, and accommodated and how local developments contributed to conversations taking place around the globe was rarely asked.

In the last few decades, however, research on Latin American law and society has undergone important transformations and experienced a spectacular growth.[2] The history of the administration of justice emerged as an important field, scholars examined the role of indigenous groups and enslaved persons in legal production both during the colonial period and thereafter, and many began to pay attention to global entanglements, which provided fascinating insights into the integration of the region into empires, commercial and intellectual networks, world economy, and international relations, to mention but a few examples.[3] Religious normativity, missionary activities,

1 On the universal projection of such experiences, see, for example, J. Adelman, "Latin American and World Histories: Old and New Approaches to the Pluribus and the Unum," *The Hispanic American Historical Review* 84(3) (2004), 399–409, 400 and 403; and M. Carmagnani, *The Other West: Latin America from Invasion to Globalization*, trans. R. M. Giammanco Frongia (Berkeley: University of California Press, 2011), for example, 3.

2 For example, J. L. Esquirol, *Ruling the Law: Legitimacy and Failure in Latin American Legal Systems* (ASCL Studies in Comparative Law) (Cambridge: Cambridge University Press, 2020); L. M. Friedman and R. Pérez-Perdomo (eds.), *Legal Culture in the Age of Globalization: Latin America and Latin Europe* (Stanford: Stanford University Press, 2003); M. García Villegas (ed.), *Normas de papel. La cultura del incumplimiento de reglas* (Bogotá: Siglo del Hombre Editores, Dejusticia, 2009); R. Gargarella, *La derrota del derecho en América Latina. Siete tesis* (Buenos Aires: Siglo Veintiuno Editores, 2020); D. E. López Medina, *Teoría Impura del Derecho. La transformación de la cultura jurídica latinoamericana* (Bogotá: Legis, 2004); C. Rodríguez Garavito (ed.), *El derecho en América Latina. Un mapa para el pensamiento jurídico del siglo XXI* (Buenos Aires: Siglo Veintiuno Editores, 2011); B. de Sousa Santos, *Refundación del Estado en América Latina. Perspectivas desde una epistemología del Sur* (Lima: Instituto Internacional de Derecho y Sociedad, Programa Democracia y Transformación Global, 2010).

3 For example, A. Agüero, *Castigar y perdonar cuando conviene a la República. La justicia penal de Córdoba del Tucumán, siglos XVII y XVIII* (Madrid: Centro de Estudios Constitucionales, 2008); D. G. Barriera, *Historia y justicia. Cultura, política y sociedad en el Río de la Plata (Siglos XVI–XIX)* (Buenos Aires: Prometeo, 2019); S. Chalhoub, "The Precariousness of

and the administration of justice through ecclesiastical institutions, long distinguished from a legal history that tended to concentrate on secular law, are now studied intensely and in their interaction with secular institutions.[4] New interpretations of the colonial legal culture have been developed and

Freedom in a Slave Society (Brazil in the Nineteenth Century)," *International Review of Social History* 56(3) (2011), 405–39; L. S. de Oliveira Coutinho Silva, *Nem teúdas, nem manteúdas: História das Mulheres e Direito na capitania da Paraíba (Brasil, 1661–1822)* (Global Perspectives on Legal History 15) (Frankfurt am Main: Max-Planck-Institut für europäische Rechtsgeschichte, 2020); N. E. van Deusen, *Global Indios: The Indigenous Struggle for Justice in Sixteenth-Century Spain* (Durham and London: Duke University Press, 2015); M. Dias Paes, *Escravidão e direito. O estatuto jurídico dos escravos no Brasil oitocentista (1860–1888)* (São Paulo: Alameda, 2019); Â. Domingues, M. L. Chaves de Resende, and P. Cardim (eds.), *Os Indígenas e as Justiças no Mundo Ibero-Americano (Sécs. XVI–XIX)* (Atlantica. Lisbon Historical Studies) (Lisbon: Universidade de Lisboa, 2019); A. L. Ferreira, *Injustos cativeiros. Os índios no Tribunal da Junta das Missões do Maranhão* (Belo Horizonte: Caravana Grupo Editorial, 2021); A. de la Fuente, "Slaves and the Creation of Legal Rights in Cuba: Coartación and Papel," *The Hispanic American Historical Review* 87(4) (2007), 659–92; K. Grinberg, "Illegal Enslavement, International Relations, and International Law on the Southern Border of Brazil," *Law and History Review* 35(1) (2016), 31–52; K. Grinberg, *A Black Jurist in a Slave Society: Antonio Pereira Rebouças and the Trials of Brazilian Citizenship* (Chapel Hill: University of North Carolina Press, 2019); T. Herzog, *Upholding Justice: Society, State, and the Penal System in Quito (1650–1750)* (Ann Arbor: University of Michigan Press, 2004); T. Herzog, *Defining Nations: Immigrants and Citizens in Early Modern Spain and Spanish America* (New Haven: Yale University Press, 2003); T. Herzog, *Frontiers of Possession: Spain and Portugal in Europe and the Americas* (Cambridge: Harvard University Press, 2015); M. McKinley, *Fractional Freedoms: Slavery, Intimacy, and Legal Mobilization in Colonial Lima, 1600–1700* (New York: Cambridge University Press, 2016); M. E. Alves de Souza e Mello, "As apelações de liberdade dos índios na América portuguesa (1735–1757)," in P. M. Sampaio and R. de Carvalho Erthal (eds.), *Rastros da memória. História e trajetórias das populações indígenas na Amazônia* (Manaus: Editora da Universidade Federal do Amazonas, 2006), 48–72; M. Monteiro Machado, *Entre fronteiras. Posses e terras indígenas nos sertões* (Rio de Janeiro, 1790–1824) (Guarapuava: Unicentro, 2012); F. Pinheiro, *Em defesa da liberdade. Libertos, coartados e livres de cor nos tribunais do Antigo Regime português (Mariana e Lisboa, 1720–1819)* (Belo Horizonte: Fino Traço Editora, 2018); J. C. de la Puente Luna, *Andean Cosmopolitans: Seeking Justice and Reward at the Spanish Royal Court* (Austin: University of Texas Press, 2018); M. Novoa, *The Protectors of Indians in the Royal Audience of Lima: History, Careers and Legal Culture, 1575–1775* (Legal History Library 19, Studies in the History of Private Law 10) (Leiden and Boston: Brill Nijhoff, 2016); B. P. Owensby, *Empire of Law and Indian Justice in Colonial Mexico* (Stanford: Stanford University Press, 2008); J. M. Portillo Valdés, *Fuero indio. Tlaxcala y la identidad territorial entre la monarquía y la república nacional. 1787–1824* (Mexico City: El Colegio de México, 2014); B. Premo, *The Enlightenment on Trial: Ordinary Litigants and Colonialism in the Spanish Empire* (New York: Oxford University Press, 2017); P. A. Revilla Orías, *Entangled Coercion: African and Indigenous Labour in Charcas (16th–17th Century)* (Work in Global and Historical Perspective 9) (Berlin and Boston: De Gruyter Oldenbourg, 2021); A. Wehling, *Direito e Justiça no Brasil Colonial. O Tribunal da Relação do Rio de Janeiro (1751–1808)* (Rio de Janeiro: Renovar, 2004); Y. Yannakakis, M. Schrader-Kniffi, and L. A. Arrioja Díaz Viruell (eds.), *Los indios ante la justicia local. Intérpretes, oficiales y litigantes en Nueva España y Guatemala (Siglos XVI–XVIII)* (Zamora: El Colegio de Michoacán, 2019).

4 For example, R. Aguirre Salvador, *Cofradías y asociaciones de fieles en la mira de la Iglesia y de la Corona: arzobispado de México, 1680–1750* (Mexico City: Real Universidad de México, 2018); J. F. Cobo Betancourt, *Mestizos heraldos de Dios. La ordenación de sacerdotes*

established historiographical notions such as *derecho indiano* have been questioned.[5] Taking to heart the vision that imagines legal production as the result of ongoing communication, scholars also began asking how developments in Latin America, for example, in the field of international law, human rights or transitional justice, participated in and contributed to global conversations.[6]

descendientes de españoles e indígenas en el Nuevo Reino de Granada y la racialización de la diferencia. 1573–1590 (Bogotá: Instituto Colombiano de Antropolgía e Historia, 2012); G. A. Mendonça dos Santos, *A justiça do bispo: o exercício da justiça eclesiástica no bispado de Pernambuco no século XVIII* (Recife: Universidade Federal de Pernambuco, 2019); B. Feitler, *Nas malhas da consciência. Igreja e Inquisição no Brasil. Nordeste 1640–1750* (São Paulo: Alamada Casa Ed, 2007); T. Duve and O. Danwerth (eds.), *Knowledge of the Pragmatici: Legal and Moral Theological Literature and the Formation of Early Modern Ibero-America* (Max Planck Studies in Global Legal History of the Iberian Worlds 1) (Leiden and Boston: Brill Nijhoff, 2020); R. Harrison, *Sin & Confession in Colonial Peru. Spanish–Quechua Penitential Texts, 1560–1650* (Austin: University of Texas Press, 2014); A. Lempérière, *Entre Dieu et le Roi, la République. Mexico, XVIe-XIXe siècles* (Paris: Belles Lettres, 2004); G. Marcocci and J. P. Paiva, *História da Inquisição Portuguesa. 1536–1821* (Lisbon: A Esfera dos Livros, 2013); G. Pizzorusso, *Governare le missioni, conoscere il mondo nel XVII secolo. La congregazione pontificia de Propaganda Fide* (Viterbo: Edizioni Sette Città, 2018); P. G. Mendonça Muniz, *Réus de Batina. Justiça Eclesiástica e clero secular no bispado do Maranhão colonial* (São Paulo: Alamada Casa Ed, 2017); C. Salinas Araneda, *Estudios históricos. El derecho canónico en Chile. Derecho canónico indiano* (Valparaíso: Pontificia Universidad Católica de Valparaíso, 2014); J. E. Traslosheros, *Iglesia, justicia y sociedad en la Nueva España. La audiencia del arzobispado de México, 1528–1668* (Mexico City: Editorial Porrúa, 2004); J. E. Traslosheros and A. de Zaballa Beascoechea (eds.), *Los indios ante los foros de justicia religiosa en la Hispanoamérica virreinal* (Mexico City: Universidad Nacional Autónoma de México, 2010).

5 For example, V. Tau Anzoátegui, *Casuismo y sistema. Indagación histórica sobre el espíritu del Derecho Indiano*, 2nd ed. (Seville: Athenaica, 2021); for a panorama of research on *derecho indiano*, including critique and defense of the notion, see the contributions in T. Duve (ed.), *Actas del XIX Congreso del Instituto Internacional de Historia del Derecho Indiano, Berlín 2016* (Madrid: Dykinson, 2017).

6 For example, F. Arocena and K. Bowman, *Lessons from Latin America: Innovations in Politics, Culture, and Development* (Toronto: University of Toronto Press, 2014); A. Becker Lorca, *Mestizo International Law. A Global Intellectual History, 1842–1933* (Cambridge: Cambridge University Press, 2014); J. L. Esquirol, "Alejandro Álvarez's Latin American Law: A Question of Identity," *Leiden Journal of International Law* 19(4) (2006), 931–56; A. McPherson and Y. Wehrli (eds.), *Beyond Geopolitics: New Histories of Latin America at the League of Nations* (Albuquerque: University of New Mexico Press, 2015); L. Obregón, "Between Civilization and Barbarism: Creole Interventions in International Law," *Third World Quarterly* 27(5) (2006), 815–32; J. P. Scarfi, *The Hidden History of International Law in the Americas: Empire and Legal Networks* (New York: Oxford University Press, 2017); K. Sikkink, "Latin American Countries as Norm Protagonists of the Idea of International Human Rights," *Global Governance* 20(3) (2014), 389–404; M. Sozzo and J. Núñez (eds.), *Los viajes de las ideas sobre la cuestión criminal hacia/desde Argentina. Traducción, lucha e innovación. 1880–1955* (Global Perspectives on Legal History) (Frankfurt am Main: Max-Planck-Institut für Rechtsgeschichte und Rechtstheorie, forthcoming). On the contribution of Latin America to the development of law more generally, see, for example, D. E. López Medina, *Teoría impura del derecho. La transformación de la cultura jurídica latinoamericana* (Bogotá: Legis, 2004); and D. Bonilla Maldonado (ed.), *Geopolítica del conocimiento jurídico (Filosofía política y del derecho)* (Bogotá: Siglo del Hombre Editores, Universidad de los Andes, 2015).

These new and exciting perspectives, opened up by innovative multidisciplinary research, have provided us with important insights. However, many of these works continue to focus on countries or regions, rarely engaging with pan-Latin American narratives, and most fail to systematically insert Latin American developments into larger contexts.[7] The result is that, presently, very few books describe what transpired in Latin America by tracing a common Latin American narrative. Nor is there a volume that places this narrative in a global perspective by showing how local law interacted continuously and resiliently with continent-wide as well as global developments and how it formed part of discussions also taking place in Europe, Africa, Asia, and North America. This book wants to provide a first step toward such a narrative.

Our first aim, therefore, is to craft a pan-Latin American narrative and insert it into a global perspective. Our second aim is to propose a new methodology that would place at the center questions rather than answers, processes rather than results, contexts rather than descriptions of solutions. We want to ask where, how, and why law materializes, who the protagonists are, and what the settings are. We also want to demonstrate the multiple levels on which law operates and how deeply it is embedded in social, political, cultural, and economic processes. This method, we hope, would connect the important literature produced by social, economic, and cultural historians, anthropologists, and linguists (to mention but a few disciplines) with the state of the art in the fields of legal history, legal theory, and legal sociology. Aiming to overcome the traditional divide between what some still perceive as a formal versus a practical vision of the law, between a "juridical" legal history with a legalistic and state-bound perspective and a history of justice and "jurispractice" that reduces law to what actors are doing, in this book, we observe the historical actors' practice in order to identify not the interests at stake but its grammar. We ask why things were done in certain ways, how knowledge of normativity was produced, and how it changed over time. Given the wealth of research on Latin American law and its history at the present moment, and the opening of the field to scholarship originating from other disciplines, we believe that such an endeavor is now possible.

While seeking to prompt interdisciplinary conversations between experts of law and history from a variety of disciplines, we also wish to facilitate the dialogue between scholars working in distinct national settings and academic

7 Exceptions exist, of course, for example, Rodríguez Garavito, *El derecho en América Latina*.

traditions. Most particularly, we wish to highlight the incredibly important contributions of scholars who work in Latin America and habitually publish in Spanish and Portuguese and bring to the forefront Latin American perspectives and interpretations, in order to avoid what some have identified as epistemicide.[8]

To achieve the above, the scholars who participated in this project were selected because they either work in Latin America or are deeply informed by the scholarship produced there. To ensure a cohesive volume, we met several times to discuss our common goals and how they could be achieved. We each read the others' chapters and commented on them extensively. Among other things, we also wanted to guarantee that all chapters would speak to several seminal themes such as the persistence of indigenous normativities throughout this long history, or the omnipresence of the Church and its legal universe. By doing so, we hoped to be able to demonstrate the complexities of Latin American legal history, tie it to larger debates, and bring it to the attention of a larger audience.

Latin America

What Latin America stands for, what it includes, where it begins and where it ends, has been a subject of debate and contestation for many years. Some tend to conceptualize Latin America as a geographical region; others refer to intense networks of communication, shared historical experiences, a common culture, religion, and language, or a combination thereof. What it meant in the past to various actors is not necessarily what it means today to others. However paradoxical this may seem, during a substantial part of that long history, many identified Latin America only with people and things originating from Europe.[9] This of course has changed radically and, presently, most tend to include in this realm a huge variety of peoples and cultures and well as their entanglements. In geographical terms, Latin America can include parts of North, Central, and South America, it can extend to the Caribbean and even the Philippines, given their insertion in Latin American networks, and the similarities in their historical trajectories.

8 B. de Sousa Santos, *Epistemologies of the South: Justice against Epistemicide* (Boulder: Paradigm Publishers, 2014). Also, see G. de Lima Grecco and S. Schuster, "Decolonizing Global History? A Latin American Perspective," *Journal of World History* 31(2) (2020), 425–46, at 431–33.

9 W. D. Mignolo, *The Idea of Latin America* (Malden: Blackwell, 2005), for example, xv; and M. Tenorio-Trillo, *Latin America: The Allure and Power of an Idea* (Chicago: University of Chicago Press, 2017).

The term Latin America as such has a long history. Until thirty years ago, it was commonly assumed that it was a European invention, explained by French imperial ambitions. However, we now have ample proof that individuals within Latin America already used this designation in the 1850s before it was taken up by the French.[10] What these individuals meant and why they chose this term depended on who they were and what their agenda was, but historians have generally conceded that the notion of "Latin America" was used mostly in response to US expansionist projects, as exemplified in the wars against Mexico, the immigration of many US individuals to Central America, and the plans for the opening of the Panama Canal. The opposition to these projects, and the defense of local sovereignty, found expression in the vindication of a "Latin race," which allegedly was different to an "Anglo-Saxon race." According to this vision, Latin America was different not only because it was "Latin" (a condition that it shared with many in Europe) but also because it was "American." Using the concept of Latin America was also a rallying cry that encouraged projects of political unification, projects that began long before Europeans invaded the continent, that continued during the colonial period, reemerged with independence, and persisted, even gained new force, in the nineteenth century – when the term Latin America was coined – and in the twentieth century under the guise of pan-Americanism, and pan-Indigenismo.

By the 1860s, identification with a Latin American community had become common among local intellectuals, who possibly wished to project their own preoccupations onto a much bigger, universal stage, which in turn transformed their struggle into one chapter in a larger confrontation also taking place in Europe between "Latins" and "Anglo-Saxons." During the second half of the nineteenth century, these claims often expressed convictions that "Latins" were superior to "Anglo-Saxons" because they espoused traditions that allowed for syncretism and were open to all. They equally pointed to an Americanness that was tied to pride at the adoption of liberal, republican, and even progressive political structures, which stood in opposition to the monarchical regimes still operating in Europe. On both these accounts, the adhesion

10 M. Quijada, "Sobre el origen y difusión del nombre 'América Latina' (o una variación heterodoxa en torno al tema de la construcción social de la verdad)," *Revista de Indias* 58(214) (1998), 595–616; A. McGuiness, "Searching for 'Latin America': Race and Sovereignty in the Americas in the 1850s," in N. P. Appelbaum, A. S. Macpherson, and K. A. Rosemblatt (eds.), *Race and Nation in Modern Latin America* (Chapel Hill: University of North Carolina Press, 2003), 87–107; and M. Gobat, "The Invention of Latin America: A Transnational History of Anti-Imperialism, Democracy, and Race," *The American Historical Review* 118(5) (2013), 1345–75.

to Latin America communicated achievement: It pointed discussants toward the legacy of old, civilized, even spiritual empires that were judged preferable to a new, barbaric, and materialistic USA. Eventually, for many locals, Latin America would also be transformed into a weapon to denounce injustices and call for reform. Some intellectuals would concentrate specifically on legal issues, as they asked whether Latin American law had its own particularities, or whether it formed part of larger systems. Was Latin America indeed exceptional, or were developments there a specific response – as well as an active contributor – to global processes?

Though most probably invented by local actors, soon thereafter the term Latin America was also taken up first by the French and then by a host of other foreign actors. The French proposed a new twist on these interpretations by advancing a new type of anti-Anglo-Saxonism, which was monarchical and based on French traditions. Other foreigners, however, tended to give the term Latin America pejorative interpretations that classified its community as backward and traditional. Thereafter, the opposition between "Anglos" and "Latins" was also translated as one contrasting Protestants with Catholics, "whites" with "mixed race persons." According to historians, by the twentieth century, some of these characterizations also influenced the way Latin America was treated by international agencies, in transnational litigation and international arbitration, in which it was often conceived as a space where there was a huge gap between law and implementation, ruled by inefficiencies, corruption, and excessive legal formalism, and where European norms were said to have been adopted but failed to materialize.[11] Under this guise, Latin America was often understood to represent a case of a failed modernization. It may have had the potential to modernize, but it never did, or did only partially.

Both locals and foreigners, in short, tended to read a particular condition into the designation "Latin America," which rendered those included in it either superior or inferior, but always different. Historically, in other words, Latin America was not a neutral term. Instead, it embodied projections and political positionings that compared locals to others and that were intended to communicate certain images. Despite, or perhaps even because of, its vagueness, imprecision, and inconsistencies,

11 Esquirol, *Ruling the Law*. On some of these issues see also D. López Medina, "The Latin American and Caribbean Legal Traditions: Repositioning Latin America and the Caribbean on the Contemporary Maps of Comparative Law," in M. Bussani and U. Mattei (eds.), *The Cambridge Companion to Comparative Law* (Cambridge: Cambridge University Press, 2012), 344–67.

and the constant changes in its meanings, "Latin America" has proved to be an extremely resilient category that has lasted from the 1850s to the present. Scholars have remarked that using this term now allows "more-than-national, thought-provoking, presently relevant" narratives and that it has the potential of stressing connections that are otherwise either ignored or undervalued.[12] Applying – albeit rarely explicitly so – a particular lens by which to organize research, some advised their readers of the need to define what it meant, what should be included and what excluded, not a priori, but according to the questions that needed answering or the topic chosen. In other words – as is often the case in history – at stake should be the question whether employing a certain term and adopting a certain circumscription is useful and what the results are: What it can illuminate and what it would hide.

This book takes this advice to heart. Rather than defining what Latin America means, each one of us adopted this vague unit to the subject matter and period under study. We did not specifically exclude the Caribbean, but we included it only where and to the degree that we found this helpful. Equally, we did not consider each and every region. Instead, we selected those places that each of us deemed most relevant to the narrative. The legacies of the past allowed us to envision Latin America as featuring a multiracial history that was the result of transcontinental migrations, forced or voluntary, a relatively early experience with colonialism, early insertion into processes of globalization and global economy, early definition of the liberal state, and so forth. For us, Latin America "represents more than a convenient label."[13] It is not the aggregate of disparate units, each with its own trajectory, but rather it is a community where the different units constantly interconnected, interacted, and were entangled internally, while also doing the same with other parts of the globe.[14] From that perspective, we found Latin America a more convenient term than Hispanoamerica, or Ibero-America, which some only identify with Spain, or which, conventionally, places the emphasis on Europe and its ambitions rather than on the Latin American region itself and its local actors of all sorts and shapes.

12 Tenorio-Trillo, *Latin America*, 168. Also, see 170.

13 J. C. Moya, "Introduction: Latin America – The Limitations and Meaning of a Historical Category," in J. C. Moya (ed.), *The Oxford Handbook of Latin American History* (Oxford: Oxford University Press, 2010), 1–26, at 4.

14 A typical study of Latin America, which divides it into discrete units and distinguishes Spanish from Portuguese America, is, for example, L. Bethell (ed.), *The Cambridge History of Latin America* (Cambridge: Cambridge University Press, 1985–2008), 12 vols.

A Global Perspective

We want to set Latin America in a global perspective so as to bring its legal history into conversation with the history of law and society elsewhere.[15] We are convinced that there were and are legal developments common to Latin America, but we are also convinced that these developments were not always nor necessarily particular to Latin America. Whether before, during, or after colonialism, Latin American law has always been both a local and a much wider affair that participated in larger conversations and developments taking place in other areas of the globe as well as in global trends. This happened not only because Latin America formed part of the "Iberian Worlds," or because of its intense interaction with European powers who were either present in the region or exercised, during the nineteenth and twentieth centuries, political, economic, cultural, and legal hegemony. Instead, global entanglements mostly originated with Latin American actors who, facing challenges similar to those that were encountered elsewhere, often tapped into a shared repository of ideas, methods, practices, and ways of thinking, analyzing, and proposing. In turn, they contributed to these repositories by adding, changing, interpreting, questioning, or affirming them.

This common repository used by actors both in Latin America and elsewhere had a mixed origin. Rather than stemming purely from one region or one historical experience, it emerged through communication and exchange, experience, and experimentation by a plethora of different individuals and communities across the globe. We presently have ample information on the Latin American contribution to the development of transitional justice, international law, and "world law" (see Sections 6.2 and 6.3 and Chapter 7), but Latin American actors and experiences have contributed to global conversations about law from the very beginnings of global networks. Sometimes, these entanglements were the result of the circulation of ideas in oral or written form; at other times, they depended on the movement of people. But whatever the media that made the flow of communication possible, the emergence of similarities and differences, and of regional, national, or transnational

15 On global perspectives in legal history, see T. Duve, "What Is Global Legal History?," *Comparative Legal History* 8(2) (2020), 73–115; on problems and opportunities of global history for Latin American history, see M. Brown, "The Global History of Latin America," *Journal of Global History* 10(3) (2015), 365–86; Lima Grecco and Schuster, "Decolonizing Global History"; for an interesting global perspective, see M. Restall, "The Americas in the Age of Indigenous Empires," in J. Bentley, S. Subrahmanyam, and M. Wiesner-Hanks (eds.), *The Cambridge World History, vol. VI: The Construction of a Global World, 1400–1800 CE, Part 2: Patterns of Change* (Cambridge: Cambridge University Press, 2015), 210–42.

law depended on continuous acts of translation, which constantly operated on multiple levels, inside and outside groups and regions. These translations of knowledge of normativity (see Sections 1.3 and 1.4) were by no means limited to translations into other languages, for example, the translation of legal institutions from Quechua to Castilian, from French law to Portuguese, or from Spanish to the Anglo-American language of international law. Instead, they happened (and still do) whenever a legal rule, or a mandate stemming from religion, or a juridical practice, is taken up and reproduced to fit specific local contexts, thus creating something new. Global legal history is, thus, a specific way of doing local legal history, which observes local solutions yet understands them as forming part of larger systems of communication.[16]

Understanding (global) legal history as an ongoing process of translations – and thus creation – of knowledge of normativity, including practices, helps overcome simplistic visions that often suggest that (mostly European) "originals" were / are "transplanted" or were / are the object of "legal transfers," and that therefore tend to classify the result as (usually Latin American) "copies" that are considered somewhat deficient or at least inferior, because they are neither original nor autochthonous.[17] Viewing these processes of local concretization as translations also has the potential to decenter the locus of production, by perceiving the different sites where norms and practices were/are translated as equal rather than hierarchically arranged. Viewing the use of law as translation can also be an important step toward a global legal history that pays attention to the geopolitics of knowledge and its asymmetries and avoids, as far as possible, the danger of historiographic neocolonialism.[18]

16 On the localization of legal knowledge in Latin American legal history, see, for example, B. Clavero, "Gracia y derecho entre localización, recepción y globalización (lectura coral de Las Vísperas Constitucionales de António Hespanha)," *Quaderni fiorentini per la storia del pensiero giuridico moderno* 41 (2012), 675; and the studies collected in V. Tau Anzoátegui and A. Agüero (eds.), *El derecho local en la periferia de la monarquía hispana. Río de la Plata, Tucumán y Cuyo. Siglos XVI–XVIII* (Buenos Aires: Instituto de Investigaciones de Historia del Derecho, 2013).

17 On the use of these metaphors in comparative law, see M. Graziadei, "Comparative Law, Legal Transplants, and Receptions," in M. Reimann and R. Zimmermann (eds.), *The Oxford Handbook of Comparative Law*, 2nd ed. (Oxford: Oxford University Press, 2019), 442–73; for a sharp critique of these Eurocentric and theoretically underdeveloped approaches, see H. P. Glenn, "Comparative Legal Families and Comparative Legal Traditions," in M. Reimann and R. Zimmermann (eds.), *The Oxford Handbook of Comparative Law*, 2nd ed. (Oxford: Oxford University Press, 2019), 423–41.

18 On this approach, see T. Duve, "Historia del derecho como historia del saber normativo," *Revista de Historia del Derecho* 63 (2022), 1–60; on the geopolitics of knowledge, see Bonilla Maldonado, *Geopolítica del conocimiento*; on the danger of historiographic neocolonialism, see B. Clavero, *Derecho global. Por una historia verosímil de los derechos humanos* (Madrid: Editorial Trotta, 2014); from the perspective of global history with regard to Latin America, see Lima Grecco and Schuster, "Decolonizing Global History."

By engaging in a global perspective, we wish to put into practice methodological postulates that, rather than privileging one tradition (mostly European) over all others, allow the incorporation of the legal experience of multiple regions and peoples, among them indigenous peoples and enslaved persons, to mention but two emblematic examples. Guided by the wish to avoid the Eurocentrism implicitly inherent to concepts such as "law" or "custom," and instead of asking "when do norms become law?," we focus on the production of knowledge of normativity by different actors and institutions. This approach also renders it possible to consider religious normativity (see Section 3.2), or normativity created and implemented in the social space of the household (see Section 3.3) or by communities living in parallel to the colonial or the modern state (see Sections 3.1 and 5.3 and Chapter 7). The analysis of processes by which knowledge of normativity is produced renders perceptible hybridizations and *mestizajes* (mixings), whose results are often invisible from the frequently static perspective of legal pluralism.[19] Considering hybridizations, and the dynamics that enable them, is incredibly important given current discussions regarding the rights of indigenous peoples and, more recently, individuals of African descent, in international law in general, and in the Inter-American system in particular.[20]

If taken seriously, a global perspective on legal history can have far-reaching consequences for the way research is organized and conducted. It does not require eliminating colonial empires or nation-states from the narrative. These can remain the primary object of inquiry, as long as they are considered within their transnational constellations. Though empires and states may remain, a global perspective requires the de-nationalization of legal historiography in conceptual as well as spatial terms. It forces legal

19 On the problematic notion of legal pluralism see T. Herzog, "Latin American Legal Pluralism: The Old and The New," *Quaderni fiorentini per la storia del pensiero giuridico moderno* 50(2) (2021), 705–36; on the invention of cultural diversity in Latin America and the danger of essentialism see S. Costa, "Freezing Differences: Politics, Law, and the Invention of Cultural Diversity in Latin America," *Revista Brasileira de Sociologia do Direito* 3 (2012), 139–56.

20 For an overview see, for example, T. Duve, "Indigenous Rights in Latin America: A Legal Historical Perspective," in M. D. Dubber and C. Tomlins (eds.), *The Oxford Handbook of Legal History* (Oxford: Oxford University Press, 2018), 817–37; V. Vadi, "Spatio-Temporal Dimension of Indigenous Sovereignty in International Law," in A. Di Blase and V. Vadi (eds.), *The Inherent Rights of Indigenous Peoples in International Law* (Rome: University of Rome III Press, 2020), 87–114; M. Monteiro de Matos, *Indigenous Land Rights in the Inter-American System. Substantive and Procedural Law* (Studies in Intercultural Human Rights 10) (Leiden: Brill Nijhoff, 2020); J. Bens, *The Indigenous Paradox: Rights, Sovereignty, and Culture in the Americas* (Philadelphia: University of Pennsylvania Press, 2020).

historians to consider a wide array of sources, and it questions the concept of law underlying a legal history that is still often shaped by the Western idea of the nation-state. It calls upon us to examine and revise canons of knowledge, periodization, and the many teleologies inherent to the grand narratives of modernization and the emergence of modern secular states as a linear historical process. The biggest challenge, however, is to write a legal history that describes the laws imposed by some, but that at the same time enables an adequate representation of the agency and the presence of normativities practiced continuously by others – in other words, to write a de-colonial legal history of people living under the conditions of formal or informal imperialism.

This book tries to adhere to these orientations. Several of its chapters make visible the histories of indigenous peoples or enslaved persons. It analyzes legal history as a history of knowledge production, and it gives weight to normative spheres traditionally not included in legal history, such as social norms emanating from the household, from religion, or informal law. We are, however, conscious that our endeavor is only a beginning. After many decades of debates about de-colonial and postcolonial perspectives on the history of Latin America, and despite the advanced socio-legal reflections about epistemic asymmetries and theories from the Global South,[21] practical proposals as to how to circumscribe it are still in their infancy.

A Legal History

Most of all, this book is a *legal* history. In recent years, legal history has become a buzzword with multiple meanings, which also means that the discipline can be pursued in multiple ways. Some scholars identify legal history as the study of a piece of legislation, doctrine, or custom, or of individuals and institutions involved in their making. Others wish to investigate how actors strategically used rules or institutions to their advantage. Yet another group looks for information about the past by reading juridical documentation, mainly legislation and court cases, while also debating their biases and

21 D. Bonilla Maldonado and M. Riegner, "Decolonization," in R. Grote, F. Lachenmann and R. Wolfrum (eds.), *Max Planck Encyclopedia of Comparative Constitutional Law* (Oxford: Oxford University Press, 2020); W. D. Mignolo, *Idea of Latin America*; E. Lander, "Ciencias sociales: saberes coloniales y eurocéntricos," in E. Lander (ed.), *La colonialidad del saber: eurocentrismo y ciencias sociales. Perspectivas latinoamericanas* (Buenos Aires: CLACSO, 2000), 11–40.

silences and how to overcome them.[22] These are frequent pursuits; however, this book takes a different approach. Rather than asking about individual solutions, or uncovering the life of individuals or groups, its goal is to understand the legal contexts in which specific answers emerged and/or operated. What was the meaning of law at different moments in time? What was it supposed to accomplish? Who was charged with making, interpreting, imposing, or changing it? And how were norms created, altered, enforced, negotiated, or eliminated?

This type of legal history – a bit like law itself – does not seek to provide solutions, such as clarifying the rules that operated in specific cases. Neither does it use only juridical documents to reconstruct the past. Rather, it concentrates on what one might compare to an operating system for a computer and strives to explain the legal setting that – though working in the background and thus mostly unseen – nonetheless enabled certain things but not others. It concentrates not on the specific results obtained in a particular case – results that can be largely accidental – but on how they were reached: What was the method, which were the procedures, and who was involved and in what way? This book views law both as a practice and as a science, where following the right itineraries is what validates the results, whatever these may be. It, therefore, seeks to reconstruct routes rather than destinations and to reveal controversies, not adhere to metanarratives or pretend to uncover a definitive truth. It is meant to help those who engage with juridical questions or juridical documents by providing them with tools to understand what was happening, often behind the scenes. It also seeks to offer a useful framework to meaningfully merge the multiplicity of voices, rules, practices, and institutions that scholars have already uncovered and to supply those who work on legal issues with the necessary information.

22 On the variety of ways to imagine legal history today see, for example, M. D. Dubber and C. Tomlins (eds.), *The Oxford Handbook of Legal History* (Oxford: Oxford University Press, 2018) which lists social history, political history, intellectual history, doctrinal history, economic history, gender history, the history of legal texts, and legal history as methods for studying law and culture. The volume also mentions quantitative legal history and enumerates several "perspectives" either by appealing to specific scholars or by observing historical or sociological jurisprudence, legal formalism, legal realism, law and society, Marxist legal history, the material turn, structuralist and post-structuralist legal history, critical legal history and critical legal studies, feminist historiography, or critical race theory. Finally, it covers various legal traditions such as Roman, medieval canon, and common law, continental civil law, Jewish law, Islamic law, Chinese law, aboriginal law, or Indian law. The aim of the volume, in other words, is to display the multiplicity of ways by which legal history can be done in terms of subject, method, approach, and sources.

This explains why this History of Latin American Law in Global Perspective does not describe how particular groups translated their interests into legal solutions or how particular topics became legally regulated. Nor does it cover the question of how contracts were made or what criminal law mandated, or examine the regimes that applied to specific groups. Instead, it hopes to explain the legal logic within which all legal regimes operated, and the legal context that made them possible and gave them specific meanings.

Summary of Contents

Given the importance of context, this volume is divided mainly according to moments of rupture or radical change: from autonomous indigenous communities (mostly pre-sixteenth century, although some groups persisted with some degree of autonomy into the twentieth century), to colony (depending on region, mostly from the sixteenth to the early nineteenth century), to experiments with building new states (mostly the first half of the nineteenth century), to the consolidation of states (mostly in the late nineteenth and early twentieth century), to the new constitutionalism and the challenges to state law (in the later part of the twentieth century and the present).

This book begins with a series of methodological questions. The first describes the historiography and agendas that have accompanied the writing of Latin American legal history over time (Section 1.1). The next asks what a legal history of Latin America is, mostly by observing what Iberian and Latin American historians have said about the similarities and differences between history and law, and how they justified the importance of legal history (Section 1.2). Section 1.3 discusses the methodological premises of our common project, which seeks to study how norms are produced by centering on processes of translation and concretization. Section 1.4 describes some of the ways by which global legal history can be accomplished by reminding us that things that qualify as "global" do not necessarily require any actual movement in space. Instead, the global can also be present in the life of an individual who experienced dislocation.

Having dealt with these methodological questions, we turn to observe the history of Latin American law. We begin by studying indigenous law in Chapter 2, which describes both what we know and what we don't about this field of inquiry, as well as the difficulties in acquiring such knowledge and the enormous transformations it has experienced over time. Because so much of the information we currently have regarding indigenous law depends on colonial records (though archaeology and anthropology have been extremely helpful), while we identify this law as precolonial, Chapter 2 also covers some of what transpired during the colonial period and thereafter. In Sections 3.1, 3.2, and 3.3, we observe the colonial period, dividing it into three parts: civil, religious, and domestic. Despite this division, all three sections speak to the same juridical universe as it is impossible to imagine a colonial Latin American civil law without considering canon law and moral theology as well as the jurisdictional powers of the *pater familias*. Together, these sections describe the entanglements typical of settler colonialism, which allowed European powers to exert control over faraway lands and their original peoples, send European colonists there and, eventually, enslave large populations mostly of African descent. Here the emphasis is on studying attempts to implement norms that were created elsewhere (i.e., in Africa or Europe) or under radically different circumstances (i.e., before Europeans invaded) but that needed to be translated and concretized so as to fit the local (and new) circumstances that included, most importantly, the presence of a large indigenous population and enslaved persons who all practiced their own laws.

Next, we turn to the construction of the Latin American states. We begin with surveying events during the revolutionary period that led from colonial to independent states, and from the Old Regime to a new one (Chapter 4). We seek to demonstrate that the revolutionary period was highly experimental in nature and featured constant struggles to define new communities and their norms, inculcate new practices, and then change it all again. Questions were asked regarding who had the authority to break the ties with the metropole, what structures the new polities would take, who their citizens would be and which their territories were, how their authorities would be chosen, and how norms would be enacted. Eventually, most of these questions would be answered in the "long nineteenth century," covered in the subsequent Sections 5.1, 5.2, and 5.3, which deal with the construction of states, the elaboration of constitutions, and legal codifications. These sections speak to issues of translations of knowledge of normativity and the participation of local actors in global conversations but also highlight the constant tensions between past and present, global and local, and survey the difficulties in adapting the aspirations of many state-makers to social realities. These sections also examine the price that various groups paid because of these state-building endeavors, as well as the constant need for compromise and reinvention, both processes that met with varying degrees of success.

By the late nineteenth century and during the twentieth century, the legal landscape of Latin America featured the rise of the administrative state (Section 6.1), experiences with dictatorships (Section 6.2), and transitional justice and demands to protect human rights (Section 6.3). Chapter 7 ends the volume with an incredibly important question, namely whether state law can survive the twenty-first century. Faced by pressures from within (to accommodate the multiple communities and multiple legalities present inside the state, including the laws of cultural communities, but also of peripheral neighborhoods and criminal organizations) and from outside (by international bodies and international law as well as other global actors), what is at stake here is the question whether this fragmentation signals the end of state law, or whether states will be able to contain these pressures and survive.

We would like to thank Raquel Razente Sirotti, who participated in our deliberations as an administrator, discussant, and advisor. We are also very grateful for the help of Vera Mark, Christina Pössel, James Thompson, and Otto Danwerth from the editorial department of the Max Planck Institute for Legal History and Legal Theory, as well as to Janina Zimmermann. This project would not have been possible without them.

We also remember Carlos Ramos Núñez, who passed away in 2021 while preparing his contribution for this book. Carlos was an outstanding legal historian and a generous colleague, whom we will greatly miss.

We dedicate this book to the memory of António Manuel Hespanha. António Manuel agreed to join this project as the third editor but passed away before it came to fruition. As always, even in the initial planning stages, he was inspirational and generously shared his wisdom, erudition, and enthusiasm. Though he is no longer with us, his scholarship, his thoughtfulness, and his kindness are our permanent companions.

1

What Is Legal History of Latin American Law in a Global Perspective?

1.1 How Was and Is Latin American Legal History Written?

CARLOS PETIT

Presenting a legal historiography of Latin America in just a few pages is a challenging task. To begin with, it is necessary to take a position on whether there actually was a geo-cultural entity with that denomination; a collective space that has existed (and continues to do so) under a normative system whose history has been the object of professional narratives. If we were to accept this point of view, we would be back, almost a hundred years later, to cherishing the dream of "the epic of Great America" that was launched in 1932 by the American Historical Association, and of a desirable "general (legal) history of America."[1] But we can also opt for the description of a plurality of territorially localized legal histories which more or less coincide with the current sovereign states. Broadly speaking, it is possible to establish the boundary between the comprehensiveness of a legal American *Ancien régime* and the "national definition" of the law at the time of the processes of independence. However, this approach, while undoubtedly useful, is in practice fraught with difficulties.

On the one hand, the *Latin* omits or silences the *American*, that is, the presence and experiences of indigenous peoples whose history rarely enters the narrative; an issue of capital importance that only began to receive attention at the end of the last century.[2] On the other hand, the traditional approach – but also the proposals intended to renovate classic historiography – leave non-Iberian America (English, French, and Dutch, but also Russian and Danish, to be precise) out of the picture, although the facts of the past reveal

1 S. Bernabéu Albert, "El universo americanista. Un balance obligado para acabar el siglo," *Revista de Indias* 60 (2000), 271–306, at 275.

2 Fortunately, in recent years, several scholars have devoted themselves to analysing the normative experiences of indigenous peoples. See also Chapter 2 in this volume.

crossed experiences and diverse spaces of influences. This was the case of Franco-Spanish Hispaniola and the Brazilian Nova Holanda as well as the Californian missions and the Russian empire's claim to territories on the northern Pacific coast. And even within the Peninsular tradition itself, the duplicity between Hispanic America and Portuguese America makes it difficult to articulate a historiographical discourse around the so-called *derecho indiano*, that great legal experience which, as António Manuel Hespanha has demonstrated, cannot simply be applied to the case of Brazil.[3]

The picture is complicated by the diverging development of local historiographies; the image of the "leopard skin" used by the well-known Americanist Peter Novick is useful in this respect, as it symbolizes the fragmentation of research topics and approaches.[4] Indeed, the sovereign nations that were born out of the processes of independence have their own traditions (histories of *derecho patrio*), with a remarkable production of narratives; only a few subjects – as is the case with the codification of private law – have received continental attention.[5] There are states with a more robust historiographical practice, where legal history has existed for a long time as a subject taught at university; they contribute to common knowledge with textbooks and journals (Argentina, Brazil, Chile, Mexico). These journals have generally been founded only recently (ranging from the 1970s in Chile and Argentina to the present day in the case of Brazil). Where there is no academic focus on the field, it is not uncommon to find studies of a nonprofessional nature, that is, research work that is undertaken by jurists and historians who specialize in other areas and occasionally take an interest in the law of the past; their methods and results are, of course, quite different.

Given the earlier-mentioned difficulties, it only seems possible to outline the circumstances in which interest in the historical research of the law(s) of Latin America – including Brazil – emerged, and its subsequent development.[6]

3 A. M. Hespanha, "O 'direito das Índias' no contexto da historiografia das colonizações ibéricas," in T. Duve (ed.), *Actas del XIX Congreso del Instituto Internacional de Derecho Indiano: Berlín 2016* (Madrid: Dykinson, 2019), vol. I, 43–83, 73–77. Nor, obviously, does it apply to British colonization: R. J. Ross, "Spanish American and British American Law as Mirrors to Each Other: Implications of the Missing *Derecho Británico Indiano*," in T. Duve and H. Pihlajamäki (eds.), *New Horizons in Spanish Colonial Law: Contributions to Transnational Early Modern Legal History* (Frankfurt am Main: Max-Planck-Institut für europäische Rechtsgeschichte, 2015), 9–28.

4 Bernabéu, "Universo americanista," 281–82.

5 C. Ramos Núñez, *El Código napoleónico y su recepción en América latina* (Lima: Pontificia Universidad Católica del Perú, 1997); A. Guzmán Brito, *La codificación civil en Iberoamérica. Siglos XIX y XX* (Santiago: Editorial Jurídica de Chile, 2000).

6 An interesting historiographical assessment was offered by V. Tau Anzoátegui, "Instituciones y Derecho Indiano en una renovada Historia de América," *Anuario de*

The Origins of Latin American Legal Historiography

The academic study of early (modern) *derecho indiano* begins in 1883, on the occasion of the celebration of the third centenary of Hugo Grotius' birth.[7] Ernest Nys' contribution on *ius belli* and the predecessors of the great Dutch humanist and writer preserved for the benefit of modern legal science the so-called *magni hispani* – until then rarely studied – as a brilliant group of Thomist thinkers who discussed the legitimacy of Castilian rule in the Indies and the conditions for a legitimate war of occupation.[8] The origins of international law of "Spanish" mold were thus mixed with the study of the Iberian domination of America and the war against the "infidel Indians," who were supposedly opposed to the *ius communicationis* imposed by the Castilian and Portuguese adventurers and justified by the theologians of Salamanca or Évora. It was in this context that the historiographical invention of the so-called *derecho indiano* took place. It consisted of a peculiar system "made up of those legal norms – royal charters, provisions, instructions, ordinances, etc. – that were dictated by the Spanish monarchs or by their delegated authorities to be applied exclusively – in a general or particular way – in the territories of Spanish America."[9] The chronological sequence of the works of Eduardo de Hinojosa y Naveros (1852–1919), the scientific father of legal history in Spain (and consequently, in Spanish America), is revealing: His acclaimed study *Influencia que tuvieron en el Derecho público de su patria, y singularmente en el Derecho penal, los filósofos y teólogos españoles anteriores a nuestro siglo* (1890) was followed by *Las Relecciones de Francisco de Vitoria*

Estudios Americanos 75 (2018), 435–58. Also, L. Nuzzo, "Between America and Europe: The Strange Case of the derecho indiano," Duve and Pihlajamäki (eds.), *New Horizons*, 161–91.

7 The expression "derecho indiano," with a strong presence in Argentina as a synonym of "colonial law" (thus, J. B. Alberdi, *Bases y puntos de partida para la organización política de la República Argentina* (Buenos Aires: Impta. Argentina, 1852), 57), penetrated academic terminology thanks to Ricardo Levene, but the syntagma is documented at least from the time of the Constitution of Cádiz (1812): J. F. de Azcárate, *Proyecto de reforma de algunos estatutos de la Real Academia de Jurisprudencia teórico-práctica, real y pública* (Mexico City: En la oficina de D. Mariano Ontiveros, 1812), 25. It seems clear that he copied the famous title of J. de Solórzano, *Política indiana* (1648): cf. *Teatro histórico, jurídico y político militar de la Isla Fernandina de Cuba y principalmente de su capital La Habana* (1791), in R. Cowley and A. Prego (eds.), *Los tres primeros historiadores de la Isla de Cuba* (Habana: Impta. y Librería de Andrés Prego, 1876), vol. II, 1876 and 18.

8 *Le droit de la guerre et les précurseurs de Grotius* (Brussels and Leipzig: Librairie Européenne C. Muquardt, Merzbach and Falk, 1882), 165–68. Cf. I. de la Rasilla del Moral, *In the Shadow of Vitoria: A History of International Law in Spain (1770–1953)* (Leiden and Boston: Brill, 2018).

9 J. M. Ots y Capdequí, *Historia del derecho español en América y del derecho indiano* (Madrid: Aguilar, 1968), 3. (Unless otherwise indicated, all tranlsations are by the autor.)

(1903) and *Los precursores españoles de Grocio* (1911). Since then, the titles to the Indies by conquest, the incorporation of the new territories to the Crown of Castile, the concept of legitimate war, the papal bulls that divided the newly (and yet to be) discovered oceanic and terrestrial regions between Castile and Portugal, the legal status of the new subjects, the evangelizing cause – all these factors have constituted the main arguments of Americanist legal historians.[10]

Meticulous Documentation: The Archivo General de Indias

The study of the theological roots of the "discovery" of America ran parallel to the first undertakings in editing and publishing documentation. The work of the Royal Academy of History (Madrid), the modern chronicler of the Indies, was decisive. Despite its errors and inexplicable omissions, the renowned *Colección de documentos inéditos relativos al descubrimiento, conquista y colonización de las posesiones españolas en América y Oceanía* (first series forty-two volumes, 1864–1884) provided an enormous mass of unpublished sources, which was completed in the twentieth century by a second series (twenty-five volumes, 1885–1932).

These were documents that, according to the subtitle of the collection, were "drawn from the archives of the kingdom, and especially from the archive of the Indies." This archive, located in Seville, the old port of the Indies, was and still is the world's main repository of documents for the history of the law and the governance of Spanish America.[11] Founded in the time of Carlos III (1785) for the custody and administrative use of the papers of the Council of the Indies, it was belatedly opened to public consultation at the end of the nineteenth century, on the occasion of the fourth centenary of the "discovery" of America (1892) and the Hispanic-Portuguese-American Congresses held at the time (conferences of Americanists, geographical, mercantile, medical sciences, legal studies,

10 From R. Levene, "La concepción de Eduardo de Hinojosa sobre la historia de las ideas políticas y jurídicas en el Derecho español y su proyección en el Derecho indiano," *Anuario de Historia del Derecho Español* 23 (1953), 259–87, to the still recent thesis by C. López Lomel, *La polémica de la justicia en la conquista de América*, Universidad Complutense de Madrid (2002). Many other doctoral theses were defended along the same lines: F. Rendón y Trova, *Condición jurídica de los indios desde el descubrimiento de América hasta la muerte de Isabel la Católica* (1898); F. Puig Peña, *La influencia de Francisco de Vitoria en la obra de Hugo Grocio* (1932); A. García Gallo, *La aplicación de la doctrina española de la guerra. Datos para su estudio*, Universidad de Madrid (1934); A. Gómez Gutiérrez, *El derecho indiano*, Universidad Complutense de Madrid (1940).

11 J. A. Calderón Quijano, *Americanismo en Sevilla, 1900–1980* (Seville: Escuela de Estudios Hispano-Americanos, 1987).

military, literary, pedagogical), which represented the first attempt at a "global" study of all things American.[12] The archive was placed in the hands of experts – professional archivists who were members of a corps of civil servants created in 1858 – and shortly after acquiring the status of "general archive" (1901) under the Ministry of Public Instruction and Fine Arts, the catalogs were made available and historians were offered professional assistance. It is not by chance that among the first historians to consult the archive were Latin American scholars, who came to Seville to document their national histories, but also to clarify the territorial limits of their countries of origin, which were often the subject of disputes. This important historical and legal question was addressed by the Ibero-American Legal Congress of 1892. Indeed, it is no coincidence that the central theme of the meeting, which was discussed from historical and geographical perspectives, was international arbitration.[13]

Spanish Heritage as Hispanidad

The fourth centenary of the "discovery" saw the birth of *hispanidad*, a hard-to-define concept that soon morphed into a Hispanoamerican holiday.[14] The royal decree of September 23, 1892 (*Gaceta* of the twenty-fifth) declared October 12 an official holiday, "without prejudice to the ability for the Crown with the *Cortes* to declare it perpetual thereafter." The Spanish government even got Italy – the disputed land of Christopher Columbus – and several transatlantic republics to establish this holiday. However, the celebration of October 12 – the day of the *Virgen del Pilar*, patron saint of *hispanidad* –[15] as a public holiday, endowed with the perpetuity that it lacked at the outset, was born years later at the initiative of Argentina, and announced as *Día de la Raza* (1917); Catholic militancy, represented by the priest Zacarías de Vizcarra,

12 S. Bernabéu Albert, *1892: El IV Centenario del Descubrimiento de América en España. Coyuntura y celebraciones* (Madrid: Consejo superior de Investigaciones Científicas, 1987).

13 Arbitration also played a role in the *Congreso Militar Hispano-Portugués-Americano. Actas I–II* (Madrid: Impta. y Litografía del Depósito de la Guerra, 1893).

14 The term *hispanidad*, which is documented in the dictionary of the Real Academia Española in 1817, meant, as an archaism, "the same as hispanismo." Its presence has been irregular (editions of 1884 and 1935) and only in the 1992 edition, celebrating the V Centenary, does it appear with the two meanings that are of interest here: (1) "generic character of all the peoples of Hispanic language and culture" and (2) "the ensemble and community of Hispanic peoples."

15 See also D. Martínez Vilches, "De patrona de la monarquía a patrona de la nación. La Inmaculada Concepción entre España y Portugal," *Historia y Política* 46 (2021), 209–35; M. Rodríguez, *Celebración de "la raza." Una historia comparativa del 12 de octubre* (Mexico City: Universidad Iberoamericana, 2004).

dominated the celebration.[16] The well-known historian Richard Konetzke, who was primarily responsible for the promotion of Ibero-Americanist studies in Central Europe, also adhered to the idea of *hispanidad*.[17]

These circumstances would seem of little relevance if it were not for the fact that they responded to a certain cultural context. I am referring to the reason for the "decline of the Latin race" – the surest proof of which was allegedly the adverse result of the Franco-Prussian (1870) and Hispano-American (1898) wars – in the face of the "Anglo-Saxon race," which was said to be "younger, more Protestant, richer, and more powerful." The ideas codified by the Italian sociologist Giuseppe Sergi in his famous work on *La decadenza delle nazioni latine* (1900) entered the mainstream – the early, multilingual experiment (French, Portuguese, Spanish, Italian) of the newspaper *La Raza Latina* (1874–1884) is significant – and this heartfelt *latinidad*, seen from America, seemed to prelude the hispanophile movement that dominated Argentina after the centenary of the May Revolution (1910). Having lost the war of arms, it was now necessary to win the war of language and culture.[18]

It is worth recalling that as late as the fourth centenary of the "discovery," the Spanish-Portuguese-American Geographical Conference (October 17 to November 4, 1891) was presented as the "congress of the race that discovered and conquered worlds and oceans," a (white and dominating) race of peoples who "constitute a great family that cannot live disunited without great prejudice to their general and private interests, and that, at a minimum, a commercial coalition is required to guarantee the future of all the states of Spanish and Portuguese origin." This way, a close ideological relationship linked the concept of *hispanidad* with the "moral superiority of the Latin race" and with the American adventure of the Iberian peoples: "The social regime that Spain established in its colonies by means of its admirable laws of the Indies is superior to all other systems of colonization, which exploit rather than civilize, and cause the extermination of the indigenous races."[19] I know of no better synthesis of the clichés that a large sector of Americanist legal

16 There was also a migration policy in favor of the reception of a "pure" race, that is, white and Catholic, free of "yellows, Turks, Jews, blacks and *mestizos*": cf. D. Pablos Papanikas, *La Iglesia de la Raza. La Iglesia católica española y la construcción de la identidad nacional en Argentina, 1910–1930*, Ph.D. thesis, Universidad Autónoma de Madrid (2012).

17 A. Sáez Arance, "Entre la «Volksgeschichte» alemana y la historiografía nacionalista del franquismo: una relectura de las primeras publicaciones de Richard Konetzke sobre España (1929–1946)," *Ayer* 69 (2008), 73–99.

18 P. F. Ledesma Fernández, *El giro hispanófilo. Configuraciones de lo hispano en Argentina*, Ph.D. thesis, Universidad Complutense de Madrid (2019).

19 Bernabéu Albert, *1892: El IV Centenario*, 82–3. But the story was a long one: A. Feros, *Nación y raza en el mundo hispánico, 1450–1820* (Madrid: Marcial Pons, 2019).

historiography has carried forward to the present day, where the "Hispanic race" (Portuguese and Castilians, and their "Creole" descendants) was clearly opposed to some "indigenous races" that only appeared in the general picture in order to show the ethical-religious, and thus civilizing, stature of Peninsular colonization as opposed to the materialistic and abusive English colonization. The Africans, who were brought to the North and South Americas by way of forced, criminal abduction and enslavement, were not even mentioned.

History Writing and Republican Culture: Brazil

The bases that inspired Hispanic racial ideology and the resulting legitimizing narrative developed differently in Brazil. A few years after the reform that introduced the study of the history of law as a subject taught at university in Spain (1883), and long before the appearance of José Caeiro da Matta's *História do Direito Português* (1911), the minister and patriot Benjamin Constant Botelho de Magalhães introduced legal history at the University of Recife in Pernambuco (1891). There, the holder of the chair, the young publicist José Izidoro Martins Junior (1860–1904), who was a disciple of Tobias Barreto and an abolitionist, published *História do Direito Nacional* (1895). A pioneer of its kind, this scientific-positivist work (Martins confessedly belonged to the "naturalistic school") conceived law as "an organic whole determined by bio-sociological fatalities," and therefore with no prior commitments to morality or the attribution of a transcendent origin to the legal experience, which was perfectly in line with republican secularism.[20] Nothing of the kind existed in the Spanish language, neither for *derecho indiano* nor for *derecho patrio*. When it finally arrived – I have the prolific Argentinean author Ricardo Levene (1885–1958) in mind – the theoretical foundations, and consequently the subject matter addressed, responded to partially different parameters.[21]

In his treatment of the legal past, Martins followed the *filiação* method (whereby the present was only understandable on the basis of the past), which led him to deal, in part one of his *História*, first with the history of Portuguese law (*Epocha dos antecedentes*) before moving on to trace the institutional history of Brazil. In doing so, he inaugurated a practice that was followed by future Latin American legal history textbooks. The past was described according to its "genetic" elements, with Portuguese (Alexandre

20 J. I. Martins Junior, *História do Direito Nacional* (Rio de Janeiro: Typographia da empresa democrática editora, 1895), 7.

21 Cf. R. Levene, *Introducción a la Historia del Derecho indiano* (Buenos Aires: Valerio Abeledo, 1924); previously, by the same author, *Notas para el estudio del Derecho indiano* (Buenos Aires: Imp. Virtus, 1918).

Herculano, Teófilo Braga) and Brazilian (Cândido Mendes) classics serving as the plinth on which then, in part two, the "national" legal experience was based (*Epocha embryogénica*). This was supported by motives and authorities imbued with the same positivist ideal of Comtian and Spencerian tradition (especially Italians: Brugi, Cogliolo, D'Aguanno). As such, Martins' *História* offered a diverse view of the colonial past.

To begin with, the so-called "ethnic-legal protoplasm" of the country was racially mixed ("the Brazilian people is currently made up of Aryan whites, Guarani Indians, blacks of the Bantu group, and *mestiços* of these three races," in the words of the writer Silvio Romero). After asserting the superiority of the white Portuguese, the discoverers, and conquerors (the *raça predominante* or "predominant race"), Martins resorted to another quotation, this time from Carlos Frederico von Martius, to warn against the error of forgetting "the forces of indigenous and imported black peoples" – a fundamental aspect, alongside the European racial substratum, for the formation of Brazilian nationality.[22] This was, in short, quite the opposite of the exclusionary *hispanidad* that was making inroads in other American lands.

Thus, the starting point for a rendition of Brazil's legal past was this racial diversity, which was reconstructed thanks to an extensive library produced by ethnographers and philologists who identified the origins, differences, and settlements of the indigenous and African populations. However, according to this version, the African populations – the authority in this case was another professor from Recife, the great Clóvis Beviláqua – did not really contribute anything to Brazilian law because of their condition as enslaved people ("without personality, without legal attributes beyond those that can emanate from a bundle of goods"). This was just the opposite of the indigenous peoples, whose customs and institutions – Beviláqua had researched those too – Martins treated with some attention. But it was clear that, both in the colonial past and in the present system, the contribution of Portugal, "a nation already in existence, which has a complete and codified legislation,"[23] had been decisive. It remained for the republican government to develop a program of "nationalization" that would succeed in synthesizing the three racial elements that made up Brazil in order to obtain "a homogeneous and compact whole, corresponding worthily to the physical and social environment in which it has to act and evolve."[24] In this way, Brazilian legal

22 Martins, História, 134.
23 Martins, *História*, 130–39 (American peoples), 143–50 (African peoples), 154–55 (European superiority).
24 Martins, *História*, 156.

historiography put itself at the service of the nation whose racial complexity was sublimated into a happy tropical "melanism." Compared to other cases – the United States, in particular – it was argued that "in no country in the world do the representatives of such different races coexist in such harmony and under such a profound spirit of equality."[25]

The Development of Literature on Derecho Indiano

The important role played by Argentina in the celebration of the *raza* – the apotheosis of a Euro-Creole super-nation – and its commitment to legal historiography through the figure of Ricardo Levene, who succeeded Carlos Octavio Bunge in the chair of "Introduction to Law" at the University of Buenos Aires, can be justified by recalling the American journey of Rafael Altamira y Crevea (1866–1951), a friend and correspondent of Levene.[26] Altamira, who stood out among the first Spanish professors of legal history, took up the chair at Oviedo in 1897 and then went on to become the protagonist of a famous cultural embassy to Latin America, where he gave seminal lectures (1909) – particularly influential and prolonged in the case of Argentina.[27] This allowed his country to strengthen ties with its former colonies and to develop a perspective for the future after the loss of the last Spanish overseas territories. Similarly to Levene in America, Altamira founded American legal historiography in Europe. His experience as a researcher of customs (including indigenous customs, 1946–1948), his skepticism toward legislation as a primary source of law, and his attention to popular legal conscience – all traits of the Krauso-positivist tradition of thought in which Altamira had been trained – coincided with the professional vision of Levene, a jurist-historian and "sociologist" concerned with the reality of law and the pluralism of normative manifestations.[28]

Altamira's move from the small town of Oviedo to the Central University (Madrid), where he held the chair of "History of the Political and Civil

25 F. J. Oliveira Vianna, "O typo brasileiro; seus elementos formadores," in *Diccionário Histórico, Geográphico e Ethnográphico do Brasil* (Rio de Janeiro: Imprensa Nacional, 1922), vol. I, 277. But the author gave a good example of racial preconceptions on 285–27 of "Psychologia do indio e do negro e do seu mestiço."

26 J. Ferrándiz Lozano and E. La Parra López (eds.), *Rafael Altamira: Idea y acción hispanoamericana* (Alicante: Instituto Alicantino de Cultura Juan Gil-Albert, 2011). On the (epistolary) relationship between Levene and Altamira, see V. Tau Anzoátegui, "Diálogos sobre derecho indiano entre Altamira y Levene en los años Cuarenta," *Anuario de Historia del Derecho Español* 67 (1997), 369–90.

27 G. H. Prado, *Las lecciones iushistóricas de Rafael Altamira (1909). Apuntes sobre historia del derecho, derecho consuetudinario y modelos formativos del jurista* (Pamplona: Analecta, 2015).

28 V. Tau Anzoátegui, "De la sociología al derecho indiano. Contrapuntos entre Ricardo Levene y Ernesto Quesada," *Revista de Historia del Derecho* 34 (2006), 357–417.

Institutions of America" from 1914 to 1936, enabled him to exert a considerable influence on the younger generation; thus, the first corpus of scientific studies on *derecho indiano* formed around him. The research focused more on the recovery and history of legal sources than on the reconstruction of the historical regime of American institutions.[29] Altamira added his own work to the magisterium, especially his late contributions. These were published when the elder Altamira, who had been a judge at the International Court of Justice (1921), went into exile in Mexico (1944–1951) following the terrible Spanish civil war.[30]

Two main developments can be traced back to Altamira. On the one hand, mention should be made of the figure and work of his first disciple, the Valencian José María Ots y Capdequí (1893–1975). A professor at the faculty of law, his tenure for several years at the University of Seville (as of 1924) allowed him to develop his research and participate in the many initiatives that arose on occasion of the great Ibero-American Exhibition (Seville, 1929). In addition to monographic studies, especially on questions of private law,[31] during his exile in Colombia, the republican Ots produced the first and most complete general exposition by a Spanish author: The *Manual de historia del derecho español en las Indias y del derecho propiamente indiano* (1943). Published in Argentina with a prologue by Levene, it served as a reference book for the teachings which, little by little, began to consolidate in several American countries. Other younger researchers belonged to the same school as Ots, such as Javier Malagón (1911–1990), a jurist and historian who was forced to

29 Many of these doctoral works were published in the law school's journal. For example, among institutional studies, J. Barrasa y Muñoz de Bustillo, "El servicio personal de los indios durante la colonización española en América," *Revista de Ciencias Jurídicas y Sociales* 6 (1923), 231–76, 361–83; 7 (1924), 5–25, 288–328, 481–517; and 8 (1925), 325–60; for the history of the sources, A. Muro Orejón, "El nuevo Código de las Leyes de Indias. Proyectos de Recopilación legislativa posteriores a 1680. Tesis doctoral," ibid. 12 (1929), 287–339; 13 (1930), 484–532, 631–60; 14 (1931), 67–112, 177–240, 416–38; 15 (1932), 5–64, 216–88, 502–31, 568–88; and 16 (1933), 130–52, 204–38 and 436–72, with a separate edition prefaced by Altamira (Madrid: Universidad Central, 1929). Muro held the chair dedicated to "Historia del Derecho Indiano" (1946–1974) at the University of Seville, in History of America; cf. A. Muro, *Lecciones de Historia del Derecho hispano-indiano, publicadas por discípulos mexicanos* (Mexico City: Porrúa, 1989).

30 Cf. R. Altamira, *Manual de investigación de la historia del derecho indiano* (Mexico City: Instituto Panamericano de Geografía e Historia, 1948).

31 His thesis, supervised by Altamira, offered a historical outline of the rights of married women in the legislation of Spanish America (*Bosquejo histórico de los derechos de la mujer casada en la legislación de Indias* (Madrid: Reus, 1920)); see also "El derecho de propiedad en nuestra legislación de Indias," *Anuario de Historia del Derecho Español* 2 (1925), 49–168, a true *pièce de résistance* of the author and the object of his courses and research. Cf. M. Valiente Ots, *José María Ots Capdequí. El americanista de la II República* (Seville: Editorial Renacimiento, 2022).

leave Spain after the war but went on to have an excellent career in Santo Domingo, Mexico, and the United States, and Juan Manzano (1911–2004), professor of legal history in Seville and Madrid, scholar of American legal sources, and well-known supporter of the theory according to which America was discovered well before Columbus "discovered" it.

On the other hand, the American followers of Altamira – beneficiaries of the boom in historical studies brought about by the Spanish Republic – created local schools of varying dimensions.[32] Besides the Chilean Aníbal Bascuñán Valdés (1905–1988), Alamiro de Ávila's teacher and an expert in legal history and public law,[33] the Mexican Silvio Zavala (1909–2014) stood out above all others. He became the reference of a school that has enjoyed, along with the Argentine school, the greatest presence in historiography. A contemporary of Zavala's who also received extensive training in Europe and North America was the Peruvian Jorge Basadre Grohmann (1903–1980). He was among the first to publish a work of general ambition that, once more, led from pre-Hispanic antecedents to Peruvian law (*Historia del derecho peruano*, 1937). From a theoretical point of view, having learned the lesson from Altamira, Latin American historiography in the 1930s and 1940s sought to establish in its studies a supposedly objective – one might say "Rankean" – truth through a very meticulous use of sources and the orderly presentation of data that was always compared and contrasted. This approach nevertheless failed, for lack of direct testimonies, when attempts were made to reconstruct institutional life prior to the conquest.[34]

The relationship of Latin American researchers with the legal past of the colonizing powers, particularly Spain, was variable and conflicted. It was closer in the cases of Chile and Argentina, and less intense in countries which, like Mexico and Peru, had highly developed indigenous presence.[35] Surely the most radical proposal came from the highly respected Alamiro de Ávila, who did not hesitate to affirm that Chileans "are Spanish and our origins are the same as those of any Spanish people," while the indigenous peoples and their

32 P. Vélez, "Política e historiografía. El americanismo español hasta 1936," *Revista de Indias* 68 (2008), 241–68, 258–63.

33 A. de Ávila, "Recuerdo de mi maestro Aníbal Bascuñán Valdés, fundador de la escuela chilena de historiadores del Derecho," *Anuario de Filosofía Jurídica y Social* (1989), 11–26. Also E. E. Palma and M. F. Elgueta, "Enseñanza de la historia del derecho centrada en el aprendizaje de los estudiantes a lo largo de 115 años de la fundación de la cátedra (Chile, 1902)," *Precedente* 12 (2018), 29–62, 49 on Bascuñán.

34 L. Mendieta y Núñez, *El derecho precolonial* (Mexico City: Porrúa hermanos y cía, 1937).

35 M. del R. González, "Silvio Zavala y la historia del derecho," *Anuario mexicano de historia del derecho* 10 (1998), 375–84.

experiences were, at most, "one of the elements, and in our case, not an important one, that inform *derecho indiano*." Consistent with such an extreme form of Eurocentrism, the reform of studies promoted by Ávila at the University of Chile (1977) allowed him to teach two courses in legal history: the first focused entirely on the history of Spanish law, from prehistory to the independence of American regions; the second, on *derecho indiano* and Chilean *derecho patrio*.[36] Latin American legal history textbooks typically began with a chapter addressing Spanish legal history in more or less detail – as Levene had written, "the history of America begins with the history of Spain" – but Ávila went so far as to reduce Chile's legal history to Spain's. I know of no other similar case.[37]

Zavala's example in Mexico did not immediately generate a legal historiography worthy of the name. In fact, the formalistic description of the great legal monuments, such as the *Siete Partidas* or the laws of Hispanic America (*Recopilación de leyes de Indias*, 1680), served to express a fundamental conception that accepted the inexorable rise of the state as a political form and the "civilizing logic" of the law as the only legal source, in a superficial and uncritical account. The renewal of studies only came in the 1970s, when Guillermo Floris Margadant (1924–2002) at the *Instituto de Investigaciones Jurídicas* (National Autonomous University of Mexico, UNAM) and the *Colegios* of Mexico and Michoacán began promoting research work and exchanges and hosting international meetings in the field. The culture that places legal positivism at the heart of legal history has been eroded by the opening up to other historiographical traditions, not only European; it is considered at present a decisive moment in the rebirth of Mexican legal history.[38]

National Celebration and Legal Historiography in Brazil

After Martins Junior's efforts in Recife at the end of the nineteenth century, no scholars of a standing equivalent to Levene or Zavala emerged in Brazil in the first half of the twentieth century. Nor was there someone like

36 A. de Ávila Martel, "La enseñanza de la Historia del Derecho Español en la Universidad de Chile," *Revista de Derecho de la Pontificia Universidad Católica de Valparaíso* 8 (1984), 31–38, at 33; on 35–38 he describes the syllabus of the "Spanish" course, which, by his own admission, he developed during his work stays in Spain.

37 For example, W. Vega Boyrie, *Historia del Derecho Dominicano*, 2nd ed. (Santo Domingo: Instituto Tecnológico, 1989), which is based on Late Fifteenth-Century Castile, 7–19.

38 J. del Arenal Fenochio, "La 'Escuela' mexicana de historiadores del derecho," *Anuario mexicano de Historia del Derecho* 18 (2006), 57–76; by the same author, "De Altamira a Grossi: presencia de historiadores extranjeros del Derecho en México," *Historia Mexicana* 55 (2006), 1467–95. Zavala's influence extended that of his master: R. Altamira, *Lecciones en América. Edition and preliminary study by Jaime del Arenal Fenochio* (Mexico City: Escuela Libre de Derecho, 1994).

Altamira to strengthen friendships and cultural relations, which were rather better between Portugal and Brazil to start with than those between Spain and Mexico or Argentina. It was not until the 1950s that another account of the *História do Direito Brasileiro* (I–IV, 1951–1956) was published, thanks to the influential lawyer, politician, and prolific writer Waldemar M. Ferreira (1885–1964).[39] The sixty years that separated Martins from Ferreira did not, however, consign the history of law to oblivion. Rather, the celebration of another event – the centenary of Brazil's independence (1822–1922) – gave impetus to historical studies, including legal studies.

In 1922, the first *Congresso Internacional de História da América* (Rio de Janeiro, September 8–15, 1922) was held, with Ricardo Levene being among the most prominent participants. It was convened by the *Instituto Histórico e Geográfico*, a venerable institution officially founded in 1838 to seek knowledge of the physical environment – the delimitation of the territory of the Brazilian states was, even with the establishment of the federal republic, merely approximate – and to write the history of the nation. "Among the interconnections of civic catechism," observed one of its members in 1912, "the study of the home country's history stands out."[40] In this historical meeting, methodologically guided by the positivist historiography of the Third French Republic (Charles Victor Langlois, Charles Seignobos), two subsections dealt with institutional history, another with constitutional and administrative history, and finally, the fifth section treated parliamentary history.

The thematic structure of the congresso was also followed in the second initiative sponsored by the Instituto Histórico e Geográfico.[41] I am referring to the Diccionário Histórico, Geográphico e Ethnográphico (1922), whose first volume, with general studies on Brazil, also contained chapters of legal interest: besides the usual constitutional ("Organização política," Max Fleiuss and Augusto Tavares de Lyra) and administrative histories (Max Fleiuss), a "História judiciaria do Brasil" (Aurelino Leal) was added, as well as a descriptive essay on "legal teaching" (Elpidio de Figueiredo). All of these authors

39 Also the author of *O direito público colonial do estado do Brasil sob o signo pombalino* (Rio de Janeiro: Editôra Nacional de Direito, 1960), Ferreira contributed a *História do direito constitucional brasileiro* (São Paulo: Max Limonad, 1954), as well as an impressive *Tratado de Direito comercial* (São Paulo: Saraiva, 1960–1966), vol. I–XV, whose first volume described "o estatuto histórico e dogmático do direito comercial."

40 J. L. Nascimento Júnior, "O Congresso, os Anais e a historiografia. Apontamentos sobre o I Congresso Internacional de História de América (1922)," *Revista Latino-Americana de História* 8 (2018), 269–84.

41 The official *Livro de Ouro*, with award-winning monographs, also coincided in content: J. Ribeiro Junqueira, "As comemorações do sete de setembro em 1922. Uma re(leitura) da história do Brasil," *Revista de história comparada* 5 (2011), 155–77.

were prominent political figures close to the Instituto. For the history of law, the contributions of Fleiuss (1868–1943), permanent secretary of the institute, and Leal (1877–1924), author of a História constitucional do Brasil (1914), stand out above all others. Both produced excellent descriptions, with bibliographical references and extensive notes, of the institutions of government and justice from the early days of the Portuguese presence in America up to the First Brazilian Republic. Their work was similar in chronology, development, and index to the legal-historical texts that were beginning to be published in Spanish-speaking countries.

The Instituto Internacional de Historia de Derecho Indiano (1966)

The academic traditions of research described in the beginning of Section 1.1 and the underlying motives that sustained them – *hispanidad*, race, religion, and universal destiny – led to the foundation, in the mid-1960s, of the "International Institute for the History of Derecho Indiano." Gathered in Buenos Aires on the occasion of the Fourth International Congress on the History of America, Alamiro de Ávila Martel (1918–1990), Ricardo Zorraquín Becú (1911–2000) and Alfonso García-Gallo (1911–1992) agreed to promote knowledge of the Latin American legal past by holding regular congresses and publishing their scientific results. This rather domestic foundational meeting in 1966 was followed by another in Santiago de Chile in 1969; since then, an uninterrupted series of conferences has taken place, which now extends to the twenty-first session (Buenos Aires, 2024). Modern historians from other traditions, such as the German (Horst Pietschmann, Enrique Otte), French (Annick Lempérière, François-Xavier Guerra), and Italian (Antonio Annino, Luigi Nuzzo, Aldo Andrea Cassi) ones, further contributed to the efforts of the institute and occasionally participated in its congresses.[42]

We already know that the Chilean Ávila was a disciple of Bascuñán. Zorraquín, like the younger José María Mariluz (1921–2018), was a disciple of Levene. García-Gallo trained in Madrid with Galo Sánchez, a medievalist expert who produced little though important work and always remained oblivious to the history of America. However, Galo Sánchez did open the

42 Former historians of the earlier-mentioned traditions studied the institutions of government in the Indies: cf. E. Schäfer, *Geschichte und Organisation des Indienrats und der Casa de la Contratación im sechzehnten Jahrhundert* (Hamburg: Iberoamerikanisches Institut, 1936); F. Chevalier, "Les municipalités indiennes en Nouvelle Espagne, 1520–1620," *Anuario de Historia del Derecho Español* 15 (1944), 352–86.

Anuario de Historia del Derecho Español, which he had helped found in 1924, to research on Latin American law with the help of his friend and colleague Ots Capdequí.[43] Although García-Gallo devoted his doctoral thesis to the Spanish "theologians-internationalists," his early research faithfully followed Sánchez' work on medieval sources.[44] His dedication to American studies came later, when he assumed the Madrid chair of "History of the Political and Civil Institutions of America" (1944), which had previously been held by Altamira. A monograph on the territorial government of the Indies, composed on that occasion, was the beginning of the very fertile Americanist production of this author.[45]

The 1966 Buenos Aires meeting was inaugural, not only because it initiated a long series of academic encounters, but because this conference laid the foundations that conditioned subsequent research. Alfonso García-Gallo was in charge of providing the methodological guidelines.[46]

The method, in this case, was hardly distinguishable from the techniques that were applied for analyzing historical sources. Since his accession to the chair of "History of Spanish Law" in 1934, García-Gallo had been rejecting any "sociological" temptation in historical-legal studies: the subject "must deal," he wrote at the time, "exclusively with legal matters and deal with all legal questions." A fundamental distinction supported his approach: whereas historical science deals with singular and unrepeatable facts, the legal fact, born of a preexisting mandate (of a norm), was destined to repeat itself as long as the rules that constrained it did not undergo changes. That was the reason why the history of law was a branch of legal science that had to be pursued "purified" of cultural, economic, or socio-political circumstances.[47]

43 In addition to the studies of Ots, the *Anuario* could count on the collaboration with Levene right from the beginning: cf. R. Levene, "Fuentes del Derecho indiano," *Anuario de Historia del Derecho Español* 1 (1924), 55–74.

44 A. García-Gallo, *La aplicación de la doctrina española de la guerra. Datos para su estudio*, Ph.D. thesis, Universidad Central de Madrid (1934). Cf. also *Anuario de Historia del Derecho Español* 11 (1934), 5–76, focused on Spanish-French relations, with documents. Nor do we find a specific section on *derecho indiano* in A. García-Gallo and R. Riaza, *Manual de Historia del Derecho Español* (Madrid: Victoriano Suárez, 1934).

45 "Los orígenes de la administración territorial de las Indias," *Anuario de Historia del Derecho Español* 15 (1944), 16–106. See A. García-Gallo, *Estudios de historia del Derecho indiano* (Madrid: Instituto Nacional de Estudios Jurídicos, 1972).

46 A. García-Gallo, "Problemas metodológicos de la Historia del Derecho indiano," *Revista del Instituto de Historia del Derecho Ricardo Levene* 13 (1967), 13–64, in an issue of the *Revista* which collected the works of that "Primera reunión de historiadores del Derecho indiano."

47 R. Medina Plana, "*Maneras de entender* o entender la manera. Las primeras Memorias de oposición a cátedras de Historia del Derecho," *Cuadernos de Historia del Derecho* 6 (1999), 19–142, at 121–36.

He further argued that "*derecho indiano* – like all law – is an ordering of social life; but in no case is it social life itself, nor can it be confused with it."[48]

The commitment to "juridicality," in the sense of an exclusively *legal* approach to research that did not take into account sociological or economic considerations, involved the rejection of the preceding tradition, in particular, that represented by Rafael Altamira. For García-Gallo, this author lacked "personal research," although he valued his role in guiding numerous disciples; and now – he wrote in 1953 – "sociological concern has begun to give way to an essentially juridical consideration of the history of *derecho indiano.*" If this went beyond Altamira's "historicist" approach,[49] it also went beyond Levene: the admired Argentinean master "in his sociological orientation of legal history … remains in the traditional line of his predecessors."[50]

A subsequent study, born out of the Buenos Aires meeting and presented at the second conference (Santiago de Chile, 1969), codified the same method, that is, working techniques and presentation of results. This is the *Metodología de la historia del Derecho Indiano* (1970), disseminated as the *vade mecum* of the discipline.[51] It does not take much effort to identify the lines of thought to which the work responded. The past was assumed as something given, which the researcher had to recover through intense study of the sources, without falling prey to subjectivity: "the personality of the scholar must yield to it."[52] The *Metodología* conceived law as an autonomous object, susceptible of separate

48 A. García-Gallo, "Problemas metodológicos," 17. The recommendation to be thoroughly familiar with the history of French and Italian law (Medina, "Entender la manera," 133) seems a remote echo of Latin "racial" consciousness.

49 "Su preocupación sociológica relegaba en él la jurídica a segundo plano … no aporta resultados originales. Pero es, en el mejor sentido de la palabra, un agitador de la conciencia histórica y un orientador de la juventud interesada en los temas americanos." A. García-Gallo, "Hinojosa y su obra," in E. de Hinojosa y Naveros, *Obras*, vol. I: *Estudios de investigación (Madrid: Instituto Nacional de Estudios Jurídicos*, 1948), XI–CXXIV, at CX–CXI.

50 A. García-Gallo, "El desarrollo de la historiografía jurídica indiana," *Revista de Estudios Políticos* 70 (1953), 163–85, at 184.

51 Among the many reviews that the *Metodología* received, the one published by A. de la Hera in the *Anuario de Historia del Derecho Español* 43 (1973), 562–67, should receive express mention because de la Hera, professor of canon law in Murcia and Seville, devoted himself extensively to the history of colonial law and even assumed the Madrid chair of "Historia de la Iglesia en América e Instituciones Canónicas indianas" (1971). With two other "indianists" he published a general work: I. Sánchez Bella, A. de la Hera, and C. Díaz Rementería (eds.), *Historia del Derecho Indiano* (Madrid: Mapfre, 1992) which added – as did Ots Capdequí before him – the exposition of the institutions of private, penal and procedural law to the more usual history of the legal sources and of the institutions of government, both temporal and spiritual.

52 It is unavoidable to remember P. Novick, *That Noble Dream: The "Objectivity Question" and the American Historical Profession* (New York: Cambridge University Press, 1988).

study: "It undoubtedly constitutes an aspect of the global culture of society, but with sufficient entity to be an object of study in its own right." To this end, García-Gallo proposed to follow the "institutional orientation": only the purely normative aspects of basic social relations were of interest to the legal historian. In reality, the pure and objective "noble dream" of the jurist-historian was in the service of a goal set fifteen years earlier: "to awaken or revive in all parts of America the interest in *derecho indiano*" and to demonstrate scientifically that it "was a decisive element in the forging of the peoples of America, in whom it inoculated the ideals of justice and liberty, who it led – by way of law – to achieve their independence; and because this Indian Law, given that it was common to all Spanish-speaking peoples, together with the language, constitutes the substratum of their cultural community."[53] The *fin-de-siècle* paradigm of Euro-Creole and Catholic *hispanidad* was still present.

New Horizons: The Casuismo *of Víctor Tau*

The rigid separation between the history of *derecho indiano* and the history of the national laws of Latin America guided the work of the *Instituto Internacional* and its conferences, although the methods used for the former did not differ much – the influence of García-Gallo on Latin American legal historiography was and is considerable –[54] from those followed to develop the latter. Changes in themes and approaches only began on the occasion of the eleventh conference in Buenos Aires (1995), thanks to Víctor Tau Azoátegui (1933–2022), a well-known Argentinean legal historian, who was a disciple of Levene and an admirer of Altamira. Tau's long trajectory as an active member of the *Instituto Internacional* revealed, indeed, an original path: he had been interested in customs (third conference, Madrid, 1972; fourth conference, Mexico, 1975; seventh conference, Buenos Aires, 1983), low-ranking norms dictated by lower authorities (sixth conference, Valladolid, 1980), and local objections to the legal orders (fifth conference, Quito-Guayaquil, 1978).[55] His sensitivity to what were, until then, considered

53 García-Gallo, "Problemas metodológicos," 61.

54 As seen in the Ph.D. theses that García-Gallo directed in Madrid: among others, M. N. Oliveros, *La condición jurídica del indio en el Derecho Indiano* (1963); G. Morazzani de Pérez-Enciso, *La reforma del gobierno indiano en el siglo XVIII* (1963); B. Bernal Gómez, *Prudencio Antonio de Palacios: notas a la Recopilación de Leyes de Indias*, Universidad Complutense de Madrid (1976); C. René Salinas Araneda, *De las instituciones de gobierno en Indias*, Universidad Complutense de Madrid (1980).

55 In particular: V. Tau Anzoátegui, *El poder de la costumbre. Estudios sobre el Derecho Consuetudinario en América hispana hasta la Emancipación* (Buenos Aires: Instituto de Investigaciones de Historia del Derecho, 2001).

minor regulations was well demonstrated. At the eleventh conference (1995), his paper was developed and published separately, and *Nuevos horizontes en el estudio histórico del derecho indiano* (1997) offered a new canon for the historical-legal studies of Latin America.

The paper was not the result of chance. Three years earlier, Víctor Tau had published *Casuismo y sistema*, an original treatise whose general theme made it resemble a manual. A basic thesis, however, distanced it from the usual description of sources and institutions: that there was tension between a case-based culture (*casuismo*) and *systematic* efforts, which for this author contained all the experience of the early modern colonial law.[56] Ortega y Gasset's distinction between *beliefs* and *ideas* served Tau to articulate his work: the belief in *casuismo* coexisted with the idea of system, as followed in four fields of analysis (namely, the jurist's apprenticeship, the creation of the law, the jurisprudential works, and the application of the rules). In fact, the culture of *derecho indiano* was always a culture of the case, although it was familiar with ideas of system which were nevertheless extrinsic to the legal object they pretended to organize in a rational manner, and therefore never altered the dominant conception. The final result could not have been more "impure," since the reactivation of "a way of thinking about law" – the dominant case-based approach – which the rationality and abstraction of modern legal conception had condemned to oblivion only seemed possible by framing the legal fact within morality, theology, and politics: "The notion of a closed and sufficient legal order, conceptualized and methodically set out in laws is inapplicable to colonial law."[57] In that operation, the old objective dream that García-Gallo had cherished also disappeared, because "the historian, whose ineludible task is to look at the past, does so from his vantage point, located in the present, where one more turn of history can be glimpsed."[58]

A general revision of the old ways of practicing the history of law soon followed. Regarding legal sources, *Nuevos horizontes* denied the leading role of the law in the face of other norms that concurred with it, but also because it was conceived as just another piece of legal culture. From the point of view of the subject matter, a new catalog of arguments – the public servants and the works of theoretical and practical jurisprudence – was offered for

56 V. Tau Anzoátegui, *Casuismo y sistema. Indagación histórica sobre el espíritu del Derecho Indiano* (Buenos Aires: Instituto de Investigaciones de Historia del Derecho, 1992).

57 Tau Anzoátegui, *Casuismo y sistema*, 571.

58 Tau Anzoátegui, *Casuismo y sistema*, 578. Cf. J. García-Huidobro and D. Pérez Lassarre, "De Altamira y Levene a Tau Anzoátegui (pasando por García-Gallo). Tres aproximaciones al derecho indiano," *Revista de Estudios Histórico-Jurídicos* 39 (2017), 195–212.

future research.[59] But Tau also challenged the temporal barriers established between colonial law and national law by drawing attention to institutional continuity. Subsequent conferences reveal the impact of these proposals, as the study of the nineteenth century has been commonplace since the Toledo conference (the twelfth, in 1998), and in La Rábida (the twentieth conference, 2019) the theme was *Pervivencias del Derecho Indiano en el siglo XIX*. In Berlin (nineteenth conference, 2016), "colonial law in the nineteenth century" was directly addressed.

Broadening Horizons

The eleventh conference held in Buenos Aires introduced a novelty: it included Brazilian historians in the list of "indianistas." Arno and María José Wehling (Rio de Janeiro) contributed a study on the *Tribunal da Relação in Rio de Janeiro*, and their names have since become a regular presence at the meetings. In those years, Arno Wehling, former president of the *Instituto Histórico e Geográfico Brasileiro*, later a member of the *Academia Brasileira das Letras* (2017), participated in the foundation (2002) of the *Instituto Brasileiro de História do Direito*. Its conferences, the latest of which was held in Curitiba (eleventh conference, 2019), bring together Brazilian, American, and European scholars of the subject, and its *Anais* – the annals – constitute a rich body of research by the younger ones.

The Wehlings' approach to Spanish-speaking Latin American legal historiography did not, however, include the communication of methods. A history of the institutions of colonial Brazil was legitimate and possible – few authors promoted it as the Wehlings did – without participating in the scheme of understanding provided by *derecho indiano*. The analysis of this point fell to António Manuel Hespanha, who was responsible for the inaugural lecture at the Berlin conference.

Spanish nationalism and Portugal's civilizing mission were the starting points of the historiographies described there. Portuguese historians have thought of the colonial adventure as an experience that was open to local contexts and the plurality of legal and institutional models; the old discussions on Lusitanian racial origins (Oliveira Martins, Sardinha) marked a vision that prioritized the gentleness and friendly character of the Atlantic nation, a romantic and traveling nation due to its geographical conditions. In contrast,

59 Another legal historian of Buenos Aires stood out in his research on these questions: J. M. Mariluz Urquijo, *El agente de la Administración pública en Indias* (Buenos Aires: Instituto Internacional de Historia del Derecho Indiano and Instituto de Investigaciones de Historia del Derecho, 1998).

drawing on the idea of *hispanidad* – also Catholic and altruistic – scholars of the Spanish expansion in America emphasized its integrating and unitarian character, as revealed, significantly, by the well-known extension of Castilian law to the new territories and their peoples ("the Indies were not colonies"); certainly, exotic circumstances and normative interventions by peripheral authorities provided specific responses to local problems, but these responses were always integrated into the dominant legal system.[60] Despite the constant testimony of diversity and *casuismo*, Spanish-American law was ultimately described as centralist, unitary, and coherent.

Hespanha's lecture concluded that the two Iberian forms of colonialism responded to an identical religious, political, and legal matrix. As such, the duplicity of historiographical traditions did not respond to appreciable differences in the historical materials. Rather, it was the respective cultural traditions of the nations – the feeling of opposition to Castile in the Portuguese case, and the exaltation of the imperial idea in the Spanish case – that allowed different visions to be developed.

Toward a Postcolonial Legal Historiography

The drawback of all this is that Latin America is presented to us as a gigantic *insula in mari nata*, empty and available for occupation by the first discoverer; "some interpretative coordinates," Luigi Nuzzo has rightly written, "from which it was possible to imagine a *derecho indiano* without Indians and without Indies, a legal history of the conquest without conquest and without conquered."[61] This warning finally brings us to the current moment in the historiography of law in Latin America. And here, the work of Bartolomé Clavero stands out in particular.[62]

The connection between "history" and "constitution" has been a constant theme in Clavero's research. Since his first reflections in *Derecho indígena*, this author has endeavored to provide an analysis in which the indigenous is the protagonist element. It is understood, in the classical manner, as a *status* – a

60 Cf. J. Barrientos Grandon, *Historia del Derecho Indiano, del Descubrimiento colombino a la codificación, vol. I: Ius commune – Ius proprium en las Indias Occidentales* (Rome: Il Cigno Galileo-Galilei, 2000).

61 L. Nuzzo, "De Italia a las Indias. Un viaje del derecho común," *Estudios Socio-Jurídicos* 10 (2008), 87–126. Also in *Rechtsgeschichte – Legal History* 12 (2008), 102–24 (in Italian). Most recently, by the same author, "Entre Derecho Indiano y Derecho Internacional. Tradición jurídica europea y crítica del eurocentrismo," in Duve, *Actas del XIX Congreso*, vol. I, 271–89.

62 B. Clavero, *Derecho indígena y cultura constitucional en América* (Mexico City: Siglo XXI, 1994); *Genocidio y justicia. La destrucción de las Indias ayer y hoy* (Madrid: Marcial Pons, 2002); *Constitucionalismo colonial. Oeconomía de Europa, Constitución de Cádiz y más acá*

specific social condition that locates its members at the heart of the unequal and hierarchical society of the *Ancien régime* – which is not merely limited to the category of the *miserable* or the *rustic* that is more frequently used by historiography. That status was the state of *ethnicity*, "legally the space that the colonizers reserved for the colonized."[63] This is undoubtedly another perspective on the term "race," which we know to be decisive in the origins and development of Latin American legal historiography.

According to Clavero, ethnicity is accompanied by another concept, the mere enunciation of which is a condemnation, and a general censure of a complacent history. The European presence in America has been a colossal genocide, committed (and partially denounced) yesterday and today, in a "now" that is only too inclined to enact a "white legend," replicating the *leyenda negra* or "black legend" invoked by mainly Protestant authors to denounce the atrocities committed by the Spanish in America.[64] This author's perspective is one of accusation. "How can we approach colonial history without taking into account the rights of the indigenous peoples who suffered colonialism and suffer its consequences?" is the question – as well as the reproach – launched by Clavero when analyzing António Manuel Hespanha's contributions to a "direito luso-brasileiro" that could result in a tropical reinvention of *derecho indiano*.[65] The question is full of disturbing implications since, in the first place, it draws attention to the omission in the historiographical narrative of the voice of the colonized, whereas philology's recent contributions now allow us to access a body of sources that enable us to hear it. Clavero's use of indigenous languages, at least to title his studies, undoubtedly responds to this new sensitivity.[66] Secondly, and more importantly, historiographical criticism is aimed at unraveling the current effects – as visible in the constitutional and international sphere – of colonial

(Madrid: Universidad Autónoma, 2016); *Europa y su diáspora. Debates sobre colonialismo y derecho* (Santiago de Chile: Olejnik, 2016). For a recent balance, see C. Garriga, "¿Cómo escribir una historia 'descolonizada' del derecho en América latina?," in J. Vallejo, S. Martín (eds.), *En antidora. Homenaje to Bartolomé Clavero* (Cizur Mayor: Thomson Reuters Aranzadi, 2019), 325–76.

63 Clavero, *Derecho indígena*, 19.

64 B. Clavero, *Genocide or Ethnocide, 1933–2007: How to Make, Unmake and Remake Law with Words* (Milano: Giuffrè, 2009).

65 A. Hespanha, *O direito dos letrados no Império português* (Florianópolis: Fundação Boiteux, 2006); also, "Porque é que existe e em que é que consiste um direito colonial brasileiro," *Quaderni fiorentini per la storia del pensiero giuridico moderno* 35 (2006), 59–81. Cf. B. Clavero, "Gracia y derecho entre localización, recepción y globalización. (Lectura coral de las Vísperas constitucionales de António Hespanha)," *Quaderni fiorentini per la storia del pensiero giuridico moderno* 41 (2012), 675–763, 700–707.

66 B. Clavero, *Ama Llunku, Abya Yala. Constituyencia indígena y código ladino por América* (Madrid: Centro de Estudios Políticos y Constitucionales, 2000).

domination, with such relevant examples as modern slavery.[67] The constitutional history of Latin America – and not only Latin America's – started from the implicit understanding and dissimulation of ethnicity to configure a deceitful citizenship; it is enough to recall the example of the Mexican state of Sonora y Sinaloa in the times of the 1824 Federal Constitution – since the state charter (1825) suspended the rights of citizens "for being in the habit of walking shamefully naked." Anthropological diversity sustained the fiction of the public law of independence, prolonging the dictates of the old *derecho indiano*. It should be pointed out that Clavero's suggestions have been passed on to recent Brazilian legal historiography, interested in *povos indígenas* whose rights, yesterday and today, are in continuous dispute.[68]

The history of Latin American law is one, if not the main form, of producing and applying law in Latin America. Or put differently, it is a "history of [Latin American] law in the present."[69] It is thus a delicate object that – negatively – invents traditions, forgets subjects, and offers culturally connoted frameworks of understanding. It also – positively – identifies peoples and pluri-national states; it defends jurisdictions, territories, and resources. Scholarly activity ultimately becomes civic engagement. It is no coincidence that this historiographical renewal coincides with a new international law attentive to indigenous peoples and with a renewed constitutionalism.[70]

. . .

1.2 What Is Legal History and How Does It Relate to Other Histories?

TAMAR HERZOG

Historians, jurists, and legal historians have long debated what legal history is, how it should be done, and what it must accomplish. These debates began long ago and continue to this day. They obscure not only important questions

67 B. Clavero, "Esclavitud y codificación en Brasil, 1888–2017. Por una historia descolonizada del derecho latinoamericano," *Revista de Historia del Derecho* 55 (2018), 27–89.

68 See S. Barbosa, "Usos da história na definição dos direitos territoriais indígenas no Brasil," in M. Carneiro da Cunha and S. Barbosa (eds.), *Direito dos povos indígenas em disputa* (São Paulo: UNESP, 2018), 125–37.

69 B. Clavero, *Constitucionalismo latinoamericano: Estados criollos entre pueblos indígenas y derechos humanos* (Santiago de Chile: Olejnik, 2019), 153.

70 Clavero, *Derecho indígena*, for an anthology of "constitutional recognitions." Specifically, Clavero, *Constitucionalismo latinoamericano*.

related to what history and law are, respectively, but also what is the point in engaging in legal history at all. Is legal history useful for jurists? What about for historians or the public at large? Moreover, what makes a history *legal*? Is it the research object being pursued, the sources used, the methodology employed? Or is it more about the questions asked?

In what follows, I deliberately take issue with how legal historians of Latin America, Spain, and Portugal answered some of these questions. I am conscious of the fact that many other scholars have debated them and that these debates greatly contributed to the emergence of the views held by the Latin American, Spanish, and Portuguese scholars whose work I study and that informs my perspective. I pursue this endeavor convinced that the scholarship I examine is insufficiently known to a wider readership, while at the same time, it has and continues to shape the way the legal history of Latin American law has developed. This analysis focuses on what transpired since the 1960s because, although older visions persist, this volume attempts to follow the lessons we have learned up to this point. In part, I do so also as a tribute to António Manuel Hespanha, whose work inspired so many of us, and who was one of the editors of this project but regretfully passed away before we could bring it to fruition. As I wrote this text, I constantly dialogued with his work as well as repeatedly asked myself: What would he have said? How would he have addressed these questions?

The relations between law and history are quite old. It is often argued that, although the realization that laws change over time reaches back to antiquity, the first inquiry that resembles present-day historical epistemology was popularized by legal humanists who in the fifteenth and sixteenth centuries set out to criticize contemporary jurists for their understanding and use of Roman law.[71] Disputing the operative premise that Roman law could serve as a matrix for a universal and atemporal science of law, legal humanists suggested instead that Roman law was a relic of the past. To study it properly, it would be necessary to develop philological and historical methods aimed

71 A very brief introduction to some of these developments can be found in P. Stein, "Legal Humanism and Legal Science," *Tijdschrift voor Rechtsgeschiedenis* 54(4) (1986), 297–306. Recent scholarship on humanism tends to question some of these conclusions, for example, B. H. Stolte, "Text and Commentary: Legal Humanism," in K. Enenkel and H. Nellen (eds.), *Neo-Latin Commentaries and the Management of Knowledge in the Late Middle Ages and the Early Modern Period (1400–1700)* (Leuven: Leuven University Press, 2012), 387–406; P. Gilli, "Humanisme juridique et science du droit au XV siècle. Tensions compétitives au sein des élites lettrées et réorganisation du champ politique," *Revue de Synthèse* 130(4) (2009), 571–93; and P. J. du Plessis and J. W. Cairns (eds.), *Reassessing Legal Humanism and Its Claims: Petere Fontes?* (Edinburgh: Edinburgh University Press, 2016).

at reconstructing the original texts while also devising ways to restore their original meaning. Among the methods legal humanists proposed was considering non-legal sources and even artifacts, studying the evolution of language, as well as imagining how readers and practitioners of that time might have comprehended things. Convinced that law was the product of society and therefore must be studied in both its temporal and geographical contexts, legal humanists also turned to observe the local customary law, which they argued was the true law of their communities. Thereafter, and using legal history both as a guide and weapon, legal humanists described Europe not only as a space for a *ius commune* but also as a patchwork of local legal solutions dependent on the time, place, and speakers involved. They envisioned a peaceful coexistence between a universal science of law and a plethora of specific arrangements that were constantly elaborated, changed, or abandoned by multiple individuals, groups, and communities who sought to define the rules that should guide their interactions.

In their quest to study law properly, fifteenth- and sixteenth-century legal humanists thus contributed to the development of historical methods. Yet, relations between law and history are not only the outcome of scholarly pursuits; they are also embedded in the very nature of juridical practice. More often than not, this practice centers on understanding the legal consequences of something that had already transpired. Evaluating the juridical meaning of both existing norms and past events necessarily involves a certain historical reconstruction, yet jurists and judges who seek to establish how to read certain texts, or how to appraise certain actions, do so in ways both similar and dissimilar to historians.[72] While the similarities are quite clear – attention to words, detail, context, and circumstances – so too are the differences. Jurists and judges have a practical reason to engage in evaluating historical evidence, namely, the need to solve conflicts. It is legitimate for them, indeed frequently even required, that they ignore all that is not essential to attaining that end. What they seek to uncover is mostly a "usable past," which can serve as a resource in the present. To draw conclusions, jurists often selectively piece together, reorganize, and reconfigure disparate events that *a priori* are not necessarily related to one another or are connected in ways other

72 The distinction between a juridical and a historical truth has been the object of many studies, perhaps most famous among them, at least for historians, is C. Ginzburg, *The Judge and the Historian: Marginal Notes on a Late-Twentieth-Century Miscarriage of Justice*, trans. A. Shugaar (London and New York: Verso, 1999). The issue, however, has been the subject of debate for a long time. See, for example, P. Calamendrei, *Il giudice e lo storico* (Milan: Giuffrè Editore, 1939).

than what they postulate. In other words, their reconstructions are not necessarily intended to uncover the truth, the whole truth, and nothing but the truth, but instead to achieve a certain goal. Jurists also inhabit an adversarial culture. There, it is completely normal to claim authority over certain interpretations, arguing that they and *only* they are correct. This same attitude is applied to their observations of the past, ascribing certainty and singularity where none existed. While historians of course also make decisions about what to include and what to ignore, or how to read what they uncover, their aim is not the attainment of a specific result but the expansion of knowledge. The conclusions and findings of their analyses normally follow the same epistemic rationale: They are not considered definitive, but instead open to rexamination, discussion, and change.[73] Most historians admit the possibility of a multiplicity of responses, and they are not particularly alarmed by ambiguity, by questions that cannot be answered, or that the past may not tell us all that we need in the present.

Jurists of course also intervene in history by writing it through pleading in the courts or delivering judicial decisions. A judge that orders the correction of a report elaborated by a truth commission, for example, deleting the name of an individual who is listed as having committed human rights violations, interferes with what is knowable and what is considered to have been proven.[74] Judges also intervene in the production of history when they sit in commissions or trials in which they adjudicate conflicts and determine what had transpired. In all these cases, the proceedings they conduct not only supply evidence that historians can use but also rulings that often illuminate – even determine, in the eyes of many – what the past contained. Juridical reconstruction of history can also be implicit, for example, when judges take

73 R. G. Ortiz Treviño, "Algo acerca del oficio del historiador del derecho," *Anuario Mexicano de Historia del Derecho* 18 (2006), 463–85, at 256–59. A (relatively) early reflection on these differences is included in J. Sankey, "The Historian and the Lawyer. Their Aims and their Methods," *History* 21(82) (1936), 97–108. I found the following most illuminating: J. M. Balkin, "Lawyers and Historians Argue About the Constitution," *Constitutional Commentary* 35 (2020), 345–400. The term "usable past" is discussed by Balkin, for example at 383–400.

74 Decision dated Recife (Brazil), Apr. 8, 2021, of the Federal Judge of 6-Vara-Pe, Hélio Silvio Querém Campos, in *Marcos Olinto Ovais de Sousa and Maria Fernanda Novais de Souza Cavalcanti v. União Federal* – União, Processo no. 0824561-44.2019.4.05.8300. The decision is available online at https://averdade.org.br/novo/wp-content/uploads/2022/02/5decd83d-jfpe.pdf (last accessed Mar. 15, 2022). On whether courts should or can decide on which past is verified, also see the most recent C. Douzinas, "History Trials: Can Law Decide History?," *The Annual Review of Law and Social Sciences* 8 (2012), 273–89; and G. Resta and V. Zeno-Zencovich, "Judicial 'Truth' and Historical 'Truth': The Case of the Ardeatine Caves Massacre," *Law and History Review* 31(4) (2013), 843–86.

"judicial notice" of allegations that involve assumptions about the past or that interpret the past in certain ways that are said to be consensual.[75] Though supposedly encapsulating common knowledge, controversies among judges, for example, regarding the history of discrimination, the meaning of family over time, or the legacies of WWII, demonstrate that such assumptions and interpretations are not uncontentious.

Expressed in different terms, behind all judicial decisions lies a narrative – implicit or explicit – on how things came to be as well as which lessons have the power to influence our vision of the past and can, therefore, be mobilized to support present-day agendas.[76] The writing of history by jurists and judges is particularly daunting because they are often ill-equipped to evaluate historical events, yet their rulings provide these events with a definitive narrative that can potentially acquire a normative value.[77]

Despite the enormous differences between historical and legal pursuits, many early historians were jurists, and they employed the techniques of exegesis, discovery, and reconstruction they acquired by studying and practicing law. Though this holds true in many different places, it is particularly illustrative of how scholarly engagement with Spanish American history has developed. In Spain, for example, many consider Eduardo Hinojosa y Naveros (1852–1919) to be the founder of historical studies. Hinojosa also trained many of those who would later go on to become historians of Spanish America. Nevertheless, Hinojosa was a jurist whose work was not particularly focused on legal questions.[78] Along similar lines, the first university chairs dedicated to the history of the Americas were established in the early twentieth

75 "Judicial notice" includes knowledge that parties do not have to prove because it is supposed to be common to all members of society, for example, what day of the week it is or the location of the court. However, it can also include more questionable facts such as the date on which colonialism ended or who was involved in a certain war. On these and other issues, see D. Barak-Erez, "History and Memory in Constitutional Adjudication," *Federal Law Review* 45(1) (2017), 1–16.

76 J. Balkin, *Constitutional Redemption: Political Faith in an Unjust World* (Cambridge: Harvard University Press, 2011), 3.

77 Presently, there is a significant debate among historians, for example, regarding how the US Supreme Court implements the doctrine of "originalism," which states that the US federal constitution should be interpreted according to the intentions of its authors. This doctrine requires that judges reconstruct what late eighteenth-century authors meant, as well as the context in which they operated. On their failure (perhaps refusal) to do so correctly, see, for example, the criticism by J. N. Rakove, "The Second Amendment: The Highest State of Originalism," *Chicago-Kent Law Review* 76(1) (2000), 103–66; and R. Piller, "History in the Making: Why Courts are Ill-Equipped to Employ Originalism," *Review of Litigation* 34(1) (2015), 187–212.

78 J. Sánchez-Arcilla Bernal, "Alfonso García-Gallo: Aportaciones metodológicas y conceptuales a la historia del derecho," *Cuadernos de Historia del Derecho* 18 (2011), 13–49, at 19–20.

century. These chairs were either situated in law faculties or their holders, among them Antonio Ballesteros Beretta, Rafael Altamira y Crevea, and José María Ots Capdequi, taught both history and law.[79] These intellectuals were also responsible for expanding the legal history of Spain (*Historia del derecho español*) to include colonial law – a law that eventually came to be identified as *derecho indiano* (see Section 1.1).

Developments in early twentieth-century Spanish America were not very distinct. The Argentinean Ricardo Levene, for example, held the chair of history before switching to legal history; the Mexican Silvio Zavala, who studied law, spent most of his career among historians; and the Brazilian Salomão de Vasconcellos, who trained as a lawyer but went on to become a prominent historian. This generation of foundational scholars, all trained in law, did not distinguish between history and legal history. Regardless of whether they were working in law faculties, history departments, studied history, or studied law, they used similar sources and pursued similar objectives to such an extent that it is often difficult to ascertain their formal education and field to which they belonged.[80]

Later generations did not continue pursuing this initial convergence of disciplines. Legal historians writing on this parting of ways usually blamed historians for having abandoned the law in favor of social and economic history, which, whether under the spell of the *Annales* school or Marxism, portrayed law as a stale and irrelevant pursuit. Historians, they argued, moved away from legal and political history, adopted quantitative methods, and embraced longer temporal periods, moves that together often resulted in the removal

79 V. Tau Anzoátegui, "Instituciones y derecho indiano en una renovada historia de América," *Anuario de Estudios Americanos* 75(2) (2018), 435–58, at 438–39; and F. Tomás y Valiente, "Escuelas e historiografía en la historia del derecho español (1960–1985)," in B. Clavero, P. Grossi, and F. Tomás y Valiente (eds.), *Hispania. Entre derechos propios y derechos nacionales. Atti dell'incontro di studio, Firenze-Lucca, 25, 26, 27 maggio 1989* (Milan: Giuffrè Editore, 1990), vol. I, 11–46, at 13 and 17–18.

80 On the influence of Spanish scholars on the development of Spanish American legal history, see, for example, J. del Arenal Fenochio, "De Altamira a Grossi: presencia de historiadores extranjeros del derecho en México," *Historia Mexicana* 55(4) (2006), 1467–95; P. Mijangos y González, *El Nuevo Pasado Jurídico mexicano. Una revisión de la historiografía jurídica mexicana durante los últimos 20 años* (Madrid: Universidad Carlos III, 2011), for example, at 19–23; and C. Villegas del Castillo, "Historia y Derecho: La interdisciplinariedad del derecho y los retos de la historia del derecho," *Revista de Derecho Público* 22 (2009), 3–22, at 9–10 who also mentions Colombian historians who had a law degree at 7. In Spain, Antonio Muro, who was trained in law, initially dedicated his attention to non-legal history: A. García-Gallo, "Antonio Muro. Historiador del derecho indiano," *Anuario de Estudios Americanos* 22 (1974), XXI–XXXIX. The same was true of many others in Spain, Portugal, and Latin America, for example, M. Habel de Vasconcellos, "Salomão de Vasconcellos. Doctor, Lawyer, Historian," *Americas* 30(5) (1978), 17–20.

of law from their list of research interests. Even if this analysis rings true, it is equally clear that legal historians have also contributed to this estrangement by abandoning history and by producing studies that mainly sought to reconstruct the genealogy of rules and institutions, a genealogy that was generally portrayed as the progressive betterment that led to present-day structures.[81] Conceiving of law in terms of an autonomous field, law faculties in Latin America, Spain, and Portugal monopolized legal history, and its practitioners were mainly interested in what some have identified as an "internal" history that looked at the law as if it had no "external" history, for example, its relationship to society.

Reacting to this growing separation, from the late 1960s onwards, many Latin American, Spanish, and Portuguese legal historians expressed their commitment to another type of legal history that also doubled as social, institutional, and political history.[82] To do so, proponents of these visions advanced a new understanding of what legal history is and ought to be. They called upon jurists to engage with the historicity of the law and appealed to historians to both acknowledge the pervasiveness of law and recognize its particularities. Yet, despite the desire to bring law and history together again, these legal historians never claimed that the two pursuits were one and the same. Instead, and as discussed later, they wanted history to improve the study of law, and the study of law to improve history. They asked questions

81 These attitudes, of course, were not particular to Latin American, Spanish, or Portuguese scholars. See, for example, P. D. Halliday, "Legal History: Taking the Long View," in M. D. Dubber and C. Tomlins (eds.), *The Oxford Handbook of Legal History* (Oxford: Oxford University Press, 2018), 323–42, at 325–26.

82 A. M. Hespanha, "Is There a Place for a Separate Legal History? A Broad Review of Recent Developments on Legal Historiography," *Quaderni fiorentini per la storia del pensiero giuridico moderno* 48 (2019), 7–29. Some of these developments are reviewed in the article. These historians responded to the contrary visions that argued that legal history was a juridical rather than a historical science. An example of this debate and its pan-European ramifications can be found in A. García Gallo, "Cuestiones de historiografía jurídica," *Anuario de Historia del Derecho Español* 44 (1974), 741–64; and the responses by F. Tomás y Valiente, "Historia del derecho e historia," in J. J. Carreras Ares, A. Eiras Roel, A. Elorza Domínguez, et al. (eds.), *Once ensayos sobre la historia* (Madrid: Fundación Juan March, 1976), 160–81; and B. Clavero, "La historia del derecho ante la historia social," *Historia. Instituciones. Documentos* 1 (1974), 239–61. The participation of Latin American scholars in these debates is examined in R. M. Fonseca, *Introducción teórica a la historia del derecho*, trans. A. Mora Cañada, R. Ramis Barceló, and M. Martínez Neira (Madrid: Universidad Carlos III, 2012), in particular the chapters on the *Annales* school and Marxism at 71–111; and A. Levaggi, "Consideraciones sobre investigación en historia del derecho," *IUShistoria Investigaciones* 5 (2012), 433–49. On a multidisciplinary vision of the law, also see M. Brutti and A. Somma (eds.), *Diritto: storia e comparazione. Nuovi propositi per un binomio antico* (Global Perspectives on Legal History 11) (Frankfurt am Main: Max-Planck-Institute für europäische Rechtsgeschichte, 2018).

about the nature of legal history, and they advanced reasons for why being familiar with it would be important for both jurists and historians.

The first target identified by this new generation of legal historians was the traditional divide; a division retained by jurists and historians alike and that distinguished "law in the books" from "law in practice." This divide, they argued, was the result of a misunderstanding of how law operates, among other things, because it assumes that law was the same as legislation and restricts its study to state-made normativity. Instead of following such a reductive reading, these legal historians defended the view that their task was to ask what the juridical value of certain phenomena was, what roles did law play in social formation, and how juridical grammar and technology affected reality. They envisioned the study of legal history as a pursuit meant to elucidate how a technology we now identify as "legal" was used to organize, arrange, and rearrange social relations, as well as grant words and actions a normative value that placed them in a hierarchy granting greater protection to some things over others. By employing methods of abstraction, and by constructing similarities and distinctions without ever losing sight of the concrete circumstances and contexts of each case, law's final aim, they argued, is to propose solutions that would guarantee a certain equilibrium between conflict and consensus by legitimizing certain things but not others, or at least not to the same extent. As a result, any study of knowledge production, social practices, or power relations, to mention but three examples, needs to reflect on law (see Sections 1.3 and 1.4 and Chapter 3).

Asking about which actors were involved in each case, their rationale, how divisions and distinctions were constructed, as well as what kinds of answers the law supplied and how prescriptive they were, these legal historians conceived of the legal field as one in which everyone participates to some degree or another. Some actors might exercise more control, possess greater agency, or have a better understanding of how the legal system works, but no one lives outside the law or completely independent of it, not even those at the social extremes: the very privileged and the heavily oppressed.

Criticizing both formalism and statism, these legal historians also rejected legal nationalism, which presupposes that law is the product (and reflection) of a particular community or nation, as the German Historical School had once argued. Like legal humanists before them, they suggested instead that law, though always attentive to local circumstances, was also a technology that crossed political, ethnic, and national borders. Finally, these legal historians argued that law should not be studied as a separate body of norms that are completely autonomous and unrelated to other normative phenomena.

Rather than imposed from the outside (as a statist formalist approach would lead us to believe), or forming a permanent and stable structure from within (as proponents of customary law presented it), they suggested that law, though varying to a great extent across time and geographies, is nonetheless a scaffold that seeks to give structure and meaning to human interactions, as well as acts as a means to arrange and rearrange them.

These views, which reflected a new understanding of the thematic field that legal history must cover, also insisted on the historicity of law. Accordingly, it is insufficient to ask about the historicity of a particular event, piece of legislation, or moment. To understand legal history, we must also consider how the legal context mutated, that is, how the legal framework in which different solutions operated differed over time. The task these legal historians adopted as their own was, therefore, to explain that law as a technology of conflict resolution had a history of its own, and that this history must be uncovered if we are to understand how law interacted with society. For example, medieval and early modern schemes for administrative work, they observed, can best be found in theories of judgment rendering and the history of the family, not in administrative correspondence or in royal decrees. Because the logic of past normative arrangements was so different from our own, to understand how they operated we must consider areas of legal research such as the juridical norms of the domestic sphere (see Section 3.3), religious normativity (see Sections 3.1 and 3.2), the legal valence of friendship and love, or even the jurisprudence tied to the various colors.[83]

Remembering that not only particular solutions but also the legal context constantly mutated would have us ask, to mention yet another example, when did *directum* (the prior term for "law" in many European languages) supersede *ius* (the ancient Roman term) as the most immediate label designating "law"? What can this transition tell us about societal expectations across Europe, where this mutation took place in some areas but not in others? Why was justice (*ius*) tied to direction (*dirigere* as in *directum*) in certain times and places but not in others?[84] How can we understand the radically

83 B. Clavero, *Antidora. Antroplogía católica de la economía moderna* (Milan: Giuffrè Editore, 1991); A. M. Hespanha, *La gracia del derecho. Economía de la Cultura en la Edad Moderna* (Madrid: Centro de Estudios Constitucionales, 1993); and A. M. Hespanha, "As cores e a instituição da ordem no mundo de antigo regime," in A. Wehling, G. Siqueira, and S. Barbosa (eds.), *História do direito. Entre rupturas, crises e descontinuidades* (Belo Horizonte: Arraes Editores, 2018), 1–18.

84 S. Cruz, *Ius. Decretum (Directum)* (Coimbra: Universidade de Coimbra, 1971). On these issues, also see A. García Gallo, "Ius y derecho," *Anuario de Historia del Derecho Español* 30 (1960), 5–48.

different ways in which certain documents were read over time, such as the emblematic Magna Carta, if we did not appreciate the constantly evolving contexts in which they were interpreted?[85]

These observations were aimed at convincing readers that law itself is not an atemporal or ahistorical construct that could be discussed in the abstract as if it were the same unchanging phenomenon. If we already recognize that the meaning of law can differ from place to place, time to time, and according to who is observing, we must also remember that the role law occupies in society does not remain static, and neither does the precise technology it proposes or what it considers prescriptive.

For this group of scholars, it was particularly important to assert the specific character of the late medieval and early modern law, which they claimed was distinct from our present-day structures, though the opposite is commonly thought to be the case. Distinctiveness was not only tied to the obvious fact that specific solutions were different, but mainly to the fact that the basic assumptions regarding what law is, how it operates, what it is supposed to accomplish, how it pretends to intervene in society, and the relations it has with other normative and cultural spheres were vastly different. Late medieval and early modern law did not dictate solutions (see Sections 3.1 and 3.2); instead, it indicated which questions should be asked and what considerations should be taken into account. What law did, therefore, was to aid in making a just decision by advancing options, explaining variations, and imagining possibilities, all while giving actors a tremendous amount of discretion as to which road they take. In other words, law was a system in which a plurality of options existed, as well as a multiplicity of sources and authorities, all of which were equally valid and none *a priori* superior to the other.

The wish to problematize the past also led this group of legal historians to rebel against portraying it as consisting of "systems" that preceded one another in an orderly fashion.[86] Such a depiction implied a degree of regularity and unity that was largely absent. A "system" presupposed a hierarchy of sources, a clear catalog of values, and/or a singular rationality. Yet, medieval and early modern law featured a casuistic universe. Furthermore, the image of various systems preceding one another portrayed the development of law as a

85 T. Herzog, *A Short History of European Law: The Last Two and a Half Millennia* (Cambridge: Harvard University Press, 2018), 1–2, 5, and 145–48.

86 V. Tau Anzoátegui, *Casuismo y sistema. Indagación histórica sobre el espíritu del Derecho Indiano* (Buenos Aires: Instituto de Investigaciones de Historia del Derecho, 1992); Tomás y Valiente, "Escuelas e historiografía," 29; and Sánchez-Arcilla Bernal, "Alfonso García-Gallo," 26–27 and 30–31.

succession of schools and centers, as in the stereotypical depiction of European law: conceived in Italy, developed in France, and improved in Holland.[87] It also sent historians to "juridical traditions" that were supposed to communicate homogeneity and permanence as well as singularity and distinction when compared to all others. These legal historians argued that such images of the legal past undermined the important role of plurality, interpenetration, flexibility, and constant updating.[88] Proposing abstractions that were perhaps necessary for lawyers in their pursuit of resolving conflicts, they nonetheless entailed a form of violence that imposed on the past our present-day desire for clarity and certitude. Instead of searching for clear answers, legal history must describe the variety of voices, contrasting positions, and alternative proposals that, rather than depicting the past as "the kingdom of what is predetermined," would demonstrate that it was "the theatre of possibilities."[89]

One of the remarkable results of this move to historicize not only legal application but also law itself was, for example, the preoccupation of this group of legal historians with the creation, administration, and imposition of categories. Who had the power to create legal categories? How prescriptive were they and how were they managed? How did the emergence of categories change society and societal processes? Identifying law as an essential instrument for creating, imposing, and debating distinctions between right and wrong, as well as between what could be considered efficient and useless, also led to the obvious observation that the greatest struggle in history was perhaps not so much for social and economic prominence but over the ability to create and impose norms. This, as Foucault would probably have argued, may seem a gentler way to order the world, but as a technique, it was no less powerful and no less violent.[90]

The proponents of these views also took issue with practitioners, whom they accused of anachronistic approaches motivated *not* by ignoring

87 F. Wieacker, *Privatrechtsgeschichte der Neuzeit unter besonderer Berücksichtigung der deutschen Entwicklung* (Göttingen: Vandenhoeck & Ruprecht, 1967), 169.

88 T. Duve, "Tradições jurídicas' e história do direito," in A. Wehling, G. Siqueira, and S. Barbosa (eds.), *História do direito. Entre rupturas, crises e descontinuidades* (Belo Horizonte: Arraes Editores, 2018), 19–41.

89 T. Duve, "Pragmatic Normative Literature and the Production of Normative Knowledge in the Early Modern Iberian Empires (16th–17th centuries)," in T. Duve and O. Danwerth (eds.), *Knowledge of the Pragmatici: Legal and Moral Theological Literature and the Formation of Early Modern Ibero-America* (Leiden: Brill Nijhoff, 2020), 1–39, at 5–9.

90 A. M. Hespanha, "Sábios e Rústicos. A doce violência da razão jurídica," *Revista Crítica de Ciências Sociais* 25–26 (1988), 31–60; and A. M. Hespanha, *Imbecillitas. As Bem-Aventuranças da Inferioridade nas Sociedades do Antigo Regime* (São Paulo: Annablume Editora, 2012).

change over time – most of them knew that laws and practices constantly mutated – but by the refusal to grant sufficient attention to what else had changed. They suggested that many jurists and historians employed a retrospective quest that mostly searched the present in the past by tracing its "roots" or "origins." Others went to extraordinary lengths to justify or legitimize their preference of present-day arrangements, in some cases rendering the past incomprehensible or even ridiculous. Either way, this regressive history, which made the past look like the present, might have questioned institutions, laws, and practices, but it did not observe the legal system itself. By going down this road, proponents of this type of history argued for continuity where none existed, and they ignored all that was no longer relevant to the present or was simply too strange or too counterintuitive to digest.

While pleading that we remember that the legal framework, and not only individual solutions, was subject to mutation, these legal historians also advocated the need to take law seriously via a close examination of its logic. Law, they argued, may use words that seem comprehensible, but like all technologies that seek to influence reality, such words carry a tremendous amount of baggage – and this baggage needs to be taken into consideration when examining legal language. In other words, though it is essential to understand the conditions that led to the emergence of certain terms, ideas, categories, or practices, it is also vital to consider that all of them have the consistency of loose sand. Like all other words, and probably more so than most words, legal terms appear immobile and immune to change; however, in reality, they are constantly shifting.

Take, for example, an apparently straightforward term like "family." While families may very well have always existed, the definition of a "family" has dramatically changed from a voluntary association of individuals in antiquity to structures we now conceive as based on blood relations. The meaning and extension of blood relations also constantly mutated: Whose blood mattered, how, why, and to what degree? Over time, law recognized radically different configurations of "family," applying to them a series of changing rights and obligations as well as intervening in them to various extents and in a multiplicity of ways. The literal continuity of terms such as family, therefore, masked deep and constant changes, with "a radical discontinuity of sense lurking beneath the ostensible uniformity of worlds."[91] To rescue family

91 A. M. Hespanha, "Legal History and Legal Education," *Rechtsgeschichte – Legal History* 4 (2004), 41–56, at 43.

law, in other words, it is insufficient to show that rules regarding the family changed. It is necessary to inquire as to what a family was, who posed the question, why, when, where did the multiplicity of answers originate, and how prescriptive or discretionary were the answers.

If "family" as a right and obligation-bearing entity was a completely different affair depending on the place and time, to rescue its history would require not only knowing a great deal about the location, period, and actors but also take into consideration how law intervened in such debates by giving different factual constellations a juridical meaning. This meaning depended on facts, but it mainly operates by attributing to these facts a normative value and by asking about their juridical significance. By using the persuasive power of language, law employs words to obtain certain goals. Though law also uses coercion and violence, it mostly seeks to convince by using language – which is why, by definition, it always includes a variety of options and involves lengthy debates that the parties use to demonstrate why they are right and the others are wrong.

To understand how the term "family" was "normalized" in the sense that at different moments in time, it was granted different normative meanings, one would have to reconstruct these debates. Family, in other words, may be a term we presently take for granted, or some consider a natural institution, but if we keep in mind that in other periods it was conceived as a constructed, artificial unit, we maybe able to liberate ourselves from considering its existence or meaning a forgone conclusion. This would also remind us that, because law has a normalizing effect, and because this effect is always part of broader discussions, the terms it uses are an open sesame that invites scholars to unfold what is otherwise unseen. Family operates in this way, but so do many other placeholders such as intention, customs, immemoriality, or consent.

Of course, one could argue that these placeholders only operate within a restricted field established by jurists or juridical experts. Yet this conclusion would defy all that we observe in society – both past and present. In this transformative process of facts to phenomena with normative value, particular traditions and practices matter, and they matter not only to jurists but also to contemporaries who use the law. How else can we explain the claims of illiterate peasants that they had to resist incursions on their territory by neighbors or else their silence would be construed as consent?[92] Alternatively, how

92 T. Herzog, *Frontiers of Possession: Spain and Portugal in Europe and the Americas* (Cambridge: Harvard University Press, 2015), 8, 34, 37–48, 106–7, 139–40, 203, and 237.

can we understand why a plethora of individuals, unable to prove what they wanted, invoked immemoriality? They knew that it was a powerful tool even if they did not know why.[93]

In this quest to refashion legal history, these Latin American, Spanish, and Portuguese scholars refuted the claim that the history of ideas was a legal history or that legal historians can stop at describing how norms evolved. They lamented the propensity by which actors invoke history to make claims in the present, and they expressed a desire for a legal history that would transcend national boundaries and be guided by the entities that were relevant in the past, not the present. They would ask questions such as: Was there a colonial law or is this law tied to our current needs and therefore a fiction of our imagination? Would it not be more appropriate to ask about transfers, translations, and exchanges as well as follow practices and processes of analysis and determination as they crossed the oceans than create categories *a priori*? (see Sections 1.3, 1.4, and 3.1 and Chapter 4).

If how to study legal history was a major issue for these legal historians, another involved the role it should play. In the past, these scholars argued, legal history mainly served either to strategically legitimize or criticize existing structures. Legal humanists strove to employ the power of local law against both universalistic tendencies and the increasing powers of kings. In nineteenth-century Germany, legal history served to justify as well as facilitate both German unification and debates regarding the character of German law. The instrumentalization of history to support political projects is, of course, a very common phenomenon. However, in the case of legal history, they argued, it has a particularly pernicious effect because this use reinforced the tendencies to portray legal evolution as linear and foretold. It often transformed the past into a repository of either better times to be recaptured or horrible times to be avoided.[94]

Rather than justifying or explaining the present – as many have done in the past – these scholars encouraged practitioners to transform legal history into a space of critical observation. They argued that recognizing legal historicity and the extreme alterity of the past should enable us to imagine alternative

93 T. Herzog, "Immemorial (and Native) Customs in Early Modernity: Europe and the Americas," *Comparative Legal History* 9(1) (2021), 1–53, 2, 22–34, 36, and 46–47.

94 Mijangos y González, *El Nuevo Pasado*, 23–25; Fonseca, *Introducción teórica*, 65–66; and S. S. Staut Júnior, "Direito e história: Algumas preocupações a partir da obra de António Manuel Hespanha," in A. Peixoto de Souza (ed.), *Estudos de história e historiografia do direito em homenagem ao professor António Manuel Hespanha* (Curitiba and Madrid: Editora Intersaberes, Marcial Pons, 2020), 31–56, at 36–42.

and unexpected routes in the present as well.[95] Instead of looking into a mirror, legal history could force us to look at familiar things from a different perspective – one that would question, rather than confirm, our present-day biases. For legal history to do so, we must seek not only to record but also to explain in the etymological sense of *ex-plicare*: the unfolding and revealing of hidden aspects that were either too obvious or too consensual for contemporaries to even mention, let alone elucidate.[96] According to this usage, it would be often more important to ask questions than to answer them, to express doubts than to look for certainties.[97] Thereafter, the goal would be to "make and unmake history" (*fazer e desfazer a história*) while also constructing and deconstructing the law.[98] This quest would transform the study of sources into an instrument rather than an end in and of itself.[99] The same could be said of episodes and events.

The extent to which these calls have been heeded remains to be seen. Though communication between jurists, historians, and legal historians has intensified in recent decades, and indeed legal history seems to be everywhere, formalist legal history remains popular, and there are still plenty of books that describe the legal past with certitude, reconstructing rules rather than possibilities, norms rather than discussions.[100] Meanwhile, many historians continue to either dismiss law altogether or consider it an external scaffolding rather than an internal spinal cord of all social interaction.[101] Perceiving law as a superstructure and believing that the social, political, or economic could be reconstructed by ignoring or at least marginalizing the law, many historians, who are otherwise extremely sensitive to historical contexts, nevertheless fail to contextualize

95 G. Silveira Siqueira, "História do direito como um olhar para o futuro: entre as experiências jurídicas e os horizontes de expectativas," in A. Peixoto de Souza (ed.), *Estudos de história e historiografia do direito em homenagem ao professor António Manuel Hespanha* (Curitiba and Madrid: Editora Intersaberes, Marcial Pons, 2020), 99–211.

96 Fonseca, *Introducción teórica*, for example, 18, 24, and 38.

97 J. Vallejo, "En busca de audiencias perdidas: a propósito de Bartolomé Clavero, 'Sevilla, Concejo y Audiencia: invitación a sus Ordenanzas de Justicia,' estudio preliminar (pp. 5–95) de *Ordenanzas de la Real Audiencia de Sevilla*, edición facsímil de las de 1603–1632, Sevilla, Audiencia/Diputación/Universidad/Fundación El Monte, 1995, 1001 pp.," *Quaderni fiorentini per la storia del pensiero giuridico moderno* 25(1) (1996), 711–27, at 715–16.

98 Â. Barreto Xavier, "António Manuel Hespanha: Fazer e desfazer a história," *Cuadernos de Historia Moderna* 44(2) (2019), 689–91. "Fazer e desfazer a história" was also the subtitle of a history journal with which A. M. Hespanha was long associated.

99 Clavero, "La historia del derecho," 247.

100 For example, I. Sánchez Bella, A. de la Hera, and C. Diaz Rementería, *Historia del derecho indiano* (Madrid: Editorial Mapfre, 1992); and M. Mirow, *Latin American Law: A History of Private Law and Institutions in Spanish America* (Austin: University of Texas Press, 2004).

101 From that perspective, little has changed since the 1970s when Tomás y Valiente lamented these attitudes: F. Tomás y Valiente, "Historia del derecho," 166–67; or in 2005 when A. M. Hespanha denounced them, *Cultura jurídica europeia: síntese de un milênio* (Florianópolis: Fundação Boiteux, 2005), 45.

and historicize the law. They adhere to a very narrow understanding of the law, equating it with present-day structures, or they implicitly use law as a synonym for state legislation in periods that, paradoxically, predated the emergence of states. Many also frequently assume that law prescribes solutions, that the words it employs have an obvious meaning, or they imagine that interpreting law to one's advantage is a form of resistance. As a result, otherwise incredibly respectful historians can confuse ancient Roman law with the Roman law that Europeans brought with them to the Americas (the revived medieval Roman law that formed part of the *ius commune* and that was largely distinct from ancient Roman law). Or, alternatively, they arrive at conclusions pointing out that certain actors (but not others) used the law as a "resource" rather than a "script" or that actors could choose and pick what to follow.[102] They suggest that the distinctions we currently maintain between state and international law (or inter-polity) had always been meaningful, and they express surprise when "internal" law affects "external" developments.[103] Many historians also routinely insist on a gap between law and its application, that is, "law in the books" versus "law in action." This allows them to see lawlessness and corruption or, on the contrary, agency where none exists. Where others see a soccer match, they only see many individuals running aimlessly after a ball.[104]

. . .

1.3 How Is Law Produced?

THOMAS DUVE

If legal history is the history of "law," the question as to what is meant by "law" needs to be addressed. Philosophers have tried to answer this question for centuries. If defining law today proves difficult, then finding a concept

102 L. Benton and B. Straumann, "Acquiring Empire by Law: From Roman Doctrine to Early Modern European Practice," *Law and History Review* 28(1) (2010), 1–38; and L. Benton, "Possessing Empire. Iberian Claims and International Law," in S. Belmessous (ed.), *Native Claims: Indigenous Law Against Empire, 1500–1920* (Oxford: Oxford University Press, 2012), 19–40, at 19 and 21–22.

103 For a particularly critical take on such anachronistic assumptions, see M. Koskenniemi, *To the Uttermost Parts of the Earth: Legal Imagination and International Power, 1300–1870* (Cambridge: Cambridge University Press, 2021).

104 See my response to a forum discussing my text *Frontiers of Possession* in M. Barbot, A. Stopani, and T. Herzog, "A proposito di 'Frontiers of Possession' di Tamar Herzog," *Quaderni Storici* 51(2) (2016), 538–87, at 586. I have to thank Thomas Duve for this image, which he included in a review of the book: T. Duve, "Grenzenlose Räume," *Rechtsgeschichte – Legal History* 23 (2015), 307–8.

determining "the law" of the past would seem to present an almost insurmountable challenge, and raises a whole host of questions: What to include into our observation of Latin American colonial law? How broadly does one draw the semantic field? Should one also take into consideration, for example, *usos, costumbres,* or *ritos*? Moreover, how should indigenous laws be included in legal history? What about rules stemming from the field categorized by Western modernity as "religion," often distinguished from "morality" and "law" but fulfilling many similar functions?

Even if these questions go unanswered, researchers are inevitably operating with a certain concept of law, or at least with a pre-understanding of what it is they are looking for in the past. Critical reflection on these assumptions is a central dimension of global legal history, given its explicit aims to overcome methodological Eurocentrism, historiographic neocolonialism, and to decenter analytical tools and perspectives (see Section 1.4).[105] No critical exercise of self-reflection, however, can replace the need to explicitly define what object of observation we actually constitute when writing legal history. For even if we pretend to limit ourselves to observing practice, we still focus on specific actors, specific actions, and describe our findings in a specific language. While these choices are perhaps unconscious, they are by no means innocent.

For a long time, as Carlos Petit and Tamar Herzog show (Sections 1.1 and 1.2), jurists writing on Latin American legal history, interested in the prehistory of the legal institutions of their times, analyzed the past by employing a concept of law taken from the present. Anachronism was a practice, not a postulate.[106] In recent decades, however, a growing number of scholars have become critical of this tradition and propose leaving aside the search for "the" concept of law. Instead, they suggest understanding law in terms of a communicative practice, focusing more on the way people actually speak and act than searching for some possible underlying concept of law. Following this approach, researchers began devoting attention to documents of legal practice and to the processes of production of law.

This change of perspective not only had an invigorating effect on legal historical research in general terms, it has also proved particularly important with regard to two fundamental methodological challenges confronting Latin American legal history. The first deals with the question of how to write a

105 T. Duve, "What Is Global Legal History?," *Comparative Legal History* 8 (2020), https://doi:10.1080/2049677X.2020.1830488 (last accessed Jan. 12, 2022), 73–115.

106 Cf. against the problematic pledge for anachronism L. Benton, "Beyond Anachronism: Histories of International Law and Global Legal Politics," *Journal of the History of International Law / Revue d'histoire du droit international* 21 (2019), 7–40.

legal history capable of doing justice to the laws of the indigenous peoples and other groups (see Chapter 2). The second challenge involves how to analyze the multiple entanglements, hybridizations, transfers, and the legal pluralism that characterized Latin American law during the colonial period – in other words, how to write a *global* legal history of Latin America (see Section 1.4). Both aspects are central to our understanding of Latin America and have tremendous political consequences.[107]

This section offers an introduction to doing legal history as a reconstruction of the production of law or, as I will explain, the production of "knowledge of normativity." It begins with a brief review of some of the pre-understandings of the object of legal history and contrasts these with the perspective developed most importantly by António Manuel Hespanha, whose seminal contributions have been one of the primary motors of innovation in legal historical research on the Iberian empires. The section then develops a perspective based on this understanding, presenting legal history as a process of the production of knowledge of normativity through "cultural translation."

Concepts of Law Underlying Legal Historical Research

Carlos Petit's review of the history of research on Latin American legal history (Section 1.1) clearly shows the extent to which the findings of legal historians working on Latin America were predetermined by their respective conceptions of law – some explicit, others implicit. Legal historians such as the Argentinean Ricardo Levene had a different concept of law at the beginning of the twentieth century than jurists such as the Spaniard Alfonso García-Gallo, whose work was formative for a large segment of the research community working on the so-called *derecho indiano* in the second half of the twentieth century. If Levene employed – at least in his methodological writings – a sociological conception of law that understood law as one mode of normativity, emanating from the pulsating social life, García-Gallo insisted that the object of legal history must be a historical legal system focusing on the institutions of the early modern state.[108] Following García-Gallo, the majority of legal historians working on colonial Latin America understood

107 On these aspects, see J. Esquirol, *Ruling the Law: Legitimacy and Failure in Latin American Law* (ASCL Studies in Comparative Law) (Cambridge: Cambridge University Press, 2019).

108 See V. Tau Anzoátegui, "De la Sociología al Derecho indiano. Contrapuntos entre Ricardo Levene y Ernesto Quesada," *Revista de Historia del Derecho* 34 (2006), 357–417; V. Tau Anzoátegui, "El tejido histórico del Derecho Indiano. Las ideas directivas de Alfonso García-Gallo," *Revista de Historia del Derecho* 21 (1993), 9–72.

law as a (somehow stable) system of norms emanating from state institutions. The laws of indigenous peoples were seen either as a residual part of a past to be overcome, or they were integrated into the colonial normative system not as "law" but as "custom," for example, when García-Gallo included them in 1975 into his vision of "legal pluralism."[109]

This legalistic and state-oriented vision of legal history and the neocolonial treatment of indigenous peoples' laws have been criticized for decades. The starting point of this criticism was the renovation of legal history in Southern Europe with regard to the early modern period. Scholars like Bartolomé Clavero and António Manuel Hespanha argued that legal history could no longer be written in a teleological manner as a history leading to the modern state with (state) institutions and (state) legislation at the center (see Section 1.2). On the contrary, early modern law should be analyzed against the background of the corporative social structures of medieval and early modern societies. Medieval and early modern legal orders originated from a variety of corporations, all characterized by a special practice of producing law, for example, the authorities and members of the guilds who produced norms pertinent to them, or religious orders, the military, and so forth. As many studies following this approach have shown, a casuistic structure characterized this early modern "jurisdictional culture," also in colonial Latin America.[110] Within the daily production of rules, various normativities were at play: not only "legal" norms but also norms grounded in religion, love, compassion, grace, and so forth. As a result, this "jurisdictional culture" needed to be analyzed in terms of a practice, and it could only be understood by paying specific attention to the legal and other kinds of knowledge that constrained and shaped an actor's actions (see Sections 3.1–3.3). First advanced by Bartolomé Clavero and António Manuel Hespanha, building on the work of Paolo Grossi, and further developed by Argentinean legal historian Víctor Tau Anzoátegui and others, this approach has stimulated researchers to write different histories of the colonial legal regime of

109 A. García Gallo, "El pluralismo jurídico en la América Española 1492–1824," in A. García Gallo, *Los orígenes españoles de las instituciones americanas. Estudios de Derecho Indiano* (Madrid: Real Academia de Jurisprudencia y Legislación, 1987), 299–310.

110 See, for example, C. A. Garriga Acosta, "Sobre el gobierno de la justicia en Indias (Siglos XVI–XVII)," *Revista de Historia del Derecho* 34 (2006), 67–160; C. A. Garriga Acosta, "Historia y Derecho. Perspectivas teóricas para una historia localizada del derecho," in J. A. Achón Insausti and J. M. Imízcoz Beúnza (eds.), *Discursos y contra-discursos en el proceso de la modernidad (siglos XVI–XIX)* (Madrid: Silex, 2019), 67–168; A. Agüero, "Las categorías básicas de la cultura jurisdiccional," in M. Lorente (ed.), *De justicia de jueces a justicia de leyes: hacia la España de 1870* (Madrid: Consejo General del Poder Judicial, *Centro de Documentación Judicial*, 2007), 19–58.

Latin America. Groups previously falling outside the purview of legal historical research, subaltern people, and local actors now entered the stage of legal history.[111] Social history and legal history, for a long time at odds, suddenly complemented each other.[112] Researchers learned how to describe legal practice and thus the dynamics of producing law as a communicative process operating under asymmetrical power relations.

Even if the original aim of Clavero and Hespanha's critique, as representatives of the "new legal history" of the 1980s and 1990s, was to deconstruct legalist and statist legal historiography in Portugal and Spain, and notwithstanding debates about the (im)possibility of speaking of an "Ancien Regime in the tropics,"[113] their critique was based on fundamental legal-theoretical considerations. Hespanha, in particular, continuously developed these theoretical foundations, critically reflecting also on the political intentions underlying this shift.[114] The blending of methodological approaches developed in cultural studies, social history, legal theory, and sociology of law, combined with a deep knowledge of early modern legal history, led him to the conclusion that law is "a communicative system, or rather, a set of related communicative systems" and needs to be analyzed historically as such.[115]

111 As an example for this tendency, see B. Premo, *The Enlightenment on Trial: Ordinary Litigants and Colonialism in the Spanish Empire* (Oxford: Oxford University Press, 2017).

112 For an excellent review of this development, see D. G. Barriera, *Historia y Justicia. Cultura, política y Sociedad en el Río de la Plata (Siglos XVI–XIX)* (Buenos Aires: Prometeo, 2019), Chapters 1–4.

113 This expression was coined by Hespanha and was the subject of intense debates; see A. M. Hespanha, "Ancien Régime in the Tropics? A Debate Concerning the Political Model of the Portuguese Colonial Empire," in C. Ando (ed.), *Citizenship and Empire in Europe 200–1900: The Antonine Constitution After 1800 Years* (Stuttgart: Franz Steiner Verlag, 2016), 157–76; see also A. M. Hespanha, "Uncommon Laws. Law in the Extreme Peripheries of an Early Modern Empire," *Zeitschrift der Savigny-Stiftung für Rechtsgeschichte: Germanistische Abteilung* 130 (2013), 180–204; for a critique of this perspective from a position that shares the basic understanding of legal history but dissents on this aspect and provides further references, see B. Clavero, "Gracia y derecho entre localización, recepción y globalización (lectura coral de Las Vísperas Constitucionales de António Hespanha)," *Quaderni fiorentini per la storia del pensiero giuridico moderno* 41 (2012), 675.

114 See on these aspects the contributions in P. Cardim, C. N. da Silva, Â. Barreto Xavier (eds.), *António Manuel Hespanha. Entre a História e o Direito* (Coimbra: Edições Almedina, 2015), and more extensively in a collection of articles published in 2018: A. M. Hespanha, *O direito democrático numa era pós-estatal. A questão política das fontes de direito* (Amazon Publishing (Kindle Edition), 2018).

115 A short summary of this perspective is found in A. M. Hespanha, "Southern Europe (Italy, Iberian Peninsula, France)," in H. Pihlajamäki, M. Dubber, and M. Godfrey (eds.), *The Oxford Handbook of European Legal History* (Oxford: Oxford University Press, 2018), 332–56.

Law as a Set of Communicative Systems

The notion of law as a set of related communicative systems relies on theoretical assumptions ranging from Wittgenstein and Foucault to Habermas, Luhmann, and more recent media and information theories. Within the scope of this section, unfortunately, we cannot explore in detail how Hespanha combined these ideas. More important, however, are the consequences for legal historiography he drew from them. For him, the decisive advantage of seeing law as a set of related communicative systems was that it allowed for an analysis not pre-structured by political entities; instead, it enabled legal historians to reconstruct the overlapping spheres in which people communicated about the law. Hespanha pointed out that the "idea of legal communicative systems (or spheres) emphasizes – and gives a sounder analytical support to – the idea of the coexistence of a plurality of laws according to factors of differentiation other than global entities, mostly related to a nation state precomprehension, such as 'races,' 'nations,' 'kingdoms'." The "shared dispositives of 'telling the law'" that made up these spheres may have corresponded to "populations speaking the same dialect or living a common practice of conviviality, to a group of monasteries sharing a similar textual heritage, or to a network of clerks or intellectuals referring to a similar cluster of texts of authority."[116] Due to this approach, communities that traditionally had not received attention, for example, subaltern groups, appear as active producers of norms. In his last major work, *Filhos da Terra* (2019), Hespanha took these concepts as a starting point for dealing with the phenomenon he identified as the "empire in the shadow" of the Portuguese: the numerous and heterogeneous people who referred to themselves as "Portuguese," traveling all over the world, sharing some basic assumptions and practices regarding law.[117]

Hespanha considered the various and overlapping communicative spheres to be relatively autonomous. Learned jurists were communicating within one sphere, whereas members of corporate bodies like guilds and religious orders mainly referred to the authorities and communicative practices of their own groups. This did not mean, however, that law was independent from political or economic influences. On the contrary, and clearly referring to systems-theoretical theories of communication, Hespanha assumed that external factors were of fundamental importance to the evolution of these spheres. However, researchers should strive to observe these external factors in terms

116 All quotations taken from Hespanha, "Southern Europe."

117 A. M. Hespanha, *Filhos da Terra. Identidades Mestiças nos Confins da Expansão Portuguesa* (Lisbon: Tinta da China, 2019).

of processes carried out within the respective subsystems, with special attention paid to the specific internal logic and mechanisms of reproduction at work within a given sphere.[118] This approach also means that the media utilized to communicate such ideas take on a central role within legal historical research.[119] Much earlier than most, Hespanha drew the attention of legal historians to the importance of mediality and materiality for legal history.[120] The understanding of legal history as a communicative practice or, as suggested in the following, as a process of production of knowledge of normativity through cultural translation, is building on these fundamental insights.

Law as (Cultural) Translation

What does it mean to understand legal history as a process of production of knowledge of normativity through "cultural translation"? A quick glance at some "classical" instances and cases, taken from the nascent period of early modern colonial Latin America legal history and from the transition to the republican period, may serve to illustrate the point.[121]

As is well known, the European invaders also brought basic concepts of law, practices, and customs with them to the shores of the Caribbean islands and later to the American continent. With the reading of the *requerimiento*, the erection of the cross, the king's coat of arms and motto, and many other acts of taking possession, a new legal order was established in the Americas – from the perspective of those who performed these acts. Just like the papal bulls

118 A. M. Hespanha, "Is There Place for a Separated Legal History? A Broad Review of Recent Developments on Legal Historiography," *Quaderni fiorentini per la storia del pensiero giuridico moderno* 48 (2019), 7 and 14. For more on his methodological reflections with regard to the jurist's law, see also A. M. Hespanha, *Como os juristas viam o mundo. 1550–1750. Direitos, estados, coisas, contratos, ações e crimes* (Lisboa: CreateSpace Independent Publishing Platform, 2015), 5–29.

119 Hespanha, "Is There Place"; Ibid., at 13: "In my opinion, one of the most promising topics in today's legal history is this stressing of the communicative nature of law and of the importance that devices of its 'telling' and 'sharing' have in its way of being. This approach allowed to diversify histories of the law, according to the communicative spheres in which law respectively circulates, emphasizing non-homologous chronological and spatial profiles of the several layers of law."

120 A. M. Hespanha, "Form and Content in Early Modern Legal Books. Bridging the Gap between Material Bibliography and the History of Legal Thought," *Rechtsgeschichte – Legal History* 12 (2008), 12–50.

121 For a more detailed account, see T. Duve, "Legal History as a History of the Translation of Knowledge of Normativity," Max Planck Institute for Legal History and Legal Theory Research Paper Series No. 2022-16 (Frankfurt am Main: Max-Planck-Institut für Rechtsgeschichte und Rechtstheorie, 2022), http://dx.doi.org/10.2139/ssrn.4229323; T. Duve, "Rechtsgeschichte als Geschichte von Normativitätswissen?," *Rechtsgeschichte – Legal History* 29 (2021), 41–68.

that had granted the Catholic kings of Spain and later the Portuguese Crown far-reaching rights to the still unknown territories, actors necessarily relied on the words, concepts, and practices of this European tradition.[122] They used the language of law inherited from Castile or Portugal, and translated this language, consisting not only of words but also of legal practices such as rituals, into new rules and practices that met the needs and requirements of the new situation. In this context, "translation" meant selection, interpretation, and adaptation to new circumstances. While a linguistic component was sometimes part of the broader translation process, "cultural translation" consisted of much more.[123] In the end, every normative statement produced – whether a court sentence, act of governance, writing of a legal text, issuing a legal opinion, and so forth – could be understood as a communicative practice or as a translation of knowledge of normativity, that is, a concretization of knowledge of normativity for the case in question. The newly created concrete normative statement then formed part of the knowledge of normativity that was again the object of translations.[124]

Not only the foundational acts but also the whole establishment and further development of the colonial legal order followed this pattern of translating knowledge of normativity according to the demands of the new situation. A prominent example for how this process transpired is the use of the term *miserabilis persona* for the integration of indigenous peoples into the colonial legal system (see also Chapter 2 and Section 3.2), the use of which has a long history.[125] The term and the legal knowledge accumulated around it originated in a privilege of jurisdiction issued by the Roman emperor Constantine, which was later included in a part of the *Corpus Iuris Civilis*, the *Codex* (Cod. 3.14).

122 "Tradition" is used here in the sense H. P. Glenn has given the term: H. P. Glenn, *Legal Traditions of the World: Sustainable Diversity in Law* (Oxford: Oxford University Press, 2014); on Glenn's current understanding, see the contributions in H. Dedek (ed.), *A Cosmopolitan Jurisprudence: Essays in Memory of H. Patrick Glenn* (ASCL Studies in Comparative Law) (Cambridge: Cambridge University Press, 2021).

123 On the concept of "cultural translation," see P. Burke, "Cultures of Translation in Early Modern Europe," in P. Burke and R. Po-chia Hsia (eds.), *Cultural Translation in Early Modern Europe* (Cambridge: Cambridge University Press, 2007), 7–38; P. Burke, "Translating Knowledge, Translating Cultures," in M. North (ed.), *Kultureller Austausch. Bilanz und Perspektiven der Frühneuzeitforschung* (Köln: Böhlau, 2009), 69–88; P. Burke, *What Is the History of Knowledge?* (Cambridge and Malden: Polity, 2015).

124 See on legal history as a history of cultural translation Duve, "Historia del derecho como."

125 See on this P. Castañeda Delgado, "La condición miserable del indio y sus privilegios," *Anuario de Estudios Americanos XXVIII* (1971), 245–335; T. Duve, *Sonderrecht in der Frühen Neuzeit. Das frühneuzeitliche "ius singulare," untersucht anhand der "privilegia miserabilium personarum," "senum" und "indorum" in Alter und Neuer Welt* (Frankfurt: Klostermann, 2008).

According to this concept, widows, orphans, the elderly, and the sick could turn directly to the imperial court. Over the centuries, this special right of privileged access to justice, issued under Christian influence, became a privilege of jurisdiction for an ever-wider group of persons. Since the High Middle Ages, many types of disadvantaged persons could claim to be "worthy of commiseration" and thus *miserabiles personae*, and these jurisdictional privileges became part of *ius commune* and its manifold regional articulations. In the Castilian tradition, people considered as such could claim that their cases were *casos de corte*, *causae curiae* in the learned law tradition, giving them immediate access to the royal court.[126] From the High Middle Ages onward, and in the context of an intensifying quarrel over jurisdiction between secular and spiritual power, the Church claimed exclusive jurisdiction over these groups. Finally, in the early modern period, an ever-widening field of special rights for a variety of different groups was derived from this tradition. At the beginning of the seventeenth century, the Neapolitan jurist Giovanni Maria Novario compiled no less than 176 privileges for the *miserabiles personae* from nearly every field of law: the law of obligations, inheritance, procedural law, and so forth. Furthermore, the range of persons who could claim these privileges also had grown enormously through casuistry and due to the extensive interpretation of privileges favoring Christian values and goals (*piae causae*). Over time, not just the poor, sick, and elderly but also clerics, pilgrims, hospices and pious foundations, traveling merchants, and other disadvantaged peoples such as prostitutes or prisoners were beneficiaries of these privileges.[127]

For this reason, it is not at all surprising that jurists and canonists of the Iberian empires used the knowledge accumulated in conjunction with this term to apply it to indigenous peoples. When Bartolomé de las Casas took office as bishop of Chiapas in 1545, for example, he and the bishops of Guatemala and Nicaragua referred to this regulatory tradition and claimed that the indigenous population as a whole should be placed under ecclesiastical – that is, their – jurisdiction.[128] In a similar manner, both the office of the

126 See Duve, *Sonderrecht*, 102–37.

127 Giovanni Maria Novarius, *Tractatus de miserabilium personarum privilegiis* (Naples, 1637), Sectio Prima, Praeludium VIII; on the privileges see also Gabriel Álvarez de Velasco's more erudite and complete deliberations, *Tractatus de privilegiis pauperum, et miserabilium personarum* (Madrid, 1630).

128 Letter dated Oct. 19, 1545, printed in F. Cantù, "Esigenze di giustizia e politica coloniale: una 'petición' inedita di Las Casas all' Audiencia de los Confines," *Ibero-Amerikanisches Archiv NF III* (2) (1977), 135–65, at 156.

Protector de indios in the Viceroyalty of Peru and a special tribunal for cases brought forward by indigenous peoples, the *Juzgado General de Indios* in the Viceroyalty of New Spain, were justified with reference to the obligation of emperors to protect the *miserabiles personae*.[129] It is very probable that direct appeal to Portuguese kings by both enslaved and free persons of African descent in colonial Brazil, that is, the "acts of grace," were also responding to this regulatory tradition.[130] As a result, the astounding number of so-called *privilegia indorum* – privileges for the members of indigenous groups – compiled in the most influential books on the laws of Hispanic America are in fact concretizations of the regulations laid down in the canon and civil law tradition that had been translated into new realities. In other words, the particular "status" of indigenous peoples was developed by translating tradition.[131] When the famous Castilian jurist Juan de Solórzano Pereira, citing the work of Novario, referred to the *miserabilis persona* in his foundational books *De Indiarum Iure* (especially in the second part, 1639) and *Política Indiana* (1647), indigenous peoples were able to appeal to one of the most respected authorities and jurists of the Spanish empire when claiming such privileges.[132] Research examining court cases has shown that actors effectively claimed and were granted this status.[133]

Were these century-old notions and the 176 privileges amassed by Novario and referred to by Solórzano applicable "law"? Unsurprisingly, many of the privileges collected in Naples to establish a legal framework for institutions of poor relief did not fit the needs of indigenous peoples.[134] The few that were deemed useful, however, especially certain privileges

129 W. Borah, *Justice by Insurance: The General Indian Court of Colonial Mexico and the Legal Aides of the Half-Real* (Berkeley: University of California Press, 1983); M. Novoa, *The Protectors of Indians in the Royal Audience of Lima: History, Careers and Legal Culture, 1575–1775* (Legal History Library 19 – Studies in the History of Private Law 10) (Leiden and Boston: Brill Nijhoff, 2016).

130 For more on this topic, see A. J. R. Russel-Wood, "'Acts of Grace': Portuguese Monarchs and Their Subjects of African Descent in Eighteenth-Century Brazil," *Journal of Latin American Studies* 32 (2000), 307–32.

131 Diego de Avendaño, *Thesaurus indicus* (Antwerp, 1668), lib. II, tit. XII.

132 Juan Solórzano Pereira, *Política indiana* (Madrid, 1647), lib. II, cap. 28, n. 25–26); more extensively also in Juan Solórzano Pereira, *De Indiarum iure sive de iusta indiarum occidentalium gubernatione, tomus secundus* (Lyon, 1672), lib. I, cap. 27.

133 See on this C. Cunill, "L'Indien, personne misérable. Considérations historiographiques sur le statut des peuples indigènes dans l'empire hispanique," *Revue d'histoire moderne & contemporaine* 64(2) (2017), https://doi.org/10.3917/rhmc.642.0021 (last accessed Jan. 12, 2022), 21–38; B. P. Owensby, *Empire of Law and Indian Justice in Colonial Mexico* (Stanford: Stanford University Press, 2008), 55–58.

134 Duve, *Sonderrecht*, 161–66.

in procedural law, were often cited and used by jurists and representatives of indigenous groups. This practice of selecting and adapting that which seemed reasonable for the case in question was standard procedure for early modern jurists. They continuously faced the need to translate legal knowledge stemming from tradition into new realities, opting for some of the authoritative statements they found and leaving out others. Roman law, *ius commune*, and medieval law books like the *Siete Partidas* were full of regulations that did not make sense as such. What they did contain, however, were deep and insightful reflections about law and a seemingly infinite number of examples as to how to resolve legal problems. In other words, they served as repositories of authoritative solutions and seemed to be expressions of a higher truth that often proved helpful in finding a just decision for any given legal question. It was precisely this quality that led early modern jurists to use their *arbitrium* and to decide in each specific case whether the regulations they found were applicable (see Section 3.1). As a result, when a 1671 *memorandum* for the reform of the office of the *Protector* addressed to the Viceroy of Peru began affirming that the "Indians of Peru, like the others of the West, are and must be counted among the persons who in law are called the *miserables*...," the author did not refer to any specific "applicable" law.[135] Instead, he simply pointed to a body of legal knowledge developed over the centuries that revolved around the idea of protecting wretched persons. This knowledge was "culturally translated" within the specific circumstances of the case at hand into the local contexts, thus producing new statements adapted to the local contexts and, once accomplished, could then be used by others.

Examples of these cultural translations of knowledge from other periods and areas abound, and not just in the colonial period. One can also find them after independences. When nineteenth-century independent Latin American states faced the need to create their own national legal orders, they did so by means of continuous cultural and lingual translations of bodies of knowledge from other areas, especially from the USA and Europe. In this period of capitalist expansion and the "transformation of the world,"[136] the intensification of communication through technological innovations like the telegraph and

135 Nicolás Matías del Campo y de la Rynaga, *Memorial histórico y iurídico que refiere el Origen del Oficio de Protector general de los Indios del Perú* (Madrid, 1671), fol 1: "Excmo Señor: Los indios del Perú, como los demas del occidente, son y deben ser reputados entre las personas que el derecho llama miserables...."

136 J. Osterhammel, *The Transformation of the World: A Global History of the Nineteenth Century*, trans. P. Camiller (Princeton: Princeton University Press, 2015).

steamships and the growing integration of Latin America into a new system of world trade created a great need for new regulations. At the same time, the exchange of goods and people, not to mention the development of new forms of communication, made a previously unseen mass of legal knowledge available to a broader audience. As the sections on codification, constitution-making, and the contestations and exclusions show (see Sections 5.1–5.3), from the early nineteenth century onwards, models of constitutions and codifications circulated between Europe and Latin America as well as within Latin America.[137] Amongst the profusion of models and drafts, the French Civil Code of 1804 proved particularly influential. Early codifications like the ones of Haiti, the Dominican Republic, Mexico, and later Bolivia and Peru, adopted important parts of the French model, and other Latin American states used these and other models for their codifications.[138] Similar processes of *bricolage* happened in criminal law, where after several decades of copying and assembling European models, lively debates between criminologists on both sides of the Atlantic emerged, giving rise to new scientific communities or – along the lines of Hespanha – to new communicative spheres that produced legal knowledge across the oceans.

In a similar manner, teaching at Latin American law faculties often relied on European – in some cases US – textbooks translated into Spanish and sometimes adapted to local realities. Thus, these seemingly "European" models became part of localized "Euro-American" law and influenced the legal language, thought, and practice in Latin America. They shaped the

137 On the circulation of models in civil and constitutional law, see F. J. Andrés Santos, "Napoleon in America? Reflections on the Concept of 'Legal Reception' in the Light of the Civil Law Codification in Latin America," in T. Duve (ed.), *Entanglements in Legal History: Conceptual Approaches* (Global Perspectives on Legal History 1) (Frankfurt am Main: Max-Planck-Institut für europäische Rechtsgeschichte, 2014), 297–314; A. Parise, "Libraries of Civil Codes as Mirrors of Normative Transfers from Europe to the Americas: The Experiences of Lorimier in Quebec (1871–1890) and Varela in Argentina (1873–1875)," in T. Duve (ed.), *Entanglements in Legal History: Conceptual Approaches* (Global Perspectives on Legal History 1) (Frankfurt am Main: Max-Planck-Institut für europäische Rechtsgeschichte, 2014), 315–84; S. P. Donlan, "Entangled Up in Red, White, and Blue: Spanish West Florida and the American Territory of Orleans, 1803–1810," in T. Duve (ed.), *Entanglements in Legal History: Conceptual Approaches* (Global Perspective in Legal History 1) (Frankfurt am Main: Max-Planck-Institut für europäische Rechtsgeschichte, 2014), 213–52; E. Zimmermann, "Translations of the 'American Model' in Nineteenth Century Argentina: Constitutional Culture as a Global Legal Entanglement," in T. Duve (ed.), *Entanglements in Legal History: Conceptual Approaches* (Global Perspectives on Legal History 1) (Frankfurt am Main: Max-Planck-Institut für europäische Rechtsgeschichte, 2014), 385–426.

138 A. Guzmán Brito, *Historia de la codificación civil en iberoamérica* (Madrid: Thomson Aranzadi, 2006).

legal imagination of the actors. An illustrative case is José María Álvarez's book *Instituciones de derecho real de Castilla y de Indias*, first published in Guatemala in three parts between 1818 and 1820, shortly before the declaration of Guatemalan independence in 1821 and Álvarez's own death.[139] The book combined linguistic and cultural translation in a variety of ways. The *Instituciones* was a Spanish translation of the *Recitationes in elementa iuris civilis secundum ordinem institutionum*, a book edited by the son of the acclaimed German jurist Johann Gottlieb Heineccius (1681–1741).[140] This German text was translated into Spanish by Álvarez and adapted to the local circumstances of pre-independence Guatemala. In the years that followed, this version of the *Instituciones* was edited in various places, and in many cases it was adapted to the volatile political circumstances experienced in these turbulent years, for example, the *nuevamente revista, corregida y aumentada* published in Mexico in 1826. Later editions were printed in Philadelphia in 1826, in New York in 1827, in Havanna in 1834 (second edition in 1841), and in many other places in the Americas. In 1829, the *Instituciones* was published in Madrid, again with amendments, now under the title *Instituciones de derecho real de España*. In this edition, all notes added in the previous editions for Hispanic American readers were taken out. Using this Spanish edition as a basis, Dalmacio Vélez Sarsfield, who three decades later penned the Argentine *Código Civil*, prepared a new edition, printed in 1834 in Buenos Aires. In his book, he eliminated the references to Spain introduced in Madrid in 1829 and reintroduced those parts of the legislation for the colonies still in use in Buenos Aires at that time. As stipulated in the preface, he corrected "errors" as well as added annotations, new topics, and appendices. For example, after the first section on persons, he inserted an appendix on the legal situation of enslaved persons after independence in Río de la Plata. Much like Vélez Sarsfield, Andrés Bello, author of the Chilean Civil Code, published a textbook based on another text written by

139 For a reconstruction of the life and work of Álvarez, as well as on the editions, see the introductory articles in the edition of J. M. García Laguardia and M. del Refugio González, J. M. Álvarez, *Instituciones de derecho real de Castilla y de Indias* (Mexico City: Universidad Autónoma de México, 1982 [1826]), vol. I, https://biblio.juridicas.unam.mx/bjv/id/388 (last accessed Jan. 12, 2022); see also A. Guzmán Brito, "La literatura de Derecho Natural Racionalista y la literatura de Derecho Indiano con especial referencia a las 'Instituciones' de José María Álvarez," in Instituto Internacional de Historia del Derecho Indiano (ed.), *XI Congreso del Instituto Internacional de Historia del Derecho Indiano. Buenos Aires, 4 al 9 de septiembre de 1995. Actas y estudios* (Buenos Aires: Instituto de Investigaciones de Historia del Derecho, 1997), vol. I, 481–98.

140 Heineccius was already well known in Spain and Latin America in the eighteenth century, see F. Pérez Godoy, "Johannes Heineccius y la historia transatlántica del ius gentium," *Revista Chilena de Derecho* 44 (2017), 539–62.

Heineccius, that is, the *Elementa iuris naturae et gentium*, which also incorporated parts of works authored by other notable jurists. Taken together, these many cultural translations and modifications constituted a dense web of legal knowledge resulting from an entangled legal history between the Americas, Europe, and even some parts of Asia – a process of global knowledge creation that transpired under the conditions of asymmetric power relations.[141]

Without delving into further examples, and as many of the chapters in this volume show, one can summarize that Latin American legal orders emerged and reproduced themselves through continuous linguistic and cultural translations of legal knowledge. These translations take place all the time, everywhere, and under varying power relations: when indigenous peoples practiced their laws, when the European invaders arrived, when the independent nations emerged, and even now in the twenty-first century, for example, when legal theories, or practices of transitional justice, are translated into different realities. In the colonial period, the translations were influenced in virtue of being part of European empires, and during the independence era, informal legal imperialism and European and US cultural, economic, and political hegemony had a huge impact on the process of state building and legislation. As a result of these multiple and ongoing processes of cultural translation, the legal orders that emerged in Latin America show considerable similarities but also marked differences, according to the flows of communication and the circumstances of the cultural translations.

Knowledge of Normativity

The vast and ongoing process of cultural translation, however, is not focused solely on "legal" knowledge as its object. Legal actors draw upon more than "legal knowledge" in a narrow sense, that is, the primary and secondary rules conceived by the legal theorist H.L.A. Hart. These primary and secondary rules are, obviously, at the core of law and thus of legal history, as the examples just given demonstrate.

In the production of a normative statement, however, legal actors necessarily rely on much more than primary and secondary rules. According to the world they live in and the legal culture they inhabit, various kinds of knowledge are drawn upon: knowledge about the concrete problem they are dealing with, knowledge about the practical consequences of their decisions,

141 Regarding these processes of global knowledge creation, see T. Duve, "The School of Salamanca: A Case of Global Knowledge Production," in T. Duve, J. L. Egío, and C. Birr (eds.), *The School of Salamanca: A Case of Global Knowledge Production* (Max Planck Studies in Global Legal History of the Iberian Worlds 2) (Leiden and Boston: Brill Nijhoff, 2021), 1–42.

about the persons involved, their status and the effects of this status on the case, and so forth. As the chapters on precolonial law (Chapter 2) and colonial law (Chapter 3) show, the varieties of knowledge – and thus the disparity and diversity of sources legal historians have to work with – is pretty much infinite. Legal actors often follow conventions, routines, and practices without being aware of them.[142] They might be guided by "grace" and "love," as Hespanha has pointed out, and by principles taken from religion and other belief systems.[143] All this knowledge has normative value in the sense that it guides the actors' operations. As such, it far exceeds what is usually considered as belonging to "legal knowledge."[144] To make this clear, it seems preferable to speak of "knowledge of normativity." This "knowledge of normativity" is operating in the process of translation of legal knowledge and other elements of knowledge, like practices, and it is itself translated – selected, adapted, transformed, and so forth – into a solution for a specific case.[145]

142 From the perspective of the history of science, see L. Daston, "The History of Science and the History of Knowledge," *Know* 1(1) (2017), https://doi:10.1086/691678 (last accessed Jan. 12, 2022), 131–54. On page 139, practices are defined as "roughly, what scientists actually do as opposed to what they say they do."

143 A. M. Hespanha, *La gracia del derecho. Economía de la cultura en la edad moderna* (Madrid: Centro de Estudios Políticos y Constitucionales, 1993); A. M. Hespanha, "La senda amorosa del Derecho: 'Amor' y 'iustitia' en el discurso jurídico moderno," in C. Petit Calvo (ed.), *Pasiones del jurista. Amor, memoria, melancolía, imaginacíon* (Madrid: Centro de Estudios Políticos y Constitucionales, 1997), 23–73.

144 The term "legal knowledge" is used by authors in many different ways. In this chapter, the term is used in a narrow sense, referring to what one might identify with H. L. A. Hart's primary and the secondary rules, see H. L. A. Hart, *The Concept of Law* (New York: Oxford University Press, 1961). Other authors like James Boyd White are using the term in a much broader sense, and much closer to what is referred to in this chapter as "knowledge of normativity" (see J. B. White, "Legal Knowledge," *Harvard Law Review* 115 (2002), 1396–1431, at 1399: "Legal knowledge is an activity of mind, a way of doing something with the rules and cases and other materials of law, an activity that is itself not reducible to a set of directions or any fixed description. It is a species of cultural competence ... for what a lawyer knows at the center is how to speak and write the language of the law, in actual situations in the world – how to use legal language to create legal meaning"). However, as I understand it, and with regard to what is explained in the following, this broad understanding is better expressed by the term "knowledge of normativity." See on this also Duve, "Legal History"; Duve, "Rechtsgeschichte."

145 Legal scholars have been addressing this broad body of knowledge toward the end of the twentieth and beginning of the twenty-first century using general terms like "legal culture." Some discussed law as either a "craft" (Scharffs) or "cultural competence" (White), while others framed it in terms of "legal imagination" (Koskenniemi) or "legal consciousness" (Kennedy), none of them really connecting their terminology to an advanced theory of cultural production taking into consideration the practice turn. Current debates in the history of knowledge and global history provide precisely this theoretical background. On "knowledge of normativity," see Duve, "Historia del derecho como"; T. Duve, "Pragmatic Normative Literature and the Production of Normative Knowledge in the Early Modern Iberian Empires (16th–17th

Some examples might help to clarify this. Research on colonial court practice in Hispanic America, for example, has shown the extent to which Christian interpretations and values guided the interpretation of legal concepts (see Sections 3.1 and 3.2). Some of these values were directly expressed in secular law, as in the case of the *miserabilis persona*, so they became part of "legal knowledge." In most cases, however, Christian values were simply tacit or implicit knowledge, and the consequences were so self-evident that they were not even mentioned.[146] The same holds true for local knowledge. In a number of sources from the colonial period, Crown or Church officials insisted on the need to know the local conditions,[147] and they emphasized the importance of practical experience.[148] What they were basically asking for was local knowledge, that is, what one "knows" without further specification. The often-misunderstood practice of non-application of a royal order by using the formula "we obey the law but we do not put it into practice" (*la ley se obedece pero no se cumple*), for example, is not a picaresque way of evading legal obligations. On the contrary, in many cases it was a way of acting legally by not implementing a decision that led to unjust results, usually because of a (perceived) lack of knowledge about the local situations, consequences,

Centuries)," in T. Duve and O. Danwerth (eds.), *Knowledge of the Pragmatici: Legal and Moral Theological Literature and the Formation of Early Modern Ibero-America* (Leiden and Boston: Brill, 2020), 1–39.

146 T. Herzog, *Upholding Justice: Society, State, and the Penal System in Quito (1650–1750)* (Ann Arbor: University of Michigan Press, 2004); A. Agüero, *Castigar y perdonar cuando conviene a la República. La justicia penal de Córdoba del Tucumán, siglos XVII y XVIII* (Madrid: Centro de Estudios Políticos y Constitucionales, 2008).

147 Domingo de Salazar, first bishop of the Philippines, for example, insisted in a letter addressed to King Philipp II on the need to know the facts, *el hecho*, and complained about the deficient way central institutions like the *Consejo de Indias* were dealing with local problems: "The problem is that information has to arrive from as far as the Spanish Philippines, … so that who has not been there must be cautious not to be deceived, because in what refers to the indigenous peoples only very few of those speaking about them are doing this without any own interests, or an interest of their friends and allies," see: Domingo de Salazar, *Tratado en que se determina lo que se ha de tener acerca de llevar tributos a los infieles de las Islas Filipinas*, cited and translated in O. R. Moutin, "'Sepamos, Señores, en que ley vivimos y si emos de tener por nuestra regla al Consejo de Indias': Salamanca in the Philippine Islands," in T. Duve, J. L. Egío, and C. Birr (eds.), *The School of Salamanca: A Case of Global Knowledge Production* (Leiden and Boston: Brill Nijhoff, 2021), 245–63, at 257, n. 47.

148 Toward the beginning of his book on contract law, published in 1569, the Dominican Tomás de Mercado wrote: "I have thought it necessary to write on the theory of businesses along the way they are practiced, because this is something that the common people know and that the very learned men ignore, or, at least, do not fully understand." On this and the value of experience, see J. L. Egío, "Travelling Scholastics: The Emergence of an Empirical Normative Authority in Early Modern Spanish America," in C. Zwierlein (ed.), *The Power of the Dispersed: Early Modern Global Travelers Beyond Imagination* (Intersections 77) (Leiden: Brill, 2022), 158–208, quotation at 169.

and so forth.[149] This conscious and selective non-implementation was itself a legal practice that emerged out of a legal culture that privileged material over formal justice and constituted an essential element of the relevant knowledge of normativity.

Political and economic interests are also important elements of the relevant "knowledge of normativity," because they guide and constrain actors' interpretations and actions, and they often end up shaping the law. An in-depth study of court cases on "political crime" during the First Brazilian Republic, for example, has shown that the classification of an offense as a "political crime" depended on various factors.[150] Apart from legal dogmatics, that is, the traditional doctrine defining this crime, translated into circumstances of late nineteenth-century Brazil, the heavily debated positivist positions in contemporary criminology, and the particular persons involved in specific cases mattered. Public opinion, in some cases orchestrated by the interested parties, backed some interpretations and delegitimized others. The decisions made under such specific conditions encoded concrete interests into seemingly abstract legal knowledge about the definition of this crime and the relevant jurisdiction used in subsequent cases. Local circumstances and contingencies, as such studies show, exerted more than an external influence on the law; this knowledge directly shaped it. They conditioned the production of law through cultural translation of the extant knowledge. Expressed in theoretical terms, cases like these confirm that the sub-system "law" absorbs external factors and processes them within its own logic of reproduction. This is why political, economic, and social circumstances cannot simply be seen as "external" influences. They need to be integrated into a legal historical analysis and analyzed as part of the knowledge of normativity people had at their disposal when they were producing law.

Finally, one field in which attention to "knowledge of normativity" far beyond the realm of "legal knowledge" in a narrow sense is of seminal importance is the history of the laws of indigenous peoples and other groups. As Caroline Cunill (Chapter 2) shows with regard to indigenous laws before and after the European invasion, the legal histories of indigenous peoples can only be appropriately written with special attention to knowledge stemming

149 V. Tau Anzoátegui, "La ley 'se obedece pero no se cumple'. En torno a la suplicación de las leyes en el Derecho indiano," in V. Tau Anzoátegui, *La ley en América hispana. Del Descubrimiento a la Emancipación* (Buenos Aires: Academia Nacional de Historia, 1992), 67–143.

150 See on this R. Sirotti, Within the Law: Criminal Law and Political Repression in Brazil (1889–1930) (Frankfurt am Main: Max-Planck-Institut für Rechtsgeschichte und Rechtstheorie, forthcoming).

from fields other than those considered "law" as traditionally understood by legal historians. The same holds for the knowledge of normativity of epistemic communities like Afro-Latin Americans, individuals from Asia working as slave labor in the Americas, or for the many corporate bodies of colonial or twenty-first-century societies that produced and enforced their regulations within their spheres of influence (see Chapters 3 and 7).[151] Speaking of "legal" knowledge in the narrow sense does not do justice to the breadth of normativities operating in these cases.

In particular, the analysis of cases often described as hybridizations or as examples of legal pluralism profits greatly from analyzing the knowledge of normativity employed by actors. Asking about the knowledge of normativity at work helps to overcome static visions of the law and avoid succumbing to the pitfall of identifying certain groups exclusively with certain bodies of knowledge of normativity, as often occurs in studies on legal pluralism. Contrary to what one might think, actors more often than not managed various registers at the same time, and the choice of the body of legal knowledge mobilized in any specific case was not necessarily limited to the jurisdiction it was made for or originally stemmed from. Especially under conditions of interlegality, that is, a legal pluralism under asymmetric power relations, use of multiple registers of knowledge of normativity seems to have been the rule rather than the exception. When indigenous actors invoked colonial justice, for example, they used colonial concepts and practices, and this use was not without repercussions for their own systems, because these concepts later shaped their own practices.[152] Research has shown that when property rights were at stake, indigenous peoples made use of property concepts from Castilian law when it was advantageous to their case.[153] And vice versa, if they considered it advantageous, Spaniards also defended themselves by invoking indigenous rights – a practice that,

151 Epistemic communities are groups of persons that share a certain *episteme*, that is, some basic assumptions with regard to values, causal beliefs, notions of validity, common practices, etc. For more on epistemic communities, including further references, see P. M. Haas, "Epistemic Communities," in J. Krieger (ed.), *The Oxford Companion to Comparative Politics* (Oxford: Oxford University Press, 2012), vol. I, 351–59; also A. Bianchi, "Epistemic communities," in J. D'Aspremont and S. Singh (eds.), *Concepts for International Law: Contributions to Disciplinary Thought* (Cheltenham and Northampton: Edward Elgar Publishing, 2019), 251–66.

152 J. C. de la Puente Luna and R. Honores, "Guardianes de la real justicia: alcaldes de indios, costumbre y justicia local en Huarochirí colonial," *Histórica* 40 (2016), 11–47.

153 K. Graubart, "Shifting Landscapes. Heterogeneous Conceptions of Land Use and Tenure in the Lima Valley," *Colonial Latin American Review* 26 (2017), 62–84; see also K. Graubart, "Learning from the Qadi: The Jurisdiction of Local Rule in the Early Colonial Andes," *Hispanic American Historical Review* 95 (2015), 195–228.

again, could have effects on the self-interpretation of this knowledge of normativity by indigenous peoples.[154] In some cases, indigenous officials invoked colonial law and used it against the "old" – that is, their own pre-colonial – law.[155] In the same vein, case studies on the interaction between colonial powers and indigenous peoples in the Americas have given insight into the "legal literacy" of participants and the different meanings these encounters produced.[156]

Glocalizations

What picture emerges when we analyze Latin American legal history as a history of the production of knowledge of normativity through cultural translation? As the chapters in this volume show, we find similarities and dissimilarities between different areas of Latin America. The perspective presented in Section 1.3 can help to explain the reasons for this. As local conditions vary, so too does the outcome of the process of translation of knowledge of normativity. Actively engaged in the types of translations described earlier, and despite the asymmetric power relations, Latin American legal actors – often as "semi-peripheral jurists"[157] – drew on legal knowledge coming from other areas. However, in translating this knowledge into their local situations, they continuously produced new originals, not copies. Thus they contributed to the emergence of normative orders that in many cases mirrored the asymmetric power relations, yet cannot be adequately understood if viewed simply as a product of European imperialism or as an extension of European legal history, as the traditional notions of "legal transplants," "legal transfer," or "reception" often insinuate.[158]

What we observe instead is a process of "glocalization," understood as the localization of transnationally circulating – "global" – legal knowledge through an infinite number of (cultural) translations in various local

154 T. Herzog, "Colonial Law and 'Native Customs': Indigenous Land Rights in Colonial Spanish America," *The Americas* 63 (2013), 303–21; T. Herzog, "Did European Law Turn American? Territory, Property and Rights in an Atlantic World," in T. Duve and H. Pihlajamäki (eds.), *New Horizons in Spanish Colonial Law: Contributions to Transnational Early Modern Legal History* (Frankfurt am Main: Max-Planck-Institut für europäische Rechtsgeschichte, 2015), 75–96.

155 Herzog, "Colonial Law and 'Native Customs'."

156 B. P. Owensby and R. J. Ross (eds.), *Justice in a New World: Negotiating Legal Intelligibility in British, Iberian, and Indigenous America* (New York: New York University Press, 2018).

157 For more on this, see A. Becker Lorca, *Mestizo International Law: A Global Intellectual History 1842–1933* (Cambridge: Cambridge University Press, 2015).

158 For an overview, see M. Graziadei, "Comparative Law, Legal Transplants, and Receptions," in M. Reimann and R. Zimmermann (eds.), *The Oxford Handbook of Comparative Law*, 2nd ed. (Oxford: Oxford University Press, 2019), 442–73.

and temporal settings.[159] These translations depended on the accumulated knowledge of normativity, and they continuously produced new knowledge. Throughout centuries of migrations of peoples and imperialism, before and after the European invasion, and due to the intense flows of communication, clear divisions between "the indigenous" and "the European" as well as between "the Spanish" and "the Portuguese" disappeared.

. . .

1.4 What Is Global Legal History and How Can It Be Done?

MARIANA DIAS PAES

What is global legal history and how can it be done? Though still a marginalized topic within the field of legal history – and one strongly overshadowed by methodological nationalism – it has nevertheless attracted more attention over the past few years.[160] Some authors have concentrated on the circulation of people – mostly throughout the Atlantic – and on the legal matters that they encountered in the course of their lives.[161] Others departed from a

159 On "glocalization" with references to Robertson and others, see V. Roudometof, *Glocalization: A Critical Introduction* (London and New York: Routledge, 2016). On "localization" and "globalization," see, for example, Clavero, "Gracia y derecho"; A. Agüero, "Local Law and Localization of Law: Hispanic Legal Tradition and Colonial Culture (16th–18th Centuries)," in M. Meccarelli and M. J. Solla Sastre (eds.), *Spatial and Temporal Dimensions for Legal History: Research Experiences and Itineraries* (Global Perspectives on Legal History 6) (Frankfurt am Main: Max-Planck-Institut für europäische Rechtsgeschichte, 2016), 101–29.

160 T. Duve, "What Is Global Legal History?," *Comparative Legal History* 8(2) (2020), 73–115. It is important to stress that the entire field of the history of international law has been booming. Nevertheless, the history of international law is not global legal history, which is capable of addressing broader topics than the norms regulating international relations. For current trends on the history of international law, see M. Koskenniemi, *To the Uttermost Parts of the Earth: Legal Imagination and International Power, 1300–1870* (Cambridge: Cambridge University Press, 2021); J. Marglin, "Nationality on Trial: International Private Law Across the Mediterranean," *Annales. Histoire, Sciences Sociales (English Edition)* 73(1) (2018), 81–113; and I. Van Hulle, *Britain and International Law in West Africa: The Practice of Empire* (The History and Theory of International Law) (Oxford: Oxford University Press, 2020).

161 C. de Castelnau-L'Estoile, *Páscoa et ses deux maris. Une esclave entre Angola, Brésil et Portugal au XVII*^e^ *siècle* (Paris: PUF, 2019); D. Galeano, *Criminosos viajantes. Circulações transnacionais entre Rio de Janeiro e Buenos Aires, 1890–1930* (Rio de Janeiro: Arquivo Nacional, 2016); J. M. Hébrard and R. J. Scott, *Freedom Papers: An Atlantic Odyssey in the Age of Emancipation* (Cambridge: Harvard University Press, 2012), 6–19; J. Marquez, "Witnesses to Freedom: Paula's Enslavement, Her Family's Freedom Suit, and the Making of a Counterarchive in the South Atlantic World," *Hispanic American Historical Review* 101(2) (2021), 231–63.

perspective that drew on the history of empires and that conflated, to some extent, the "imperial" with the "global." Even fewer works embrace a more explicit claim that includes global perspectives in the analysis of specific regions of the world.[162]

In Section 1.4, I argue that writing legal history in a global perspective has the potential to overcome theoretical blind spots and put forward less Eurocentric perspectives on how law is made. When it comes to legal histories of regions in the Global South, the most common approaches depart from theoretical assumptions that place the production of law outside these regions themselves. The Global South is often depicted as a recipient of law, that is, places to which law is transplanted, transferred, adapted, and so on. According to these assumptions, inspired by their foreign counterparts, elite jurists in these locations lay the groundwork for this reception and adaptation of foreign law.[163]

Placing the production of norms primarily outside the Global South reflects origin myths that still pervade scholarship on legal history. For scholars with a legal or historical background, it is still commonplace to identify the origins of legal categories and institutions in Roman law, the French Civil Code, the US Constitution, Savigny's work, and so on. These origin myths are usually

162 See, for example, L. Benton, "The Legal Regime of the South Atlantic World, 1400–1750: Jurisdictional Complexity as Institutional Order," *Journal of World History* 11(1) (2000), 27–56; Duve, "Global Legal History;" T. Green, "Baculamento or Encomienda? Legal Pluralisms and the Contestation of Power in the Pan-Atlantic World of the Sixteenth and Seventeenth Centuries," *Journal of Global Slavery* 2(3) (2017), 310–36; W. L. Silva Júnior, "No limiar da escravidão: uma mirada global sobre os debates em torno de *coartados* em Cuba (1856) e *statuliberi* no Brasil (1857)," *Revista de História* 179 (2020), 1–33.

163 For a summary on the debates concerning legal transplants, transfer, adaptation, hybridization, etc. that still inform most of the research on Latin America legal history, see M. Graziadei, "Comparative Law, Transplants, and Receptions," in M. Reimann and R. Zimmermann (eds.), *The Oxford Handbook of Comparative Law*, 2nd ed. (Oxford: Oxford University Press, 2019), 442–73. More recently, scholars have been calling attention to the innovative production of norms taking place in Latin America. The fields of constitutional law, international law, and legal anthropology are especially thriving. See, for example, J.-M. Barreto (ed.), *Human Rights From a Third World Perspective: Critique, History and International Law* (Newcastle Upon Tyne: Cambridge Scholars Publishing, 2013); A. Becker Lorca, *Mestizo International Law: A Global Intellectual History 1842–1933* (Cambridge Studies in International and Comparative Law 115) (Cambridge: Cambridge University Press, 2014); D. Bonilla Maldonado, "El constitucionalismo radical ambiental y la diversidad cultural en América Latina. Los derechos de la naturaleza y el buen vivir en Ecuador y Bolivia," *Revista Derecho del Estado* 42 (2018), 3–23; L. Obregón, "Between Civilisation and Barbarism: Creole Interventions in International Law," *Third World Quarterly* 27(5) (2006), 815–32; L. Obregón, "Peripheral Histories of International Law," *Annual Review of Law and Social Science* 15 (2019), 437–51.

accompanied by a strict dichotomy separating "law" from "practice." This dichotomy, in turn, leads to the clear distinction between the "production of law" and the "use of law." Production is often associated with jurists and government agents. Usage, on the other hand, usually encompasses a wider spectrum of social groups, frequently ones able to resort to courts in order to claim rights and better living conditions.

In what follows, I demonstrate that a global perspective can shed light on how law was made in regions of the Global South, going beyond hegemonic paradigms such as "transplant." To do so, I will present a set of conceptual tools that might help to highlight the role of other agents and places outside the traditional ones in the making of law. This perspective goes beyond the habitual analysis that considers jurists and politicians as the main agents in producing norms within solemn places, such as state institutions and law schools. In the first section, I will discuss the "production of norms" as a process assigning "concrete meanings" to legal categories and institutions – a process consisting of many layers. While some of them have long been the object of historiographical attention, such as the role of early modern jurists in building conceptual legal frameworks, others have not yet received sufficient attention.[164] The most important among them are the role of "practice," of reiterated habits, the reproduction of formalities, and the reinforcement of worldviews in the making of law.[165]

Assuming the engagement of a wide array of agents in the making of law, I use "memories" and "zones of shared production of norms" as conceptual tools to bring "the global" to the analysis of the law. "Memories" – understood as shared cultural backgrounds – can potentially highlight the role that non-Western normative systems and diverse worldviews might have played in assigning concrete meanings to legal categories and institutions. In this sense, "the global" can exist within the experiences of a single person or within a group of individuals that share common cultural backgrounds.[166] "Zones of shared production of norms"

164 A. M. Hespanha, *Como os juristas viam o mundo. 1550–1750. Direitos, estados, pessoas, coisas, contratos, ações e crimes* (Lisboa: CreateSpace Independent Publishing Platform, 2015), 3–24.

165 For a discussion of the role of practice in normative production, see T. Duve, "Historia del derecho como historia del saber normativo," *Revista de Historia del Derecho* 63 (2022), 1–60. See also M. Dias Paes, "Legal Files and Empires: Form and Materiality of the Benguela District Court Documents," *Administory – Zeitschrift für Verwaltungsgeschichte* 4 (2019), 53–70.

166 D. Sachsenmaier, *Global Entanglements of a Man Who Never Traveled: A Seventeenth-Century Chinese Christian and His Conflicted Worlds* (New York: Columbia University Press, 2018). See also M. J. M. de Carvalho, F. dos Santos Gomes, and J. J. Reis, *The Story of Rufino. Slavery, Freedom, and Islam in the Black Atlantic*, trans. H. S. Gledhill

are, in turn, inductively defined geographical spaces that may or may not coincide with imperial or national boundaries. They indicate that "the global" entails a geography that encompasses connections between places where norms can be produced outside and independent of European spaces.

Although Section 1.4 and volume focus on the legal history of Latin America, its theoretical and methodological claims also apply to the writing of legal histories of other regions of the Global South, for example, Africa.[167] While I will make explicit references to Latin America throughout the text and use mostly examples drawn from the scholarship on Latin American legal history, my broader aim is to contribute to the elaboration of new ways of writing legal history. In this sense, this section is not addressed exclusively to legal historians focused on Latin America but to legal historians in general.

Myths of Origin in Latin American Legal History

As Tamar Herzog emphasizes (see Section 1.2), a multiplicity of ways of doing legal history have been pursued over the last few decades. When it comes to the history of law in Latin America, despite many attempts to promote interdisciplinarity, a fairly harsh institutional, theoretical, and methodological division still exists between legal historians with a background in law and those with a background in history. Though exceptions exist, especially among younger scholars making a real effort to engage in debates with peers from different disciplinary backgrounds, such scholars are by no means the rule.

This institutional division minimizes the role that historians have played in the building of legal history scholarship. In recent years, social history in particular has been extremely important in the writing of the legal history of Latin America. Though the contribution of social historians is not adequately acknowledged in narratives on the history of the field, their work has, nonetheless, played a crucial role in promoting core debates on methodological issues when analyzing law, as well as on stressing the engagement of subaltern groups with legal matters. That subaltern groups, such as enslaved

(Oxford: Oxford University Press, 2020); Castelnau-L'Estoile, *Páscoa et ses deux maris*; Hébrard and Scott, *Freedom Papers*; B. G. Mamigonian, "José Majojo e Francisco Moçambique, marinheiros das rotas atlânticas: notas sobre a reconstituição de trajetórias da era da abolição," *Topoi. Revista de História* 11(20) (2010), 75–91; Marquez, "Witnesses to Freedom."

167 It is important to stress that "Africa" is a highly diverse continent, within which societies with different cultural backgrounds exist: *hausa, somali, berber, akan, fulani, igbo, kikongo, yoruba, zulu, shona, ovimbundo*, etc. Nevertheless, for the sake of reading fluidity, I will employ "Africa" the same way I do with "Europe" and "Latin America," that is, to refer to a geographical space within which diverse societies exist.

persons, women, workers, indigenous populations, and children, made their way into historical research on law is due in large part to social history. Besides directing attention to new agents, the work of social historians also made it clear that researchers interested in law should analyze sources other than the writings of jurists and enactments by state institutions. Social historians also contested many theoretical and methodological assumptions of the more traditional scholarship on law and history. They were, for example, the main party responsible for claiming that the writing of legal history should rely on extensive archival research, encompassing a broad array of sources in addition to legislation and legal doctrine.[168]

Though some progress has been made toward combining legal and historical training, when it comes to addressing global issues, scholars in both "groups" tend to disregard non-jurists and non-government agents as producers of norms and tend to place innovative production of norms outside Latin America.

Carlos Petit (see Section 1.1) explains how legal historians with a legal background wrote over the years the history of law in Latin America. As he clarifies, for many years, this way of doing legal history privileged official sources and focused mostly on legislation and legal doctrine.[169] This scholarship

168 E. Azevedo, *O direito dos escravos. Lutas jurídicas e abolicionismo na província de São Paulo* (Campinas: Editora da Unicamp, 2010); P. Cantisano and M. Dias Paes, "Apresentação: processos judiciais e escrita da história na América Latina," *Varia Historia* 37(74) (2021), 353–60; S. Chalhoub, *Visões da liberdade. Uma história das últimas décadas da escravidão na corte* (São Paulo: Companhia das Letras, 1990); M. A. Corva, "Rastreando huellas: la búsqueda de documentos judiciales para la investigación histórica," *Revista Electrónica de Fuentes y Archivos* 6 (2015), 43–65; M. Dantas and F. N. Ribeiro, "A importância dos acervos judiciais para a pesquisa em história: um percurso," *LexCult. Revista Eletrônica de Direito e Humanidades* 4(2) (2020), 47–87; K. Grinberg, *A Black Jurist in a Slave Society: Antonio Pereira Rebouças and the Trials of Brazilian Citizenship* (Chapel Hill: University of North Carolina Press, 2019); T. Herzog, *Upholding Justice: Society, State, and the Penal System in Quito (1650–1750)* (Ann Arbor: University of Michigan Press, 2007); S. H. Lara, *Campos da violência. Escravos e senhores na Capitania do Rio de Janeiro. 1750–1808* (Rio de Janeiro: Paz e Terra, 1988); S. H. Lara and J. M. N. Mendonça, "Apresentação," in S. H. Lara and J. M. N. Mendonça (eds.), *Direitos e justiças no Brasil. Ensaios de história social* (Coleção Várias Histórias 22) (Campinas: Editora da Unicamp, 2006), 9–22; S. Mallo, C. Mayo, and O. Barreneche, "Plebe urbana y justicia colonial: las fuentes judiciales, notas para su manejo metodológico," *Frontera, sociedad y justicias coloniales: Estudios-Investigaciones* 1 (1989), 47–53; B. Premo, *The Enlightenment on Trial: Ordinary Litigants and Colonialism in the Spanish Empire* (Oxford: Oxford University Press, 2017); M. Yangilevich, "Normas, rupturas y continuidades: la administración de justicia y los ataques contra la propiedad en la Provincia de Buenos Aires (2ª mitad del siglo XIX)," *Revista de Historia del Derecho* 38 (2009), 1–11.

169 For further discussion of this legal history historiography, see T. Duve, "Rechtsgeschichte als Geschichte von Normativitätswissen?," *Rechtsgeschichte – Legal History* 29 (2021), 41–68; and A. M. Hespanha, "Is There a Place for a Separated Legal History? A Broad Review of Recent Developments on Legal Historiography," *Quaderni fiorentini per la storia del pensiero giuridico moderno* 48 (2019), 7–28.

traced the origins of Latin America's legal categories and institutions mostly to Iberian colonial law and Roman law. Norms were either a transplant or subject to the influence of foreign legal debates, such as those posed by the Historical School, and foreign legislation, such as the French Civil Code. The places of innovative norm production were, therefore, mostly outside of Latin America. Global perspectives were virtually absent since this historiography was framed largely by methodological nationalism.[170] The "global" appeared mostly as the myths of origin created by Roman or colonial law that somehow linked Latin America to European traditions.[171]

The Eurocentrism characteristic of this way of doing legal history was influenced by the assumption that the "law of jurists" was the primary object of research in the field.[172] It presupposed that the only actors who produced norms were part of a narrow elite, learned group. These were the actors influenced by foreign legal debates and responsible for adapting them to Latin American realities. Other historical actors were considered irrelevant to legal history. An eloquent example of this perspective is given by Petit (Section 1.1): "[T]he African populations – the authority, in this case, was another professor from Recife, the great Clóvis Beviláqua – did not really contribute anything to Brazilian law because of their condition as enslaved people."[173]

As emphasized in other chapters in this volume, the work of António Manuel Hespanha, Víctor Tau Anzoátegui, and Bartolomé Clavero criticized this tradition and proposed other ways of writing the legal history of the Iberian empires (see Section 1.2). More recent works incorporated much of what the aforementioned authors proposed regarding the relative autonomy of law; the role of local practices and customs; the importance of other normative spheres, such as religion, affection, and so forth; and the necessity to broaden the range of primary sources. Yet, the relation of Latin America to other parts of the Global South occupied only a marginal space in their work or was altogether absent. In this sense, the "global" was again embodied in ideas such as "circulation," "reception," "transfer," "adaptation," "comparison," which seemed to lead only to the protagonism of some places but not others. Moreover, jurists and government agents are still depicted in many studies as the main producers of norms, though some scholars broaden the array of actors, including in

170 On "methodological nationalism," see Duve, "Global Legal History," 3–11; Duve, "Rechtsgeschichte als Geschichte."

171 On ideological grounds of linking colonial law to European traditions, see A. M. Hespanha, "O direito de Índias no contexto da historiografia das colonizações ibéricas," in T. Duve (ed.), *Actas del XIX Congreso del Instituto Internacional de Historia del Derecho Indiano. Berlín 2016* (Madrid: Dykinson, 2017), vol. I, 43–85.

172 Duve, "Rechtsgeschichte als Geschichte."

173 See Section 1.1.

their analysis the lower echelons of colonial bureaucracies and people who constantly interacted with the law but did not necessarily have a formal legal education.[174] And while subaltern groups, such as women, indigenous people, and enslaved persons, have indeed been the subject of more recent research, they are usually portrayed as "users" of the law who mobilize legal categories in order to resist, claim rights, or achieve better living conditions. They are not considered, however, producers of norms.

Though taking a different route, legal historians with a background in history usually end up falling into the same trap. The contribution of social history to the field of Latin American legal history is immeasurable. However, in most of these works, a very traditional idea of law continues to persist, that is, associating law with written legislation. In this sense, everything that happens contrary to, or in the absence of, written legislation is considered "custom" or "practice." An example of this narrow conception of law are the debates over enslaved persons' *peculium*. Having shown that enslaved people went to court to pay for their manumission well before the Free Womb laws came into existence was undoubtedly a significant innovation on the part of social historians. Forming a *peculium* and later claiming the right to pay for manumission, however, was characterized by these historians as a "customary practice" that was eventually recognized by legislation. In other words, though these scholars acknowledge that enslaved people were aware of and engaged with the law, their actions were situated in the realm of custom and *not* law – certainly not in the sense of the Free Womb legislation. According to this view, courts were therefore an "arena of struggle" where law was "mobilized." The engagement of subaltern groups with norms was depicted in terms of "practice" and often contrary to "law." The result of such perspectives is the reproduction of narrow conceptions regarding the places and agents of the production of norms. As for "the global," transplanted paradigms and related perspectives often make their way into this scholarship. One such "classic" misconception is to tie the roots of slavery law to Roman law. The result of this assumption is that the law "used" by subaltern groups has its origins mostly outside of Latin America. Again, Europe plays a central role in the innovative production of norms, resulting in the exclusion of other geographies of production.[175]

174 See, for example, O. Danwerth and T. Duve (eds.), *Knowledge of the Pragmatici: Legal and Moral Theological Literature and the Formation of Early Modern Ibero-America* (Max Planck Studies in Global Legal History of the Iberian Worlds 1) (Leiden: Brill Nijhoff, 2020).

175 See also, M. Dias Paes, "Direito e escravidão no Brasil Império," in S. Barbosa and M. Dantas (eds.), *Constituição de poderes, constituição de sujeitos: caminhos da história do direito no Brasil (1750–1930)* (Cadernos do IEB 14) (São Paulo: Instituto de Estudos Brasileiros, 2021), 182–203.

Over the last few years, social historians have produced an amazing body of scholarship showing the entanglement between different cultural backgrounds – notably the highly diverse cultural practices of African societies – in the making of Latin American societies.[176] Why exclude law from this perspective? Why should law be considered something primarily made in regions of the Global North by elite groups? Why should the legal systems of the societies of the Global South and of subaltern groups be classified as "customs" – a label that clearly reproduces the perspective framed by colonial agents?[177] In Section 1.4, I propose that Latin American legal history would benefit from a global perspective that enables a broadening of the places and agents of the production of norms, rendering a more complex answer to the question: How is law made?

The Production of Norms and Concrete Meanings

The "production of norms" is a conceptual tool that allows us to overcome dichotomies such as "law" and "reality," "law" and "practice," "law-in-action" and "law-in-the-books," and "law" and "custom." "Production" emphasizes that law is not a given; it is not a monolithic thing transplanted from one place to another in an atemporal and decontextualized fashion. Law is produced in a specific historical context by a variety of historical agents. It is not

176 C. Alfagali, "'Capazes de trabalhar': domínio, política e cultura nas relações de trabalho do Atlântico Sul (séculos XVII e XVIII)," *Topoi. Revista de História* 22(47) (2021), 387–407; Carvalho, Santos Gomes, and Reis, *The Story of Rufino*; A. Chira, *Patchwork Freedoms: Law, Slavery, and Race Beyond Cuba's Plantations* (Cambridge: Cambridge University Press, 2022); Hébrard and Scott, *Freedom Papers*, 6–19; S. H. Lara, *Palmares & Cucaú. O Aprendizado da Dominação* (São Paulo: Edusp, 2021); I. L. Miller, *Voice of the Leopard: African Secret Societies and Cuba* (Jackson: University Press of Mississippi, 2012); J. J. Reis, *Slave Rebellion in Brazil: The Muslim Uprising of 1835 in Bahia*, trans. A. Brakel (Baltimore: Johns Hopkins University Press, 1993); J. J. Reis, *Divining Slavery and Freedom: The Story of Domingos Sodré, an African Priest in Nineteenth-Century Brazil* (New Approaches to the Americas), trans. H. S. Gledhill (Cambridge: Cambridge University Press, 2015); R. Slenes, "'Malungo, ngoma vem!': África coberta e descoberta do Brasil," *Revista USP* 12 (1992), 48–67; R. Slenes, *Na senzala, uma flor. Esperanças e recordações na formação da família escrava: Brasil Sudeste, século XIX* (Campinas: Editora da Unicamp, 2011).

177 For a discussion of how "custom" is a concept framed within colonialism, see M. Chanock, *Law, Custom, and Social Order: The Colonial Experience in Malawi and Zambia* (Cambridge: Cambridge University Press, 1985); T. Ranger, "The Invention of Tradition in Colonial Africa," in E. Hobsbawm and T. Ranger (eds.), *The Invention of Tradition* (Cambridge: Cambridge University Press, 1983), 211–62. See also T. Herzog, "Immemorial (and Native) Customs in Early Modernity: Europe and the Americas," *Comparative Legal History* 9(1) (2021), 3–55; F. Salomon, "Collquiri's Dam: The Colonial Re-Voicing of an Appeal to the Archaic," in E. Hill Boone and T. Cummins (eds.), *Native Traditions in the Postconquest World: A Symposium at Dumbarton Oaks, 2nd through 4th October 1992* (Cambridge: Harvard University Press, 1998), 265–93.

an abstract entity that "came from Roman law," but rather it is produced by people on a daily basis and is deeply entangled with local cultural backgrounds, worldviews, social structures, and political struggles. Moreover, using the concept of "norms" instead of "law" prevents us from considering only state-produced written legislation as that which belongs to the legal sphere. "Norms" is a broader concept that can shed light on other forms of normative behavior as well as knowledge of normativities that are crucial to understanding the various layers of complexity that regulating societies and solving conflicts entail.[178]

The production of norms is a broader process that entails much more than creating legislation, legal categories, or institutions that will at a later point in time be applied or used by historical agents. Producing norms means assigning concrete meanings to legal categories. This assignment of concrete meanings happens through the reproduction and enforcement of different knowledge of normativity.[179] Therefore, legal history scholarship gains complexity when focusing on the way people act when it comes to normative matters. Moreover, people's knowledge of normativity is a key aspect of the making of law, as the examples later illustrate. Paying close attention to what people say about norms and to how they behave on a daily basis, informed by certain normative ideas, makes it clear that this process of assigning concrete meanings to norms does not solely occur in solemn places such as the state. This process takes place in an extremely diffuse way, both on a local and global level. In order to explain how this process occurs, let us look at the example of possession.

"Possession" is a structural legal category of European societies. Before the advent of codification, it was hardly defined in written legislation; its formal definition was mostly found in doctrinal texts. A widespread definition of "possession" among learned jurists was: "the natural faculty to apprehend a thing with the intention of having it as one's own."[180] But what does it concretely mean to have something as one's own? The doctrinal definition per se does not really explain what possession is. Therefore, if we only looked to written legislation or to doctrinal texts, we lose some of the fundamental dimensions of this legal category.

The concrete meaning of possession – what it actually meant to have something as one's own – varied with regard to a given time and space. For

178 Duve, "Global Legal History." 179 See Section 1.3 in this volume.

180 P. J. Mellii Freirii, *Institutionum juris civilis lusitani cum publici, tum privati* (Lisboa: Typographia Ejusdem Academiae, 1800), lib. III, 14. See also, Hespanha, *Como os juristas*, 352–60.

example, to possess a piece of land in nineteenth-century Brazil meant things like building houses corresponding to specific patterns of "quality," usually associated with Portuguese colonial architecture (*casas de vivenda*); cultivating certain crops, for example, coffee; planting specific kinds of trees such as guava trees; having enslaved persons, free workers, or dependents working one's land and reverting part or the entire production to the "legitimate master and possessor", allowing free dependents to occupy the land, and so on. These acts, and many others, constituted the concrete meanings of possession in nineteenth-century Brazil because local communities recognized them as patterns of behavior that would ground land rights and, therefore, constantly repeated and enforced them. It is worth noting that jurists also recognized these actions as acts imbued with legal value, placing them at the center of judicial disputes over land and of public policies.[181] For years, however, most of the scholarship considered such acts of possession "practices" and "customs" that unfolded outside of or even in opposition to law. By restricting norms to written legislation or even juridical doctrine, such perspectives tend to obscure other aspects of the production of norms. Acts such as those listed earlier were not just social practices but also legal ones. Informed by specific knowledge of normativity, they were normative behaviors capable of generating law.

The well-known legal category of *indio* is another instance of how paying attention to the creation of concrete meanings attributed to norms highlights a richer and more complex picture of Latin America legal history. Let's take as an example the case of enslaved persons of Asian origin in colonial Mexico. During the sixteenth and the seventeenth centuries, various enslaved persons reached Mexico from different regions of the Indian subcontinent and Southeast Asia. Initially categorized by Spanish colonial officials as *chinos*, many enslaved persons and some jurists argued they were actually *indios*, that is, vassals of the Spanish Crown. Throughout the centuries, different historical agents disputed and assigned a wide array of concrete meanings to the legal category of *indio* when referring to Asian populations. To some, the indigenous people of the Philippines – with the exception of those coming from Muslim societies – were vassals of the Spanish Crown and therefore classified as *indios chinos*, a group that could not be enslaved. Asians from

181 M. Dias Paes, "Ser dependente no Império do Brasil: terra e trabalho em processos judiciais," *Población & Sociedad* 27(2) (2020), 8–29; M. Dias Paes, *Esclavos y tierras entre posesión y títulos. La construcción social del derecho de propiedad en Brasil (siglo XIX)* (Global Perspectives on Legal History 17) (Frankfurt am Main: Max-Planck-Institut für europäische Rechtsgeschichte, 2021).

regions not subject to Spanish colonial power, on the other hand, were *chinos* that could be enslaved. Under certain circumstances, colonial officials considered all *chinos* to be "free *indios*." The assignment of concrete meanings to the legal category of *indio* within the context of Asian slavery in Mexico was clearly a process that occurred in different places and involved a variety of actors: well-known jurists who wrote legal treatises; legal officials and judges who acted on the ground and in local courts; religious authorities who took part in global and local debates over the legitimacy of slavery; enslaved persons of different Asian origins who self-identified as *indios* in their everyday lives and filed court cases; and indigenous individuals who had personal relations and eventually established family ties with people from the other side of the Pacific.[182]

Understanding the production of norms as a process that creates concrete meanings assigned to legal categories is a theoretical perspective that also applies to postcolonial and contemporary societies. The case of "contemporary slavery" makes it very clear. There is no consensus in the international community on what currently constitutes "slave labor."[183] Thus, the meaning of this legal category can change dramatically depending on specific contexts. The Brazilian Penal Code defines the crime of reducing someone to a condition analogous to that of a slave as follows: (a) submitting someone to forced labor, (b) submitting someone to exhausting working hours, (c) subjecting someone to degrading working conditions, (d) restricting someone's mobility due to a debt with the employer, (e) to curtail the employer from using means of transportation with the goal of keeping the worker at the workplace, (f) to employ ostensible vigilance at the working place and to retain workers' documents, or (g) personal objects with the goal of keeping them at

182 T. Seijas, *Asian Slaves in Colonial Mexico: From Chinos to Indians* (Cambridge: Cambridge University Press, 2014). The historiography analyzing the different meanings of *indio* in Latin America is enormous. For bibliographic references on this topic, see ch. 2, 3.3, 5.3, and 7 in this volume. In the chapter on Global Legal History, it is also important to stress that the legal category of *indio* was not particular to Latin America. In the context of Portuguese colonialism in Africa, the legal category of *indígena* also acquired concrete meanings that had commonalities and differences with the legal meanings it acquired in Latin America. See, for example, L. Macagno, *A invenção do assimilado. Paradoxos do Colonialismo em Moçambique* (Lisboa: Edições Colibri, 2020); I. Monteiro, "A cidadania e o Indigenato: uma confrontação sociopolítica e cultural no Cabo Verde colónia (1820–1960)," Ph.D. thesis, Universidade de Coimbra (2017); C. Nogueira da Silva, *Constitucionalismo e império. A cidadania no ultramar português* (Coimbra: Almedina, 2009).

183 Scholars, jurists, and activists have been trying to address this lack of consensus in order to make the repression to this crime more effective. See, for example, J. Allain (ed.), *The Legal Understanding of Slavery: From the Historical to the Contemporary* (Oxford: Oxford University Press, 2012).

the workplace. According to the letter of the law, any and all of these actions constitute the crime. They do not need to all happen at the same time, nor is one more relevant than the other in constituting the offense.[184] But, as I have been arguing, assigning concrete meanings to norms is a much more complex process than enacting a penal code.

Despite the letter of the law as found in the Brazilian Penal Code, for a crime to have occurred, judges tend to consider that the employer or someone acting on his behalf must restrain the mobility and the autonomy of the worker. This understanding resonates with narratives found in legal doctrine that traces "slavery" to common sense ideas regarding transatlantic slavery – ideas that do not take into consideration the huge body of knowledge about this topic produced by historians and legal historians over the last few decades.[185] On the other hand, activists and some jurists have a different conception of what constitutes contemporary slavery. They argue that the actual meaning of the Brazilian Penal Code's article is that slavery is related to labor conditions against or incommensurate with human dignity.[186] Workers subjected to degrading working conditions also have their own conceptions about what constitutes slavery, how working conditions should be, and what actions by their employers are and are not permissible.[187] In this sense, even in the twenty-first century, we can see that different actors, each with different knowledge of normativity, interact and dispute the concrete meanings of norms. In these disputes, they create law.

184 M. Dias Paes, "La esclavitud contemporánea en la doctrina jurídica brasileña: un análisis desde la perspectiva de la historia del derecho," *Revista Electrónica del Instituto de Investigaciones Ambrosio L. Gioja* 17 (2016), 6–34; M. Dias Paes, "L'histoire devant les tribunaux: la notion d'esclavage contemporain dans les décisions judiciaires brésiliennes," *Brésil(s). Sciences humaines et sociales* 11 (2017).

185 Dias Paes, "La esclavitud contemporánea"; Dias Paes, "L'histoire devant les tribunaux;" R. Scott, "O trabalho escravo contemporâneo e os usos da história," *Revista Mundos do Trabalho* 5(9) (2013), 129–37.

186 L. A. de Andrade Barbosa, C. H. Borlido Haddad, and R. J. Scott, "How Does the Law Put a Historical Analogy to Work? Defining the Imposition of 'A Condition Analogous to That of a Slaver' in Modern Brazil," *Duke Journal of Constitutional Law & Public Policy* 13 (2017), 1–46; R. Rezende Figueira, E. M. Galvão, and A. Antunes Prado (eds.), *Discussões contemporâneas sobre trabalho escravo: teoria e pesquisa* (Rio de Janeiro: Mauad X, 2017); R. Rezende Figueira, E. M. Galvão, V. Jacob, and A. Antunes Prado (eds.), *Estudos sobre as formas contemporâneas de trabalho escravo* (Rio de Janeiro: Mauad X, 2018); M. Gomes Silva Lopes, M. C. Fernandes Oliveira, and T. Souza Rodrigues (eds.), *Quanto vale a dignidade? Estudos contemporâneos sobre trabalho escravo* (Belo Horizonte: RTM, 2021).

187 R. Rezende Figueira, *Pisando fora da própria sombra. A escravidão por dívida no Brasil contemporâneo* (Rio de Janeiro: Civilização Brasileira, 2004); R. Rezende Figueira, R. F. Palmeira, and A. Antunes Prado, *A escravidão na Amazônia. Quatro décadas de depoimentos de fugitivos e libertos* (Rio de Janeiro: Mauad X, 2021).

Shared legal understandings, habitual practices, and daily reiteration of forms and procedures are therefore an essential dimension of the production of norms; they are not something related to yet nevertheless occurring outside of it.[188] When the role of practice as constitutive of law itself is taken into consideration, adopting global perspectives in the writing of legal history become almost inevitable.

Memories as Shared Cultural Backgrounds

Assigning concrete meanings to norms takes place through different mechanisms. Some of them have long been the object of historiographical attention, such as the construction and reproduction of learned legal knowledge within law schools, courts' jurisprudence, codification debates, and so forth. Given the dimensions involved, the role of global processes might seem fairly evident since learned jurists and governmental agents traveled from one place to the next, had access to foreign literature, and explicitly claimed the authority of foreign influence to justify their arguments and proposals. The global dimension of the participation of other groups in the production of norms is, however, not that explicit.[189]

"Memories" is another concept that can help to highlight other dimensions of the entanglement of global processes in the production of norms. When studying enslaved families in nineteenth-century Brazil, historian Robert Slenes argued that the great majority of enslaved persons in the southeast region were either from West Central Africa or their direct descendants. Despite the existence of different ethnic groups in West Central Africa, most of them shared a common cultural background that had a direct impact on how enslaved persons shaped their ways of life and strategies of resistance in Brazil. This common cultural background could be considered "memories" that informed the actions of West Central African enslaved persons and their descendants in Brazil. Enslaved persons did not lose their cultural "memories" when forced to cross the Atlantic. On the contrary, they kept these memories and were able to disseminate them among their descendants.[190]

Slenes' idea that "memories" – understood not as individual and subjective experiences, but instead as shared cultural backgrounds – shaped the ways of life of enslaved Africans and their descendants in Brazil can be extended to law

188 Duve, "Rechtsgeschichte als Geschichte."

189 For a discussion on how to include global perspectives when analyzing the lives of people "who never travelled," see Sachsenmaier, *Global Entanglements*.

190 Slenes, "'Malungo, ngoma vem';" Slenes, *Na senzala, uma flor*.

and, more broadly, normative behavior. It is a useful concept for approaching the production of norms in a more complex fashion. Norms exist in any society, and they shape people's behavior and daily actions. Not only cultural practices as the structure of families, modes of resistance, culinary habits, and artistic manifestations are part of "memories." Knowledge of normativities and normative behavior also constitute people's "memories." Digging through these memories makes it possible to uncover the more complex backgrounds underlying certain patterns of normative behavior, repetitive practices, and reiterated habits that help assign concrete meanings to norms. Taking "memories" seriously in writing the legal history of Latin America could challenge the origins that are often attributed to legal categories and institutions, namely Europe or the United States. It inserts Africa and Asia into the equation and suggests entanglements that are quite different from "reception" or "imitation." It also puts the legal history of Latin America in a truly global perspective.[191]

An example of what including "memories" can do to the writing of Latin American legal history in a global perspective is the recent scholarship that discusses the presence of African Muslims in the Americas during the era of the transatlantic slave trade. Although the exact numbers are difficult to estimate, data suggests that during the nineteenth century, most of enslaved Muslims left from ports in Upper Guinea and disembarked in the Spanish Caribbean and in the Amazon region.[192] Some enslaved persons who arrived in Mexico were Muslims from the Philippines.[193] There is also a substantive body of scholarship that analyzes the social practices and modes of resistance of enslaved Muslims in the northeast of Brazil.[194]

As was the case with the West Central African enslaved persons who were the focus of Slenes' research, Muslim Africans did not lose their "memories" (cultural background) when forcibly trafficked to the Americas. Since the

191 In addition to the existence of a common cultural background, scholars have been showing how subaltern groups actively produced written documents that attest to a literacy that also extended into the realm of "the law." J. Rappaport and T. Cummins, *Beyond the Lettered City: Indigenous Literacies in the Andes* (Narrating Native Histories) (Durham and London: Duke University Press, 2012); Premo, The Enlightenment on Trial; G. Ramos and Y. Yannakakis (eds.), *Indigenous Intellectuals: Knowledge, Power, and Colonial Culture in Mexico and the Andes* (Durham and London: Duke University Press, 2014).

192 D. Eltis, N. Khan, P. Misevich, O. Ojo, and D. B. Domingues da Silva, "The Transatlantic Muslim Diaspora to Latin America in the Nineteenth Century," *Colonial Latin American Review* 26(4) (2017), 528–45.

193 Seijas, *Asian Slaves in Colonial Mexico*, 61–67.

194 Carvalho, Santos Gomes, and Reis, *The Story of Rufino*; Reis, *Slave Rebellion in Brazil*; Reis, *Divining Slavery and Freedom*.

seventeenth century, the perseverance of their beliefs in Cartagena de Indias posed constant challenges to the projects of Catholic missionaries.[195] Apart from being a religion that shapes cultural manifestations and modes of resistance, Islam is also a legal system. Therefore, the presence of such individuals in Latin America raises the question of how "memories" of Islamic legal systems,[196] that is, a shared legal background, might have impacted these enslaved Muslims and their descendants' patterns of normative behavior and thus formed part of the history of law in the Americas. To what extent might the fundamental and even magical role that written words possess in Islam have affected how enslaved persons approached manumission papers?[197] To what extent might their previous familiarity with the possibility of claiming rights and freedom in courts have shaped their judicial behavior before Latin American tribunals?[198]

It is well known among historians of Latin America that enslaved persons resorted to courts in order to complain about abuse and misconduct on the part of owners. Moreover, enslaved persons in Cuba made strong claims to have acquired rights through the practice of *coartación*, that is, an agreement between them and their owners to pay for freedom in installments. The lawsuits originating from these kinds of disputes show that enslaved people had their own shared conceptions about the law, about practices that were legal or illegal, and about their rights and their owners' obligations.[199] It is

195 T. H. Mota, "Wolof and Mandinga Muslims in the Early Atlantic World: African Background, Missionary Disputes, and Social Expansion of Islam Before the Fula *Jihads*," *Atlantic Studies. Global Currents* 20(1) (2021), 150–76.

196 Similar to *ius commune* legal tradition, Islamic legal systems rely heavily on doctrinal writings. There are four main schools of jurisprudence within Islamic Law: *Maliki* (predominant in North Africa), *Hanafi*, *Shafi'i* (predominant in East Africa), and *Hanbali*. A. A. Sikainga, "Shari'a Courts and the Manumission of Female Slaves in the Sudan, 1898–1939," *The International Journal of African Historical Studies* 28(1) (1995), 1–24.

197 On the role of writing among Muslim African diaspora, see Carvalho, Santos Gomes and Reis, *The Story of Rufino*; Reis, *Slave Rebellion in Brazil*. See also the hypothesis raised by Hébrard and Scott, *Freedom Papers*, 6–19. On the selling of Korans in nineteenth-century Rio de Janeiro, see A. da Costa e Silva, "Buying and Selling Korans in Nineteenth-Century Rio de Janeiro," *Slavery & Abolition* 22(1) (2001), 72–82.

198 Sikainga, "Shari'a Courts;" E. R. Toledano, *As If Silent and Absent: Bonds of Enslavement in the Islamic Middle East* (New Haven: Yale University Press, 2007); E. R. Toledano, *Slavery and Abolition in the Ottoman Middle East* (Publications on the Near East) (Seattle and London: University of Washington Press, 1998); J. M. White, "Slavery, Manumission, and Freedom Suits in the Early Modern Ottoman Empire," in S. Conermann and G. Şen (eds.), *Slaves and Slave Agency in the Ottoman Empire* (Ottoman Studies / Osmanistische Studien 7) (Bonn: Bonn University Press, 2020), 283–320.

199 A. de la Fuente, "Su 'único derecho': los esclavos y la ley," *Debate y Perspectivas* 4 (2004), 7–21; A. de la Fuente, "Slaves and the Creation of Legal Rights in Cuba: *Coartación* and *Papel*," *Hispanic American Historical Review* 87(4) (2007), 659–92. See also E. Pérez

noteworthy that enslaved persons in Muslim communities made similar legal claims. Muslim judges (*qadi*) could decide to sell or manumit someone whose owner was not treating them appropriately. Manumission agreements such as the establishment of a fixed sum the slave would pay to buy his freedom, or the commitment the slave would be free after the owner's death, were also present in Muslim societies.[200] When dealing with similar claims for rights in Latin America, it would be fruitful to take into account other cultural backgrounds in addition to tracing norms that regulated slavery to Roman law.[201]

The case of enslaved Muslims in the Americas is an example of how "memories," shared cultural backgrounds, have the potential to add new layers of complexity to the writing of legal history. This shift in the theoretical paradigm also requires reconsidering the methodology. In order to grasp how knowledge of normativities other than the European ones might have played a role in the making of law in Latin America, it is important to rethink our toolkit of research skills and broaden the types of documents we analyze. As for research skills, it would be fundamental to learn languages other than European ones. This would allow legal historians to engage with other kinds of documents and even conduct interviews or ethnographic fieldwork. Moreover, it would open a dialogue with the scholarship produced in non-European languages. In order to get at "memories" through empirical research, it is also necessary to consider other kinds of primary sources that are of common use among historians but have not yet made their way to legal history, such as iconography and photography, interviews, travel accounts, etc.[202]

Taking the "memories" of historical agents seriously when writing the history of law in Latin America makes evident the limitation of national or imperial boundaries when defining the geographical scope of our research. It also highlights the existence in the field of "myths of origin" that only look to some actors and some places but not others. Determining that a legal category or institution came from one foreign place – primarily regions of the Global North – obscures not only the local production of norms but also a varied set of backgrounds that shapes local legal processes.

Morales, "Manumission on the Land: Slaves, Masters, and Magistrates in Eighteenth-Century Mompox (Colombia)," *Law and History Review* 35(2) (2017), 511–43.

200 Sikainga, "Shari'a Courts."

201 For a parallel between the *qadi* and the *cacique*, see K. B. Graubart, "Learning from the Qadi: The Jurisdiction of Local Rule in the Early Colonial Andes," *Hispanic American Historical Review* 95(2) (2015), 195–228.

202 About different sources for writing the law of subaltern groups, see Chapter 2 in this volume.

Zones of Shared Production of Norms

Much has been debated about just how "global" global legal history should be. Should it encompass the entire world, all the territories of an empire, or all the territories of a specific legal tradition? When deciding to adopt a global perspective in our research, the memories of historical agents have shown that an inductive approach should be taken with respect to the geographical scope. In other words, this decision should be sensitive to the spaces within which the production of norms takes place in entangled ways. These "zones of shared production of norms" change over time and may or may not correspond to imperial or national boundaries. For example, the South Atlantic experienced a strong interconnectedness between the sixteenth and nineteenth centuries, which gradually diminished after this period.[203]

The legal category of *agregados* is a good example of how the production of norms takes place in entangled geographical areas that can extrapolate imperial and national boundaries. In some regions of West Africa and the Americas, there was a socio-legal category of dependency called *agregados*. The *agregados* were part of a household, and they performed different kinds of labor within this context. It was not the kind of work they performed that was constitutive of the relationship, but rather the fact that these people were taken in as *agregados* on the basis of the alleged favor and goodwill of the head of the household. Ideas of "favor," "protection," and "being part of a family" were what determined this dependency relation, framed its labor configuration, and shaped its legal aspects.[204]

Despite being a noun defined in well-known Portuguese dictionaries of that period,[205] to this day, *agregados* do not appear in the scholarship on land and dependency relations on the Iberian Peninsula, and its role as a structural legal category with direct impact on the acquisition of land rights is largely ignored. Nevertheless, most would tend to explain its existence in the Americas as the direct consequence of the "transplantation" of Iberian law and family structures to colonial territories. It is well known that "grace," "liberality," "mercy," and "gratitude" were principles that structured society, shaped normative behavior, and pervaded law in the Iberian Peninsula.[206]

203 On South Atlantic interconnectedness, see L. F. de Alencastro, *The Trade in the Living: The Formation of Brazil in the South Atlantic, Sixteenth to Seventeenth Centuries* (Albany: State University of New York Press, 2018).

204 Dias Paes, *Esclavos y tierras*, 53–71.

205 Raphael Bluteau, *Vocabulario portuguez e latino* (Coimbra: Collegio das Artes da Companhia de Jesu, 1712), vol. I, 168.

206 B. Clavero, *Antidora. Antropología católica de la economía moderna* (Milano: Giuffrè, 1991); A. M. Hespanha, "La senda amorosa del derecho: amor e iustitia en el discurso jurídico

Thus, it is beyond question that the *oeconomia católica* contributed to the reproduction of extended families and consequently to the existence of *agregados* in Latin America.[207] Recounting the legal history of *agregados* in Latin America giving consideration only to the Iberian legal perspective, however, would overshadow other aspects of this legal category and of how it was produced. Adopting a perspective that takes "memories" into consideration, on the contrary, would help to broaden the global aspects of the processes that enabled the existence of *agregados* in Latin American jurisdictions.

Research indicates that although *agregados* could be from any ethnic background, it was relatively common for formerly enslaved persons – during the time of slavery – to engage in this kind of dependency relationship after acquiring manumission.[208] Continuous repetition and daily enforcement of these connections gave this institution a particular social significance. The transformation of formerly enslaved persons into *agregados* might have played a central role in transforming this legal category into a constitutive and structural feature of Latin American societies. It is obvious that such relationships were a consequence of the violence rooted in racial relations in these jurisdictions and the constant menace of re-enslavement people of color faced that dependency ties could help to prevent. Nevertheless, it is also noteworthy that formerly enslaved persons sought to "acquire" *agregados*, perhaps as a strategy of social ascension.[209]

Yet, beyond explanations that sends us to Iberia or to the local circumstances, the engagement of people of African descent in *agregado* relationships also had a "memory" component. Africanist historians have been debating for decades the concept of "wealth in people." In West African societies, they showed that accumulating dependents could be key to controlling labor and, consequently, to acquire patrimony and prestige.[210] In this sense, Iberian

moderno," in C. Petit (ed.), *Pasiones del jurista. Amor, memoria, melancolía, imaginación* (Historia de la Sociedad Política) (Madrid: Centro de Estudios Constitucionales, 1997), 23–74.

207 R. Zamora, *Casa poblada y buen gobierno. Oeconomia católica y servicio personal en San Miguel de Tucumán, siglo XVIII* (Buenos Aires: Prometeo Libros, 2017).

208 A. Chira, "Uneasy Intimacies: Race, Family, and Property in Santiago de Cuba, 1803–1868," Ph.D. thesis, University of Michigan (2016), 218–30; E. Guimarães, *Terra de preto. Usos e ocupação da terra por escravos e libertos (Vale do Paraíba mineiro, 1850–1920)* (Niterói: Editora da Universidade Federal Fluminense, 2009).

209 Chira, "Uneasy Intimacies," 218–30.

210 For a summary of the debate over the concept of "wealth in people," see J. I. Guyer, "Wealth in People, Wealth in Things – Introduction," *The Journal of African History* 36(1) (2009), 83–90. For a critique on the harsh separation between "wealth in people" and "wealth in things," see M. Candido, "Understanding African Women's Access to Landed Property in Nineteenth-Century Benguela," *Canadian Journal of African Studies* 54(1) (2020), 1–23.

social structures linked to *oeconomia católica* would not be strange to enslaved persons coming from these regions – quite the contrary. Recent scholarship also stressed that enslaved Africans and their descendants reproduced African family structures and dependency relations in Latin America. Therefore, the history of the legal category of *agregado* would gain complexity by taking these "memories" into consideration.[211] It would also force the conclusion that the production of norms takes place in truly diffused ways. Norms do not necessarily have clear origins, or at least these are very hard to identify. *Agregados* are an example of this diffusiveness. It is a legal category relatable to *oeconomia católica*, to African "wealth-in-people" social structures, to consequences of local practices of manumission, and so on.

But the history of *agregado* as a legal category is not exhausted by tracing back enslaved Africans' and their descendants' memories. It also points to the existence of zones of shared production of norms. *Agregados* existed in various jurisdictions of Latin America,[212] but in some of them, whether or not one was an *agregado* was crucial to the success of a person in claiming land rights in court. In Brazil and Argentina, if a person claimed land and the adversary could prove that he was an *agregado*, chances were that the claimant would lose the case. In these jurisdictions, the legal category of *agregado* gained specific meanings that embodied and strengthened the idea that dependents could not acquire ownership rights, even if they exercised possession over a piece of land.[213]

Considering the current state of the scholarship, it seems that the concrete meanings of the legal category of *agregado* that limited the possibility of acquiring rights over land were produced in various regions of Latin America. These territories were connected by certain kinds of economic and labor relations, especially intensive forms of slavery and coerced labor. Southern Brazil,

211 Chira, "Uneasy Intimacies," 218–30; Dias Paes, "Ser dependente no Império"; F. Schleumer, *Laços de família. Africanos e crioulos na capitania de São Paulo colonial* (São Paulo: Alameda, 2020), 290–94.

212 D. Bonnett Vélez and M. Herrera Ángel, "Ordenamiento espacial y territorial colonial en la 'región central' neogranadina. Siglo XVIII. Las visitas de la tierra como fuente para la historia agraria del siglo XVIII," *América Latina en la Historia Económica* 8(16) (2001), 11–32; Chira, "Uneasy Intimacies," 218–30; H. R. S. Mejía, "De esclavos a campesinos, de la 'roza' al mercado: tierra y producción agropecuaria de los 'libres de todos los colores' en la gobernación de Santa Marta (1740–1810)," *Historia Crítica* 43 (2011), 130–55; M. de los Ángeles Meriño Fuentes and A. Perera Díaz, *Familia, agregados y esclavos. Los padrones de vecinos de Santiago de Cuba (1778–1861)* (Santiago de Cuba: Editorial Oriente, 2011).

213 Dias Paes, *Esclavos y tierras*, 53–71; C. M. Poczynok, "Los procesos civiles como fuente para el estudio de las luchas por los derechos de propiedad de la tierra (Buenos Aires, 1776–1822)," *Varia Historia* 37(74) (2021), 393–427.

La Plata basin, and West Central Africa are not usually studied together, and legal historical research was no different in this respect. Yet, these regions were nevertheless bound together until the mid-nineteenth century. West Central African ports, such as Luanda and Benguela, were the places of departure of the majority of slave ships transporting the enslaved workforce to southern Brazil and the Río de la Plata basin.[214] Circulation promoted by the slave trade was, however, wider than this commerce. As Atlantic history has shown over the years, commercial routes very often promoted wider cultural entanglements.[215] Because law is a cultural practice, commercial routes also promoted legal entanglements between different regions of the world. The case of the *agregado* is just such an example that allows us to think of the southern Atlantic as a zone of shared production of norms.

The concrete meanings that *agregado* acquired in the South Atlantic were the result of processes that mostly took place outside the metropolitan territories of the Spanish and Portuguese empires and which did not "respect" imperial borders. There is no doubt that the production of norms was strongly determined by imperial experiences and by the asymmetrical power relations inherent to them. However, more than being circumscribed to imperial geographies, the production of norms took place within entangled spaces inside and beyond Latin America. Zones of shared production of norms are dynamic, change over time, and depend on material conditions and on economic configurations.

Zones of shared production of norms is a conceptual tool that helps to frame the geographical space of one's research, even when the object of study extrapolates the Latin American colonial period. Constitutional review is a good example of how legal history research could profit from this concept in order to complexify the analysis of the making of law.

It is by no means unusual to find texts tracing the "origins" of judicial and constitutional review in Latin American countries to the US Supreme Court's *Marbury v. Madison* case or to Hans Kelsen's work. The history of this institution is, however, more intricate. Over the last century, many constitutions adopted some sort of judicial review. In this global expansion, constitutional

214 Alencastro, *Trade in the Living*; A. Borucki, D. Eltis, and D. Wheat, "The Size and Direction of the Slave Trade to the Spanish Americas," in A. Borucki, D. Eltis, and D. Wheat (eds.), *From the Galleons to the Highlands: Slave Trade Routes in the Spanish Americas* (Albuquerque: University of New Mexico Press, 2020), 15–46.

215 R. Ferreira, *Cross-Cultural Exchange in the Atlantic World: Angola and Brazil During the Era of the Slave Trade* (African Studies 121) (Cambridge: Cambridge University Press, 2012), 1–19.

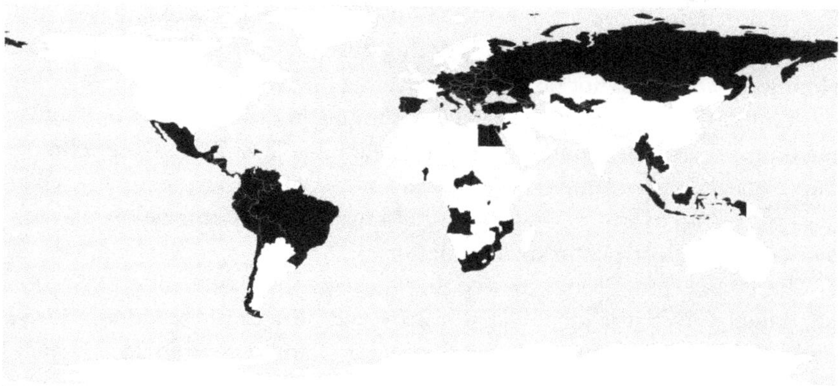

Map 1 Uninterrupted experiences of constitutional review.
Source: J. Mariano Silva, "Jurisdição constitucional em Espanha (1981–1992) e Brasil (1988–1997)," Ph.D. dissertation, Universidade do Estado do Rio de Janeiro, 2016, p. 63. Reproduction authorized by the author.

review (the "abstract" judicial control of legislation and other normative acts equivalent to legislation) spread mostly to countries in the Global South, the Colombian case being one of the oldest uninterrupted cases of constitutional review.[216]

Map 1 clearly highlights that, when it comes to the history of constitutional review, "diffusion" or "transplant" perspectives might not be the best way to explain its existence in various regions of the world.[217] Instead, "zones of shared production of norms" might be a more appropriate conceptual tool that would complexify the analysis of the production of this legal institution, shifting the attention of legal historians to other parts of the world other than the United States or certain European countries.

Final Remarks

Many aspects of the interaction of global processes with local experiences frame the production of norms. Abandoning fictions of origins and instead assuming the blurred dynamics that underlies the production of norms can push forward research that takes seriously the need to overcome

216 T. Ginsburg and M. Versteeg, "Why Do Countries Adopt Constitutional Review?," *The Journal of Law, Economics, and Organization* 30(3) (2013), 587–622; J. Mariano Silva, "Jurisdição constitucional em Espanha (1981–1992) e Brasil (1988–1997)," Ph.D. thesis, Universidade do Estado do Rio de Janeiro (2016), 48–63.

217 Ginsburg and Versteeg, "Countries Adopt Constitutional Review."

Eurocentrism in global legal history. European conceptions of law were disseminated around the world both during and after the colonial expansion. However, we should not take for granted that they were the exclusive or the most important normative framework operating in Latin America or in other regions of the Global South. If not always, then at least there were multiple moments and opportunities where local population agency, their vernacular understandings of law, as well as non-European legal systems clearly played a pivotal role in the daily production of norms.

These conceptual tools answer the question that is the title of Section 1.4, namely, "What is global legal history and how can it be done?" These tools are not exclusive to research focused on Latin American legal history. "Production of norms," "concrete meanings," "memories," and "shared zones of production of norms" can also shed light on still unexplored aspects of the making of law in other geographical areas. In addition to space, these conceptual tools blur time. Production of norms can take place in chronologies that are not bound to categories such as the "pre-colonial," "colonial," and "post-colonial" periods. Thus, the conceptual tools I am proposing can be useful to research framed by various chronologies while, at the same time, highlighting that the temporal and geographical scopes should not be determined in advance but instead depend on the object of inquiry.

2

How to Approach Indigenous Law?

CAROLINE CUNILL

It is important to remember that both the term "indigenous peoples" and the concept of "precolonial past" were created as categories only at the time of the European invasion. This does not mean that the people so described did not have their own ways for defining themselves and registering the past, but rather that transforming the conquest into a turning point in the historical narrative was part of an epistemological colonial setting per se. The issue is especially acute when dealing with precolonial law because most the available written sources on this topic were recorded during the colonial period and were therefore drafted from the perspective and in the language of their time. How then to approach indigenous law?

For many years, this question was mostly ignored by legal historians. As Carlos Petit points out in Section 1.1, "the *Latin* omits or silences the *American*, that is, the presence and experiences of indigenous peoples" in the history of law. It is therefore necessary to first shed some light on the factors that might explain this lack of interest in indigenous law, which prevailed in legal history from the nineteenth century until the 1920s and explain why this law acquired increasing relevance from that moment on. The first section of this chapter will highlight the links between the treatment of the indigenous component in Latin American legal history and the position that both the indigenous peoples and the law were thought to occupy in the societies in which those narratives were written. The second section will provide a dynamic picture of precolonial law and show that to study this topic requires questioning the relations and boundaries between various disciplines such as archaeology, history, and anthropology. Writing the history of indigenous law from precolonial times is especially challenging, not only because of the diversity of human groups that occupied the continent but also because of the disparity of sources available according to the cultures and periods under consideration. Not all the indigenous peoples have left lasting material traces throughout America over the centuries. Moreover, although the Olmecs, the Maya, the

Mixtecs, and the Aztecs created systems of writing, only a few precolonial texts have survived to the present day. A similar observation can be made with regard to the *khipus*, a system of cords with different colors and knots that were produced in the Andean region from the time of the Wari culture. Nevertheless, the progress made in the fields of epigraphy, archaeology, and ethnohistory sheds new light on indigenous law.

The last section will propose a reflection on the relations between indigenous and European law in the aftermath of the Spanish and Portuguese conquests. We will show that, after the Iberian conquests, a wide range of alphabetic texts focusing on precolonial indigenous normative orders was produced. These records were diverse in authorship, languages, formats, degree of accuracy, and sources selected. Not only the Spaniards but also indigenous peoples and *mestizos* (individuals of mixed descent) wrote – sometimes in their own languages – historical narratives, accounts of deeds and services, and requests to the king. Furthermore, indigenous people participated as litigants in a number of lawsuits in which they gave their own vision of law and justice according to their own interests. It is therefore necessary to ask what this evidence tells us about precolonial normative orders and the way in which they intersected with colonial law after the Iberian imperial conquests.

Indigenous Law in Historiographical Perspective

Although, as will be shown later, the indigenous past was an essential component in writings from the colonial period, the rise of nation-states in the first decades of the nineteenth century marked a shift in the position that both indigenous peoples and their law were held to occupy in Latin America. As was common at that time, the society in which the modern state was going to be built was expected to share a homogenous national identity. Defining national identity as white and European led the Latin American elite either to ignore indigenous peoples or to consider them a problem to be solved through assimilation or, in some extreme cases, physical elimination.[1] Furthermore, the contradiction between a universalist and egalitarian understanding of law and a hierarchical and racialized conception of society was "solved" by creating unequal forms of citizenship within the first Latin American constitutions

1 P. López Caballero and C. Giudicelli (eds.), *Régimes nationaux d'altérité. États-nations et altérités autochtones en Amérique latine, 1810–1950* (Rennes: Presses Universitaires de Rennes, 2016); C. R. Larson, *The Conquest of the Desert* (Albuquerque: University of New Mexico Press, 2020).

on the basis of cultural, moral, socioeconomic, or racial grounds.[2] According to José María Portillo, a definition of the citizen as an autonomous individual closed the doors of political inclusion not only to women but also to "the plebeian sector of those societies, mainly *mestizo* and indigenous."[3]

This is not to say that the precolonial indigenous past was hidden, since its monuments were brought into the spotlight by the consolidation of archaeology as a scientific field, but rather that the dead "indians" and their ancient civilizations were separated from the living. Antiquarians and scholars considered that "contemporary nineteenth-century American Indians were not direct descendants of the enlightened dwellers of ancient America; or if they were, their stock had degenerated beyond recognition."[4] In other words, interest in the indigenous past was articulated around the issue of the origins of humanity and ancient world civilizations, through racist, diffusionist, and evolutionist approaches. In doing so, archaeology emerged as partipant in a political project that followed the exclusionary national model, as evidenced by its close links with the museums as well as by the enactment of the first laws intended to protect the patrimony of the Latin American countries.[5]

2 According to Silvia Sebastiani, the nineteenth-century emergence of racial anthropology took place in "a new Atlantic and trans-imperial perspective" in which "the Enlightenment debate about the 'science of man'" was transformed into "a dispute about the inferiority of human races versus the equality of human beings." S. Sebastiani, "Anthropology beyond Empires: Samuel Stanhope Smith and the Reconfiguration of the Atlantic World," in L. Kontler, A. Romano, et al. (eds.), *Negotiating Knowledge in Early Modern Empires: A Decentered View* (London: Palgrave MacMillan, 2014), 207–33.

3 See Section 5.1; B. Clavero, *Derecho indígena y cultura constitucional en América* (Mexico City: Editorial Siglo XXI, 1995); A. M. Hespanha, "Le Droit et la domination coloniale européenne. Le cas de l'Empire oriental portugais," in J. C. Garavaglia and J.-F. Schaub (eds.), *Lois, justice, coutumes. Amérique et Europe latines, 16e-19e siècles* (Paris: Editions de l'Ecole des Hautes Etudes en Sciences Sociales, 2005), 203–26; Y. Miki, *Frontiers of Citizenship: A Black and Indigenous History of Postcolonial Brazil* (Cambridge: Cambridge University Press, 2018); J. Harrington, *The Uses of Imperial Citizenship: The British and French Empires* (London: Rowman & Littlefield Publishers, 2020); E. Isin (ed.), *Citizenship after Orientalism: Transforming Political Theory* (London: Palgrave Macmillan, 2015).

4 M. Achim, *From Idols to Antiquity: Forging the National Museum of Mexico* (Lincoln and London: University of Nebraska Press, 2017), 253. On the distinction between the dead and the living "Indians," see also E. Sanz Jara, *Los indios de la nación. Los indígenas en los escritos de intelectuales y políticos del México independiente* (Madrid and Berlin: Iberoamericana, Vervuert, 2011).

5 Achim, *From Idols to Antiquity*; S. Gänger, *Relics of the Past: The Collecting and Study of Pre-Columbian Antiquities in Peru and Chile, 1837–1911* (Oxford: Oxford University Press, 2014), 250–53; O. Chinchilla Mazariego, "Archaeology in Guatemala: Nationalist, Colonialist, Imperialist," in D. L. Nichols and C. A. Pool (eds.), *The Oxford Handbook of Mesoamerican Archaeology* (New York: Oxford University Press, 2012), 55–68. On the changing importance that Latin American elites gave to the precolonial past in the nineteenth-century process of nation-building, see R. A. Earle, *The Return of the Native: Indians and Myth-Making in Spanish America, 1810–1930* (Durham and London: Duke University Press, 2007), especially Chapter 6, "Citizenship and Civilization: The 'Indian Problem'."

Furthermore, in line with the desire for a state monopoly over normative production, it was not really possible for contemporaries to see "law" without also taking into account the notion of state itself; or, to put it differently, "law" was defined by them as the written systems of norms decreed by a state. With the existence of precolonial states not even deemed worthy of consideration, legal historians manifested little if any interest in any hypothetical precolonial law. In fact, the very idea of a precolonial indigenous history was questioned, since historical science was thought to be the study of written, and preferentially alphabetic, texts. As Petit points out in Section 1.1, the disintegration of the Spanish empire and the perception of the United States as a threat also played a key role in constituting transatlantic networks of intellectuals around the notions of *raza* and *hispanidad*.[6] Accordingly, the history of law in Latin America was thought to begin with Spanish and Portuguese law, in an area covered by the *derecho indiano*.[7] As for the *derecho patrio*, which emerged in the newly created Latin American nation-states after the wars of independence, this was formulated within a national framework that barely considered indigenous peoples and excluded precolonial law altogether (see Section 1.1).

However, there were alternative, although marginal, narratives. In 1864, a Mexican lawyer called Francisco León Carbajal wrote a dissertation on the "legislation of the ancient Mexicans" in which he argued that "if we want to give fair, beneficial and efficient laws to our homeland, not only the few European elements that Mexico possesses, but also particularly the

6 On the role played by the pan-American conferences in the construction of transatlantic networks, see C. Marichal (ed.), *México y las Conferencias Panamericanas 1889–1938. Antecedentes de la globalización* (Mexico City: Secretaría de Relaciones Exteriores, 2002). See also I. Sepúlveda Muñoz, *El sueño de la madre patria: hispanoamericanismo y nacionalismo* (Madrid: Marcial Pons, 2005); L. López-Ocón Cabrera, J.-P. Chaumeil, and A. Verde Casanova (eds.), *Los americanistas del siglo XIX. La construcción de una comunidad científica internacional* (Madrid: Iberoamericana, 2005); L. López-Ocón Cabrera, "El papel de los primeros congresos internacionales de americanistas en la construcción de una comunidad científica," in M. Quijada and J. Bustamante García (eds.), *Elites intelectuales y modelos colectivos. Mundo ibérico, siglos XVI-XIX* (Madrid: Consejo Superior de Investigación Científica, 2002), 271–84.

7 On the difficulties of applying the concept of *derecho indiano* in the Portuguese empire, see A. M. Hespanha, "O 'direito das Índias' no contexto da historiografia das colonizações ibéricas," in T. Duve (ed.), *Actas del XIX Congreso del Instituto Internacional de Derecho Indiano. Berlín 2016* (Madrid: Universidad Carlos III de Madrid, 2019), 43–83. On the reasons that help explain the absence of this concept in the history of the British Empire, see R. J. Ross, "Spanish American and British American Law as Mirrors to Each Other: Implications of the Missing Derecho Britanico Indiano," in T. Duve and H. Pihlajamäki (eds.), *New Horizons in Spanish Colonial Law: Contributions to Transnational Early Modern Legal History* (Frankfurt am Main: Max-Planck-Institut für europäische Rechtsgeschichte, 2015), 9–28.

indigenous ones have to be taken into account."[8] The author made use of the early colonial pictographic manuscript known as the *Codex Mendoza*, published by Lord Kingsborough in 1831, which he described as "a judicial lawsuit in Aztec hieroglyphs."[9] In Peru, some oral traditions regarding the "just laws and moral values of the Incas" were recorded by Cesare Cantú, in his *Historia Universal*, and by Gabino Pacheco Zegarro in his translation of the Quechua play *Ollantay*.[10] In Brazil, José Izidoro Martins Junior warned against "the error of forgetting the forces of indigenous and imported black peoples," alongside the European racial substratum, for the formation of Brazilian nationality in his *História do Direito Nacional* (1895).[11]

In order to better understand this marginal trend in Latin American legal history, one should look at it in a larger political and intellectual context. In the nineteenth-century United States, a number of scholars became interested in the indigenous past, with a clear prevalence of a museum-based archaeology. They also sought to find, by studying the recollections of a few indigenous men, a past that they felt was in danger of disappearing. It is worth noting that this movement was closely linked to nationalism.[12] Moreover, it aimed to achieve a continental dimension, as was demonstrated by the interest shown by North American intellectuals such as Daniel G. Brinton or John Lloyd Stephens for precolonial Central American past and ruins.[13] The "Native American tradition" therefore offered an alternative to the concepts of *raza* and *hispanidad* in Latin American national discourses and was echoed in legal history.

In the twentieth century, however, under the influence of Franz Boas, anthropology's primary institutional basis changed "from museum to university."[14] Not only was the notion of "museum anthropology based on

8 F. León Carbajal, *Discurso sobre la legislación de los antiguos mexicanos, 1864 con estudio preliminar de A. L. Izquierdo y de la Cueva* (Mexico City: Instituto Nacional de Ciencias Penales, 2014), 4 (unless otherwise indicated, all translations are by the author).

9 Carbajal's description of the *Codex Mendoza* points not only to the content of the document but also to its origins, while drawing a subtle line between the Aztec and the Egyptian civilizations through the designation of the system of writing.

10 R. Cerrón Palomino, "Sobre el carácter espurio de la trilogía moral incaica," in L. Regalado and F. Hernández (eds.), *Sobre los Incas* (Lima: Instituto Riva-Agüero, Pontificia Universidad Católica del Perú, 2011), 69–76.

11 Petit, Section 1.1.

12 L. Philips Valentine and R. Darnell, *Theorizing the Americanist Tradition* (Toronto: University of Toronto Press, 1999).

13 T. Evans, *Romancing the Mayas: Mexican Antiquity in the American Imagination, 1820–1915* (Austin: University of Texas Press, 2004).

14 S. E. Murray, "The Non-Eclipse of Americanist Anthropology during the 1930s and 1940s," in Philips Valentine and Darnell, *Theorizing the Americanist Tradition*, 52–74, at 56.

evolution and diffusion of items of material culture" questioned, but anthropology also moved out of the shadow of archaeology. Its main objective went from seeking in a few men's recollections a past in danger of disappearing to the study of living communities.[15] From this perspective, the historical approach became one factor among many in the understanding of any given community.[16] British functionalist anthropologists such as Alfred Radcliffe-Brown even called into question the pertinence of history in the analysis of "social laws."[17] These debates, which transcended national boundaries, had critical consequences not only for the understanding of normativity but also for the place contemporary indigenous peoples occupied in the academic field, since their "social laws" became the subject of anthropological studies. Moreover, anthropological studies aimed to be useful in forging state policies within and outside national boundaries, either to address indigenous issues or to implement imperialist views.[18]

Mexican intellectuals such as Manuel Gamio or Moisés Sáenz, who both studied at Columbia University in the 1910s, were in contact with Boas and the sociologist and advocate for "Native American matters" John Collier, who played a key role in shaping the "Indian policy" in the United States in the 1930s.[19] They also had close ties with other Latin American scholars.[20]

15 Ibid.

16 R. Darnell, "Theorizing Americanist Anthropology: Continuities from the B. A. E. to the Boasians," in Philips Valentine and Darnell, *Theorizing the Americanist Tradition*, 38–51, at 50.

17 Murray, "The Non-Eclipse of Americanist Anthropology," 52–54.

18 In *Forjando Patria*, Mexican anthropologist Manuel Gamio lamented that "it was erroneously thought that … the diverse laws of our continent addressed the lifestyle of native people, whereas the text and the spirit of almost all of them are only inspired by the tendencies, needs, and aspirations of the American groups of European race, culture, and language.... It is thus unfair that the criteria of the Social Sciences, which are supposed to and have to give form to the law … are unilaterally imposed on the indigenous groups." M. Gamio, *Forjando Patria* (Mexico City: Editorial Porrúa, 1960 [1918]), 199.

19 S. Rico Monge, "Manuel Gamio Martínez entre México y América Latina: Indigenismo, nacionalismo y poder," *Pacarina del Sur* 25 (2015); T. Blanchette, "Applied Anthropology and Indigenous Administration in the United States: 1934–1945," *Desacatos* 33 (2010), 33–52; W. T. Ahlstedt, "John Collier and Mexico and the Shaping of U.S. Indian Policy: 1934–1945," Ph.D. thesis (Lincoln, Nebraska: University of Nebraska-Lincoln, 2015); D. Robichaux, "Del Indian New Deal al indigenismo interamericano: Moisés Sáenz y John Collier," *Cahiers des Amériques latines* 95 (2020), 165–84.

20 The literature on *indigenismo* has increased substantially in recent years. For an excellent historiographical synthesis, see L. Giraudo, "Indigenismo en las Américas: balance provisional y perspectivas en los estudios," the introduction to the dossier "Relire l'indigénisme aujourd'hui. Sources, pratiques, acteurs," *Cahiers des Amériques latines* 95 (2020), [Online], 95 | 2020, Online since 14 September 2021, connection on 01 August 2023. URL: http://journals.openedition.org/cal/12404; DOI: https://doi.org/10.4000/cal.12404. See also J. Coronado, *The Andes Imagined: Indigenismo, Society,*

The Congresos Indigenistas Interamericanos and especially the first one held in Patzcuaro in 1940, which lead to the creation of the Instituto Indigenista Interamericano, were also critical in structuring the field of *indigenismo*, which oscillated between an "inter-American scope and national trajectories."[21] Although anthropology was central to *indigenismo*, it is essential to ask what the place of history and, especially, the indigenous past was in order to understand how precolonial law was being addressed during this period.

Mexican sociologist Lucio Mendieta y Núñez, who founded the Instituto de Investigaciones Sociales at the National Autonomous University of Mexico in 1930, stated that law was "nothing but one of the expressions of the culture of a specific group and transforms itself depending on the group who creates it, following his historical and social contingencies." According to him, it was "necessary to deal with the law observed by the indigenous peoples before the conquest … because … the actual population of the [Mexican] Republic, in its aboriginal groups, has many cultural contact points with its primitive inhabitants."[22] In other words, law was now conceived as a cultural product and a connection was drawn between the indigenous present-day social life and precolonial past, therefore justifying a dialogue between anthropology and history. Moreover, knowledge of indigenous law, past and present, was now expected to be part of the "national identity" and to be used in the implementation of the nation's legal policies.

It is thus not surprising that during this period precolonial law was studied by anthropologists or sociologists whose interest in indigenous contemporary life extended to the ancient past, with a view to applying anthropological

and Modernity (Pittsburgh: University of Pittsburgh Press, 2009); S. E. Lewis, *Rethinking Mexican Indigenismo: The INI's Coordinating Center in the Highland Chiapas and the Fate of a Utopian Project* (Albuquerque: University of New Mexico Press, 2018); T. A. Diaccon, *Stringing Together a Nation: Candido Mariano da Silva Rondon and the Construction of a Modern Brazil, 1906–1930* (Durham and London: Duke University Press, 2004); J. Pacheco de Oliveira (ed.), *Sociedades indígenas e indigenismo no Brasil* (Rio de Janeiro and São Paulo: EdUFRJ, Marco Zero, 1987); A. C. de Souza Lima, "El indigenismo en Brasil: migración y reapropiaciones de un saber administrativo," in J. P. de Oliveira (ed.), *Hacia una antropología del indigenismo* (Rio de Janeiro and Lima: Contra Capa, Centro Amazónico de Antropología y Aplicación Práctica, 2006), 97–125; C. Briones (ed.), *Cartografías argentinas. Políticas indigenistas y formaciones provinciales de alteridad* (Buenos Aires: Antropofagia, 2008).

21 L. Giraudo and J. Martín-Sánchez (eds.), *La ambivalente historia del indigenismo. Campo interamericano y trayectorias nacionales, 1940–1970* (Lima: Instituto de Estudios Peruanos, 2011); L. Giraudo and S. E. Lewis, "Pan-American Indigenismo (1940–1970): New Approaches to an Ongoing Debate," in L. Giraudo and S. E. Lewis (eds.), Special issue "Rethinking Indigenismo on the American Continent," *Latin American Perspectives* 39(5) (2012), 3–11.

22 L. Mendieta y Núñez, *El Derecho precolonial* (Mexico City: Editorial Porrúa, 1992 [1937]), 26.

knowledge to state policies. In this respect, it is important to note that a preliminary version of Mendieta y Núñez's work was published in *Ethnos*, a review edited by Gamio, and that the anthropologist Carlos H. Alba's *Estudio comparado entre el derecho azteca y el derecho positivo mexicano* was published a few years later by the Instituto Indigenista Interamericano with a prologue by Gamio.[23] In Peru, the anthropologist Luis Valcárcel, who had close ties with the intellectuals José María Arguedas and José Carlos Mariátegui, played a key role in promoting Inca laws as a subject for study in the 1920s and 1930s. He became the director of the Instituto Indigenista Peruano in 1948.[24]

Given this context, precolonial law, which had previously been of marginal or no interest at all, took on significantly more importance in the writings of Latin American legal historians. A number of Mexican jurists began writing texts on the "judicial institutions of the civilized indigenous people of Mexico before the conquest," to use Alfonso Toro's expression.[25] Moreover, "Aztec law" was included in the lessons on the "History of National Law" that were given in the Escuela Libre de Derecho, an institution created in Mexico City in 1912. Josef Kohler's *El derecho de los aztecas*, first published in German in 1892 as an exercise in comparative law, was translated into Spanish and published by the *Revista jurídica de la Escuela libre de derecho* in 1924 and circulated widely throughout Latin American.[26] A similar trend can be observed in Peru, as recently shown by Carlos Ramos Núñez.[27] The relation between academic knowledge and state policies, and the tensions between the wish not only to recognize and protect but also to integrate and assimilate, were reflected in contemporary Latin American national institutions, as evidenced

23 C. Alba, *Estudio comparado entre el derecho azteca y el derecho positivo mexicano*, with an introduction by M. Gamio (Mexico City: Instituto Indigenista Interamericano, 1949).

24 L. Valcárcel, *Del ayllu al imperio: la evolución político-social en el antiguo Perú y otros estudios* (Lima: Edición Garcilaso, 1925); O. Gonzales, "The Instituto Indigenista Peruano: A New Place in the State for the Indigenous Debate," *Latin American Perspectives* 39(5) (2002); H. Urteaga, *La organización judicial en el imperio de los incas y en la colonia. Contribución al estudio del derecho peruano* (Lima: Imprenta Gil, 1938). The first version of the book, focused on Inca law, was published in 1928.

25 Ramón Prida, Manuel Moreno, Alfonso Toro, Roque Cevallos Novelo, Salvador Toscano, and Toribio Esquivel Obregon can be included among the Mexican jurists who showed an interest in precolonial law in the 1930s. J. de Cervantes y Anaya, *Introducción a la historia del pensamiento jurídico en México* (Mexico City: Tribunal Superior de Justicia del Distrito Federal, 2002), 393–447.

26 J. Kohler, *El Derecho de los aztecas*, trans. C. Rovalo y Fernández, cia (Mexico City: Compañía Editora Latinoamericana, 1924).

27 C. Ramos Núñez, *Historial del derecho civil peruano, siglos XIX y XX: los signos del cambio* (Lima: Fondo Editorial de la Pontificia Universidad Católica del Perú, 2006), tome 5, vol. II, 215–30. As for Brazil, see R. Otávio, *Os Selvagens americanos Perante o direito* (São Paulo: Companhia Editorial Nacional, 1946).

by the creation in Brazil of the Serviço de Proteção aos Índios (1910) and of the Conselho Nacional de Proteção aos Índios (1939).[28]

Because sources for legal history are "invented" by legal historians, in a sense that they fit their own idea of what the law is in the first place, it is also legitimate to ask what sources were used to write the history of precolonial law in the early 1900s.[29] The majority consisted of Spanish texts from the colonial period that had been found and published by nineteenth-century scholars such as Joaquín García Icazbalceta.[30] In Peru, significant work was undertaken by Horacio Urteaga and Carlos Romero.[31] Indigenous and *mestizo* chronicles, however, were almost absent. More critically, the legal historians mentioned earlier did not take into account the imperial context of how these sources were produced. It was as if those texts faithfully "reflected" the precolonial indigenous past and as if colonial policies had had no impact on indigenous peoples' history – thus justifying the drawing of a connection between their precolonial past and their contemporary life.

However, the Cold War and the struggles against colonial regimes brought about a change among anthropologists and helped create "a sense of how the changing world order … affected the imperatives of their work."[32] According to Brian K. Axel, before World War II, "within anthropology, the primary concern with history was in evaluating its use as a technique of reconstruction – the viability of which relied upon whether it might successfully yield an image

28 A. C. de Souza Lima, "Poder tutelar y formación del Estado en Brasil: notas a partir de la creación del Servicio de Protección a los Indios y Localización de Trabajadores Nacionales," *Desacatos* 33 (2010), 53–66. For a reflection on the ambiguities that resulted from the applied dimension of anthropology in Latin American *indigenismo*, see L. Giraudo, "Neither 'Scientific' nor 'Colonialist': The Ambiguous Course of Inter-American Indigenismo in the 1940s," *Latin American Perspectives* 39(5) (2012), 12–32.

29 On the "invention" of sources for the colonial law, see Tamar Herzog, Section 3.1. See also T. Duve and O. Danwerth (eds.), *Knowledge of the Pragmatici: Legal and Moral Theological Literature and the Formation of Early Modern Ibero-America* (Leiden: Brill, 2020).

30 R. Martínez Baracs, "Los estudios sobre Joaquín García Icazbalceta," *Historias, Revista de la Dirección de Estudios Históricos del INAH* 99 (2018), 109–21. Of particular relevance were the sources published in the *Colección de documentos para la historia de México*, 2 vols. (Mexico City: Antigua Librería, 1858–1866) and the *Nueva colección de documentos para la historia de México*, 5 vols. (Mexico City: Antigua Librería de Andrade y Morales, Sucesores, 1886–1892), but also see J. de Mendieta, *Historia eclesiástica indiana* (Mexico City: Antigua Librería, 1870); M. Mould de Pease, "Historia del Perú en traducción: un comentario a las primeras versiones en español de la obra de William Prescott," *Histórica* 9(1) (1985), 15–34.

31 *Colección de Libros y Documentos referentes a la Historia del Perú, anotados y concordados con las Crónicas de Indias* (1916–1921).

32 This sense of a change did not extend, however, to anthropologists being "willing to make explicit the relationship of their work to colonial violence." B. K. Axel, "Introduction: Historical Anthropology and Its Vicissitudes," in B. K. Axel (ed.), *From the Margins. Historical Anthropology and Its Future* (Durham and London: Duke University Press, 2002), 1–44, at 5.

of primitive society prior to the advent of colonialism," a tendency he also called the "prewar fetish of precolonial purity."[33] In the post-World War II era, however, the awareness that communities were "enclosed in, and form part of great historical societies" became critical.[34] This shift affected the relation between anthropology and history, insofar as they were now concerned with the changes that affected human groups within complex societies. In the 1960s, those new concerns gave rise to the advent of "ethnohistory," an academic and intellectual movement that can be defined as the study of the indigenous peoples from an interdisciplinary perspective seeking to bridge the gaps between archaeology, history, and anthropology.[35]

For ethnohistorians it was especially important to analyze the history of indigenous peoples during the colonial period, an aspect that had previously been neglected. The question of continuity of and rupture with precolonial indigenous practices under European colonial domination became a key topic in ethnohistorical studies. This trend also emerged alongside the "invention" of new sources, placing at center stage the publication and study of indigenous chroniclers, archival material, and texts written in local languages or in local scripts.[36] John V. Murra's career and his interest in the precolonial, colonial, and contemporary indigenous peoples of the Andes are emblematic of

33 Axel, "Introduction," 3 and 7.

34 E. E. Evans-Pritchard, "Anthropology and History," in *Social Anthropology and Other Essays* (New York: The Free Press of Glencoe, 1962), 147, cited by Axel, "Introduction," 6.

35 As early as 1962, Adams outlined the main characteristics of Latin American ethnohistory. R. N. Adams, "Ethnohistoric Research Methods: Some Latin American Features," *Ethnohistory* 9(2) (1962), 179–205. For a general discussion on the rise and limits of ethnohistory, see S. Krech, "The State of Ethnohistory," *Annual Review of Anthropology* 20 (1991), 345–75. On the development of ethnohistory in Mexico, see A. Araujo Pardo, "La Etnohistoria en México: Un intento por normar las relaciones entre la Historia y la Antropología," in G. Marín Guardado and G. Torres Mazuera (eds.), *Antropología e Historia en México. Las fronteras construidas de un territorio compartido* (Mexico City: El Colegio de Michoacán, Universidad Nacional Autónoma de México, 2016), 97–126. On Argentina, see A. Ramos and C. Chiappe, *En la trama de la etnohistoria americana* (Buenos Aires: Editorial La Pluma del Escribano, Universidad de Buenos Aires, 2018).

36 To give only a few examples regarding the publication of ethnohistorical sources, see M. León-Portilla, *Literatura del México antiguo: los textos en la lengua náhuatl* (Caracas: Biblioteca Ayacucho, 1978); A. Recinos, *Crónicas indígenas de Guatemala* (Guatemala: Academia de Geografía e Historia de Guatemala, 1984); F. Pease, *Las crónicas y los Andes* (Lima: Pontificia Universidad Católica del Perú, Instituto Riva-Agüero and Mexico City: Fondo de Cultura Económica, 1995); A. Porro, *As Crônicas do Rio Amazonas. Notas Etno-históricas sobre as Antigas Populações Indígenas da Amanzônia* (Petrópolis: Vozes, 1993); and *O Povo das Águas: Ensaios de Etno-História Amazônica* (Petrópolis: Vozes, 1996). Since Barlow's, Dibble's, Galarza's, or Espinoza Soriano's pioneering studies, an increasing knowledge on the Andean and Mesoamerican systems of writing has accumulated in the last decades. R. Barlow, "Una nueva lámina del Mapa Quinatzin," *Journal de la Société des Américanistes* 39 (1950), 111–24; J. Galarza, *Codex mexicains. Catalogue. Bibliothèque Nationale de Paris* (Paris: Musée de l'Homme, Société des Américanistes,

the rise of ethnohistory among Latin Americanists. In 1978, he stated that "the living continuities of the Andean world, especially in agriculture, the reciprocity in the working relationships ... make the use of ethnological evidence indispensable for the understanding of the pre-European organization."[37]

Not only did Murra participate in excavations in Ecuador financed by the Institute of Andean Research in the 1940s, but he also attached great importance to Spanish chronicles as well as to archival material. The *Proyecto de Huanuco* (1964–6), for example, combined archaeological prospection, fieldwork, and information resulting from a *visita,* that is, an inspection made by colonial authorities in the region in 1562.[38] Through his correspondence, the organization of congresses and teaching seminars, and the publication and exchange of books and archival material, Murra created a network of personal and institutional ties with scholars throughout Latin America, Europe, and the United States. As Ramos has shown, mobilizing this network was crucial to the consolidation of both ethnohistory as an academic field and the definition of the Andes as a regional and cultural area (one that went beyond the national boundaries of Peru), thus establishing a counterpart to the concept of "Mesoamerica."[39]

There is little doubt that the accumulation of archaeological and archival data, the publication of texts written in local languages in the early colonial

1974); C. Dibble, *Códice Xolotl* (Mexico City: Universidad Nacional Autónoma de México, 1980); W. Espinoza Soriano, "Los Huancas, aliados de la Conquista. Tres informaciones inéditas sobre la participación indígena en la conquista del Perú. 1558–1560–1561," *Anales Científicos de la Universidad del Centro del Perú* 1 (1971), 5–47. On the research regarding the Maya script, see M. Coe, *Breaking the Maya Code* (London: Thames and Hudson, 1992). For the Andean region, see G. Urton, *Signs of the Inka Khipu: Binary Coding in the Andean Knotted-String Records* (Austin: University of Texas Press, 2003).

37 J. Murra, *La organización económica del Estado Inca* (Mexico City: Siglo XXI, 1978), 20, cited by C. Zanolli, "La antropología, la historia, la antropología histórica. De la teoría al caso," in C. Zanolli, J. Costilla, D. Estruch, and A. Ramos (eds.), *Los estudios andinos hoy. Práctica intelectual y estrategias de investigación* (Buenos Aires: Prohistoria ediciones, 2013), 123–46, at 126: "las continuidades vividas en el mundo andino, particularmente en la agricultura, reciprocidades en el trabajo ... hacen indispensable el uso de la evidencia etnológica para comprender la organización pre europea."

38 This investigation gave rise to the publication of the article focused on the economic organization of the Inca empire, "El control vertical de un máximo de pisos ecológicos en la economía de las sociedades andina," in J. Murra, *Formaciones Económicas y Políticas del Mundo Andino* (Lima: Instituto de Estudios Peruanos, 1975), 59–115.

39 A. Ramos, "John Murra y la formación de una 'comunidad andina'," in A. M. Lorandi (ed.), *El Ocaso del Imperio. Sociedad y cultura en el centro-sur andino* (Buenos Aires: Antropofagia, 2013), 259–72. To mention only a few examples, Murra was one of the founders of the *Instituto de Estudios Peruanos* (1964), and he encouraged José María Arguedas and Pierre Duviols to publish the Huarochiri manuscript and other archival materials (1966). See *Dioses y hombres de Huarochiri. Narración quechua recogida por Francisco de Ávila [ca. 1598]*, bilingual edition, trans. J. M. Arguedas, bibliographical studies by P. Duviols (Lima: Fondo Editorial del Instituto de Estudios Andinos, 1966). In

period, and the progress in deciphering the Mesoamerican and Andean writing systems largely contributed to a renewed understanding of precolonial law during the 1970s and 1980s.[40] But what did this bulk of works on Mesoamerica and on the Andes have in common? In what theoretical and methodological frameworks were these texts written? The hypothesis of the cultural continuity from precolonial past to present-day social life was a key issue, since it allowed, and even encouraged the combined use of archaeological, historical and ethnographic data. It also enabled the incorporation of theories developed in the field of legal anthropology, not only in America, but also in Africa or Oceania. Jerome A. Offner used the concept of the "reasonable men" – introduced by Max Gluckman in 1955 to refer to judges in the British colony of Barotseland in Africa who "used implied standards of behavior in reaching decisions" – to describe the Texcocan legal system.[41]

As Murra pointed out in 1978, it was of equal importance to draft an "integrative description of a specific society, avoiding its classification according to categories borrowed to the European economic and social history."[42] The

1978, he edited a special issue of the *Annales* with Nathan Wachtel and Jacques Revel. In Argentina, he also had close ties with Ana María Lorandi, who would assume a key role in the institutionalization of ethnohistory in this country, thanks to the construction of "colonial Tucuman colonial as a subject of inquiry," and the organization of the first *Congreso Internacional de Etnohistoria* in Buenos Aires in 1989. A. Ramos and C. Chiappe, "Ana María Lorandi y el Primer Congreso Internacional de Etnohistoria," *Diálogo andino* 56 (2018), 9–15, at 10. On Murra's influence on Chilean studies, see L. Núñez, "Sobre los comienzos de los estudios andinos y sus avances actuales en el norte de Chile," in Zanolli, Costilla, Estruch, and Ramos, *Los estudios andinos*, 79–122. For a discussion on the development of ethnohistory in the United States, see S. Krech, "The State of Ethnohistory," *Annual Review of Anthropology* 20 (1991), 345–75.

40 A. López Austin, *La constitución real de México-Tenochtitlan* (Mexico City: Universidad Nacional Autónoma de México, 1961); N. Wachtel, *La vision des vaincus. Les Indiens du Pérou devant la Conquête espagnole, 1530–1570* (Paris: Editions Gallimard, 1971); P. Carrasco and J. Broda (eds.), *Estratificación social en la Mesoamérica prehispánica* (Mexico City: Instituto Nacional de Antropología e Historia, 1976); P. Carrasco and J. Broda (eds.), *Economía política e ideología en el México prehispánico* (Mexico City: Instituto Nacional de Antropología e Historia, 1978); J. Offner, *Law and Politics in Aztec Texcoco* (Cambridge: Cambridge University Press, 1983).

41 Offner, *Law and Politics*, 70. Of particular influence were works by M. Gluckman and L. Pospisil, namely *The Judicial Process among the Barotse of Northern Rhodesia* (Manchester: Manchester University Press, 1955) and *The Kapauku Papuans of West New Guinea* (New York: Holt, Rinehart and Winston, 1963). On legal anthropology, see L. Nader, "Antropología legal," in T. Barfield (ed.), *Diccionario de antropología* (Mexico City: Siglo XXI Editores, 2000), 54–57; E. Krotz (ed.), *Antropología jurídica: perspectivas socioculturales en el estudio del derecho* (Mexico City: Anthropos, Universidad Autónoma Metropolitana-Iztapalapa, 2002).

42 Murra, *La organización económica*, at 19: "una descripción integradora de una sociedad especifica, y no su clasificación según categorías que surgen de la historia económica y social de Europa."

concepts of "reciprocity and redistribution" and of discontinuous territorial control sought to describe the relations between the "Inca state" and its subjects.[43] In his prologue to Alfredo López Austin's *La constitución real de México*, Miguel León-Portilla outlined that one of most important achievements of the book was to have outlined "the indigenous people's own vision of their laws" and the "Aztec world's idiosyncratic legal categories."[44] Quite paradoxically, however, another critical idea in ethnohistorical studies was the existence of precolonial states, which were perceived as being similar to their European counterparts, probably with the purpose to go beyond previous hierarchizations. The word "constitution," defined as the "statal organization generated by the social manifestations that structure the relations … between individuals," was used, for example, by Alfredo López Austin to describe the Aztec state: The author considered that "any state is structured by a constitution, whether or not a systematic body of juridic norms exists."[45]

While some scholars described indigenous states, others instead suggested that at least some indigenous societies were built "against the state," to use the title of Pierre Clastres' influential study based on the ethnography of the Awé of Brazil.[46] His work offered an alternative interpretation to the growing bulk of literature focused on the Maya "city-states," the Muisca "confederation" or the Inca and Aztec "states" or "empire." Clastres described a society with little centralization, ruled by chiefs who maintained their authority through speeches and were accountable to their people. Some archaeologists projected this vision into the precolonial past of some indigenous groups on the basis of two main arguments: the absence of significant archaeological vestiges, on the one hand, and the reliance on the European chronicles in which the notion of *behetría*, defined in Sebastián de Covarrubias' 1611 Castilian dictionary as "the freedom to change *señores*, thus generating great confusion," was used to define several communities.[47] Archaeologists Betty J. Meggers and Clifford Evans, for example, developed the theory of the "tropical forest culture" to describe the Amazonian precolonial indigenous past.

43 N. Wachtel, "La réciprocité et l'Etat Inca: de Karl Polanyi a John V. Murra," *Annales Histoire Sciences Sociales* 6 (1974), 1346–57. See also F. Pease, *Curacas, reciprocidad y riqueza* (Lima: Pontificia Universidad Católica del Perú, 1992).

44 M. León-Portilla's prologue to López Austin, *La constitución real*, IX.

45 López Austin, *La constitución real*, at 3.

46 P. Clastres, *La Société contre l'État. Recherches d'anthropologie politique* (Paris: Les Editions de Minuit, 1974), translated into Spanish in 1978. See *La sociedad contra el Estado* (Caracas: Monte Ávila Editores, 1978). On the way in which Clastres constructed his theory, see O. Allard, "Faut-il encore lire Clastres?," *L'Homme* 236 (2020), 159–76.

47 Sebastián de Covarrubias, *Tesoro de la lengua castellana o española*, ed. Felipe Maldonado (Madrid: Editorial Castalia, 1995 [1611]), 177–78.

They emphasized the "lack of cultural traits," the "environment-based explanation," and the "peripheral perspective" with respect to the Andean culture.[48] The result was the gradual building of an alleged opposition between Mesoamerica and the Andes and "other areas" of the continent.[49]

The 1990s, however, were marked by "a persistent critique of the legacies of colonialism in the formation of the modern nation-states and institutions of knowledge production like the area studies."[50] In other words, scholars became interested in exploring not peoples, but rather "the production of a people," not territories, but rather "the production of space and time."[51] This line of inquiry gave rise to a questioning of national frameworks and center-periphery relations. By contrast, the interplay between the local and the global became a central category of analysis.[52] As instrumental were the shifts in approaching the history of science, which advocated taking into account the Iberian experiences, on the one hand, and bridging the gap between the local and the global scale in the production

48 See, for example, B. J. Meggers, *Amazonia. Un paraíso ilusorio* (Mexico City: Siglo XXI Editores, 1989 [1976]). On this trend in archaeological studies, see E. O. Neves, "Changing Perspectives in Amazonian Archaeology," in G. Politis and B. Alberti (eds.), *Archaeology in Latin America* (London and New York: Routledge, 1999), 219–27.

49 On the construction of Mesoamerica and the Andes as area studies, see C. Battcock and A. Ramos, "Mesoamérica y Andes: un debate necesario sobre las áreas de investigación," draft paper. I am grateful to the authors for giving me the opportunity to read their work. See also B. Cumings, "Boundary Displacement: Area Studies and International Studies during and after the Cold War," *Bulletin of Concerned Asian Scholars* 29(1) (1997), 6–26; C. Clados and E. Halbmayer, "Between Mesoamerica, the Central Andes, and Amazonia: Area Conceptions, Chronologies, and History," in E. Halbmayer (ed.), *Amerindian Socio-Cosmologies between the Andes, Amazonia and Mesoamerica: Toward an Anthropological Understanding of the Isthmo–Colombian Area* (London and New York: Routledge, 2020), 123–57.

50 Axel, "Introduction," 9.

51 Ibid., 3; T. Asad, *Anthropology and the Colonial Encounter* (Atlantic Highlands: Humanities Press, 1973); J. Clifford and G. Marcus (eds.), *Writing Culture: The Poetics and Politics of Ethnography* (Berkeley: University of California Press, 1986); A. Appadurai, "Theory in Anthropology: Center and Periphery," *Comparative Studies in Society and History* 28(2) (1986), 356–61 and *Modernity at Large: Cultural Dimensions of Globalization* (Minneapolis: University of Minnesota Press, 1996); W. Mignolo, *Local Histories/Global Designs: Coloniality, Subaltern Knowledges and Border Thinking* (Princeton and Oxford: Princeton University Press, 1999).

52 This interpretation benefited from the research on the construction of *americanismo*, *indigenismo*, ethnohistory, and area studies as academic fields in a global perspective. Special emphasis has been put on formal and informal ties between scholars, the impact of personal trajectories, the institutional evolutions, and on the "invention" of new sources such as personal correspondence. A. Ramos, "Consultando archivos, haciendo archivos. La epistolar como fuente para investigación de prácticas académicas," in C. Cunill, D. Estruch, and A. Ramos (eds.), *Actores, redes y prácticas dialógicas en la construcción de archivos en América Latina, siglo XVI-XXI* (Mérida: Universidad Nacional Autónoma de México, Centro Peninsular en Humanidades y Ciencias Sociales, 2021), 221–47.

of knowledge, on the other. These changes had an impact on the history of law, now understood as a process of legal knowledge production, in which a wide range of actors participated in dialogic and conflictive ways (see Section 1.4).[53]

When Laura Nader proposed to carry out an anthropological study of the state, she expressed the wish to break the "North / South" line that marked the division between state and non-state societies, between legal and extra-legal cultures that was reproduced in the boundaries between legal sociology and legal anthropology.[54] As explained by Jonas Bens and Larissa Vetters, until those years,

> as sociology investigated those societies characterized by the "modern" nation state, legal sociology was consequently responsible for law in the Global North. As anthropology investigated those societies where the state was presumed to be absent, legal anthropology was consequently responsible for the law of "premodern" non-state societies in the Global South.[55]

Boaventura Sousa Santos also called attention to the overlaps, coexistence, and interpenetration of different normative orders in a same society, a phenomenon he defined as "interlegality." And Sally E. Merry engaged with the concept of legal pluralism and the relation between law and colonialism, thereby rendering more complex the understanding of how knowledge of normativity was produced in a world marked by local / global dynamics and by colonial domination both in the past and in the present.[56]

Thanks to the contributions of scholars such as António Manuel Hespanha or Víctor Tau Azoátegui, in recent years our understanding of early modern legal cultures has gone through a complete renewal, marked by a growing distance with respect to the nineteenth-century paradigms. As Tamar Herzog points out in this volume (see Section 3.1), early modern law "featured discussions rather than solutions, guiding ideas rather than rules" and if "there was never a single authoritative answer ... neither was there a single jurisdiction,"

53 T. Duve (ed.), *Entanglements in Legal History: Conceptual Approaches* (Frankfurt: Max-Planck-Institut für europäische Rechtsgeschichte, 2014).

54 L. Nader, *Law in Culture and Society* (Chicago: Aldine, 1969); M. Goodale, "A Life in the Law: Laura Nader and the Future of Legal Anthropology," *Law and Society Review* 39(4) (2005), 945–55.

55 J. Bens and L. Vetters, "Ethnographic Legal Studies: Reconnecting Anthropological and Sociological Traditions," *The Journal of Legal Pluralism and Unofficial Law* 50(3) (2018), 239–54.

56 B. de Sousa Santos, *Toward a New Legal Common Sense: Law, Globalization and Emancipation* (London: Butterworths LexisNexis, 2002 [1985]); S. E. Merry, "Legal Pluralism," *Law and Society Review* 22(5) (1988), 869–96 and "Law and Colonialism," *Law and Society Review* 25(4) (1991), 889–922.

since early modern "jurisdictional states" were formed by "a conglomerate of communities and corporations," each one of these units having "authorities endowed with jurisdiction, that is, the capacity to declare and apply the law."[57] These changes affected how historians, anthropologists and archaeologists approached not only Iberian imperial law, but also precolonial law. Indeed, they treated the dichotomy between "state" and "non-state" societies more cautiously and paid increasing attention to legal pluralism.[58]

In the field of Amazonian archaeology, the tropical forest culture theory was abandoned in the 1990s, and the "environment-based explanation" and "peripheral perspective" with respect to the Andes were replaced by an insistence on the "political character" of late Amazonian precolonial societies and the idea that the Amazonian landscape was a "cultural artefact."[59] According to Eduardo G. Neves, this shift was due to the re-evaluation of colonial sources, as well as the "warning against the indiscriminate use of ethnographic analogies in the interpretation of the archaeological record."[60] In the same period, as noted by Oscar Calavia Sáez, the historiography on indigenous people benefited from a more complex approach to the notion of power and of the pre-modern "states" in both European and extra-European spaces.[61] Moreover, the idea of cultural contact, understood as the influence

57 See Section 3.1. In 1986, A. M. Hespanha proclaimed the death of the state in "A historiografia jurídico-institucional e a morte do estado," *Anuario de Filosofía del Derecho* 3 (1986), 191–227; A. M. Hespanha, *A cultura jurídica europeia: Síntese de um milénio* (Lisbon: Almedina, 2012); V. Tau Anzoátegui, *Casuismo y sistema: Indagación histórica sobre el espíritu del Derecho Indiano* (Buenos Aires: Instituto de Investigaciones de Historia del Derecho, 1992) and *El poder de la costumbre. Estudios sobre el Derecho Consuetudinario en América hispana hasta la Emancipación* (Buenos Aires: Instituto de Investigaciones de Historia del Derecho, 2001). On those developments, see T. Herzog, *A Short History of European Law: The Last Two and a Half Millennia* (Cambridge: Harvard University Press, 2018).

58 T. Herzog, "Latin American Legal Pluralism: The Old and the New," *Quaderni fiorentini per la storia del pensiero giuridico moderno* 50(1) (2021), 705–36; L. Benton and R. Ross, *Legal Pluralism and Empires, 1500–1850* (New York: New York University Press, 2013); A. M. Hespanha, "The Legal Patchwork of Empires," *Rechtsgeschichte – Legal History* 22 (2014), 303–14; P. Schiff Berman (ed.), *The Oxford Handbook of Global Legal Pluralism* (London: Oxford University Press, 2020); L. Benton, *Law and Colonial Cultures: Legal Regimes in World History, 1400–1900* (Cambridge: Cambridge University Press, 2000).

59 Neves, "Changing Perspectives," 227.

60 Ibid., 228. Manuela Carneiro da Cunha's editorial project, called *Núcleo de história indígena e do indigenismo*, played a key role in this evolution. See also E. Viveiros de Castro and M. Carneiro da Cunha (eds.), *Amazônia. Etnología e História Indígena* (São Paulo: Universidad de São Paulo, 1993); A. C. Roosevelt (ed.), *Amazonian Indians from Prehistory to the Present. Anthropological Perspectives* (Tucson: University of Arizona Press, 1994), 79–94; N. L. Whitehead, "Ethnic Transformation and Historical Discontinuity in Native Amazonia and Guayana, 1500–1900," *Homme* 126–28 (1993), 285–305.

61 O. Calavia Saez, "La jefatura indígena, hoy," *Indiana* 27 (2010), 47–62. See also M. Abensour (ed.) *El espíritu de las leyes salvajes. Pierre Clastres o una nueva antropología política* (Buenos Aires: Ediciones del Sol, 2007); B. Alcántara Rojas and F. Navarrete

of the European colonizers on indigenous peoples, was reframed in terms of "dialogical relation that constituted both metropole and colony, the European and the other, as indissociable."[62]

Already in the 1980s, Bernard Cohn stated that

> the anthropological "other" are part of the colonial world.... Whites everywhere came into other peoples' world with models and logics ... with which they adapted the construction of new environments, peopled with new "others." By the same token, these "others" had to restructure their models to encompass the fact of white domination and their powerlessness.[63]

Cohn therefore considered that the "colonial situation" had to be viewed "as a situation in which the European colonist and the Indigene [were] united in one analytic field."[64] From this perspective, historians outlined that the colonial sources are not an exact reflection of precolonial indigenous past, but rather reconstructions elaborated from the perspective of a "colonial situation."[65] Some even asked whether or not it is possible to capture the pre-Hispanic past through colonial sources, even those written by indigenous authors in their own languages in the aftermath of the Iberian conquests.[66]

But this perspective regarding the past also enables us to put increasing emphasis on indigenous agency, understood as the indigenous people's capacity to respond to imperial domination either with their own epistemological tools or with Europeans ones. For specialists of indigenous history, the indigenous people's agency in using or, even, forging the law under imperial rule thus became an especially challenging issue.[67] There is little doubt that present-day struggles for the recognition of indigenous normative orders

Linares (eds.), *Los pueblos amerindios más allá del Estado* (Mexico City: Universidad Nacional Autónoma de México, 2011).

62 Axel, "Introduction," 8.

63 B. Cohn, *An Anthropologist among the Historians and Other Essays* (Delhi: Oxford University Press, 1987), cited by Axel, "Introduction," 9.

64 Axel, "Introduction," 9.

65 See, for example, Germán Morong Reyes' excellent work on the colonial discourses focused on the Incas. G. Morong Reyes, *Saberes hegemónicos y dominio colonial. Los indios en el Gobierno del Perú de Juan de Matienzo (1567)* (Buenos Aires: Prohistoria, 2016) and "Lo que conviene a la república: el orden del inca, la condición colonial de los indios y el buen gobierno," in G. Morong Reyes and M. Gloël (eds.), *Gobernar el virreinato del Perú, S. XVI-XVII. Praxis Político-Jurisdiccional, redes de poder y usos de la información oficial* (Santiago de Chile: Ediciones Sindéresis y UBO ediciones, 2020), 95–124.

66 J. Szeminski, "Los estudios andinos hoy. Practica intelectual y estrategias de investigación. ¿Es posible investigar la historia del Tawantin Suyu anterior a la conquista española?," in C. E. Zanolli, J. Costilla, D. Estruch, and A. Ramos, *Los estudios andinos*, 19–30.

67 F. Salomon and S. B. Schwartz (eds.), *The Cambridge History of the Native Peoples of the Americas* (Cambridge: Cambridge University Press, 1999).

and jurisdictions within the legal systems of the Latin American nations, as shown by Daniel Bonilla Maldonado in Chapter 7 of this volume, constitute another key factor that helps explaining the increased interest of scholars in precolonial law and its evolution under Iberian imperial domination.[68] According to Alexandra Huneeus, Javier Couso and Rachel Sieder, the analysis of the conditions in which legal pluralism emerged in Latin America requires additional work "on the political role of law and courts in political struggles in Latin American history, as well as the legal history of particular struggles."[69] Obviously, these changes, which occurred on a global scale, are affecting our understanding of the role that indigenous peoples have played and still play in forging the law and writing Latin American legal history.

Precolonial Indigenous Law

Given the diversity of the peoples that lived throughout Latin America over time, the following passages offer a study of indigenous law as allocated to specific groups and moments, with special emphasis on the period that preceded the European conquests. Any such study must begin by affirming the obvious, namely, that these legal orders changed over time, since they were designed to meet the needs of the society in which they were produced. Drawing on the interpretation of ancient "painted histories and annals," the indigenous intellectual Alva Ixtlilxochitl, who wrote in seventeenth-century Tezcoco, stated that shortly after establishing his people in the Valley of Mexico in the tenth century, the Acolhua ruler Xolotl enacted a series of laws to regulate agricultural and hunting practices. According to the chronicler, "burning the fields and the mountains was forbidden without the ruler's

68 See also S. Garfield, *Indigenous Struggles at the Heart of Brazil. State Policy, Frontier Expansion and the Xavante Indians, 1937–1988* (Durham and London: Duke University Press, 2001); I. Bellier (ed.), *Peuples autochtones dans le monde. Les enjeux de la reconnaissance* (Paris: L'Harmattan, 2013); M. Carneiro da Cunha and S. Barbosa, *Direitos dos povos indígenas em disputa* (São Paulo: Fundação Editora da Unesp, 2018); T. Duve, "Indigenous Rights: Latin America," in M. Dubber and C. Tomlins (eds.), *The Oxford Handbook of Legal History* (Oxford: Oxford University Press, 2018), 817–37 (https://doi.org/10.1093/oxfordhb/9780198794356.013.42, last accessed Sep. 15, 2022).

69 A. V. Huneeus, J. Couso, and R. Sieder, "Cultures of Legality: Judicialization and Political Activism in Contemporary Latin America," in J. Couso, A. V. Huneeus, and R. Sieder (eds.), *Cultures of Legality. Judicialization and Political Activism in Latin America* (Cambridge: Cambridge University Press, 2010), 11. The authors define legal cultures as "contested and ever-shifting repertoires of ideas and behaviors relating to law, legal justice, and legal systems" that include "representations, ideologies, norms, conceptions, beliefs, values, and discourses about law," as well as "language, informal institutions, and symbolic actions (such as mimicry)." Ibid., 6.

license and, if appropriate, punishable by death"[70] and "taking the prey that had been caught in someone else's nets was forbidden and punished by the confiscation of one's bow and arrow."[71] A few generations later, however, Nezahualcóyotl developed a complex legal system in which justice was administered by specialized courts and a series of crimes and punishments defined and recorded.[72]

A similar emphasis on the historical dimension of precolonial law can be found in the *Royal Commentaries,* in which Garcilaso de la Vega, known as "El Inca," a *mestizo* from both Spanish and Inca descent, stated that Inca rulers brought "natural law" and "urbanity" to the people they conquered. According to Garcilasco,

> as these people were living, or dying, in the way we have seen [*behetría*, or barbarism], God our Lord permitted that from amongst them there should arise a morning star; someone who would illuminate that extreme darkness and offer people some notion of natural law, and of urbanity, and of the respect, that men should have for one another; so that the descendants of that prophet, proceeding from good to better, would tame the savages and convert them into men, capable of reason, and of receiving any good doctrine: so that when this same God, the sun of justice, finally decided it was the right time to send the light of his divine rays to those idolaters, he would find them no longer savage, but more docile and capable of accepting the Catholic faith.[73]

It is true that this account was influenced by the concepts and language of the imperial world in which Garcilaso lived, since he used the contrast between "urbanity" and "barbarism" to compare the Incas with other Andean cultures.[74]

70 F. de Alva Ixtlilxochitl, *Obras históricas* (Mexico City: Universidad Nacional Autónoma de México, 1985), vol. II, 24. See also Offner, *Law and Politics*, 47–49.

71 Ixtlilxochitl, *Obras*, vol. I, 526.

72 C. Battcock and M. Aguilar, "Nezahualcóyotl. Paradigma de justicia y rectitud," *Arqueología Mexicana*, 24(142) (2016). A complete list of crimes and punishments was also drawn up by the Maya Gaspar Antonio Chi in 1582. See M. Strecker and J. Artiega, "La 'Relación de algunas costumbres (1582)' de Gaspar Antonio Chi," *Estudios de Historia Novohispana* 6 (1978), 89–107; A. L. Izquierdo y de la Cueva, "El delito y su castigo en la sociedad maya," in J. L. Soberanes Fernández (ed.), *Memoria del II Congreso de Historia del Derecho Mexicano* (Mexico City: Universidad Nacional Autónoma de México, Instituto de Investigaciones Jurídicas, 1980), 57–68.

73 Inca Garcilaso de la Vega, *Royal Commentaries of the Incas* [1609], book I, chapters XV, f. 13v., translated and quoted by J. A. Mazzotti, "A Syncretic Tropology: Semantic and Symbolic Aspects of the *Comentarios*," in S. Castro-Klarén and C. Fernández (eds.), *Inca Garcilaso and Contemporary World-Making* (Pittsburgh: University of Pittsburgh Press, 2016), 65.

74 Archaeologist Luis Lumbreras has shown that, contrary to the one-way vision proposed by Garcilaso, the Incas had drawn on the Wari culture. L. Lumbreras, *Los orígenes del Estado en el Perú* (Lima: Instituto de Estudios Peruanos, 1972) and *Arqueología de la América andina* (Lima: Editorial Milla Batres, 1981).

Although Garcilaso might have exaggerated the differences between various indigenous cultures in an attempt to idealize the Inca rule to Christian readers, it is nonetheless plausible that the Inca imposed new laws on other population groups in the Andes and that the expansion of Quechua played a key role in this process.[75] Inca Garcilaso went a step further when he compared Quechua to the "civilizing impact of Latin in the Roman Empire." According to him, the Incas

> domesticated and united a great variety of different nations of conflicting religion and customs whom they brought into their empire, welding them, thanks to the use of a common language, into such union and friendship that they loved each other like brothers.[76]

Garcilaso's objective was not only to claim legitimacy for the descendants of the Incas to govern the Andean region, but also to defend Quechua as the language of evangelization, since the clerics were supposed to speak the language of the parishes in which they exercised their pastoral duties. Some local languages became "general languages" in extended territories of the Iberian empires.[77]

However, the imposition of vehicular languages, the emergence of bilingual mediators, and the formulation of dominant linguistic ideologies might also have been common practices in precolonial times.[78] Long

75 A. Torero, *El quechua y la historia social andina* (Lima: Universidad Ricardo Palma, 1974) and *Idiomas de los Andes: lingüística e historia* (Lima: Instituto Francés de Estudios Andinos, 2002); B. Mannheim, *The Language of the Inka since the European Invasion* (Tucson: University of Texas Press, 1991); R. Howard, *Por los linderos de la lengua: ideologías lingüísticas en los Andes* (Lima: Institut Français d'Etudes Andines and Instituto de Estudios Peruanos, 2007); P. Heggarty and A. J. Pearce, *History and Language in the Andes* (London: Palgrave Macmillan, 2011).

76 I. Garcilaso, *Comentario reales*, in *Obras completas del Inca Garcilaso de la Vega*, ed. C. Saenz de Santa María (Madrid: Atlas, 1960), vol. II, 247, quoted and translated by S. Maccormack, "'The Discourse of My Life': What Language Can Do (Early Colonial Views on Quechua)," in A. Durston and B. Mannheim (eds.), *Indigenous Languages, Politics, and Authority in Latin America. Historical and Ethnographic Perspectives* (Notre Dame: University of Notre Dame Press, 2018), 25–58, at 29.

77 D. Moore, "Historical Development of Nheengatu (Lingua Geral Amazônica)," in S. S. Mufwene (ed.), *Imperialism and Language Evolution in Latin America* (Chicago: University of Chicago Press, 2014), 108–42; J. C. Estenssoro and C. Itier (eds.), "Dossier Langues indiennes et empire dans l'Amérique du Sud coloniale," *Mélanges de la Casa de Velázquez* 45(1) (2015); A. Durston, "Standard Colonial Quechua," in Mufwene, *Iberian Imperialism*, 225–44; C. Itier (ed.), *Del siglo de Oro al siglo de las luces. Lenguaje y sociedad en los Andes del siglo XVIII* (Cusco: Centro de Estudios Regionales Andinos "Bartolomé de las Casas", 1995); Y. Yannakakis, "Introduction: How Did They Talk to One Another? Language Use and Communication in Multilingual New Spain," in R. Schwaller (ed.), "A Language of Empire, a Quotidian Tongue: The Uses of Nahuatl in New Spain," *Ethnohistory* 59(4) (2012), 667–74.

78 On the expansion of the Guarani, see I. Telesca and A. Vidal (eds.), *Historia y lingüística guaraní. Homenaje a Bartolomé Meliá* (Buenos Aires: Paradigma Inicial, 2021). For a general overview of the linguistic history of Brazil from precolonial to present times, see G. Urban, "História da cultura brasileira segundo as línguas nativas," in C. da Cunha (ed.),

before the Portuguese and Spanish conquests, the Valley of Mexico was a mosaic of diverse ethnic groups that spoke different languages, but Nahuatl was the lingua franca even in distant territories such as Oaxaca and Guatemala.[79] In the southwestern coastal areas of Guatemala, El Salvador, and Nicaragua, a Nahuatl dialect called Pipil had been spoken since 900 AD due to "trade and diplomacy prior to the rise of the Aztec State," a phenomenon reinforced by Aztec expansion.[80] Alva Ixtlilxochitl's and Garcilaso's narratives suggest that law was used to govern multiethnic and plurilingual societies that were constantly involved in wars and processes such as migrations, territorial reorganization, and ethnicization. In other words, language policy, diplomacy, matrimonial alliances with members of the local ruling elites, the dispatch of agents and, eventually, migrants through distant regions, and the privileged status of merchants were part of precolonial indigenous legal cultures.[81] According to Tsubasa Okoshi Harada, the post-classic Maya *cúuchcabal*, which the Spaniards translated as "province" in Castilian, did not designate territories with continuous

História dos Índios (São Paulo: Companhia das letras, 1992), 87–103. On the K'ichee' Maya, see S. Romero, *Language and Ethnicity among the K'ichee' Maya* (Salt Lake City: University of Utah Press, 2015). A global perspective on linguistic policies and imperialism over time in Latin America can be found in Mufwene, *Iberian Imperialism*, and Durston and Mannheim, *Indigenous Languages*.

79 M. Swanton, "Multilingualism in the Tocuij Ñudzaviu Region," in M. Jansen and L. van Broekhoven (eds.), *Mixtec Writing and Society (Escritura de Ñuu Dzaui)* (Amsterdam: Koninklijke Nederlandse Akademie van Wetenschappen, 2008), 363–73.

80 L. Matthew and S. Romero, "Nahuatl and Pipil in Colonial Guatemala: A Central American Counterpoint," *Ethnohistory* 59(4) (2012), 765–81.

81 P. Carrasco, *Estructura político-territorial del Imperio Tenochca* (Mexico City: Fondo de Cultura Económica, 1996); C. Brokmann Haro, *La estera y la silla. Individuo, comunidad e instituciones jurídicas nahuas; Hablando fuerte. Antropología jurídica comparativa de Mesoamérica; La fecha dorada. Pluralismo y derechos humanos en los sistemas jurídicos de Mesoamérica* (Mexico City: Comisión Nacional de Derechos Humanos, 2006, 2008, and 2018); M. A. Malpass and S. Alconini (eds.), *Distant Provinces in the Inka Empire : Toward a Deeper Understanding of Inka Imperialism* (Iowa City: University of Iowa Press, 2010); C. Townsend, "Polygyny and the Divided Altepetl: The Tetzcocan Key to Pre-Conquest Nahua Politics," in J. Lee and G. Brokaw (eds.), *Texcoco. Prehispanic and Colonial Perspectives* (Boulder: University of Colorado Press, 2014), 93–116; A. Coley, *How the Incas Built Their Heartland. State Formation and the Innovation of Imperial Strategies in the Sacred Valley, Peru* (Ann Arbor: University of Michigan Press, 2006); C. Battcock, *Construcciones y significaciones de un hecho histórico. La guerra entre México-Tenochtitlan y Azcapotzalco* (España, Editorial Académica Española, 2011); F. Berdan, et al. (eds.), *Aztec Imperial Strategies* (Cambridge: Harvard University Press, 1996); M. Castañeda de la Paz, "Historia de una casa real. Origen y ocaso de un linaje gobernante en México-Tenochtitlan," *Nuevo Mundo, Mundos Nuevos* 2011; R. Hassig, *Trade, Tribute, and Transportation. The Sixteenth-Century Political Economy of the Valley of Mexico* (Norman: University of Oklahoma Press, 1985); M. Kobayashi, *Tres estudios sobre el sistema tributario de los mexicas* (Mexico City: CIESAS, 1993).

frontiers, but rather the people who depended on a local ruler by alliances, kinship, or war.[82]

The accumulation of information about other peoples, natural resources, and territories might also have been characteristic of the way in which law was forged and adapted to local situations in precolonial times. For a long time, insufficient knowledge of pre-Hispanic systems of writing and the assumption that, before the European conquests, justice was delivered orally – an interpretation in part supported by the fact that, during the colonial period, indigenous "uses and customs" were not habitually written down – led scholars to assume that indigenous law was unwritten. Nevertheless, we now know that the use of *khipus* was widespread in the Andes even before the Inca period. Scholars also suspect that these records contained not only tributary, but also historical evidence (see Section 3.1).[83] The *lámina* 3 of the *Mapa Quinatzin*, in which a series of crimes and punishments were depicted, could be considered as an early colonial pictographic reminiscence of the "written laws" decreed under Nezahualcóyotl's rule in Texcoco.[84] This document, now kept at the Bibliothèque Nationale de France, is thought to have been one of Alva Ixtlilxochitl's main sources for describing precolonial law.[85]

The nobleman Motelchiuhtzin, who was in charge of the Aztec estate under Moctezuma II and was baptized under the Spanish name of Andrés de Tapia, kept a number of pictographic records in his house in Tenochtitlan. According to the Spanish conqueror Bernal Díaz del Castillo, Tapia kept a record of "all the tributes due to Moctezuma; he did so with the help of [old] books made of a paper called *amatl*, which filled a big house."[86]

82 T. Okoshi Harada, "El *cúuchcabal* de los Xiu: análisis de su formación y consolidación," *Contributions in New World Archaelogy* 4 (2012), 231–50. Pedro Carrasco had shown that in Mesoamerica the urban space was organized according to ethnic diversity in the so-called "intertwined neighborhoods."

83 G. Urton, *Inka History in Knots. Reading Khipus as Primary Sources* (Austin: University of Texas Press, 2017).

84 "Mexicain 396," Bibliothèque Nationale de France, Paris, https://gallica.bnf.fr/ark:/12148/btv1b10303825m (last accessed Sep. 15, 2022). An analysis and a facsimile edition of this document were published by L. M. Mohar Betancourt, *Códice Mapa Quinatzin. Justicia y derechos humanos en el México antiguo* (Mexico City: Comisión Nacional de Derechos Humanos, 2004).

85 In his *Historia de la nación chichimeca*, the indigenous chronicler mentioned the collection of pictographic records that he had in his house in Tezcoco. Fernando de Alva Ixtlilxóchitl, *Historia de la nación chichimeca* (Madrid: Editorial Dastin, 2000 [ca. 1620]), cap. XXXVIII, 156–161. On this topic, see A. Brian, *Alva Ixtlilxochitl's Native Archive and the Circulation of Knowledge in Colonial Mexico* (Nashville: Vanderbilt University Press, 2016).

86 Bernal Díaz del Castillo, *Historia verdadera y cierta de la conquista de México*, 254, quoted by R. Rovira Morgado, "Lengua, identidad y residencialidad indígenas en la ciudad de México de la primera centuria virreinal: el caso del *nahuatltato* Hernando de Tapia," in

Rossend Rovira Morgado points out that this archive in the Tapia family's possession might well have been one of the reasons why the Spanish authorities promoted Don Andrés' son to make him one of the most influential indigenous interpreters of the Audiencia of Mexico.[87] According to a 1576 source, the Tapia family kept in one of their houses "boxes and feathers, and ancient paintings in which his Majesty's [Moctezuma's] tributes were recorded."[88] Ethelia Ruiz Medrano and, more recently, Ana Pullido Rull have shown that "the use of paintings for litigation was a constitutive element of the Aztec legal system."[89] Written records of precolonial law were not produced only by the Aztecs or Incas. The social pre-eminence of Maya scribes, observable in the classic and the postclassic iconography, indicates that Maya codices might have been used in registering and keeping normative knowledge.[90]

Vasco de Quiroga, judge of the high court (*audiencia*) of Mexico between 1531 and 1535, recognized that precolonial pictographic records of the Valley of Mexico contained "legal cases" that might have served as jurisprudence in the resolution of conflicts.[91] In his *Información en derecho* (1535), Quiroga claimed that

> the Indians did not have ordinances, but paintings similar to annals that contained the cases and the facts like they had happened and occurred fairly or unfairly and they painted them and considered them not as laws, but

C. Cunill and L. M. Glave Testino (eds.), *Las lenguas indígenas en los tribunales de América Latina: intérpretes, mediación y justicia, siglos XVI-XXI* (Bogotá: Instituto Colombiano de Antropología e Historia, 2019), 17–40, at 28–29.

87 Rovira Morgado, "Lengua, identidad," 26–29.

88 Archivo General de la Nación, México, Tierras, vol. 37, exp. 2, f. 99, quoted by Rovira Morgado, "Lengua, identidad," 29. León-Portilla explains that the use of the *tequiamatl* (book of tributes) required specialized, technical knowledge. M. León-Portilla, *Códices. Los antiguos libros del nuevo mundo* (Mexico City: Aguilar, 2003), 250. On the existence of archives in precolonial times, see J. E. Ramírez López, *Catálogo de fuentes para la historia franciscana de Tezcoco* (Mexico City: Diósesis de Texcoco, 2018), 25–50; J. Á. Vázquez Martínez, "El amoxcalli o la casa de los libros," *Acalán* (2011), 5–9.

89 A. Pulido Rull, *Mapping Indigenous Land. Native Land Grants in Colonial New Spain* (Norman: University of Oklahoma Press, 2020), at 45. See also E. Ruiz Medrano, *Mexico's Indigenous Communities. Their Lands and Histories, 1500–2010* (Boulder: University Press of Colorado, 2010), at 2 and 13.

90 M. Coe and J. Kerr, *The Art of the Maya Scribe* (New York: Harry N. Abrams, 1998). It must be said that the few precolonial Maya codices that have survived to the present day have been studied predominantly for their historical, genealogical, and religious content. See G. Vail and A. Aveni (eds.), *The Madrid Codex: New Approaches to Understanding an Ancient Maya Manuscript* (Boulder: University Press of Colorado, 2004).

91 See also Ruiz Medrano, *Mexico's Indigenous Communities*; and Pulido Rull, *Mapping Indigenous Land*.

> as examples of what others did badly or well, which is, according to law, reproved since *non exemplis sed legibus in [ju]dicandum est.*[92]

These practices might explain why, during the early colonial period, extensive use was made of both *khipus* and pictographic records in Spanish courts of justice (see Section 3.1).[93] Equally, the systematic destruction of pre-Hispanic codices in the sixteenth century, although traditionally explained as part of the attempt to eradicate indigenous belief systems, could also have been motivated by the Spaniards' wish to erase their legal content.[94]

The intertwining of religious beliefs with the normative order, which was typical of the Iberian legal cultures, also operated among the indigenous peoples. According to Friar Bernardino de Sahagún, from 1524 on the Spaniards sought to

> destroy the objects of idolatry, and even the customs of the republic [of the Indians] since they were entangled with their rites and associated with their ceremonies of idolatry, which happened to almost all the customs by which this republic was ruled; and, for that reason, it was necessary to dismantle everything and establish another kind of *policía* (regime) that had nothing to do with their objects of idolatry.[95]

92 Vasco de Quiroga, *Información en derecho* (Madrid: Biblioteca Nacional de España, 1535), ms. 7369, f. 81r, quoted by C. Cunill and R. Rovira Morgado, "'Lo que nos dejaron nuestros padres, nuestros abuelos': retórica y praxis procesal alrededor de los usos y costumbres indígenas en la Nueva España temprana," *Revista de Indias* 81 (2021), 283–313, at 288.

93 E. Ruiz Medrano and P. Valle, "Los colores de la justicia: códices jurídicos del siglo XVI en la Biblioteca Nacional de Francia," *Journal de la Société des Américanistes* 84(2) (1998), 228–35; B. Mundy, *The Mapping of New Spain: Indigenous Cartography and the Maps of the Relaciones Geográficas* (Chicago: University of Chicago Press, 1996); M. Curatola Petrocchi and J. C. de la Puente Luna (eds.), *El quipu colonial. Estudios y materiales* (Lima: Fondo Editorial Pontificia Universidad Católica del Perú, 2007); C. B. Loza, "El quipu y la prueba en la práctica del Derecho de Indias, 1550–1581," *Historia y cultura* 26 (2000), 11–38; M. Medelius and J. C. de la Puente Luna, "Curacas, bienes y quipus en un documento toledano (Jauja, 1570)," *Histórica* 28(2) (2004), 35–82; J. C. de la Puente Luna, "That Which Belongs to All: Khipus, Community, and Indigenous Legal Activism in the Early Colonial Andes," *The Americas* 72(1) (2015), 19–59.

94 On the destruction of the Maya records in Yucatan, see P. Sullivan, "Los archiveros mayas de lo Sagrado," in Cunill, Estruch, and Ramos, *Actores, redes y prácticas*, 107–46; J. Chuchiak, "Pre-Conquest *Ah Kinob* in a Colonial World: The Extirpation of Idolatry and the Survival of the Maya Priesthood in Colonial Yucatán, 1563–1697," in U. Hostettler and M. Restall (eds.), *Maya Survivalism* (Markt Schwaben: A. Saurwein, 2001), 135–60; R. Vainfas, *A heresia dos índios. Catolicismo e rebeldia no Brasil colonial* (São Paulo: Companhia das Letras, 1995).

95 Bernardino de Sahagún, *Historia general de las cosas de la Nueva España* (Madrid: Editorial Dastin, 2003 [1577]), vol. 2, book 10, cap. 27, 815–16, quoted by Cunill and Rovira Morgado, "Lo que nos dejaron," 286.

Even through Sahagún preferred the term "customs" to that of "law," probably in an attempt to create a hierarchy between indigenous and Spanish legal orders, he recognized the existence of "a kind of *policía,*" that is to say, a series of rules according to which the precolonial republic was governed. The Nahua word *tlamanitiliztli*, defined by Sahagún as "the laws and the customs that the ancients in the republic bequeathed," certainly conveys the idea of a normative order.[96]

The intertwining of indigenous law with indigenous belief systems and their ceremonial dimensions might explain the zeal manifested by Europeans not only in destroying precolonial records but also in prohibiting or re-signifying pre-Hispanic dances in the early colonial period. Nonetheless, in some cases, the Spanish religious and civil authorities sought to make use of local linguistic expressions and written or visual traditions as well as rituals, and to insert them into the new religious, political and legal order.[97] The translation of the word *tlamanitiliztli* as (Christian) "*policía*" in colonial bilingual dictionaries is a paradigmatic example of this kind of processes.[98] When Friars Andrés de Olmos, Juan Bautista Viseo and Bernardino de Sahagún decided to save the *huehuetlatolli* – a textual tradition that gathered the norms governing all matters related to the household and literally meant "the ancient word" in Nahuatl – from destruction, they reframed the norms contained therein according to Christian sensibility.[99] Illustration 8 of the *Tlatelolco Codex* also

96 Sahagún, *Historia*, vol. 1, book 6, cap. 43, at 610; M. León-Portilla, *La filosofía náhuatl estudiada en sus fuentes* (Mexico City: Universidad Nacional Autónoma de México, 2006 [1956]), 233–36.

97 B. Alcántara Rojas, "El canto-baile nahua del siglo XVI: espacio de evangelización y subversión," in A. Ciudad Ruiz, M. J. Iglesias Ponce de León, and M. Sorroche Cuervas (eds.), *El ritual en el mundo Maya de lo privado a lo público* (Madrid: Sociedad española de Estudios Mayas, 2010), 377–93; E. Ruiz Medrano, "Fighting Destiny: Nahua Nobles and the Friars in the Sixteenth-Century Revolt of the *Encomenderos* against the King," in S. Kellogg and E. Ruiz Medrano (eds.), *Negotiation within Domination: New Spain's Indian Pueblos Confront the Spanish State* (Boulder: University Press of Colorado, 2010), 45–78; P. A. Scolieri, *Dancing in the New World. Aztecs, Spaniards and the Choreography of Conquest* (Austin: University of Texas Press, 2013); J. Fernandes, "Feast and Sin: Catholic Missionaries and Native Celebrations in Early Colonial Brazil," *Social History of Alcohol and Drugs* 23(2) (2009), 111–27.

98 Alonso de Molina, *Vocabulario en lengua castellana y mexicana* (Mexico City: Casa de Antonio Espinola, 1571), f. 125v. An equivalent was also found in Yucatec Maya language. See R. Arzápalo Marín (ed.), *Calepino de Motul. Diccionario Maya-Español* (Mexico City: Universidad Nacional Autónoma de México, 1995), vol. I, 199.

99 On the normative knowledge relative to the domestic sphere in colonial law, see R. Zamora, Section 3.3; *Huehuetlatolli. Testimonios de la antigua palabra, estudio introductorio de M. León-Portilla, transcripción del texto náhuatl y traducción al castellano de L. Silva Galeana* (Mexico City: Fondo de Cultura Económica, 1991); L. Silva Galeana, "Los *huehuehtlatolli* recogidos por Sahagún," in M. León-Portilla (ed.), *Bernardino de Sahagún. Quinientos años de presencia* (Mexico City: Universidad Nacional Autónoma de México, 2002), 117–35. On the household as sphere of normativity in the Portuguese and Spanish cultures and its imperial projections, see Romina Zamora, Section 3.3.

shows how dances imitating precolonial styles and traditions were organized in Mexico City to celebrate King Philip II's ascension to the throne in 1556.[100]

Although colonial records must be treated with extreme caution, in order to avoid assuming as pre-Hispanic concepts that might have been either imposed, superposed, or co-invented after the European conquests, they do offer a path for research on precolonial law. In the dictionaries of local languages produced in the early colonial period, for example, several terms referred to the assemblies through which governance and justice were enacted. In the *Calepino de Motul*, a Yucatec Maya-Spanish dictionary from ca. 1580, the verbs *mul-can/mul-than*, derived from *mul* ("something that has been gathered") and *can/than* ("conversation"/"word, language, speech"), meant "to deal with some affair between several persons in community."[101] Moreover, *mul-tumtah* is registered with the meaning of "to decide, to deliberate, or to determine in council, in audience, or between several persons, even though they are only the two of them, to make an agreement, as well as the agreement and decision taken in this manner," and *molay* with that of "assembly, congregation, college and gathering."[102]

It is true that Spaniards were familiar with collegial decision-making, as reflected in the Castilian words *junta*, *ayuntamiento* or *concejo*. Yet, in Maya Yucatec language, emphasis was put as much on the gathering as on the talking. The relevance of oral exchanges in Maya political thought can be inferred by the widespread use of the terms *can/than* in the substantives that designed a large range of offices relative to both governance and justice.[103] They also appear in *nuch-can/nuc-than*, from *nuch* "to gather things together," which meant "to confer, to confederate, to ally" and therefore apparently referred to diplomacy.[104] Those expressions were frequently used in early colonial texts written in Maya

100 Illustration 8 of the *Codex Tlatelolco*. Biblioteca Nacional de Antropología e Historia, México. P. Valle, "La sección VIII del Códice de Tlatelolco. Una nueva propuesta de lectura," in X. Noguez and S. Wood (eds.), *De tlacuilos y escribanos. Estudios sobre documentos indígenas coloniales* (Zamora: El Colegio de Michoacán, 1998), 33–48.

101 *Mulcan/multan*: "tratar entre muchos de comunidad algún negocio," *Calepino*, vol. I, 533–34.

102 *Multumtah*: "acordar, deliberar o determinar en concejo, en audiencia o entre muchos, aunque no pasen de dos, convenir y hacer conveniencia así y el tal acuerdo o determinación." From *tumtah* "to demonstrate, to experience, to deliberate, to put in order an affair and to think about it properly and this consideration, deliberation, and order" ("probar, experimentar, arbitrar, deliberar, ordenar, trazar y dar orden en algún negocio y pensarlo bien y la tal consideración, deliberación y orden"). *Molay*: "junta, congregación, colegio y ayuntamiento," *Calepino*, vol. I, 524–25 and 730.

103 C. Cunill, "El pensamiento político maya en el Yucatán del siglo XVI: reflexiones sobre *can* y *than* (la plática/la palabra)," *Estudios de Cultura Maya* 52 (2018), 117–37.

104 *Nuchcan/nucthan:* "concertarse, confederarse, aliarse" and *nuchah:* "juntar una cosa con otra," *Calepino*, vol. I, 533–34.

Yucatec language that narrated how indigenous governors fixed the limits of their town's jurisdiction in the context of the territorial reorganization imposed by the Spanish authorities. Sentences such as *nuchpah ci u canob* or *hop'i u mulcantoob can,* translated as "they gathered to find an agreement" and "they began to agree in community" by Okoshi Harada, can be found in the *Códice de Calkiní*.[105]

Daniel Graña-Behrens has recently pointed out that a "class of distinguished men, and even women" were referred to as "wise men and women" in precolonial times. These individuals were called *itz'aat* in classic Maya inscriptions from the sixth to the tenth century, and *tlamatini* in early alphabetic records from Central Mexico; they "served as keepers of the collective memory in royal courts as well as within small-scale political units and communities."[106] There is little doubt that the Spaniards built on the tradition of precolonial indigenous assemblies when they established indigenous town councils or *cabildos*. In the translation into Nahuatl of the "ordinances for the indigenous republics" decreed by Viceroy Antonio de Mendoza in the 1540s, an impressive number of Nahua words were conserved to describe the "new" councils' officials.[107] It is also worth noting that, in precolonial times, those councils gathered in specific edifices, such as the *tecpan calli*, the house of governance, in central Mexico and, in some cases, there was a continuity in the use of these political and presumably judicial spaces in the early colonial period. According to Rovira Morgado, Andrés de Tapia's house in Tenochtitlan still served as a *tecpan calli* when he was appointed governor by viceroy Antonio de Mendoza in the 1530s.[108]

105 T. Okoshi Harada, *Códice de Calkiní* (Mexico City: Universidad Nacional Autónoma de México, 2009), 60 and 70: "se juntaron para concertarse"; "comenzaron a tratar en comunidad." The same expressions were used in documents elaborated in Mani in 1557. S. Quezada and T. Okoshi Harada, *Los papeles de los Xiu de Yaxá, Yucatán* (Mexico City: Universidad Nacional Autónoma de México, 2001).

106 D. Graña-Behrens, "*Itz'aat* and *Tlamatini*: The 'Wise Man' as Keeper of Maya and Nahua Collective Memory," in A. Megged and S. Wood (eds.), *Mesoamerican Memory: Enduring Systems of Remembrance* (Norman: University of Oklahoma Press, 2012), 15–32. Among the high-ranking persons who surrounded the supreme ruler (*ajaw*), some late classic Maya stone monuments and ceramics also mentioned the scribe (*aj tz'ib*), the sculptor (*aj[?]-lu*), a religious interpreter called *chilam*, the *aj k'uhuun* ("he of the holy books," or "one who keeps, guards"), and the *sajal* ("one who fears"), a subordinate lord who governed "smaller sites within the realm of the larger city-states." Ibid., 16. See also E. Hill Boone, "In *Tlamatinime*: The Wise Men and Women of Aztec Mexico," in E. Hill Boone, et al. (eds.), *Painted Books and Indigenous Knowledge in Mesoamerica: Manuscript Studies in Honor of Mary Elizabeth Smith* (New Orleans: Tulane University, 2005), 9–25.

107 S. Kellogg and B. Sell, "We Want to Give Them Laws. Royal Ordinances in a Mid-Sixteenth Century Nahuatl Text," *Estudios de Cultura Nahuatl* 27 (1997), 325–67.

108 Rovira Morgado, "Lengua, identidad," 28–29. See also B. Mundy, *The Death of Aztec Tenochtitlan, the Life of Mexico City* (Austin: University of Texas Press, 2015).

The Spanish showed some tolerance toward indigenous forms of political organization because they understood that maintaining these could facilitate the implementation of imperial order. However, they also engaged in an ongoing process of marginalizing a wide range of precolonial indigenous "officials" and reducing their positions. Many members of traditional indigenous councils did not receive any official recognition and were categorized under the general concept of *principales*, a Castilian word created to describe and, simultaneously, erase the specificities of local rule. According to Graña-Behrens, "Spanish colonialism did not extinguish the concept of the wise one in either culture zone," but rather made them invisible in the official records.[109] Owen H. Jones has shown, for example, that in Guatemala the *chinamitales* – although they were not officially recognized by the Spanish authorities – acted as lawyers for *K'ichee'* indigenous communities.[110]

The precolonial indigenous councils might have been more or less specialized, depending on the region and the period. In *lámina* 3 of the *Mapa Quinatzin*, four councils were represented inside Nezahualcóyotl's palace.[111] Both the pictographic and alphabetic sources suggest that one of these councils could have served as a "legal supreme council."[112] Building on Toribio de Benavente Motolinía's memorials, Offner described this council as "made up of six sets of two judges responsible for six territories. The judges, located in two rooms, were presided over by two supreme judges and the ruler."[113] The indigenous chronicler Juan Bautista de Pomar reported that it was composed of twelve judges, "six of royal blood and an equal number of commoners" who had to respect an eighty-day limit for the duration of the cases.[114] Offner's use of the concept of territoriality, however, must be treated with some caution, since in early modern European law jurisdiction was conceived in relation to the people rather than to the territory. A similar situation might have prevailed in precolonial times, as suggested by Okoshi Harada's investigations of the post-classic Maya *cúuchcabal*, for example. According to Luz María Mohar Betancourt,

109 Graña-Behrens, "*Itz'aat*," 15.

110 O. H. Jones, "*Chinamitales*: defensores y justicias k'ichee' en las comunidades indígenas del altiplano de Guatemala colonial," *Revista Histórica* 40(2) (2016), 81–109.

111 Mohar Betancourt, *Mapa*, 107–8.

112 Offner, *Law and Politics*, 55.

113 T. de Motolonía, *Memoriales de fray Toribio de Motolinia, manuscrito de la colección del señor don Joaquín García Icazbalceta* (En casa del editor, Editorial Luis Garcia Pimentel, 1903), quoted by Offner, *Law and Politics*, 55.

114 J. B. Pomar, "Relación de la ciudad y provincia de Tezcoco," in *Relaciones geográficas del siglo XVI, VIII* (Mexico City: Universidad Nacional Autónoma de México, 1983), 23–113, quoted by Offner, *Law and Politics*, 56.

the council's composition might have had to do with ethnic diversity rather than with territoriality.[115]

Furthermore, the use of Castilian words to describe precolonial law tends to project European concepts onto indigenous ones. In this respect, the distinction between "nobles" and "commoners" in Pomar's report is interesting. Although indigenous peoples did not lack a social hierarchical order – in the Valley of Mexico, the *macehualli* or "commoner" category was distinct from the *pilli* or "nobles" – these concepts were built on values that were erased by the use of Castilian in Pomar's text. Such semantic substitutions were also accompanied by legal mechanisms that sought to recognize an indigenous nobility according to colonial criteria, even if some of them were said to ensure a supposed continuity with the pre-Hispanic past.[116] Giving some room to indigenous law yet reframing it into a new legal and political order were thus simultaneous processes. In doing so, the Portuguese and Spanish Crowns hoped to avoid major social discontent, to consolidate their legitimacy, and to maintain political stability in their imperial realms.[117]

Indigenous Law in Iberian Imperial Settings

During the early colonial period, the official historic narratives were characterized by the practice of comparing indigenous and European legal orders – and, more opportunistically, contrasting royal justice with an alleged tyrannical precolonial rule. Indeed, they were at the core of the enterprise of legitimizing Iberian imperial authority.[118] In the second half of the eighteenth century,

115 Mohar Betancourt, *Mapa*, 68.

116 B. Benton, *The Lords of Tetzcoco: The Transformation of Indigenous Rule in Postconquest Central Mexico* (Cambridge: Cambridge University Press, 2017); J. Ramírez López (ed.), *De Catemahco a Tezcoco: origen y desarrollo de una ciudad indígena* (Texcoco: Diócesis de Texcoco, 2017); A. Argouse, "¿Son todos caciques? Curacas, principales e indios urbanos en Cajamarca (siglo XVII)," *Bulletin de l'Institut français d'études andines* 37(1) (2008), 163–84; S. Quezada, *Maya Lords and Lordship: The Formation of Colonial Society, 1350–1600* (Norman: University of Oklahoma Press, 2014).

117 It must be pointed out that, according to the present state of the research on the field, and although the union of the Crowns of Castille and Portugal in 1580 favored the project to implement the Spanish law in colonial Brazil, it appears that the indigenous people's relationship with the courts of justice remained more marginal than it was in Spanish America during most of the colonial period. S. Schwartz, *Sovereignty and Society in Colonial Brazil* (Berkeley: University of California Press, 1973) and "The Iberian Atlantic to 1650."

118 F. Montcher, "Archives and Empires: Scholarly Archival Practices, Royal Historiographers and Historical Writing across the Iberian Empire (Late 16th and Early 17th century)," *History of Historiography/Storia della Storiografia* 68–72 (2015), 21–35. For a comparison with other imperial powers, see E. Bury and F. Montcher, "Savoirs et Pouvoirs à l'âge de l'humanisme tardif," *Dix-septième siècle* 266(1) (2015), 5–16.

the indigenous past and its manifestations in contemporary life in the empire proved to be essential also to the defense of something else: an American identity, known as *patriotismo criollo*. By adopting the indigenous past as their own, the *criollos* – but also, in some cases, the European subjects of the Spanish and Portuguese monarchies – were reacting to French or British characterizations of the New World as decadent in a context of increasing imperial rivalries.[119] During the colonial period, the indigenous past was important also because the king's justice was not only supposed to be the expression of natural and divine law, but that it was also expected to be grounded in the general consent of his vassals, including the indigenous ones.[120]

On several occasions, King Philip II of Spain expressed his desire that the new rules imposed on the indigenous peoples would be perceived as "fairer" than the ones they had in precolonial times. In written exchanges with his counsellors in the 1580s, the Spanish monarch manifested his interest in being informed about precolonial rules, languages, territories, and warfare not only in order to select the "customs" that would be either conserved or erased within the colonial order, but also because he was concerned about his own image as a "king of justice."[121] The fairness of the law was defined in comparative terms (with respect to a precolonial past reconstructed from an imperial present), and this process played a key role in consolidating colonial authority over indigenous peoples.

But the Iberian Crowns also sought a balance between political obedience and labor obligations owed by their indigenous subjects, on the one hand, and a sense of justice and reciprocity, on the other. In this sense, knowledge of indigenous legal culture proved to be useful for finding a degree of compromise with the indigenous elite, for whom a series of privileges were preserved (provided they could prove that their preeminence in society predated Hispanic

119 J. Cañizares-Esguerra, *How to Write the History of the New World. Histories, Epistemologies, and Identities in the Eighteenth-Century Atlantic World* (Stanford: Stanford University Press, 2001); S. Sebastiani, "Las escrituras de la historia del Nuevo Mundo: Clavijero y Robertson en el contexto de la Ilustración europea," *Historia y Grafía*, 37 (2011), 203–36; D. A. Brading, *The First America. The Spanish Monarchy, Creole Patriots, and the Liberal State, 1492–1867* (Cambridge: Cambridge University Press, 1991); A. More, *Baroque Sovereignty. Carlos de Sigüenza y Góngora and the Creole Archive of Colonial Mexico* (Philadelphia: University of Pennsylvania Press, 2013); M. Almagro Gorbea and J. Maier Allende (eds.), *De Pompeya al Nuevo Mundo. La Corona española y la arqueología en el siglo XVIII* (Madrid: Real Academia de Historia, 2012).

120 P. Ragon and A. Exbalin (eds.), *Roi de justice aux Indes espagnoles* (Nanterre: Presses Universitaires de Paris Nanterre, 2020); B. Owensby, "Pacto entre rey lejano y súbditos indígenas. Justicia, legalidad y política en Nueva España, siglo XVII," *Historia Mexicana* 61(1) (2011), 59–106.

121 C. Cunill, "Philip II and Indigenous Access to Royal Justice: Considering the Process of Decision-Making in the Spanish Empire," *Colonial Latin American Review* 24(4) (2015), 505–24.

times), and with the commoners, whose tributary obligations were decreed by law (after inquiries were made to determine the modalities and amount of the tribute they had had to deliver in pre-Hispanic times). Therefore, although indigenous law tended to be either depreciated or marginalized in Portuguese and Spanish official histories, generating knowledge of precolonial normative orders was critical for the purpose of imperial governance. The missionaries, as well as a wide range of civil agents, were required to undertake historical research and what today we would call ethnographic studies on diverse indigenous groups in order to implement efficient policies at the local level.

Knowing according to which rules goods and riches were accumulated and exchanged, how warfare was conducted, on which grounds alliances were forged, how political authority was constructed, exercised and manifested itself, and what the belief systems were, was indeed instrumental in developing efficient strategies in the conquest, governance and evangelization of the New World.[122] In the 1570s, indigenous law was still at the core of the questionnaires that the Council of the Indies sent to Americas, and the Spanish

122 Recent studies have indeed highlighted that indigenous expertise was crucial in the hybridization of warfare techniques and political alliances, the implementation of mail systems, the drafting of religious and linguistic policies, the cultivation of plants, the silver extraction, the organization of labor, and the repartition of tributary obligations. L. Matthew and M. Oudijk (eds.), *Indian Conquistadors: Indigenous Allies in the Conquest of Mesoamerica* (Norman: University of Oklahoma Press, 2007); A. Covey, *Inca Apocalypse: The Spanish Conquest and the Transformation of the Andean World* (Oxford: Oxford University Press, 2020); F. Asselbergs, *Conquered Conquistadors: The Lienzo de Quauhquechollan: A Nahua Vision of the Conquest of Guatemala* (Boulder: University Press of Colorado, 2008); J. P. Galvão Ramalho et al., "Os grupos nativos e a morfologia da conquista na América Portuguesa," *Nuevo Mundo Mundos Nuevos*, Jun. 25, 2020, https://journals.openedition.org/nuevomundo/80168 (last accessed Feb. 1, 2023); B. R. Ferguson, and N. L. Whitehead (eds.), *War in the Tribal Zone: Expanding States and Indigenous Warfare* (Santa Fe and New Mexico: School of American Research Press, 1999); N. González Martínez, "Communicating an Empire and Its Many Worlds: Spanish American Mail, Logistics and Postal Agents, 1492–1600," *Hispanic American Historical Review* 101(4) (2021), 567–96; J. O'Malley et al. (eds.), *The Jesuits. Culture, Science, and the Arts (1540–1773)* (Toronto: University of Toronto Press, 1999); A. Bigelow, "Incorporating Indigenous Knowledge into Extractive Economies: The Science of Colonial Silver," *The Extractive Industries and Society* 3(1) (2016), 117–23; K. Lane, *Potosi. The Silver City That Changed the World* (Berkeley: University of California Press, 2021); R. Gil Montero and P. Zaglasky, "Colonial Organization of Mine Labor in Charcas (Present-Day Bolivia) and Its Consequences (Sixteenth to the Seventeenth Centuries)," *International Review of Social History* 61 (2016), 71–92; J. Lee, "The Aztec Triple Alliance: A Colonial Transformation of the Pre-Hispanic Political and Tributary System," in Lee and Brokaw, *Texcoco*, 63–91; S. Declercq, "'Siempre peleaban sin razón'. La Guerra Florida como construcción social indígena," *Estudios de Cultura Náhuatl* 59 (2020), 97–130; M. Pastrana Flores, *Historias de la Conquista. Aspectos de la historiografía de tradición náhuatl* (Mexico City: UNAM-Instituto de Investigaciones Históricas, 2004) and "La entrega del poder de Motecuhzoma. Una propuesta crítica," *Estudios de Historia Novohispana* 62 (2020), 111–44; D. E. Chipman, *Moctezuma's Children. Aztec Royalty under Spanish Rule, 1520–1700* (Austin: University of Texas Press, 2005).

king's literate indigenous vassals were encouraged to participate in the drafting of some of the answers, a process that would give birth to the reports known as the *relaciones geográficas*.[123]

The question of whether and how this bulk of local knowledge was incorporated into the Iberian monarchies' legal production in relation to their overseas territories is still under debate today.[124] The historian José Luis Egío considers that judge Alonso de Zorita's accounts on the Aztec tributary system tells us not only about "the extensive translation of European or Castilian normativities into the viceroyalty of New Spain," but also "about the complex ways in which the highly developed Nahua juridical and institutional culture influenced the legal evolution in the Mexican high plateau."[125] There is little doubt that the "translation" of indigenous law into colonial textual experience participated in the "localization" of the early modern European law in America. At the same time that data on indigenous law was accumulated, it was also reframed into a new legal language and order in a wide range of texts, including lawsuits.

Colonial courts of justice played an important role in the process of legal knowledge production in the Iberian empires. Recent studies have stressed the need to understand how indigenous peoples interacted with both civil and ecclesiastic courts of justice during the colonial period. They showed that a wide range of indigenous actors engaged with colonial courts as litigants, plaintiffs or witnesses, and that the mechanisms through which imperial justice was administered cannot be fully understood without taking their agency into account. Of particular importance in this context was the way in which

123 F. de Solano (ed.), *Cuestionarios para la formación de las relaciones geográficas de Indias, siglos XVI-XIX* (Madrid: Consejo Superior de Investigaciones Científicas, 1988).

124 A. Brendecke, *Imperio e información. Funciones del saber en el dominio colonial español* (Madrid and Berlin: Iberoamericana, Vervuert, 2012); A. Agüero, "Local Law and the Localization of Law: Hispanic Legal Tradition and Colonial Culture (16th-18th centuries)," in M. Meccarelli and M. J. Solla Sastre (eds.), *Spatial and Temporal Dimensions for Legal History. Research Experiences and Itineraries* (Frankfurt: Max-Planck-Institut für europäische Rechtsgeschichte, 2016), 101–29; A. Masters, "A Thousand Invisible Architects: Vassals, the Petition and Response System, and the Creation of Spanish Imperial Caste Legislation," *Hispanic American Historical Review* 98(3) (2018), 377–406; F. Ruan, "Prudent Deferment: Cosmographer-Chronicler Juan López de Velasco and the Historiography of the Indies," *The Americas* 74(1) (2017), 27–55.

125 J. L. Egío, "From Castilian to Nahuatl to Castilian? Reflections and Doubts about Legal Translation in the Writing of Judge Alonso de Zorita (1512–1585)," *Rechtsgeschichte – Legal History* 24 (2016), 122–53, at 123. On the concept of legal translation, see T. Duve, "European Legal History – Concepts, Methods, Challenges," in T. Duve (ed.), *Entanglements*, 29–66; L. Foljanty, "Legal Transfers as Processes of Cultural Translation: On the Consequences of a Metaphor," *Max Planck Institute for European Legal History Research Paper Series No. 2015–09* (Frankfurt am Main: Max-Planck-Institut für europäische Rechtsgeschichte, 2015).

indigenous peoples mobilized their legal cultures and their past in order to defend their interests at court and how those interpretations and reformulations of their law gave rise to the emergence of an ever-shifting and contested legal order in the Iberian empires.[126] In this context, one must bear in mind that the judicial strategies in which indigenous legal concepts were used were designed to defend their authors' views, interests or sense of belonging.

It is therefore not surprising that, from the sixteenth to the eighteenth century, some narratives on precolonial law aimed to convey criticisms against the colonial authority and that their authors claimed a wider access to political life. The "eighty-day limitation on the duration of the cases" invoked by Pomar might well have been a way of criticizing the length of the legal procedures in the vice-regal courts of justice, which – in cases that involved indigenous people – were supposed to follow a summary procedure.[127] In Peru, colonial authorities thought that the use of the precolonial indigenous

126 See D. Gonzales Escudero, "*Capacocha*, praxis y saber: Los saberes normativos en un ritual inca en el valle del río Chillón prehispánico (ca. 1500–1520s)," draft paper. I am grateful to the author for giving me the opportunity to read his work. S. Kellogg, *Law and Transformation of Aztec Culture, 1500–1700* (Norman: University of Oklahoma Press, 1995); J. E. Traslosheros, "El tribunal eclesiástico y los indios en el arzobispado de México, hasta 1640," *Historia Mexicana* 51(3) (2002), 485–516; B. Owensby, *Empire of Law and Indian Justice in Colonial Mexico* (Stanford: Stanford University Press, 2008); Ruiz Medrano, *Mexico's Indigenous Communities*; J. Traslosheros and A. de Zaballa Beascoechea (eds.), *Los indios ante los foros de justicia religiosa en la Hispanoamérica virreinal* (Mexico City: Universidad Nacional Autónoma de México, 2010); R. Honores, "Una aproximación a la hiperlexia colonial: caciques, cultural legal y litigación en los Andes (1550–1640)," *Nueva Crónica* 1 (2013), 1–8; B. Premo, *The Enlightenment on Trial. Ordinary Litigants and Colonialism in the Spanish Empire* (Oxford: Oxford University Press, 2017); Y. Yannakakis, M. Schrader-Kniffi, and L. A. Arrioja Díaz Viruell (eds.), *Los indios ante la justicia local. Intérpretes, oficiales y litigantes en Nueva España y Guatemala (siglos XVI-XVIII)* (Zamora: El Colegio de Michoacán, 2019); H. Cuevas Arenas (ed.), *Conflictos indígenas ante la justicia colonial: los hilos entrelazados de una compleja trama social y legal, siglos XVI-XVIII* (Cali: Universidad de Santiago de Cali, 2021); J. Gamboa, *El cacicazgo muisca en los años posteriores a la conquista: del* psihipkua *al cacique colonial, 1537–1575* (Bogotá: Instituto Colombiano de Antropología e *Historia*, 2013); S. Muñoz Arbeláez, *Costumbres en disputa. Los muiscas y el Imperio español en Ubaque, siglo XVI* (Bogotá: Universidad de los Andes, 2015).

127 W. Connell, "'De sangre noble y hábiles costumbres': etnicidad indígena y gobierno en México Tenochtitlan," *Histórica* 40(2) (2016), 111–33; H. Costilla Martínez, "La reinvención de Nezahualcóyotl desde el discurso jurídico en *Historia de la nación chichimeca* de Fernando de Alva Ixtlilxóchitl," *eHumanista* 33 (2016), 425–38; J. R. Romero Galván (ed.), *Historiografía novohispana de tradición indígena* (Mexico City: Universidad Nacional Autónoma de México, Instituto de Investigaciones Históricas, 2003), 313–51. Similar "idealizations" of precolonial law were used to denounce colonial dysfunctions in Gaspar Antonio Chi's *relación* about the "customs" of the Maya, in Guaman Poma de Ayala's *Coronica de buen gobierno*, as well as in Inca Garcilaso's *Comentarios reales de los Incas;* Strecker and Artiega, "La Relación," 89–107; R. Adorno, *Guaman Poma: Writing and Resistance in Colonial Peru* (Albuquerque: University of Texas Press, 2000); R. Adorno, "Court and Chronicle: A Native Andean's Engagement with Spanish Colonial Law," in S. Belmessous (ed.), *Native Claims: Indigenous Law Against*

past for political purposes had constituted one of the factors that led to the uprising in the 1780s known as the "Inca National movement."[128] After this rebellion, copies of Inca Garcilaso's *Royal Commentaries*, which contained information on precolonial law and were widely circulated in the eighteenth century, were confiscated.[129]

Sometimes, the narratives on precolonial law sought to consolidate the prestige of one indigenous city above another or to legitimize a particular indigenous family in the search for political power.[130] According to Offner, "law occupied a special position in Texcocan history: emphasis on its antiquity and continuity served to legitimize Texcoco's claim to a superordinate position in valley politics as well as to enhance the majesty of the law of Texcoco under later rulers."[131] It is also worth noting that, similarly to the lawsuits in which diverse actors were involved, much of the material gathered on indigenous law by royal demand was multiple in authorship, formats, degree of accuracy, and sources selected.[132] Europeans were not the only ones to participate in these epistemological and political challenges. Several *mestizos* and indigenous intellectuals produced their own interpretations of indigenous legal orders. These actors' capacity to travel to and meet in specific places, such as the house of the

Empire, 1500–1920 (Oxford: Oxford University Press, 2012), 63–85; M. Zamora, *Language, Authority, and Indigenous History in the Comentarios Reales de los Incas* (Cambridge: Cambridge University Press, 1988); G. Lamana, "Signifyin(g), Double Consciousness, and Coloniality: The *Royal Commentaries* as Theory of Practice and Political Project," in Castro-Klarén and Fernández, *Inca Garcilaso*, 297–315; J. Godenzzi and C. Garatea (eds.), *Literaturas orales y primeros textos coloniales* (Lima: Pontificia Universidad Católica del Perú, Casa de la Literatura, 2017).

128 A. Flores Galindo, *In Search of an Inca: Identity and Utopia in the Andes* (Cambridge: Cambridge University Press, 2010); F. Macchi, *Incas ilustrados. Reconstrucciones imperiales en la segunda mitad del siglo XVIII* (Berlin and Madrid: Vervuert, Iberoamericana, 2009); C. Walker, *Smoldering Ashes: Cuzco and the Creation of Republican Peru, 1780–1840* (Durham and London: Duke University Press, 1999).

129 P. Guibovich Pérez, "The Dissemination and Reading of the *Royal Commentaries* in the Peruvian Viceroyalty," in Castro-Klarén and Fernández, *Inca Garcilaso*, 129–53; S. Thomson, *We Alone Will Rule: Native Andean Politics in the Age of Insurgency* (Madison: University of Wisconsin Press, 2002).

130 A. Díaz Serrano, "La República de Tlaxcala ante el Rey de España durante el siglo XVI," *Historia Mexicana* LXI(3) (2012), 1049–107; J. Baber, "Empire, Indians and the Negotiation of the Status of City in Tlaxcala, 1521–1550," in Kellogg and Ruiz Medrano, *Negotiation within Domination*, 19–44.

131 Offner, *Law and Politics*, 47.

132 F. Montcher, "Écriture polyphonique de l'histoire. Archives et communication politique dans la monarchie hispanique (c. 1580–1640)," in M. Pia Donato and A. Saada (eds.), *Pratiques d'archives à l'époque moderne. Europe, mondes coloniaux* (Paris: Classiques Garnier, 2019), 323–49; N. L. Whitehead, *Histories and Historicities in Amazonia* (Lincoln: Unversity of Nebraska Press, 2003); and "Historical Writing about Brazil, 1500–1800," in J. Rabasa, M. Sato, E. Tortarolo, and D. Woolf (eds.), *The Oxford History of Historical Writing* (Oxford: Oxford University Press, 2012), vol. III, 641–61.

indigenous town council in Lima, or the Royal court in Madrid, contributed to the configuration of interethnic and transatlantic networks through which information circulated and pressure was put on the Crown.[133]

Consequently, the frontiers between distinct types of documents were often blurred, since some ideas that appeared in treaties could also be used in the trials filed before colonial courts of justice.[134] There is little doubt that indigenous peoples and their allies often succeeded to obtain royal decrees that met their demands, thus showing that they played a role in forging the law in the Iberian empires, even beyond the local sphere.[135] The academic literature focused on these topics largely contributes to complexifying the overall discussions on the polycentric nature of the Iberian empires, the challenges of governing distant territories and diverse populations, and the idea of legal orders being constantly negotiated by a wide range of actors, including the indigenous ones.[136]

The historian Fransico Quijano Velasco has shown, for example, how the Mendicant friar Alonso de la Veracruz used the concept of natural law to

133 A. Dueñas, *Indians and Mestizos in the 'Lettered City': Reshaping Justice, Social Hierarchy, and Political Culture in Colonial Peru* (Boulder: University Press of Colorado, 2010); J. C. de la Puente Luna, *Andean Cosmopolitans: Seeking Justice and Reward at the Spanish Royal Court* (Austin: University of Texas Press, 2018); C. Cunill and F. Quijano, "Los procuradores de las Indias en el Imperio hispánico: reflexiones en torno a procesos de mediación, negociación y representación," *Nuevo Mundo Mundos Nuevos*, https://journals.openedition.org/nuevomundo/79934?lang=pt (last accessed Feb. 1, 2023).

134 L. M. Glave Testino, "La gran vejación: manuscritos reivindicativos de Incas, caciques y defensores de la población indígena," *Revista Andes. Revista de la facultad de derecho y ciencias sociales* 4 (2020), 35–60; F. Ruan, "Language, Genealogy, and Archive: Fashioning the Indigenous Mother in the *Comentarios reales* and in Sixteenth-Century Mestizo Petitions," *Revista Canadiense de Estudios Hispánicos* 41(1) (2016), 35–64; Brian, *Alva Ixtlilxochitl's Native Archive*; J. Charles, "Felipe Guaman Poma de Ayala en los foros de justicia eclesiástica," in A. de Zaballa Beascoechea (ed.), *Los indios, el Derecho canónico y la justicia eclesiástica en la América virreinal* (Madrid and Berlin: Iberoamericana, Vervuert, 2011), 203–22.

135 S. Albiez-Wieck, "Indigenous Migrants Negotiating Belonging: Peticiones de cambio de fuero in Cajamarca, Peru, 17th–18th centuries," *Colonial Latin American Review* 26(4) (2017), 483–508; C. Cunill, "La negociación indígena en el Imperio ibérico: aportes a su discusión metodológica," *Colonial Latin American Review* 21(3) (2012), 391–412; Y. Yannakakis, "Indigenous People and Legal Culture in Spanish America," *History Compass* 11(11) (2013), 931–47 and "Beyond Jurisdiction: Native Agency in the Making of Colonial Legal Cultures. A Review Essay," *Comparative Studies in Society and History* 57(4) (2015), 1070–82.

136 P. Cardim, T. Herzog et al. (eds.), *Polycentric Monarchies. How Did Early Modern Spain and Portugal Achieve and Maintain a Global Hegemony?* (Brighton: Sussex Academic Press, 2012); G. Gaudin and R. Stumpf (eds.), *Las distancias en el gobierno de los imperios ibéricos. Concepciones, experiencias y vínculos* (Madrid: Casa de Velázquez, 2022); J. Fragoso and N. G. Monteiro (eds.), *Um reino e suas repúblicas no Atlântico. Comunicações políticas entre Portugal, Brasil e Angola nos séculos XVII e XVIII* (Rio de Janeiro: Civilização Brasileira, 2017).

describe the indigenous legal order to defend the indigenous people's "dominion" over their lands, as well as their political legitimacy at the local level. This – among other arguments and motives – led to the institutionalization of the indigenous town councils and the recognition of their jurisdiction.[137] Because during the Renaissance language was associated with the political ability of the people who spoke it and with the laws according to which they ruled themselves, debates on local languages' *policía* became central in the defense of indigenous governance under imperial rule. To put it in other terms, the *policía* of a language had much to do with the *policía* of the people who used it. According to Sabine MacCormack, "among Nebrija's concerns was to show that the Castilian vernacular of which he composed the very first grammatical analysis was as orderly and systematic as Latin."[138] In America, several friars applied the same argument to the local languages that they put into *artes* (grammars). In the dedication of his work to King Philip II, Friar Domingo de Santo Tomás insisted on the "exceptional order and *policía*" of Quechua and claimed that "such being the language, the people who use it should be counted not as barbarous but as possessing *policía*."[139]

Linguistic ideologies, convenient reconstructions of precolonial indigenous past, European traditions of legal pluralism, and the Iberian Crowns' political interests therefore played a crucial role in many respects: the creation of the indigenous town councils (with jurisdiction over their people at the local level), the recognition of indigenous "customs" (as long as they did not contradict Christian principles) (see Section 3.1), and the use of local languages not only in matters of evangelization (by training priests to become bilingual), but also in court, thanks to the mediation of official interpreters. Like their Spanish counterparts, the indigenous town councils conducted legal inquiries and administered justice in their own languages at the local level. If the case matter was serious, they were obliged to advise the higher authorities thereof

137 F. Quijano Velasco, "Alonso de la Veracruz: Natural Law, Dominion and Political Legitimacy in Native American Governance," in J. Paul (ed.), *Governing Diversity: Democracy, Diversity and Human Nature* (London: Cambridge Scholars Publishing, 2012), 89–106 and *Las repúblicas de la Monarquía. Pensamiento constitucionalista y republicano en Nueva España 1550–1610* (Mexico City: Universidad Nacional Autónoma de México, 2017).

138 S. MacCormack, "The Discourse of My Life: What Language Can Do (Early Colonial Views on Quechua)," in Durston and Mannheim, *Indigenous Languages*, 25–58, at 29. See also K. A. Woolard, "Bernardo de Aldrete and the Morisco Problem: A Study in Early Modern Spanish Language Ideology," *Comparative Studies in Society and History* 4 (2002), 446–80.

139 D. de Santo Tomas, *Grammatica o arte de la lengua general de los indios de los reynos del Peru* (Lima: Universidad Nacional de San Marcos, 1951), fol. Av, r-v, quoted by MacCormack, "The discourse," at 30.

and to send them the documentation they had produced. Key sources for investigating the issue of indigenous jurisdiction in the Iberian empires are the royal instructions that were given to indigenous town councils, the rules (*actas*) which these town councils wrote to organize their internal political life, and the local inquiries that were led by indigenous authorities and were inserted (after being translated into Castilian) as evidence in lawsuits.[140]

Although only a few documents of this kind have survived to date, which makes it difficult to understand according to which rules this jurisdiction was exercised, researchers have shown that the members of the Mendicant orders played a crucial role in forging and translating the first royal instructions given to the indigenous town councils into local languages. Moreover, we know that these councils did not hesitate to take advantage of the jurisdictional conflicts that arose between the ecclesiastic and civil authorities, in order to forge opportunistic alliances that enabled them to defend their own interests and jurisdiction.[141] As Herzog correctly points out, however, "[T]he existence of a plurality of jurisdictions did not produce distinct legal regimes. What existed instead was a universal common law that had to be localized."[142] In this sense, the Iberian experience in the Americas differed from its British counterpart, where a neat frontier was drawn between English colonists and indigenous

140 The records of the indigenous city of Tlaxcala are a perfect illustration of this ongoing indigenous legal production under Spanish rule. E. Solís, A. Valencia, and C. Medina Lima (eds.), *Actas de Cabildo de Tlaxcala, 1547–1567* (Mexico City: Archivo General de la Nación, 1985); J. Lockhart, F. Berdan, and A. Anderson (eds.), *The Tlaxcalan Actas: A Compendium of the Records of the Cabildo of Tlaxcala, 1545–1627* (Salt Lake City: University of Utah Press, 1986). On the Royal instructions given to the indigenous town councils in the Valley of Mexico, see Kellogg and Sell, "We Want to Give" and R. Rovira Morgado, *San Francisco Padremeh. El temprano cabildo indio y las cuatro parcialidades de México-Tenochtitlan, 1549–1599* (Madrid: Consejo Superior de Investigaciones Científicas, 2017).

141 A. Díaz Serrano, "Las poco y las más repúblicas. Los gobiernos indios en la América española," in F. Palomo, Â. Barreto, and R. Stumpf (eds.), *Monarquías Ibéricas en perspectiva comparada (siglos XVI-XVIII)* (Lisbon: Universidade de Lisboa, 2018), 237–69; J. C. Puente Luna and R. Honores, "Guardianes de la real justicia: alcaldes de indios, costumbre y justicia local en Huarochirí colonial," *Histórica* 40(2) (2016), 11–47; A. Dueñas, "Cabildos de naturales en el ocaso colonial: jurisdicción, posesión y defensa del espacio étnico," *Histórica* 40(2) (2016), 135–67; C. Cunill, "'Nos traen tan avasallados hasta quitarnos nuestro señorío': cabildos mayas, control local y representación legal en el Yucatán del siglo XVI," *Histórica* 40(2) (2016), 40–80; J. Munford, "Las llamas de Tapacarí: un documento judicial de un alcalde de indios en la Audiencia de Charcas, 1580," *Histórica* 40(2) (2016), 171–85; M. R. C. de Almeida, *Metamorfoses indígenas. Identidade e cultura nas aldeias coloniais do Rio de Janeiro* (Rio de Janeiro: Arquivo Nacional, 2003); K. B. Graubart, "'Ynuvaciones malas e rreprouadas': Seeking Justice in Early Colonial Pueblos de Indios," in B. Owensby and R. Ross (eds.), *Justice in A New World. Negotiating Legal Intelligibility in British, Iberian, and Indigenous America* (New York: New York University Press, 2018), 151–80.

142 Herzog, Section 3.1.

peoples. The latter were not incorporated into the empire under the category of vassals embedded with their own jurisdiction operating within the imperial system of justice but were instead considered as "sovereign nations." Consequently, diplomacy and treaties, rather than courts, were the instruments through which indigenous peoples and British colonists confronted and negotiated their respective conception of the law.[143]

In the Spanish empire, a comparable situation can only be found in the Chilean frontiers zone, where the relationships with the Mapuche were handled through diplomacy and the mechanism of the so-called *parlamentos*.[144] Differences between the Iberian and British empires were also due to how land tenure was handled. In the Spanish and Portuguese empires, the monarchs held titles over the Americas, but they did recognize the legitimacy of indigenous people's dominion over their land, thus enabling them to have access to property through royal bestowal (mercy) or sale. As a

143 B. Owensby and R. Ross, "Making Law Intelligible in Comparative Context," in Owensby and Ross, *Justice in a New World*, 1–58; C. L. Tomlins, "The Legalities of English Colonizing: Discourses of European Intrusion upon the Americas, c. 1490–1830," in S. Dorsett and I. Hunter (eds.), *Law and Politics in British Colonial Thought: Transposition of Empire* (New York: Palgrave, 2000), 51–70; J. Glover, *Paper Sovereigns: Anglo-Native Treaties and the Law of Nations, 1604–1644* (Philadelphia: University of Pennsylvania Press, 2014). According to most of those treaties, indigenous people had the right to attend colonial trials and, eventually, to be part of "mixed juries" when indigenous individuals were involved in a case. Furthermore, indigenous individuals who lived in English plantations or towns and had no tribal ties were subjected to British law. J. Smolenski, "The Death of Sawantaeny and the Problem of Justice on the Frontier," in W. A. Pencack and D. K. Richter (eds.), *Friends and Enemies in Penn's Woods: Indians, Colonists, and the Racial Construction of Pennsylvania* (University Park: Pennsylvania State University Press, 2004), 104–28; K. Hermes, "'Justice Will Be Done Us': Algonquian Demands for Reciprocity in the Courts of European Settlers," in C. L. Tomlins and B. H. Mann (eds.), *The Many Legalities of Early America* (Chapel Hill and London: University of North Carolina Press, 2001), 123–49. In New France, the recognition of the indigenous nations' sovereignty, the extension of citizenship (the status of *régnicoles* or natural French) to those who accepted Christianity, and the grant of royal "protection" varied depending on time and place. According to Gilles Harvard, "far from being an affirmation of sovereignty, protection was understood as an unequal alliance, a greater power being able to take a secondary power under its wing upon request." G. Harvard, "'Protection' and 'Unequal Alliance': The French Conception of Sovereignty over Indians in New France," in R. Englebert and G. Teasdale (eds.), *French and Indians in the Heart of North America, 1630–1815* (East Lansing: Michigan State University Press, 2013), 113–38, at 117. See also G. Harvard and C. Vidal, *Histoire de l'Amérique française* (Paris: Flammarion, 2003), 170–250.

144 A. Levaggi, *Paz en la frontera. Historia de los tratados con las comunidades indígenas en la Argentina, siglos XVI-XIX* (Buenos Aires: UMSA, 2000) y *Diplomacia hispano-indígena en las fronteras de América. Historia de los tratados entre la Monarquía española y las comunidades aborígenes* (Madrid: Centro de Estudios Políticos y Constitucionales, 2002); J. M. Zavala Cepeda, J. M. Díaz Blanco, and G. Payàs, "Los parlamentos hispano-mapuches bajo el reinado de Felipe III: la labor del padre Luis de Valdivia (1605–1617)," *Estudios Ibero-Americanos* 40(1) (2014), 23–44.

result, discussions on precolonial law regarding land tenure were relevant for both the preservation and the incorporation of indigenous relations to land within the new legal order. These discussions were also invoked in trials over land that confronted indigenous peoples with settlers and, in the Valley of Mexico, visual evidence was produced to support the indigenous litigants' arguments.[145] By contrast, the British Crown considered that empty land was *terra nullius*, which any sovereign able to settle would be entitled to govern.[146]

Closely intertwined with indigenous jurisdiction was the recognition of the legal valence of indigenous peoples' customs. In a 1555 royal decree, the category of "laws and customs" included not only the norms that indigenous peoples had applied in the past and that were still in use within indigenous communities but also the ones that had been produced after Spaniards arrived. The Spanish king decreed that he would

> approve and consider as good your good laws and good customs that you had in the past and that you currently have for your good governance and civility (*policía*), as well as the ones you have newly made and ordered altogether, provided that we can add what we want and what seems to us convenient for God our lord's service and ours and for your conservation and Christian civility (*policía*), as long as they do not prejudice neither

145 On land tenure in the Iberian empires, see T. Herzog, *Frontiers of Possession. Spain and Portugal in Europe and the Americas* (Cambridge: Harvard University Press, 2015) and "Colonial Law and 'Native Customs': Indigenous Land Rights in Colonial Spanish America," *The Americas* 69(3) (2013), 303–21; Pulido Rull, *Mapping Indigenous Land*; Ruiz Medrano, *Mexico's Indigenous Communities*; M. Bastias Saavedra, "The Normativity of Possession. Rethinking Land Relations in Early-Modern Spanish America, ca. 1500–1800," *Colonial Latin American Review* 29(2) (2020), 223–38; J. Holston, "The Misrule of Law: Land and Usurpation in Brazil," *Comparative Studies in Society and History* 33 (1991), 695–725; J. Cañizares-Esguerra, "The 'Iberian' Justifications of Territorial Possession by Pilgrims and Puritans in the Colonization of America," in J. Cañizares-Esguerra, *Entangled Empires. The Anglo-Iberian Atlantic, 1500–1830* (Philadelphia: University Press of Pennsylvania), 161–77; J. Baber, "Law, Land, and Legal Rhetoric in Colonial New Spain: A Look at the Changing Rhetoric of Indigenous Americans in the Sixteenth Century," in Belmessous, *Native Claims*, 41–63; M. E. Matsumoto, *Land, Politics, and Memory in Five Nija'ib' k'iche' titulus. 'The Title and Proof of Our Ancestors'* (Boulder: University Press of Colorado, 2017).

146 C. L. Tomlins, "The Legal Cartography of Colonization, the Legal Polyphony of Settlement: English Intrusions on the American Mainland in the Seventeenth Century," *Law and Social Inquiry* 26(2) (2006), 315–72. Tomlins considers that those differences between Iberian and English colonialism not only stem from a distinct legal thought but also in the socioeconomic model that the British Crown and its settlers sought to implement in the Americas. According to him, "the English colonial project was one more of accumulation through clearance and settlement than through extraction, a transference of population rather than the seizure of one." C. L. Tomlins, "Introduction: The Many Legalities of Colonization: A Manifesto of Destiny for Early American Legal History," in Tomlins, *The Many Legalities*, 1–24, at 12.

what you have done nor the good customs and statutes when they are fair and good.[147]

This text demonstrates how the treatment of indigenous "customs" was paradigmatic of imperial ambiguities toward indigenous normative orders. The king's invocation of "your good laws and good customs" referred to the town councils' ability to draft their own norms at the local level. However, their content could be modified at any moment to serve God and king, that is to say, according to imperial political rhetoric, to Christianization, and to the conversion of the indigenous people. Furthermore, in court, the recognition of "customs" depended on how successfully the lawyers argued and, above all, on the judges' decisions, which could be based on a series of imprecise criteria such as the customs' antiquity, their current social value, and the conflicts in which they were invoked.[148] The invocation of these customs in court could therefore give rise to unpredictable jurisprudence. In some cases, the settlers' lawyers appealed to this concept to defend their own practices, such as the use of indigenous porters called *tamemes* for transporting the tributes, which indigenous peoples sought to abolish.[149]

Local Languages as an Arena for Ever-Shifting and Contested Normative Orders

Language also played a key role in enforcing or contesting legal orders in the Iberian empires. In this context, it is important to note that the use of local

147 D. de Encinas, *Cedulario Indiano*, Book IV, f. 355–56, decree approving the good customs that the "indios" had in the past and have for their good governance and civility, Valladolid, 1555 (Cédula en que se aprueba a los indios las buenas costumbres que antiguamente han tenido y tienen para su buen regimiento y policía): "aprobamos y tenemos por buenas vuestras buenas leyes y buenas costumbres que antiguamente entre vosotros habéis tenido y tenéis para vuestro buen regimiento y policía y las que habéis hecho y ordenando de nuevo todos vosotros juntos con tanto que nos podamos añadir lo que fuéremos servido y nos pareciere que conviene al servicio de Dios nuestro señor y nuestro y a vuestra conservación y policía cristiana no perjudicando a lo que vosotros tenéis hecho ni a las buenas costumbres y estatutos vuestros que fueren justos y buenos."

148 Y. Yannakakis, *Since Time Immemorial: Native Custom and Law in Colonial Mexico* (Durham: Duke University Press, 2023). T. Herzog, "Immemorial (and Native) Customs in Early Modernity: Europe and the Americas," *Comparative Legal History* (2021), 1–53; B. Premo, "Custom Today: Temporary, Customary Law, and Indigenous Enlightenment," *Hispanic American Historical Review*, 94(3) (2014), 355–79; Y. Yannakakis, "Costumbre: A Language of Negotiation in Eighteenth-Century Oaxaca," in Kellogg and Ruiz Medrano, *Negotiation within Domination*, 137–73; T. Okoshi Harada, "Tenencia de la tierra y territorialidad: conceptualización de los mayas yucatecos en vísperas de la invasión española," in L. Ochoa (ed.), *Conquista, transculturación y mestizaje: raíz y origen de México* (Mexico City: Universidad Nacional Autónoma de México, 1995), 67–94.

149 Cunill and Rovira, "Lo que nos dejaron," 290.

languages was tolerated in court. Lawyers and interpreters who were tasked with representing indigenous people or translating their statements before the judges were essential to these dynamics. Discussions around unequal access to royal justice for indigenous persons in comparison with Spaniards and the subsequent decision to consider them as *personae miserabiles* were decisive for the appointment of *defensores de indios*, lawyers specialized in representing the indigenous people in the colonial courts of justice.[150] As for the interpreters, as bilingualism was not a general practice – neither among the judges nor among the indigenous people – their presence in court was required. In the Spanish empire, abuses committed by some interpreters – and the dramatic consequences for the indigenous peoples – led to the institutionalization of this position. As early as 1540, official interpreters were appointed for the court of Mexico. They had to follow a series of rules and were regularly inspected by higher officials. Eventually, the same norms would be used in other jurisdictions as the Spanish Crown expanded its control over other territories.[151]

Although in Brazil interpreters did not receive official recognition until the nineteenth century, recent scholarship has highlighted the key role that the so-called *linguas* played during the entire colonial period.[152] Along the imperial frontiers, translating and interpreting played a different role. This

150 W. Borah, *Justice by Insurance: The General Indian Court of Colonial Mexico and the Legal Aides of the Half-Real* (Berkeley: University of California Press, 1983); C. Cunill, *Los defensores de indios de Yucatán y el acceso de los mayas a la justicia colonial, 1540–1600* (Mérida: Universidad Nacional Autónoma de México, Centro Peninsular en Humanidades y Ciencias Sociales, 2012); M. Novoa, *The Protector of Indians in the Royal Audience of Lima: History, Careers and Legal Culture, 1575–775* (Leiden: Brill, 2016). For a historiographical overview on this topic, see C. Cunill, "La protectoría de indios en América: avances y perspectivas entre historia e historiografía," *Colonial Latin American Review* 28(4) (2019), 478–95. It is worth noting that, after being abolished, this institution resurfaced in some Latin American nations in the nineteenth century. See J. Pavez Ojeda, G. Payàs, and F. Ulloa Valenzuela, "Los intérpretes mapuches y el Protectorado de Indígenas (1880–1930): constitución jurídica de la propiedad, traducción y castellanización del Ngulumapu," *Boletín de Filología* 55(1) (2020), 161–98.

151 On the interpreters of local languages, see Cunill and Glave Testino, *Las lenguas indígenas en los tribunals*; Y. Yannakakis, "Making Law Intelligible: Networks of Translation in Mid-Colonial Oaxaca," in G. Ramos and Y. Yannakakis (eds.), *Indigenous Intellectuals. Knowledge, Power and Colonial Culture in Mexico and the Andes* (London and Durham: Duke University Press, 2014), 79–106; C. Cunill, "Un mosaico de lenguas: los intérpretes de la Audiencia de México en el siglo XVI," *Historia Mexicana* 269 (2018), 7–48; J. C. de la Puente Luna, "The Many Tongues of the King: Indigenous Language Interpreters and the Making of the Spanish Empire," *Colonial Latin American Review* 23(2) (2014), 143–70; C. Jurado, "Dar a entender. Prácticas de interpretación y saberes jurídicos en las revisitas. El corregimiento de Chayanta (Charcas, Virreinato del Perú) en el siglo XVII," in Cunill and Glave Testino, *Las lenguas indígenas*, 165–79; J. Gamboa, "El primer 'lengua indígena' de los naturales de la real audiencia de Santa Fe: el mestizo Lucas Bejarano, mediador y protagonista en los tribunales reales (s. XVI)," in Cunill and Glave Testino, *Lenguas indígenas*, 97–120.

152 B. Mariani, "Quando as línguas eram corpos: sobre a colonisação linguística portuguesa na África e no Brasil," in E. P. Orlandi, *Política linguística no Brasil* (Campinas: Pontes

is exemplified by the case of the Mapuche, who fulfilled a function similar to that of the intermediaries along the Spanish-Arab frontier in the context of the late medieval *Reconquista*.[153] Both interpreters and lawyers were situated at the intersection between the indigenous peoples and the judges. They not only articulated diverse regimes of justice but also brought to the fore different expectations of what justice meant for the actors engaged with the colonial justice system. The images, concepts, and categories that languages convey were, indeed, instrumental to the translation of normative orders in the Iberian empires (and probably also in pre-Hispanic America).[154]

The linguistic work on local languages undertaken by the members of the Mendicant orders largely contributed to the imposition of new legal concepts on indigenous peoples. The friars introduced loanwords and neologisms, and they re-signified a selection of indigenous words so that they could fit well with Christian concepts. Because – as shown by Thomas Duve in Section 3.2 of this volume – in early modern European legal culture, ecclesiastical and civil law were intertwined, the friars' linguistic accomplishments had an impact not only on indigenous religious beliefs but also on their view on governance, justice, and law. The colonial dictionaries and grammars, as well as the sermons, catechisms, and confessionals were vivid manifestations of the conceptual translation work performed by these friars on the indigenous languages.[155] The friars, helped by indigenous specialists, were also in charge

Editora, 2007); D. Silva-Reis and J. Milton, "The History of Translation in Brazil through the Centuries: In Search of a Tradition," in Y. Gambier and U. Stecconi (eds.), *A World Atlas of Translation* (Amsterdam and Philadelphia: John Benjamins Publishing Company, 2019), 395–417; A. C. Metcalf, *Go-betweens and the Colonization of Brazil, 1500–1600* (Austin: University of Texas Press, 2008); A. Rodrigues, "As outras línguas de colonização do Brasil," in S. Cardoso, J. Mota, R. V. Matos Silva (eds.), *Quinhentos anos de história linguística do Brasil* (Salvador: Funcultura, 2006); M. C. Barros, "The Office of Lingua: A Portrait of the Religious Tupi Interpreter in Brazil in the Sixteenth Century," *Itinerario – European Journal of Overseas History* 25(2) (2001), 110–40.

153 G. Payàs and I. Alonso Araguás, "La mediación lingüística institucionalizada en las fronteras hispano-mapuche e hispano-árabe: ¿un patrón similar?," *Historia* 42(1) (2009), 185–201; M. A. Samaniego López and G. Payàs, "Traducción y hegemonía: Los parlamentos hispano-mapuches de la Frontera araucana," *Atenea: revista de ciencias, artes y letras* 516 (2017), 33–48; G. Payàs and J. Manuel Zavala (eds.), *La mediación lingüístico-cultural en tiempos de guerra: cruce de miradas desde España y América* (Temuco: Ediciones la Universidad Católica de Temuco, 2012).

154 For an interesting comparison with how Persia acquired the "status of a language of Islamic law" in premodern India, see N. Kanalu, "Prefatory Notes on Persian Idioms of Islamic Jurisprudence: Reasoning and Procedures of Law-Making in Premodern Islamicate India," *Manuscript Studies* 4(1) (2019), 93–112.

155 B. Melià, *El guaraní conquistado y reducido. Ensayos de etnohistoria* (Asunción: Universidad Católica del Paraguay, 1993); G. Wilde, *Religión y poder en las misiones de guaraníes* (Buenos Aires: SB Editores, 2009); C. Pompa, *Religião como tradução. Missionários, Tupi e "Tapuia" no Brasil colonial* (Bauru: EDUSC, 2003); C. Castelnau-L'Estoile, *Operários de*

of translating the New Laws of 1542 as well as the first royal ordinances for the indigenous town councils into local languages, and they used linguistic strategies to introduce European legal concepts to indigenous languages. Similarly, the struggles between early modern and revolutionary conceptions of the law manifested themselves in indigenous languages during the Spanish–American wars of independence.[156]

Nonetheless, as Capucine Boidin and Angélica Otazù Melarejo put it, drawing offensive parallels "between Amerindian language and Amerindian identity and culture" must be set aside to avoid an essentializing approach to indigenous lexicography.[157] Equally problematic would be the use of categories created by colonial agents, for example, the aforementioned *principales*, to describe indigenous realities, as that would ignore the fact that these categories largely contributed to rendering some members of indigenous councils invisible. Although the use of such terms did not mean that these actors completely disappeared during the colonial period, it deprived them of official recognition and subjected them to indigenous governors' arbitrary decisions regarding

uma vinha estéril. Os jesuítas e a conversão dos índios no Brasil, 1580–1620 (Bauru: EDUSC, 2006); S. MacCormack, *Religión en los Andes. Visiones e imaginación en el Perú colonial* (Lima: Ediciones El Lector, 2016); A. Durston, Pastoral Quechua. *The History of Christian Translation in Colonial Peru, 1550–1650* (Notre Dame: University of Notre Dame Press, 2007); M. Schrader-Kniffki and Y. Yannakakis, "Sin and Crimes: Zapotec-Spanish Translation in Catholic Evangelization and Colonial Law in Oaxaca, New Spain," in O. Zwartjes, K. Zimmermann, and M. Schrader-Kniffki (eds.), *Translation Theories and Practices: Selected Papers from the Seventh International Conference on Missionary Linguistics* (Amsterdam and Philadelphia: John Benjamins Publishing Company, 2014), 161–200; S. Dedenbach-Salazar Sáenz, "Idolatría y sexualidad: Métodos y contextos de la transmisión y traducción de conceptos cristianos en los confesionarios ibéricos y coloniales de los siglos XVI-XVIII," *Indiana* 35(2) (2018), 9–27; W. Hanks, *Converting Words: Maya in the Age of the Cross* (Berkeley: University of California Press, 2010); M. Christensen, *Translated Christianities: Nahuatl and Maya Religious Texts* (Philadelphia: Pennsylvania State University Press, 2014); L. Burkhart, *The Slippery Earth: Nahua-Christian Moral Dialogue in Sixteenth-Century Mexico* (Tucson: The University of Arizona Press, 1989); B. Alcántara Rojas, "Evangelización y traducción. La vida de san Francisco de San Buenaventura vuelta al náhuatl por fray Alonso de Molina," *Estudios de Cultura Náhuatl* 46 (2013), 89–158 and "Los textos cristianos en lengua náhuatl del periodo novohispano: fuentes para la historia cultural," *Dimensión Antropológica* 74 (2018), 64–94.

156 C. Boidin, C. Itier, and J. Chassin, "Presentación del suplemento especial sobre la propaganda política en lenguas indígenas en las Guerras de Independencias sudamericanas," *Ariadna Histórica. Lenguajes, conceptos, metáforas* (2016); M. Morris, "Language in Service of the State: The Nahuatl Counterinsurgency Broadsides of 1810," *Hispanic American Historical Review* 87(3) (2007), 433–70; A. Durston, "Quechua Political Literature in Early Republican Peru (1821–1876)," in Heggarty and Pearce, *History and Language*, 165–85; R. M. Laughlin, *Beware of the Great Horned Serpent! Chiapas under the Threat of Napoleon* (New York: Institute for Mesoamerican Studies, University at Albany, 2003).

157 C. Boidin and A. Otazù Melarejo, "Toward a Guarani Semantic History: Political Vocabulary in Guarani (Sixteenth to Nineteenth Centuries)," in Durston and Mannheim, *Indigenous Languages*, 125–60, at 126.

their presence at the meetings of town councils. Conversely, a Castilian loanword that appears in a text written in a local language might convey different indigenous representations perfectly.[158] Colonial texts, either in Castilian or in local languages, must thus be understood as spaces of "cultural oscillation," in which both European and indigenous views could be entangled.

According to José Antonio Mazzotti, when Inca Garcilaso wrote of the "sun of justice" in the fragment of the *Royal Commentaries* mentioned earlier, he referred to the Christian God, but also suggested "meanings within the context of an Incan imagery."[159] The fact that "the medieval Christian church began to wield the image of the *Sol Iustitiae* in an effort to replace the pagan Sol Invictus of the Roman Empire" may not have gone unnoticed by Garcilaso.[160] The inclusion of Quechua words as well as the comparisons between Latin and Quechua and between the Roman and the Inca empires were also part of a rhetorical strategy intended to defend the indigenous jurisdiction under the imperial rule.[161] To put it differently, language was an arena in which legal concepts were constantly negotiated through the mediation of specialized agents, whose linguistic work depended on their sociopolitical position. From this perspective, the use of local languages in colonial courts of justice might have contributed to creating *loci* in which diverse interpretations of the law could be expressed and, eventually, discussed thanks to the cultural and linguistic mediation of interpreters.

Glave Testino has shown that the Quechua word *landi*, which among Andean peoples had a meaning close to the ideas of alienation and slavery, was used by the interpreter of the *corregidor* of Cuzco (a high-ranking judicial

158 C. Cunill, "Emprunts lexicaux au castillan en langue maya yucatèque. Une approche historique à partir de textes du XVIe siècle," *HispanismeS. Revue de la société des Hispanistes Français* 12 (2019), 7–24. See also D. Zaslavsky, G. Payàs, and I. Carreño, "Vicisitudes de algunas equivalencias en el discurso de la diplomacia hispano-mapuche en el Chile colonial," *Meta: Journal des traducteurs* 64(3) (2019), 648–67; M. A. Mendoza Posadas, "La retraducción colonial al español de dos testamentos nahuas del siglo XVI: adaptaciones de una tradición discursiva," in M. L. Arnal Purroy et al. (eds.), *Actas del X Congreso Internacional de Historia de la Lengua Española* (Zaragoza: Institución Fernando El Católico, 2018), vol. II, 1965–982; D. Silva-Reis and M. Bagno, "A tradução como política linguística na colonização da Amazônia brasileira," *Revista Letras Raras* 7(2) (2018), 8–28; T. Brignon, "Los falsos Tupãs: censura, traducción y recepción del concepto de idolatría en las reducciones jesuíticas de guaraníes (s. XVII-XVIII)," in Telesca and Vidal, *Historia y lingüística guaraní*, 81–114.

159 Mazzotti, "A Syncretic Tropology," 78. 160 Ibid., 66.

161 S. MacCormack, *On the Wings of Time: Rome, the Inca, and Peru* (Princeton: Princeton University Press, 2007); C. Townsend, "The Politics of Aztec History," in Durston and Mannheim, *Indigenous Languages*, 105–25; D. Tavárez, "Aristotelian Politics among the Aztecs: A Nahuatl Adaptation of a Treatise by Denys the Carthusian," in J. Mander, D. Midgley, and C. Beaule (eds.), *Transnational Perspectives on the Conquest and Colonization of Latin America* (London and New York: Routledge, 2019), 141–55.

official in the viceroyalty of Peru in the 1560s) to refer to the "perpetuity" of the *encomienda*, a royal grant given to the conquerors in the form of indigenous tributes. For such a translation, which contributed to fuel the indigenous opposition to a political project that would have undermined their interests, the interpreter was prosecuted in a trial in which the issue of "legal translation" proved to be crucial.[162] Although discussions ultimately took place in Castilian, thus enhancing the asymmetric coexistence of different legal orders that characterized the imperial situation, the relevance of using local languages in the judicial sphere, and the weight of some indigenous legal concepts in political debates must not be underestimated.[163] Their use in court must be interpreted in the light of ideologies of language, power relationships, and cultural oscillations.[164]

Final Comments

The main challenges in the study of indigenous law are not only the disparity of the sources available depending on the groups, areas, or times under consideration but also their diversity. They range from material vestiges, ethnographic surveys, historical narratives, iconographic and pictographic documents to dictionaries, and notarial and judicial texts. In general, the exclusion

162 L. M. Glave Testino, "*Simiachi*: traductor o lengua en el distrito de la Audiencia de Lima," in Cunill and Glave Testino, *Las lenguas indígenas*, 121–66; C. Cunill, "Indigenous Interpreters on Trial in the Spanish Empire: The Rise and Fall of the Maya Interpreter don Hernando Uz in Seventeenth-Century Yucatán," in L. Ruiz Rosendo and J. Baigorri Jalón (eds.), *Towards an Atlas of the History of Interpreting* (Amsterdam and Philadelphia: John Benjamins Publishing Company, 2023).

163 On this topic, see also T. Herzog, "Dialoging with Barbarians: What Natives Said and How Europeans Responded in Late-Seventeenth- and Eighteenth-Century Portuguese America," in Owensby and Ross, *Justice in a New World*, 61–88. For a comparison with the role that language and linguistic mediation played in other imperial settings, see R. M. Morrissey, "The Terms of Encounter: Language and Contested Visions of French Colonization in the Illinois Country, 1673–1702," in Englebert and Teasdale, *French and Indians*, 43–76; Hermes, "'Justice Will Be Done Us'."

164 During the wars of independence, indigenous peoples – as well as Afro-Latin Americans – continued to engage in politics, and a significant bulk of the political literature was produced in local languages with the aim of introducing new legal concepts such as "citizenship" among these sectors of the population. See Herzog, Chapter 4. M. Echeverri Muñoz, *Indian and Slave Royalists in the Age of Revolution. Reform, Revolution and Royalism in the Northern Andes, 1780–1825* (Cambridge: Cambridge University Press, 2016); J. Malerba (ed.), *A independência brasileira. Novas dimensões* (Rio de Janeiro: Editora FGV, 2006). On the political literature in indigenous languages produced during the wars of independence, see C. Boidin, C. Itier, and J. Chassin, "Presentación del suplemento especial sobre la propaganda política en lenguas indígenas en las Guerras de Independencias sudamericanas," *Ariadna Histórica: Lenguajes, Conceptos, metáforas* (2016); Morris, "Language in Service"; Laughlin, *Beware of the Great Horned Serpent*.

or inclusion in the analysis of specific sources has been intertwined with the conception of law that prevailed in the writing of legal history and the place that indigenous people were expected to occupy in society. Among the factors that have contributed to change the history of indigenous law over the last decades were reflections on the multiple actors who engaged with the production of legal knowledge; the consideration of the local and global dynamics in which legal knowledge emerged in an Atlantic and imperial perspective; and the criticism of the use of European concepts in describing the indigenous peoples' normative orders.

These changes have led scholars to take into account the historical processes through which different precolonial legal orders were intertwined before the Iberian conquests. From this perspective, the contact with European law can be placed within a long history of contested and ever-shifting legal accommodations. It also enables an understanding of how indigenous peoples experienced these negotiations according to their own legal culture. Furthermore, it is crucial to acknowledge the fact that precolonial law did not survive Iberian rule without alteration, but rather that it was subjected to complex changes following the engagement by a wide range of actors with law at different levels. The exercise of the indigenous town councils' jurisdiction, the engagement with the courts of justice, the sending of claims, memorials, and agents throughout the empire were avenues through which indigenous peoples participated in forging Iberian imperial law.

Obviously, this must not supersede the need to take into account the asymmetries in the power relations and to discern distinct degrees of agency when analyzing these questions. When indigenous, *mestizos*, or European peoples, who all occupied diverse sociopolitical positions, reported on indigenous law, they produced legal knowledge, in the sense that they situated indigenous law within a new linguistic, social, epistemological, and judicial setting. In this sense, approaches focused on local languages, translation, and linguistic policies help us go beyond the model of a dominant legal culture spreading and local normative orders resisting or disappearing, and take us closer to the negotiation, disputes, and misunderstandings that underpin the production of law in the Iberian empires.

3

How to Approach Colonial Law?

3.1 A Civil Law for a Religious Society

TAMAR HERZOG

To inquire on Latin American colonial law requires remembering a time before the institution of national legal systems and before legislation became the primary tool for legal creation. Understanding that time, so foreign to our contemporary experience, mandates that we take a journey into a past that was vastly different than our present. This journey will show that the main issue in understanding early modern alterity is not revealing the obvious fact that specific norms were different, but instead shedding light on a legal universe that was profoundly distinct from our own.[1] It will also demonstrate the enormous difficulties in imagining a colonial law as many scholars have described it in the past: clearly distinguishable from a metropolitan law, mainly resulting from legislation, and with a certain unity or intentionality (for the details of the relevant historiographical discussions, see Section 1.1).

To understand how Europeans implemented legal systems in the colonies and how these operated, it is essential to begin in Europe, our first stop. In the chapter's first section, we will observe what early modern European law consisted of, and how it functioned, including the relations between civil and canon law and the existence of a multiplicity of jurisdictions, that is, of authorities endowed with the capacity to declare and apply the law (*juris-dictio*). Moving ahead, our second stop will be to examine how this pan-European matrix

1 A. M. Hespanha, "The Law in the High and the Late Middle Ages: The Learned *Ius Commune* and the Vernacular Laws: Southern Europe (Italy, Iberian Peninsula, France)," in H. Pihlajamäki, M. D. Dubber, and M. Godfrey (eds.), *The Oxford Handbook of European Legal History* (Oxford: Oxford University Press, 2018), 332–57. See also J. L. Halpérin, "Est-il temps de déconstruire les mythes de l'histoire du droit français?," *Clio@Thémis* 5 (2012), 1–19, who criticizes the move to equate the history of medieval and early modern law with the history of the state.

operated in Spain and Portugal. Here, among other things, we will see that royal orders were jurisdictional acts that declared and applied the law but did not create it. Iberian kings did not invent new rules; they applied rules allegedly already in existence to concrete situations. The third stop of our journey focuses on how, starting in the sixteenth century, this matrix was transported to the Americas, where both the Spanish and the Portuguese faced the questions of how to adapt their own laws to the colonial situation and how to deal with what they perceived as local variations, including indigenous and African legalities. To explain how all this operated, the fourth stop will be a close examination of the case of customary law. After surveying its role in Europe, and then in Spain and Portugal, we will observe how it operated in the Iberian American colonies in general, and *vis-à-vis* indigenous and Afro-Latin American legalities in particular. Our journey will end with the practical questions of how we can reconstruct colonial law and how we can set Iberian colonial law in the larger global context of European early modern colonialism.

The Early Modern European Legal Universe

The first stop on our journey is to understand that the early modern European law (*derecho, direito, diritto, droit*) that shaped developments in the colonies was not a collection of legal solutions but an assortment of suggestions – some more prescriptive than others – regarding how to analyze social phenomena so as to identify a just solution. The basic assumption that guided this legal universe was that a preset divine order existed, indicating how things must transpire. All members of society, including the authorities but also a plethora of other actors such as jurists, theologians, judges, officials, and many others, had the obligation to defend this divine order.[2] To uncover what it prescribed, they considered multiple sources.[3] Those who attended university looked for indications in texts of Roman, canon and feudal law, as well as theology, all of which they learned to analyze and debate during their academic training. They, and others who had no university training, also appealed to Scripture, customs, common sense, as well as royal and local enactments.

2 The classical definition of justice during this period was "to give each person their due." This definition originated in antiquity. It was already mentioned by Cicero (*iustitia suum cuique distribuit*) and was later reproduced in the *Corpus Iuris Civilis*, where students were told, for example., in the *Institutes*, lib. I, title I "concerning justice and law," that "justice is the constant and perpetual desire to give each man his due right." This definition was then taken on by medieval jurists.

3 J. Vallejo, "El cáliz de plata: Articulación de órdenes jurídicos en la jurisprudencia del *ius commune*," *Revista de Historia del Derecho* 38 (2009), 1–13; and A. M. Hespanha, *Como os juristas viam o mundo. 1550–1750. Direitos, estados, pessoas, coisas, contratos, ações e crimes* (Lisbon: CreateSpace Independent Publishing Platform, 2015).

The plurality of actors who engaged in these efforts at discovery, the variety of situations they discussed, and the multiplicity of sources they considered, ensured that this hermeneutical effort led to constant debates and disagreements, with different actors and authors often proposing distinct, sometimes even outright contradictory, solutions. Some solutions were considered more trustworthy than others, either because of the reputation of those who proposed them, or because they had successfully stood the test of extensive debate. However, no solution was ever considered final, because at stake was not who made the pronouncement, but whether it correctly captured what contemporaries considered the ultimate truth.

This understanding of the law was widely disseminated both socially and geographically. In the past, many scholars appealed to what they described as a gap between law and its application, "law on the books" versus "law in action," an erudite and a popular sphere of legal knowledge and practice. Yet, these descriptions mostly depended on a very narrow and often anachronistic understanding that equated law with legislation. This understanding assumed that early modern kings enacted rules that their subjects were obliged to follow.[4] But this was not how early modern European law operated. Indeed, when the activities of contemporary actors are compared not only to royal enactments or the opinion of a single jurist, but instead to the compound world of legal debates and its multiplicity of suggestions, it becomes astonishingly clear that even illiterate actors living in remote communities fully participated in this universe.[5] These actors knew, for example, that in order to use communal pasture, they needed to be members of the community, and that, to achieve recognition as such, they had to demonstrate their loyalty to it. They were equally aware that their usage of the land gave them rights to continue doing so, and they understood that if others invaded their territories, they needed to protest immediately, else their silence would be interpreted as consent. Though less erudite actors were not always clear about why this was the case, or what plethora of options were available in

4 From this perspective, to argue, as does L. Benton, "Possessing Empire: Iberian Claims and International Law," in S. Belmessous (ed.), *Native Claims: Indigenous Law Against Empire, 1500–1920* (New York: Oxford University Press, 2012), 19–40, at 19 and 21–22, that actors did not always adhere to the letter of the law, or that they used law as a resource rather than as a script, is both anachronistic and a misunderstanding of how law operates generally, even today.

5 T. Herzog, *Defining Nations: Immigrants and Citizens in Early Modern Spain and Spanish America* (New Haven: Yale University Press, 2003), also available in Spanish and French translations; and T. Herzog, *Frontiers of Possession: Spain and Portugal in Europe and the Americas* (Cambridge: Harvard University Press, 2015), also available in Spanish, Portuguese, and Brazilian Portuguese.

legal debates, nonetheless, individuals of very different social, educational, and economic backgrounds were cognizant of how they had to behave to obtain or guard rights.

Historians have yet to explain how these processes of communication between a juridical and a popular sphere took place. Most actors, convinced that these practices were so self-evident as to require no explanation, seldom discussed them explicitly. When asked by neighbors, the authorities, or judges why they thought these behaviors awarded them rights, most suggested that they followed them because this was how god created the universe: The practices reflected the way things were, and had always been, everywhere.[6] These responses point to legal knowledge acquired by processes of socialization. These likely included informal observation and conversations, texts read or read out in public by town criers, as well as participation in public rituals and ceremonies in which certain ideas and structures were created, manifested, and reproduced. Clergymen also had a major role in inculcating this implicit normative knowledge in their Christian flock by intervening in local conflicts, giving advice, hearing confessions, explaining and telling the law, and preaching sermons.[7]

Europe: Civil and Canon Law

Though the sources considered by those seeking to reach a just solution were diverse and a multiplicity of persons was engaging in these discussions, we tend to divide the European legal universe into two branches, distinguishing civil from canon law. This distinction, intuitively dependent on a split between the material and the spiritual, was nevertheless also based on a particular vision of the law, one that placed the sources studied, as well as jurisdiction – that is, the faculty to declare and apply the law – at the center of the legal universe.[8] This vision organized legal knowledge not according to purely thematic divisions, as we do today (such as "contract law" or "criminal law"), and not even according to what pertained to the spiritual (everything

6 Herzog, *Defining Nations*, 18–25 and 166–69; and Herzog, *Frontiers of Possession*, 33–40.

7 T. Duve and O. Danwerth (eds.), *Knowledge of the Pragmatici: Legal and Moral Theological Literature and the Formation of Early Modern Ibero-America* (Leiden: Brill, 2020), particularly 1–39. See also C. Cunill, "La circulación del derecho indiano entre los mayas: escritura, oralidad y orden simbólico en Yucatán, siglo XVI," *Jahrbuch für Geschichte Lateinamerikas* 52 (2015), 15–36; and P. Cardim and M. Baltazar, "A difusào da legislação régia (1621–1808)," in J. Fragoso and N. Gonçalo Monteiro (eds.), *Um reino e suas repúblicas no Atlântico. Comunicações políticas entre Portugal, Brasil e Angola nos séculos XVII e XVIII* (Rio de Janeiro: Civilização Brasileira, 2017), 161–207, at 174.

8 P. Costa, *Iurisdictio. Semantica del potere politico nella pubblicistica medievale (1100–1433)* (Milan: Giuffrè Editore, 1969).

did), but according to the texts consulted, as well as by whether they originated with or were likely to be required by secular or religious authorities.

Despite this separation, however, early modern actors believed that both civil and canon law worked together to guarantee justice and that, together, they formed the common law of the Christian community, its *ius commune*.[9] Contemporaries referred to this understanding when they described civil and canon law as "the one and the other law" (*utrumque ius*) and expected most university-trained jurists to have studied both. Monarchs also acknowledged this when they ruled that if an answer could not be found in "one of the two laws," it could be sought in the other. Thus, though both rulers and jurists distinguished civil from canon law, they also considered them to be mutually supportive and to form a unified legal universe together.[10]

The co-penetration between civil and canon law, and often moral theology, was not only the domain of theory but also clear in the treatment of specific questions. For example, the *Decretum*, the mid-twelfth-century compilation of canon law, instructed users to follow civil law where canon law was silent. Canon law practitioners constantly looked to civil law for answers to questions such as whether a heretic had a valid legal personality and could administer a valid baptism, or to affirm that rules about communal life must be approved by all (*quod omnes tangit debet ab omnibus approbari*), a principle derived from classical Roman law.[11] Jurists of civil law followed the same procedure when they debated the categorization of certain individuals as *miserabilis* (in need of special protection due to poverty, sickness, old age, or similar) (see Sections 1.3 and 3.2), a classification that originated in canon law but was soon after also taken up by civil law.[12] Debates regarding how judges must proceed to collect and weigh evidence and to reach conclusions, initially conducted in the context of ecclesiastical courts, also affected the ways

9 The literature on *ius commune* is enormous. I found the following most useful: M. Bellomo, *The Common Legal Past of Europe, 1000–1800*, trans. L. G. Cochrane (Washington: Catholic University of America, 1995); P. Grossi, *A History of European Law*, trans. L. Hooper (Chichester and Malden: Wiley-Blackwell, 2010); and A. M. Hespanha, *A cultura jurídica europeia. Síntese de um milénio* (Coimbra: Almedina, 2018). For an abbreviated history of *ius commune*, see T. Herzog, *A Short History of European Law: The Last Two and a Half Millennia* (Cambridge: Harvard University Press, 2018), 75–92.

10 First developed in the twelfth century and subsequently refined during the early modern period, a special literary genre named *differentiae iuris civilis et canonici* helped practitioners overcome the differences between both laws: J. Portemer, *Recherches sur les Differentiae juris civilis et canonici au temps du droit classique de l'Église: l'expression des differentiae* (Paris: Jouve, 1946).

11 P. Stein, *Roman Law in European History* (New York: Cambridge University Press, 1999), 50–52.

12 B. Tierney, *Medieval Poor Law: A Sketch of Canonical Theory and Its Application in England* (Berkeley: University of California Press, 1959).

secular courts operated.[13] The pope's efforts to affirm his supremacy within the Church and *vis-à-vis* the bishops contributed to the development of legal and political models that would eventually lead to the birth of states, and the emergence of the concept of sovereignty.[14] The Church also intervened in matters we today associate with civil law, such as contract law.

This close association between civil and canon law, as well as moral theology, allowed actors as late as the eighteenth century to conclude that a theologian's education qualified him to serve as a judge also in civil courts.[15] What he lacked was not knowledge or an understanding of the relevant normative debates, only experience in the courts, which he could easily obtain while exercising the office. Thus, although in this volume we treat civil and canon law separately, it is important to remember that during the medieval and early modern periods, they were not considered independent of each other, but instead seen as together forming the *ius commune* of Christian Europe.

Europe: A Multiplicity of Jurisdictions

Early modern European law thus featured discussions rather than solutions, guiding ideas rather than rules. In such a universe, there was never a single authoritative answer, but rather a variety of possibilities that actors had to consider. If there was no single answer, neither was there a single authority that could decide what it would be. Early modern European states were not the unitary structures headed by a king or a republican authority that historians once imagined them to be. Instead, historians of European law now define these states as "jurisdictional states" consisting of a conglomerate of communities and corporations, including cities and villages, confraternities and guilds, families and congregations, religious and ethnic groups.[16] Each of these units was considered

13 K. Pennington, "Due Process, Community, and the Prince in the Evolution of the *Ordo iudiciarius*," *Rivista internazionale di diritto commune* 9 (1989), 9–47.

14 The classic work of H. Berman, *Law and Revolution: The Formation of the Western Legal Tradition* (Cambridge: Harvard University Press, 1983) has over the years won both admirers and critics, but there is much to it that still holds true.

15 T. Herzog, "¿Letrado o teólogo? Sobre el oficio de Justicia a principios del siglo XVIII," in J. M. Scholz (ed.), *Fallstudien zur spanischen und portugiesischen Justiz. 15.–20. Jahrhundert* (Frankfurt am Main: Vittorio Klostermann, 1994), 697–714.

16 These ideas can be traced back to Otto von Gierke and Otto Brunner. For a more recent reiteration, see A. M. Hespanha, "A historiografia jurídico-institucional e a *morte do estado*," *Anuario de Filosofía del Derecho* 3 (1986), 191–227; M. Fioravanti, "Stato e costituzione," in M. Fioravanti (ed.), *Lo Stato moderno in Europa: Istituzioni e diritto* (Rome and Bari: Laterza, 2002), 4–36; C. Garriga, "Orden jurídico y poder político en el antiguo régimen," *ISTOR: Revista de Historia Internacional* 4(16) (2004), 1–21; and A. Agüero, "Las categorías básicas de la cultura jurisdiccional," *Cuadernos de Derecho Judicial* 6 (2006), 19–58, at 41.

a "republic," that is, a body politic, and each had authorities endowed with jurisdiction, that is, with the capacity to declare and apply the law.

Thus, despite the conviction that a universal Christian and Roman ecumene existed, in practice this ecumene was divided into communities, each having a natural right to regulate itself. As the famous jurist Baldus de Ubaldi (1327–1400) once argued, this right was inherent to all groups and functioned "like spirit and soul in animated creatures."[17] Communal organs intervened in the local order by pronouncing sentences that rendered determinations about the past or by announcing norms that would apply in the future. Legal historians have thus asserted that, although the norms applying to the future may seem legislative to us – and indeed many historians have interpreted them as "legislation" – in reality, they were jurisdictional: Rather than inventing new rules, their goal was to declare and apply rules that were said to have predated the need to use them.[18] Furthermore, whether the authorities of corporations were resolving past conflicts or enacting instructions regarding the future, their decisions had to be just, that is, they had to reflect the preexisting divine order and thus to preserve the status quo that allegedly reproduced it.

Though the commonly agreed goal was to preserve the status quo, the various authorities could bitterly disagree about how this should be done, because, among other things, the indications they found in the sources were multiple rather than singular, and because each situation was considered distinct and thus meriting a detailed examination. Aiming to come to a just decision in accordance with the divinely ordained order, rather than to follow a particular rule or guarantee legal certainty, the authorities had a great degree of discretion. Indeed, discretion was considered essential to ensuring a just solution, as it allowed adapting existing norms and ideas to the specific case in hand. Royal orders did not limit this discretion, as they mostly indicated not how a case was to be resolved but emphasized the primacy of the duty to decide the matter justly. Given these characteristics of early modern European law, to expect decisions to be constant across cases and authorities is to misunderstand how this legal universe operated.

17 For example, Baldus in his commentary on the *Digesta* (D.1.1.5): Baldo degli Ubaldo, *Lectura super Digesto Novo* (Lyon: Johannes Sibert, 1498), fol. 9r. Jurists often referred to the right of communities to jurisdiction by arguing *ubi societas, ibi ius* ("wherever there is a society, there is law").

18 L. Mayali, "*Lex animata*: Rationalisation du pouvoir politique et science juridique (XIIème-XIVème siècles)," in A. Gouron and A. Rigaudière (eds.), *Renaissance du pouvoir législatif et genèse de l'État* (Montpellier: Société d'Histoire du Droit et des Institutions des Anciens Pays de Droit Écrit, 1988), 155–64, at 161–62; and J. Vallejo, *Ruda Equidad: Ley Consumada. Concepción de la Potestad Normativa (1250–1350)* (Madrid: Centro de Estudios Constitucionales, 1992).

The early modern normative world in Europe was thus both deeply united and highly fractured. It was united because all social actors were committed to upholding the preset divine order, and they all engaged in discussing how this could be done by relying on similar sources and employing similar vocabularies and techniques. It was fractured because within it there were multiple authorities competent to declare and apply the law, and these could, and did, easily produce different, even contradictory, solutions. As a result, while there was a shared framework and extensive communication between different jurisdictions and authorities, the norms in each could vary dramatically.

The main task of jurists was to ensure that despite conflicting indications as to which was the correct solution, or even conflicting results, the legal system would remain united. To achieve this goal, jurists developed vocabularies, techniques, and ways of arguing. They also adopted important rules regarding interpretation, which mandated, for example, that the local be preferred to the general, and the newer to the older, unless the general and the older were considered more just.[19]

The legal order thus operated simultaneously on a pan-European level and in a highly particularistic way. This said, it would be erroneous to consider this universe as featuring legal pluralism, as some historians have argued.[20] The existence of a plurality of jurisdictions did not produce distinct legal regimes. What existed instead was a universal common law that had to be localized. In other words, though this legal universe operated on multiple levels and with a plurality of sources and authorities, it remained one single system.

The European Legal Matrix as It Operated in Spain and Portugal

Most present-day historians of Spanish, Portuguese, and Latin American law subscribe to these interpretations. They explain that, as elsewhere in Europe, the laws of the Iberian kingdoms were composed of multiple sources, discussed by multiple agents, and implemented by multiple authorities endowed

19 Juan de Hevia Bolaños, *Curia Philipica* (Madrid: Imprenta de Ulloa, 1790 [1603]), 16–17.
20 Criticizing this use are Vallejo, "El caliz," 3–5 and 11–12; A.M. Hespanha, "The Legal Patchwork of Empires," *Rechtsgeschichte – Legal History* 22 (2014), 303–14; A. Agüero, "Local Law and the Localization of Law: Hispanic Legal Tradition and Colonial Culture (16th–18th centuries)," in M. Meccarelli and M. J. Solla Sastre (eds.), *Spatial and Temporal Dimensions for Legal History: Research Experiences and Itineraries* (Frankfurt am Main: Max-Planck-Institut für europäische Rechtsgeschichte, 2016), 101–29, at 102. See also T. Herzog, "Latin American Legal Pluralism: The Old and The New," *Quaderni fiorentini per la storia del pensiero giuridico moderno* 50(2) (2021), 705–36; and T. Herzog, "Legal Pluralism," in M. Mirow and V. Uribe (eds.), *A Companion to the Legal History of Latin America* (Leiden: Brill, 2023), 553–72.

with jurisdiction. Though the decisions of the various authorities could differ from each other, sometimes radically so, they nonetheless confirmed the existence of a *ius commune* that featured the universal search to uncover and preserve the preset divine order by discussing ancient and religious texts, by studying customs and the activities of multiple jurisdictional bodies, and by employing "common sense."[21]

These features were pan-European, yet scholars of Spanish and Portuguese legal history also stress the important connections between developments in the different kingdoms of the Iberian Peninsula. They argue that scholars and practitioners in Southern Europe, also including Italy and France, formed part of a particularly intensive communication system, whose members read and cited one another with great frequency (see Section 1.3). These exchanges led to striking similarities in the ways they debated questions and proposed solutions. Spain and Portugal also shared legal traditions that emerged not only because of their common adherence to *ius commune* or due to a shared communication network but also because of their common historical trajectory, including Roman, Visigoth, and Muslim occupation, the so-called Reconquest, overseas expansion, temporary periods of unity during the Middle Ages and the early modern period, similar experiences concerning state formation and liberal revolutions, French occupation, and so forth. These commonalities sustained the existence of a "customary Iberian law" and explain, for example, why, until the seventeenth century and possibly even later, Portuguese actors could use the Castilian *Siete Partidas*, a thirteenth-century restatement of *ius commune*, as if it were their own.[22]

21 On the reception of *ius commune* in the Iberian Peninsula, see J. M. Font Rius, "La recepción del derecho romano en la península ibérica durante la edad media," *Recueil des mémoires et travaux publiés par la Société d'Histoire du Droit et des Institutions des Anciens Pays de Droit Écrit* 6 (1967), 85–104; B. Clavero, *Historia del derecho: Derecho Común* (Salamanca: Universidad de Salamaca, 1994), 31–59; A. J. Torrent Ruiz, "La recepción del derecho justinianeo en España en la baja edad media (siglos XII–XV). Un capítulo en la historia del derecho europeo," *RIDROM: Revista internacional de derecho romano* 10 (2013), 26–119; A. Vitória, *Legal Culture in Portugal from the Twelfth to the Fourteenth Centuries* (Porto: Universidade do Porto, 2013); Hespanha, *Cultura jurídica europeia*, 114–75; and J. Domingues, "Recepção do *ius commune* medieval em Portugal, até às Ordenações Afonsinas," *Initium: Revista catalana d'historia del dret* 17 (2012), 121–67, at 123–24.

22 B. Clavero, "Lex Regni Vicinioris. Indicio de España en Portugal," *Boletim da faculdade de direito de Coimbra* 58(1) (1983), 239–98; and P. Cardim and J. Domingues, "A tradição Jurídica," in *Entre Portugal e a Galiza (Sécs. XI a XVII). Um Olhar Peninsular sobre uma Região Histórica* (Porto: Fronteira do Caos, 2014), 385–99. On the *Siete Partidas*, and *ius commune* more generally, in Portugal, see G. Braga da Cruz, "O direito subsidiário na história do direito português," in *Obras Esparsas: Estudos de História do Direito. Direito Moderno* (Coimbra: Biblioteca Geral da Universidade de Coimbra, 1981), vol. II, pt. 2, 245–436; Domingues, "Recepção do *Ius Commune*"; J. Domingues, "As Partidas de Castela e o Processo Medieval Português," *Initium: Revista catalana d'historia del dret*

Spain and Portugal: The Status of Royal Enactments

A key question in understanding how this legal universe dealt with new situations – such as those raised by the establishment of colonies and the resultant encounter with non-European normativities – is to understand the status and role attributed to royal orders in it. In the older historiography, royal legislation was often seen as the key ingredient of colonial law. However, as has become clear in the preceding discussion, in the early modern legal universe, monarchs were just one of a plurality of authorities who could declare the law, and all these authorities searched for a just solution by referring to a common set of texts, techniques, and practices.

Over the course of the early modern period, Spanish and Portuguese monarchs, like their counterparts elsewhere in Europe, did attempt to bolster their powers by insisting on their authority to declare and apply the law, and by demanding that their decisions be preferred to all other legal sources. In Castile, the *Ordenamiento de Alcalá* (1348) and the *Leyes de Toro* (1505) attempted this by instructing that royal orders be accorded the greatest authority, followed by customs (*fueros*), and only then by *ius commune*. Castilian monarchs also elaborated rules regarding which jurists should be favored. For example, in 1499, the Catholic kings expressed a preference for the works of the Italian civil jurist Bartolus of Sassoferrato (1313–1357) and his student Baldus de Ubaldis, and the Italian canon law jurists Johannes Andreas (1270–1348) and Niccolò de Tudeschi, alias Panoramitanus (1386–1445). In Portugal, royal pronouncements similarly established the rule that *ius commune* was to serve as a subsidiary source and be consulted only when royal law, courtly practice (*estilo da nossa corte*), and ancient customs of the kingdom (*costume dos nossos reinos antigamente usado*) were insufficient.[23] If no solution could be found in these, experts were first to appeal to canon law, then to the interpretations offered by the Italian jurist Franciscus Accursius (1182–1263), and as a last resort to the work of Bartolus of Sassoferrato, because, as the Portuguese kings put it, even if other jurists disagreed with him, most held his opinions to be most reasonable.

18 (2013), 237–88; J. Domingues, "O elemento castelhano-leonês na formação do direito medieval português," *Cuadernos de Historia del Derecho* 14 (2021), 213–27, at 218–24; J. Domingues, "Códices medievais de *ius commune* em Portugal: *Status quaestionis*," *Anuario de estudios medievales* 46(2) (2016), 725–50, at 740; and J. Domingues, "As Partidas de Castela na Sistemática Compilatória do Livro I da Reforma das Ordenações," *Initium: Revista catalana d'historia del dret* 21 (2016), 39–108.

23 *Ordenações Afonsinas* (1446–447) liv. 2, tit. 9. The *Ordenações Manuelinas* (1521) liv. 2, cap. 5 include similar provisions. See also Jorgede Cabedo, *Decisiones supremi lusitanici senatus regni* (Lisbon: J. Rodríguez, 1602–1604) pt. 1, dec. 211; and Álvaro Valasco, *Decisiones consultationum ac rerum judicatarum in regno Lusitaniae* (Venice: Baptistam & Bernardum Sessam, 1597), cons. 117, n. 24.

As far as we can tell, however, in practice, Spanish and Portuguese jurists and practitioners mostly ignored these royal attempts to establish a hierarchy of sources of law or developed legal presumptions that rendered them irrelevant. Presumptions were legal techniques that allowed jurists to assume the existence of a fact without having to prove it first. One such presumption was that royal orders were never intended to modify either *ius commune* or customary law.[24] Jurists also insisted that *ius commune* featured a complex system of organization, interpretation, and discussion that embodied a "natural reason" and could therefore be applied irrespective of whether the king allowed the use of *ius commune* or not.[25] Furthermore, as we saw earlier, in the early modern legal universe, it was undisputed that judges must rule by employing *arbitrium*, that is, the power (and the obligation) to decide correctly, rather than simply obeying a particular norm.[26]

Thus, although royal orders mattered, it is essential for understanding early modern law – and the development of colonial law in particular – that we appreciate that they were never perceived as external to the existing order, nor as capable of modifying it – at least until theories of sovereignty won the day in the eighteenth century. Like the pronouncements made by other authorities endowed with jurisdiction, royal orders were directed at finding a just solution for a particular case. Royal enactments themselves explicitly acknowledged this understanding of their status and purpose. As early as the thirteenth century, royal jurists stated that the final aim of all legislation (*ley*) was to demonstrate the things of God, provide a guide to living well, be a source of discipline, show the law (*derecho*) and what the good customs were, and to love justice.[27] Royal orders, therefore, were not legislation as we would understand this term today. Most did not deal with matters generally,

24 For example, Jerónimo Castillo de Bobadilla, *Política para corregidores y señores de vasallos en tiempo de paz, y de guerra y para jueces eclesiásticos y seglares* (Madrid: Instituto de Estudios de la Administración Local, 1978 [1704]), lib. 3, cap. 8, n. 195, argued in 1597 that customs were preferable to both *ius commune* and statutes. See also lib. 2, cap. 10, ns. 25 and 39, lib. 5, cap. 3, n. 51, lib. 3, cap. 8, ns. 194–95, and lib. 1, cap. 5, ns. 9–10. The same was true of Juan de Solórzano y Pereira, *Política Indiana*, ed. F. Ramiro de Valenzuela (Madrid: Compañía Ibero-Americana de Publicaciones, 1972 [1647]), lib. 2, cap. 6, n. 14. For a discussion arguing against authors who considered that a clear hierarchy of norms existed in Spain and its empire, see L. Nuzzo, "Dall'Italia alle Indie: Un viaggio del diritto comune," *Rechtsgeschichte – Legal History* 12 (2008), 102–24, at 109–10.

25 Hevia Bolaños, *Curia Philipica*, 15.

26 M. Meccarelli, *Arbitrium. Un aspetto sistematico degli ordinamenti giuridici in età di diritto comune* (Milan: Guiffrè, 1998).

27 This was what the *Fuero Juzgo*, enacted in 1241 by King Fernando III, stated, and was probably derived from the Hispano-Roman-Visigothic *Liber Iudiciorum* (654), lib. I, title II, law 2. By the early modern period, the *Fuero Juzgo* was considered a collection of kingdom-wide customs.

but were instead jurisdictional acts, produced to resolve a particular situation that required royal intervention. They usually included information on the specific circumstances of the case and often also mentioned the existence of conflicting possibilities as to how it could be solved.

Compilations of royal orders, such as the famous Castilian *Nueva Recopilación* of 1567 and *Novísima Recopilación* of 1805, the Spanish-American *Recopilación de Indias*, and the Portuguese *Ordenações*, openly discussed the limited enforceability of royal orders. They instructed readers to obey the latter, yet also acknowledged that they were not final (as new solutions might be required), that local norms and norms pertaining to corporations and communities, even if contradictory, must be respected, and that, in cases of legal *lacunae*, when no answers could be found in royal instructions, other sources must be consulted.[28] It is therefore not surprising that authorities in both Madrid and Lima agreed that instructions of the *Recopilación de Indias* that went against local practices should be ignored.[29]

Because they were the easiest to find and use, particularly when included in *Recopilaciones*, royal orders were often the most visible part of the legal system, both to contemporaries and to later historians. However, they were neither superior to other sources of law nor did they stand on their own. Furthermore, *recopilaciones* omitted most of the information regarding the case that the royal orders had been intended to resolve, as well as the legal reasoning that underlay the original decision. Despite this silence, contemporaries were aware of the fact that compilations furnished only the tip of the iceberg: Hidden from view was the huge volume of discussions that underlay royal decisions and was essential for understanding their correct meaning. This was particularly the case in compilations of royal orders that served as indices rather than law books. While *recopilaciones* were thus meant to facilitate the work of jurists and interested parties by letting them know which cases had already been resolved by the monarch, they still needed to consult the original decisions to know whether a case could serve as a precedent, or indeed why it had been decided as it was.

Furthermore, royal compilations were not the only instruments that jurists and litigants could use. Many jurists also authored legal recompilations, which

28 *Recopilación de Indias*, lib. 2, title 1, laws 1 and 4. See also C. Ramos Núñez, "Ius Commune y derecho real en la práctica forense de Manuel Lorenzo de Vidaurre," in L. E. González Vales (ed.), *XIII congreso del Instituto Internacional de Historia del Derecho Indiano: Actas y estudios* (San Juan de Puerto Rico: Academia Puertorriqueña de la Historia, 2003), vol. I, 403–30.

29 V. Tau Anzoátegui, *El Poder de la Costumbre. Estudios sobre el Derecho Consuetudinario en América hispana hasta la emancipación* (Madrid: Fundación Mapfre, 2000), 32–33.

they believed were necessary to facilitate knowledge of the legal system. While only a few were sanctioned by the kings, others – which we would nowadays perhaps consider mere personal projects – also aided contemporaries as they navigated this complex legal universe.[30] Whether privately prepared or sanctioned by the monarchs, however, all compilations of royal orders followed the same procedure, with original decisions being stripped of their context and the reasons that had led to their adoption. Thus, even in the case of authoritative compilations, contemporaries insisted that the validity of the precedents enumerated in a *recopilación* did not depend on their insertion in the collection, but on the validity of the original decision. Early modern jurists often criticized even the formal *recopilaciones* that won royal approval for failing to reproduce the precedents correctly, for assembling precedents that were unrelated, for rearranging royal orders incorrectly, and for neglecting to mention the facts that had led to the royal decision – criticisms echoed by many modern scholars. Some of the latter have even gone as far as to characterize the processes of selection and summation involved in the production of royal *recopilaciones* as capricious.[31] Given these concerns, litigants and jurists who were able to cite the original royal decisions tended to do so. The *Siete Partidas*, a work that collected juridical opinions and acquired an extended gloss, was similarly often ignored by more erudite discussants, who preferred to consult the original texts.[32]

In the Portuguese world, too, collections of royal orders were drawn up. Though the Portuguese monarchs did not sanction compilations other than the various *Ordenacões* (most famous among them, the *Ordenações Afonsinas*, *Manuelinas*, and *Filipinas*), individual jurists and institutions labored to remedy

30 M. Galán Lorda, "La relación entre la tarea recopiladora de Encinas, León Pinelo y Paniagua en algunos títulos de la Recopilación de Leyes de Indias," in T. Duve (ed.), *Actas del XIX Congreso del Instituto de Historia del Derecho Indiano* (Madrid: Dykinson, 2017), vol. I, 423–51; and W. Ahrndt, *Edición crítica de la Relación de la Nueva España y de la Breve y Sumaria Relación escritas por Alonso de Zorita*, trans. L. F. Segura (Mexico City: Instituto Nacional de Antropología e Historia, 2001), 27–28.

31 A. García Gallo, *Estudios de historia del derecho indiano* (Madrid: Instituto Nacional de Estudios Jurídicos, 1972), 55–93; E. Martiré, "Guión sobre el proceso recopilador de las leyes de Indias," in F. Icaza Dufour (ed.), *Recopilación de leyes de los reinos de Indias. Estudios históricos jurídicos* (Mexico City: Miguel-Ángel Porrua, 1987), 27–41; A. Muro Orejón, *Estudio general del nuevo código de las leyes de Indias* (Seville: Universidad de Sevilla, 1979); A. Bermúnez Aznar, "Las ordenanzas de audiencias en la recipilación de 1680," in *Memoria del X Congreso del Instituto Internacional de Historia del Derecho Indiano* (Mexico City: Universidad Autónoma de México, 1995), 161–68; and A. Lira, "El derecho y la historia social," *Relaciones. Estudios de historia y sociedad* 15(57) (1994), 33–48, at 37–39.

32 On the relationship between the *Partidas* and their gloss, see, for example, D. Alberto Panateri, "Uso, costumbre y fuero en relación al discurso medieval de la soberanía. Alfonso X el sabio y la glosa de Gregorio López," *Temas Medievales* 20 (2012), 147–96.

this lack by providing their own. Yet the Portuguese jurists, too, acknowledged that these compilations had no normative value, because they were tools rather than laws.[33]

The Immigration of European Law to the Americas

Together with European people, religion, and social, cultural, and economic institutions, this legal universe was exported overseas. Its immigration into the colonial territories was promoted by Iberian monarchs who ordered the implementation of Castilian or Portuguese law overseas, but it was mainly a by-product of the way early modern European normativity, which largely ignored political divisions, functioned. Implementing the European legal universe in the colonies meant that not only the belief in a preset divine order was imported but also the technologies developed over time as to how to discover and protect it. These technologies led to debates rather than to unique solutions and revealed guidelines rather than rules.[34]

Similarities between Spanish and Portuguese law in Europe and in the Americas also extended to the existence of a multiplicity of jurisdictions. Like the Iberian territories in Europe, Spanish and Portuguese America were divided into multiple communities (which contemporaries identified as "republics"), each with authorities endowed with the right (and the obligation) to declare and apply the law. These communities were multiple because each locality, group, and household was one (see Section 3.3). There were

33 Cardim and Baltazar, "A difusào da legislação régia," 188–90.

34 A. Pérez Martín, "Derecho común, derecho castellano, derecho indiano," *Rivista internazionale di diritto comune* 5 (1994), 43–90; J. Barrientos Grandón, *Historia del derecho indiano: Del descubrimiento colombino a la codificación. Ius commune – ius proprium en las Indias occidentales* (Rome: Il Cigno Galileo Galilei, 2000); V. Tau Anzoátegui, "La doctrina de los autores como fuente del derecho castellano-indiano," *Revista de Historia del Derecho* 17 (1989), 351–408; V. Tau Anzoátegui, "El derecho indiano en su relación con los derechos castellano y común," in B. Clavero, P. Grossi, and F. Tomás y Valiente (eds.), *Hispania entre derechos propios y derechos nacionales: atti dell'incontro di studio Firenze-Lucca 25, 26, 27 maggio 1989* (Milan: Giuffrè, 1990), vol. II, 573–59; H. Nébias Barreto, "Legal Culture and Argumentation in the Vice-Reign of Peru from the 16th to the 18th Centuries," *Clio@Themis 2* (2009); B. Bravo Lira, "Vigencia de las partidas en Chile," *Revista de estudios histórico jurídicos* 10 (1985), 43–105; A. M. Hespanha, "Modalidades e limites do imperialismo jurídico na colonização portuguesa," *Quaderni fiorentini per la storia del pensiero giuridico moderno* 41 (2012), 101–35, at 122–23; L. S. de Oliveira Coutinho Silva, *Nem teúdas, nem manteúdas: História das mulheres e direito na capitania da Paraíba (Brasil, 1661–1822)* (Frankfurt am Main: Max-Planck-Institut für europäische Rechtsgeschichte, 2020); T. Herzog, "Colonial Law: Early Modern Normativity in Spanish America," in J. Tellkamp (ed.), *A Companion to Early Modern Iberian Imperial Political and Social Thought* (Leiden: Brill, 2020), 105–27; and T. Herzog, "Rights of People in Spain and Its Empire," in R. Hammersley and A. Fitzmaurice (eds.), *Cambridge History of Rights III: The Sixteenth and Seventeenth Centuries* (Cambridge: Cambridge University Press, forthcoming).

hundreds of Portuguese, Spanish, and indigenous "republics," "republics" that were based on locality, and others that embraced individuals who exercised the same profession, professed the same creed, or lived in the same household. Though multiple, all these republics belonged to the "republic of republics," the Christian ecumene.

A paradigmatic example of how the European legal system operated in the colonies is provided by the work of Juan de Solórzano y Pereira (1575–1655). Solórzano was a judge in Lima and the author of a mid-seventeenth-century manual of legal matters arising from colonial situations that was extremely popular, particularly in its abbreviated Spanish translation.[35] In this manual, Solórzano included questions that a colonial judge or administrator might encounter and provided a number of possible answers. While he did give his opinion as to which of the possible options was the most just, he nonetheless showcased the multiplicity of questions that needed asking and the variety of possible answers, as well as the need to consult a wide range of authors. He referenced no less than 30,000 works written by over 3,000 authors, many of whom were born, had studied, or resided outside Spain.

Solórzano never imagined that the questions he asked had a simple, definitive answer.[36] Neither did he believe that such an answer could be found in royal enactments or in royal recompilations. When he did use the medieval *Siete Partidas*, he treated it not as a royal command, but as an encyclopedia of *ius commune*. Although most historians consider Solórzano to have authored a manual of colonial law, Solórzano himself never conceived of his work as describing a new or separate law for the colonies. He was clearly conscious of the fact that conditions in the Americas presented new questions and new challenges and therefore warranted discussion, but nowhere in his writing does he conclude that a colonial law, distinct from European law, existed. Instead, Solórzano articulated a synthesis of what he observed as a practicing judge, what he read, what was already established, and of new solutions that he formulated using existing techniques. He employed the knowledge he gathered

35 Solórzano y Pereira, *Política Indiana*. On how other colonial judges dealt with such realities, see, for example, A. Casagrande, "Forensic Practices and the 'History of Justice' in the 17th and 18th Centuries: A View from a Spanish American Periphery," in Duve and Danwerth, *Knowledge of the Pragmatici*, 350–78.

36 On Solórzano's methodology, see, for example, T. Duve, "Los privilegios de los indios: ¿Derecho local?," in M. Torres Aguilar (ed.), *Actas del XV Congreso del Instituto Internacional de historia del Derecho Indiano* (Córdoba: Universidad de Córdoba, 2005), 112–30; and S. Scafidi, "Old Law in the New World: Solórzano and the Analogical Construction of Legal Identity," *Florida Law Review* 55 (2003), 191–204. On Solórzano's life, œuvre, and working methods, see also E. García Hernán, *Consejero de ambos mundos: vida y obra de Juan de Solórzano* (Madrid: Fundación Mapfre, 2007).

by residing in the Americas and working as a magistrate, but he also constantly relied on his training as a jurist and his familiarity with both civil and canon law. His manual aimed at systematizing a huge array of often contradictory solutions, which he applied to his specific time and place – mid-seventeenth-century Peru – and arranged into a logical edifice that was plausible but, as always, only one proposal among many. Despite Solórzano's efforts and enormous erudition, the edifice he created, like early modern law itself, was replete with contradictions, ambiguities, and inconsistencies.

Thus, regardless of what we may think about early modern actors and their values today, the conviction that law must provide a just solution that fitted the specific circumstances of each case, place, and time, was as pervasive in the colonies as it was in Europe. Ibero-America neither had a distinct colonial law nor was it a zone of lawlessness, as Carl Schmitt argued. Instead, it was a highly legalistic space where both the Spanish and the Portuguese implemented legal systems that formed part of European law, in which debates were more frequent than agreements, and where a general *ius commune* coexisted with a mosaic of specific solutions.[37]

When the authorities failed to adapt the solutions to the specific context, locals protested. Among the most famous mechanism enabling them to do so was to "obey but not comply" (*obedecer y no cumplir*).[38] This faculty, long seen by historians as permitting abuses, was nevertheless a legitimate legal procedure practiced in medieval and early modern Iberia as well as being present elsewhere in Europe. It allowed locals to suspend obedience to orders that were against local practices, customs, or privileges, or that were considered in other ways unjust, and to advocate for a different, sounder solution. Procedures similar to *obedecer y no cumplir* also existed in Portuguese America, where royal orders were considered binding only as long as they

37 Carl Schmitt, *The Nomos of the Earth in the International Law of Jus Publicum Europaeum*, trans. G. L. Ulmen (New York: Telos Press, 2003).

38 V. Tau Anzoátegui, "La ley 'se obedece pero no se cumple'. En torno de la suplicación de las leyes en el derecho Indiano," in V. Tau Anzoátegui, *La ley en América hispana del descubrimiento a la emancipación* (Buenos Aires: Academia Nacional de la Historia, 1992), 69–143. On how this worked in the Iberian Peninsula, see, for example, B. González Alonso, "La fórmula 'obedézcase, pero no se cumpla' en el derecho castellano de la Baja Edad Media," *Anuario de historia del derecho español* 50 (1980), 469–88; and J. M. Fernández Hevia, "El ejercicio de la fórmula 'obedecer y no cumplir' por parte de la Junta General del Principado durante el siglo XVI," *Boletín del Real Instituto de Estudios Asturianos* 55(157) (2001), 123–50. On its presence elsewhere, see the somewhat related French institution of *remontrances*, for example, F. Bidouze, "Remontrances contre lettres de cachet, ou l'*habeas corpus* à la française en 1788," *Parliaments, Estates and Representation* 31(2) (2011), 137–54; O. Chaline, "La pratique des remontrances au XVIIIe siècle: Paris, Rouen, Rennes," *Annales de Bretagne et des Pays de l'Ouest* 122(3) (2015), 89–105.

were compatible with local norms. When royal precepts did not seem appropriate to local conditions or contradicted local privileges, actors could ignore them.[39] The conviction that the norms must fit the circumstances of place and time was also expressed by royal officials; the fifth viceroy of Peru, Francisco de Toledo (1515–1582), for example, pointed out the danger of giving the same rules to communities that were different.[40]

As in Europe, royal attempts to control this diversity and to subject law to the royal will mostly failed. On multiple occasions in the sixteenth and seventeenth centuries, the Spanish kings insisted on the applicability of Castilian law in the "New World" and pointed out that the overseas territories should be governed according to the preferences expressed in the 1505 *Leyes de Toro*, which placed royal orders at the top of the hierarchy of norms. Legal historians have shown that these efforts were as unsuccessful in colonial Latin America as they had been in Europe. Equally moot was a royal attempt to ensure that Peninsular law won the approval of the Council of the Indies before being applied in the Americas. As a result, looking to the royal law to understand Iberian colonial law is incorrect and anachronistic, as is the assumption of a separation of colonial from metropolitan law.[41]

39 A. Wehling, "Sem embargo da ordenação em contrário. A adaptação da norma portuguesa à circunstância colonial," in N. Mello Souza (ed.), *Brasil: Construindo uma Nação* (Brasilia: Confederação Nacional do Comércio de Bens, Serviços e Turismo, 2014), 115–35, at 132 specifically mentions the Spanish American *obedecer y no cumplir* as a similar institution.

40 "Ordenanzas particulares para los pueblos de indios del distrito de La Paz, Arequipa, 6 de noviembre de 1575," in G. Lohmann Villena (ed.) and M. J. Sarabia Viejo (trans.), *Francisco de Toledo: Disposiciones gubernativas para el Virreinato del Perú, 1569–1574* (Seville: Escuela de Estudios Hispanoamericanos, 1989), vol. II, no. 63, 203–16, at 203.

41 As early as the 1940s, R. Altamira, "Autonomía y descentralización legislativa en el régimen colonial español: Siglos XVI a XVIII," *Boletim da Faculdade de Direito* 20 (1944), 1–71, warned against equating colonial law with royal legislation (26). Also criticizing authors who argued as much is Nuzzo, "Dall'Italia alle Indie," 108–12. The same is true for Portuguese America: A. M. Hespanha, "Porque é que existe e em que é que consiste um direito colonial brasileiro," *Quaderni fiorentini per la storia del pensiero giuridico moderno* 35 (2006), 59–81, at 59–60; N. Camarinhas, "Administração da justiça em espaços coloniais: A esperiência imperial portuguesa e os seus juízes, na época moderna," *Jahrbuch für Geschichte Lateinamerikas* 52 (2015), 109–24, at 112 and 120–24; A. Slemian, "A primeira das virtudes; justiça e reformismo ilustrado na América portuguesa face à espanhola," *Revista complutense de historia de América* 40 (2014), 69–92, at 70, 80, and 85; G. C. Machado Cabral, "Senhores e ouvidores de capitanias hereditárias: uma contribuição ao estudo das fontes do direito colonial brasileiro a partir da literatura jurídica (séculos XVI a XVIII)," in G. Silveira Siqueira and R. M. Fonseca (eds.), *História do direito: olhares diacrônicos* (Belo Horizonte: Arraes Editores, 2015), 97–118, at 112–15; G. C. Machado Cabral, "*Ius Commune* in Portuguese America: Criminal Issues on Local Canon Law in the 'First Constitutions of the Diocese of Bahia' (1707)," *Glossae: European Journal of Legal History* 13 (2016), 308–27; and G. C. Machado Cabral, "Pegas e Pernambuco: notas sobre o direito comum e o espaço colonial," *Revista Direito & Práxis* 9(2) (2018), 697–720.

Present-day legal historians, therefore, conclude that colonial Latin American law was an American version of *ius commune* or, as contemporaries sometimes classified it, a "municipal" law in a legal universe that admitted both a pan-European framework as well as local variations.[42] These historians reject the view of earlier generations who portrayed Spanish colonial law as a unitary and systematic body of law developed specifically by the monarchs for overseas rule (see Section 1.1). They also question older views that identified such a unified body of law as *derecho indiano*, arguing that this term, rather than reflecting early modern realities, was the product of historiographical and political ambitions in the nineteenth and early twentieth centuries, which sought to identify a particular (and superior) Spanish mode of colonialism.[43]

Paradoxically, although historians of Portuguese America never pretended that Portuguese overseas territories were ruled by a single, unitary colonial law, they, too, engaged in the effort of presenting the Portuguese imperial endeavor as exceptional. An older generation of historians argued that, in contrast to other colonial empires, the Portuguese were willing to adapt to local realities, developing legal regimes that were highly flexible. However, this portrayal, sometimes called Luso-Tropicalism, also responded to twentieth-century ideological pressures that reflected political goals rather than history. In fact, Luso-American law formed part of the general European *ius commune*: the *Ancien régime*, as António Manuel Hespanha put it, also extended to the tropics.[44]

How Early Modern European Law Operated I: The Example of Customary Law

How all this operated in Europe (first) and the colonies (second) can be demonstrated by observing customary law, which has been on the minds of

42 Altamira, "Autonomía y descentralización," 26; and Tau Anzoátegui, *El Poder de la Costumbre*, 51–54 refer to this law as "municipal." C. Petit, "El caso del derecho indiano," *Quaderni fiorentini per la storia del pensiero giuridico moderno* 22 (1993), 665–77, at 665 refers to it as a version of *ius commune*.

43 On how the concept of *derecho indiano* was born and the type of political work it was supposed to perform, see (besides Section 1.1) L. Nuzzo, "Between America and Europe: The Strange Case of the *derecho indiano*," in T. Duve and H. Pihlajamäki (eds.), *New Horizons in Colonial Spanish Law: Contributions to Transnational Early Modern Legal History* (Frankfurt am Main: Max-Planck-Institut für europäische Rechtsgeschichte, 2015), 161–91; and A. M. Hespanha, "O 'direito de índias' no contexto da historiografia das colonizações ibéricas," in Duve, *Actas del XIX Congreso*, vol. I, 43–83.

44 A. M. Hespanha, "Antigo Regime nos trópicos? Um debate sobre o modelo político do império colonial português," in J. Fragoso and M. F. Gouvêa (eds.), *Trama das redes: Política e negócios no império português, séculos XVI–XVIII* (Rio de Janeiro: Civilização Brasileira, 2010), 43–94; and A. M. Hespanha, *Filhos da terra. Identidades mestiças nos confins da expansão portuguesa* (Lisbon: Tinta de China, 2019).

legal historians in recent years.[45] Customs are an interesting example because the older colonial historiography assumed that they were an authentic reflection of communal traditions, that they did not form part of the "law" but were external to it, or were particular to certain groups but not others (such as the alleged distinction between a written legal system followed by the colonists and the unwritten customs of the indigenous populations). Recent scholarship has questioned these conclusions, pointing out that customs were an important part of European law, too, and that they operated similarly in Europe and its colonies. The study of customs, therefore, allows us to examine how early modern European law operated, while also demonstrating the need to understand the functioning of European law in order to grasp developments in the colonies.

The European background, with which I begin this section, shows why older interpretations that suggested that indigenous customs included an autochthonous normativity that either reflected ancient traditions or at least stood for a distinct culture that might have served to delay or resist the implementation of European law, are problematic. A better grasp of the development of the European understanding of customary law explains how, on the contrary, it was possible for indigenous customs in the American territories to be relatively recent, change over time, and be affected by imperial law and colonial conditions. How indigenous and Afro-Latin American customary law interacted with the imported Iberian legal universe to create a colonial law will be the subject of the following two sections.

Customs were an important source of European law from as early as the second century AD and throughout late antiquity, the Middle Ages, and the early modern period. During this long timespan, jurists viewed customs as norms reproducing local particularism that could differ from and sometimes even contradict the general law, yet complemented rather than stood in opposition to it.

This understanding of customs was particularly clear in the thirteenth and fourteenth centuries, when university-trained jurists began categorizing existing European local law as "customary."[46] They argued that each

45 T. Herzog, "Immemorial (and Native) Customs in Early Modernity: Europe and the Americas," *Comparative Legal History* 9(1) (2021), 1–53.

46 M. Ascheri, *The Laws of Late Medieval Italy (1000–1500): Foundations for a European Legal System* (Leiden: Brill, 2013). The involvement of jurists in the creation of "customary law" is discussed, among others, by A. Gouron, "Sur les plus anciennes rédactions coutumières du Midi: Les 'chartes' consulaires d'Arles et d'Avignon," *Annales du Midi* 109(218) (1997), 189–200, at 196; A. Gouron, "Aurore de la Coutume," in A. Gouron, *Droit et coutume en France au XIIe et XIIIe siècles* (Abingdon-on-Thames: Routledge,

community had norms that constituted its "customs." These local norms could originate in statutes, constitutions, acts of authority, jurisprudence, or in repeating acts that community members believed prescriptive. What distinguished customs from other laws, then, was not the way they were created, but the fact that they were particular to a locality. Though such local norms could vary from community to community, jurists saw no contradiction between the diversity of customs and the unity of *ius commune*. They believed that they mutually reinforced rather than opposed one another.[47] To them, customs were an essential component of the legal universe because they guaranteed just solutions by being highly attuned to the specific context of place, time, and group. They were also the natural product of the process of concretization required of legal practitioners, who, as we saw earlier, found just solutions not by following abstract rules but by weighing different norms anew for each individual case. Meanwhile, *ius commune* guaranteed that, despite these local variations, all Christians would share a basic understanding of what justice mandated.

Customs, in other words, might have been created locally by either the authorities or community members, but they also won the approval and support of jurists, who labored both to identify local norms as customary and to integrate them into a wider legal universe. The interconnectivity between customs and legal thought was especially evident during campaigns to write down the local law, in which jurists abandoned the axiom that customs must be oral and produced written collections of customary law. Such campaigns took place across Europe in the late Middle Ages and the early modern period. In the Iberian world, when collections of customs covered a wide range of activities, they obtained the status of *fuero* or *foro*. There were *fueros* and *foros* of towns, certain guilds or occupations, and groups, such as the *fuero militar*, which applied to soldiers.

While the efforts of writing down the local customs were supposedly motivated by the wish to better know and conserve them, the resulting collections demonstrate that those recording customs often dramatically changed them.

1993) ch. 20, 181–87; K. Pennington, "Learned Law, Droit Savant, Gelehrtes Recht: The Tyranny of a Concept," *Syracuse Journal of International Law and Commerce* 20 (1994), 205–15; L. Mayali, "La coutume dans la doctrine romaniste au moyen âge," *Recueils de la Société Jean Bodin Pour l'Histoire Comparative des Institutions* 52(2) (1990), 11–31; and E. Conte, "Consuetudine, Coutume, Gewohnheit and Ius Commune: An Introduction," *Rechtsgeschichte – Legal History* 24 (2016), 234–43.

47 P. Ourliac, "Coutume et mémoire: Les coutumes françaises au XIIIe siècle," in B. Roy and P. Zumthor (eds.), *Jeux de mémoire: Aspects de la mnémotechnie médiévale* (Montreal: Presses de l'Université de Montréal, 1985), 111–22, at 114.

In their attempts to systematize and rationalize local laws, jurists decontextualized and de-historicized what they observed and made unique solutions into general rules. The modifications introduced by them were so extensive that some scholars have likened the process to the forced acculturation that colonizers inflicted on the colonized.[48] In choosing what to record as custom, jurists also developed the rules regarding what custom was. They distinguished practices that were compulsory (customs) from others that were not (which they called *usos*, "uses"), and set rules as to how long a norm needed to have existed for it to become prescriptive. As a result of these processes of recording and definition, customary law as scholars tend to think about it today came into being. The image of customary law as community-based and ancient has become so pervasive and so evident that we tend to forget how it emerged. Thus, while we remember that customs might have originated in communities or with their authorities, we no longer recall that they underwent juridical reinvention from the thirteenth and fourteenth centuries and were deeply affected by the dominating presence of *ius commune*.

Juridical intervention in customary law was so successful that, by the fourteenth century, customs (*consuetudo*) and customary law (*ius consuetudinarium*) had become an integral part of European law. One of the main reasons for the growing significance of customs was that they came to be considered a useful tool not only for affirming local autonomy but also for defining the relations between the different units that together constituted the emerging states, as well as between them and the developing central authorities. Members of different groups, alleging that customs were part of their communal heritage,

48 R. Jacob, "Les coutumiers du XIIIe siècle ont-ils connu la coutume?," in M. Mousnier and J. Poumarède (eds.), *La coutume au village dans l'Europe médiévale et moderne: Actes des XXe Journées internationales d'histoire de l'Abbaye de Flaran, Septembre 1998* (Toulouse: Presses Universitaires du Mirail, 2001), 102–19. On efforts to write down French customary law, see J. P. Dawson, "The Codification of the French Customs," *Michigan Law Review* 38(6) (1940), 765–800; M. Petitjean, "La coutume de Bourgogne: Des coutumiers officieux à la coutume officielle," *Mémoires de la société pour l'histoire du droit et des institutions des anciens pays bourguignons* 35 (1972), 13–20; A. Gouron, "Aux origines de l' 'émergence' du droit: glossateurs et coutumes méridionales (XIIe-milieu du XIIIe siècle)," in *Religion, société et politique: Mélanges en hommage à Jacques Ellul* (Paris: Presses Universitaires de France, 1983), 255–70; M. Grinberg, "La rédaction des coutumes et les droits seigneuriaux," *Annales HSS* 52(5) (1997), 1017–38; and M. Seong-Hak Kim, "Custom, Community, and the Crown: Lawyers and the Reordering of French Customary Law," in C. H. Parker and J. H. Bentley (eds.), *Between the Middle Ages and Modernity: Individual and Community in the Early Modern World* (Lanham: Rowman & Littlefield, 2007), 169–86. On developments elsewhere, see, for example, J. Gilissen, "La preuve de la coutume dans l'ancien droit belge," in *Hommage au professeur Paul Bonenfant 1899–1965: Études d'histoire médiévale dédiées à sa mémoire* (Brussels: Universa, 1965), 564–94, at 591–93.

used them to make demands on kings. Kings, in turn, invoked custom both to signal their respect for the liberties of their subjects and, on the contrary, to impose limits on them.[49]

Although by the fifteenth and sixteenth centuries, many customs could be found in written compilations, those not recorded in writing could still be substantiated by the declaration of witnesses, who tended to describe them as "immemorial." Many historians have assumed that immemoriality was the same as antiquity or even authenticity, yet such was not the case. Rather than necessarily attesting to the antiquity of customs, "immemoriality" was an instrument designed and implemented by jurists: It was a presumption, that is, a category of proof that jurists invented to solve difficult cases.

Presumptions mostly reproduced conclusions that seemed commonsensical to contemporaries.[50] A typical presumption was the inference that a child born in wedlock was the offspring of both spouses. Most presumptions only acted to reverse the burden of proof. Instead of placing it on the plaintiff (to show that the child was the offspring of both spouses, e.g., in cases of alimony), they shifted it to the defendant, who had to produce evidence to contradict the presumption (in this case, showing that the child could not be the offspring of the husband by proving, for example, that he was absent when the child was conceived). Immemoriality, however, used by jurists to prove the existence of a custom, was a special type of presumption, called a *praesumptio juris et de jure*. In contrast to other presumptions, it admitted of no rebuttal.[51] Even if there was solid evidence showing that it led to the wrong conclusion, jurists still adhered to the presumption, allowing a party to prove something that they knew was incorrect.

49 This is why Castillo de Bobadilla, *Política para corregidores*, lib. 3, cap. 8, n. 195, could think about local customs as "privileges." Also, see M. Toch, "Asking the Way and Telling the Law: Speech in Medieval Germany," *Journal of Interdisciplinary History* 16(4) (1986), 667–82; and A. Wood, *The Memory of the People: Customs and Popular Senses of the Past in Early Modern England* (Cambridge: Cambridge University Press, 2013). On the relationship between customs and contracts, see W. Ullmann, "Bartolus on Customary Law," *Judicial Review* 52 (1940), 265–83, at 269–70 and 280–81.

50 The literature on presumptions is enormous. For a brief description of how they operated at different times and in different settings, see R. H. Helmholz and W. D. Sellar (eds.), *The Law of Presumptions: Essays in Comparative Legal History* (Berlin: Dunker and Humblot, 2009).

51 Aimone Cravetta, *Tractatus de antiquitatibus temporum* (Lyon: Haeredes Iacobi Iuntae, 1559) part I, argument 1, ns. 1 and 3, part IIII, argument 3, ns. 23, 40, and 60; Miguel de Reinoso, *Observationes practicae* (Lisbon: Typis Petri Craesbeeck Regii Typographi, 1625), observation 65, 357–65, most particularly ns. 1 and 3; António Cardoso do Amaral, *Liber utilissimus judicibus, et advocatis, additionatus ad Fratre Josepho Leitam Telles* (Coimbra: Franciscum de Oliveyra, 1733) vol. I, 155; and Hieronymus de Monte, *Tractatus de finibus regundis ciuitatum, castrorum, ac praediorum, tam vrbanorum, quam rusticorum*

The juridical assertion that customs could be classified as immemorial is therefore a powerful proof of jurists' desire to support and legitimize them. Jurists not only accepted local law as customary and proceeded to record it, but they were also willing to adopt extreme solutions to enable locals to argue (by invoking immemoriality) for the existence of customs even when information was scarce or wholly absent. The presumption of immemoriality converted local norms for which no one remembered how and why they had originated into "the best title in the world" (*consuetudo immemoriabilis praestat meliorem titulum de mundo*) that could not be refuted.[52] Juridical support of customs also included the argument that it was plausible to assume that the authorities, both civil and ecclesiastical, and/or the community at large, had agreed to what was immemorial, else they would have prohibited it. And, because immemorial practices were presumed to have won broad social acceptance, some jurists argued that they could be assumed to be reasonable and good.

Jurists might have curated customs into powerful tools, but jurisdictional authorities and litigants also supported them. Comparing, for example, what litigants said to what jurists argued demonstrates the surprising degree to which most litigants described not their individual experiences, but instead what was legally required.[53] Incorporating and domesticating juridical categories as their own – without being necessarily aware of their full implications, and most probably following the advice of notaries, judges, lawyers, or other experts or peers – witnesses in late medieval and early modern Europe constantly argued that their customs were immemorial.[54] They understood that this term was a powerful one, and they employed it in order to ensure a result to their liking.

Historians have asserted that, paradoxically, recourse to immemoriality enabled change, with newer customs being easily characterized as

(Cologne: Johann Gymnich, 1614 [1565]) 48–49. See also J. P. Lévy, *La hiérarchie des preuves dans le droit savant du Moyen Âge depuis la Renaissance du Droit Romain jusqu'à la fin du XIVe siècle* (Paris: Librairie du Recueil Sirey, 1939), 62–66; and J. Franklin, *The Science of Conjecture* (Baltimore: Johns Hopkins University Press, 2001), 31.

52 Reinoso, *Observationes practicae*, 65 and 357–65, most particularly ns. 1 and 3.

53 J. A. Jara Fuente, "'Que memoria de onbre non es en contrario': Usurpación de tierras y manipulación del pasado en la Castilla urbana del siglo XV," *Studia Historica: Historia Medieval* 20–21 (2002–2003), 73–104; and P. Miceli, "La costumbre en perspectiva histórica: desde el consenso populi a la voluntad popular," *Anales de historia antigua, medieval y moderna* 44 (2012), 277–304, at 142 and 152–65.

54 On the role of notaries, see Francisco González de Torneo, *Práctica de escribanos que contiene la judicial y orden de examinar testigos* (Madrid: Antonio Vázquez, 1640 [1587]), lib. 4, fols. 102v–103r and fols. 124v–125r, as well as lib. 5, tit. 5, fols. 141r–142v; and José Febrero, *Librería de escribanos e instrucción jurídica teórico-práctica* (Madrid: Imprenta de Pedro Martin, 1789), vol. III, part I, cap. 8 (1), at 56 and 66 n. 49.

immemorial. In addition, immemoriality was invoked even when the customs described had a clear point of departure that the witnesses remembered, and the presumption was thus not strictly necessary. While immemoriality, ironically, allowed for constant change, the writing down of customs did the opposite. Though recording customs in writing did modify what was remembered and how, after customs had been written down, they became fixed. As a result, they could no longer easily cater for changes.

The study of customs thus reveals the interdependency between customs and juridical debates as well as between customs and royal attempts to control them. It demonstrates the importance of presumptions and commonsense assertions, and the plurality of options that existed at each given moment. It also displays the pan-European character of these legal entanglements because the dynamics unleashed by the processes of defining, addressing, and proving customs were common to many European countries. They were certainly impactful also in Spain and Portugal, where the presence of customs was recorded in antiquity, where kings attempted to control local normativity mainly by writing it down, and where local compilations of *ius commune* – such as the *Siete Partidas* – dealt extensively with customs.[55] As would eventually happen also in the Americas, Spanish monarchs ordered their subjects and officials to obey customary law as long as its instructions did not contradict the mandates of god or reason, did not require improvement or change, and did not contradict royal instructions.[56] Spanish and Portuguese practitioners, theologians, and jurists did the same, describing different customs, explaining their origins, and advocating their importance.[57]

55 *Siete Partidas*, partida 1, título 2. On developments in the kingdom of Aragon, see A. Iglesia Ferreirós, "La creación del derecho en Cataluña," *Anuario de Historia del Derecho Español* 47 (1997), 99–423; A. Iglesia Ferreirós, "Ley y costumbre en la Cataluña medieval," in A. Iglesia Ferreirós (ed.), *El Dret Comú i Catalunya: Actes del V Simposi Internacional* (Barcelona: Fundació Noguera, 1996), 207–22; J. A. Obarrio Moreno, "El valor de la costumbre en el reino de Valencia," *Anuario da facultade de direito da Coruña* 9 (2005), 637–62; and A. Planas Rosselló, "La costumbre en el derecho histórico de Mallorca," *Cuadernos de Historia del Derecho* 22 (2015), 101–16. On Portugal, see, for example, M. J. Brito de Almeida e Costa, "Foros ou costumes," in J. Serrão (ed.), *Dicionário de história de Portugal* (Porto: Livraria Figueirinhas, 1985), vol. III, 59–60; A. Tavares, "Direito local português na Idade Média: Os Costumes e foros (Guarda, Évora, Santarém e Beja)," *Quiroga: Revista de Patrimonio Iberoamericano* 13 (2018), 80–90, at 82 and 86–87; and J. Domingues, "Os foros extensos na Idade Média em Portugal," *Revista de Estudios Histórico-Jurídicos* 37 (2015), 153–74.

56 See, for example, *ley* 1 of the *Leyes de Toro*, 1505.

57 Castillo de Bobadilla, *Política para corregidores*, lib. 1, cap. 5, n. 9, lib. 2, cap. 10, ns. 34–58 and lib. 3, cap. 8, ns. 194–97; and Francisco Suárez, *Tractatus de legibus ac deo legislatore: in decem libros distributus* (Coimbra: G. de Loureyro, 1612), lib 7.

How Early Modern Law Operated II: Customary Law in the Iberian Colonies

The interaction between local customary and global law, and between customary law and jurists, which emerged in late medieval and early modern Europe, was central to developments also in the colonies. In both Spanish and Portuguese America, a huge plethora of customs was recognized by jurists and practitioners as prescriptive: local customs as well as customs of corporations, communities, households, and groups, and customs of Spanish, indigenous, and Afro-Latin American communities.[58] As in Europe, these customs were understood as representing a local legal specificity operating alongside the common framework that united them all, a true *ius commune*. Often written down, customs could also be supported by the declarations of witnesses who frequently classified them as immemorial, though this did not mean that they were necessarily ancient. Finally, customs were perceived as belonging to certain groups and could become a powerful instrument to resist external imposition and affirm local autonomy to declare and apply the law, but this did not make them external to the law itself, only an important, indeed an essential, part thereof.

Because customs – in the colonies as in Europe – could be integrated into the early modern legal universe only after jurists declared them "good" and in harmony with religious precepts, the question which customs could be recognized as valid greatly preoccupied contemporaries. Also important was the need to decide which practices were *usos* that had no normative valence and which were customs (*costumbres* and sometimes *fueros*) and therefore binding.[59]

The Particular Case of Indigenous Customs

These findings challenge previous historians' understanding of custom in the colonies. Historians tended to concentrate their attention mostly on indigenous customs – seen either as authentic practices or a colonial invention – but

58 R. Levene, "El derecho consuetudinario y la doctrina de los juristas en la formación del derecho indiano," *Hispanic American Historical Review* 3 (1920), 144–51; Tau Anzoátegui, *El poder de la costumbre*, 15–16; T. Duve, "La pragmatización de la memoria y el trasfondo consuetudinario del Derecho Indiano," in R. Folger and W. Oesterreicher (eds.), *Talleres de la memoria: reivindicaciones y autoridad en la historiografía indiana de los siglos XVI y XVII* (Münster: Lit, 2005), 77–97; M. R. Pugliese, "Apuntamientos sobre la aplicación del derecho indiano local en el Río de la Plata," *Revista de Historia del Derecho* 33 (2005), 219–95; Agüero, "Local Law," 117–23; V. Tau Anzoátegui, "Provincial and Local Law of the Indies: A Research Program," *New Horizons in Spanish Colonial Law* 3 (2015), 235–55. Customs were explicitly addressed by Solórzano y Pereira, *Política Indiana*, lib. 4, cap. 3, n. 6 and lib. 5, cap. 14, n. 18.

59 C. Cunill and R. Rovira-Morgado, "'Lo que nos dejaron nuestros padres, nuestros abuelos': retórica y praxis procesal alrededor de los usos y costumbres indígenas en la Nueva España temprana," *Revista de Indias* 81(282) (2021), 283–313.

always as different from "the law." However, as we have seen, customs – including, but not restricted, to indigenous customs – were part of the legal order.[60] Furthermore, customs were always extremely local: Rather than belonging, for example, to all Spanish or all indigenous communities (as in the idea of "Spanish customs" or "indigenous customs"), each group and each locality had its own. Multiple rather than unique, complex rather than simple, customs included an enormous range of practices and norms that could vary dramatically from place to place, group to group, and over time.

Given the importance of customary law to European and Iberian legal traditions, it is not surprising that colonial actors turned their attention to indigenous customs. They did so as clergymen who wished to guarantee indigenous conversion, as administrators looking for feasible solutions, but also as jurists whose task it was to cater for local variations as long as they did not contradict the *ius commune*. Royal officials made efforts to find information about indigenous normativities by sending out questionnaires throughout the territories, asking which indigenous customs, good or bad, pre- or post-conquest, existed.[61] Aware of the enormous diversity in indigenous customs, the local officers and indigenous individuals who answered the questionnaires sent back information regarding governmental structures, taxation, laws, and the administration of justice.[62] Royal magistrates also participated in these efforts of discovery and documentation by conducting their own surveys and writing down what they identified as indigenous customary law.[63] The resulting copious records are what enables modern historians to

60 The Spanish formally acknowledged the validity of indigenous customs in 1530, 1542 and 1555, long before this acknowledgement was inserted in the *Recopilación de Indias*: Tau Anzoátegui, *El Poder de la Costumbre*, 70–74 and 135–37. See also J. Manzano, "Las leyes y costumbres indígenas en el orden de prelación de fuentes del derecho indiano," *Revista del Instituto de Historia del Derecho Ricardo Levene* 18 (1967), 65–71; C. J. Díaz Rementería, "La costumbre indígena en el Perú hispánico," *Anuario de estudios americanos* 33 (1976), 189–215; M. A. González de San Segundo, "El elemento indígena en la formación del derecho indiano," in M. A. González de San Segundo, *El mestizaje jurídico: el derecho indiano de los indígenas (estudios de historia del derecho)* (Madrid: Universidad Complutense de Madrid, 1995), 1–54, at 5–6, 12 and 16–19; T. Herzog, "Indiani e cowboys: il ruolo dell'indigeno nel diritto e nell'immaginario ispanocoloniale," in A. Mazzacane (ed.), *Oltremare: Diritto e istituzioni dal colonialismo all'età postcoloniale* (Naples: Cuen, 2006), 9–44; and Herzog, "Immemorial (and Native) Customs."

61 Ahrndt, *Edición crítica*, 25–27 describes some of these efforts. As for the type of questions that had to be answered, see, for example, Francisco de Solano, *Cuestionarios para la formación de las relaciones geográficas de Indias, siglos XVI–XIX* (Madrid: CSIC, 1988), 23 and 82.

62 See, for example, M. Strecker and J. Arteaga, "La 'Relacion de algunas costumbres' (1582) de Gaspar Antonio Chi," *Estudios de historia novohispana* 6 (1978), 1–21.

63 For more detail on the various methods employed by those recording indigenous customs, see Herzog, "Immemorial (and Native) Customs," 40–43.

imagine what indigenous law might have looked like even before Europeans invaded the continent (see Chapter 2).

Although the motivation of those collecting and writing down data on indigenous customs could vary, the jurists and ecclesiastics who took part in these endeavors largely followed the same procedures as their European equivalents in the preceding centuries.[64] Judging their task as essential to the integration of multiple communities into a "jurisdictional state" – which, in the colonial setting, also included a variety of ethnicities – jurists and clergymen gathered information, observed what they could, and wrote down what seemed most relevant, appropriate, and just, while also endeavoring to transform it into something familiar and comprehensible. In the surveys they conducted, they sometimes used indigenous informants and witnesses, as well as indigenous mnemonic devices. However, they often relied on the expertise of Spaniards, either settlers or ecclesiastics, who were said to be familiar with indigenous peoples and their customs.

Some colonial actors clearly advocated in favor of indigenous customs, which they believed were an antidote to chaos; others criticized them bitterly, believing them pagan, unjust, or simply unwise. But whatever their attitude, like their predecessors in Europe, all those recording customs in the colonies tended to decontextualize and de-historicize the evidence they collected. They distinguished good customs (which should persist because they were compatible with divine and natural law and the main tenets of *ius commune*) from bad ones (which should be prohibited). Although colonial

64 Polo Ondegardo, "Informe del licenciado Juan Polo Ondegardo al licenciado Briviesca de Muñatones sobre la perpetuidad de las encomiendas en el Perú," Lima, December 12, 1561; and "Las razones que movieron a sacar esta relación y notable daño que resulta de no guardar a estos indos sus fueros," Lima, June 26, 1571, in G. Lamana Ferrario (ed.), *Pensamiento colonial crítico: Textos y actos de Polo Ondegardo* (Cuzco and Lima: Centro Bartolomé de las Casas and Instituto Francés de Estudios Andinos, 2012), 139–204 and 217–330; A. de Zorita, "Breve y sumaria relación de los señores y maneras y diferencias que había de ellos en la Nueva España," in J. García Icazbalceta (ed.), *Nueva colección de documentos para la historia de México* (Mexico City: Liechtenstein Kraus, 1971 [1886]), vol. III, 71–227, at 73–78; "Carta de don Francisco de Toledo al rey, fecha en los Reyes, 18 de abril de 1578," in J. Toribio Medina, *La Imprenta en Lima (1584–1824)* (Lima: Casa del Autor, 1904), vol. I, 187–99; and Gaspar de Escalona Agüero, *Gazofilacio real del Perú* (La Paz: Editorial del Estado, 1941 [1647]), lib. 2, part 2, cap. 20, n. 1, 239–40, and n. 15, 252. Francisco de Toledo, viceroy of Peru from 1569 to 1581, was particularly active in both recording and changing indigenous customs. See, for example, "De lo que han de guardar los indios de cada pueblo en general y en particular," in *Relaciones de los virreyes y audiencias que han gobernado el Perú: Memorial y ordenanzas de D. Francisco de Toledo* (Lima: Imprenta del Estado, 1867) vol. 1, 204–17. On how Zorita proceeded to record indigenous law, see J. L. Egío, "From Castilian to Nahuatl to Castilian? Reflections and Doubts about Legal Translation in the Writing of Judge Alonso de Zorita (1512–1585)," *Rechtsgeschichte – Legal History* 24 (2016), 122–53.

recorders acknowledged the existence of a huge variety of customs among indigenous peoples, as their European equivalents had done in the "Old World," they nonetheless tended to reduce the customs' complexity, and to portray them as belonging to a single normative universe by turning concrete examples into general rules. The result was that, in the process of recording, these actors also modified what they had found. They allowed European law as applied in the colonies to absorb indigenous customs but, in the aftermath, neither indigenous customs nor European law were ever the same.

The Spanish officials who engaged in these campaigns were driven by a bias in favor of European alphabetical writing and believed that this was the only technology that would enable the conservation of indigenous customs. They expressed their fear that, unless they proceeded as they did, many indigenous customs would be "lost," because indigenous peoples had no system to write down their own laws.[65] According to this view, due to the lack of written collections, indigenous people could not account for their customs; they could only repeat what their ancestors had done. Some Spaniards concluded that it was "almost impossible" to find out the truth about indigenous customs, because an authoritative compilation – a "general history of the customs of the Indians of Peru," for example – was lacking.[66]

The belief that indigenous customs must be recorded led Spaniards to pay attention also to indigenous methods of recollection. In testimonies collected in Cuzco in 1582, for example, multiple witnesses explained that the indigenous peoples of Peru had their own systems of registration, which had "secretaries" sing (!) the information on laws and ordinances while holding a Khipu in their hands.[67] Khipus were colorful knotted cords that, as far as we presently know, included information that was numerical, legal, and perhaps also literary and historical. It identified kinship organization and communities and

65 Strecker and Artiega, "La Relación de Algunas." See also Bernabe de Cobo, *Inca Religion and Customs*, trans. R. Hamilton (Austin: University of Texas Press, 1990 [1653]), lib. 1, cap. 1, 9. Vasco de Quiroga, for example, stated that the Spanish must record indigenous customs because this was the best as well as the most appropriate thing to do: P. B. Villella, "'For So Long the Memories of Men Cannot Contradict It.' Nahua Patrimonial Restoration and the Law in Early New Spain," *Ethnohistory* 63(4) (2016), 697–720, at 698.

66 J. A. Guevara Gil, "Los caciques y el 'señorío natural' en los andes coloniales (Perú, siglo XVI)," in J. A. Guevara Gil, *Diversidad y complejidad legal: Aproximaciones a la antropología e historia del derecho* (Lima: Pontificia Universidad Católica del Perú, 2009), 301–18, at 311–12, citing Alonso Fernández de Bonilla, a doctor in canon law and *visitador* and *juez de residencia* of Viceroy Toledo. Present-day scholars express similar disappointment; see, for example, J. Ravi Mumford, "Litigation as Ethnography in Sixteenth Century Peru: Polo de Ondegardo and the Mitimaes," *Hispanic American Historical Review* 88(1) (2008), 5–40, at 8.

67 "Carta de don Francisco," 192, 194, and 196–98.

narrated their privileges.[68] According to several colonial testimonies, Khipus sometimes included information on Inca law, and not only reflected reality but contributed to its making, because they allowed not only the preservation of the memory of the past but also planning and distribution of resources in the future.[69]

Precolonial in origin, Khipus continued to be produced during the colonial period, though their presence somewhat diminished from the 1590s, and starkly decreased from the mid-seventeenth century onwards. In the early period, the Spanish authorities often ordered that the contents of Khipus be transcribed into Spanish-type documentation, and colonial judges routinely accepted Khipus as valid proof. To admit Khipus as evidence, indigenous experts (*Khipucamayocs*) who had them in their possession testified to their contents in the courts. We know that litigants and judges who heard these expert testimonies assumed that Khipus contained facts about past events, but they also tended to believe that these historical accounts had normative dimensions. Khipus were thus seen in the early modern period as reflecting the indigenous management of justice and order, perhaps even law, and as records of decisions that were categorized as jurisdictional because they declared and applied the law. Belief in the veracity of Khipus was such that, on occasions, Spanish judges demanded to hear what Khipus, which they described as "truthful and correct," indicated. In 1575, Viceroy Toledo ordered Khipus to be collected, and instructed the *Khipucamayocs*, who by that stage were considered notaries (*escribanos*), to write down their contents so that the information would be "more certain and durable."[70]

Andeans were not the only indigenous peoples to record information in forms that appeared alien to the colonizers yet were considered reliable. Mayan elites presented colonial magistrates with information recorded using traditional hieroglyphic scripts that captured historical accounts as well as evidence regarding communities and land rights.[71] During the colonial period,

68 G. Urton, "From Knots to Narratives: Reconstructing the Art of Historical Record Keeping in the Andes from Spanish Transcriptions of the Inka Khipus," *Ethnohistory* 45(3) (1998), 409–39; C. B. Loza, "El quipu y la prueba en la práctica del derecho de Indias, 1550–1581," *Historia y cultura* 26 (2000), 11–37; and J. C. de la Puente Luna, "That Which Belongs to All: Khipus, Community, and Indigenous Legal Activism in the Early Colonial Andes," *The Americas* 72(1) (2015), 19–53. On the presence of Khipus in the post-colonial Andes, see F. Salomon, *The Cord Keepers: Khipus and Cultural Life in a Peruvian Village* (Durham: Duke University Press, 2004).

69 José de Acosta, *Historia natural y moral de las indias*, ed. Edmundo O'Gorman (Mexico City: Fondo de Cultura Económica, 1940 [1590]), lib. 6, cap. 8, 465.

70 "Ordenanzas generales para la vida común en los pueblos de indios, Arequipa, 6 de noviembre de 1575," in *Francisco de Toledo: Disposiciones*, vol. II, no. 64, 217–66, at 238.

71 J. F. Chuchiak IV, "Writing as Resistance: Maya Graphic Pluralism and Indigenous Elite Strategies for Survival in Colonial Yucatan, 1550–1750," *Ethnohistory* 57(1) (2010), 87–116.

those trained to read these scripts were recognized as notaries. Many of them produced both Spanish and Maya documentation, as well as mixed texts that, written in Spanish, incorporated Maya style, forms of address, measurements, numerals, and classifiers, or that, though written in indigenous languages, used Spanish alphabetical script.

Aztec authorities and litigants relied on indigenous painted histories to keep information safe.[72] Considered faithful recollections of the past, these paintings were admissible in colonial courts and accepted as reliable evidence for claims regarding the rights of communities to certain lands, or of families to certain leadership positions.[73] Perhaps because these instruments seemed so foreign, Spaniards sometimes questioned whether they only included facts or also normative knowledge. Vasco de Quiroga (1477/78–1565), for example, argued in 1535 that the indigenous peoples of Mexico did not have "ordinances" nor laws and that their paintings only represented records of past events.[74] By contrast, his contemporary Bernardino de Sahagún (*c.* 1499–1590) believed that Aztec paintings were like writing and contained information on litigation, laws, and customs.[75]

72 On Nahua writing systems and their interaction with Spanish alphabetical record keeping, see J. Lockhart, *The Nahua after the Conquest: A Social and Cultural History of the Indians of Central Mexico, Sixteenth through Eighteenth Centuries* (Stanford: Stanford University Press, 1992), 326–73. See also J. Galarza, *Estudios de escritura indígena tradicional Azteca-Nahuatl* (Mexico City: Archivo General de la Nación, 1980); E. Hill Boone, "Pictorial Documents and Visual Thinking in Postconquest Mexico," in E. Hill Boone and T. Cummins (eds.), *Native Traditions in the Postconquest World: A Symposium at Dumbarton Oaks 2nd through 4th October 1992* (Washington: Dumbarton Oaks, 1998), 149–99; and E. Hill Boone, *Stories in Red and Black: Pictorial Histories of the Aztecs and Mixtecs* (Austin, University of Texas Press, 2000).

73 T. de Benavente, *Historia de los indios de la nueva España*, ed. M. Serna Arnaz and B. Castany Prado (Madrid: Real Academia Española, 2014), 5. On the usage of indigenous record keeping in Spanish courts, see, for example., A. Megged, "Between History, Memory, and Law: Courtroom Methods in Mexico," *The Journal of Interdisciplinary History* 45(2) (2014), 163–86; and, more generally, J. Rappaport and T. Cummins, *Beyond the Lettered City: Indigenous Literacies in the Andes* (Durham: Duke University Press, 2012), 175–88. See also Egío, "From Castilian to Nahuatl," 145–48.

74 Vasco de Quiroga, "Información en derecho" (Mexico, July 24, 1535), in *Colección de documentos inéditos relativos al descubrimiento, conquista y organización de las antiguas posesiones españolas en América y Oceanía* (Madrid: Bernaldo de Quinós, 1868), vol. 10, 333–513, at 423.

75 Bernardino de Sahagún, *Historia general de las cosas de la Nueva España* (Mexico City: Imprenda de Alejandro Valdés, 1829 [1540]), lib. VI, cap. 43, vol. II, 241, lib. XVIII, cap. 15, vol. II, 304, cap. 24, vol. II, 314, and lib. X, cap. 13, vol. III, 30. Historians tend to believe that Aztec records did indeed include normative information, yet they also argue that this information had to be explained, justified, and interpreted by expert decoders. They thus highlight the dynamic relations between rules, principles, and implementation. See, for example, J. A. Offner, "The Future of Aztec Law," *The Medieval Globe* 2(2) (2016), 1–32, at 2–3 and 6.

Despite preference for written over oral transmission, and despite the push to record indigenous customs in (alphabetical or other) writing, colonial courts, both Spanish and indigenous, were constantly called upon to apply indigenous law as reconstructed by the declarations of witnesses. However, historians who have studied how this worked in practice argue that Spanish officials who claimed to decide cases according to indigenous customary law actually curated a new law that no indigenous individual would have easily recognized (see also Chapter 2).[76] These officials were not ethnographers seeking to discover what indigenous law mandated, but behaved as early modern judges did elsewhere, namely, they searched for what they considered was the just result, using the methods discussed earlier. They thus applied to indigenous law their own judgment of what justice required. For example, they supported the nomination of heirs to leadership positions according to patriarchal principles and linked the right to land with possession. The Spanish administrative authorities followed suit, despite frequently insisting – even as they sought to control or alter indigenous customs – that their orders were not meant to change the customary law. Instead, they claimed that colonial administrators and judges were merely continuing and repeating "ancient" indigenous legal practices.[77]

Indigenous judges and litigants were often similarly creative in inventing or shaping customs according to present needs while at the same time claiming to be following long-established practices. Rather than focusing on preserving their ancient traditions or expressing allegiance to the past, they translated and adapted old practices to new realities in pursuit of what they considered just and followed the strategies to which they attributed the greatest chances of success.[78] Indigenous judges, influenced by colonial conditions

76 W. Borah, *Justice by Insurance: The General Indian Court of Colonial Mexico and the Legal Aides of the Half-Real* (Berkeley: University of California Press, 1983), 3–4, 35, 47, 49–50, and 57–58; C. J. Díaz Rementería, *El cacique en el virreinato del Perú. Estudios histórico jurídico* (Seville: Universidad de Sevilla, 1977), 47 and 113 n. 2; B. Lavallé, *Al filo de la navaja. Luchas y derivas caciquiles en Latacunga, 1740–1790* (Quito: Corporación Editora Nacional, 2002), 184–87; and T. Herzog, "Colonial Law and 'Native Customs': Indigenous Land Rights in Colonial Spanish America," *The Americas* 63(3) (2013), 303–21.

77 See, for example, T. Cummins, "Let Me See! Reading Is for Them: Colonial Andean Images and Objects 'como es costumbre tener los caciques Señores,'" in Hill Boone and Cummins, *Native traditions*, 91–148, at 110–11.

78 B. Premo, "Custom Today: Temporality, Law, and Indigenous Enlightenment," *Hispanic American Historical Review* 94(3) (2014), 355–79; Y. Yannakakis and M. Schrader-Kniffki, "Between the 'Old Law' and the New: Christian Translation, Indian Jurisdiction, and Criminal Justice in Colonial Oaxaca," *Hispanic American Historical Review* 96(3) (2016), 517–48; F. Salomon, "Collquiri's Dam: The Colonial Re-Voicing of an Appeal to the Archaic," in Hill Boone and Cummins, *Native Traditions*, 273–74; S. Muñoz Arbeláez, *Costumbres en disputa: Los muiscas y el imperio español en Ubaque, siglo*

as well as Christianity, and often presiding over communities composed of members from a plurality of origins, mixed elements from various traditions. In the process, they created a law that was certainly local but was neither authentic nor necessarily old – in contrast to what they sometimes argued and what historians used to assert.

Indigenous authorities also contributed to disseminating knowledge about Spanish law.[79] On occasions, they or local scribes were responsible for translating Spanish norms into local languages, or preparing collections of law for local use.[80] Comparison of what they produced with the Spanish originals demonstrates that, while their work enabled Spanish concepts and norms to penetrate locally, it also ensured their adaptation to local concepts, idioms, and possibilities, for example, by stressing orality, by adding commentaries, or by referring to customs, distinguishing between those that should be maintained (because they were "good") from those which must not. In other words, like Spanish judges, indigenous judges were involved in processes of cultural (and legal) translation and searched for a just solution (see Sections 1.3 and 1.4).

Indigenous litigants learned to use the colonizers' language of "customs" to refer to their own normativity. They defended some customs as "good" and thus valid and classified others as "bad" and therefore no longer prescriptive.[81] They invoked custom, which they often categorized as "immemorial," to justify new habits and argued – in line with the European understanding of the term – that immemoriality required that there would be "nothing in human memory to contradict it." Thus, indigenous judicial practices and concepts substantially changed during the colonial period not just due to the adherence to Spanish law but also through the transformation of indigenous normativity into a European style "customary law."[82]

XVI (Bogotá: Universidad de los Andes, 2015), 27–67; and M. Deardorff, "Republics, Their Customs and the Law of the King: *Convivencia* and Self-Determination in the Crown of Castile and Its American Territories, 1400–1700," *Rechtsgeschichte – Legal History* 26 (2018), 162–99, at 162 and 165–66.

79 C. Cunill, "La circulación del derecho indiano entre los mayas: escritura, oralidad y orden simbólico en Yucatán, siglo XVI," *Jahrbuch für Geschichte Lateinamerikas* 52 (2015), 15–36, at 27–35.

80 B. D. Sells and S. Kellogg, "We Want to Give Them Laws. Royal Ordinances in a Mid-Sixteenth Century Nahuatl Text," *Estudios de cultura Náhuatl* 27 (1997), 325–67.

81 Villella, "For So Long the Memories"; and Cunill Rovira-Morgado, "Lo que nos dejaron nuestros padres."

82 Such transformations were described, for example, in the pioneering work of S. Kellogg, *Law and the Transformation of Aztec Culture, 1500–1700* (Norman: University of Oklahoma Press, 1995). See also M. Á. Romero Frizzi, "The Power of the Law: The Construction of Colonial Power in an Indigenous Region," in E. Ruiz Medrano and

In other words, whether written down or applied by the courts, in Spanish America as in Europe, customs were both a means of preserving local normativity and a motor for change. The early modern European concept of customary law allowed for the integration of a wide range of jurisdictions – in this case, indigenous communities and their laws – into a *ius commune*, but both customs and the common law were modified as a result. Historians have thus concluded that one can consider colonial indigenous customs as the outcome of complex processes involving local agency, juridical mediation, and an ongoing conversation regarding what was local and what was global, what was permissible and what was prohibited, what was written down, and what remained oral. Customs both European and indigenous, new or old, communally based, reimagined by jurists, or mandated by kings, formed part of a complex legal universe in which a great variety of norms competed but also, according to the contemporary understanding of *ius commune*, cohered.

While there is ample information on how these processes operated in Spanish America, we still lack data regarding the equivalent developments in Luso-America. Nonetheless, there is reason to believe that similar processes occurred. Unlike the Spanish, the Portuguese did not formally acknowledge the validity of indigenous jurisdictions or indigenous law.[83] However, in Portuguese territories, too, indigenous leaders (*principais*) substantially contributed to the maintenance of order within indigenous communities and therefore must also have engaged in declaring and applying the law.[84] This

S. Kellogg (eds.), *Negotiation within Domination. New Spain's Indian Pueblos Confront the Spanish State* (Boulder: University Press of Colorado, 2010), 107–35; Y. Yannakakis, "*Costumbre*: A Language of Negotiation in Eighteenth-Century Oaxaca," in Ruiz Medrano and Kellogg, *Negotiation within Domination*, 37–173; and J. C. de la Puente Luna and R. Honores, "Guardianes de la real justicia: alcaldes de indios, costumbre y justicia local en Huarochirí colonial," *Revista Histórica* 40(2) (2016), 11–47.

83 In Africa, however, the Portuguse took into account, and sometimes formally recognized, indigenous customs: see, for example, C. Madeira Santos, "Entre deux droits: Les lumière en Angola (1750–v.1800)," *Annales HSS* 60(5) (2004), 817–48; C. Madeira Santos, "Esclavage africain e traite atlantique confrontés: transactions langagière et juridiques (à propos du tribunal de *mucanos* dans l'Angola des XVIIe et XVIIIe siècles)," *Brésil(s). Sciences humaines et sociales* 1 (2012), 127–48.

84 M. R. Celestino de Almeida, *Metamorfoses indígenas: Identidade e cultura nas aldeias coloniais do Rio de Janeiro* (Rio de Janeiro: Arquivo Nacional, 2003), 134 and 145–68; V. M. Losada Moreira, "Territoriality, Mixed Marriages, and Politics among Indians and Portuguese," *Revista brasileira de história* 25(70) (2015), 17–39, at 17–19 and 21; V. M. Losada Moreira, "Casamentos indígenas, casamentos mistos e política na América portuguesa: amizade, negociação, capitulação e assimilação social," *Topos* 19(39) (2018), 29–52, at 31; P. P. Langer, *A Aldeia de Nossa Senhora dos Anjos: a resistência do guarani-missioneiro ao processo de dominação do sistema colonial luso (1762–1798)* (Porto Alegre: Est Edições, 1997), 3; and M. C. Coelho, "O Diretório dos Índios e as chefias Indígenas: Uma inflexão," *Campos* 7(1) (2006), 117–34, at 121–22.

must have been the case throughout the colonial period, though indigenous jurisdictional powers possibly intensified after the mid-eighteenth-century reforms that tasked indigenous village councils and justices of the peace (*juiz ordinário*) with adjudicating conflicts.[85] Though this theoretically transformed the indigenous population into vassals and subjected them to Portuguese law, there is some evidence that indigenous judges continued to be influenced by indigenous legal concepts.[86] Our ignorance of how this transpired is mostly explained by the limitations of the source material, which is either scarce or nonexistent.

Afro-Latin American Customs in Colonial Latin America

Whereas indigenous law has been the object of ample research, at least with respect to Spanish America, the literature has yet to ask questions regarding the presence of African law in the Iberian empires' American colonies. The current assumption among historians of both Spanish and Portuguese America is that enslaved Afro-Latin Americans lacked opportunities to exercise their laws and that those who achieved freedom mostly sought to integrate into colonial society by, among other things, abandoning their distinct traditions.[87] However, colonial documentation often demonstrates the persistence among Afro-Latin Americans of a wide

85 On these issues, see also P. Cardim, "Os povos indígenas, a dominação colonial e as instâncias de justiça na América portguesa e espanhola," in Â. Domingues, M. L. Chaves de Resende, and P. Cardim (eds.), *Os indígenas e as justiças no mundo ibero-americano (sécs. XVI–XIX)* (Lisbon: Universidade de Lisboa, 2019), 29–84, at 55, 58–59, and 65–67. These reforms have been studied by many scholars; see, for example, M. Carneiro Cunha and N. Farage, "Caráter da tutela dos índios: origens e metamorfoses," in M. Carneiro Cunha (ed.), *Os Direitos dos Índios: ensaios e documentos* (Rio de Janeiro: Brasiliense, 1987), 103–18; R. H. de Almeida, *O Diretório dos Índios: um projeto de civilização no Brasil do século XVIII* (Brasilia: Editora Universidade de Brasília, 1997); Â. Domingues, *Quando os índios eram vassalos: colonização e relações de poder no norte do Brasil na segnda metade do século XVIII* (Lisbon: Comissão Nacional para as Comemorações dos Descobrimentos Portugueses, 2000); P. Melo Sampaio, "Fronteras de la libertad: Tutela indígena em el directorio pombalino y em la carta regia de 1798," *Boletin Americanista* 64 (2012), 13–23; M. C. Coelho and R. R. Nascimento dos Santos, "'Monstruoso systema (…) intrusa e abusiva jurisdição': O diretório dos índios no discurso dos agentes administrativos coloniais (1777–1798)," *Revista de História* 168 (2013), 100–30, at 103–7; Á. De Araújo Antunes, "As paralelas e o infinito: uma sondagem historiográfica acerca da história da justiça na América portuguesa," *Revista de História* 169 (2013), 21–52, at 50; and Coelho, "O Diretório dos Índios," 123–26.

86 Losada Moreira, "Territoriality, Mixed Marriages, and Politics," 24–26.

87 D. Wheat, *Atlantic Africa and the Spanish Caribbean, 1570–1640* (Durham: University of North Carolina Press, 2016), 216–52; G. C. Machado Cabral, "Normative Orders in a Seaborn Empire: Sources of Law in Portuguese America (16th–18th Centuries)," unpublished paper presented at the Seminaire "Franco-Brazilian Chair of Legal History," 31 May 2021.

variety of African legal practices, originating in different groups and areas, or sometimes developed in colonial cities in Africa where enslaved persons could spend years before they were sent to the Americas (on these issues, see Section 1.4). One of the elements that can be traced to specific regions in Africa is the use in colonial Latin America of rituals of divination and ordeals to decide who committed a crime or to discover stolen goods. In these instances, spiritual specialists functioned as judges in settings comparable to trials.[88] Similarly, social problems, including what was considered social deviance, could be solved by using a "cult of affliction," which involved communicating with spirits said to both cause the problem and be in a position to solve it.[89] These rites justified many of the powers held by leaders and explained why their instructions were followed. It is also possible that the formation of colonial families was greatly influenced both by a particular African definition of family and by their openness to integrate outsiders, including former enslaved persons or their offspring, into them. This likely also affected experiences how and when freedom could be achieved, and what it entailed.[90] Afro-Latin Americans, in other words, used as well as manipulated their multifaceted heritage to cope with slavery as well as with living in a colonial society.[91]

There is also reason to believe that specifically African legal notions might have operated in maroon communities, where escaped enslaved persons and freed Afro-Latin Americans created new political, social, and judicial structures, and followed their own norms. Though we still know very little about how these communities operated, there are plenty of indications that they were led by specific individuals or kin groups, who managed them as true

88 J. H. Sweet, *Recreating Africa: Culture, Kinship, and Religion in the African-Portuguese World, 1441–1770* (Chapel Hill: University of North Carolina Press, 2003), 119–37 and 228–30. See also J. C. Bristol, *Christians, Blasphemers, and Witches: Afro-Mexican Ritual Practices in the Seventeenth Century* (Albuquerque: University of New Mexico Press, 2007). It is possible that these dynamics continued into the nineteenth and twentieth centuries: R. W. Slenes, "Like Forest Hardwoods: Jongueiros *Cumba* in the Central-African Slave Quarters," in P. Meira Monteiro and M. Stone (eds.), *Cangoma Calling. Spirits and Rhythms of Freedom in Brazilian Jongo Slavery Songs* (Dartmouth: University of Massachusetts, 2013), 49–64, at 55.

89 R. W. Slenes, "L'arbre *nsanda* replanté. Cultes d'affliction kongo et identité des esclaves de plantation dans le Brésil du sud-est (1810–1888)," *Cahiers du Brésil Contemporain* 67–68 (2007), 217–313.

90 H. M. Mattos de Castro, *Das cores do silêncio: os significados da libertade no sudeste escravista, Brasil século XIX* (Rio de Janeiro: Arquivo Nacional, 1993), 162–63. Though this study focuses on the nineteenth century, there is no reason to assume that the colonial period was different.

91 R. W. Slenes, *Na senzala, uma flor: esperanças e recordações na formação da família escrava. Brasil Sudeste, século XIX* (Rio de Janeiro: Editora Nova Fronteira, 1999), 148.

"republics."[92] At least, both the Spanish and the Portuguese believed such was the case and treated maroon leaders as "governors" who controlled both people and territory. According to the colonial sources' portrayal, these leaders had power over subjects, distributed work, and administered criminal justice, either personally or through judges. Many maroon communities seem to have had norms distinguishing members from outsiders, as well as procedures for accommodating and integrating newcomers.

Of course, we do not know if these legal arrangements were based on European, indigenous, or African notions, or perhaps some combination of them all, but it is hard to imagine that the African heritage of the communities' leaders or members, most particularly in the first generations, did not affect their choices.[93] A number of historians have suggested this might have been the case, pointing to similarities between what transpired in maroon communities and normative systems in some parts of Africa.[94] For example, ritual behavior that recognized subjection to local leaders identified as kings, such as prostration at their feet or applauding, was common in Congo and Angola, and has also been reported for maroon communities in Ibero-America. Equally striking is the presence in some maroon communities of African *kilombo*, a custom that enabled the social, religious, political, and perhaps also legal integration of younger males by mandating their temporary separation from the community in order to prepare them to become warriors and full community members. It is also clear that African linguistic

92 F. dos Santos Gomes and H. S. Gledhill, "A 'Safe Heaven': Runaway Slaves, Mocambos, and Borders in Colonial Amazonia, Brazil," *Hispanic American Historical Review* 82(3) (2002), 469–98, at 488; J. G. Landers, "Cimarrón and Citizen: African Ethnicity, Corporate Identity, and the Evolution of Free Black Towns in the Spanish Circum-Caribbean," in J. G. Landers and B. M. Robinson (eds.), *Slaves, Subjects, and Subversives: Blacks in Colonial Latin America* (Albuquerque: University of New Mexico Press, 2006), 111–45; S. Hunold Lara, "Marronnage et pouvoir colonial: Palmares, Cucaú et les frontières de la liberté au Pernambuc à la fin du XVIIe siècle," *Annales HSS* 62(3) (2007), 639–62; C. Beatty-Medina, "Caught between Rivals: The Spanish-African Maroon Competition for Captive Indian Labor in the Region of Esmeraldas during the Late Sixteenth and Early Seventeenth Centuries," *The Americas* 63(1) (2006), 113–36; C. Beatty-Medina, "Between the Cross and the Sword: Religious Conquest and Maroon Legitimacy in Colonial Esmeraldas," in S. K. Bryant, R. S. O'Toole, and B. Vinson III (eds.), *Africans to Spanish America: Expanding the Diaspora* (Urbana Champaign: University of Illinois Press, 2012), 95–113, at 97; S. Hunold Lara, "Com fé, lei e rei: um sobado africano em Pernamuco no século XVII," in F. Gomes (ed.), *Mocambos de Palmares. História e fontes (séc. XVI–XIX)* (Rio de Janeiro: Viveiros de Castro Editora, 2010), 100–18; and A. C. Viotti, "Revisitar Palmares: histórias de um mocambo do Brasil colonial," *Trashumante. Revista Americana de Historia Social* 10 (2017), 78–99, at 83 and 90–91.

93 H. L. Bennett, *Colonial Blackness: A History of Afro-Mexico* (Bloomington: Indiana University Press, 2009), 105, calls upon us to remember generational differences as well as change over time.

94 Hunold Lara, "Marronnage et pouvoir colonial," 647 and 652–53.

elements were present in many maroon communities, and it seems reasonable to assume that these also communicated values and concepts, including some pertaining to the law.

Afro-Latin Americans living in maroon communities could both rely on normative knowledge obtained before enslavement and utilize what they had learned after they had been captured while waiting for the ships in African ports; second-generation enslaved persons could gather information from newcomers, or they could depend on diasporic customs that evolved in the Americas.[95] Yet, most historians warn us against concluding that maroon communities were true African states where renegades sought to revive African traditions, as some have argued. Clearly, these communities were new creations in which new African diasporic customs – with roots in multiple locations and social or ethnic groups – might have emerged, and where a diversity of customs of African origin came into intense contact with Iberian and possibly also indigenous legal traditions.[96]

Customs: European, Indigenous, and Afro-Latin American Entanglements

It is therefore fair to say that, though indigenous peoples clearly had their own laws before Europeans invaded the continent, as did Afro-Latin Americans before they endured enslavement, during the colonial period these normativities underwent dramatic transformations. These substantial and dynamic changes mean that, while colonial documentation can help us to imagine the precolonial indigenous order (see Chapter 2) and to explain what transpired during the colonial period (and may even, on occasion, illuminate what occurred during the nineteenth and twentieth centuries), it cannot give us definitive answers as to what originated from where. Like all normativities, indigenous and African laws changed over time, but in addition, they were also greatly modified by the intense dialogue with other legal traditions,

95 On some of these issues, though focusing on the nineteenth century, see M. Dias Paes, "Ser dependente no Império do Brasil: terra e trabalho em processos judiciais," *Población & Sociedad* 27(2) (2020), 8–29, at 13–16 and 21–24; and M. Dias Paes, "Direito e escravidão no Brasil Império: Quais caminhos podemos seguir?," in M. Duarte Dantas and S. Barbosa (eds.), *Constituição de poderes, constituição de sujeitos: caminhos da História do Direito no Brasil (1750–1930)* (São Paulo: Universidade de São Paulo, 2021), 182–203. On the shared legal culture of Portuguese posts in Africa and Brazil, see M. Dias Paes, "Shared Atlantic Legal Culture: The Case of a Freedom Suit in Benguela," *Atlantic Studies: Global Currents* 17(3) (2020), 419–40.

96 R. W. Slenes, "'Malungu, ngoma vem!' África coberta e descoberta no Brasil," *Revista USP* 12 (1991–1992), 48–67; R. S. O'Toole, "To be Free and Lucumí. Ana de la Calle and Making African Diaspora Identities in Colonial Peru," in Bryant, O'Toole and Vinson, *Africans to Spanish America*, 73–92; Beatty-Medina, "Between the Cross."

regardless of whether this dialogue was imposed (as many have rightly observed) or voluntary, and regardless of asymmetries in power relations.

More easily traceable in the Spanish territories, but most likely to some degree also taking place in Portuguese America, processes of change, hybridization, translation, concretization, and reinvention had their local and group particularities, yet they also shared much in common with similar processes transpiring elsewhere in the Iberian world. On both sides of the ocean, in both Spanish and Portuguese territories, communal authorities – but also outsiders, such as the central authorities in the Peninsula or the colonizers in America – sought to identify, control, and change the customary law. By pronouncing what this law included and, on occasion, by writing it down, multiple agents confirmed both the existence of local variations, which they identified as "customary," and the importance of a common framework.

Indigenous and Afro-Latin Americans, of course, also greatly contributed to the formation of colonial law – not only by inserting their own customs, but also by engaging with European Spanish and Portuguese law. They did so as authorities endowed with jurisdiction and as individuals in their daily activities or in court. Their contributions to the development of colonial law of European origin cannot be overestimated. Interpretations of European law by local actors introduced a huge variety of new understandings and customs – perhaps not necessarily of indigenous or African origin, but nonetheless colonial (see Sections 1.3 and 1.4 and Chapter 2). Indigenous litigants and agents, for example, redefined the meaning and extent of their status as protected individuals.[97] They extended the use of entailed estates to cover situations in which indigenous leaders argued for historical rights to land based on their nobility. These and other actions led to the development of a corpus of jurisprudence regarding indigenous leadership positions (*cacicazgo*) that relied on European debates and notions but took them in novel directions. Some indigenous individuals gained sufficient literacy to intervene in Spanish courts on behalf of their communities, pushing for solutions that used Spanish terminology and Spanish frameworks, yet promoted new ideas.[98] Freed

97 C. Cunill, "Philip II and Indigenous Access to Royal Justice: Considering the Process of Decision-Making in the Spanish Empire," *Colonial Latin American Review* 24(4) (2015), 505–24; and A. Dueñas, "Indian Colonial Actors in the Lawmaking of the Spanish Empire in Peru," *Ethnohistory* 65(1) (2018), 51–73.

98 The literature on these questions is enormous. I found the following particularly useful: S. J. Stern, *Peru's Indian Peoples and the Challenge of Spanish Conquest: Huamanga to 1640* (Madison: The University of Wisconsin Press, 1982); B. P. Owensby, *Empire of Law and Indian Justice in Colonial Mexico* (Stanford: Stanford University Press, 2008); S. Belmessous (ed.), *Native Claims: Indigenous Law against Empire 1500–1920* (Oxford and New York: Oxford University Press, 2011); K. Burns,

Afro-Latin Americans did the same, arguing against their discrimination, for example, by advancing different interpretations of what being worthy of the rights and duties of vassals, Spaniards, or Portuguese, meant.[99] Particularly fascinating is the contribution of enslaved persons who, by appealing to the courts, greatly affected the meaning of the legal concepts of both slavery and freedom. They did so by using legal arguments to claim a space between one status and the other, by living as free despite their status as enslaved persons, and by following practices that allowed them to gradually free themselves.[100] These contributions not only clarified what the different statuses were, they also brought about new ideas regarding the obligations and rights of different members of society.

In addition to colonized indigenous individuals' contributions to and entanglements with colonial law, indigenous law also existed side-by-side with colonial law. This was the case in indigenous communities that maintained their autonomy and independence during the colonial period, including those inhabiting much of the Southern Cone as well as the Chocó and Amazon regions. These communities continued to use their own laws, laws that until the present have not been sufficiently studied. From records produced by the Spanish and the Portuguese when they attempted to befriend or enter into alliances with these groups, it is evident that Europeans generally failed to appreciate the diverse legal traditions of these independent communities, believing instead that European law should apply because, according to them, it had universal validity.[101]

"Making Indigenous Archives: The Quilcaycamayoc of Colonial Cuzco," *Hispanic American Historical Review* 91(4) (2011), 665–89; and J. Charles, "'More *Ladino* than Necessary': Indigenous Litigants and the Language Policy Debate in Mid-Colonial Peru," *Colonial Latin American Review* 16(1) (2007), 23–47.

99 See, for example, M. Dantas, "Humble Slaves and Royal Vassals: Free Africans and Their Descendants in Eighteenth-Century Minas Gerais, Brazil," in A. B. Fisher and M. D. O'Hara (eds.), *Imperial Subjects: Race and Identity in Colonial Latin America* (Durham: Duke University Press, 2009), 115–40; and T. Herzog, "The Colonial Expansion and the Making of Nations: The Spanish Case," in C. Carmichael, M. D'Auria, and A. Roshwald (eds.), *Cambridge History of Nationhood and Nationalism* (Cambridge: Cambridge University Press, 2022), vol 1, 145–62.

100 A. de la Fuente, "Slaves and the Creation of Legal Rights in Cuba: Coartación and Papel," *Hispanic American Historical Review* 87(4) (2007), 659–92; M. McKinley, *Fractional Freedoms: Slavery, Intimacy and Legal Mobilization in Colonial Lima, 1600–1700* (Cambridge: Cambridge University Press, 2016); and A. Chira, *Patchwork Freedoms: Law, Slavery, and Race beyond Cuba's Plantations* (Cambridge: Cambridge University Press, 2022).

101 T. Herzog, "Dialoging with Barbarians: What Natives Said and How Europeans Responded in Late-Seventeenth- and Eighteenth-Century Portuguese America," in B. P. Owensby and R. J. Ross (eds.), *Justice in the New World: Negotiating Legal Intelligibility in British, Iberian, and Indigenous America* (New York: New York University Press, 2018), 61–88.

Conclusion: How to Reconstruct Colonial Law

The previous discussion has shown that to understand colonial law, we need to place it in dialogue with European law. We also need to know more about both indigenous American precolonial law and Afro-Latin American law and trace the processes that led to their reinvention under imperial rule. However, though consideration of these longer and larger contexts is vital, so is attention to place, time, and the specific parties involved: We need to explore how these frameworks operated in a particular setting. It is therefore clear that we can neither imagine colonial law as entirely separate and distinct from European law nor simply equate it with royal orders.[102] Neither can we forget the role of normative sources such as juridical discussions, canon law, theology, or customary law. To imagine a *derecho indiano* that was particularly Spanish, to envision a distinct Portuguese colonial law, or to separate royal decision-making from the principles that it sought to implement, is to give life to a strawman.

These findings enable us to assess the validity of the various methods by which historians have previously tried to reconstruct colonial law (see Section 1.1). Studying the royal decrees, as many have done in the past, is of course possible, but only if we take into account that these were jurisdictional acts that reflected not only royal objectives or social, economic, and political interests (as has often been asserted) but also normative debates. Examining what the various *Recopilaciones* included is equally plausible, but it requires bearing in mind that these compilations were indexes or summaries, and that the fragments they reproduced were taken out of context, might not have been cited correctly, and lacked references to the debates that led to their enactment. Studying Solórzano is a must, but this, too, can be done only as long as one recalls that his work, like the *Siete Partidas* in the thirteenth century, was no more than an attempt – ingenious, informed, and logical, yet still only a suggestion – as to how to fit a pan-European *ius commune* to the demands of place and time. Interrogating case law is just as important, but this, too, requires considering the juridical debates and disagreements upon which it relied. As Vasco de Quiroga argued already in 1535, listing examples (in his case, solutions adopted by case law or in royal orders) is not the same

102 As recently as 2004, some authors still equated colonial law with royal orders: M. C. Mirow, *Latin American Law: A History of Private Law and Institutions in Spanish America* (Austin: University of Texas Press, 2004), 45–46. On earlier reiterations of these ideas despite recognition of the role not only of written law but also of doctrine, customs, and equity, see C. R. Cutter, *The Legal Culture of Northern New Spain, 1700–1810* (Albuquerque: University of New Mexico Press, 1995), for example, 31–43.

as understanding the principles that governed them. Only by placing all these pieces of evidence of a long-gone juridical past in their early modern legal context will we be able to understand what they tell us.

A Final Word about the Global Context

These characteristics of early modern law operated in colonial Latin America, but – as mentioned throughout this text – they were also typical of Europe. As a result, it is easy to imagine that other European powers that colonized parts of the Americas, Asia, or Africa during the early modern period equally followed them. These powers also asked whether metropolitan law could be implemented in the colonies and how it must be adapted to colonial conditions. They discussed whether it was advisable and/or possible to incorporate indigenous law and how to distinguish what of the latter could be integrated from what must be rejected. While many similarities are evident, the biggest difficulty in inserting Latin American narratives into the larger story of law and European colonialism is not that the various imperial pasts were different, but the huge differences in the relevant historiographical traditions, which focus on different questions and use different methodologies. Scholars of colonial North America, for example, have concentrated on understanding the laws that applied to settlers, traditionally saying relatively little about other normativities, which they sometimes assumed were in some profound way external to the colonial legal system.[103] The literature on New France largely follows this approach, though it is somewhat more open to recognizing the existence of indigenous communities and their laws.[104] Meanwhile, the most recent literature on Portuguese colonialism in Asia and Africa has been particularly focused on recuperating a colonial law that was neither European nor indigenous, but extremely entangled.[105] These studies narrate,

103 For example, A. M. Plane, *Colonial Intimacies: Indian Marriage in Early New England* (Ithaca: Cornell University Press, 2018); and T. A. Midtrød, *The Memory of All Ancient Customs: Native American Diplomacy in the Colonial Hudson Valley* (Ithaca: Cornell University Press, 2012).

104 See, for example, H. Dewar, *Disputing New France: Companies, Law and Sovereignty in the French Atlantic, 1598–1663* (Montreal: McGill-Queens University Press, 2022); and B. Rushforth, *Bonds of Alliance: Indigenous and Atlantic Slaveries in New France* (Chapel Hill: University of North Carolina Press, 2012). On how such questions continued to be invoked even in the twentieth century, see, for example, K. E. Hoffman, "Berber Law by French Means: Customary Courts in the Moroccan Hinterlands, 1930–1956," *Comparative Studies in Society and History* 52(4) (2010), 851–80.

105 For example, Madeira Santos, "Entre deux droits" and "Esclavage africain"; Â. Barreto Xavier, *A invenção de Goa: Poder imperial e conversões culturais nos séculos XVI e VII* (Lisbon: Imprensa de Ciências Sociais, 2008); C. Nogueira da Silva, *A construção jurídica dos territórios ultramarinos portugueses no século XIX: Modelos, doutrinas e leis* (Lisbon: Imprensa

for example, how Portuguese law interacted with African and Asian laws in Portuguese enclaves (such as Angola or Goa, for example), and with what results, and how the authorities and residents of these locations responded. They highlight not only important commonalities but also the prevalence of local norms.

Given these historiographical differences, it is currently impossible to productively compare the legal experiences of colonizers and colonized in the different European powers' overseas territories. Indeed, where such a comparison has been attempted, the results, by repeating what the existing literature described without subjecting it to critical examination, have often reified the differences rather than the commonalities between different colonial experiences, or have focused on what transpired during the colonial period, without necessarily understanding the principles that enabled it.[106] Thus, although scholars working on European colonialism in Latin America and elsewhere have asked many important questions regarding colonial law, we still have much to ask, learn, and understand.

. . .

3.2 Religious Normativity for Colonial Empires

THOMAS DUVE

Many legal histories of colonial Latin America begin with the bulls issued by Alexander VI in May of 1493. A member of the notorious Borgia family, and born near Valencia, he granted special rights and duties to the so-called Catholic Kings in relation to territories known today as Latin America and the Caribbean.[107] Modeled on previous privileges granted to the Portuguese

de Ciências Sociais, 2017); J. Flores, *Unwanted Neighbours: The Mughals, the Portuguese and Their Frontier Zones* (New Delhi: Oxford University Press, 2018); Hespanha, *Filhos da terra*; and M. Bastias Saavreda (ed.), *Norms beyond Empire. Law-Making and Local Normativities in Iberian Asia, 1500–1800* (Leiden: Brill, 2022).

106 For example, J. H. Elliott, *Empires of the Atlantic World: Britain and Spain in America, 1492–1830* (New Haven: Yale University Press, 2006).

107 On the bulls and how they were modeled on the preceding bulls granted to Portugal, see the still foundational studies of A. García-Gallo, "Las bulas de Alejandro VI y el ordenamiento jurídico de la expansión portuguesa y castellana en África e Indias," *Anuario de Historia del Derecho Español* 27–28 (1957–1958), 461–829. For a general overview over the legal instruments, the institutional framework, and the main ideas of the evangelization and the history of the Church, see the various chapters in P. Borges (ed.), *Historia de la Iglesia en Hispanoamérica y Filipinas (siglos XV–XIX), vol. I: Aspectos generales* (Madrid: Biblioteca de Autores Cristianos, 1992). Many papal privileges have

Crown and to the Portuguese Order of Christ for expansion (*extra territorium*) along the African coast and into Asia, these bulls were based on the idea that the pope exercised *dominium* over the entire world. To substantiate this claim, the papacy could draw on a century-old juridical debate about the rights of the pope, the legal status of non-Christians, and the legitimacy of war, the so-called *bellum iustum*.[108] While the Treaty of Tordesillas, concluded between the Portuguese and Spanish Crowns in 1494, did introduce some changes, it was based on the same foundation, followed medieval juridical practices, and was confirmed by Pope Julius II in 1506.[109] Spreading the gospel, missionizing *infideles*, as well as developing, sustaining, and protecting the Church thus became a central justification for the Iberian empires' imperial politics. For centuries, and notwithstanding the famous debates about the juridical titles of the Spanish Crown triggered by Francisco de Vitoria and other theologians from the School of Salamanca, both empires claimed the papal donation as the primary legitimation of their imperial rule in the Americas, the Caribbean, and the Pacific.[110]

been printed in collections such as Cyriaci Morelli, *Fasti Novi Orbis et ordinationum apostolicarum ad Indias pertinentium breviarium cum adnotationibus* (Venice: Antonium Zatta, 1776); P. F. J. Hernáez, *Colección de bulas, breves y otros documentos relativos a la Iglesia en América latina y Filipinas* (Vaduz: Kraus Reprint, 1964 [1879]), vol. I; others can be found in R. Konetzke (ed.), *Colección de documentos para la historia de la formación social de Hispanoamérica. 1493–1810* (Madrid: Consejo Superior de Investigaciones Científicas, 1953–1962), 3 vols.; and in J. Metzler, *America Pontificia primi saeculi evangelizationis 1493–1592. Documenta pontificia ex registris et minutis praesertim in Archivo Secreto Vaticano existentibus* (Vatican City: Libreria Editrice Vaticana, 1991), 2 vols.; J. Metzler, *America Pontificia primi saeculi evangelizationis, vol. III: Documenti pontifici nell'Archivio Segreto Vaticano riguardanti l'evangelizzazione dell'America 1592–1644* (Vatican City: Libreria Editrice Vaticana, 1995).

108 On the previous experiences, see F. Fernández-Armesto, *Before Columbus: Exploration and Colonization from the Mediterranean to the Atlantic, 1229–1492* (Philadelphia: University of Pennsylvania Press, 1987); on the tradition in canon law, see J. Muldoon, *Popes, Lawyers, and Infidels: The Church and the Non-Christian World, 1250–1550* (Philadelphia: University of Pennsylvania Press, 1979); J. Muldoon, *The Americas in the Spanish World Order: The Justification for Conquest in the Seventeenth Century* (Philadelphia: University of Pennsylvania Press, 1995).

109 On the Treaty of Tordesillas, see with further references T. Duve, "Spatial Perceptions, Juridical Practices, and Early International Legal Thought Around 1500: From Tordesillas to Saragossa," in S. Kadelbach, T. Kleinlein, and D. Roth-Isigkeit (eds.), *System, Order, and International Law: The Early History of International Legal Thought from Machiavelli to Hegel* (The History and Theory of International Law) (Oxford: Oxford University Press, 2017), 418–42.

110 The literature on these issues is endless. For a good overview of the theories in Spanish, see P. Castañeda Delgado, *La teocracia pontifical en las controversias sobre el Nuevo Mundo* (Instituto de Investigaciones Jurídicas Serie C: Estudios Históricos 59) (Mexico City: Universidad Nacional Autónoma de México, 1996); on the legal problem of *dominium* and the debates in the School of Salamanca, see M. Koskenniemi, *To the Uttermost Parts of the Earth: Legal Imagination and International Power, 1300–1870* (Cambridge: Cambridge University Press, 2021), 117–211.

The fact that European expansion to Latin America and the subsequent empire-building was legitimized with reference to papal bulls – not to mention that the harshest criticism of this legitimation came from theologians – points to the importance of religion for the legal history of Latin America. Even more than in the European territories, the kings of Spain and Portugal saw themselves as patrons of the Catholic Church in their overseas dominions, and thus they felt obliged to foster missionary activities and act as protectors of the Church. If the idea of a *Respublica Christiana* was deeply rooted in medieval political theory and had already legitimized the war against the Arabs on the Iberian Peninsula during the High Middle Ages, the entitlement to christianize the so-called infidels in the Americas made it a guiding principle of the entire colonial enterprise.[111]

However, it was not only the religious legitimation of the expansion as such or the patronage of the kings over the Church that made religion a central facet of colonial rule. Religious symbols, language, and practices – that is, knowledge of normativity from the religious sphere (see Section 1.3) – shaped everyday life. Sacraments structured one's life from birth to death. Catalogs of sins and virtues contained norms for behavior, confession was a regular practice, and religious celebrations were essential elements of urban and rural conviviality. Long before they ever crossed paths with a jurist or a Crown official, many indigenous peoples had already encountered and, in many cases, lived amongst missionaries and priests. Through religious precepts and prohibitions – in catechesis, in the confessional, in school, in images, in pictographs, in performances like processions, and in choral singing – indigenous peoples, Afro-Latin Americans, and Asian Americans learned the language and the culture of the European colonizers. They were introduced to what Christian faith presented as good and evil, just and unjust, permissible and impermissible. Sexual behavior, marital practices, and food consumption were all subject to and regulated by religious norms. Moreover, many cultural and social categories stemmed from religion and established social and political hierarchies. Whether one was classified as a neophyte, as an old or

111 The importance of religion for the early modern Iberian empires, their law, and imperial governance has been emphasized by Spanish and Portuguese legal historians, most notably by B. Clavero, *Usura. Del uso económico de la religión en la historia* (Colección Derecho, Cultura y Sociedad) (Madrid: Tecnos, 1984); A. M. Hespanha, *As vésperas do Leviathan. Instituições e Poder Político. Portugal – séc. XVII* (Coimbra: Almedina, 1994), 227–58; C. A. Garriga Acosta, "Sobre el gobierno de la justicia en Indias (Siglos XVI–XVII)," *Revista de Historia del Derecho* 34 (2006), 67–160. For a study of the *Respublica Christiana* as a guiding principle of governance in colonial Mexico, see for example, A. Lempérière, *Entre Dieu et le Roi, la République. Mexico, XVIe–XIXe siècles* (Histoire 65) (Paris: Belles Lettres, 2004).

new Christian, was a member of the clergy, or was granted privileges and dispensations, had a profound impact on one's opportunities in life.[112] Church courts presided over cases concerning marital violence, alimony claims, and even crimes. Because ecclesiastical institutions provided loans and sometimes partook in large business enterprises, some disputes taken to the ecclesiastical courts involved substantial amounts of money. Religion also influenced and shaped secular law: Punishment could be more lenient if one was considered a good Christian, and what was just or unjust was determined according to the precepts of religion and with the help of the doctrines of moral theology.[113] Bishops, religious orders, ecclesiastical judges, confessors, confraternities,

112 Most studies on the emergence of racial and social classifications point to the importance of religion and Church institutions for the negotiation and classification, for example, N. von Germeten, *Black Blood Brothers: Confraternities and Social Mobility for Afro-Mexicans* (The History of African American Religions) (Gainesville: University Press of Florida, 2006); H. L. Bennett, *Colonial Blackness: A History of Afro-Mexico* (Blacks in the Diaspora) (Bloomington and Indianapolis: Indiana University Press, 2009); J. F. Cobo Betancourt, *Mestizos heraldos de Dios. La ordenación de sacerdotes descendientes de españoles e indígenas en el Nuevo Reino de Granada y la racialización de la diferencia, 1573–1590* (Colección Cuadernos Coloniales) (Bogotà: Instituto Colombiano de Antropolgía e Historia, 2012); J. Rappaport, *The Disappearing Mestizo: Configuring Difference in the Colonial New Kingdom of Granada* (Durham and London: Duke University Press, 2014); B. Premo, *The Enlightenment on Trial: Ordinary Litigants and Colonialism in the Spanish Empire* (New York: Oxford University Press, 2017); R. S. O'Toole, *Bound Lives: Africans, Indians, and the Making of Race in Colonial Peru* (Pittsburgh: University of Pittsburgh Press, 2012); R. C. Schwaller, *Géneros de Gente in Early Colonial Mexico: Defining Racial Difference* (Norman: University of Oklahoma Press, 2016); S. B. Schwartz, *Blood and Boundaries: The Limits of Religious and Racial Exclusion in Early Modern Latin America* (Waltham: Brandeis University Press, 2020). On the role of the Church and religious orders in the formation of the slave society in Brazil, for example, see C. A. de Moura Ribeiro Zeron, *Linha de Fé. A Companhia de Jesus e a Escravidão no Processo de Formação da Sociedade Colonial (Brasil, Séculos XVI e XVII)* (São Paulo: EDUSP, 2011); C. A. Zeron, "O governo dos escravos nas Constituições Primeiras do Arcebispado da Bahia e na legislação portuguesa: separação e complementaridade entre pecado e delito," in B. Feitler and E. Sales Souza (eds.), *A Igreja no Brasil. Normas e Práticas durante a Vigência das Constituições Primeiras do Arcebispado da Bahia* (São Paulo: Editora Unifesp, 2011), 323–54; C. de Castelnau-L'Éstoile, "'Os filhos obedientes da Santíssima Igreja.' Escravidão e estratégias de casamento no Rio de Janeiro do início do século XVIII," in M. Cottias and H. Mattos (eds.), *Escravidão e subjetividades. No Atlântico luso-brasileiro e francês (séculos XVII–XX)* (Marseille: OpenEdition Press, 2016). On *mestizaje*, specifically from the perspective of canon law regulation, see P. Castañeda Delgado, *El mestizaje en Indias. Problemas canónicos* (Madrid: Editorial Deimos, 2008); on indigenous peoples and the ecclesiastical courts, see J. E. Traslosheros and A. de Zaballa Beascoechea (eds.), *Los indios ante los foros de justicia religiosa en la Hispanoamérica virreinal* (Mexico City: Universidad Nacional Autónoma de México, 2010); on the concept of "neophyte," see T. Duve, "Derecho canónico y la alteridad indígena: los indios como neófitos," in W. Oesterreicher and R. Schmidt-Riese (eds.), *Esplendores y miserias de la evangelización de América. Antecedentes europeos y alteridad indígena* (Pluralisierung & Autorität 22) (Berlin and New York: De Gruyter, 2010), 73–94.

113 See T. Herzog, *Upholding Justice: Society, State, and the Penal System in Quito (1650–1750)* (Ann Arbor: University of Michigan Press, 2004); and the case study by A. Agüero,

and many other institutions of the Church ceaselessly produced knowledge of normativity via ecclesiastical courts, at synods and councils, through ordinances, statutes, catechesis, preaching, counseling, and in the confessional.

Even in the late eighteenth century – when the influence of the Church in many places was on the wane, the Jesuits were expelled, and Enlightenment thinking questioned the role of religion – public discourse and the law remained profoundly shaped by religious semantics. After independence, "political catechisms" served to teach the new citizens the ten commandments of the republic, symbolizing the ambivalent secularization of religious forms under the conditions of modern states.[114] More than a few states declared themselves "Catholic" nations, and some constitutions have retained privileges for the Catholic Church to this day. The fact that the Catholic Church, and increasingly other Christian confessions, played an important role in political life in the twentieth century shows the long-lasting effects of the religious dimension of Iberian imperial politics (see Chapter 4 and Sections 5.1 and 6.2).

All of this has not gone unnoticed. Since Robert Ricard wrote about the *conquête spirituelle* almost a century ago, scholars have been very aware of the importance of religion, especially for building up colonial society.[115] Yet in the literature on legal history, very few references to canon law and moral theology are found, or to the importance of secular clergy and religious orders. Even less common are references to the role of the Roman Curia and to globally active religious orders. This lack of attention is probably due to the legalistic character of both the historiography on the so-called *Derecho indiano* and Portuguese colonial legal history, and their focus on state institutions. Just as the theory of the *patronato* – and later *vicariato* – placed the monarchy above the Church, Church institutions and thus knowledge of normativity from the religious sphere seemed to have been absorbed by secular institutions and law.[116] However, this has

Castigar y perdonar cuando conviene a la República. La justicia penal de Córdoba de Tucumán, siglos XVII y XVIII (Historia de la Sociedad Política) (Madrid: Centro de Estudios de Políticos y Constitucionales, 2008).

114 See, for example, R. Sagredo Baeza, "Actores políticos en los catecismos patriotas y republicanos americanos, 1810–1827," *HMex XLV* 3 (1996), 501–38.

115 R. Ricard, *The Spiritual Conquest of Mexico: An Essay on the Apostolate and the Evangelizing Methods of the Mendicant Orders in New Spain, 1523–1572*, trans. L. B. Simpson (Berkeley and Los Angeles: University of California Press, 1966 [1933]).

116 Most of the literature on the relations between Church and state until the 1990s was written from this perspective. Although in the meantime the perspective has changed considerably, much of this literature still contains valuable information, for example, J. M. García Añoveros, *La Monarquía y la Iglesia en América* (La Corona y los pueblos americanos 6) (Valencia: Asociación Francisco Lopez de Gomara, 1990); I. Sánchez Bella, *Iglesia y Estado en la América Española* (Pamplona: Ediciones Universidad de Navarra, 1990);

all started to change as a result of new interpretations on the role of religion in early modern Iberian (legal) history, understanding colonial society in terms of a jurisdictional culture based on ideas of material justice deeply rooted in Christian discourse (see Sections 1.1, 1.2, and 3.1), and in no small part due to the research findings of cultural and social history. Legal historians are beginning to discover the role of institutions such as charitable confraternities, church courts, synods, and provincial councils for legal history.

Notwithstanding these developments, the way these institutions operated and the knowledge they built upon is not easy to understand. There are only a handful of introductions to the history of canon law dedicated to the early modern period, and even fewer to Latin America. Research on the history of mission and (moral) theology is often unknown to legal historians. Therefore, this section aims to provide some basic information about the bodies of knowledge of normativity from the religious sphere, about techniques of localizing canon law, and the institutional framework within which actors moved. It assumes that legal history can best be understood as a huge process of translation of knowledge of normativity, as explained in Section 1.3, and thus provides introductory information about the institutions – or "epistemic communities" – that produced knowledge of normativity relevant for the religious sphere, as well as on the knowledge of normativity from the religious sphere as such.

Though other religions were of course present in Latin America, this Section's focus is on the Catholic Church. Indigenous peoples, Afro-Latin Americans, and Asian Americans brought to the Americas as captives or enslaved persons, as well as people of Jewish ancestry, practiced their religions and followed the laws and precepts of their beliefs in the Americas.[117]

P. Castañeda Delgado and J. Marchena Fernández, *La jerarquía de la Iglesia en Indias. El episcopado americano, 1500–1850* (Colección Iglesia Católica en el Nuevo Mundo 9) (Madrid: Editorial MAPFRE, 1992); A. de la Hera, "El patronato y el vicariato regio en Indias," in P. Borges (ed.), *Historia de la Iglesia en Hispanoamérica y Filipinas (siglos XV–XIX), vol. I: Aspectos generales* (Madrid: Biblioteca de Autores Cristianos, 1992), 63–79; C. Maqueda Abreu, *Estado, Iglesia e Inquisición en Indias. Un permanente conflicto* (Madrid: Centro de Estudios Políticos y Constitucionales, 2000). For a survey of early modern canonists' perspective, see A. González-Varas Ibañez, "Derecho de patronato," in T. Duve and P. Mejía (eds.), *Diccionario Histórico de Derecho Canónico en Hispanoamerica y Filipinas, Siglo XVI–XVIII (DCH)*, https://dch.hypotheses.org/.

117 A succinct overview of Afro-American religions and their relationships to the Catholic faith can be found in J. Bristol, "The Church, Africans, and Slave Religion in Latin America," in V. Garrard-Burnett, P. Freston, and S. C. Dove (eds.), *The Cambridge History of Religions in Latin America* (New York: Cambridge University Press, 2016), 198–206; on cryptojudaism, see A. A. Faria de Assis, *Macabeias da Colônia. Criptojudaísmo feminino na Bahia* (São Paulo: Alameda, 2012); for insights into religious dissidents in

Despite severe immigration controls, even some Protestants came to the Americas starting in the sixteenth century, and their numbers increased with the acceleration of trade in the late eighteenth century. However, as indigenous religions, crypto-Judaists, and Protestants were persecuted, and non-Catholic religious practices classified as superstition, their impact on public life was limited. Similarly, while Protestant communities in Dutch Brazil even held a synod in 1642, their presence between 1621 and 1654 ultimately remained an interlude.[118] This is why the focus of the following analysis is on the bodies of knowledge of normativity stemming from the Catholic Church. Within this context, the oldest and richest repository of knowledge of normativity was the *ius canonicum*, that is, the law of the Catholic Church. Without some basic information about canon law, it is neither possible to understand the administration of justice in the Church nor the emergence of moral theology as a powerful second layer of knowledge of normativity in the sixteenth century.

The Repository of Knowledge of Normativity: Universal Canon Law

Canon law goes back to the beginnings of the Church and consisted over the course of the first few centuries primarily of texts by Church fathers, constitutions of Church councils, and fragments from Scripture.[119] Soon, papal responses to inquiries in legal matters (so-called decretals) and, since the eleventh century, canon law scholars furthered its development. With the mass of authoritative statements growing continuously, scholars, bishops, and later the

colonial Brazil, see C. A. Myscofski, *Amazons, Wives, Nuns, and Witches: Women and the Catholic Church in Colonial Brazil, 1500–1822* (Louann Atkins Temple Women & Culture 32) (Austin: University of Texas Press, 2013); for a wide range of studies on institutions and practices of control, see Yllan de Mattos, P. Gouveia Mendonça Muniz, A. A. Faria de Assis, and A. C. Rodrigues (eds.), *Edificar e Transgredir: Clero, Religiosidade e Inquisição no espaço ibero-americano (séculos XVI–XIX)* (Jundiaí: Paco Editorial, 2016).

118 On the Church in Dutch Brazil, see F. L. Schalkwijk, *Igreja e Estado no Brasil Holandês (1630 a 1654)* (São Paulo: Soc. Religiosa Ed. Vida Nova, 1989).

119 For a general introduction to the history of canon law, see M.A. Eichbauer and J.A. Brundage, *Medieval Canon Law*, 2nd ed. (New York: Longman Group Limited, 2022); A. Winroth and J. C. Wei, *The Cambridge History of Medieval Canon Law* (Cambridge: Cambridge University Press, 2022); R. H. Helmholz, *The Spirit of Classical Canon Law* (The Spirit of the Laws) (Athens: University of Georgia Press, 1996); G. Le Bras, C. Lefebvre, and J. Rambaud, *L'âge classique. 1140–1378. Sources et théorie du droit* (Histoire du Droit et des Institutions de l'Eglise en Occident 7) (Paris: Sirey, 1965); C. Lefebvre, M. Pacaut, and L. Chevallier, *L'époque moderne (1563–1789). Les sources du droit et la seconde centralisation romaine* (Paris: Éditions Cujas, 1976), vol. XV; on the modern period C. Fantappiè, *Chiesa romana e modernità giuridica. L'edificazione del sistema canonistico (1563–1903)* (Milan: Giuffrè, 2008), vol. I–II.

Roman Curia selected and integrated parts of this heritage into collections of canons. An important part of this legacy was included in the *Decretum Gratiani* from the first half of the twelfth century and supplemented by the *ius novum*, that is, law from the period of "classical" canon law between the twelfth and mid-fourteenth centuries. In 1234, a part of this new canon law was selected, integrated into a systematic structure, and edited as *Liber extra*, which was a particularly influential, authoritative collection of more recent papal decretals. Other collections eventually followed (*Liber Sextus*, *Clementinae*).

Between the eleventh and fourteenth centuries, scholarship on canon law flourished. Canonists wrote glosses and extensive treatises on specific problems. Their writings enjoyed a high level of authority, not least because in practice papal decretals and even collections required recognition by scholars for their acceptance. Popes sent the collections containing "new law" to universities, where it was up to the scholars to integrate them into their writings and teaching. One consequence of this practice was that the opinion of scholars acquired the status of a source of law. At the beginning of the sixteenth century, a complex body of knowledge of normativity had emerged that was comparable to the so-called *ius civile*, that is, the "civil" or secular law elaborated by medieval jurisprudence based on Roman law. Even if the *ius canonicum* was clearly distinguished from the *ius civile*, together with this and some other bodies of knowledge of normativity, it formed the *ius commune*.[120]

Shortly after 1500, the most important elements of this canon law tradition were compiled by a publisher to form the *Corpus Iuris Canonici*, which, as the designation indicates, was to stand alongside the *Corpus Iuris Civilis*. Many printed editions from the late sixteenth and early seventeenth centuries also included a short textbook modeled on the institutions of Roman law, the *Institutiones Iuris Canonici* by Giovanni Paolo Lancelotti (1522–90). This convergence of the forms was no accident. The relationship between canon and secular law was complex. Though their evolution over the centuries involved constant exchange, they were nevertheless quite distinct. Partly as the result of this co-evolution and mutual interdependence, a popular introduction to the study of law published in Salamanca at the beginning of the seventeenth century compared secular and canon law to a pair of gloves: having just one is of very little use.[121]

120 On the relation between civil and canon law see Section 3.1 in this volume.

121 Francisco Bermúdez de Pedraza, *Arte legal para estudiar la iurisprudencia* (Madrid: Editorial Civitas, 1992 [1612]), "El buen Iurista ha de saber entrambos Derechos: porque son como vn par de guantes, que el vno sin el otro es de poco prouecho: no basta saber el Derecho Ciuil para ser perfecto Iurista, es preciso, que sepa tambien el Canonico…," 59.

Given that the Council of Trent (1545–1563) was marked by the Catholic Church's attempts to counter the Reformation and implement reforms in the Church and the Roman Curia, and bishops from Hispanic America had asked the king in vain for permission to participate, the Council did not explicitly dedicate itself to the mission in Latin America. Nonetheless, important areas of canon law were discussed and further developed, and the decisions of the Council are actually of great relevance to Latin American legal history. The Council took place during a period in which the Church was consolidating its structures in Latin America, and it simultaneously produced both centralizing and pluralizing effects in the Catholic Church at the global level. It both strengthened the centrality of the Roman Curia, for example, by attempting to monopolize the interpretation of canon law through the prohibition of commenting on the Council's canons. At the same time, it fortified the position of local bishops and created the framework for Catholicism as a world religion. In many respects, it was through the provincial councils and synods that Tridentine canon law was translated into Latin American realities.[122]

As part of the attempts to centralize the administration of justice in the realm of the Catholic Church in the aftermath of the Council, an official edition of the *Corpus Iuris Canonici* was produced. This *Editio Romana*, the work of a group of cardinals and scholars known as the *Correctores Romani*, was part of the move to reformulate important normative texts of Church life in the post-Tridentine period. These texts included the *Catechismus Romanus* (1566), the *Breviarium Romanum* (1568), the *Missale Romanum* (1570), the *Pontificale Romanum* (1596), the *Caeremoniale Episcoporum* (1600), and the *Rituale Romanum* (1614). These texts were tools for evangelization and counter-reformation, and they also served as normative foundations for a renewal of the symbolic power of the Catholic Church. The publication of the *Catechismus Romanus* was particularly important for Latin America, as it influenced the numerous catechisms written in the late sixteenth- and throughout the seventeenth century, especially those by provincial councils in Lima and Mexico and by religious congregations. These catechisms were translated into many different indigenous languages. Despite the fact that they are full of rules,

122 S. Ditchfield, "Tridentine Catholicism," in A. Bamji, G. H. Janssen, and M. Laven (eds.), *The Ashgate Research Companion to the Counter-Reformation* (Farnham and Burlington: Ashgate, 2013), 15–31; S. Ditchfield, "De-centering Trent: How 'Tridentine' Was the Making of the First World Religion?," in W. François and V. Soen (eds.), *The Council of Trent: Reform and Controversy in Europe and Beyond (1545–1700), vol. III: Between Artists and Adventurers* (Refo500 Academic Studies 35,3) (Göttingen: Vandenhoeck & Ruprecht, 2018), 185–208.

prohibitions, and commandments, little attention has been paid to them as a source for legal history.[123]

The Council of Trent also brought about important changes in the role of legal scholarship on canon law in the production of knowledge of normativity. At first glance, however, not too much appeared to have changed. Since commentaries on the decrees of the Council of Trent were forbidden, canonists' writings, and to some extent Church practice, followed the structure of the *Liber extra* and, in some cases, in the later period the order of Lancelotti's *Institutiones*. The *Cursus iuris canonici, hispani, et indici* by the Jesuit Pedro Murillo Velarde from the Philippines – printed in 1743, 1763, and 1791 – represented the most comprehensive account of canon law in the Spanish empire and was still based on the order of the *Liber extra*.[124] Some synods and provincial councils also arranged their decisions in accordance with this structure. Thus, medieval canon law had not only shaped the order of knowledge before Trent, it also continued to provide the intellectual structure into which the increasingly specialized proto-national variations and appropriations of universal canon law were integrated.

In a similar vein, the reference to pre-Tridentine authorities remained an important scholarly practice. The general opinion of scholars (*communis opinio doctorum*) and recognized authors (*probati auctores*) were still important sources of law for the practice of canon law in Latin America as well as in Europe. This is why, for example, Gaspar de Villarroel, bishop of Santiago de Chile, pointed

123 On catechisms in Hispanic America, see the collection of J. G. Durán, *Monumenta catechetica hispanoamericana* (Buenos Aires: Facultad de Teología de la Pontificia Universidad Católica Argentina, 1984–2017), 3 vols.; an example for a pictorial catechism is E. Hill Boone, L. M. Burkhart, and D. Tavárez (eds.), *Painted Words: Nahua Catholicism, Politics, and Memory in the Atzaqualco Pictorial Catechism* (Dumbarton Oaks Pre-Columbian Art and Archaeology Studies Series 39) (Dumbarton Oaks: Trustees for Harvard University, 2017); on the translations see L. M. Burkhart, *The Slippery Earth: Nahua-Christian Moral Dialogue in Sixteenth-Century Mexico* (Tucson: University of Arizona Press, 1989); G. Urton, "Sin, Confession, and the Arts of Book- and Cord-Keeping: An Intercontinental and Transcultural Exploration of Accounting and Governmentality," *Comparative Studies in Society and History* 51(4) (2009), 801–31; A. Durston, *Pastoral Quechua: The History of Christian Translation in Colonial Peru, 1550–1650* (South Bend: University of Notre Dame Press, 2007); R. Harrison, *Sin & Confession in Colonial Peru: Spanish Quechua Penitential Texts, 1560–1650* (Austin: University of Texas Press, 2014); especially on the translation of concepts like "sin" for example, L. K. Pharo, "Transfer of Moral Knowledge in Early Colonial Latin America," in H. Wendt (ed.), *The Globalization of Knowledge in the Iberian Colonial World* (Max Planck Research Library for the History and Development of Knowledge: Proceedings 10) (Berlin: Edition Open Access, 2016), 53–94.

124 Pedro Murillo Velarde, *Cursus iuris canonici, Hispani et Indici* (Madrid, 1763), 2 vols.

out in the introduction to his treatise on good governance of the Church in the Indies, the *Govierno eclesiastico pacifico* (1656–1657), that the purpose of his book was to put "a whole library" at the reader's disposal. He did so because he was convinced that a decision could only be reached in a responsible manner if it was based on a thorough examination of the authorities of canon law.[125] A century later, in 1744, Pope Benedict XIV chided the archbishop of Santo Domingo in a response to a practical legal question raised by the archbishop that the *opinio communis doctorum* could not simply be dismissed.[126] The practical need for arguments and orientation in legal matters – perhaps also the interest of the Curia in counteracting the centrifugal tendencies in canon law associated with the formation of what were eventually referred to as "national" Churches – was also served by reference works such as Lucio Ferraris' *Prompta bibliotheca canonica*. First published in 1746 (and many times thereafter), it assembled the opinions of the most relevant scholars on matters of canon law and was organized around hundreds of entries in alphabetical order. These and other, less erudite media served as repositories for the knowledge of normativity required to find the right solution to a specific case. Research on the circulation of books and on holdings of libraries has shown that many of these works were available in Latin America in monasteries, seminaries, and universities.

Notwithstanding this apparent stability of scholarly practices and content, the Council of Trent also introduced important changes. Many of these reforms went into effect in the decades that followed. Most importantly, the Council of Trent sought to monopolize the interpretation of canon law and to centralize the amendment and reform process at the Curia, especially in the newly founded Congregation of the Council. From that point onward, the most important new scholarly books, such as the commentary on the *Liber Extra* by Prospero Fagnani (who was himself active in the Congregation of the Council) or the *Theatrum veritatis et iustitiae* (1669–1673) by Giovanni Battista de Luca, drew primarily on the sentences of the *Rota Romana*, that is, the so-called *decisiones* of the highest court of the Roman Catholic Church. Not least the Congregation *Propaganda Fide*, founded in 1622 to promote evangelization all across the globe, issued numerous regulations that became the basis for the growing missionary law.[127] Its impact, however, was different in

125 Gaspar de Villarroel, *Govierno eclesiastico pacifico* (Madrid, 1656 / 1657), 2 vols.

126 C. H. F. Meyer, "Probati auctores. Ursprünge und Funktionen einer wenig beachteten Quelle kanonistischer Tradition und Argumentation," *Rechtsgeschichte – Legal History* 20 (2012), 138–54.

127 G. Pizzorusso, *Propaganda Fide. La Congregazione Pontificia e la Giurisdizione sulle Missioni* (Rome: Edizioni di Storia e Letteratura, 2022), vol. I.

the Spanish and the Portuguese empires. As the mission in Spanish America had already started and been well developed prior to the foundation of the *Propaganda Fide*, due to the *patronato regio* and the fact that the Tridentine reforms had already been introduced, the Hispanic American territories were not considered to be under the jurisdiction of the Congregation. With regard to Portuguese America, however, the Holy See often considered the *patronato regio* to be ineffective and claimed jurisdiction over these territories, granting authority to the *Propaganda Fide*.[128] In addition to these institutions, a *Nunciatura Apostólica de las Españas* had been created in 1529, replaced in 1769 by the *Tribunal de la Rota de la Nunciatura Apostólica en España*. Both institutions exercised jurisdiction over and continuously created knowledge of normativity for the Spanish empire.[129] These are but a few examples of how the Roman Curia developed institutions and practices for the governance of what was becoming a world religion.

In terms of content, however, not much changed. Canon law most notably contained regulations for the core areas of Church life such as sacramental law, that is, norms on baptism, marriage, the Eucharist, and priestly ordination. It regulated ecclesiastical offices, property law, criminal law, and procedural law. The ecclesiastical judge, that is, the bishop or his delegate in the *forum externum*, decided such cases that were considered *causae spirituales*. The Church also claimed exclusive jurisdiction over several groups of persons, especially over the broad group of persons considered clerics. This competence was characterized as jurisdiction *ratione personarum*. Under specific circumstances, the Church also asserted its jurisdiction in cases of mixed jurisdiction, the so-called *causae mixti fori*, and it insisted on its competence to judge any behavior that constituted a sin (*ratione peccati*). For this reason, one finds in canon law important norms relating to contract or property law, yet each instance of a breach of contract, fraud, or usury constituted a sin and therefore could be tried, according to this doctrine, before an ecclesiastical court.

128 G. Pizzorusso, *Governare le missioni, conoscere il mondo nel XVII secolo. La Congregazione Pontificia de propaganda fide* (Studi di storia delle istituzioni ecclesiastiche 6) (Viterbo: Edizionei Sette Città, 2018); G. Pizzorusso, "The Congregation de Propaganda Fide and Pontifical Jurisdiction Over Non-Tridentine Church," in M. Catto and A. Prosperi (eds.), *Trent and Beyond: The Council, Other Powers, Other Cultures* (Mediterranean Nexus 1100–1700 4) (Turnhout: Brepols, 2017), 423–42.

129 On this see M. Calvo Tojo, "Aportación del Tribunal de la Rota de la Nunciatura a la iglesia española," in F. R. Aznar Gil (ed.), *La administracion de la justicia eclesiástica en España. Jornadas celebradas en Salamanca, 5 y 6 de febrero de 2001* (Salamanca: Universidad Pontificia de Salamanca, 2001), 111–79.

Particularly important for understanding canon law is that most of the provisions it contained derived from concrete practical problems. Canon law was meant to facilitate the administration of the Church and was first and foremost created for the salvation of souls. Of course, general statements exist, especially in the texts of the Church fathers and in the decisions of councils that were included in the collections of laws. Scholarship strove to establish coherent doctrines and to resolve contradictions, and it was eventually able to fill in some gaps that remained when papal collections were compiled. However, almost all of the decretals, that is, the papal responses to concrete legal questions, and many scholarly opinions concerned individual cases. While geared toward specific addressees, they at the same time served as authoritative statements to be consulted in similar cases. It is because of this specific technique of legislating in a casuistic manner that we find "cases" that were created to clarify certain practical problems, for example, the question whether a marriage was valid if the spouses gave their consent in a church ceremony but it later came to light that the husband was an impostor or an enslaved person (*Causa* 29 of the *Decretum Gratiani*). Such situations served as occasions for deliberation about the relevance of false or misrepresented identity (*error in persona*) and, more importantly for later Latin American legal history, the need for permission of the enslaved person's "owner" to contract a valid marriage (which canon law did not require).[130] In this respect, one can speak of a casuistic structure of canon law shaped by principles of theology and legal doctrine. In the ambiguity of this principle-oriented case law lies an important functional mechanism for the adaptability of canon law to particular times and circumstances. But it was primarily a consequence of the conviction that the ultimate goal of administration of justice consisted in reaching a suitable decision for the case at hand, and that this decision could only be reached by having all the concrete circumstances in mind. Decisions in previous cases thus could serve as a guideline, they could serve to reflect about important aspects to take into account, but they did not impose a decision.

However, not only this structural ambiguity of a casuistic order left margins for interpretation and adaptation to specific situations and circumstances. The most important instruments for concretizing canon law with regards to

130 On this case from the Causa 29 of the *Decretum Gratiani*, see A. Winroth, "Neither Slave nor Free: Theology and Law in Gratian's Thoughts on the Definition of Marriage of Unfree Persons," in W. P. Müller and M. E. Sommar (eds.), *Medieval Church Law and the Origins of the Western Legal Tradition: A Tribute to Kenneth Pennington* (Washington: The Catholic University of America Press, 2006), 97–109.

certain persons, situations, or regions were legal institutions known as dispensations, privileges, and customary law.

Tools for Concretization: Dispensations, Privileges, and Customary Law

Dispensations and privileges were among the most important forms of action in canon law in everyday life. A "dispensation" basically meant that a norm should not be applied because it would lead to an unjust result in a concrete case. Dispensations were particularly common in Latin America with regard to impediments to marriage – for example, exemption from the minimum age or from the marital impediment of kinship – or to receiving the sacrament of priestly ordination. Similarly, many practices considered in historical research to be part of a culture of non-application were based on the same material understanding of law underlying the possibility (or obligation) of granting dispensations. Thus, non-application of a norm does not necessarily mean that there was a gap between "theory" and "practice." Rather, the contemporary understanding of justice could require that a law not be applied. Dispensations were a legal means of putting this into practice.

Privileges (*privilegia*), in contrast to dispensations, contained a special regulation made with a particular addressee or group of persons in mind. In principle, they did not suspend the applicability of a norm, but instead created a new, more specific norm. Accordingly, privilege usually was defined as a *lex specialis*, the opposite of a *lex generalis*. However, because privileges were used in many distinct ways, there is a fair amount of overlap with other terms, for example, with the *ius singulare* and *dispensatio*. Though the widely known bull *Altitudo Divini Consilii* (1537), for instance, is often referred to as a privilege – because it made special provisions for the marriage of so-called neophytes, that is, recently baptized persons and more or less a synonym in Latin America for members of indigenous groups – it is actually a dispensation. And while *privilegium* often denoted the special regulation itself, it sometimes simply referred to the form of conferral. Some privileges were already included in texts of the *ius commune*, that is, in Roman and canon law, but in line with this tradition, scholarship could also establish privileges. Moreover, and contrary to later understandings, *privilegium* did not always mean an improved position for all parts involved; there were also *privilegia odiosa*, that is, privileges that favored one person to the detriment of others.

Privileges were used to implement many of the fundamental measures for the organization of the Church in Latin America. The pope himself established dioceses, appointed bishops – in agreement with the Crowns – and founded universities by means of privileges. Both the power of local actors as well as the *patronato regio* relied on rights acquired through privileges granted by the pope. In most cases, the privileges were given in the form of a bull, often retaining the form of earlier models, and in some instances even repeating the same initial words. For example, as mentioned at the beginning of this text, the pope had granted the Portuguese Crown far-reaching powers for expansion into Africa and Asia via the *Ordem de Cristo* in 1455, and the Alexandrian bulls of 1493 granted to the Catholic kings were modeled on this structure. With the bull *Universalis Ecclesiae* (1508), the Spanish Crown was given the right of patronage, and with the bulls *Eximiae Devotionis* (first in 1501 and again in 1510), it was given a series of other rights. These rights were confirmed and extended through other important bulls (e.g., *Praecelsae devotionis*, 1514). Particularly important was the delegation to the Spanish Crown of the power to organize and supervise the sending of missionaries (*Exponi nobis*, also called *Omnimoda*, 1522). Notwithstanding these rights granted to the Crowns, privileges also endowed the missionary orders with jurisdictional powers in the *forum internum*, namely, the authority to hear confessions. Privileges were also granted to the many lay confraternities in Latin America. When a confraternity of indigenous nobles from Cuzco, with a Jesuit acting as a courier, asked for recognition and a series of special rights, not only were the privileges conferred, but they were written in both Latin and Quechua.[131] While this is the only known case of a papal bull in Quechua, it was certainly not the only privilege granted to confraternities of indigenous peoples.

A great number of special regulations relating to members of indigenous peoples in Latin America were issued, often referred to as *privilegios de los indios*. Lists of these privileges can be found in texts written for catechesis, missions, pastoral work, preparation for confession, and other practical purposes. Examples of this include the *Confesionario para los curas de indios*, approved by the Third Council of Lima in 1585, and the *Gramatica o Vocabulario de la lengua general de todo el Perú llamada lengua quichua…*, written by the Jesuit Diego González Holguín (1608).[132] While some of these privileges

131 M. Gnerre, "Una Bula Pontificia de 1603 en quechua," in L. Laurencich Minelli and P. Numhauser (eds.), *Sublevando el Virreinato. Documentos contestatorios a la historiografía tradicional del Perú colonial* (Quito: Ediciones Abya-Yala, 2007), 339–50.

132 See the *Sumario de algunos privilegios y facultades concedidas para las indias por diversos Sumos Pontifices*, approved at the Third Council of Lima, in J. G. Durán, *Monumenta catechetica hispanoamericana (siglos XVI–XVIII), vol. II: Siglo XVI* (Buenos Aires: Facultad de Teología de la Pontificia Universidad Católica Argentina, 1990), 590–94; on the context: J. G. Durán, *Monumenta catechetica hispanoamericana (siglos XVI–XVIII), vol. I: Siglo XVI* (Buenos Aires: Facultad de Teología de la Pontificia Universidad Católica

had been enacted by the pope, many others were derived from classical canon law. For example, Diego de Avendaño's *Thesaurus indicus* (1668) contains the chapter *De privilegiis indorum* in a folio format of 150 pages. After a discussion of some general considerations, Diego de Avendaño enumerated a large number of privileges: special rights regarding baptism, confirmation, the Eucharist, confession, as well as ordination and marriage. He also detailed regulations regarding the observance of Church holidays, the fasting commandments, marital obligations, and other such subject matters.[133] He thus assembled privileges of various origins – some granted by a sovereign, others developed by legal scholars or created by his own interpretation of the legal tradition.

While privileges served to adapt the general rules to special cases and thus ensure the ultimate goal of canon law, namely, the salvation of the soul, they were also quite profanely a means of generating revenue. The *Bula de la Santa Cruzada* – distributed by a *Comisario de la Santa Cruzada* on behalf of the Crown and regularly issued for Hispanic America from 1574 onwards – is a good example of this combination of spiritual and financial purposes. The bull granted a number of privileges or dispensations in exchange for a payment. It was one of the Spanish Crown's most important revenue sources during the colonial period, and for this reason, among others, it was regulated in a separate title in the *Recopilación de Indias*. Its theological and canonical aspects have been discussed at length in numerous books and treatises by canon lawyers and theologians.[134]

The *Bula de la Santa Cruzada* itself consisted of various parts. The so-called *Bula de lacticinios* could exempt individuals from some food prohibitions, for example, the prohibition on consuming animal products such as eggs, milk, and fat, especially during Lent. Such prohibitions could become important in everyday life when alternative products were either not available or expensive. Exemptions from such food prohibitions were by no means

Argentina, 1984). See also the appendix with the *Summario* [sic] *de los privilegios y facultades concedidas para los indios* in Diego de Gónzales Holguín, *Vocabulario de la Lengua General de Todo el Perú Llamada Lengua quichua o del Inca* (Lima: Universidad Nacional Mayor de San Marcos, 1952 [1608]), following the index to the main work.

133 Diego de Avendaño, *Thesaurus indicus* (Antwerp, 1668), lib. II, tit. XII.

134 On the *Bula* in New Spain see M. del Pilar Martínez López-Cano, *La Iglesia, los fieles y la Corona. La bula de la Santa Cruzada en Nueva España, 1574–1660* (Mexico City: Universidad Nacional Autónoma de México, 2017); in Peru J. A. Benito Rodríguez, *Historia de la Bula de la Cruzada en Indias* (Madrid: Fundación Universitaria Española, 2002); in Brazil C. M. F. Figueiredo, "Os esmoleiros do rei: a Bula da Santa Cruzada e seus oficiais na Capitania de Minas Gerais (1748–1828)," Ph.D. thesis, Universidade Federal Fluminense (2014).

uncommon. In 1522, for instance, Pope Hadrian VI had authorized the clergy sent to America to be exempted from some food prohibitions, mainly meat, eggs, and dairy products during the forty-day Lent. In later papal bulls, the indigenous population was almost completely exempt from observing the abstinence commandments altogether.[135]

Beyond the exemption from food prohibitions, another part of the *Bula de la Cruzada*, the so-called *Bula de Composición*, exempted those who acquired its privileges and dispensations from the obligation to restitute something they had obtained in an illegitimate way should the beneficiary of the restitution not be locatable. This was of considerable practical relevance, for example, if one had amassed booty in the course of unjustified warlike conflicts (i.e., in a *bellum inustum*), exploited indigenous peoples beyond the "legitimate measure," or gained unjustified advantages in business, such as through usury. Since restitution was a precondition for absolution in confession, a major problem would arise if the beneficiary of the restitution could not be located. To compensate this unresolved debt by means of the bull was, therefore, a convenient solution to this problem – and as the revenues of the *Bula* were shared between the Church and the Crown, it was profitable for both. Of course, this exemption was quite controversial and criticized not only in the Protestant world but also by Catholic moral theologians. Francisco de Vitoria, for example, claimed that this possibility for compensation by paying a minimum of what one owed was "the biggest joke on earth."[136]

In addition to privileges and dispensations as tools for adapting the legal framework to specific needs, custom was also able to establish or derogate rights (on customary law, see also Section 3.1). According to early modern doctrine, a repeated practice that was reasonable under certain conditions could become a legally recognized custom. It was then considered "unwritten law" (*lex non scripta*) and had the same weight as written law. The requirements for the recognition of a practice as a custom were intricate and had been disputed for centuries. By the beginning of the seventeenth century, however, a consolidation of doctrine had occurred, in part through the Spanish Jesuit Francisco Suarez' epoch-making work *De legibus*.

135 On food prohibition, see C. Ferlan, "Ayuno Eclesiástico (DCH)," *Max Planck Institute for European Legal History Research Paper Series No. 2018–09* (Frankfurt am Main: Max-Planck-Institut für europäische Rechtsgeschichte, 2018), http://dx.doi.org/10.2139/ssrn.3260582 (last accessed Jan. 13, 2022).

136 T. Duve, "¿'La mayor burla del mundo'? Francisco de Vitoria y el *dominium* del Papa sobre los bienes de los pobres," in J. Cruz-Cruz (ed.), *Ley y dominio en Francisco de Vitoria* (Pamplona: Ediciones Universidad de Navarra, 2008), 93–106.

In both empires, people frequently invoked custom as a means to legitimize their behavior or legal titles, or to derogate laws. For example, it was discussed at length whether the aforementioned prohibitions on the consumption of milk, eggs, fat, or other animal products during Lent were not derogated by customary law. If so, it would not have been necessary to pay for the *Bula de la Cruzada* in order to be exempt from these prohibitions. Gaspar de Villarroel devoted an entire chapter to this problem in his *Govierno eclesiastico pacifico*, and referring to Francisco Suárez' doctrine of customary law, he came to precisely this conclusion. In other words, the legitimate practice was a *lex non scripta* and thus would even supersede a papal privilege that seemed to suppose that the custom did not exist. Given the remaining uncertainty, however, the bishop of Santiago de Chile concluded his deliberations with a pragmatic recommendation: Though not strictly necessary, it was nevertheless better to err on the side of caution and acquire the dispensation granted in the *Bula de la Cruzada*. While perhaps an astonishing recommendation from today's perspective, it is characteristic of the early modern *modus operandi*: Insecurity about the legal framework and its interpretation, and the need to maintain a peaceful coexistence between Church and state, compelled him to recommend avoiding a conflict by making a prudent decision.[137]

Dispensations, privileges, and customary law thus provided universal canon law with effective techniques to tailor appropriate solutions to individual cases. They could also serve to make canon law more flexible and more specific with regard to particular situations or groups of persons. An expression of the economy of grace that came to characterize the Iberian monarchies as well as other Catholic societies, they were used for very different purposes: to achieve justice, as an instrument of control, and to generate revenue. They also contributed to a regionalization of universal canon law. For instance, when bishops or missionary orders requested numerous privileges for specific territories for an extended period of time, when the inhabitants of entire regions were meant to be freed from certain obligations in conjunction with local customs, or when bishops and missionaries tended to grant dispensations in special cases, distinct regional normative orders would emerge.[138] This dialectic between universal and particular canon law, formed by the

137 On this case, see T. Duve, "Algunas observaciones acerca del modus operandi y la prudencia del juez en el Derecho Canónico Indiano," *Revista de Historia del Derecho* 35 (2007), 195–226.

138 Many of these regulations are contained in collections such as Hernáez, *Colección de bulas*; Morelli, *Fasti Novi Orbis*; Metzler, *America Pontificia*; Simon Marques, *Brasilia Pontificia* (Lisbon, 1749).

lawgiver as well as in daily practice, was one of the fundamental principles of the global governance of the Church that also shaped the legal landscape of Latin America.

Nonetheless, the most important agents in the concretization of universal canon law and the development of regional canon law were the various corporate bodies of the Church at the local level. For even if the Church is understood ecclesiologically in terms of a unity, from a historical-sociological perspective, it consisted of a variety of bodies or communities of practice, and these exercised jurisdiction and produced knowledge of normativity in their own spheres. They translated the knowledge of normativity stemming from tradition into their specific worlds.

Church-Made Law: Corporate Bodies and Ecclesiastical Jurisdictions

Like early modern monarchies, the early modern Church was a composite and multilayered institution.[139] It was hierarchically organized into different spaces. Church provinces and archdioceses formed the supreme organizational unit.[140] Every archdiocese contained multiple dioceses, which were further divided into parishes. The first Hispano-American dioceses in the

139 On this notion, see the classic considerations of J. H. Elliot, "A Europe of Composite Monarchies," *Past & Present* 137 (1992), 48–71; with regard to early modern Catholicism, C. Windler, "Early Modern Composite Catholicism in a Global Perspective: Catholic Missionaries and the English East India Company," in A. Badea, B. Boute, and B. Emich (eds.), *Pathways Through Early Modern Christianities* (Köln: Böhlau, 2023); See also the overall picture sketched by A. Maldavsky and F. Palomo del Barrio, "La misión en los espacios del mundo ibérico: conversiones, formas de control y negociación," in A. Barreto Xavier, F. Palomo, and R. Stumpf (eds.), *Monarquias Ibéricas em Perspectiva Comparada (Sécs. XVI–XVIII). Dinâmicas Imperiais e Circulação de Modelos Administrativos* (Lisbon: Universidade de Lisboa, 2018), 543–90.

140 For an overview of the history of the Church in Hispanoamerica, see the contributions in Borges, *Historia de la Iglesia*, vol. I; and A. de Zaballa Beascoechea, "Las Instituciones eclesiásticas en la Monarquía Hispánica," in A. Barreto Xavier, F. Palomo, and R. Stumpf (eds.), *Monarquias Ibéricas em Perspectiva Comparada (Sécs. XVI–XVIII). Dinâmicas Imperiais e Circulação de Modelos Administrativos* (Lisbon: Universidade de Lisboa, 2018), 481–512. On the history of the Church and its structures in Brazil, see E. Sales Souza, "The Construction of a Tridentine Christianity in Portuguese America (Sixteenth and Seventeenth Centuries)," in A. Prosperi and M. Catto (eds.), *Trent and Beyond: The Council, Other Powers, Other Cultures* (Mediterranean Nexus 1100–1700 4) (Turnhout: Brepols, 2017), 479–500; E. Sales Souza, "Estruturas eclesiásticas da Monarquia portuguesa. A Igreja diocesana," in A. Barreto Xavier, F. Palomo, and R. Stumpf (eds.), *Monarquias Ibéricas em Perspectiva Comparada (Sécs. XVI–XVIII). Dinâmicas Imperiais e Circulação de Modelos Administrativos* (Lisbon: Universidade de Lisboa, 2018); E. Sales Souza "Ecclesiastical Geography of Colonial Brazil," in W. Beezley (ed.), *Oxford Research Encyclopedia of Latin American History* (Oxford: Oxford University Press, 2020), 1–20; and D. R. Vieira, *História do Catolicismo no Brasil, vol. I: 1500–1889* (Aparecida: Editora Santuário, 2016).

Caribbean, established in 1504, belonged to the archdiocese of Seville until 1546. When later the archdioceses of Santo Domingo, Mexico, and Lima were erected, they became the first archdioceses in Latin America and the Caribbean. In present-day Brazil, the diocese of San Salvador de Bahía was originally established in 1551 as part of the archdiocese of Lisbon. However, once the dioceses of Río de Janeiro and Olinda were founded, San Salvador de Bahía was elevated to the status of archdiocese in 1676. These differences in chronology point to the different dynamics in Portuguese overseas expansion, as institutional structures in Portuguese America consolidated only once Brazil's importance grew within the Portuguese empire, and thus later than they did in Hispanic America.

The Church-made law within the jurisdictional spaces defined by this hierarchy. Of particular importance was lawmaking at provincial councils and synods.[141] At the provincial councils, the bishops of a province deliberated on important aspects of Church life, and in many cases, they also addressed questions submitted externally to the council. In particular, the provincial councils of Mexico and Lima were responsible for far-reaching decisions about the organization of the Church. The particularly important third provincial councils of Lima (1582/1583) and Mexico (1585) played decisive roles in the implementation of the decisions made at the Council of Trent.[142] In Brazil, the decisions of the synod of the archdiocese of Bahía of 1707 – the *Constituições Primeiras do Arcebispado da Bahia of* 1707 – were the first synodal

141 For a useful list of the synods and provincial councils in the Hispanic World, see M. Deardorff, "Synods and Councils of the Hispanic World, 1300–1700," *Max Planck Institute for Legal History and Legal Theory Research Paper Series No. 2022–14: subsidia et instrumenta* (Frankfurt am Main: Max-Planck-Institut für Rechtsgeschichte und Rechtstheorie, 2022), http://dx.doi.org/10.2139/ssrn.4131300; a very helpful overview and index to the issues raised in a South American diocese (Arquidiócesis de la Plata) between the sixteenth and eighteenth centuries is N. C. Dellaferrera and M. P. Martini (eds.), *Temática de las constituciones sinodales indianas (s. XVI–XVII). Arquidiócesis de La Plata* (Buenos Aires: Instituto de Investigaciones de Historia del Derecho, 2002). See also M. T. Fattori, "Districts, Metropolitans and Ecclesiastical Territories: Geo-Local Aspects of Ecclesiastical Territorial Evolution," *Zeitschrift für Kirchengeschichte* 132(2) (2021), 218–62.

142 The texts of the provincial councils and other materials have been edited by a group of Mexican and Spanish scholars. Regarding the Third Provincial Council of Lima, see L. Martínez Ferrer (ed.), *Tercer Concilio Limense (1583–1591). Edición bilingüe de los Decretos*, trans. J. L. Gutiérrez (Lima and Rome: Facultad de Teología Pontificia y Civil de Lima, 2017); regarding the Third Provincial Council of Mexico, see L. Martínez Ferrer, *Decretos del Concilio Tercero Provincial Mexicano 1585. Edición histórica crítica y estudio preliminar por Luis Martínez Ferrer* (Zamora: El Colegio de Michoacán, Universidad de la Santa Cruz, 2009). The materials of the Mexican Council have been edited by A. Carrillo Cázares, *Manuscritos del Concilio Tercero Provincial Mexicano (1585)* (Zamora and Mexico City: El Colegio de Michoacán, Universidad Pontificia de México, 2006–2011), 5 vols.

legislation by a local bishop and were motivated by the need to create a legal framework for the Brazilian archdiocese established three decades earlier.[143]

In nearly all synods and provincial councils, the members of the councils discussed matters of Church discipline, the regulation of local Church life, but also questions that went far beyond these issues. In the Third Provincial Council of Mexico, for example, the council fathers debated at length whether the war against the so-called Chichimeca, a group of indigenous peoples, was a legitimate "just war" (*bellum iustum*). After intense deliberations, they concluded that this was not the case and that the use of force against them could not be justified.[144] At the same council, the bishops and their advisors also dealt with the legitimacy of contracts and financial transactions and answered a large variety of questions from laypeople. While some of the decisions reached led to dispositions in the council constitutions (*canones*), other results of the deliberations were included in a manual for confessions.[145] Catechisms were drafted in the provincial councils in Lima and in Mexico, and the catechisms redacted in Lima were published in Spanish and Quechua.

At the diocesan level, the bishop held the power of jurisdiction (*potestas iurisdictionis*).[146] He could convene synods to discuss any and all affairs related to the diocese, and it was his authority as bishop that meant the decisions of the synods were considered binding law. We now have access to a great number of synodal decisions, especially from Hispanic America and, to a lesser extent, from Portuguese America. Their importance lies above all in the concretization of the normative options made available by universal canon law and in the special regulation with regard to indigenous people. Last but not least, synodal decisions also played an important role in the repetition and thus reaffirmation and implementation of norms. Most synods in Hispanic America

143 See the contributions in B. Feitler and E. Souza Sales (eds.), *A Igreja no Brasil. Normas e Prácticas durante a Vigência das Constituições Primeiras do Arcebispado da Bahia* (São Paulo: Editora UNIFESP, 2011). On the implementation of Trent in Brazil, in particular, see B. Feitler, "Quando chegou Trento ao Brasil?," in A. Camões Gouveia, D. Sampaio Barbosa and J. P. Paiva (eds.), *O Concílio de Trento em Portugal e nas suas conquistas. Olhares novos* (Lisbon: Centro de Estudos de História Religiosa, Universidade Católica Portuguesa, 2014), 157–73.

144 The deliberations have been transcribed and commented on by A. Carrillo Cázares, *El debate sobre la guerra Chichimeca, 1531–1585. Derecho y política en la Nueva España* (Zamora and San Luis: El Colegio de Michoacán, El Colegio de San Luis, 2000), 2 vols.

145 On the making of the Third Provincial Council of Mexico, see O. R. Moutin, *Legislar en la América hispánica en la temprana edad moderna: Procesos y características de la producción de los Decretos del Tercer Concilio Provincial Mexicano (1585)* (Frankfurt am Main: Max-Planck-Institut für europäische Rechtsgeschichte, 2016).

146 For an overview about the institutions of the secular church in Mexico, see J. F. Schwaller, *The Church and Clergy in Sixteenth-Century Mexico* (Albuquerque: University of New Mexico Press, 1987).

took place in the late sixteenth and early seventeenth centuries. After 1769, during an extended period of synodal inactivity, a number of important synods and provincial councils took place in Hispanic America and the Philippines.

In his diocese, the bishop exercised his office as chief judge in the so-called *forum externum* through a commissioner (*provisor y vicario general*) in the ecclesiastical court and in his regular visitations, especially important in Latin America due to the vast distances.[147] A wide variety of matters were submitted to the bishop. He – or his delegate judges – decided on all matters involving members of the clergy, especially crimes and property disputes, in part because religious institutions, confraternities, and others were the main creditors in colonial society. Ecclesiastical courts exercised jurisdiction over matrimonial law, wills and trusts, and disputes over Church tithes.[148] They also had jurisdiction over the indigenous population, including matters that would have fallen under the jurisdiction of the Inquisition if Spaniards or Portuguese had been involved. Because ecclesiastical jurisdiction was open to any baptized person, members of indigenous peoples, women, Afro-Latin Americans, and members of other ethnic minorities pursued their causes in Church courts, which enabled an important legal mobilization of these groups.[149] For instance, cases in which ecclesiastical courts required slaveholders to allow married slaves to live together were quite common.[150] The cathedral chapter (*cabildo ecclesiástico*), which regulated the affairs of the

147 Individual studies on ecclesiastical jurisdiction are available, for example, on New Spain by J. E. Traslosheros, *Iglesia, justicia y sociedad en la Nueva España. La audiencia del arzobispado de México, 1528–1668* (Mexico City: Editorial Porrúa, 2004); on Pernambuco by G. A. Mendonça dos Santos, *A justiça do bispo: O exercício da justiça eclesiástica no bispado de Pernambuco no século XVIII* (Recife: Universidade Federal de Pernambuco, 2019); on Marañao see P. Gouveia Mendonça Muniz, *Réus de Batina. Justiça Eclesiástica e clero secular no bispado do Maranhão colonial* (São Paulo: Alamada Casa Ed, 2017). On ecclesiastical offices, see J. R. Gouveia, "Ministros De Los Tribunales (DCH)," *Max Planck Institute for Legal History and Legal Theory Research Paper Series No. 2021–11* (Frankfurt am Main: Max-Planck-Institut für Rechtsgeschichte und Rechtstheorie, 2021), http://dx.doi.org/10.2139/ssrn.3862514 (last accessed Jan. 13, 2022).

148 On the procedural law, offices, and institutions, see various entries in the *DCH*, https://dch.hypotheses.org/category/publicaciones (last accessed Jan. 13, 2022).

149 K. B. Graubart, *With Our Labor and Sweat: Indigenous Women and the Formation of Colonial Society in Peru, 1550–1700* (Stanford: Stanford University Press, 2007); R. S. O'Toole, *Bound Lives*; M. A. McKinley, *Fractional Freedoms: Slavery, Intimacy, and Legal Mobilization in Colonial Lima, 1600–1700* (Studies in Legal History) (New York: Cambridge University Press, 2016); Premo, *Enlightenment on Trial*; C. Cunill and L. M. Glave Testino (eds.), *Las lenguas indígenas en los tribunales de América Latina. Intérpretes, mediación y justicia (siglos XVI–XXI)* (Bogotá: Instituto Colombiano de Antropología e Historia, 2019).

150 On Africans in colonial Mexico and their use of ecclesiastical courts, see H. L. Bennett, *Africans in Colonial Mexico: Absolutism, Christianity, and Afro-Creole Consciousness, 1570–1640* (Blacks in the Diaspora) (Bloomington: Indiana University Press, 2003); in Brazil Castelnau-L'Éstoile, "Os filhos obedientes."

diocese when no bishop was in office, also had its own jurisdiction and regulated its activity in documents that in many cases contained detailed rules (e.g., *consuetas*).[151]

Apart from this spatially organized jurisdiction, there were many other jurisdictional spheres not defined by territory. Within the Church, many corporate bodies were granted specific rights for taking care of their own affairs and thus exercised jurisdiction in the wider sense this term had in the premodern world. The religious confraternities (*cofradías*), in Brazil *misericórdias*, were particularly important institutions in colonial daily life.[152] They enjoyed a certain degree of autonomy and were of significance not only for the elite but also for the population groups much lower down the social hierarchy, such as the indigenous peoples, Afro-Latin Americans, people of mixed ethnicity (*mestizos*), and others. Confraternities served the interests of their members and advocated, for example, for the status and rights of people of mixed ethnicity, but they were also a means of internal differentiation within the group itself.[153] A variety of other institutions with their own jurisdictions also existed. Of particular relevance were the *Tribunal de la Santa Cruzada*, the *Juzgado de testamentos*, and the *Juzgado de capellanias y obras pías*.

The missionary orders, divided into provinces and answering to their central authorities, largely remained independent of the secular clergy.[154] Of the many religious orders that existed in Europe, the Dominicans, Franciscans, Augustinians, Mercedarians, and – especially in today's Argentina, Brazil, and Paraguay – Jesuits were particularly important in Latin America. They exercised jurisdiction, elaborated their own statutes, and decided on the affairs

151 For an example from late sixteenth-century Lima, see M. L. Grignani, "La legislación eclesiástica de Toribio Alfonso de Mogrovejo, segundo arzobispo de Lima: la Regla Consueta y los sínodos diocesansos," in O. Danwerth, B. Albani and T. Duve (eds.), *Normatividades e instituciones eclesiásticas en el virreinato del Perú, siglos XVI–XIX* (Frankfurt am Main: Max-Planck-Institut für europäische Rechtsgeschichte, 2019), 19–42.

152 See R. Aguirre Salvador, *Cofradías y asociaciones de fieles en la mira de la Iglesia y de la Corona: arzobispado de México, 1680–1750* (Mexico City: Real Universidad de México, 2018).

153 See J. J. Hidalgo and M. Valerio (eds.), *Indigenous and Black Confraternities in Colonial Latin America: Negotiating Status Through Religious Practices* (Amsterdam: Amsterdam University Press, 2022). On Brazil, see E. W. Kiddy, *Blacks of the Rosary: Memory and History in Minas Gerais, Brazil* (University Park: Pennsylvania State University Press, 2005); Germeten, *Black Blood Brothers*. On Peru, see K. B. Graubart, "'So color de una cofradia': Catholic Confraternities and the Development of Afro-Peruvian Ethnicities in Early Colonial Peru," *Slavery & Abolition* 33(1) (2012), 43–64.

154 See the overview in Maldavsky and Palomo del Barrio, "*La misión en los espacios del mundo ibérico*," 543–90; for Spain R. A. Gutiérrez, "The Spanish Missions of North and South America," in V. Garrard-Burnett, P. Freston, and S. C. Dove (eds.), *The Cambridge History of Religions in Latin America* (New York: Cambridge University Press, 2016), 173–97.

of the members of the order; only the convents of nuns were subject to the jurisdiction of the local bishop. In many cases, members of missionary orders acted as judges, deciding on disputes and setting rules. Within the Portuguese realm, a *Junta Geral das Missões*, sometimes called *Junta da Propagação da Fé*, was established in Lisbon in 1655. Another was established in Brazil (located first in Pernambuco, then in Rio de Janeiro and Marañao) in 1680 and was staffed mainly by the secular clergy. In addition to serving as an appeal instance, these *juntas* also decided cases in which members of indigenous peoples defended themselves against illegal enslavement or deprivation of liberty.[155] Also worth noting were *doctrinas*, administrative units created for missionary purposes with the indigenous population in mind.

The Inquisition was an independent institution with its own jurisdiction and a remarkable degree of power over both Church and Crown officials.[156] In both Iberian empires, supervision of the courts of the Inquisition rested with the king; unlike in practically all other matters in Hispano-America, appeals against the decisions by the Inquisition could not be lodged with the Council of the Indies but with the *Supremo Consejo de la Inquisión* in Madrid. Only for members of indigenous peoples did local bishops have jurisdiction to prosecute what were considered crimes against the faith. In a few cases, the Inquisition's jurisdiction also seems to have been used strategically, for instance, by enslaved persons who feigned heretical practices in order to protect themselves from mistreatment.[157]

The corporative structure of the Church, and the fact that many corporations were able to produce and enforce special rights, led to numerous disputes within the ecclesiastical sphere. Even if traditional historiography

155 See on Maranhão, for example, A. L. Ferreira, *Injustos cativeiros. Os índios no Tribunal da Junta das Missões do Maranhão* (Belo Horizonte: Caravana, 2021).

156 For an overview, see F. Bethencourt, *The Inquisition: A Global History, 1478–1834*, trans. J. Birrell (Past and Present Publications) (Cambridge and New York: Cambridge University Press, 2009); for the Portuguese Inqusition G. Marcocci and J. P. Paiva, *História da Inquisição Portuguesa (1536–1821)* (Lisbon: A Esfera dos Livros, 2013); on Brazil, B. Feitler, *Nas malhas da consciência. Igreja e Inquisição no Brasil. Nordeste 1640–1750* (São Paulo: Alamada Casa Ed, 2007); B. Feitler "Continuidades e rupturas da Igreja na América Portuguesa no tempo dos Áustrias. A importância da questão indígena e do exemplo espanhol," in P. Cardim, L. Freire Costa, and M. Soares da Cunha (eds.), *Portugal na Monarquia Hispânica. Dinâmicas de Integração e de Conflito* (Colecção Estudos & Documentos, 18) (Lisbon: CHAM, 2013), 203–30; B. Feitler, "The Inquisition in the New World," in V. Garrard-Burnett, P. Freston, and S. C. Dove (eds.), *The Cambridge History of Religions in Latin America* (New York: Cambridge University Press, 2016), 133–42; A. C. Rodrigues, *Igreja e Inquisição no Brasil. Agentes, carreiras e mecanismos de promoção social (século XVIII)* (São Paulo: Alamada Casa Ed, 2014).

157 J. Villa-Flores, "To Lose One's Soul': Blasphemy and Slavery in New Spain, 1596–1669," *The Hispanic American Historical Review* 82(3) (2002), 435–68.

places the Church and state in opposition to one another, the tension between holders of jurisdictional powers *within* these spheres was often more pronounced. Striking examples of the fierce, sometimes even violent, conflicts in the first decades of the construction of ecclesiastical structures in today's Mexico between the 1530s and 1560s are the numerous legal disputes by Vasco de Quiroga, first bishop of Michoacán. His lawsuits against neighboring dioceses (New Galicia and Mexico), against the religious orders of the Franciscans and Augustinians, as well as against secular officials, private individuals, and the indigenous inhabitants of Tzintzuntzan document not only his own litigiousness but also the shaping of the political constitution in the Iberian empires and the Catholic Church.[158] Disputes between the official Church and the religious communities in which the boundaries of jurisdictions were negotiated remained on the agenda until the end of the colonial period and beyond.

On the local level, however, not only were conflicts within the Church at issue but also numerous conflicts between Church and Crown officials. Fruitful cooperation was an explicit aim, and both Crowns had an interest in mutual control of the secular and the ecclesiastical officeholders. Nevertheless, cooperation was difficult to implement in everyday life, even though the king had appointed the Church officials and required them to swear an oath of allegiance to him. The main source of the manifold conflicts could be traced back to the king's patronage over the Church in Latin America, which meant that a number of issues were regulated by both secular and canon law.

Various factors contributed to this overlap and to the conflicts that resulted from contested jurisdictions. On a very basic level, one must bear in mind that the extent of the *patronato regio* was not easy to determine, as the rights of the Crown had been conferred not in one document but through a series of privileges. The existence and exact wording of many of these privileges were simply not widely known at the time. Even Juan de Solórzano Pereira, one of the most important jurists of his time and author of the *De Indiarum Iure* and the *Politica Indiana*, did not have firsthand knowledge of the Alexandrian bulls.[159] This uncertainty about the exact wording or even existence of such fundamental legal documents is the reason one finds transcriptions of important privileges not only in Solórzano Pereira's books but

158 See P. Serrano Gassent, *Vasco de Quiroga. Utopía y derecho en la conquista de América* (Madrid: Fondo de Cultura Económica, 2001); A. Carrillo Cázares (ed.), *Vasco de Quiroga: La pasión por el derecho y el pleito con la orden e San Agustín (1558–1562)* (Zamora: El Colegio de Michoacán, 2003), 2 vols.

159 Juan Solórzano Pereira, *Política Indiana* (Madrid, 1647), 4.2.

also in manuals for the mission and in the books on the good government of the Church, including those by José de Acosta, Diego de Avendaño, Alonso de la Peña Montenegro, and others.

In addition to the uncertainty about the wording of such privileges, the proliferation of privileges and special legislation made consulting and remembering all of them difficult. The Jesuit Domingo Muriel from Córdoba de Tucumán in what is today Argentina, for example, compiled more than 600 special regulations in his *Fasti novi orbis et ordinationum apostolicarum ad Indias pertinentium breviarium*. Muriel explained the need for this publication stating that there were so many peculiarities in the canon law of overseas territories that one could not decide anything without first having knowledge of these.[160] A similar line of reasoning motivated Simon Marques, a Jesuit living in Río de Janeiro, to write his *Brasilia Pontificia, sive speciales facultates pontificiae, quae Brasiliae Episcopis conceduntur*, printed in Lisbon in 1749.

Even in cases in which the relevant texts from both secular and ecclesiastical authorities were available, it was nevertheless difficult to interpret their content and judge the legitimacy of contradictory claims. In theory, the patronage of the Crowns over the Church did not empower them to legislate, act against, or regulate matters reserved to canon law. However, as long as the Crowns did not make regulations that openly deviated from canon law, even a regulation clearly aimed at sacramental matters or relating to fundamental aspects of the Church could be interpreted as a confirmation of rather than an interference in canon law. Such was the case, for example, in 1564 when the Spanish king Philip II decreed that the decisions of the Council of Trent should be applicable in Hispanic America.

A peaceful coexistence, however, was more difficult when the Crown claimed rights that had not been conferred on it or that were clearly contrary to canon law. Such usurpations of power became increasingly common from the mid-sixteenth century onwards. Both Crowns began, no later than under King Philip II, who also ruled Portugal from 1580 as Philip I, to regulate vast areas of ecclesiastical life by invoking their rights as patrons of the Church. The resulting ecclesiastical law, that is, the law set by the state with regard to religion, was not part of canon law, yet it shaped the conditions under which Church institutions operated, and it guided and constrained the actions of Church officials to the same extent as canon law.

160 Morelli, *Fasti Novi Orbis*, prologus. The collection itself was based, as he reports in the preface, on the preliminary work done by Antonio León Pinelo. This work was also used by B. de Tobar, *Compendio bulario indico* (Seville: Escuela de Estudios Hispanoamericanos de Sevilla, 1954–1966), 2 vols.

Crown-Made Church Law: Ecclesiastical Law

As mentioned at the beginning of Section 3.2, the pope had granted both the Spanish and the Portuguese Crowns extensive rights regarding the organization and shaping of the Church in Latin America. Within the framework of patronage law (*ius patronatus*), which had its roots in medieval canon law, it was common for secular rulers to promote christianization and mission, to establish churches, to provide the financial means necessary for their operation, and to physically construct them (*fundatio, dotatio, aedificatio*). In return, secular rulers received a number of rights and benefits, most notably, the right to propose candidates to fill ecclesiastical offices and to share in the revenues from Church tithe.[161]

The distinctive feature of the *patronato regio* by the Iberian monarchies in Latin America consisted in the fact that, over time, the Crowns obtained or claimed for themselves ever more powers. The extremely unspecific and wide-ranging rights granted by the first papal bulls were followed by a series of specific and much more concrete privileges. In the case of Brazil, in 1551, the Portuguese Crown obtained the transfer of the rights originally granted to the *Ordem de Cristo* and to the *Mesa de Consciência e Ordens*,[162] making this institution the highest instance of ecclesiastical jurisdiction. A similar gradual process of extension can be found with regard to Hispanic America in a royal decree of 1574, which hearkened back to a failed larger project of legislation (the so-called *Código de Ovando*) and concerned patronage rights, later incorporated into the *Recopilación de Indias*.[163]

161 See recent overviews in I. Fernández Terricabras, "El Patronato Real en la América Hispana: fundamentos y prácticas," in A. Barreto Xavier, F. Palomo, and R. Stumpf (eds.), *Monarquias Ibéricas em Perspectiva Comparada (Sécs. XVI–XVIII). Dinâmicas Imperiais e Circulação de Modelos Administrativos* (Lisbon: Universidade de Lisboa, 2018), 97–122; A. Barreto Xavier and F. Olival, "O padroado da coroa de Portugal: Fundamentos e práticas," in A. Barreto Xavier, F. Palomo, and R. Stumpf (eds.), *Monarquias Ibéricas em Perspectiva Comparada (Sécs. XVI–XVIII). Dinâmicas Imperiais e Circulação de Modelos Administrativos* (Lisbon: Universidade de Lisboa, 2018), 123–60; and G. Pizzorusso, "Il padroado régio portoghese nella dimensione 'globale' della Chiesa romana. Note storico-documentarie con particolare riferimento al Seicento," in G. Pizzorusso, G. Platania, and M. Sanfilippo (eds.), *Gli archivi della Santa Sede come fonte per la storia del Portogallo in età moderna* (Viterbo: Sette Città, 2012), 177–219.

162 See on the *Mesa da Consciência e Ordens* G. Marcocci, "Conscience and Empire: Politics and Moral Theology in the Early Modern Portuguese World," *Journal of Early Modern History* 18(5) (2014), 473–94; and M. do Carmo Dias Farinha and A. Azevedo Jara (eds.), *Mesa da Consciência e Ordens* (Lisbon: Instituto dos Arquivos Nacionais da Torre do Tombo, 1997). On the role of the military orders in the expansion, see F. Olival, *The Military Orders and the Portuguese Expansion (15th to 17th Centuries)* (Peterborough: Baywolf Press, 2018).

163 On this, see R. C. Padden, "The Ordenanza del Patronazgo of 1574: An Interpretative Essay," in J. F. Schwaller (ed.), *The Church in Colonial Latin America* (Wilmington: Scholarly Resources, 2000), 27–47; J. F. Schwaller, "The ordenanza del Patronazgo

From the Spanish Crown's perspective, Church patronage included powers beyond the traditional rights to present incumbents and maintain churches. Among other things, the Crown insisted that all papal orders be directed to their recipients through the Crown (*pase regio* or *exequatur*), that ecclesiastical officeholders swear allegiance not only to the pope but also to the Crown, on a general appeal against the decisions of ecclesiastical courts to secular courts (*recurso de fuerza*), the routing of communications between bishops and Rome through the Crown, and on control over the activities of religious orders.[164] This comprehensive catalog was justified in the seventeenth century by appeal to the theory that in Latin America the Catholic kings had become deputies of the pope (*vicariato*). Juan de Solórzano Pereira was an advocate of this theory, which is why his *De Indiarum Iure* was placed on the Index of Prohibited Books by the Church. Despite this prohibition, several ecclesiastical authors supported this interpretation.

In Brazil, the Crown controlled, directly or indirectly, all the most important ecclesiastical appointments.[165] The *Ordenações Filipinas*, enacted during the personal union between the Portuguese and Spanish Crowns in 1595 and put into force with its publication in 1603, contained numerous provisions that affected Church life. Especially in the course of the Pombaline reforms in the second half of the eighteenth century, the Portuguese Crown enforced its policy of strengthening its rights as a patron, a pursuit very similar to the Spanish idea of *regalismo* – both with regard to the secular clergy and the religious orders.[166] The Portuguese and Spanish Crowns thus exerted influence on the regulation of ecclesiastical affairs in Latin America that far exceeded what they had been granted in their European territories. Not until the Concordat of 1753 did the Spanish Crown gain the right of patronage over its territories on the Iberian Peninsula.

Notwithstanding these many rights and attributions, the picture researchers have long painted of the Church in Latin America as completely under

in New Spain, 1574–1600," in J. F. Schwaller (ed.), *The Church in Colonial Latin America* (Wilmington: Scholarly Resources, 2000), 49–69; S. Poole, *Juan de Ovando. Governing the Spanish Empire in the Reign of Philip II* (Norman: University of Oklahoma Press, 2004), 144–50; as well as A. Martín González, *Gobernación espiritual de Indias. Código Ovandino, Libro 1* (Guatemala: Instituto Teológico Salesiano, 1977).

164 Compare the overview in Sánchez Bella, *Iglesia y Estado*; García Añoveros, *La Monarquía*, 68–136; briefly also De la Hera, "El patronato."

165 A. R. Disney, *A History of Portugal and the Portuguese Empire, vol. II: The Portuguese Empire* (Cambridge: Cambridge University Press, 2009), 160.

166 See A. Wehling, "Absolutismo e regalismo: a alegação jurídica do bispo Azeredo Coutinho," in J. L. Soberanes Fernández, R. M. Martínez de Codes (eds.), *Homenaje a Alberto de la Hera* (Mexico City: Universidad Autónoma de México, 2008), 867–84.

the control of the Portuguese and Spanish Crowns may not be entirely accurate.[167] Research has primarily been oriented toward legislation and the discussions surrounding the theory of *patronato regio* and vicariate, giving too much weight to programmatic political discourses. Moreover, most research by legal historians has focused on state archives, almost to the exclusion of the holdings in ecclesiastical archives, especially those of the religious headquarters and the Roman Curia. Yet the intensive communication between local churches, members of religious orders, and their central offices can only be found in these archives. We also know today not only much more about how extensive the exchange actually was but also more about how it took place, for example, through missionaries and secular clerics carrying letters, reports, and books with them on their journeys.

It is in this context that moral-theological and pastoral literature that circulated in great numbers between the Old and New Worlds gained particular importance. Together with spiritual and juridical books, this literature made up a large portion of the books that were imported to the Americas.[168] A title like the *Manual for Confessors* by Martín de Azpilcueta, for example, had more than ninety editions published in Portuguese, Latin, Spanish, and later in Italian during the author's lifetime, making it a bestseller in the book trade.[169] Each edition of this work was updated, and the revised edition then served as a model for other books printed to help guide the clergy in their duties. These books, together with the many manuscripts and excerpts that traveled with missionaries and priests, contributed to the emergence of a dense web

167 B. Albani, "Nuova luce sulle relazioni tra la Sede Apostolica e le Americhe. La pratica della concessione del 'Pase regio' ai documenti pontifici destinati alle Indie," in C. Fernal (ed.), *Eusebio Francesco Chini e il suo tempo. Una riflessione storica* (Trento: F. B. K. Press, 2012), 83–102; B. Albani, "Un nuncio per il Nuovo Mundo. Il ruolo della nunciatura di Spagna come istanza di giustizia per i fedeli americani tra Cinque e Seicento," in P. Tusor and M. Sanfilippo (eds.), *Il papato e le Chiese locali. Studi/The Papacy and the Local churches. Studies* (Viterbo: Sette Città, 2014), 257–86; B. Albani and G. Pizzorusso, "Problematizando el Patronato Regio. Nuevos acercamientos al gobierno de la Iglesia Ibero-Americana desde la perspectiva de la Santa Sede," in T. Duve (ed.), *Actas del XIX Congreso del Instituto Internacional de Historia del Derecho Indiano, Berlín 2016* (Madrid: Editorial Dykinson, 2017), 519–43.

168 On this see O. Danwerth, "The Circulation of Pragmatic Normative Literature in Spanish America (16th–17th Centuries)," in T. Duve and O. Danwerth (eds.), *Knowledge of the Pragmatici: Legal and Moral Theological Literature and the Formation of Early Modern Ibero-America* (Leiden and Boston: Brill Nijhoff, 2020), 89–130.

169 See on this M. Bragagnolo, "Managing Legal Knowledge in Early Modern Times: Martín de Azpilcueta's Manual for Confessors and the Phenomenon of Epitomisation," in T. Duve and O. Danwerth (eds.), *Knowledge of the Pragmatici: Legal and Moral Theological Literature and the Formation of Early Modern Ibero-America*, (Leiden and Boston: Brill Nijhoff, 2020), 187–242.

of communication between Europe, the Americas, and Asia, far beyond the control of the communication between Rome and its dioceses.

The high demand for moral theological literature points to a jurisdictional sphere that has largely been overlooked by legal history, but which was of paramount importance in practice: the *forum internum*. The knowledge of normativity generated and used in this *forum* came primarily from moral theology. Its importance increased so much between the sixteenth and the eighteenth centuries that moral theology has been called a "second canon law."[170]

A Second Canon Law: Moral Theology

The reasons for the rise of moral theology as a body of knowledge of normativity are manifold and closely connected with the multiple historical transformations in world history during the sixteenth century, not least the rise of the early modern state and European expansion.[171] In a certain sense, royal patronage and the successive absorption of jurisdictional competencies by the Crowns in Latin America was simply an early case of what was happening in both Catholic and Protestant territories in Europe after the Reformation and the emergence of confessional states on a larger scale. These confessional states had a strong tendency to establish churches that responded to the political geography and differentiated themselves from each other. In response to these developments, the Roman Curia had attempted to standardize knowledge of normativity, for example, by regulating the production of catechetical works, through devotional literature, and through the requirement of curial approval of synodal decrees. The *Editio Romana*, that is, the official text of the *Corpus Iuris Canonici*, mentioned at the beginning of this section, stems from this same context.

At the same time, and even more importantly, the Church strengthened its jurisdiction in the so-called *forum internum*, often related to the practice of confession. The revitalized theological discipline of moral theology provided knowledge of normativity for this *forum internum*, which was regarded as no less juridical than the *forum externum*.[172] The confessor was considered a

170 P. Legendre, "L'inscription du droit canon dans la théologie. Remarques sur la Seconde Scolastique," in S. Kuttner and K. Pennington (eds.), *Proceedings of the Fifth International Congress of Medieval Canon Law, Salamanca, 21–25 September 1976* (Vatican City: Biblioteca Apostolica Vaticana, 1980), 443–54.

171 On the history of Moral Theology, see J. I. Saranyana (ed.), *Teología en América Latina* (Frankfurt and Madrid: Iberoamericana Vervuert, 1999–2005), 3 vols.

172 See J. Mahoney, *The Making of Moral Theology: A Study of the Roman Catholic Tradition* (Oxford: Clarendon Press, 1987); for the significance of the *forum internum* for

judge of souls, a *iudex animarum*, and confession was equated with a judicial procedure: The decrees of the Council of Trent explicitly called the granting of absolution an *actus iudicialis*.[173] In a certain sense, the Church tried to strengthen its control over the souls in the *forum internum* because it was losing its power in the *forum externum*.[174]

Of particular importance for Latin America was the knowledge of normativity produced by the so-called School of Salamanca. This intellectual movement is usually associated with the Dominican convent and the University of Salamanca because prominent theologians such as Francisco de Vitoria, Domingo de Soto, and others taught there. In reality, however, this phenomenon was by no means limited to Castile. In Coimbra, Évora, México, Lima, and many other places, attempts were made to find answers to the burning questions of the time by employing the scholastic method and by working mainly with Thomas Aquinas' *Summa Theologiae*. Although the School of Salamanca is today best known for its great systematic treatises *De iustitia et iure* and *De legibus*, its real aim was to offer Christians guidance on how to live and act properly so as not to endanger their salvation.[175] In various passages of his *De iustitia et iure*, which many consider to be the foundational text of the School of Salamanca, Domingo de Soto stated that he wrote the treatise primarily to offer people guidance, in particular with regard to the then common problem of usury.[176] The more

example, P. J. O'Banion, *The Sacrament of Penance and Religious Life in Golden Age Spain* (Pennsylvania: Pennsylvania State University Press, 2013); G. Marcocci, "Conscience and Empire: Politics and Moral Theology in the Early Modern Portuguese World," *Journal of Early Modern History* 18 (2014), 473–94.

173 In the text from the session of the Council of Trent dedicated to the sacrament of confession, the penitents are seen as the accused facing a trial, *ante hoc tribunal tanquam reos*, the confession is equated to a trial, and the confessor considered a judge: *ad instar actus iudicialis, quo ab ipso velut a iudice sententia pronunciatur*; see Council of Trent, sessio XIV, 25.11.1551, doctrina, cap. II, VI, in the edition of J. Alberigo, J. A. Dossetti, P. P. Joannou et Al. (eds.), *Conciliorum Oecumenicorum Decreta*, 3rd ed. (Bologna: Edidit Istituto per le Scienze, 1973), cited according to the text in J. Wohlmuth (ed.), *Dekrete der ökumenischen Konzilien, vol. III: Konzilien der Neuzeit* (Paderborn: Ferdinand Schöningh, 2002), 704 and 707.

174 See on this process P. Prodi, *Una historia de la justica. De la pluralidad de fueros al dualismo moderno entre conciencia y derecho* (Buenos Aires: Katz, 2008 [2000]), 247–97.

175 See T. Duve, "The School of Salamanca: A Case of Global Knowledge Production," in T. Duve, J. L. Egío and C. Birr (eds.), *The School of Salamanca: A Case of Global Knowledge Production* (Leiden and Boston: Brill Nijhoff, 2021), 1–42; T. Duve, "Law," in H. Braun, E. De Bom and P. Astorri (eds.), *A Companion to Spanish Scholastics* (Brill's Companions to the Christian Tradition 102) (Leiden and Boston: Brill Nijhoff, 2021), 57–84.

176 Domingo de Soto, *De iustitia et iure* (Salamanca, 1553), *Prooemium*, fol. 5.

difficult the case, the greater the need for an expert's opinion. Francisco de Vitoria had stated this clearly at the beginning of his famous *Relectio* on the Indies: "Effectively, for an act to be good, if there is cause for doubt, it is necessary to do it according to a wise man's advice."[177] The wise men he refers to were the theologians.

Such statements express not only a methodological conviction but also what could be called a culture of consultation prevalent in the Iberian monarchies during the sixteenth and seventeenth centuries. One sees this culture at the highest hierarchical level in the *juntas* held before the king, in the important role of confessors, in the many questions posed by the Crowns to moral theologians in Coimbra, Évora, or Salamanca, and in institutions such as the Portuguese Crown's *Mesa da Consciência*, which was "one of the two pillars of Portuguese colonial society."[178] Priests and moral theologians were confronted with an abundance of requests also in their daily lives.[179] Although this naturally elevated their status and placed them in a position of power, they were not always enthusiastic about it. At the beginning of one of his answers to questions about the permissibility of certain commercial customs, Francisco de Vitoria wrote: "I do not really feel like answering the cases brought by the traders of finance without knowing who wants information and why. After all, many only ask in order to have an advantage, and to be happy when you give them permission. And if one says something that goes against their interests, they do not care and make fun of the doctrine and its author."[180]

This practical dimension of moral theology – an orientation toward the solution of concrete cases – meant that moral theologians dealt with

177 Francisco de Vitoria, in T. Duve and M. Lutz-Bachmann (eds.), *Francisco de Vitoria, Relectiones Theologicae XII* (Mainz: Akademie der Wissenschaften und der Literatur, 2018 [1557]), vol. II; *The School of Salamanca. Eine Digitale Quellensammlung*, https://id.salamanca.school/texts/W0013, "Relectio … quam habuit … anno a dominica incarnatione millesimo quingentesimo trigesimo nono…," 289, "Ad hoc enim ut actus sit bonus, oportet si aliâs non est certum, ut fiat secundum diffinitionem & determinationem sapientis. Haec enim est una conditio boni actus…," 288.

178 C. R. Boxer, *The Portuguese Seaborne Empire, 1415–1825* (Lisbon: Carcanet, 1991 [1969]), 273. On the *Mesa de Consciência e Ordens*, see Carmo Dias Farinha and Azevedo Jara, *Mesa da Consciência*.

179 See A. González Polvillo, *El gobierno de los otros. Confesión y control de la conciencia en la España Moderna* (Seville: Universidad de Sevilla, 2010); O'Banion, *Sacrament of Penance and Religious Life*.

180 Francisco de Vitoria, "Disensiones del reverendo padre maestro fray Francisco de Vitoria sobre ciertos tratos de mercaderes," in Z. Huarte and M. Idoya (eds.), *Francisco de Vitoria. Contratos y usura* (Colección de Pensamiento Medieval y Renacentista) (Pamplona: Ediciones Universidad de Navarra, 2006), 302.

many practical legal problems. The fundamental reflections on the *ius gentium*, on the status of indigenous peoples, or on the legitimacy or illegitimacy of slavery are found in texts written by moral theologians because they felt a responsibility to judge these issues.[181] Since precise knowledge of the local circumstances was crucial to adequately address such matters, ready-made answers were simply insufficient, especially in Latin America, where many situations were new and at least perceived to be different. Offering advice without knowledge of local circumstances was considered extremely dangerous. Written at the request of the merchants in Seville, and based on his experience in Mexico, the Dominican Tomás de Mercado emphasized this point in his 1569 manual on contract law: "In this little book, I have thought it necessary to write on the theory of businesses along the way they are practiced, because this is something that the common people know and that the very learned men ignore, or, at least, do not fully understand."[182]

The results of moral theologians' reflections on these questions of everyday life were disseminated in a variety of ways: through individual advice, artistic representations, sermons as well as manuals for confessors and for confession, catechisms, and other texts of a pragmatic nature.[183] Unlike legal books, confessional manuals and catechisms were frequently translated into indigenous languages. Both pictograms and printed translations of texts were of major importance for evangelization and thus for the teaching and implementation of knowledge of normativity.[184] Indigenous believers and Afro-Latin Americans who participated in confraternities helped disseminate this knowledge of normativity in their communities. In this way, too, knowledge of normativity from the religious sphere was translated into the diverse and multiple situations of everyday life and became localized.

181 See on *ius gentium* Koskenniemi, *Uttermost Parts of the Earth*, 117–211; on slavery the overview in J. M. García Añoveros, *El pensamiento y los argumentos sobre la esclavitud en Europa en el siglo XVI y su aplicación a los indios americanos y a los negros africanus* (Madrid: CSIC, 2000), vol. VI.

182 J. L. Egío, "Travelling Scholastics: The Emergence of an Empirical Normative Authority in Early Modern Spanish America," in C. Zwierlein (ed.), *The Power of the Dispersed: Early Modern Global Travelers Beyond Integration* (Intersections: Interdisciplinary Studies in Early Modern Culture 77) (Leiden and Boston: Brill Nijhoff, 2022), 169.

183 D. Rex Galindo, *To Sin No More: Franciscans and Conversion in the Hispanic World, 1683–1830* (Stanford: Stanford University Press, 2017).

184 Pharo, "Transfer of Moral Knowledge," 53–94; Hill Boone, Burkhart and Tavárez, *Painted Words*; G. C. Machado Cabral, D. X. de Farias, and S. K. Limão Papa (eds.), *Fontes do Direito na América Portuguesa. Estudos sobre o fenômeno jurídico no período colonial (séculos XVI–XVIII)* (Porto Alegre: Editora Fi, 2021).

Translating and Localizing Religious Knowledge of Normativity

The localization of knowledge of normativity from the religious sphere via cultural translation (with the concrete situation in mind) occurred each time a normative statement was produced (see Section 1.3). This production of a normative statement could take place in the ecclesiastical court, in the confessional, in writing a legal opinion, or in advising merchants, soldiers, or kings.[185]

A prominent example for how this process of continuous cultural translation occurred is the knowledge of normativity that had accumulated over the centuries around the term *miserabilis persona*. In Latin America, this knowledge was used to create normative options to deal with specific problems related to the integration of indigenous peoples into Christianity.[186] As shown more extensively in Section 1.3, the term had been employed by jurists and canonists since the Middle Ages to designate a person who was, according to Christian principles, in a situation worthy of commiseration, and thus deserved privileged treatment. The broad field of normative options that emerged over the centuries around this notion was used in colonial Latin America in quite flexible ways. It also served, for example, to claim ecclesiastical jurisdiction over indigenous peoples. When Bartolomé de las Casas took office as bishop of Chiapas, he and the bishops from Guatemala and Nicaragua jointly claimed in a letter to the *Audiencia* in 1545 that the indigenous population as a whole should be placed under ecclesiastical – that is, their – exclusive jurisdiction. Though well-founded in medieval canon law, the bishops' argument was unsuccessful. However, what they were proposing was anything but far-fetched. Ten years later, the prominent Castilian jurist Gregorio López – who was involved in the deliberations on the "new laws" (*Leyes Nuevas*) and was familiar with the peculiarities of the New World as a member of the Council of the Indies – also dealt with

185 On localization, see B. Clavero, "Gracia y derecho entre localización, recepción y globalización (lectura coral de Las Vísperas Constitucionales de António Hespanha)," *Quaderni fiorentini per la storia del pensiero giuridico moderno* 41 (2012), 675; A. Agüero, "Local Law and Localization of Law: Hispanic Legal Tradition and Colonial Culture (16th-18th Centuries)," in M. Meccarelli and M. J. Solla Sastre (eds.), *Spatial and Temporal Dimensions for Legal History: Research Experiences and Itineraries* (Global Perspectives on Legal History 6) (Frankfurt am Main: Max-Planck-Institut für europäische Rechtsgeschichte, 2016), 101–30.

186 On the following, see T. Duve, *Sonderrecht in der Frühen Neuzeit. Studien zum ius singulare und den privilegia miserabilium personarum, senum und indorum in Alter und Neuer Welt* (Frankfurt: Vittorio Klostermann, 2008).

the problem of ecclesiastical jurisdiction over *miserabiles personae* in his gloss on the *Siete Partidas*. Though he concluded that no realistic case under the current circumstances would justify the application of such a doctrine, one exception seemed possible to him. In rare circumstances, he wrote, one might accept a subsidiary jurisdictional power of the bishop in instances of negligence on the part of secular judges regarding cases of *miserabiles personae* in areas where it was not easy to access royal justice (*defectus iustitiae*). This would be the case, he added, for bishops of provinces of "particularly remote areas," as in the case of the New World, "where there are Indians recently converted to the faith, who are also called *miserabiles personae*."[187] In short, a doctrine developed in medieval canon law was used to find a solution to a problem in Latin America, where vast distances generated challenging practical problems when it came to large parts of the population. The knowledge accumulated over centuries was selected, adapted, translated into new circumstances.

Though reference to centuries-old traditions and extensive quotations of medieval canon law were not uncommon in the Indies, this was obviously a phenomenon of erudite elite practice. Yet the mechanism of translating a normative option taken from the tradition was by no means restricted to the elite. When cases of superstition (*superstitio*) were examined as part of the Inquisition proceedings at Cartagena de Indias, for example, the officials naturally referred to an offense that had been dealt with in a plethora of texts over centuries. However, there were some difficult questions to be decided in the concrete cases, and given the distances involved, it was not always easy to call in an expert to judge the case. For example, it was important to determine whether a given superstitious practice should be sanctioned as a major cause or only as a very slight deviation (*causas leves y levísimas*). A number of criteria could be taken into account, such as the frequency with which the superstitious practice was carried out, the persons involved, and so on. These and many other questions had to be resolved by relying on the knowledge available in handbooks for the Inquisition and similar resources, but these sources nevertheless left many open questions. In order to resolve this situation, leaflets (*cartillas*) and small treatises (*obritas*) summarized the answers developed in the practice of the tribunal. Doing so meant producing a specific (or even new) meaning of the offense, as well as introducing

187 Gregorio López, *Las Siete Partidas del Sabio Rey don Alonso el nono, nuevamente Glosadas por el Licenciado Gregorio Lopez del Consejo Real de Indias de su Magestad* ... (Salamanca, 1555), ad 1.6.48, glos. g, ad v. Rey.

new distinctions and categories. Repetition of this practice could lead to entrenched meanings and thus to different legal situations in different places, not to mention that this production of norms in specific cases simultaneously defined the content and limits of popular religiosity.[188] Here again, what occurred was a translation of knowledge of normativity from tradition or previous practical experience to solve new concrete cases under specific conditions. This translation produced new knowledge that could then be used to resolve the future cases, eventually leading to a local or regional practice distinct from other places'. However, if this knowledge was stored in media, for example, leaflets or small handbooks, it could circulate and have an impact on other areas, too.

Especially when it came to the indigenous population, the need to establish special regulations and new meanings was enormous. A central problem was marriage law. The privileges granted by the pope recognizing the validity of certain marriages prior to baptism solved many, though not all, of the important problems. How should one deal with cultural practices that were difficult to interpret, for example, with celebrations and rituals preceding the wedding or work performed by the future son-in-law in the household of the future parents-in-law? Did such celebrations already constitute a promise of marriage and the work a dower?[189] Here again, the indigenous practices had to be translated, now into the Catholic mindset.

Intense discussion also arose about how long members of indigenous peoples should be regarded "neophytes," that is, as "still young plants" in the faith. Certain privileges, for example, with regard to religious duties, and exclusions, for example, the exclusion from the sacrament of priestly ordination, were attached to this category. Once this issue was concluded, for example, because enough time had passed and the category "neophytes" was no longer applicable, the main point of contention focused on whether the so-called *mestizos*, descendants of mixed marriages, should have access to the

188 P. Mejía, "'Just Rules' for a 'Religiosity of Simple People?': Devotional Literature and Inquisitory Trials in Cartagena de Indias (17th–18th Centuries)," in T. Duve and O. Danwerth (eds.), *Knowledge of the Pragmatici: Legal and Moral Theological Literature and the Formation of Early Modern Ibero-America* (Leiden and Boston: Brill Nijhoff, 2020), 328–48.

189 A. de Zaballa Beascoechea, "Matrimonio (DCH)," *Max Planck Institute for European Legal History Research Paper Series No. 2018-15* (Frankfurt am Main: Afro-Latin Americans, 2018), http://dx.doi.org/10.2139/ssrn.3299914 (last accessed Jan. 13, 2022); on marriage of indigenous people and African-Americans C. de Castelnau-L'Éstoile, *Un catholicisme colonial. Le mariage des Indiens et des esclaves au Brésil, XVIe–XVIIIe siècle* (Paris: Presses Universitaires de France, 2019).

priesthood and could enter religious orders.[190] Though these disputes were partly motivated by the social and economic significance of holding these offices, the results shaped the interpretation of canon law, for example, with regard to the category *neophytus*. According to the traditional interpretation, certain requirements had to be met to be admitted to the sacrament of ordination, but in many cases a dispensation was possible. In the end, if the personal conditions were met and the necessary qualification proven, any baptized male was eligible to become a priest. In Latin America, however, the situation was far from clear, not least due to the different strategies employed by the Church and the Crown. While Pope Gregory XIII had dispensed the so-called *mestizos* from the ordination prohibition of illegitimate descent in 1576, enabling them to become priests, the Spanish Crown issued a general prohibition of ordination against them in 1578. Echoing the sentiments of the Crown, and following the Jesuit José de Acosta's advice in his authoritative work *De procuranda indorum salute*, the Provincial Council of the Jesuits in Lima also decided in 1582 not to admit *mestizos* to the order.

Before the Third Provincial Council of Lima in 1582/83, however, a group of *mestizos* conducted a sort of trial (*proceso*) to collect evidence for their claim to be admitted to ordination. They successfully obtained the Council's permission to question witnesses and obtain detailed opinions to make the king revoke the previous disposition banning them. Their collective action, supported by confraternities of *mestizos* in various cities of the Viceroyalty of Peru, was ultimately successful. After at least two envoys presented their arguments and handed over the material to the king, the ban was lifted in 1588. The royal decree stating that *mestizos* were allowed to enter the priesthood was even included in the *Recopilación de Indias* a century later. In this case, collective action by *mestizos* before the council in Lima eventually led to the repeal of a royal norm contradicting the principles of universal canon law ten years after its enactment, and the publication in the *Recopilación* meant that this law could be invoked beyond the Viceroyalty of Peru. Not only did local action on the part of *mestizos* before the church council in Peru result in the amendment of royal legislation, it also created arguments applicable to other cases, that is, about the children of members of indigenous peoples

190 A. J. Machado de Oliveira, "Dispensa da cor e clero nativo: poder eclesiástico e sociedade católica na América Portuguesa," in A. J. Machado de Oliveira and W. de Souza Martins (eds.), *Dimensões do catolicismo no Império português (séculos XVI–XIX)* (Rio de Janeiro: Garamond, 2014), 199–229. For a broad overview, see M. C. Giannini, "Il problema dell' esclusione dei non bianchi dal sacerdocio e dagli ordini religiosi nei cattolicesimi dell' età moderna (XVI–XVII secolo)," *CrSt* 42(3) (2021), 751–92.

with people of African descent, or of so-called *mestizos* with so-called *mulatos*, both in Latin America and beyond.[191] Local action thus transformed the laws of the empire and reinforced and localized the universal canon law.

The case also illustrates the deep entanglements between the Church, secular institutions, and their respective laws. Church and secular institutions were part of the same political empires: They shared the idea of a *Respublica Christiana*, operated under the conditions of a "jurisdictional culture," and cooperated in many ways. Much more so than in the case of knowledge of normativity from the secular sphere, however, knowledge of normativity from the religious sphere must be understood in terms of the tension between the claim to universality, on the one hand, and the necessity of localization, on the other. The global outreach of the Catholic Church, together with the need to localize its precepts, thus turns out to be a showcase for the process of "glocalization."

Glocalizations

Notwithstanding the many instruments for accommodation and localization, the challenge involved in translating the knowledge of normativity stemming mainly from canon law and moral theology into seemingly new situations was enormous. The numerous overlapping jurisdictions inside the Church as well as between it and the state added further complexity, forcing actors to continuously negotiate boundaries. The methods used to cope with this need were firmly rooted in European juridical culture and scholarly practices, and a multiplicity of consolidated local practices of juridical conviviality emerged. Knowledge of normativity stemming from the religious sphere was stored in different media and activated in different forums. It played an essential role in the continuous construction of society and its law, going far beyond the realm of Church institutions, and was deeply entangled with secular knowledge of normativity.

A comparison of the Spanish and Portuguese spheres indicates that the institutional variations, different temporalities, and individual strategies of settlement in Latin America (as well as in the Philippines and the Caribbean) did not result in two completely dissimilar historical paths. As soon as the role of Brazil within the Portuguese empire changed over the course of the seventeenth century, both the institutional setting and state actions with regard to religion in Portuguese and Spanish America start to converge. As a result of the personal union between the Spanish and Portuguese Crowns,

191 Castañeda Delgado, *El mestizaje en Indias*.

the similarity of their reform efforts during the Pombaline and Bourbon eras, the strong presence of the missionary orders and their moral theologies, and the significant role of the Curia after the Council of Trent, knowledge of normativity from the religious sphere operated under increasingly similar conditions in both colonial empires. At the same time, the knowledge of normativity was translated under local conditions in numerous places throughout the world, leading to what has been called an "early modern composite Catholicism" and the "making of Roman Catholicism as a world religion."[192]

Despite secularization, the Catholic Church maintained its influence in many parts of Latin America well into the twentieth century. In some places, this influence continues to this day. The growing political influence of evangelical movements in some parts of Latin America within the past few decades, as well as heated debates about topics like the criminalization of abortion, show the enduring presence and legal significance of religion and its normativity for Latin American law.

. . .

3.3 The Domestic Sphere*

ROMINA ZAMORA

The historical regime of normativity that took shape in colonial Latin America consisted of several orders which developed in a complementary manner. While each of those normative spheres applied to people's everyday lives to regulate a wide range of realities – including interactions between persons of different social classes, possession and ownership, effective governance over a specific territory, and the implementation of shared principles of justice and punishment – the domestic normative sphere remained the most immediate and often the most relevant in people's lives.[193]

192 See Windler, "Early Modern Composite Catholicism"; S. Ditchfield, "'Provincializing Europe': The Circulation of the Sacred and Reciprocity in the Making of Roman Catholicism as a World Religion," in K. von Greyerz and A. Schubert (eds.), *Reformation und Reformationen. Kontinuitäten, Identitäten, Narrative/Reformation and Reformations. Continuities, Identities and Narratives* (Schriften des Vereins für Reformationsgeschichte 221) (Gütersloh: Gütersloher Verlagshaus, 2022), 177–206.

* Translated from Spanish by Jean-Paul Calderón.

193 C. Garriga, "¿Cómo escribir una historia 'descolonizada' del derecho en América Latina?," in J. Vallejo Fernández de la Reguera and S. Martín Martín (eds.), *En Antidora. Homenaje a Bartolomé Clavero* (Madrid: Thomson Reuters Aranzadi,

Following the invasion of American lands, Spanish and Portuguese colonizers reorganized territorial and political structures.[194] Cities functioned as scattered islands with their own governance structures within a territory that was only partially explored and controlled.[195] That being said, ruling over such an extensive territory also required assistance from other normative transmission channels, such as the *pueblos de indios* (indigenous towns / communities established by the Spanish Crown) and the European *casas grandes* (literally: big houses or large households).[196]

In this section, I will analyze the *casa grande's* role, and most importantly, the person in charge thereof – the *pater familias* – in shaping the colonial normative landscape. I will demonstrate that the *casa grande* was a key institution that played a highly complex, recognized, and predominant role in governing a territory's economic production, social interactions, and political and legal organization.[197] I will focus on the householder, *hacendado*, or *fazendeiro*

2019), 325–76; C. Ramos Nuñez, *Historia del derecho peruano* (Lima: Palestra, 2019); D. Barriera, *Historia y justicia. Cultura, política y sociedad en el Río de la Plata (Siglos XVI–XIX)* (Buenos Aires: Prometeo, 2019); A. M. Hespanha, "Fazer um império com palabras," in Â. Barreto Xavier and C. Nogueira da Silva (eds.), *O Governo dos Outros. Poder e Diferença no Império Português* (Lisbon: ICS, 2016), 67–100; B. Clavero, "¿Es que no hubo genocidio en las Américas?," *Quaderni fiorentini per la storia del pensiero giuridico moderno* 47 (2018), 647–87.

194 "L'histoire de la formation territoriale de la monarchie espagnole a conféré à la république urbaine une importance politique considérable." A. Lempérière, *Entre Dieu et le Roi, la République. Mexico, XVIe–XIXe siècle* (Paris: Les Belles Lettres, 2004), 6; A. Pereira Sousa, *Poder político local e vida cotidiana: a Câmara Municipal da cidade de Salvador no séc. XVIII* (Bahía: Universidad Estatal del Sudoeste de Bahía, 2013); P. Sanz Camañes, *Las ciudades en la América Hispanha. Siglos XV al XVIII* (Claves históricas) (Madrid: Silex, 2004); R. Morse, "El desarrollo urbano de la Hispanoamérica colonial," in L. Bethell (ed.), *Historia de América Latina* (Barcelona: Ed. Crítica, 1990), vol. III, 15–48; J. Hardoy and R. Schaedel (eds.), *Las ciudades de América Latina y sus áreas de influencia a través de la historia* (Buenos Aires: Siap, 1975).

195 D. Barriera, "Archipiélagos de gobierno: distancias y discontinuidades territoriales como problemas para el análisis histórico de los territorios americanos de la monarquía española," keynote speech, VI Congreso Internacional de Historia de la América Hispánica (Siglos XVI–XIX), Coahuila (3 Nov. 2021).

196 J. Erbig, *Entre caciques y cartógrafos. La construcción de un límite interimperial en la Sudamérica del siglo XVIII* (Buenos Aires: Prometeo, 2022); C. Mayo, *Estancia y sociedad en la pampa (1740–1820)* (Buenos Aires: Biblos, 1995); E. A. Davis, *Louisiana: A Narrative History* (Baton Rouge: Claitor's Publishing, 1971); E. Florescano, "Formación y estructura de la hacienda en Nueva España," in L. Bethell (ed.), *Historia de América Latina* (Barcelona: Ed. Crítica, 1990), vol. III, 92–122.

197 There is a wealth of research on the *casa grande* and plantations. Researchers from North America, Mesoamerica, the Caribbean, and all over South America have covered the topic and analyzed it through different perspectives. It is, among others, identified as a space of social reproduction and economic production. Research has also focused on the *casa grande's* linkages with slavery and the work of servants; some authors have looked into the matter from a possession and property point of view, and others have inquired into its archaeological and architectural dimensions and

(*senhor da terra*) who concurrently played the roles of father, neighbor, and master, and held a central position in people's everyday lives, in a context where at least 80 percent of the populace still lived in the countryside.[198] This focus will provide a clearer understanding of those domestic spaces that contributed to the transmission, creation, and recreation of norms while also highlighting that a wealth of knowledge of normativity was produced, shared, and applied by a myriad of actors with different backgrounds, social positions, and motivations.[199]

also on its environmental impact. See: C. Shammas, "Anglo-American Household Government in Comparative Perspective," *The William and Mary Quarterly* 52(1) (1995), 104–44; E. Adams Davis, R. A. Suarez, and J. Gray Taylor, *Louisiana: The Pelican State* (Louisiana: Louisiana State University Press, 1985); P. E. Hoffman, *Luisiana* (Madrid: Mapfre, 1992); B. Wyatt-Brown, "The Plantation Household Revisited," *The Mississippi Quarterly* 65(4) (2012), 591–612; A. J. Bauer, "Millers and Grinders: Technology and Household Economy in Meso-America," *Agricultural History* 64(1) (1990), 1–17; M. D. Groover, "Creolization and the Archaeology of Multiethnic Households in the American South," *Historical Archaeology* 34(3) (2000), 99–106; J. Handler and D. Wallman, "Production Activities in the Household Economies of Plantation Slaves: Barbados and Martinique, Mid-1600s to Mid-1800s," *International Journal of Historic Archaeology* 18 (2014), 441–66; J. Gelman, *Campesinos y estancieros. Una región del Río de la Plata a fines de la época colonial* (Buenos Aires: Los libros del Riel, 1998); J. C. Garavaglia, *Pastores y labradores de Buenos Aires. Una historia agraria de la campaña bonaerense, 1700–1830* (Buenos Aires: Instituto de Estudios Histórico Sociales, Ediciones La Flor, Universidad Pablo de Olavide, 1999); L. Flores García, *La casa y el territorio* (Zacatecas: Texere, 2013). – see: F. Chevalier, *La formación de los latifundios en México. Hacienda y sociedad en los siglos XVI, XVII y XVIII*, 3rd rev. enl. ed. (Mexico City: Fondo de Cultura Económica, 2013); E. Van Young, *La ciudad y el campo en el México del siglo XVIII. La economía rural de la región de Guadalajara, 1675–1820* (Mexico City: Fondo de Cultura Económica, 1989); E. A. Kuznesof, *Household Economy and Urban Development. São Paulo, 1765 to 1836* (New York: Routledge, 2019); J. A. Guevara Gil, *Propiedad agraria y derecho colonial. Los documentos de la hacienda Santotis. Cuzco (1543–1822)* (Lima: PUCP, 1993); T. Halperín Donghi, *La formación de la clase terrateniente bonaerense* (Buenos Aires: Prometeo, 2007); D. Brading, *Mineros y comerciantes en el México Borbónico* (Mexico City: Fondo de Cultura Económica, 1979); H. Prem, *Milpa y hacienda. Tenencia de la tierra indígena y española en la cuenca del Alto Atoyac, Puebla, México (1520–1650)* (Mexico City: Fondo de Cultura Económica, 1988); N. Sibill, *Ayllus y haciendas. Dos estudios de caso sobre la agricultura colonial en los Andes* (La Paz: HISBOL, 1989); H. S. Klein, *Haciendas and "Ayllus." Rural Society in the Bolivian Andes in the Eighteenth and Nineteenth Centuries* (Stanford: Stanford University Press, 1993); M. Dubber, "The Power to Govern Men and Things: Patriarchal Origins of the Police Power in American Law," *Buffalo Law Review* 52(4) (2004), 1277–345; A. M. Hespanha, *Filhos da Terra. Identidades Mestiças nos Confins da Expansão Portuguesa* (Lisbon: Tinta da China, 2019); V. Tau Anzoátegui, *Nuevos horizontes en el estudio histórico del Derecho Indiano* (Buenos Aires: Instituto de Investigaciones de Historia del Derecho, 1997); T. Duve and H. Pihlajamäki (eds.), *New Horizons in Spanish Colonial Law: Contributions to Transnational Early Modern Legal History* (Global Perspectives on Legal History 3) (Frankfurt am Main: Max-Planck-Institut für europäische Rechtsgeschichte, 2015).

198 M. Dubber, *The Police Power: Patriarchy and the Foundations of American Government* (New York: Columbia University Press, 2005).

199 Hespanha, *Filhos da Terra*; Tau Anzoátegui, *Nuevos horizontes*; Duve and Pihlajamäki (eds.), *New Horizons*.

I will start by offering a descriptive account of the challenges experienced by colonizers in their attempts to establish and recreate a European normative model within the complexities of the American landscape. I will then comment on that model's ability to organize society, particularly relating to the establishment of social status within a multiethnic and diverse population. This is followed by a discussion of the linkages between the householder's domestic governance capacity and the recognition of his role in local governance. The section ends with some general and specific questions – admittedly without providing many answers – on the extent of the *casa grande*'s normative reach in the colonial Latin American legal landscape. To what extent and how did the *pater familias*' actions and decisions in the domestic sphere become broadly applicable rules?[200] This leads me to wonder how norms were developed based on issues arising in the domestic sphere, including obedience to the father, social status within multiethnic populations, work, ownership of land and authority over those living thereon, slavery, or domestic service. Given that theoretical knowledge and practical solutions to everyday problems (emerging under specific, but also changing and contingent circumstances) are both necessary components of casuistic systems, it is worth asking to what extent they had an impact on other norm-production spheres.[201]

The Casa Grande *in Latin America. Creation, Recreation, and the Originality of a Model*

As a social institution, in Latin America, the *casa grande* was instrumental in ensuring the occupation and control of the territory, just as it was for British America. This was not only true for the colonial period but also – and with particular significance – when colonies became independent. It was a basic unit of social reproduction, and most importantly, it was the primary traditional corporate governance structure and played an extraordinarily powerful role in regulating different aspects of everyday life such as micropolitics, and the internalization of discipline and faith.[202] A closer look at the *casa grande* shows

200 Cesare Beccaria argued that the privileges of the nobles, that is, of the particular interests of the leading families, form a large part of the laws of nations. Cesare Beccaria, *De los delitos y las penas*, trans. and annot. F. Tomás y Valiente (Buenos Aires: Hyspa, 2005 [1764]), 90.

201 T. Duve, "What Is Global Legal History?," *Comparative Legal History* 8(2) (2020), 73–115.

202 Otto Brunner pioneered historiographic research on the matter with his study on "das ganze Haus": O. Brunner, "La 'casa grande' y la 'Oeconomia' de la vieja Europa," in O. Brunner, *Nuevos caminos de la historia social y constitucional*, trans. A. F. de Rodríguez (Buenos Aires: Alfa, 1976 [1948]), 87–123; G. Freyre, *Casa-Grande y Senzala* (Madrid: Marcial Pons, 2010 [1933]).

how it contributed to regulating domestic relationships, sexuality, health care, religious education, and the transmission of values within the domestic community. A broader view shows a political system where the legitimacy of a person's functions in the public sphere rested on domestic authority. The function and authority of the *pater familias* was the central pillar of different forms of power, ranging from the parental relationships to the most feudal and asymmetric ones. The main role in the *casa grande* was undoubtedly played by the father: He was the cornerstone of internal dynamics, discipline, property-related rules, and political relationships.[203]

Lawyers and jurists focusing on Spanish America, such as Juan de Matienzo, Miguel de Agía, or Juan Solórzano Pereira, argued that governing the *casa* was equivalent to ruling over the republic. These jurists lived in Latin America and had firsthand knowledge of the issues that arose there. They contended that some had to command and others to obey to ensure order and harmony within the mystical body of the republic, for the sake of its preservation and perpetuity. Similar to the human body, composed of parts with different complementary properties and functions, the republic's body needed different parts to fulfill a variety of roles. This was held to be such an absolute truth that Agía suggested that "it would not be difficult to convince those who know about governance of this truth, and of the republic's need for different classes of people."[204]

Large areas of territory were under the direct governance of a *casa grande*, which included authority over large populations that extended far beyond the *casa*'s biological family. The *casa* thus became a central locus of governance.[205] The main figure was the father, or both the patriarch and

203 P. Laslett, "La famiglia e l'aggregato domestico come grupo di lavoro e gruppo di parenti: aree dell' Europa tradizionale a confront," in R. Wall, J. Robin, and P. Laslett (eds.), *Family Forms in Historic Europe* (Cambridge: Cambridge University Press, 1983), 253–304; B. Clavero, *Freedom's Law and Indigenous Rights: From Europe's Oeconomy to the Constitutionalism of the Americas* (Studies in Comparative Legal History) (Berkeley: Robbins Collection, 2005).

204 Miguel de Agia, "Tratado que contiene tres pareceres graves en Derecho. Primer parecer," in Miguel de Agia, *Servidumbres personales de indios*, F. J. de Ayala (ed.) (Seville: Escuela de Estudios Hispanoamericanos, 1946), 43; A. Flores Galindo, *La ciudad sumergida. Aristocracia y plebe en Lima, 1760–1830* (Lima: Editorial Horizonte, 1986).

205 D. Frigo, *Il padre di famiglia. Governo della casa e governo civile nella tradizione dell'economica tra cinque e seicento* (Rome: Bulzoni, 1985); T. Duve, "Der blinde Fleck der 'Oeconomia'? Wirtschaft und Soziales in der frühen Neuzeit," in H. Mohnhaupt and J.-F. Kervégan (eds.), *Wirtschaft und Wirtschaftstheorie in Rechtsgeschichte und Philosophie* (Frankfurt: Vittorio Klostermann, 2004); A. Seelaender, "A longa sombra da casa. Poder doméstico, conceitos tradicionais e imaginário jurídico na transição brasileira do antigo regime à modernidade," *Instituto Histórico y Geográfico Brasileño* 473 (2017), 327–418; R. Zamora, *Casa poblada y buen gobierno. Oeconomia católica y servicio personal en S. M. Tucumán, siglo XVIII* (Buenos Aires: Prometeo, 2017).

matriarch, since the *casa* could fall under the control of either the father alone or the father and mother together.[206] Because marriage was the bedrock of the *casa grande*, women were not merely relegated to a lesser role. The mother played an undeniably relevant role, which was reinforced by the Latin American culture – but also Iberian, to a certain extent – of matrilocality.

The house itself did not only accommodate the married couple and its children, but also all their next of kin and other people close to them (i.e., illegitimate children, members of the extended family, and guests) "[who were] under their protection and were familiar with them, and all those who supported and remained [in] their *casas* … providing assistance, services or care for their family or domestic matters."[207] The servants were also included in the household, under the generic designation of *criados*.[208] In addition, temporary laborers, enslaved persons, and *agregados* (see Section 3.1) also lived on the *casa grande*'s extensive lands. The father – as well as the mother – exercised their authority over these individuals by setting their expectations, including moral and obedience standards but also knowledges of normativity relating to notions of right and wrong, on social status, work, wealth production, and on land possession and ownership. In the *casa grande*, the mother was in charge of female servants, child-rearing, health care, food preparation, representing the family's moral character in public, but also of relationships with other women of the principal families in order to establish influential connections in the political sphere.[209] Many *haciendas* also had *obrajes* (textile and other workshops) where women and men worked under harsh conditions, including – in some places and times – with shackles on their feet to prevent them from escaping.[210] In addition to these people, the

206 R. Zamora, "Oeconomia," in J. Vallejo Fernández de la Reguera and C. Garriga (eds.), *Manual de Historia del Derecho español* (Madrid: Tirant lo Blanch, in press).

207 *Recopilación de Leyes de Indias [Compilation of the Laws of the Indies]* (1680), vol. I, lib. 2, tit. 2, law XXVIII: "Que por criados, allegados y familiares sean tenidos todos los que esta ley declara."

208 *Recopilación [Compilation]*, vol. I, lib. 2, tit. 2, law XXVIII: "Que por criados sean tenidos todos los que llevaren salario o acostamiento."

209 S. Stern, *La historia secreta del género. Mujeres, hombres y poder en las postrimerías del período colonial* (Mexico City: Fondo de Cultura Económica, 1999); A. Becker, "Gender in the History of Early Modern Political Thought," *The Historical Journal* 60(4) (2017), 843–63.

210 E. de la Torre Villar, *Los pareceres de don Juan de Padilla y Diego de León Pinelo acerca de la enseñanza y buen tratamiento de los indios* (suplemento al Boletín del Instituto de Investigaciones Bibliográficas 6) (Mexico City: UNAM, 1979); K. Graubart, *With Our Labor and Sweat: Indigenous Women and the Formation of Colonial Society in Peru, 1560–1700* (Stanford: Stanford University Press, 2007); A. Carabarín Gracia, *El trabajo y los trabajadores del obraje en la ciudad de Puebla. 1700–1710* (Mexico City: Centro de Investigaciones Históricas y Sociales, 1984).

Latin American *casa grande* was in need of an indigenous labor force, which required specific forms of incorporation.

The Encomienda: A Form of Casa Grande?

The *encomienda* was the first form of *casa grande* to emerge in Latin America.[211] It was based on a royal grant "entrusting" a specific number of the local indigenous population to a Spanish *vecino* (a person of high status and good reputation who owned a house in a town or city; this title was usually bestowed on those relocating to populate the colonies on behalf of the Crown). The *vecino* was in charge of evangelizing indigenous peoples and also entitled to use their labor for a set period of time that could last anywhere from two years to two generations.[212] Gradually, this labor was conflated with the tribute exacted from indigenous peoples by the king. An *encomienda's* duration varied according to time and location, but following the New Laws of 1542 issued by Carlos I of Spain and the Manila Codicil of 1545, it was more or less settled at a period of two generations before it reverted to the Crown, which could decide whether the indigenous peoples subject to the *encomienda* would be entrusted to a *vecino* again.[213]

Pursuant to these grants, indigenous communities would retain possession and use of their land, as the person in charge – the *encomendero* – was not allowed to live there and had no rights over a specific territory.[214] However,

211 Originally called *repartimiento*, this form of service "emerged in the Antilles, almost at the same time as – but independent from – the payment of tribute to the king. Its objective was to fulfill the labor needs of colonial and royal agricultural and mining enterprises. Legally, it was a system of forced labor." As its legal status solidified, it became an *encomienda*. S. Zavala, *La encomienda indiana* (Madrid: Junta para la ampliación de estudios e investigaciones históricas, 1935), 4.

212 The dispute between the *encomenderos* and the Crown regarding the perpetuity of the *encomiendas* lasted throughout the sixteenth and part of the seventeenth centuries until no more *encomiendas* were granted. J. de la Puente Brunke, *Encomiendas y encomenderos del Perú* (Seville: Diputación de Sevilla, 1992).

213 S. Zavala, *El servicio personal de los indios en Nueva España*, 8 vols. (Mexico City: Colegio de México, 1995); S. Zavala, *El servicio personal de los indios en el Perú*, 3 vols. (Mexico City: Colegio de México, 1978–1980); C. Gibson, *Los aztecas bajo el dominio español 1519–1810* (Mexico City: Siglo XXI, 1996); M. Mörner, "La hacienda Hispanoamericana. Examen de las investigaciones y debates recientes," in E. Florescano (ed.), *Haciendas, latifundios y plantaciones en América Latina* (Mexico City: Siglo XXI, 1975), 15–48; G. Madrazo, *Hacienda y encomienda en los Andes. La Puna de Jujuy bajo el marquesado de Tojo, siglos XVII–XIX* (Buenos Aires: Fondo Editorial, 1982).

214 T. Herzog, "Colonial Law and 'Native Customs'. Indigenous Land Rights in Colonial Spanish America," *The Americas* 9 (2013), 303–21; M. Menegus Bornemann, "Títulos Primordiales de los pueblos de indios," in M. Menegus Bornemann (ed.), *Dos décadas de investigación en historia económica comparada en América Latina. Homenaje a Carlos Sempat Assadourian* (Mexico City: Colegio de México, UNAM, CIESAS, Instituto Mora, 1999),

Spanish colonizers were permitted to settle on uninhabited indigenous territories or bordering regions. This often resulted in the taking of such lands by the Spanish, especially given that many territories were vacant and unoccupied due to the decline of indigenous populations.[215] Philip II issued a royal *cédula* in 1591 – known as *de los baldíos* (of the wasteland), which sought to resolve this issue and to curb settlers' abuses against both indigenous communities and the king. The implementation of this decree (including its misuses and improper applications), however, produced varying results.[216]

The *encomendero* exercised "paternal dominion" over the entrusted community.[217] This meant he not only had a right, but also the duty to protect the *encomendados* and to care for them in the event of illness. The *encomienda* did not establish a *casa grande* per se; rather, the *casa grande* became the subject of manifold discussions and prompted the crafting of many (varied and sometimes even contradictory) norms, which generally revolved around the status of indigenous peoples and the scope of Christian freedom.[218] For jurists

137–62; D. Bonnett Vélez, "De la conformación de los pueblos de indios al surgimiento de las parroquias de vecinos. El caso del Altiplano cundiboyansense," *Revista de Estudios Sociales* 1 (2001), 9–19; I. Goicovic and A. Armijo, "Tierras en disputa. El traslado de los pueblos de indios de Melipilla, Chile, siglos XVIII–XIX," *Historia y Sociedad* 39 (2020), 24–50; J. Farberman, "Las márgenes de los pueblos de indios. Agregados, arrendatarios y soldados en el Tucumán colonial. Siglos XVIII y XIX," *Nuevo Mundo, Mundos Nuevos* (2009) https://doi.org/10.4000/nuevomundo.57474 (last accessed Jan. 12, 2022); L. M. Glave, "El arbitrio de tierras de 1622 y el debate sobre las propiedades y los derechos coloniales de los indios," *Anuario de Estudios Americanos* 71(1) (2014), 79–106; C. Jurado, "Las reducciones toledanas a pueblos de indios: aproximación a un conflicto," *Cahiers des Amériques latines* (2004), 123–37; G. P. Lopera Mesa, "Creando posesión vía desposesión. Visitas a la tierra y conformación de resguardos indígenas en la Vega de Supía, 1559–1759," *Fronteras de la Historia* 25(2) (2020), 120–56.

215 J. V. Mumford, *Vertical Empire: The General Resettlement of Indians in the Colonial Andes* (Durham: Duke University Press, 2012); S. A. Wernke, *Negotiated Settlements: Andean Communities and Landscapes under Inka and Spanish Colonialism* (Gainesville: University Press of Florida, 2013); E. Noli, "Pueblos de indios, indios sin pueblos: los calchaquíes en la visita de Luján de Vargas de 1693 a San Miguel de Tucumán," *Anales Nueva Época* 6 (2005), 330–63.

216 S. Stern, *Los pueblos indígenas del Perú y el desafío de la conquista española. Huamanga hasta 1640* (Madrid: Alianza Editorial, 1982).

217 "Ordenanzas dadas por Gonzalo de Abreu para el buen tratamiento de los indios en las provincias de Tucumán. Santiago del Estero, 10 de abril 1576," in R. Levillier (ed.), *Correspondencia de la ciudad de Buenos Aires con los reyes de España. Documentos del Archivo de Indias. Cartas del Cabildo; memoriales presentados en la corte por los procuradores, apoderados y enviados de la ciudad* (Buenos Aires: Municipalidad de Buenos Aires, 1915), vol. 2, 291–332.

218 It is in this context that Francisco de Vitoria's suggestion to use the principle of *ius gentium* emerged. This idea was closely linked to the Christian aspects of the old *ius commune*, which had recognized the freedom of indigenous communities. L. Nuzzo, "Between America and Europe: The Strange Case of the derecho indiano," in T. Duve and H. Pihlajamäki (eds.), *New Horizons in Spanish Colonial Law* (Global Perspectives on Legal History 3) (Frankfurt am Main: Max-Planck-Institut für europäische Rechtsgeschichte, 2015), 161–91, at 171.

and theologians, it was an indisputable fact that the conversion of indigenous peoples to Catholicism not only spread the faith but also obligated them to serve.[219] This link between indigenous people and the services they had to render became a legal ground to justify their work in the *casas grandes*.

Nevertheless, the fact that the *encomienda* was not perpetual meant that no genuine feudal ties with indigenous populations could be established under the *encomienda*; these relationships were limited to the – quite imperfect – evangelization of indigenous peoples and their exploitation by the *encomendero*. It is also worth noting that for different reasons, the *encomenderos* became increasingly less desirable to the Crown, which stopped granting *encomiendas* in the Andean and Mesoamerican central regions during the seventeenth century.[220] With the decline of *encomiendas*, the *haciendas* gained prominence as units of production and cultural transmission, as well as spaces that supported the reproduction of order.[221]

The Casa *as Land Management Institution*

As a consequence of the significant distances between cities – but also between production and distribution centers and ports, and even more so between colonial cities and the metropole – there were large tracts of land that were only intermittently known and controlled. While one would think that those "interstitial gaps" would be filled by a wide range of government and ecclesiastical agents, the truth is that the only existing authorities in those areas were the Spanish and Portuguese living in the countryside, who either received land grants from the Crown, or had successfully sought the recognition of a right of possession and thus became lords of a *casa* and controlled some land.

It took centuries to clarify how this territorial and social assemblage would be governed. First, an institution and a specific place were required, and these were provided by a family and the *casa*. The Spanish Crown required that those leaving Spain to colonize the Americas had to establish a *casa poblada* (inhabited house) in an urban settlement.[222] While holding a

219 R. Zamora, "Consapevolezza dello spazio e plasticità giuridica. Due fasi nella regolazione delle encomiendas indigene a Tucumán (regione andina meridionale, XVI e XVII secolo)," *América Crítica* 5(1) (2021), 55–61.

220 In marginal regions such as New Granada and Tucumán, the *encomenderos* managed to maintain their positions at least until the end of the eighteenth century.

221 L. M. Glave and I. Remy, *Estructura agraria y vida rural en una región andina. Ollantaytambo entre los siglos XVI y XIX* (Cusco: Centro de Estudios Regionales Andinos, 1986).

222 *Recopilación [Compilation]*, vol. II, lib. 4, tit. 10, law VI: Que para los oficios se elijan vecinos: "El que tuviere casa poblada, se entienda por vecino."

casa poblada was necessary to have political and jurisdictional rights, it was not – with very few exceptions – an immediate source of wealth for those who had a *casa*. Until well into the latter part of the eighteenth century, most of the goods and wealth – save for the sale of goods made in Castile or by enslaved persons – was produced in the countryside in mines, *obrajes*, *encomiendas*, or *haciendas*. This is why the Spanish *casa grande* in America can be seen as a discontinuous territorial puzzle comprising three parts: the *casa poblada* in the city, the *hacienda* in the countryside, and the *encomienda* of indigenous peoples.

Most of the early Spanish *vecinos* requested and were granted lands located in areas neighboring the cities in which they lived or near their *encomiendas*. As land was only valuable as long as people would work on it, householders attracted landless indigenous peoples, people of lower lineage (*casta*), and poorer Spaniards to farm land, work in the *obrajes*, and care for cattle. By virtue of orders by Philip II that were later codified in the *Recopilación de Leyes de Indias* of 1680, the Spaniards could take indigenous peoples to farm lands as long as they were not attached to a *casa* or assigned to an *encomienda* (unless they had the *encomendero*'s permission).[223] Over time, some indigenous people fled, others were taken from their villages to work, free labor was authorized, and racial mixing (*mestizaje*) became widespread. It became increasingly difficult to identify a worker's ethnic status, as well as the reasons why he or she was in the *hacienda*, and the landholders thus progressively became less interested in clarifying those questions.[224]

The relocation of indigenous populations to the *encomendero*'s *hacienda* was also a common practice. Other indigenous people escaped from their own communities and found shelter in *haciendas* in exchange of their labor. These indigenous peoples – who were usually christianized and westernized (*ladinizados*) and lived on lands held by Spaniards – were known in the Andean

223 *Recopilación [Compilation]*, vol. IV, lib. 3, tit. 5, law III: Que para labradores y oficiales, se puedan llevar indios voluntarios.

224 A. M. Lorandi, "El servicio personal como agente de desestructuración en el Tucumán colonial," *Revista Andina* 6(1) (1988), 135–73; G. Doucet, "La encomienda de servicio personal en el Tucumán, bajo régimen legal: comentarios a las ordenanzas de Gonzalo de Abreu," in A. Levaggi (ed.), *El Aborigen y el Derecho en el Pasado y el Presente* (Buenos Aires: Universidad del Museo Social Argentino, 1990), 141–244; Q. Aldea Vaquero, *El Indio peruano y la defensa de sus derechos* (Madrid: Consejo Superior de Investigaciones Científicas, 1993); I. Castro Olaneta, "Servicio personal, tributo y conciertos en Córdoba a principios del siglo XVII: La visita del gobernador Luis de Quiñones Osorio y la aplicación de las ordenanzas de Francisco de Alfaro," *Memoria Americana* 18(1) (2010), 101–27.

regions of South America as *yanaconas de españoles*.[225] They were entire families living in relatively stable conditions on the land of the Spanish lord who were in general not paid for their work, but were provided with a plot of land, sometimes under a lease contract, or with no legal protection against evictions. In different places, they were also called *agregados a la tierra, arrimados,* or *huasipungos*. These people were part of an indigenous or mixed population undergoing a "peasantization" or *macehualización* process (from the Mexican term *macehual*, i.e., indigenous commoner).[226]

The three spheres comprised under the Spanish *casa grande* in Latina America – the *casa poblada* in the city, the *hacienda* in the countryside, and the *encomienda* of indigenous peoples – were not static; they varied significantly through time. Once the *encomiendas* reverted to the Crown, the Spanish *casa* was reduced to two realms: the urban *casa* and the rural *hacienda*, which is a reality that persisted until the early nineteenth century.[227] Only the wealthiest traders of goods produced in Castile or the masters of foreign enslaved persons could subsist on only an urban *casa*. Paradoxically, those traders were not always considered as *vecinos* by local Spanish urban societies, but only as residents with no right to full participation in local political life. The *casas grandes* held by some of the main Spanish families comprised an urban *casa poblada* (which granted political rights) and the countryside *hacienda*, where wealth was produced. This complex arrangement caused serious governance challenges to the Crown, the *audiencias*, *gobernaciones*, and *cabildos*, but these issues were

225 C. Díaz Rementería, "En torno a la institución del yanaconazgo en Charcas," *Congresos del Instituto de Historia del Derecho Indiano. Actas y publicaciones* (Madrid: Digibis Publicaciones Digitales, D.L., 2000), vol. IV, 305–22; P. Revilla Orías, "Historizando al Yanacona. Decisiones metodológicas, implicancias y desafíos," in M. F. Fernández Chaves and R. M. Pérez García (eds.), *Tratas atlánticas y esclavitudes en América. Siglos XVI–XIX* (Seville: Universidad de Sevilla, 2021), 229–47.

226 V. Tau Anzoátegui, *El poder de la costumbre. Estudios sobre el derecho consuetudinario en américa hispana hasta la Emancipación* (Buenos Aires: Instituto de Investigaciones de Historia del Derecho, 2001); K. Spalding, *De indio a campesino. Cambios en la estructura social del Perú colonial* (Lima: Instituto de Estudios Peruanos, 1970); C. López de Albornoz, *Los dueños de la tierra, economía, sociedad y poder, Tucumán, 1770–1820* (Tucumán: Universidad Nacional de Tucumán, 2002); G. Doucet, "Génesis de una visita de la tierra. Los orígenes de la visita de las gobernaciones de Tucumán y Paraguay por el licenciado Don Francisco de Alfaro," *Revista del Instituto de Investigaciones de Historia del Derecho* 14 (1986), 123–215; F. Chevalier, "Servidumbre de la tierra y rasgos señoriales en el Alto Perú prehispánico, apuntes comparativos sobre los yanaconas," *Revista de Historia de América* 115 (1993), 7–22.

227 G. Tío Vallejo, "El ocaso del Imperio, sociedad y cultura en el centro sur andino," *Revista de Historia del Derecho* 49 (2015), 259–64; A. Annino, "Imperio, constitución y diversidad en la América Hispana," *Mundo Nuevo, Nuevos Mundos* (2008) https://doi.org/10.4000/nuevomundo.33052 (last accessed Jan. 12, 2022).

mainly resolved by those concurrently holding the roles of *pater familias*, master, and lord. Until the early nineteenth century, both peasant and urban societies located in the Portuguese regions of Latin America continued to be structured around families as the householder remained responsible for those living in his *casa*.[228]

In the Portuguese *casa grande*, the *fazendeiros* (plantation owners) were not required to have a *casa* in the city in order to be part of the political community.[229] By contrast to the Spanish colonial context, the Portuguese cities were inhabited more by traders and urban lower classes than landholders. The *casa*, as a land management mechanism, operated differently in Portuguese American territory because the *fazenda* was established on a more unified (but not less diverse) territory. The plantation and *hacienda* landholders controlled a certain amount of people of different legal status and ethnic backgrounds. Those workers lived in the *senzalas* (plantations) but were also scattered throughout the countryside. These people used the land under unclear and precarious arrangements as *agregados*.[230]

Serving Within and Outside the Casa

The challenges posed by the diverse Spanish American population had to be resolved both in the government and normative spheres. Legal structures were needed to define principles such as the concept of order and different social positions. Population was hierarchically organized around different statuses, which each entailed different sets of rights and duties.[231] Being granted the status of Spanish or Portuguese – the apex of the social pyramid – required more than mere Peninsular origins or a specific skin color, but also the ability to be recognized as such. In the early beginnings of the conquest, the *conquistadores* and settlers were recognized as Spanish *hijosdalgos* (lower-level nobles), which is a status that was passed on to their descendants.[232] The

228 B. J. Barickman, "Reading the 1835 Parish Censuses from Bahia: Citizenship, Kinship, Slavery, and Household in Early Nineteenth-Century Brazil," *The Americas* 59(3) (2003), 287–323.

229 A. Comissoli, "Os 'homens bons' e a Câmara de Porto Alegre (1767–1808)," unpublished master's thesis, Universidade Federal do Rio de Janeiro (2006).

230 M. Dias Paes, *Esclavos y tierras, entre posesión y títulos. La construcción social del derecho de propiedad en Brasil (siglo XIX)* (Global Perspectives on Legal History 17) (Frankfurt am Main: Max-Planck-Institut für Rechtsgeschichte und Rechtstheorie, 2021).

231 T. Herzog, "La vecindad: entre condición formal y negociación continua. Reflexiones en torno a las categorías sociales y las redes personales," *Anuario IEHS* 15 (2000), 123–31.

232 *Recopilación [Compilation]*, vol. II, lib. 4, tit. 4, law VI. Que los pobladores principales y sus hijos y descendientes legítimos sean hijosdalgos en las Indias: "... y les concedemos todas las honras y preeminencias que deben gozar todos los hijosdalgos y caballeros de estos Reynos de Castilla, según fueros, leyes y costumbres de España."

hijosdalgos and the *caballeros* (a nobility title based on wealth and military activity) were exempted from paying tribute to the king, which only had to be paid by indigenous peoples.

Peninsular and American Spaniards regarded themselves as the main and most respectable component of Hispanoamerican societies; they were the ones who should generally settle in the cities and ideally have a *casa grande*.[233] Those Peninsulars who, for different reasons, were not considered *vecinos* or residents of a city were usually not identified as Spaniards and were not considered part of the elite. They were rather associated to their respective homeland (e.g., *Castellanos, Navarros, Vizcaínos*). In other words, they remained foreigners to the political community. Devoid of any right to participate in local governance and administration of justice, they were part of the multiethnic lower classes living in the cities and the countryside.[234]

Indigenous peoples of America were first deemed to be "slaves of war." That being said, since 1503, indigenous people had to be recognized as free vassals, which had significant consequences on later theological and legal debates, including key issues such as whether indigenous people had souls, and questions relating to how they should be treated. Those questions laid the foundations of a new way of understanding relationships between peoples: the law of nations.[235]

In the early days of colonization, *repartimiento*, *encomienda*, and personal service were synonymous; by virtue of the right of conquest, indigenous people under the *repartimiento* and *encomienda* had to work for the conquerors. Joseph de Acosta indicated that personal service "generally covered any advantage that we hope to get from [indigenous people's] work and services relating to farming, livestock, house building, mining, errands, chores, and other public and domestic works."[236]

The living conditions of indigenous peoples under the *encomienda* were exposed by many who were close to the king as well as by ecclesiastics such as Bartolomé de Las Casas, who was likely one of their most famous advocates.

233 T. Herzog, "The Appropriation of Native Status: Forming and Reforming Insiders and Outsiders in the Spanish Colonial World," *Rechtsgeschichte – Legal History* 22 (2014), 140–49.

234 Zamora, *Casa Poblada*.

235 D. Brading, "El gran Debate," in D. Brading, *Orbe indiano. De la monarquía católica a la república criolla, 1492–1667* (Mexico City: Fondo de Cultura Económica, 1993); J. López de Palacios Rubios, *De las islas del Mar Océano. Del dominio de los Reyes de España sobre los indios* (Mexico City: Fondo de Cultura Económica, 1954).

236 Juan Solórzano Pereira, *Política Indiana*, vol. I, lib. 2, cap. II, § 1, 140.

The focus of their concerns eventually shifted toward the living conditions of those serving within and outside the *encomienda*. In 1609, Miguel de Agía took part in discussions with Peru's viceroy on the servitude of indigenous people; the ecclesiastic contended that it was necessary, as indigenous labor was required to preserve the Indies and to ensure the expansion of Christianity. By contrast, Juan de Padilla, a magistrate (*alcalde*) of the criminal chamber of Lima's *Real Audiencia* (a royal body with appellate and first instance judicial functions, among others), raised concerns regarding the abuses carried out toward indigenous people condemned to servitude, and the resulting vulnerability of communities. According to Padilla, as indigenous people were taken from their lands to work in the *encomenderos*' fields, *casas* and *obrajes*, indigenous lands were left vacant and communities would therefore lose their land-related rights.[237] With no land, he argued, indigenous communities would inevitably break up and disappear; to survive, indigenous people would have no other choice than to serve in Spanish *casas*, and the king would thus lose the tribute of indigenous communities.[238]

Juan Solórzano Pereira devoted considerabe thought to the issue of indigenous people's personal service. In his monumental work *Política Indiana*, he discussed indigenous labor and documented the Crown's efforts to ensure the survival and adequate treatment of indigenous people by establishing restrictions to and punishments for abuses perpetrated by the *encomenderos*, *corregidores de indios* (local administrative and judicial officials who ruled indigenous communities), and missionaries, including the prohibition of all forms of forced labor. The jurist identified those royal *cédulas* in which the king confirmed that indigenous people were only obligated to pay a specific amount as tribute in currency or in kind but were allowed to make use of the remaining part of their time to engage into other endeavors, as free persons. They should only be serving Spaniards of their own volition. This was also confirmed by *visitadores* (officials of the *Real Audiencia* commissioned by the Crown to monitor colonial authorities) in the early seventeenth century and included in the 1680 *Recopilación de Leyes*.[239] It is worth noting that these laws, as well as the *visitadores*' prescriptions, authorized indigenous people to work freely. Indigenous people – as free vassals but under conditions of servitude – had a legal status that put them at a disadvantage. Finding balance was only

237 Torre Villar, *Los pareceres*; Agia, "Tratado"; S. Zavala, "Orígenes coloniales del peonaje en México," *El Trimestre Económico* 10(40) (1944), 711–48.

238 A. M. Lorandi, "El servicio personal como agente de desestructuración en el Tucumán colonial," *Revista Andina* 6(1) (1988), 135–73.

239 Zamora, "Consapevolezza."

possible by establishing service linkages with someone who would be their *pater familias*, lord, and master.

Personal service became more of a social position than a type of work. It was a mode of social integration and an identity for an elusive, malleable, and very broad range of people which included not only indigenous people but also *mestizos*. The complex system of *castas* was the result of countless instances of hybridization of cultures, languages, customs, religions and rites among the European, American, African, and Asian populations that settled in the continent since the sixteenth century.

Enslaved persons had a different status.[240] Indigenous warriors who were captured by the colonizers were considered enslaved persons, as were the African people sold into the New World. African people were not utilized as temporary workforce outside of the *casas*, but they were rather considered as "part" of the *casa*. With some exceptions – such as in Minas Gerais toward the late eighteenth century – enslaved persons were not connected to a *casa*. Depending on the region, slavery took place in plantations or referred to urban service relationship.

Enslaved persons who escaped from their masters gathered in *palenques* or *quilombos*. Some took risks and traveled long distances to reach remote *haciendas* where masters sought workers to farm their land and would not send back the fugitives to their previous, far-off, and often unknown masters.[241] The following generations blended with indigenous people and Spaniards, thus giving rise to a broad spectrum of *castas*, from which many attempted to draw up taxonomies based on degrees of whiteness, indigeneity, and negritude. Some "*casta* paintings" depicted up to sixteen degrees to which blood was considered mixed, whose labels provided progressively animalistic and disturbing analogies as the proportions of indigenous and African blood

240 M. Candioti, "Nuevos horizontes en la historia de la esclavitud en América Latina," *Páginas. Revista Digital de la Escuela de Historia* 13(33) (2021), 1–4; M. Morrissey, *Slave Women in the New World: Gender Stratification in the Caribbean* (Lawrence: University Press of Kansas, 1989); A. J. Finley, *An Intimate Economy: Enslaved Women, Work, and America's Domestic Slave Trade* (Chapel Hill: University of North Carolina Press, 2020); H. S. Burton and F. Todd Smith, "Slavery in the Colonial Louisiana Backcountry: Natchitoches, 1714–1803," *The Journal of the Louisiana Historical Association* 52(2), 133–88; M. McKinley, *Fractional Freedoms: Slavery, Intimacy, and Legal Mobilization in Colonial Lima, 1600–1700* (New York: Cambridge University Press, 2016); J. W. Parkhurst, "The Role of the Black Mammy in the Plantation Household," *The Journal of Negro History* 23(3) (1938), 349–69.

241 Galindo, *La ciudad*; D. E. Kanter, 'Their Hair Was Curly': Afro-Mexicans in Indian Villages, Central Mexico, 1700–1820," in T. Miles and S. P. Holland (eds.), *Crossing Waters, Crossing Worlds: The African Diaspora in Indian Country* (Durham: Duke University Press, 2006), 164–80.

increased. Those included terms such as *lobezno* (wolf pup), *pantera* (panther), *caboclo* (copper-colored skin), and *salta-atrás* (a jump backward).

Owing to the fact that they went almost unnoticed by Spanish authorities, the treatment reserved for Asian populations migrating across the Pacific Ocean was different. Only a small portion of this population was enslaved, but a considerable number of free people arrived in Latin America from the Philippines, Malaysia, China, and Japan aboard the Manila galleons, the ships that traveled the only official route between America and the Philippines. Deborah Oropeza has accounted for at least eight thousand "Chinese" people legally arriving through the port of Acapulco in Mexico and staying in New Spain between the sixteenth and eighteenth centuries. The number of Asian immigrants arriving illegally through other means may have been ten times higher.[242] Similarly, the same occurred in the port of Callao, in Peru, which was an important hub for the trafficking of goods, merchandise, knowledge, and persons traveling illegally from Asia. Those people moved into *casas* to work as servants, and were registered as such in colonial files.[243] The masters of a significant number of people known as *indios chinos* in seventeenth-century Lima considered them as "Chinese indigenous peoples of service."[244]

The *chino* status was particularly confusing for the reason that it was associated to the status of enslaved persons. In her work on indigenous vassals, Tatiana Seijas highlights how the *indio* and *chino* labels were not only given based on place of origin. The Crown decided that those born in the Philippines should be called *indios*, but the masters of enslaved Asian persons advocated to call them *chinos* to ensure that they would not be granted the freedom associated to the *indio* status.[245]

Be they *mestizos, zambos, indios chinos*, or *negros libertos*, the entire racially mixed Latin American population fell under the concepts of *pardos, castas*, or the general populace. This raised a normative and governance concern not so

242 D. Oropeza, *La migración asiática en el virreinato de la Nueva España: Un proceso de globalización (1565–1700)* (Mexico City: Colegio de México, 2020).

243 M. Bonialian, "Relaciones económicas entre China y América Latina. Una historia de la globalización, siglos XVI–XXI," *Historia Mexicana* 70(3) (2021), 1231–74; S. Gruzinski, *Las cuatro partes del mundo. Historia de una mundialización* (Mexico City: Fondo de Cultura Económica, 2010).

244 J. J. Vega Loyola, "El padrón y lista de los indios de la China y el Xapon e India de Portugal en Lima de 1613," *Tipshe Revista de Humanidades* (2015), 197–210; J. J. Vega Loyola, "Asiáticos en Lima de inicios del siglo XVII," in J. Olveda (ed.), *Relaciones intercoloniales. Nueva España y Filipinas* (Jalisco: El Colegio de Jalisco, 2017), 221–42.

245 T. Seijas, "Native Vassals: Chinos, Indigenous Identity and Legal Protection in Early Modern Spain," in C. H. Lee (ed.), *Western Visions of the Far East in a Transpacific Age, 1522–1657* (London: Routledge, 2012), 153–64.

much because racial mixedness was an issue per se, but because these mixes did not lead to clear social distinctions. Racially mixed people were poor and free and had no specific social position. In the eighteenth century, as ethnic pedigree became less helpful to organize differences, the *cabildo* (municipal council) authorities indicated that "the poor and free people whose only livelihood is to serve, those part of the 'serving class', or those 'serving'" (the *gente de servicio*) had the duty to find a master who would be accountable for them.[246] The "serving class" did not only comprise indigenous people or *mestizos*, but also every poor and free person who could only survive by working for a more powerful person.

This did not, however, mean that the *casa grande* absorbed the shantytowns, the rural hamlets scattered on unowned land, or the *palenques*: These informal spaces did not cease to exist, because they were the *casa grande's* main source of labor. A person from a lower class with no fixed abode could alternate between those informal spheres and the *casa grande*. On the one hand, the *casa grande* entailed living under a normative sphere, but on the other hand, the urban and rural marginal spaces were regulated by different social and solidarity codes; there, people worshipped different gods, spoke different languages, and different normative codes regulated everyday life. An important challenge for the lower classes was that their life was intrinsically shaped by the fact that they were generally invisible to the law: They were safe as long as they went unnoticed. Both the marginalized and the regulated spheres – which referred to specific places of residence and relationships – coexisted with forts, indigenous villages, *reducciones* (Jesuit missions), convents, and monasteries; they existed along with a set of normative spaces separated by empty rural or tropical spaces, which could extend over hundreds of kilometers.[247]

Being part of the *casa* meant food, shelter, and clothing for the poor and free people who had no property or other source of income. Being linked to a *casa* also involved some form of protection against the legal system; having a master who was accountable for them meant that the *alcaldes* and *alguaciles* (constables or bailiffs) could not see them as "vagrants and lingerers" (*vagos y*

246 R. Zamora, "La polvareda periférica. Los bandos de buen gobierno en el Derecho indiano provincial y local. El caso de San Miguel de Tucumán en el siglo XVIII," in V. Tau Anzoátegui and A. Agüero (eds.), *El derecho local en la periferia de la Monarquía hispana. Siglos XVI–XVIII. Río de la Plata, Tucumán y Cuyo* (Buenos Aires: Dunken, 2013), 215–34.

247 Flores Galindo, *La ciudad*; N. Websdale, *Policing the Poor: From Slave Plantation to Public Housing* (Northeastern Series on Gender, Crime, and Law) (Boston: Northeastern University Press, 2001).

malentretenidos) and thus had no authority to force them to labor in different public works, ports, or in forts.[248]

The Casa *and the Governance of the Republic*

The strategy of the Castilian Crown to control New World territory was the same used to conquer Granada: establishing cities pursuant to a royal license (*licencia real*) and granting *encomiendas* to those leading the expedition.[249] Establishing a city with a *cabildo* as well as building the main church and immediately populating the city with Spanish families were necessary steps to control a specific place. To be part of the *cabildo*, men were required to own a *casa poblada* in the city.[250]

Family men legitimized their political role in the republic by resorting to an *oeconomic* rationale, drawing from their role in ensuring good governance over their respective *casas* and in managing relationships among peers. As the *casa* was the backdrop of all these power relationships, the community of *casas* was the *raison d'être* of the local republics: It justified the gathering of all families under a political community, gave shape to the structures of the republics, and informed their need for good governance. The *casa* and the local republic were thus intertwined: The former justified the existence of the latter, whose purpose was the good governance for the benefit of the community of *casas* and the pursuit of common good. As mentioned by Justus Lipsius (1589), "encompassing and restraining so many people under the same body was a heavy burden";[251] that burden was no other than that of governing. Therefore, a *pater familias'* domestic – or *oeconomic* – power was a required and necessary condition to access jurisdictional power, and only the most deserving family men could be in charge of the community's political governance.[252]

The Latin American *cabildo*, similarly to the Spanish one, combined both justice and governance functions, as the *alcaldes* were those in charge of

248 F. Alonso, M. Barral, R. Fradkin, and G. Perri, "Los vagos de la campaña bonaerense. La construcción histórica de una figura delictiva (1730–1830)," *Prohistoria* 5 (2001), 171–202; A. Araya Espinoza, *Ociosos, vagabundos y malentretenidos en Chile colonial* (Santiago: LOM Ediciones, 1999).

249 P. A. Porras Arboleda, *La orden de Santiago en el siglo XV* (Madrid: Dykinson, 1997).

250 *Recopilación [Compilation]*, vol. II, lib. 4, tit. 4, law VI. Que para los oficios se elijan vecinos (Apr. 21, 1554): "el que tuviere casa poblada, aunque no sea encomendero de indios, se entienda ser vecino."

251 P. Rosanvallon, *El buen gobierno* (Buenos Aires: Manantial, 2015), 175.

252 I. Atienza Hernández, "Pater familias, señor y patrón: oeconomia, clientelismo y patronato en el Antiguo Régimen," in R. Pastor (ed.), *Relaciones de poder, de producción y parentesco en la Edad Media y Moderna* (Madrid: Consejo Superior de Investigaciones Científicas, 1990), 411–58.

adjudication and the *regidores* (councilors) were overseeing political and *hacienda*-related relations within the city. Governing the city was equated with managing a *casa*: The *regidores* were called to rule over people pertaining to different social classes and had to command obedience with the same authority they exerted over their *casas*; they were also in charge of protecting property to ensure the *people* could enjoy its benefits.

In mid-seventeenth-century New Spain, the *hacendados* of Tepeaca succeeded in getting the king to issue a royal *provisión* of immunity so that the local legal authorities were not allowed to enter within the limits of their *casas grandes*.[253] This provision was endorsed by the *Real Audiencia*, and its application was extended, in practice, to the entire territory of the viceroyalty. Its scope and application in the other Hispanic territories remain to be studied.

While it also established cities with political institutions, the Portuguese Crown prioritized the establishment of *fazendas* and the settling of Portuguese people in the countryside. To be a member of the *câmara* (city council), men were not required to be *vecinos* of the city but had to be considered to be "good men," Old Christians, with no mixed blood, honest; they were chosen among those "[persons] who care for the public interest and value good morals."[254]

Politically organizing Latin America in this manner was useful to the Crown as it provided the king with some – but minimal – control over the local republics. Spaniards had to establish a *casa poblada* in a Spanish city to be part of the political life and to be granted lands by the Crown, while the Portuguese had to prove that they were Old Christians, cared for the public interest, were respected by their community, and had to demonstrate skill in managing the land and people under their control.

In this context, householders were those managing the *cabildos*, whose function was to ensure the common good of the notables of the city, and they also decided who could (and could not) be considered a member of the community.[255] Seeing the republic as the self-governance of the city's polity meant that the *ius commune* had to adjust to *domestic* realities and to the needs of local day-to-day decision-making. This conception of the republic informed how

253 F. Chevalier, *La formación de los latifundios en México. Haciendas y sociedad en los siglos XVI, XVII y XVIII*, rev. and enl. ed. (Mexico City: Fondo de Cultura Económica, 2013), 29.

254 Alvará [decree], 12 Nov. 1611, *Em que se declarou a forma de fazer as eleições de Juizes e Procuradores*; C. R. Boxer, *The Portuguese Seaborne Empire, 1415–1825* (London: Hutchinson, 1969).

255 Lempérière, *Entre Dieu et le Roi*; Jean Bodin, *Los seis libros de la República*, ed. and trans. P. Bravo Gala (Madrid: Tecnos, 2006 [1576]).

society was ordered through law and also determined how the laws applicable to corporations – for example, the city, which comprised families – were coordinated with the kingdom's different laws.

The Pater Familias

The concept of *pater familias* referred less to a biological link than to authority, responsibility, and control and subjection of all those falling under the *casa*. It was therefore an important legal concept. The father's authority gave shape to a religiously inspired cultural structure, which informed different institutions such as family, marriage, lineage, inheritance, and servitude. Those qualified to develop norms, rule over a territory, and achieve justice through local political structures had to be – first and foremost – family men valued by the community. For most people, those men were invariably members – directly or indirectly – of the political entity in charge of governing and administrating justice.

Both having a *casa poblada* in the city and being recognized as a notable were requirements established to consolidate existing Latin American elites and to curb the ambitions of those leaving the Iberian Peninsula to settle in the New World. Not every *pater familias* disposed of the material and intangible resources to meet such standards: They were not all regarded as *vecinos*, nor were all the *senhores da terra* seen as *homens bons*. The elites within the local republics sought – with variable results – to prevent the "poor with no privilege" from being granted *encomiendas* or land by the Crown, which could ultimately allow them to be recognized as members of the community.[256]

While the householders were those holding the reigns of local government, neither the *alcaldes* nor the judges or any other officeholder could interfere in matters relating to a *vecino*'s *casa*, that is, in issues of discipline and domestic governance that fell under the father's exclusive purview. Other jurisdictions could only meddle in matters relating to the *casa* when some outrageous or violent events could not be contained within the domestic sphere. Rather, public authorities had to protect the privacy of that space. Within the household, authority could not be challenged and

256 Incomplete letter from the Tucumán governor Juan Ramírez de Velasco to his majesty the King on administrative and governance matters, Santiago de Estero, October 2, 1590, in R. Levillier, *Gobernación del Tucumán. Papeles de Gobernadores en el siglo XVI. Documentos del AGI* (Madrid: Imprenta de Juan Peyo, 1920), vol. I, 294. J. Marchena Fernández and C. Gómez Pérez, "Los señores de la guerra en la conquista," *Anuario de Estudios Americanos* 42 (1985), 127–215; R. Douglas Cope, *The Limits of Racial Domination: Plebeian Society in Colonial Mexico City, 1660–1720* (Madison: University of Wisconsin Press, 1994).

was backed by domestic values such as love and loyalty toward the next of kin. But it is well known that romantic love was not the primary driver behind marriage in the main families; these were usually arranged and domestic violence was often exposed to public view and brought before courts. Similarly, cases of intergenerational violence between parents and children were documented by colonial courts.[257] Even more so, claims against masters abusing servants, laborers, and enslaved persons were brought before the highest royal courts.[258]

In contrast, in the Portuguese context, the *meirinho mor* (main bailiff) had jurisdiction over the great lords but his right to enter into their houses remained unsettled.[259] This bailiff was a very important person, chosen among the oldest and most distinguished members of the community. Social prestige vested him with the authority to impart justice with more clout than other notables. In other words, *oeconomic* rationale and jurisdictional authority were linked just as they were in the Spanish colonies, even if institutional structures were slightly different.[260]

The analogy between the city and *casas* – "the casa is a small town and the city is a casa grande"[261] – highlighted the significance of paternal authority and the binding character of some elements of domestic power structures. That authority and structure provided the strongest rationale for compliance and supported solid and lasting obedience. The political arena mirrored domestic power structures: Binding linkages based on private principles such as love could not be confused with administrative or public

257 "Cultural factors amplified the frequency with which accounts of murderous children and child martyrs were told and retold." B. Hamann, "Child Martyrs and Murderous Children. Age and Agency in Sixteenth-Century Transatlantic Religious Conflicts," in T. Arden and S. Hutson (eds.), *The Social Experience of Childhood in Ancient Mesoamerica* (Boulder: University Press of Colorado, 2006), 205–6; B. Premo, *Children of the Father King: Youth, Authority, and Legal Minority in Colonial Lima* (Chapel Hill: University of North Carolina Press, 2005); B. Premo and O. González (eds.), *Raising an Empire: Children in Early Modern Iberia and Colonial Latin America* (Albuquerque: University of New Mexico Press, 2007).

258 H. J. Nickel and M. E. Ponce Alcocer (eds.), *Hacendados y trabajadores agrícolas ante las autoridades. Conflictos laborales a fines de la época colonial documentados en el Archivo General de Indias* (Mexico City: Universidad Iberoamericana, 1996); Websdale, *Policing*.

259 *Ordenaçoes, e leis do Reino de Portugal. Recopiladas per mandado do muito alto catholico, e poderoso rei dom Philippe o Primeiro*, lib. 1, tit. XVII, Do Meirinho Mór: "E a seu Officio pertenece prender pessoas de stado, e grandes Fidalgos e Senhores de terras, e taes, que as outras Justiças não possam bem prender."

260 A. Almeida Santos de Carvalho Curvelo, *O senado da câmara de Alagoas do Sul. Governança e poder local no Sul de Pernambuco (1654–1751)* (Recife: O autor, 2014).

261 Jeronimo Castillo de Bovadilla, *Política para corregidores y señores de vassallos, en tiempos de paz y de guerra y para juezes eclesiásticos y seglares, juezes de comisión, regidores, abogados y otros oficiales públicos (1597)*, lib. I, cap. I, n. 29, 13.

relations considerations. Love was the main source of unity, cohesion, and respect that gave shape to obedience and tutelage relationships within the *casa* and the family, which also provided a model of discipline applicable in the political sphere.[262]

Conversely, the *cabildo* – the city's main political body – was in charge of regulating and establishing norms to define the nature of relations between persons or between persons and things. The *cabildo* had the authority to regulate work, including the *distribución de mitayos* (forced labor draft) among the *vecinos* who did not hold *encomiendas*, and also to facilitate the hiring of seasonal workers and setting salaries for the *casas'* domestic servants.[263] *Cabildos* were also in charge of providing land grants in the cities and in the territories falling under their jurisdiction.[264] The *cabildo* – a political body made up of the masters of the *casas grandes* – thus had authority to regulate two core elements of the *casa grande*'s operations: land possession and the establishment of servant-like relationships.

The Casa Grande *as a Normative Sphere*

The safeguards applicable to those governing were not based on principles of division of powers, but on conceptions of good governance and common good, which were closely linked to good morals and the cardinal virtue of justice. Both virtues had to inform the behaviors of both a *good judge* and a *good father*. The notion of common good provided guidance to those ruling over both the household and the city. Common good did not go against the concept of individual interest because it referred to both the public administration of common goods and to the management of private privileges to achieve the well-being of all the *pater familias* and their respective households.

Royal governance institutions were transplanted to Latin American soil and contributed to breaking up the territory in to large patches of land with undefined (and sometimes overlapping) borders.[265] In parallel, a religious structure was also brought to the New Continent: The Church played a key role in

262 P. Cardim, "'Governo' e 'política' no Portugal de seiscentos," *Penélope: revista de história e ciências sociais* 28 (2003), 59–92.

263 R. Zamora, "De la 'servidumbre y clausura' al 'trabajo asalariado para la felicidad pública'. Las normativas sobre el conchabo en el Río de la Plata y en San Miguel de Tucumán en el siglo XVIII," *Prólogos* 6 (2013), 15–40.

264 J. M. Ots Capdequí, *Manual de historia del Derecho Español en las Indias y del derecho propiamente Indiano* (Buenos Aires: Losada, 1945); Zamora, *Casa*.

265 V. Tau Anzoátegui, "La monarquía. Poder central y poderes locales," *Nueva Historia de la Nación Argentina* (Buenos Aires: Planeta, 2000), vol. III, 211–50.

shaping colonial control. The European seigniorial mindset was also transposed to Latin America, which did not, however, lead to the establishment of a feudal order but required the imposition of Western and Christian standards on indigenous populations. This mindset also entailed that indigenous peoples had to submit to the notion that the benefit of their work would be reaped by the lords, those holding *encomiendas*. The same applied to the settlers' notions relating to property and use of land.

Mestizos, *mulatos*, *zambos*, *indios chinos*, and Afro-Latin Americans had social, religious, and discipline-related knowledges which drew on a variety of sources and were thus different from European perspectives. These people were therefore compelled to conform to European structures by forsaking their cultural patterns, languages, and gods, with varying results depending on levels of coercion, on the one hand, and of resistance, on the other. The source of coercion was generally not jurisdictional, but domestic: Knowledge of normativity was conveyed within the Spanish *casas*. The following generations of members of the *pardos* or *castas* internalized Spanish or Portuguese normative standards as a way to relate to others but also – and most importantly – as a way to survive. Depending on available opportunities, they could be regarded as members of the main family when the *pater familias* recognized them as such or if he allowed them to remain in his *casa*. It is worth noting that there was a high level of tolerance toward miscegenation, when Spanish men reproduced with women pertaining to other *castas*. They could also be considered as *indios* if they were accepted within an indigenous community or village. Generally speaking, the lower *castas* were part of a diverse and very elusive population that could work in a Spanish *casa*, *obraje*, or *hacienda* for a certain period of time under the authority of the *pater familias* who simultaneously played the role of master, father, and lord.[266]

For Latin American indigenous and common people, joining a *casa grande* meant entering into the most important normative space. This is where they would learn to obey, speak Spanish or Portuguese, pray, respect authority, and to internalize the rules applicable to their social class.

It may be worth coming back to the questions raised earlier in this section: To what extent did the knowledges developed in the *casas grandes* become normative principles, and how did the *casa* contribute to the implementation of legal principles? Archives provide little more than

266 B. Ares Queija, "Mestizos en hábito de indios. ¿Estrategias transgresoras o identidades difusas?," in R. M. Loureiro and S. Gruzinski (eds.), *Passar as Fronteiras* (Lagos: Centro de Estudos Gil Eanes, 1999), 133–46.

silence on these points.[267] Víctor Tau Anzoátegui highlighted this gap and emphasized that no law, not even the *bandos de buen gobierno* (proclamations of good government) referred to the domestic sphere until well into the eighteenth century. He demonstrated how municipal norms remained silent on what happened within the *casas* owned by the main families, which contrasted with how spaces inhabited by ordinary people were regulated as well as with how laws were permanently meddling in the affairs of common households.[268]

This silence is due to the fact that the *casa grande*, which comprised the *hacienda* and the *casa poblada*, was governed by its own order and authorities without being bothered by the *cabildo*. The *casa* was the forum where household- and family-related normative principles were implemented, adapted, and recreated. While those were longstanding normative principles, they underwent modifications in the New World. For example, rules applicable to inheritance were adapted to the Latin American context, and the relationships with servants and enslaved persons may have appeared similar to European practices but still remained different.[269]

From a normative standpoint, the first half of the sixteenth century was probably the part of the colonial period most significantly marked by legal hybridization. As indicated by Tau Anzoátegui, there were only a handful of Spaniards to rule over millions of indigenous peoples.[270] The most complex issues probably emerged in situations involving indigenous institutions or normative principles which progressively evolved, but some were accepted as compromises required during this early colonial period.[271] These were likely the "least Catholic" times of colonization: a period where many indigenous religious traditions (along with their worldviews) persisted and often

267 J. Derrida, *Mal de archivo. Una impresion freudiana*, trans. P. Vidarte (Madrid: Editorial Trotta, 1997).

268 "The late appearance of certain precepts regarding the domestic order, resulting from the silence of the previous era, probably serves to prove the condition of the 'big house,' exempt from any jurisdiction alien to it in everyday life, where the civil authority could not enter." V. Tau Anzoátegui, "Provincial and Local Law of the Indies," in T. Duve and H. Pihlajamäki (eds.), *New Horizons in Spanish Colonial Law: Contributions to Transnational Early Modern Legal History* (Global Perspectives on Legal History 3) (Frankfurt am Main: Max-Planck-Institut für europäische Rechtsgeschichte, 2015), 235–55, at 245.

269 B. Clavero, "El mayorazgo indiano," in B. Clavero, *Mayorazgo: Propiedad feudal en Castilla (1369–1836)* (Madrid: Siglo XXI, 1974), 181–207; F. Cuena Boy, "Yanaconazgo y derecho romano: ¿una conjunción extravagante?," *Revista de Estudios Histórico-Jurídicos XXVIII* (2006), 401–24.

270 V. Tau Anzoátegui, "La costumbre jurídica en la América española (siglos XVI–XVIII)," *Revista de Historia del Derecho* 14 (1986), 355–425.

271 Herzog, "Native customs"; V. Tau Anzoátegui, *El poder de la costumbre* (Buenos Aires: Instituto de Investigaciones de Historia del Derecho, 2000).

conflicted with Christian morals and rituals. The Spaniards had to negotiate with existing indigenous structures to establish institutions that were acceptable to everyone.

To ensure they were respected and obeyed during that period – that is, when most of the active population was indigenous and under an *encomienda* – *encomenderos* had to acknowledge some of the underlying principles of local traditions. This was basically how the *in situ* integration of global and local knowledges of normativity was conceptualized. Obedience had to be negotiated.[272] The most skilled *encomenderos* knew they had no other choice than securing agreements with the *curacas*, *tlatoques*, and the leaders of different ethnic lordships to ensure the payment of tribute and to prevent escapes.[273] Rules alone were not sufficient to subject whole populations to servitude and to ensure the payment of tribute; neither could direct and violent compulsion be considered the single means to control people who used to be free. The early *encomenderos* and Portuguese *senhores da terra* had to continuously negotiate payment conditions, relocation of scattered populations into villages and *reducciones*, compliance with work shifts, conversion to Catholicism, alignment of indigenous family structures with European standards, and respect for a social hierarchy and religious morality. The settlers had to engage in such negotiations with the traditional leadership of people who were forced to undergo a radical change in mentality.

Over time and due to factors such as the decline of indigenous populations, the demise of the *encomienda*, the emergence of *Afrolatinos* (and, to a lesser extent, people of Asian descent), and to the general demographic hybridization, the Spanish and Portuguese were able to implement more Western normative principles in the spheres falling under the *hacienda* and the *casa*. As noted by António Manuel Hespanha, the breakdown or re-articulation of traditional power and justice arrangements was not solely determined by political and normative authorities; the impact of demographics played a peripheral role that those authorities had to reckon with.[274] In this case, a growing and increasingly mixed and adaptable population gradually adjusted to the *casa* and the *hacienda*'s territorial structure and thus contributed to developing their full potential.

272 M. Zuloaga Rada, *La conquista negociada: guarangas, autoridades locales e imperio en Huaylas, Perú (1532–1610)* (Lima: Instituto de Estudios Peruanos, Instituto Francés de Estudios Andinos, 2012).

273 Stern, *Los pueblos*, 59–77: "Ascensión y caída de las alianzas postincaicas."

274 A. M. Hespanha, *Vísperas del Leviatán. Instituciones y poder político (Portugal, siglo XVII)* (Madrid: Taurus Humanidades, 1989).

Thomas Duve argues that these domestic fora generated and implemented norms, as they were in fact the expression of the diversity of collective decision-making mechanisms (see Section 1.3). At this point, one could wonder what was the relationship between legal doctrine and those scattered and plural – but highly binding – knowledges of normativity that were produced, appropriated, and recreated by different epistemic communities in specific and contingent contexts where no jurists or written procedures were involved.[275] Similarly, customs did not require legislative validation or judicial recognition to be recognized as such and to have binding force. Custom did not go hand in hand with the idea of uniformity and much less with the conception of law as a closed system:

> The doctrinal jurist expects certainty and formality from custom, but custom does not have such features and cannot provide them; trying to meet such expectations would put it at risk of losing its identity. In turn, the doctrinal jurist will ruin his own system if he appreciates custom as it is.... There is thus a dialectical interplay, a vicious argument, a dilemma between different essences.[276]

Both the Spanish and Portuguese *casa grande* developed their own normativity – their customs – to achieve the levels of order and obedience needed to bind those falling under their purview. As householder and *vecino* of the city, the *pater familias* could demand these norms be recognized as customs by local authorities insofar as he was part of the local political institutions and could be a member of the *cabildo* or the *cámara* (city council). While the administration of the *casa* and the city were different, normative solutions were often determined by the *pater familias* and then confirmed by the *cabildo* before being implemented in other cases falling under the *cabildo's* jurisdiction. In other words, practices established by families did not require having the force of law to be effective within the household, but some could be accepted as local uses and customs by institutions and be wielded to protect local interests against royal authorities.[277] Both casuistry and the weight of specific local custom served as safety valves and fostered normative plasticity without entailing some form of transgression or distortion; they rather meant that rules were being adapted to the facts to reach the most equitable results.[278]

275 T. Duve, "Historia del derecho como historia del saber normativo," *Revista de Historia del Derecho* 63 (2022), 1–60.

276 Tau Anzoátegui, *El poder*, 29–30.

277 Tau Anzoátegui, *El poder*, 96.

278 V. Tau Anzoátegui, *Casuismo y sistema. Indagación histórica sobre el espíritu del Derecho Indiano* (Buenos Aires: Instituto de Investigaciones de Historia del Derecho, 1992).

Conversely, abusive domestic practices could be challenged and reported by local authorities. Under the influence of Enlightenment thought and with written law taking a predominant role, abusive customs were increasingly challenged during the latter part of the eighteenth century. These customs thus generally began to be questioned in Spanish and Portuguese territory and more specifically in the *cabildos*, *audiencias*, or in the *câmaras* and *tribunais da relação*. Some actors also sought to put an end to practices they considered to be *contra legem*. Most of the records of such customs show discussions relating to litigation, which (in some cases) gave rise to new rules similar to the *bandos de buen gobierno*; these proclamations sought to delineate the confines of domestic customs and authorities, which were progressively less protected by public authorities.[279]

Those joining or remaining for some time on a *hacienda* or in an urban *casa* owned by the main families were subjected to strict rules. This regime was imposed by the father and master, who was also in charge of implementing rules directly or with the support of other members of the *casa*.

These rules referred to a specific field of action: the tenant's rent payments, land tenure regimes, and the regulation of labor. They also referred to a significant amount of information relating to ways of organizing the domestic life of workers and their families, observing the sacraments, attending mass, while implicitly tolerating indigenous, Asian, or African rituals and allowing consensual and *de facto* unions and the burial of the dead at traditional sites (not only in church graveyards). All this knowledge gave a normative content to everyday life and could vary depending on regions, cities, *haciendas*, or *casas*. Every case reflected how global knowledge was locally absorbed depending on the background and the distinct traditions of those who were part of a *casa grande*, but also on the normative wishes of the father and master of the household.

Many *haciendas* had their own detention and punishment spaces to sanction deviant behaviors and transgressions. Part of domestic discipline fell under the father's exclusive jurisdiction. The father could set himself up as

279 V. Tau Anzoátegui (ed.), *Los Bandos de buen gobierno del Río de la Plata, Tucumán y Cuyo (época hispánica)* (Buenos Aires: Instituto de Investigaciones de Historia del Derecho, 2004); D. Apaolaza Llorente, *Los Bandos de Buen Gobierno en Cuba. La norma y la práctica (1730–1830)* (Inéditos de Historia 11) (Bilbao: Universidad del País Vasco, 2016); L. González Pujana, *El libro del cabildo de la ciudad de Cuzco* (Lima: Instituto Riva-Agüero, 1982); R. Zamora, "Acerca de las discusiones sobre el salario de las criadas: Algunas reflexiones sobre el orden jurídico local en San Miguel de Tucumán a fines del siglo XVIII," *Revista de Historia del Derecho* 39 (2010), 1–20; B. Bandecchi, "O município no Brasil e sua função política (I)," *Revista de História* 44(90) (1972), 495–530.

the judge within his own household.[280] Those living in the *hacienda* could be subject to punishment related not only to theft, attempted escapes, or altercations, but more generally also for threatening social hierarchy and morality when practices and knowledge were not sufficient to internalize the principles of order.[281] By contrast, in the urban *casas pobladas*, it was the mothers who ensured the internalization of behaviors and effective punishment, as those spaces were mainly inhabited by women. Mothers were in charge of the discipline of the *criadas*, sons and daughters, and those living in the *casa*.[282]

As there was an infinite range of differences from one *casa* and domestic group to the other, enforcement had to go hand in hand with norm transposition and recreation processes. As the *casa*'s inhabitants carried different types of knowledges and mindsets that came from different places, knowledges from diverse origins had to be blended to provide a shared normative understanding of the *casa* (see Section 1.4). In the case of Asian knowledges, Confucianism was accepted – or at the very least not rejected – in Latin America due to the clarity of its standards relating to obedience to family and political subjection. These standards had significant impact on the *casas grandes* that were inhabited by *indios chinos*, but these knowledges were also disseminated by Asian traders and travelers. Missionaries who had spent time in the East Indies before arriving in Spanish America (mainly Jesuits or Franciscans, such as Martín Ignacio de Loyola y Mallea) also contributed to the circulation of such knowledges, which were furthermore shared by American jurists such as Juan Egaña, Pedro Murillo Velarde, or Ignacio de Castro.[283]

280 M. Fargas Peñarrocha, "La práctica de la justicia en el orden doméstico: el padre de familia en Domingo de Soto y su tiempo," *Studia Historica: Historia Moderna* 40(2) (2018), 271–304.

281 B. Garnot, "Justice, infrajustice, parajustice et extrajustice dans la France d'Ancien Régime," *Crime, History & Societies* 4(1) (2000), 103–20. Quoted in Fargas Peñarrocha, "La práctica," 273.

282 P. Gonzalbo Aizpuru, "La historia de la familia en Iberoamérica," in F. Chacón Jiménez, A. Irigoyen López, E. de Mesquita Samara, and T. Lozano Armendares (eds.), *Sin distancias. Familia y tendencias historiográficas en el siglo XX* (Murcia: Universidad de Murcia, Universidad de Colombia, 2002), 47–60.

283 R. Carrillo, "Asia llega a América. Migración, influencia cultural asiática en Nueva España (1565–1815)," *Asiadémica. Revista universitaria de estudios sobre Asia oriental* (2014), 81–98; A. C. Hosne, *Entre la fe y la razón. La Doctrina y el Catecismo del Tercer Concilio Limense (1584–85) de José de Acosta SJ como autor principal del texto en castellano, y la Verdadera Doctrina del Señor del Cielo (Tianzhu shiyi) de Matteo Ricci SJ en China (1603)*, unpublished Ph.D. thesis, Universidad de Buenos Aires (2009); D. Sola, *El cronista de China. Juan González de Mendoza, entre la misión, el imperio y la historia* (Barcelona: Universidad de Barcelona, 2018); A. Dougnac Rodríguez,

For their part, Afro-Latin Americans preserved the memory of their earlier domestic life and cohabitation practices, which they hoped to revert to once they became freedpeople, and sometimes even while remaining legally enslaved persons. This was possible when the *fazendas* were not organized in collective *senzalas* or *bohíos* but rather as pieces of land held in precarious tenure where they built homes, lived with their families, and farmed on small plots of land whose harvests could be claimed by the lords as consideration for using the land (similarly to what was the practice with *agregados*: see Section 3.1).[284]

The *casa* acted as a catalyst for those diverse knowledges by creatively mixing them to facilitate the cohabitation of people of different origins, with varying motivations, and who were subject to differentiated rights and duties based on their class. The most difficult interactions between persons or communities and the law emerged in cases where social classes were defined in a colonial context where non-Spanish and non-Portuguese were *a priori* considered as lesser and as having deficient capacity, if not lacking it altogether.[285]

Knowledges of normativity available to those living in a *casa* were actualized in a particular way under specific socioeconomic conditions, based on specific power relations, and on the distinct *savoir faire* of the social group that was involved in both the production and implementation of those knowledges. This meant that the structure of each historical normative regime differed in many aspects, including conceptions of ethnic hierarchies, possession and use of land, labor, family structure, and also regarding Christian precepts, which were – contrary to glorifying narratives – malleable, vague, and contingent.

These knowledges of normativity were conveyed orally within the *casas*. They did not have to be developed by jurists or to be written laws in order to be effectively valid. But these knowledges had force of law in the mainly illiterate communities with only a rough command of the Spanish language that were delimited by the *haciendas'* boundaries and the cities' *ejidos* (suburban land available for the common use of the *vecinos*), and surrounded by borders, as though they were scattered normative islands.

"El pensamiento confuciano y el jurista Juan Egaña (1768–1836)," *Revista de Estudios Histórico-Jurídicos* 20 (1998), 143–93; P. Murillo Velarde, *Curso de derecho canónico hispano e indiano* (Mexico City: El Colegio de Michoacán, 2004), 4 vols.; Martín Ignacio de Loyola y Mallea, *Viaje alrededor del Mundo (1585)* (Barcelona: Red Ediciones, 2021); Ignacio de Castro, *Relación de la fundación de la Real Audiencia de Cuzco en 1788* (Madrid: imprenta de la viuda de Ibarra, 1794).

284 Dias Paes, *Esclavos y tierras*.

285 Duve, "What is Global Legal History?," 94: "Emancipating from hegemonic concepts."

This leaves open the question of the extent to which practical issues relating to labor, land tenure, social positions, the principles of obedience in a hierarchic, multiethnic, and multicultural society as well as the practical solutions developed within Latin American *casas grandes* reflected the existence of a standalone and diverse normative system. Those solutions were haphazard attempts to establish a social structure with ties to the greater Catholic community. All of this unfolded in the context of chaotic, changing, and immeasurably vast territories, lands with varied and infinite characteristics, a population in constant social and territorial motion due to its diverse backgrounds, hybridizations, and evolving social hierarchies.

This is not just a matter of demonstrating that norms that were created and recreated within the Spanish *casas grandes* forayed into other normative production spheres (which they did). It is rather a question of whether it is possible to conceptualize these normative knowledges as part of a legal, hierarchic, and political system. Regardless of their legitimacy, these normative knowledges were part of the main challenges that constitutional lawyers and codifiers encountered during the nineteenth century.

4

Independence(s): What Is a Revolutionary Law?

TAMAR HERZOG

Like all revolutionary processes, those that led to Latin American independence were highly volatile and experimental in nature. If the French revolution is noteworthy for having produced several, radically different constitutions in only a few years, no less dramatic were the upheavals that in Latin America accompanied the search for a new consensus regarding what the process of emancipation from colonial domination should lead to. Often accompanied by extreme violence, even open warfare, the formation of the new Latin American states in the early nineteenth century required imagining what form and shape the new entities would take, what their citizen body and territory would be, and what their institutions and laws.[1] The need, often urgency, to transform colonial domains into various independent units often coincided with the desire to end (or at least modernize) the *Ancien régime*. Yet, the wish to supersede the past did not guarantee rupture. Instead, it initiated a period of questioning more often than answering, of experimenting more often than finding solutions.

For many years, analysis of this period was mostly geared toward justifying the breakup with Spain and Portugal and the formation of new polities. This political motivation produced standard accounts that sought to demonstrate the pre-existence of communities, mostly identified as "nations," which naturally and logically fought against the injustices of imperial rule by outsiders. For the independent Latin American states, this way of telling their history supplied both a narrative of origins (that explained how the states came to be) and a confirmation of previously prevailing identities (that vindicated their creation). In the last decades, however, most historians have

1 J. Adelman, "Ritos de estado: Violencia y soberanía en Hispanoamérica, 1789–1821," in M. Irurozqui and M. Galante (eds.), *Sangre de ley. Justicia y Violencia en la institucionalización del estado en América Latina, siglo XIX* (Madrid: Polifemo, 2011), 25–63, discusses some of these issues.

gradually abandoned these teleological accounts. Instead, they have started to present Latin American independence as the outcome of a long and complex process, the results of which were neither natural, nor could they have been foretold.[2] Rather than attributing the independence movements only to internal pressures, many historians now look to external developments, and ask important questions about the larger contexts in which Latin American independence took place.

The Larger Contexts

The complex unfolding that eventually led to the independence of Latin American states began with imperial crises in both the Spanish and Portuguese monarchies. In 1807, Napoleon invaded the Iberian Peninsula, forcing actors in Portugal, Spain, and their overseas territories to decide how they should react. Some were willing to collaborate with the new French regime, either because they believed it would improve their societies by modernizing them, or because they feared the consequences of a confrontation.[3] Yet many others rejected the French-imposed governments that were instituted in Portugal and Spain and proceeded to imagine new political arrangements. The first to do so was the Prince Regent of Portugal who, acting for his mother the queen, sailed in 1807 with his family, members of his entourage, and his ministers – a total of some 10,000, perhaps even 15,000 people – to Rio de Janeiro. He left Portugal in the hands of a regency, whose members he instructed to conserve the traditional laws and structures of government, yet without antagonizing the French occupiers.[4] In the Spanish territories, news regarding the forced

2 See for example, the survey by H. Sábato, "La ciudadanía en el siglo XIX: Nuevas perspectivas para el estudio del poder político en América Latina," in H. J. König, T. Platt, and C. Lewis (eds.), *Estado-nación, comunidad indígena, industria. Tres debates al final del milenio* (Cuadernos de Historia Latinoamericana 8) (s.l.: Ahila, 2000), 49–70, at 49–51.

3 J. R. Aymes, "Españoles al servicio de Napoleón," *Historia* 16(20) (1977), 49–60; L. Barbastro Gil, *Los afrancesados: primera emigración política del siglo XIX español (1813–1820)* (Madrid: CSIC, Instituto de Cultura Juan Gil-Albert, 1993); J.–B. Busaall, "Los afrancesados: el estado como modernidad política," in M. A. Cabrera and J. Pro (eds.), *La creación de las culturas políticas modernas, 1808–1833* (Historia de las culturas políticas en España y América Latina 1) (Madrid: Marcial Pons Historia, 2014), 347–73; and A. C. Araújo, "Confluencias políticas en el trienio liberal: el proceso de la revolución portuguesa de 1820 y el modelo constitucional gaditano," *Historia y política* 45 (2021), 53–83, at 56–58. On how the French-led government tried to sway Spanish Americans in its direction, see M. Artola, "Los afrancesados y América," *Revista de Indias* 9 (1949), 541–67.

4 V. Alexandre, *Os sentidos do império. Questão nacional e questão colonial na crise do antigo regime português* (Porto: Afrontamento, 1993); K. Schultz, *Tropical Versailles: Empire, Monarchy, and the Portuguese Royal Court in Rio de Janeiro, 1808–1821* (New World in the Atlantic World) (New York: Routledge, 2001); M. Halpern Pereira, "Crown, Empire,

abdication of the Spanish king and the coronation of Napoleon's brother as the new monarch of Spain led municipal actors on both sides of the Atlantic to constitute local committees (*juntas*) that were to act as sovereign entities in the absence of the legitimate monarch (on the sovereignty of *pueblos*, see also Sections 5.1 and 5.3).[5] Back in Portugal, after the French dissolved the regency and instituted their own (1808), many municipalities also moved to form *juntas* that either collaborated with the regency or acted autonomously. As in Spain, these municipal *juntas* claimed jurisdiction over their district or province.

The resulting fragmentation, with each *junta* claiming to be fully sovereign, led to the search for alternative solutions. In northern Portugal, the *junta* of Porto, having achieved the allegiance of a series of municipalities located north of the river Douro, declared itself *Junta Suprema do Governo do Reino*, as did the *junta* of Faro in the Algarve. In the Spanish territories, the search for a coordinated government produced first an organ that was to coordinate the distinct *juntas* (the so-called *Junta Central*), then a regency (that stood for the absent king), and eventually a meeting of the parliament, the *Cortes*, that declared itself a constituent assembly and that, in 1812, adopted the Constitution of Cádiz. During this period, Spain was *de facto* divided into a French-controlled territory, where a French-inspired (and -imposed) constitution (the Constitution of Bayonne, 1808) and government prevailed, and a so-called free territory, controlled by *juntas*, the regency, and the *Cortes*.[6]

and Nation (1807–1834)," *e-Journal of Portuguese History* 11(1) (2013), 43–60; and A. C. Araújo, "Confluencias políticas," 53–83, at 56–88. On how locals reacted to the royal decision, see A. C. Araújo, "O 'reino unido de Portugal, Brasil e Algarves' 1815–1822," *Revista de História das Ideias* 14 (1992), 233–61. A general description of the transfer of the court to Rio, the ensuing debate about its return, and the resulting constitutional changes in both Portugal and Brazil can be found in G. Paquette, *Imperial Portugal in the Age of Atlantic Revolutions: The Luso-Brazilian World, c.1770–1850* (Cambridge: Cambridge University Press, 2013).

5 B. R. Hamnett, *La política española en una época revolucionaria, 1790–1820* (Mexico City: Fondo de Cultura Económica, 1985); F.-X. Guerra, *Modernindad e independencias. Ensayos sobre las revoluciones hispánicas* (Mexico City: Fondo de Cultura Económica, 1993); F.-X. Guerra, "The implosion of the Spanish American Empire: Emerging Statehood and Collective Identities," in L. Roniger and T. Herzog (eds.), *The Collective and the Public in Latin America: Cultural Identities and Political Order* (Brighton: Sussex Academic Press, 2000), 71–93; J. E. Rodríguez O., *The Independence of Spanish America* (Cambridge: Cambridge University Press, 1998); J. E. Rodríguez O., "We Are Now the True Spaniards." *Sovereignty, Revolution, Independence, and the Emergence of the Federal Republic of Mexico, 1808–1824* (Stanford: Stanford University Press, 2006); and J. E. Rodríguez O., *La revolución política durante la época de la independencia. El Reino de Quito, 1808–1822* (Quito: Universidad Andina, 2006).

6 On what transpired under the French government of Spain, see for example., C. Muñoz de Bustillo Romero, *Bayona en Andalucía: El estado bonapartista en la prefectura de Xerez* (Historia de la Sociedad Política) (Madrid: Centro de Estudios Constitucionales, 1991).

Portugal was similarly ruled by several governments: the military government first of France and then of Britain, whose troops either invaded or liberated (depending on whom was speaking) the country, a regency, and various *juntas*. The king in Rio de Janeiro also tried to control the Peninsula by issuing a series of orders to local officials, though his success in doing so was limited.

In 1814, as the power of Napoleon was waning, the Spanish king, Fernando, returned to Spain, where he declared the Cádiz Constitution, and all that was enacted by the *Cortes* of Cádiz, void. A liberal uprising in 1820 forced the king to reinstall the constitution, but in 1823 it was again repealed. Meanwhile, the Portuguese Prince Regent remained in Brazil where, crowned as King João VI in 1815 after the death of his mother, he declared the formation of the United Kingdom of Portugal and Brazil. Under enormous pressure, probably linked to fears that Brazil would colonize Portugal, and after an uprising in Porto in 1820 that protested "the status of a colony to which Portugal in effect is reduced," the regency in Portugal agreed to call a meeting of a constituent *Cortes*. Threatened by these developments, João VI returned to Portugal in 1821, leaving his heir behind as regent. As he was departing, crowds in Rio de Janeiro forced him to swear allegiance to the Spanish Constitution of Cádiz, which they believed would ensure that the United Kingdom of Portugal and Brazil would become a constitutional monarchy that would protect equal relations between the Portuguese territories on both sides of the ocean.[7]

The Portuguese *Cortes*, which met from 1820 to 1822, in 1822 adopted a new constitution for the United Kingdom of Portugal and Brazil. Yet, in response to these developments as well as pressures from locals, the heir to the throne, Dom Pedro, who remained in the Americas, declared Brazilian independence in 1822. He convoked a constituent assembly in 1823 but, ignoring most of its work, proceeded to impose a new constitution on Brazil in 1824. In Portugal, João VI began purging Portuguese liberal legislation of elements that according to him did not conform to the customs and will of the nation and, in 1824, declared the return to the *Ancien régime*, that is, all which existed before the imperial crisis.

These European events greatly affected developments in Latin America. In Spanish territories, while some remained loyal to the captive king despite his deposition in 1808 and refused to adopt any measure that might amount to innovation, others formed local *juntas*, which, although swearing allegiance

7 M. R. Berbel, "Os sentidos de Cádis em Portugal e no Brasil," in A. Annino and M. Ternavasio (eds.), *El laboratorio constitucional iberoamericano: 1807/1808–1830* (Estudios AHILA de Historia Latinoamericana 9) (Madrid and Frankfurt am Main: Ahila, Iberoamericana, Vervuert, 2012), 119–235.

to the deposed Spanish monarch and claiming to use the traditional powers of local communities, did not necessarily form part of the traditional political repertoire (on traditional claims to sovereignty as voiced during the monarchical crises by local communities, see Section 5.1).[8] After the Spanish *Cortes* had passed the new liberal constitution in 1812, the populations of the Spanish American territories were called upon by the *Cortes* to express their adherence to it. In many places, the constitution was joyfully received in public ceremonies, and, obeying its instructions, elections to a variety of representative bodies took place.[9] The constitution was also welcomed by many indigenous communities, where the constitutional text was read and discussed during church services as well as translated into local languages.[10] In Portuguese America, the 1822 Portuguese constitution was accepted, but because of the declaration of independence, it was soon replaced by the Brazilian constitution of 1824.[11]

As one historian put it, like Humpty Dumpty in the famous English nursery rhyme, after the pre-Napoleonic political order had fallen and broken to pieces, "all the king's horses and all of the king's men" could not put it "together again."[12] Or, as another historian has shown, the imperial crisis itself was transformative. It was an opportunity for Latin American actors – both elites and

8 On royalists, see for example, S. Chambers, "Rewarding Loyalty after the Wars of Independence in Spanish America: Displaced Bureaucrats in Cuba," in A. Forrest, K. Hagemann, and M. Rowe (eds.), *War, Demobilization and Memory: The Legacy of War in the Era of Atlantic Revolutions* (New York: Palgrave Macmillan, 2016), 238–53; and M. Echeverri Muñoz, *Indian and Slave Royalists in the in the Age of Revolution: Reform, Revolution, and Royalism in the Northern Andes, 1780–1825* (Cambridge Latin American Studies 102) (New York: Cambridge University Press, 2016). On royalist political ideas, see J.–P. Luis, "La construcción inacabada. Una cultura política realista," in M. A. Cabrera and J. Pro (eds.), *La creación de las culturas políticas modernas, 1808–1833* (Historia de las culturas políticas en España y América Latina 1) (Madrid: Marcial Pons Historia, 2014), 319–45.

9 M. Rodríguez, *El experimento de Cádiz en Centroamérica, 1808–1826* (Cuadernos de Historia 7) (Mexico City: Fondo de Cultura Económica, 1984); M. Chust (ed.), *Doceañismo, constituciones e independencias. La Constitución de 1812 y América* (Madrid: Mapfre, 2006); and S. Eastman and N. Sobrevilla Perea (eds.), *The Rise of Constitutional Government in the Iberian Atlantic World: The Impact of the Cádiz Constitution of 1812* (Atlantic Crossings) (Tuscaloosa: University of Alabama Press, 2015). On some of these questions, see also T. Herzog, *Defining Nations: Immigrants and Citizens in Early Modern Spain and Spanish America* (New Haven: Yale University Press, 2003), 141–63.

10 G. Chiaramonti, *Ciudadanía y representación en el Perú (1808–1860). Los itinerarios de la soberanía* (Lima: Universidad Nacional Mayor de San Marcos, 2005), 117.

11 For the types of questions facing Brazilians at that time, see for example, I. Jancsó, "Brasil e brasileiros – Notas sobre modelagem de significados políticos na crise do Antigo Regime português na América," *Estudos Avançados* 22(62) (2008), 257–74.

12 F. Fernández-Armesto, *The Americas: A Hemispheric History* (New York: The Modern Library, 2003), 5. The Humpty-Dumpty metaphor had already been used earlier in the context of the historiography of the British empire by D. Fieldhouse, "Can Humpty-Dumpty be Put Together Again? Imperial History in the 1980s," *Journal of Imperial and Commonwealth History* 12(2) (1984), 9–23.

non-elites – Spaniards, Portuguese, indigenous and Afro-Latin Americans, to engage with politics. At the end of the imperial crisis, they emerged as very different political actors than they had been before it took place.[13]

According to this interpretation, in the period between 1807 and 1823, different actors in Latin America had to respond to unfolding events as the war situation in the Iberian Peninsula deteriorated and political upheavals intensified. In Spanish America, some disliked the *Junta Central*, others the regency. Yet another group criticized the *Cortes* of Cádiz for not including a sufficient number of Latin American representatives, or for enacting a constitution either too liberal or insufficiently liberal, or they agreed or disagreed with King Fernando who, after his return to Spain in 1814, sought to reinstitute the pre-crisis status quo, or they agreed with or refused to follow the liberals who, in 1821, had obtained from Fernando an oath of allegiance to the 1812 Cádiz constitution, or they advocated for or disliked the second annulment of the Cádiz constitution in 1823. In many areas of Spanish America, the focus was on how to obtain or conserve (depending on who was speaking) autonomy from Spain. In others, what was at stake was the need to ensure autonomy *vis-à-vis* other American enclaves, as was famously the case in Río de la Plata, where relations between the city of Buenos Aires and other regional capitals quickly deteriorated, and in Central America, where the various political centers wished to renegotiate their relations with Mexico City. In both these cases, the crisis was an opportunity to rearrange relations not only with the Spanish monarchy but also with other Latin American political centers.

In Luso-America, actors faced the questions whether to obey the *juntas*, provincial assemblies, or the king, and how to position themselves with

13 On politicization in Spanish America, see for example, Echeverri Muñoz, *Indian and Slave Royalists* and her article "'Sovereignty Has Lost its Rights': Liberal Experiments and Indigenous Citizenship in New Granada, 1810–1819," in B. P. Owensby and R. Ross (eds.), *Justice in a New World: Negotiating Legal Intelligibility in British, Iberian, and Indigenous America* (New York: New York University Press, 2018), 238–69; P. Blanchard, *Under the Flag of Freedom: Slave Soldiers and the Wars of Independence in Spanish South America* (Pittsburgh: University of Pittsburgh Press, 2008). On politicization in Luso-America, see for example, J. P. G. Pimenta, "A política hispano-americana e o império português (1810–1817): Vocabulário político e conjuntura," in I. Jancsó (ed.), *Brasil: Formação do estado e da nação* (Estudos Históricos 50) (São Paulo: Editora Hucitec, 2003), 123–39; A. C. Araújo, "Um império, um reino e uma monarquia na América: as vésperas da independência do Brasil," in I. Jancsó (ed.), *Independência. História e Historiografia* (São Paulo: Editora Hucitec, 2005), 235–70; L. M. Bastos Pereira das Neves, *Corcundas e constitucionais. A cultura política da independência (1820–1822)* (Rio de Janeiro: Editora Revan, 2003); and H. Kraay, "Muralhas da independência e liberdade do Brasil: a participação popular nas lutas políticas (Bahia, 1820–25)," in J. Malerba (ed.), *A independência brasileira. Novas dimensões* (Rio de Janeiro: Editora FGV, 2006), 303–41.

regards to the 1822 Portuguese constitution. As in Spanish territories, they disagreed about the form of government and the policies to adopt, but they also engaged in heated debates regarding the appropriate relations between the metropole and its American territories. Historians point out that the transfer of the Portuguese court to Brazil was itself revolutionary, as it exposed the prince regent to new pressures and politicized the Brazilian society. By the 1820s, much of the debates centered around the question whether Portugal and Brazil would remain united under a central government, or each have a separate and autonomous government, or whether Brazil would again be subjected to Portuguese interests, as had been the case before the imperial crisis.[14] For some Brazilians, a united government, even if unequal, was preferable, as they feared control by Rio de Janeiro and São Paulo more than they feared supervision by Portugal. Others felt that the contrary was true. Fragmentation within Luso-America was also evident. Several Brazilian provinces participated in the Portuguese *Cortes* of 1820 despite royal disapproval, others did not. Confrontations between the various regions in Luso-America that predated the imperial crisis and the creation of the independent kingdom of Brazil in 1822 continued into the 1840s.[15] As in Spanish America, disagreement as to how to respond to European developments led to civil wars, as different factions and different regions clashed as to which was the best way to react.

Regardless of these disagreements, at the initial stages of these imperial crises, almost no one – either in Spanish or in Portuguese America – imagined independence to be the solution. Instead, actors wished to preserve or enhance their autonomy. When separation did become a possibility, it was not always evident whether the aim was to sever the links with the monarchy or with the Spanish and Portuguese Peninsular communities. Was the rebellion directed against the monarch or the metropole? Even among those in favor of independence, different answers were given to the question of the kind of relations the new polities would have with the former colonial power (confederation, commonwealth, association, or none of the above?) If finding a common answer was difficult, identifying who should give it was

14 M. R. Berbel, "Nación portuguesa, Reino de Brasil y autonomía provincial," in J. E. Rodríguez O. (ed.), *Revolución, independencia y las nuevas naciones de América* (Madrid: Mapfre, 2005), 397–423; and C. Nogueira da Silva, "Empire, Federalism, Nation(s) and Homeland(s) in the First Portuguese Constitutionalism (1821–1822)," *Giornale di storia costituzionale* 40(2) (2020), 57–82. On the question how revolutionary these processes were, see J. P. G. Pimenta, "La independencia de Brasil como revolución: historia y actualidad sobre un tema clásico," *Nuevo Topo: Revista de Historia y Pensamiento Crítico* 5 (2008), 69–98.

15 J. C. Mosher, *Political Struggle, Ideology, and State Building: Pernambuco and the Construction of Brazil, 1817–1850* (Lincoln: University of Nebraska Press, 2008).

just as problematic. In this process of renegotiation, reorganization, perhaps imperial disintegration, who would be the legitimate political actors? How to identify the territories that could become new polities? Would the old viceroyalties become new states? Would colonial provinces? Colonial towns? And who could legitimately represent them?

Attempts at answering the fundamental question of which new states would be instituted in the former colonial territories led to confrontations and internal struggles, even civil wars.[16] Different polities were proposed, experimented with, and sometimes eliminated. Attempts to conserve viceregal structures in both North and Central America, and in the territory of Nueva Granada, soon failed. This was partly the result of the growing powers of municipal corporations, which had increased their autonomy during the imperial crisis. Whether because their authorities assumed sovereignty to replace the captive king, or because the 1812 Cádiz constitution had mandated the creation of new municipalities and established electoral procedures that increased municipal control (by allowing parish *juntas* to decide on who had the right to vote), by the time independence was declared, municipal bodies were the main political actors. In some places, for example, present-day Ecuador, alliances between cities acting as sovereign bodies constituted new states. In others, such as Río de la Plata, alliances between cities were harder to achieve, and took various shapes and a very long time to cohere.[17] Several cities, such as Montevideo, proclaimed themselves independent states. In Brazil, separate colonial units, such as the State of Brazil and the State of Grão Pará, which had been directly tied to Lisbon rather than to one another, were joined together to create a new country (the state / empire of Brazil), sometimes to the displeasure of local actors who had sought autonomy (or independence) not so much from Lisbon

16 See for example, N. Goldman and M. Ternavaio, "Construir la república: Semántica y dilemas de la soberanía popular en Argentina durante el siglo XIX," *Revista de Sociologia e Política* 20(40) (2012), 11–19; and S. C. Chambers, "'Drying Their Tears': Women's Petitions, National Reconciliation and Commemoration in Post-Independence Chile," in K. Hagemann, G. Mettele, and J. Rendall (eds.), *Gender, War and Politics: Transatlantic Perspectives, 1775–1830* (London: Palgrave Macmillan, 2010), 343–60. On what transpired in Brazil, see for example, J. Malerba, "As independências do Brasil: ponderações teóricas em perspetiva historiográfica," *História (São Paulo)* 24(1) (2005), 99–126, at 101.

17 J. C. Chiaramonte, "El federalismo argentino en la primera mitad del siglo XIX," in M. Carmagnani (ed.), *Federalismos latino-americanos: México/Brasil/Argentina* (Mexico City: El Colegio de México, Fondo de Cultura Económica, 1992), 81–132; and J. C. Chiaramonte, "Autonomía e independencia en el Río de la Plata, 1080–1810," *Historia Mexicana* 58(1) (2008), 325–68. Chiaramonte criticizes the lack of attention to natural law in the historiography that studies these political debates. On natural law (though failing to identify it as such), see also F. J. Tavarez, "Viscardo's Global Political Economy and the First Cry for Spanish American Independence, 1767–1798," *Journal of Latin American Studies* 48(3) (2015), 537–64.

as from Rio de Janeiro or São Paulo. During the first half of the nineteenth century, and sometimes even later, in both Spanish and Portuguese America, new polities who claimed to represent new or old communities were formed, transformed, reformed, dismantled, and constructed yet again.

As the first answers to the most basic question – what new states would emerge out of the implosion of the colonial regime – began surfacing, the challenges in transitioning from colony to independent state became obvious. The transition required thousands of specific decisions regarding practically every aspect of collective life. The future was to be built on the ruins of the past, yet, despite the desire for change, the past often served as a foundation for the present.

In this chapter, I survey some of the questions that had to be answered, mostly by identifying debates that had to be settled and the difficulties entailed in achieving this goal. While the specific solutions that were adopted will be described in Sections 5.1–5.3, the aim here is to imagine a revolutionary period that required profound mutations and presented enormous challenges, and in which both continuity and change played major roles.[18] I also wish to demonstrate that, despite local differences, there was a common Latin American story, and that, moreover, the various options that were considered often formed part of a larger repertoire that actors on other continents also discussed.

The Challenges

If the first question that had to be answered was which polities could demand autonomy or independence, no less problematic was the definition of their citizen body (on this, see also Section 5.1). As the imperial crises unfolded and local actors moved to declare independence (roughly in the period from 1807 to the 1830s), some of the new Latin American states decreed the expulsion of the citizens of the former colonial powers, which they now considered dangerous foreigners.[19] Others admitted them into citizenship if they were willing to swear allegiance to the new order. In Brazil, already resident Portuguese were transformed into "Brazilians" under the presumption that if they remained in

18 On this period as featuring constant experimentation on multiple levels, see also H. Sábato, *Republics of the New World: The Revolutionary Political Experiment in Nineteenth-Century Latin America* (Princeton: Princeton University Press, 2018).

19 As happened in Lima, Mexico, and Argentina. See for example, T. Herzog, "Communities Becoming a Nation: Spain and Spanish America in the Wake of Modernity (and Thereafter)," *Citizenship Studies* 11(2) (2007), 151–72, at 161–63; and T. Herzog, "Nosotros y ellos: españoles, americanos y extranjeros en Buenos Aires a finales de la época colonial," in J. I. Fortea and J. E. Gelabert (eds.), *Ciudades en conflicto (Siglos XVI–XVIII)* (Valladolid: Junta de Castilla y León, 2008), 241–57.

the country after 1822, they had agreed with the move to declare independence. Yet, in many localities, hostility to these Portuguese was evident, as was their *de facto* exclusion from the community. Loyalty was required not only of these former compatriots, but also from all other residents, who were implicitly or explicitly to agree to the new emerging structures. During this period, some disagreements regarding the measures and laws that the new states should adopt were perceived as legitimate (and were thus tolerated), while many others were classified as treason and their proponents punished.[20]

Equally complex was the status the new states bestowed on their indigenous inhabitants and populations of African descent, including both free and enslaved persons.[21] Individuals belonging to these groups were either granted theoretical legal and/or political equality, or they were outright discriminated against by their exclusion from the nation's body politic or citizenship (or both). Often, inclusion – declaring all those born locally citizens, regardless of race or ethnicity – survived only a few decades before such declarations were repealed or exclusion was exercised indirectly by eliminating the participation of those considered unfree or dependent. In other places, theoretical inclusiveness did not stop or diminish anti-indigenous violence and the intensification of slavery.[22] New legal categories were invented, distinguishing "civilized" persons from so-called "savages," to whom the laws assigned differential treatment. The legal capacity of those classified as belonging to the second category was limited, such as their ability to enter into contracts,

20 See for example, I. Polastrelli, *Castigar la disidencia. Juicios y condenas en la élite dirigente rioplatense, 1806/1808–1820* (Buenos Aires: Academia Nacional de la Historia, 2019); J. L. Ossa Santa Cruz, *Armies, Politics, and Revolution: Chile, 1808–1826* (Liverpool: Liverpool University Press, 2014).

21 The literature on these questions is enormous. I found the following most useful: B. Larson, *Trials of Nation Making: Liberalism, Race and Ethnicity in the Andes, 1810–1910* (New York: Cambridge University Press, 2004); A. Sleiman, "'Seriam todos cidadãos?': Os impasses na construção da cidadania nos primórdios da constitucionalismo no Brasil (1823–1824)," in I. Jancsó (ed.), *Independência. História e Historiografia* (São Paulo: Editora Hucitec, 2005), 829–47; and C. Nogueira da Silva, "Da 'carta de alforria' ao 'alvará de assimilação': a cidadania dos 'originários de África' na América e na África portuguesas, séculos XIX e XX," in M. Berbel and C. H. de Salles Oliveira (eds.), *A experiência constitucional de Cádis. Espanha, Portugal e Brasil* (São Paulo: Alameda, 2012), 109–35.

22 Y. Miki, *Frontiers of Citizenship: A Black and Indigenous History of Postcolonial Brazil* (Cambridge and New York: Cambridge University Press, 2018); J. A. Erbig, Jr., *Where Caciques and Mapmakers Met: Border Making in Eighteenth-Century South America* (The David J. Weber Series in the New Borderlands History) (Chapel Hill: UNC Press, 2020); and C. R. Larson (ed.), *The Conquest of the Desert: Argentina's Indigenous Peoples and the Battle for History* (Albuquerque: University of New Mexico Press, 2020). On projects of granting equality to all, regardless of race or ethnicity, and their demise in the second half of the eighteenth century, see for example, T. H. Schaefer, *Liberalism as Utopia: The Rise and Fall of Legal Rule in PostColonial Mexico, 1820–1900* (Cambridge Latin American Studies 106) (Cambridge: Cambridge University Press, 2017).

or they were attributed diminished criminal responsibility, allegedly in order to protect and "civilize," rather than punish, them.[23] Treating these individuals and groups as potential, rather than actual, members of the body politic, some Latin American states eventually began to disregard their presence. Indigenous and Afro-Latin American individuals and groups disappeared from the official records, as state authorities no longer mentioned their existence or counted them. This elimination enabled some states, most notably Argentina, to claim that these groups were extinct.

If the composition of the new national communities was debated, no less contentious was the extent of their territories. The literature on the new Latin American states tends to center on the juridical doctrine of *uti possedetis*, which allegedly permitted continuity between the colonial and the postcolonial period by determining that the borders of the former colonial entities, now states, would remain as they had been before independence.[24] More recently, however, various historians have demonstrated that this continuity was easier to imagine than implement, as actors in most Latin American states disagreed as to what the situation at the end of the colonial period had been. Such disagreements often degenerated into conflicts which, according to most contemporaries, were not directed at expansion but only at allowing each of the new polities to possess what was rightfully theirs. As a result of these repeated confrontations, and despite vociferous claims to the contrary, by the mid-twentieth century most Latin American borders did not derive from the old colonial demarcations but had been fixed either as a result of war or in bilateral treaties.[25]

23 T. Herzog, "Latin American Legal Pluralism: The Old and The New," *Quaderni fiorentini per la storia del pensiero giuridico moderno* 50(2) (2021), 705–36, at 713–19. Also see T. Herzog, "Percibir el otro: El código penal de 1924 y la división de los peruanos en personas 'civilizadas', 'semi-civilizadas' y 'salvajes'," in J.-M. Scholz and T. Herzog (eds.), *Observation and Communication: The Construction of Realities in the Hispanic World* (Ius Commune Sonderheft 101) (Frankfurt am Main: Vittorio Klostermann, 1997), 399–414.

24 S. Lalonde, *Determining Boundaries in a Conflicted World. The Role of Uti Possidetis* (Montreal: McGill-Queen's University Press, 2002), 24–60; J. Castellino and S. Allen, *Title to Territory in International Law: A Temporal Analysis* (Burlington: Ashgate, 2003), 7 and 57–89; and M. G. Kohen, *Possession contestée et souveraineté territoriale* (Paris: Presses Universitaires de France, 1997), 426–28. On the original use of this doctrine in international law, see K. Touri, "The Reception of Ancient Legal Thought in Early Modern International Law," in B. Fassbender and A. Peters (eds.), *The Oxford Handbook of the History of International Law* (Oxford: Oxford University Press, 2012), 1012–33, at 1029–30.

25 It has been estimated that as much as 75 percent–90 percent of present-day Latin American borders were the result of post-independence conflicts: T. Herzog, "Historical Rights to Land: How Latin American States Made the Past Normative and What Happened to History and Historical Education as a Result," in M. Carretero, S. Berger, and M. Grever (eds.), *Palgrave Handbook on Historical Culture and Education* (London: Palgrave Macmillan, 2017), 91–107; and T. Herzog, "The Meaning of Territory: Colonial Standards and Modern Questions in Ecuador," in L. Roniger and

In part, the difficulty in fixing the new states' territories can be explained by the constant changes in colonial jurisdictions, and the constant disagreement regarding their definition even during the colonial period.[26] However, complexity was also aggravated by the prevalence of territories – including large tracts of the continent's interior as well as its Southern Cone – that had *de facto* been external to the colonial system. The conquest of these territories by the post-independence states during the nineteenth century unleashed violent campaigns of occupation and extermination that continued well into the twentieth century.[27]

Another fundamental issue that contemporary actors had to resolve was the nature of the political system to be established. Would the new states be monarchies? Republics? Perhaps even empires? All these forms were attempted, some producing regimes more stable than others. Supporters of centralism fought against federalists, and in both factions, many disagreed about what centralism and federalism actually were, and how they should best be designed and implemented (for a more detailed discussion, see Sections 5.1, 5.3, and 6.1).[28] Regions clashed with each other, rural and urban interests competed, liberals faced conservatives, and each of these groups was internally divided on multiple issues. Instability was permanent, as different projects were experimented with, polities were constituted and broken up, constitutions were drawn and redrawn, and governments constantly changed.

Despite these disagreements, to most of those contemporaries whose opinions are preserved in the written record, it was clear that the transition from colony to independent state required a new legal regime. In various declarations and in early legislation, the polities that declared their independence formally espoused the idea of a legal order in which parliaments would have a monopoly over legal creation. This required the drastic modification of the old order. As described in Section 3.1, instead of the multiplicity of legal sources (ranging from canon and Roman law to customs, royal decrees, and "common sense," all of which had to be weighed anew in each case to be decided) and a variety of different powers, each with its own jurisdiction, many actors in the postcolonial

C. H. Waisman (eds.), *Globality and Multiple Modernities: Comparative North American and Latin American Perspectives* (Brighton: Sussex Academic Press, 2002), 162–82.

26 T. Herzog, *Frontiers of Possession: Spain and Portugal in Europe and the Americas* (Cambridge: Harvard University Press, 2015).

27 S. E. Lewis, "Myth and History of Chile's Araucanians," *Radical History Review* 58 (1994), 112–41; V. N. César de Carvalho, "Soberanía e confronto na fronteira amazónica (1850–1910)," *Anuario de Estudios Americanos* 52(2) (1995), 121–50; and P. García Jordán and N. Sala i Vila (eds.), *La nacionalización de la Amazonía* (Barcelona: Universitat de Barcelona, 1998).

28 See for example, J. L. Ossa, "No One's Monopoly: Chilean Liberalism in the Post-Independent Period, 1823–1830," *Bulletin of Latin American Research* 36(3) (2017), 299–312.

states imagined a system in which there would be a single sovereignty that would be undivided, exclusive, and monopolistic. They also imagined a new normative system where legislation enacted by the representatives of the people would be the only legitimate legal source. The aim was to abandon the old system that allowed for the existence of multiple distinct authorities that declared and applied the law, and to instead institute a single authority and a single normativity. As Francisco de Paula Santander, who championed the cause of independence in the territory of present-day Colombia, famously stated "[w]eapons have given you independence: laws will guarantee you liberty."[29]

Yet, how was this to be achieved? Could colonial law persist in some matters, or must it be completely abolished, and new laws adopted instead? How would the transition from the old to the new system be organized, and how fast could it be realized? If the system required a true overhaul, what areas should be prioritized? And how to deal with colonial law that was contradictory to the new constitutional arrangements? Should older norms that were in conflict with the new order be automatically repealed, or should this require formal revocation? Here too, opinions varied. Some leaders urged their contemporaries to abandon Spanish or Portuguese law, which they believed was deeply flawed and inadequate for the needs of the early nineteenth century, and to adopt a better system, often by imitating legal developments elsewhere. Others rejected the idea of looking to foreign law for inspiration and imagined a homegrown legislation, modeled according to local conditions and local desires by rational actors meeting and discussing the various solutions in parliament. In the end, most of the new Latin American countries opted to uphold the colonial law as long its provisions did not stand in direct or indirect opposition to the "freedom" and "independence" that had been achieved.[30] What this meant in practice, of course, was a matter of debate.[31]

29 "Las armas os han dado independencia: las leyes os darán la libertad." This famous saying, contained in a message Santander sent to congress on December 2, 1821, is now reproduced on the walls of the Palacio de Justicia in Bogotá. For the full text, see "El general Santander se dirige a los pueblos de Colombia…" in J. F. Blanco (ed.), *Documentos para la historia de la vida pública del libertador de Colombia, Perú y Bolivia* (Caracas: Imprenta de "La Opinión Nacional", 1876), n. 1954, vol. VIII, 223–24.

30 J. C. Chiaramonte, "The 'Ancient Constitution' After Independence (1808–1852)," *Hispanic American Historical Review* 90(3) (2010), 455–88, at 471; R. Breña, "The Emancipation Process in New Spain and the Cádiz Constitution: New Historiographical Paths Regarding the *Revoluciones Hispánicas*," in Eastman and Sobrevilla Perea, *The Rise of Constitutional Government*, 42–62, at 57.

31 M. Candioti, "'Reformar útilmente la justicia': Jueces y leyes en la construcción del estado en Buenos Aires en la década de 1820," in Irurozqui and Galante, *Sangre de ley*, 97–130, for example, at 121–22.

This continuity explains why legal education, too, remained largely unchanged in most Latin American countries, and legal textbooks from the colonial period continued to be used. The process of changing the legal order that began in the early nineteenth century, in some areas as early as the imperial crisis of 1807/8 and during the wars of independence, did not culminate until the second half, sometimes the end, of the nineteenth century (codification, e.g., mostly got underway only from the 1850s onwards; see Section 5.2). As we shall see later, the result was that for almost a century, the new independent structures that emerged in Latin America often stood on shaky grounds not only socially, politically, or economically, but also legally. As one historian has observed, they were in a "permanently provisional" state.[32]

This reality produced extraordinary situations. For example, in many places, citizens were to vote before the laws defining who citizens were had been enacted or lists of citizens had been drawn. This enabled members of "voting tables" – or sometimes local priests or *juntas* – to decide whom they considered a citizen and thus permitted to vote. Those who wished to vote did not know whether they would be able to before they attempted to exercise this right.[33] Confusion also reigned in other ways. While the general assumption was that colonial law of Iberian inspiration should continue in place at least until the new states had consolidated their legal regime, less attention was given to the question of the status of indigenous customary law, practiced by indigenous peoples, which had been recognized *de iure* in Spanish territories, and *de facto* operated also in Portuguese America (see Section 3.1). Would it continue to be considered valid under the new legal order, or automatically revoked? Equally problematic was the status of other customary laws, created by locals and Afro-Latin American communities. Another issue to be resolved was the interaction of local law with state-wide normativity. Would the previous system that permitted the existence of both a general pan-European law and local adaptations persist, or should a single legality apply to all the new states' inhabitants, irrespective of their place of residence and group belonging?

32 J. C. Chiaramonte, cited in M. Ternavasio, *La revolución del voto. Política y elecciones en Buenos Aires, 1810–1852* (Buenos Aires: Siglo Veintiuno Editores, 2002), 33.

33 G. Chiaramonti, "Andes o nación: la reforma electoral de 1898 en Perú," in A. Annino (ed.), *Historia de las elecciones en Iberoamérica, siglo XIX* (Buenos Aires: Fondo de Cultura Económica, 1995), 315–46, at 320; A. Annino, "The Ballot, Land and Sovereignty: Cádiz and the Origins of Mexican Local Government, 1812–1820," in E. Posada-Carbó (ed.), *Elections before Democracy: The History of Elections Europe and Latin America* (London: Institute of Latin American Studies, 1996), 61–86, at 66 and 69–70; Sábato, "La ciudadanía en el siglo XIX," 83.

Challenges from within were matched by challenges from the outside. As they transitioned to independent status, the new Latin American polities strove to obtain international recognition.[34] Spanish American states mostly achieved this in 1833, when Spain renounced its claims to the continent and recognized them as sovereign and independent. Yet, even before this date, the need to deal with these new polities led to the invention of new doctrines, based on natural law, which allowed a *de facto* treatment of them as sovereign even before they had been granted formal recognition. These new doctrines were championed by many of the new Latin American states, which paradoxically pushed for a more inclusive and formally equal international order at the same time as they domestically intensified, rather than questioned, social hierarchies.[35] Thus, while opposing European supremacy in the international sphere, Spanish American actors continued in their quest to "conquer" the Americas, efforts which they justified by Eurocentric notions based on hierarchies in what they identified as "levels of civilization." Some Latin American actors even reversed the European argument regarding levels of civilization that discriminated against the American continent in the international sphere and suggested that Spanish American polities were superior to European ones because of their rejection of monarchical rule and their adherence to the wave of liberal revolutions that had swept the Atlantic World.[36]

Meanwhile, in 1820s and 1830s Portugal, a conflict regarding the succession to the Portuguese Crown – first between Dom Pedro, the heir who remained in Brazil, and his younger brother Miguel, and then between Miguel and Pedro's daughter Maria (as will be discussed in more detail later) – led to a civil war (1828–34) during which a regency acting for Maria strove to secure international recognition first from her father, the emperor of Brazil, and only then from other countries.[37] Portugal recognized Brazilian independence in 1825, but, somewhat ironically, by the late 1820s, it was the Peninsular

34 N. Carillo-Santarelli and C. Olarte-Bácares, "From Swords to Words: The Intersection of Geopolitics and Law, and the Subtle Expansion of International Law in the Consolidation of the Independence of the Latin American Republics," *Journal of the History of International Law* 21(3) (2019), 378–420; and G. S. Ribeiro, "Legalidade, legitimidade e soberania no reconhecimento da independência," in G. S. Ribeiro (ed.), *Brasileiros e cidadãos. Modernidade política, 1822–1930* (São Paulo: Alameda, 2008), 17–35.

35 T. Long and C. A. Schulz, "Republican Internationalism: The Nineteenth-Century Roots of Latin American Contributions to International Order," *Cambridge Review of International Affairs* 35(5) (2021), 1–23.

36 J. E. Sanders, "The Vanguard of the Atlantic World: Contesting Modernity in Nineteenth-Century Latin America," *Latin American Research Review* 46(2) (2011), 104–27.

37 G. Paquette, "In the Shadow of Independence: Portugal, Brazil, and Their Mutual Influence after the End of Empire (late 1820s-early 1840s)', *e-Journal of Portuguese History* 11(2) (2013), 101–19, at 106–17.

Portuguese government that, fighting against Miguel, sought recognition as well as military and economic support from Brazil.

Spanish America: An Old Constitution for a New Society?

In the post-independence period, the question whether the new polities should be constructed *ex nihilo* or retain at least some of the old institutions was also widely debated across the continent. Some suggested that the imperial breakup provided an opportunity for redrawing even the most basic social rules. Others argued that, as with the legal system, it was impossible to change the entire social, economic, and political order quickly, and that continuity – at least of some aspects, and temporarily – was beneficial. Yet others insisted that the new states lacked the power to undo or redo society. As the famous Argentinean intellectual Juan Bautista Alberdi (1810–1884) argued in 1853, governments came and went, but the old laws not only continued in place, the new governments were also called to abide by them.[38] Because humans could not change the nature of things, a representative assembly could enact laws, but these laws could not be invented at will. They had to derive from both nature and history, and to take existing legal precedents into consideration.

The struggle between those advocating for continuity and those pressing for change, those imagining a slow transition and those preferring it rapid, as well as disagreements regarding what to change and how, led to a power struggle between social groups, political factions, and powerful individuals. One of the first and most fundamental questions these actors had to answer was how to transform an *Ancien régime* based on loyalty to a king to a new regime whose legitimacy would originate in the consent of community members. Those declaring independence often claimed to speak for units – the people? the nation? – not yet in existence, and their legitimacy as their representatives was not generally recognized. As a result, debates regarding retaining the old or inventing a new constitution also involved preliminary considerations as to what kind of political body could legitimately decide on such elemental issues as independence and the drawing up of a new constitution. Should municipal *juntas*? A constitutional assembly? Should political leadership be limited to the capital city, or should other towns or even

38 J. B. Alberdi, *Bases y puntos de partida para la constitución de la República Argentina* (Valparaíso: Imprenta de Mercurio, 1852), esp. at 92–94, 119–21, and 150–51.

villages participate? Would representation in the new assemblies be limited to corporate bodies or should it include all citizens? And what would a just and proportional representation be? Most agreed that voting was the best way to elect representatives, but how would voting be organized, and how would representation be distributed?

The case of Buenos Aires is illuminating.[39] In the 1810s and 1820s, locals debated how to square the existence of multiple local communities, each demanding recognition as a sovereign body, with the formation of new central authorities also endowed with sovereignty. Could Buenos Aires represent the villages inside its province, or must each village send its own representative to a general assembly? Should voting take place in open meetings in which all citizens could participate and vote (similar to the traditional *cabildo abierto*, as during the 1810 election of deputies to the *junta* of Buenos Aires), or was there to be an assembly of elected representatives who would vote on behalf of their electorates (as in the 1811 elections)? Should each local community be represented individually by one or several of its citizens, or should representation be general to the entire province and elections be organized in the province as a whole? If communities were to be represented, how many delegates should each have? If each community were to be represented by the same number of delegates, the largest city, Buenos Aires, would lose its hegemony. Was it fair for small settlements to be accorded the same weight as the capital? If not, should representation be proportional to the number of inhabitants? To a community's economic importance? And once elected, would those chosen represent their particular town or village, or the provincial or national community at large? Among other things, the answer to this last question was of prime importance, because it also touched on the question whether delegates would have a free mandate, or would, by contrast, be limited to the power and instructions received from their local community.[40]

The flurry of elections that took place in Buenos Aires after independence (of deputies to the general congress, of governors, members of various *juntas*, and town councils), did not mask these disagreements. Neither did it solve the question of who had the right to vote. The general assumption was that this

39 See Ternavasio, *La revolución del voto*; M. Ternavasio, "The Impact of Hispanic Constitutionalism in the Río de la Plata," in Eastman and Sobrevilla Perea, *The Rise of Constitutional Government*, 133–49; and M. Ternavasio, *Gobernar la revolución. Poderes en disputa en el Río de la Plata, 1810–1816* (Buenos Aires: Siglo Veintiuno Editores, 2007).

40 This was reminiscent of how the Old Regime *Cortes* had functioned, where representatives of cities had met to discuss different issues, and where debate about whether they had the power to take decisions or required the pre-authorization of their municipality had been frequent.

right should be granted to all *vecinos,* or at least to those who were "free" and "patriots," but there was no consensus either on what this category (*vecino*) or these conditions ("free" and "patriot") meant, nor on whether all those voting were equal. In 1815, members of the voting table in Arrecife, in the province of Buenos Aires, declared a person who had not received the majority of votes to have won the election because, according to them, he had been backed by "better" and "freer" voters, whose votes should not be counted as one but as 100 votes each, because they also represented their family, dependents, and employees.[41] In the minds of those taking this decision, *Ancien régime* configurations that gave heads of household the power to represent all members of the household justified these conclusions, and quality – however they defined it – had to come before quantity, or at least quantity could be readjusted to what it allegedly represented. In 1817, after many elections had already taken place in the province, a provisional enactment by the government specified twenty-five years as the minimum age for voting. It also determined that the right to vote should be granted to those "born and residing" in the territory, unless they were dependent, had no property, and/or no "useful" office or occupation. These arrangements largely reproduced *Ancien régime* perceptions that considered vagabonds and other individuals without fixed domicile or economic independence as having no political rights. As mentioned earlier, these vague definitions, as well as the absence of electoral or other registers, led to the extraordinary situation in which members of voting tables were able to decide who had the vote and who did not (on the definition of citizenship in early constitutions, see also Section 5.1).[42]

The wish to adopt a new system that would embody a new, postcolonial "general will," thus met with resistance from those who had upheld the old system, in which only heads of households or municipal corporations had been enfranchised, and only they had had the right to represent and speak for the community. These disagreements also unleashed a power struggle between the new central authorities that were to replace the king, on the one hand, and the municipal corporations that declared themselves sovereign, on the other. In Buenos Aires, this power struggle resulted in provincial legislation that abolished the autonomy of existing municipalities and their representative assemblies. The central organs of the province, who took this decision, argued that while municipal corporations had been important

41 Ternavasio, *La revolución del voto*, 50.

42 Ternavasio, *La revolución del voto*, 41–42, 83 and 95, showing that as a result he who controlled the identity of those sitting at the voting table, also controlled the results of the elections.

under monarchical rule as representatives of their community, they were superfluous under the new representative system.[43] The suppression of the traditional representative bodies and their officials and judges, however, led to legal uncertainty, because no new law regulating the municipal regime was enacted until 1854.[44] The result were continuous conflicts between officeholders at different levels. Many of those whose offices were theoretically suppressed *de facto* proceeded as if this suppression had not taken place. Locals, who frequently refused to collaborate with the new officials named by the provincial authorities, preferred the previous officeholders, because they believed that they were more likely to respect their traditional rights and privileges. Similarly, as had been the case during the colonial period, local judges (*alcaldes*) continued to both declare and implement the law, as well as to act as magistrates with the authority to govern their communities. Attempts to limit their political and legislative power mostly failed, as locals continued to consider villages and towns as moral entities that not only merited representation in provincial and national assemblies, but should also be headed by local, traditional, magistrates.

Developments in other parts of Latin America were somewhat similar to what transpired in Buenos Aires.[45] In Central America, frequent debates took place between 1808 and 1823 regarding municipal sovereignty and its role in the transition to new republican structures.[46] National and local sovereignty often clashed rather than cohered, making the transition from the *Ancien régime* model of sovereignty (with a plurality of local powers) to a new model with a single (central) sovereignty extremely difficult. In what is now Mexico, municipalities that had traditionally been subjected to the city of Tlaxcala sought to protect – and probably increase – their autonomy by opposing attempts by the city's elites to have Tlaxcala province be declared

43 Similar arguments were invoked in Mexico, where actors debated how to maintain old, corporate representation, while also enabling a new form of representation of the nation as a whole. See for example, C. A. Hale, *El liberalismo mexicano en la época de Mora (1821–1853)* (Mexico City: Siglo Veintiuno Editores, 1972), 118.

44 M. Ternavasio, "Entre el cabildo colonial y el municipio moderno: los juzgados de paz de campaña en el Estado de Buenos Aires, 1821–1854," in M. Bellingeri (ed.), *Dinámicas de antiguo régimen y orden constitucional. Representación, justicia y administración en Iberoamérica, siglos XVIII–XIX* (Turin: Otto Editore, 2000), 295–336, for example, 308–9.

45 These questions have recently been studied in a special thematic issue of the journal *Nuevo Mundo, Mundos Nuevos* 23 (2023), edited by G. Verdo and V. Ayrolo.

46 M. Molina Martínez, *Los cabildos y la independencia de Iberoamérica* (Granada: CEMCI, 2002); J. Dym, "La soberanía de los pueblos: ciudad e independencia en Centroamérica, 1808–1823," in Rodríguez O., *Revolución, independencia*, 309–37; and J. Dym, *Politics, Economy, and Society in Bourbon Central America, 1759–1821* (Boulder: University Press of Colorado, 2007).

a state within the Mexican federal structures. As the capital of such a new state, the city of Tlaxcala's control over the surrounding municipalities would have been not just cemented, but also augmented.[47] At the opposite end of the spectrum, other Mexican actors asked how civil equality could coexist with distinctions and privileges attached to corporate municipal structures, and argued for their suppression and the creation of a single, united, central sovereignty and a single, general law.[48]

Similar processes also took place in the territory of the *Audiencia de Quito* (present-day Ecuador) in the 1810s, 1820s, and 1830s. There, municipal corporations, whose powers had increased substantially during the late eighteenth-century Bourbon reforms, struggled to maintain their hegemony inside and outside their territories, as well as to coordinate their activities with one another during and even after independence.[49] This has led some historians to conclude that in this *Audiencia,* independence led to federalization with cities, rather than citizens, as political actors. The configurations that emerged during this period did not imagine the state as an assembly of citizens. Instead, they accentuated *Ancien régime* structures that viewed the polity as an assembly of corporations that, paradoxically, were now more powerful than had been under colonial rule. After independence, municipal elections usually allowed members of the old elite to remain in power, with their positions now legitimized not only by their place in the local hierarchy, but also by their ability to mobilize supporters. Here as in Buenos Aires, the vote was granted to *vecinos*, and until an electoral law was introduced in 1861 and civil registries were formed, parish *juntas* had the power to decide who held citizenship and could vote, and who did not.

During and after the imperial crises, the sovereignty of local entities augmented rather than diminished also in other ways. One of the most important changes introduced in Spanish America with the Cádiz constitution – but which continued also after independence – was the "municipalization" of indigenous communities. Giving them the status of *municipio* turned these communities, which had previously been governed by traditional elites, into constitutional entities with new, elected authorities endowed with new administrative powers. The Cádiz delegates had initiated municipalization as a way to ensure the

47 M. Galante, "Municipios y construcción del estado (Tlaxcala, 1824–1826): Definición ante la ley y administración de justicia," in Irurozqui and Galante, *Sangre de ley*, 169–201.

48 Hale, *El liberalismo mexicano*, for example, at 123–25.

49 F. Morelli, *Territorio o nación. Reforma y disolución del espacio imperial en Ecuador, 1765–1830*, trans. A. Hermosa Andújar (Madrid: Centro de Estudios Políticos y Constitucionales, 2005).

modernization of indigenous communities as well as their integration into the nascent constitutional structures. Given that the constitution equated local citizenship (*vecindad*) with kingdom-wide citizenship, transforming indigenous villages into municipalities could potentially also ensure the integration of their local citizens in the national community. For local indigenous individuals, municipalization opened the road not only for greater local autonomy and formal equality with nonindigenous individuals and municipalities, but also for changes within indigenous communities, desired by some, disliked by others.

We have ample information on how this process of municipalization unfolded in various locations.[50] In some, it led residents to request the authorities to grant the status of *municipio* to residential conglomerates or villages founded on private lands that formed part of colonial *haciendas* or *estancias*.[51] The affected landowners frequently challenged these requests, because they feared losing not only ownership of their land but also their – *de facto* even if not *de iure* – political power over those living on their land. Many of the resulting legal issues were hotly debated. Would the municipalization of settlements on private land change the status of their residents from tenants to citizens, that is, *vecinos*? If so, would the landlords lose the ability to remove tenants who failed to pay their rent because, as local citizens, they would have the right to remain in the community? Could they be compelled to sell parts of their land to the community, because it would now include not only private land but also municipal territory? On occasions, landlords employed a racialized argument that their indigenous tenants were not yet ready to become members of self-ruling communities and that only they, the landlords, could ensure social and political order and obedience to the law.

In many places, the municipalization of indigenous communities led to power struggles between traditional indigenous elites and newly elected officials, yet, in many others, formal changes masked continuities. Frequently, despite legal reforms, indigenous communities maintained many of their organs and customs almost intact.[52] The constitutional redefinition of indigenous

50 Rodríguez O., *La revolución política*, 109–23 and Morelli, *Territorio o nación*, 159–87. On how Cádiz reinforced rather than undermined municipal structures also among the indigenous peoples and in rural areas, see M. Guzmán Pérez, "Cádiz y el ayuntamiento constitucional en los pueblos indígenas de la Nueva España, 1820–1825," in Centro de Investigaciones de América Latina (ed.), *De súbditos del rey a ciudadano de la nación (Actas del I Congreso Internacional Nueva España y las Antillas)* (Castelló de la Plana: Universitat Jaume I, 2000), 305–24.

51 T. H. Schaefer, "Law of the Land? Hacienda Power and the Challenges of Republicanism in Postindependence Mexico," *Hispanic American Historical Review* 94(2) (2014), 207–36. Also see Schaefer, *Liberalism as Utopia*, 97–128.

52 Schaefer, *Liberalism as Utopia*, 129–60.

villages, furthermore, did not necessarily mean that the constitution's egalitarian ethos was adopted, as well. In some communities, traditional service obligations that resulted from membership status were not distributed equally: Mostly on the basis of hereditary distinctions between nobles and commoners, some community members managed to avoid these duties altogether.[53] In other instances, general suffrage was rejected in favor of giving the vote only to elders and *principales*. Equally important in maintaining traditional hierarchies was the continuing presence of common landholding, despite constitutional and legal changes that favored private ownership. Common lands were frequently managed by the local authorities that, despite the abolition of traditional village structures and the institution of constitutional municipalities, still functioned as sovereign corporate bodies that could exclude those whom they identified as "foreign," even when they resided locally, from enjoying the rights of members. Traditional elites also continued to represent their communities in negotiations with other authorities and in the courts, as they and many members of indigenous communities insisted that the traditional structures continued to exist parallel to and independently of the new constitutional structures and their officeholders.

If the difficulties in converting colonial and monarchical governance to one based on new constitutional and legal arrangements were clear with respect to the role and organization of municipal bodies, the same was true for the judiciary. The colonial judiciary had been an important instrument both for enhancing state hegemony and for limiting its reach (see Section 3.1). Most cases were decided locally by locally elected, non-jurist judges, who considered their principal task to be what we would now call peace and justice making.[54] Despite the new constitutional arrangements, in most polities, these practices remained largely unchanged, as did the identity of those occupying the bench.[55] Alongside the persistence of most colonial law into the second half of the nineteenth century in both Spanish and Portuguese

53 P. Guardino, "Community Service, Liberal Law and Local Custom in Indigenous Villages, Oaxaca, 1750–1850," in S. Caufield, S. C. Chambers, and L. Putnam (eds.), *Honor, Status, and Law in Modern Latin America* (Durham: Duke University Press, 2005), 50–65; N. Sobrevilla Perea, "Loyalism and Liberalism in Peru, 1810–1824," in Eastman and Sobrevilla Perea, *The Rise of Constitutional Government*, 111–32.

54 T. Herzog, *Upholding Justice: Society, State, and the Penal System in Quito (1650–1750)* (History, Languages, and Cultures of the Spanish and Portuguese Worlds) (Ann Arbor: University of Michigan Press, 2004).

55 S. C. Chambers, "Citizens Before the Law: The Role of Courts in Postindependence State Building in Spanish America," in M. A. Centeno and A. E. Ferrao (eds.), *State and Nation Making in Latin America and Spain: Republics of the Possible* (Cambridge: Cambridge University Press, 2013), 356–74. On attempts to reform the system, see for example, Candioti, "Reformar útilmente la justicia," 101–21.

America (given the slow pace of legal change and codification, discussed in Section 5.2) and the ongoing dependence on wide judicial discretion, this has led historians to conclude that there was extensive continuity in jurisprudence from the late colonial to the early national period.[56] Even though the basic assumptions of colonial legislation were in theory radically different from (and sometimes even incompatible with) the new values that independence and revolution sought to implement, in the absence of new legislation, both judges and litigants continued to uphold the old norms. This was true both in Spanish America and in Brazil, where conflicts between the new constitutional powers and the judiciary were constant, and where, despite the legal changes introduced in the early nineteenth century, legal culture remained more or less untouched.[57] It is possible, however, that some of the new values did find recognition in the courts, where they were sometimes imposed by judges rendering decisions that endorsed them.[58] Among these was the demand to hold public officers accountable when they ignored the law (rather than when they upset social harmony, as had been the case before), or the introduction of new measures to evaluate the honorability of individuals, where old criteria based on traditional hierarchies were now accompanied by the new languages of citizenship and equality, patriotism, and civic virtue.

Portuguese America: A Unique Yet Ordinary Case?

When compared to developments in Spanish America, the untangling of Portugal and Brazil leading to Brazilian independence was a particularly convoluted affair. Acting as regent of Brazil, Dom Pedro, heir to the Portuguese throne, first refused to obey the order of the Portuguese *Cortes* to return to Portugal in 1821 and, in 1822, declared Brazilian independence. Yet, the story of Brazilian independence did not end there.[59] Though

56 C. Hünefeldt, *Paying the Price of Freedom: Family and Labor among Lima's Slaves, 1800–1854* (Berkeley: University of California Press, 1994) and the works of S. C. Chambers, for example, in "'To the Company of a Man Like My Husband, No Law Can Compel Me': The Limits of Sanctions Against Wife Beating in Arequipa, Peru, 1780–1850," *Journal of Women's History* 11(1) (1999), 31–52. Several of the contributions to V. M. Uribe-Urban (ed.), *State and Society in Spanish America during the Age of Revolution* (Wilmington: Scholarly Resources, 2001) also describe these continuities.

57 A. Slemian, "A administração da justiça nas primeiras décadas do império do Brasil: instituições, conflitos de jurisdições e ordem pública (c.1823–1850)," *Revista do Instituto Histórico Geográfico Brasileiro* 172(452) (2011), 225–72.

58 R. Zahler, *Ambitious Rebels: Remaking Honor, Law, and Liberalism in Venezuela, 1780–1850* (Tuscon: University of Arizona Press, 2013).

59 Paquette, "In the Shadow of Independence," 103–6.

crowned as the new Brazilian emperor, Dom Pedro was still the legitimate successor to the Portuguese throne, to which he ascended after his father's death in 1826. Acclaimed as the rightful monarch in both Portugal and Brazil, he controlled Portugal through a regency. Within months of succeeding his father, however, growing pressure in both Portugal and Brazil led Dom Pedro to abdicate the Portuguese throne in favor of his seven-year-old daughter Maria – on certain conditions: First, when Maria came of age, she was to marry Dom Pedro's younger brother Miguel and rule Portugal alongside her husband; second, in place of the 1822 constitution embraced by the *Cortes*, Portugal was to adopt a new constitutional charter that Dom Pedro would dictate.

The constitution that Dom Pedro imposed on Portugal in 1826 was extremely similar to the one he had instituted in Brazil in 1824.[60] In both cases, he proceeded without consulting representative assemblies, creating a constitutional monarchy that granted the monarch strong executive power. Though the 1826 constitution was received with public celebrations in Portugal, by 1828 the struggle between monarchists, who backed these developments, and liberals, who opposed them, between the supporters of absolutism and those in favor of the constitutional monarchy, had degenerated into a civil war. During this conflict, many of those who criticized the 1826 constitution argued that while the need to draft a new constitution for Brazil had been evident – after all, it had emerged as a new polity in 1822 – the same was not true for Portugal, which already had its own traditions. Furthermore, they argued, as Portugal had recognized Brazilian independence in 1825, Brazil was now a foreign country, even if it was ruled by the same monarch as Portugal. That both countries should have an almost identical constitution was, in the eyes of such critics, inconceivable. The constitution was also criticized by some because it was seen as an instrument to secure continued relations between Portugal and Brazil as well as the continuous domination of the house of Braganza on both sides of the Atlantic Ocean.

The conflict over constitutional issues was compounded by a war of succession. Miguel, Pedro's brother and his daughter Maria's supposed future husband, first declared himself regent and then, in 1828, claimed to be the lawful Portuguese king, arguing that his brother Pedro had lost his rights to the throne after he had become the sovereign of an independent Brazil and therefore could not abdicate in favor of his daughter.

60 G. Paquette, "The Brazilian Origins of the 1826 Portuguese Constitution," *European History Quarterly* 41(3) (2011), 444–71.

In 1831, under public pressure from his Brazilian subjects, Dom Pedro also renounced the Brazilian Crown, this time in favor of his son, Dom Pedro II. He then returned to Portugal and declared himself regent and the guardian of his daughter. Queen Maria's reign, however, was established firmly only in 1834, when her uncle and fiancé, Miguel, was finally defeated. Maria also retained rights to the Brazilian throne, until the Brazilian parliament excluded her from the list of possible heirs in 1835, following a 1834 vote to prohibit the return of her father, the former emperor, to Brazil. In 1836, the constitution imposed by Dom Pedro on Portugal in 1826 was abolished and the 1822 constitution restored, but two years later, in 1838, Maria approved a new constitution for Portugal, which had been proposed by the *Cortes*. Only four years later, however, the constitution imposed by Dom Pedro in 1826 was reinstituted. It remained in force, albeit with modifications, until the declaration of a republic in Portugal in 1910.

Some contemporaries in both Portugal and Brazil remarked on the absurdity of these entanglements. In 1826, they asked how the Portuguese could support the crowning of the emperor of Brazil as their king.[61] Others pointed to Pedro's constant attempts to control both Portugal and Brazil and argued that these violated the 1824 Brazilian constitution, which mandated that Portugal and Brazil never again be unified under the same monarch. On both sides of the ocean, factions debated whether or not to trust the Braganza dynasty, and how to manage the relations between Portugal and Brazil: Some supported total separation, others favored a union, and most preferred one of multiple other options between these two extremes. As one historian has remarked, even after Brazilian independence, it was difficult, perhaps even impossible, to separate colonial from national history.[62] Indeed, contrary to what had taken place in Spanish America, the continuing presence of the king and the involvement of the different Braganza family members in ruling both sides of the ocean made the breakup between Portugal and Brazil particularly convoluted.

Despite these particularities, common threads linked the Spanish and the Portuguese experience in the 1810s, 1820s, and 1830s. In both empires, relations between the old metropole and the Americas were central to the debates regarding the new shape of the "national" political and legal systems. In both, the role of the monarch, both when present and when absent (either because he had been forced to abdicate, as in Spain/Spanish America, or

61 Paquette, "In the Shadow of Independence," 108–10.

62 Paquette, "In the Shadow of Independence," 117. See also Paquette, *Imperial Portugal*, for example, 2–3 and 9–11.

because he was residing elsewhere, as in the case of Portugal/Brazil), was pivotal, as was the assumption of sovereignty by municipal *juntas*, central *juntas*, and regencies. In both monarchies, the questions whether the absence of the king and the war situation justified calling a meeting of the *Cortes* (a task normally performed by the king, who, however, could or would not issue such a call throughout the 1810s and 1820s), and what these *Cortes* could do (could they propose a new constitution?), as well as who should be represented in them and how (municipalities? citizens? and how many?), were equally debated. Legally, the wish to enact new constitutions met with the response that these either must innovate and reform or, on the contrary, must respect the "ancient constitution" or *lei fundamental*.[63] Regardless of the innovations the various constitutions introduced, even the most ardent revolutionaries argued that their aim had only been to ensure respect for an ancient constitution that a tyrannical regime had violated. In both monarchies, in short, the separation of colonies from metropole and the adoption of a new, constitutional, regime was easier to conceive than to execute, as legal and political ties and traditional social structures often proved more resilient than the declarations that announced their rupture.

The Global Context: Imitation or Convergence?

Latin American actors who had to answer these questions were not the only ones facing such dilemmas. Many of the issues they were called to consider formed part of larger Atlantic conversations, fueled by revolutions that sought to change the social order (according to some historians), or independence movements that only wished to end the colonial regime (according to others). Obviously, Latin American actors were propelled into action by an international crisis that engulfed large parts of Europe, which were equally affected by the so-called Napoleonic wars. Traditionally, historians have also suggested that Iberian responses to the Napoleonic invasion of the Iberian Peninsula were heavily influenced by the events of the previous decades in British North America, where thirteen colonies had declared their independence in 1776, and the French revolution of 1789, which, among other things, had also fueled the Haitian revolution and subsequent independence (1791–1804).[64] But

63 On this debate in Portugal and Brazil, see Paquette, *Imperial Portugal*, 17–34.

64 For example, J.-R. Aymes, "Le débat idéologico-historiographique autour des origins françaises du libéralisme espagnol: Cortes de Cadix et constitution de 1812," *Historia Constitucional* 4 (2003), 45–102, http://hc.rediris.es/04/index.html (last accessed Mar. 12, 2022); P. G. Carozza, "From Conquest to Constitutions: Retrieving a Latin American Tradition of the Idea of Human Rights," *Human Rights Quarterly* 25(2)

other researchers have asked whether, irrespective of issues of influence or reception, similar responses could possibly also be explained by the similarities of the challenges facing those trying to limit the consequences of the war, or striving to create a new order. Some historians have also rejected the conclusion that Latin American actors imitated revolutions taking place elsewhere by pointing out that the solutions adopted in Iberia and Latin America might have been in some regards even more radical, precisely because of their truly Atlantic dimensions.[65]

The challenges facing contemporary actors in the future United States of America, in Haiti, and in Latin America were indeed strikingly similar. The initial goal of those responding to the imperial crises was not independence but to reform the colonial order and/or obtain greater autonomy from the metropole. Yet, their responses to the imperial crises, and the discussions, and the degree of violence they unleashed, were transformative. They politicized colonial actors, many of whom went on to demand independence. In all these cases, the move from the *Ancien* to a new *régime* produced formal declarations of independence that, first proposed by North American actors, thereafter became the standard procedure by which new polities claimed sovereignty and international recognition.[66] Independence also required the elaboration of new constitutions and laws, although, as described earlier, constitutions changed faster than other areas of law, a situation that often resulted in a lack of legal certainty or even chaos.[67]

(2003), 281–313, at 300; K. Racine, "'This England and This Now:' British Cultural and Intellectual Influence in the Spanish American Independence Era," *Hispanic American Historical Review* 90(3) (2010), 423–54, at 429; and M. Rodríguez, "The Impact of the American Revolution on the Spanish- and Portuguese- Speaking World," in Library of Congress Symposia on the American Revolution (ed.), *The Impact of the American Revolution Abroad* (Washington: Library of Congress, 1976), 101–25. For a critique of such interpretations, see Paquette, *Imperial Portugal*, 3–5.

65 A. Rivero, "The Portuguese Uprising of 1820: A Forgotten Atlantic Revolution," in F. Colom González and A. Rivero (eds.), *The Traditions of Liberty in the Atlantic World: Origins, Ideas and Practices* (Leiden: Brill, 2016), 55–69, citing (at 60–62) Abbé de Pradt, Karl Marx, Jeremy Bentham, and Antonio Gramsci.

66 D. Armitage, *The Declaration of Independence: A Global History* (Cambridge: Cambridge University Press, 2008); and J. Gaffield (ed.), *The Haitian Declaration of Independence: Creation, Context, and Legacy* (Charlottesville: University of Virginia Press, 2016). On the declarations of independence in Latin America, see a.o. J. Malagón (ed.), *Las actas de independencia de América* (Washington: Pan-American Union, 1955).

67 On the role of the US constitution as a model for Latin American ones, see E. Zimmermann, "Translations of the 'American Model' in Nineteenth Century Argentina: Constitutional Culture as a Global Legal Entanglement," in T. Duve (ed.), *Entanglements in Legal History: Conceptual Approaches* (Global Perspectives on Legal History 1) (Frankfurt am Main: Max-Planck-Institut für europäische Rechtsgeschichte, 2014), 385–425; and Section 5.1.

In North as in Latin America, those moving to declare independence and adopting constitutional changes suggested that their activities were justified by loyalty to an "ancient constitution," which they accused their monarch and European compatriots of having infringed. Their struggle, they argued, involved a fight to restore the "good old order," and was an act of legitimate resistance against tyranny and oppression. Yet, in both cases, as well as in France and Haiti, actors also appealed to a natural law that, according to them, included the right to form new communities and endow them with institutions and norms. Moreover, in their view, natural law also authorized them to rebel in order to protect their individual rights. The new regime they instituted, therefore, had to abide by these rights, and the best method to do so was by adopting a written declaration of rights. The connection between independence and the institution of a new regime based on both natural law and natural rights was made explicitly in Haiti's 1804 declaration of independence. It included not only the pledge to end French domination, but also an oath by those declaring independence that, in the new state, all would be not only independent but also enjoy personal freedoms.[68]

In France, the future United States, Haiti, and Latin America, actors favoring independence battled to define the new political entities, draw their boundaries, and delineate their citizenry. Institutionally, however, the transfer from the *Ancien régime* to the new regimes was more contentious in France and Latin America than it had been in North America. During the revolutionary years in Latin America, the identification of the units that would become independent was extremely convoluted. Different cities, provinces, and territories could not agree on how to proceed, whether to unite or remain separate (see also Section 5.1). Disagreements regarding which political structures would ensure the "greatest happiness" led the French to change constitutions as often as many Latin American states would do over the course of the nineteenth and even twentieth centuries. Meanwhile, the transition from colony to statehood in the future United States in the 1770s was relatively simple, as separate colonies declared themselves states and adopted their own, new constitutions. As far as we currently know, no serious debate took place in the future USA regarding which communities could declare their independence, nor on whether each of the old colonies would

68 D. Armitage and J. Gaffield, "Introduction: The Haitian Declaration of Independence in an Atlantic Context," in Gaffield, *The Haitian Declaration of Independence*, 1–22, at 11. The text of the declaration (translated into English) is available online at https://today.duke.edu/showcase/haitideclaration/declarationstext.html (last accessed Mar. 20, 2023).

become a single new state or be divided into several – or whether various colonies would be united to form one state, as was often the case in Spanish America. Moreover, the new North American states' constitutions, enacted in that emancipatory moment, retained their validity, rather than repeatedly changing throughout the nineteenth and twentieth centuries, as happened in France and in the former Iberian colonies. Yet, in the USA, the new states nonetheless found it difficult to coordinate their activities and create federal structures. Various types of alliances were considered, discussed, espoused, or discarded.

Despite these differences, the processes that led to independence in the future United States and in Latin America did share many similarities. For example, the story of the North American British colonies' independence could be told – though it mostly is not – as involving the gradual rise of local assemblies that limited royal powers and extended colonial autonomy, even freedoms. In Latin America, too, cities obtained greater powers over time, which had them refashion themselves as autonomous, if not outright sovereign. In both cases, while independence had initially been almost inconceivable, it eventually became the desired goal, though not everywhere at the same pace. Historians have linked this development, among other things, to changes in political culture and a growing political involvement by colonists as a result of Enlightenment thought as well as the social and economic changes wrought by the imperial crises.

In France and Latin America, contemporaries invoked the general will of a nation – but who constituted that nation was far from obvious (see also Sections 5.1–5.3). The US constitution spoke for "we the people," without defining whom this included. Yet, neither in the United States not in France and in the new Latin American polities was the "national" community for whom the political actors claimed to speak truly inclusive. In France and most Latin American countries, all those who opposed the revolutionary measures or were considered unfree were excluded from the body politic. In France, the USA, and Latin America, the general principle of legal equality and the declaration that humans were born free did not guarantee the end of enslavement. In the USA and the new Latin America states, discrimination often extended also to members of indigenous groups, who were either classified as not yet ready for citizenship or were viewed as both domestic and foreign, both belonging to the state and in some important ways external to its body politic.

Debates regarding whom to include or exclude from political participation and other rights continued throughout the nineteenth and twentieth centuries (see also Section 5.3). In many of the new polities, after an initial period in which most male inhabitants were granted political rights, those in power increasingly tended to restrict these to a smaller group. Despite these exclusions, popular participation in political action was evident in France, Haiti, and Latin America. Whether achieved through the celebration of popular assemblies, appeals to the courts, involvement in uprisings, or in other ways, those lacking the right to vote found means of expressing their opinions and to influence decision-making, at least to some degree. We have fewer studies on how this was done in the United States, but historians nonetheless suggest that many subaltern actors were also active there, even if the literature has not yet described their contributions fully.

Confronted with huge neighboring territories that had been largely outside colonial control – the continental interiors, as well as the Southern Cone – the USA and many Latin American countries expanded their boundaries at the expanse of indigenous peoples in the course of the nineteenth century. They claimed indigenous territory as their own by arguing that the land was either vacant or insufficiently or inappropriately occupied (because only intense agriculture – which according to them, indigenous peoples did not practice – produced a valid title), or by claiming that it already formed part of their territory, even though in practice (and in most cases even *de iure*) it never had.

Though American independence, both in the North and in the South, would eventually inspire homegrown normativity, the enactment of new constitutions did not immediately produce a flurry of legislation (on the particular case of codifications, see Section 5.2). The old colonial law continued in force on most matters, the residents of the new polities mainly debating which part should be applied and which repealed because it was not appropriate, or even repugnant, to the local conditions, which now also included the new regime.

Battling against regional differences, post-revolutionary France and Latin America also had to decide whether some measure of local distinctions would be allowed, or whether "national" homogenization and legal unification – required by the principle of legal equality – must be complete. And, despite massive changes in the way law – now the product of the "general will" as expressed by parliament – was conceived, in practice, the new legislation, while enshrining some of the principles of the revolutions, also allowed great continuity with the *Ancien régime* (on these issues, see also Section 5.3). In post-revolutionary France, despite the desire for a complete overhaul of the legal system, the *Code Napoléon*, enacted in 1804, included many traditional elements (on this code's influence on American codifications, see Section 5.2). In Haiti, despite the revolutionaries' harsh criticism of French despotism, the wish to establish a completely new regime with laws that would guarantee freedoms did not preclude continuing French legal influence.[69] Indeed, to break with the powerful legacies of slavery inherited from France, the Haitian constitution of 1805 sought to ensure equality not by imagining a new system that would disregard racial categories, but instead by accepting these and simply declaring all citizens of Haiti black.

Though apparent in both France and Latin America, legal continuity was even more pronounced in the USA, where independence hardly affected law, other than public and administrative law. From that perspective, the move for independence in the USA was much less of a legal rupture than it is often claimed. The "nation" might have emancipated itself from colonial and monarchical domination, but its social and economic order continued mostly unchanged.

Obviously, many Latin Americans political actors closely followed debates and developments taking place elsewhere. In the 1810s, Jeremy Bentham's (1748–1832) various proposals for constitution and codification were published in Venezuela, and many of his other essays were translated and sold. Abridged versions of Thomas Paine's (1737–1809) *Rights of Man* (1791) were translated into Spanish in various locations across the continent. A Spanish translation of the French Declaration of the Rights and Duties of Man and Citizen (1789) was produced in 1794 and circulated in Nueva Granada and Venezuela.[70] Simón Bolívar was an avid reader of a huge variety of such works, as were many of his contemporaries.[71]

If one way to think about these connections between American independence, the French Revolution, the independence of Haiti, and Latin America is to argue for imitation and influence (as many historians have done in the past), another is to suggest that Latin American actors participated in the same republic of letters as other contemporaries did (see also Sections 5.1 and 5.2).[72]

69 M.W. Ghachem, "Law, Atlantic Revolutionary Exceptionalism, and the Haitian Declaration of Independence," in Gaffield, *The Haitian Declaration of Independence*, 95–114.

70 Carozza, "From Conquest," 297–99.

71 Carozza, "From Conquest," 301–2.

72 On such issues, see for example, J. Simon, *The Ideology of Creole Revolution: Imperialism and Independence in American and Latin American Political Thought* (Cambridge: Cambridge University Press, 2017), who highlights the similarity in the dilemmas faced and in the horizon of possible solutions between actors in the thirteen British colonies in North America and Latin America. Both Sábato, *Republics of the New World* (e.g., 5–6 and 22–49); and J. A. Aguilar Rivera, *Ausentes del universo. Reflexiones sobre el pensamiento politico hispanoamericano en la era de la construcción nacional, 1821–1850* (Mexico City: Fondo de Cultura Económica, 2012), also study the plethora of ideas and options that

Many among the leaders of the new states had resided for some time in London, Paris, or the USA, where they took part in local conversations and corresponded with local leaders.[73] Others remained in Latin America but published their work also in Europe. The leaders of the independence movements and the resulting states might have looked at the questions raised by independence and revolutions differently from their counterparts in Europe, or the events that they experienced might have led them to adopt different strategies. Regardless of these variations, however, their responses were nonetheless part of wider conversations, which focused on why, when, and how to form new political communities, institute new states, define their borders and citizens, and develop new legal regimes. The answers to these questions involved innovations and change, as well as continuity and preservation. As the Sections 5.1–5.3 and 6.1–6.3 and Chapter 7 will trace in more detail, decisions taken by Latin American actors not only formed part of global conversations, they also influenced them. The discussions that took place and the solutions adopted in Latin America during this period were known and debated in Europe and the USA and, according to some, contributed to the formation of new ideas and practices in such important areas as humanitarian law and international law more widely (see Section 6.3).[74] Some historians have also argued that the positions taken by Latin American actors during the independence period and the construction of the new Latin American states reinforced the international recognition of the importance of constitutions, the need to adapt states to what was perceived as their "natural borders," and the importance of guaranteeing the freedom of the seas. Others point out that Latin American actors who expressed a desire for a new *ius gentium* in which the former colonies would play a major role might have contributed to

contemporary actors in Latin America considered, and which formed part of a larger repertoire of ideas and options that also inspired others.

73 Racine, "This England and This Now;" Paquette, *Imperial Portugal*, for example, 107, 114–17, and 124–27; C. Banko, "Influencia de la revolución francesa en la constitución de Barcelona, Venezuela del año de 1812," *Boletín de la Academia Nacional de la Historia* 81(318) (1997), 43–57; and S. Alberro, A. Hernández Chávez, and E. Trabulse Atala (eds.), *La revolución francesa en México* (Mexico City: El Colegio de México, 1992).

74 For example, J. J. Urbana, "La aportación latinoamericana al desarrollo del derecho internacional humanitario," in E. R. Tristán and P. Calvo González (eds.), *Actas XIV Encuentro de Latioamericanistas españoles. Congreso Internacional. 1810–2010: 200 años de Iberoamérica Santiago de Compostela, 15–18 de septiembre de 2010* (Santiago de Compostela: Universidade, Servizo de Publicacións e Intercambio Científico, 2010), 2238–58, https://halshs.archives-ouvertes.fr/halshs-00531620/document (last accessed Mar. 10, 2022); and L. O. Castaño Zuluaga, "Antecedentes del derecho humanitario bélico en el contexto de la independencia hispanoamericana (1808–1826)," *Revista de Estudios Histórico-Jurídicos* 34 (2012), 323–68.

widening the list of legitimate participants in the international legal arena.[75] Beyond direct influence, it is also clear that Latin American developments impacted debates taking place elsewhere, as foreign observers compared and contrasted their own experiences to that of Latin America and sought to draw important conclusions from this comparison.[76]

75 See, for example, the writing of Abbé de Pradt as described in M. Aguirre Elorriaga, *El abate de Prad en la emancipación hispanoamericana (1800–1830)* (Caracas: Universidad Católica Andrés Bello, 1983); L. Bornholdt, "The Abbé de Pradt and the Monroe Doctrine," *The Hispanic American Historical Review* 24(2) (1944), 201–21; D. Todd, *A Velvet Empire: French Informal Imperialism in the Nineteenth Century* (Princeton: Princeton University Press, 2021), at 25–71; J. C. Benassy-Berling, "Notes sur quelques aspects de la vision de l'Amérique hispanique en France pendant la première moitié du XIXe siècle," *Caravelle* 58 (1992), 39–48, at 45–47. Interestingly, the abbé is credited with both influencing Latin American independence and learning from it. See for example, G. Jiménez Codinach, *México en 1821: Dominique de Pradt y el Plan de Iguala* (Mexico City: Ediciones El Caballito, 1982); M. Morel, "O caminho incerto das Luzes francesas: o abade De Pradt e a Independência brasileira," *Almanack* 13 (2016), 112–29; and J. M. Portillo, *Una historia atlántica de les orígenes de la nación y el estado. España y las Españas en el siglo XIX* (Madrid: Alianza Editorial, 2022), 195–202.

76 On the way in which Latin American Independence affected discussions elsewhere, see for example, C. Fitz, *Our Sister Republics: The United States in an Age of American Revolutions* (New York: W.W. Norton, 2016).

5
The Coming of States? The Nineteenth Century

5.1 Constitutions

JOSÉ MARÍA PORTILLO

In 1856, the Peruvian liberal jurist José Silva Santisteban published a *Course on Constitutional Law*, motivated by the idea that Latin American youth needed to be educated with a locally written treatise instead of translated European manuals. By the time that he published its second edition in 1874, events in Europe had convinced him that that continent was not any longer the constitutional oracle it used to be during the first half of the century: it was time for Latin America to take over. He opened his manual with a sentence that neatly summarized the spirit of the century: "The destinies of humanity are largely entrusted to constitutional law."[1]

When considering the origins and subsequent evolution of constitutionalism in the new Latin American republics, we should bear this sentence in mind. As in other parts of the Western world, constitutions became one of the central axes of political life in nineteenth-century Latin America, and protagonists debated and fought over numerous issues – to be discussed later – ranging from the very meaning of emancipation to the scope of national sovereignty, the organization of the state, the latter's relationship with the Catholic Church, and the government of complex societies characterized by ethnic, gender, and class differences.

Constitutionalism in the Iberian world was conditioned by two circumstances: First, by earlier debates, especially during the late eighteenth century, on whether Catholic culture was able to assimilate the ideas of moral philosophy and political economy generated by European Enlightenment

1 J. Silva Santisteban, *Curso de Derecho Constitucional* (Lima: Centro de Estudios Constitucionales, 2015 [1856]), prologue. All translations are the author's unless otherwise stated.

thought; and second, by the specific historical contexts that produced the first constitutional texts in the Spanish and Portuguese realms. As in other Atlantic spaces, such as the British or French empires, the emergence of constitutions in the Iberian world was closely linked to imperial crises. As will be discussed later, these crises had unique characteristics that significantly shaped the earliest constitutions drafted in their territories (see Chapter 4). In the case of the Portuguese monarchy, this was the transfer of the imperial center to Brazil in 1807. In the Spanish empire, the coincidence of an imperial with a dynastic and a monarchic crisis (in the form of the conflict between King Carlos IV and his son and heir, Crown Prince Fernando), created highly complex scenarios both in the Peninsular kingdom and the various American colonies because of the novelty of the absence of the king (both father and son agreed to move to France, at Napoleon's behest) and the necessity of setting up new emergency institutions. A variety of constitutional projects emerged as attempts to resolve this critical situation.[2]

Section 5.1 will first consider the more distant origins of Iberian and Latin American constitutionalism by revisiting the most relevant aspects of Enlightenment thinking. The second part will focus on the "first constitutional moment" in Latin America, from the 1810s to the 1820s, and analyze how the crises of the Portuguese and Spanish monarchies resulted in the emergence of new political spaces with their own constitutional proposals. The third part is devoted to the "second constitutional moment," exploring the constitutional issues that the new, independent Latin American republics had to address and resolve from their foundations in the 1820s and 1830s until the end of the nineteenth century. While the third part focuses on Latin America, the discussion in the first two parts concerns both the European and the American territories of the Portuguese and Spanish empires, because the most decisive debates and historical processes took place within this larger context. The Spanish constitutions of 1808 (drafted by Napoleon) and the *Constitución política de la monarquía española* of 1812 (discussed and approved by an imperial parliament in Cádiz) were intended to be in force in all Spanish dominions around the world. Despite its official name, the Cádiz text should be taken not only as a Spanish but as a Hispano-American constitution for two reasons. First, together with smaller constitutional projects in Venezuela, Chile, and Nueva Granada (modern-day Colombia), it was one of the earliest

2 J. Viejo, *Amor propio y sociedad comercial en el siglo XVIII hispano* (Bilbao: Universidad del País Vasco, 2018); A. M. Hespanha and J. M. Portillo Valdés, "Portugal and Spain Under the Newly Established Liberal Regimes," in F. Bouza, P. Cardim, and A. Feros (eds.), *The Iberian World 1450–1820* (London: Routledge, 2020), 656–71.

constitutions in force in Latin America. Second, and more importantly, many American representatives who contributed to the preparation of the Cádiz constitution, went on to play important roles in the debates and drafting of the constitutions of the first independent republics in Latin America. Thus, the 1812 text can be viewed as one of the first links in the constitutional chain in the Iberian world, and arguably the most influential.[3]

The first Portuguese constitution of 1822 can similarly be seen as both a European and an American constitution. Like the Cádiz text, it took for granted that empire and nation coincided. However, after the proclamation of Brazilian independence by Dom Pedro I in Ipiranga (1821) and the definitive departure of Spanish troops from America after the Battle of Ayacucho (1824), the Latin American space was reorganized into new republics (in the formerly Spanish territories) and into a constitutional monarchy (in Brazil). Among other things, this meant the divergence of constitutional history in the Iberian worlds, with Portugal and Spain following their particular constitutional paths independently from their former American dominions. Section 5.1 ends when, following the intense debates on the separation of Church and state and on whether federalism or centralism represented the ideal form of state organization during the mid-nineteenth century, other conflicts emerged over the need to equip the new republics and the Brazilian monarchy with solid administrative structures (discussed in Sections 5.2, 5.3, and 6.1).

Constitutional Thought in the Iberian Enlightenment

The Iberian empires were anything but removed from the major philosophical and political debates that took place in Europe in the eighteenth century, particularly in the second half. Enlightenment thought was not only received in the Iberian monarchies; enlightened thinkers elsewhere were also interested in the developments and debates in the two largest European empires at the time.

With the term "Iberian monarchies," we describe two empires that exhibited similarities, but whose significant differences should also be borne in mind. Both had initiated a process of major territorial expansion at the end of the fifteenth century. In the case of the Portuguese monarchy, however,

3 For an English-language publication on this topic, see M. C. Mirow, *Latin American Constitutions: The Constitution of Cádiz and Its Legacy in Spanish America* (New York: Cambridge University Press, 2013). The relationships between Spanish and Portuguese first constitutions was analyzed by G. Paquette, "In the Shadow of Cádiz? Exogenous and Endogenous Factors in the Development of Portuguese Constitutionalism, c. 1780–1825," *Bulletin for Spanish and Portuguese Historical Studies* 37 (2012), https://doi.org/10.26431/0739-182X.1131 (last accessed Mar. 31, 2023).

this process, taking place during the fifteenth and sixteenth centuries, was more intermittent, and spread across different continents. The expansion of the Spanish monarchy, meanwhile, was a phenomenon that was principally – though not exclusively – American. In terms of the organization of government, the Portuguese monarchy combined the structured system of viceregal government, as in Brazil, with more flexible systems of military forts and agreements with local rulers, as practiced in various of its African and Asian territories. The vast Spanish dominions in America and Asia, meanwhile, were governed by a system of viceroyalties, *audiencias* (regional courts), and *capitanías generales* ("general captaincies," regional governments partially independent of the viceregal administration). Along with cities and, most notably, religious jurisdictions, these were the instruments of territorial control that enabled the Iberian monarchies to expand in such a dramatic fashion.

There were also differences between the two monarchies that could be described as constitutional, which became more visible after 1640, when Portugal separated from the Spanish monarchy (with which it had been linked since 1581). In contrast to Castile, the Portuguese kingdom – as represented by the *Cortes*, the meeting of the three estates: clergy, nobility, cities – acquired a political significance that became particularly visible in the crisis provoked by the removal of Alfonso VI from government in 1667, after the *Cortes* had declared him insane. In both 1640 and 1667, the Kingdom of Portugal, in the form of the *Cortes*, was an active political protagonist. In the second half of the seventeenth century, the *Cortes* also included representatives from overseas viceroyalties, such as Goa or Brazil. From the end of that century onwards, however, the Portuguese *Cortes* gradually lost its political significance, as had previously occurred in Castile. In Portugal, no meetings of the *Cortes* were convened during the whole of the eighteenth century. Instead, in both monarchies, there were other, far more effective forms of political representation of the different groups and units (cities, nobility, clergy, viceroyalties, provinces, merchants, etc.), which sent their agents to the court to take care of their own specific interests in direct and individual communication.[4]

The loss of the constitutional relevance of the Portuguese kingdom as represented by the *Cortes* resulted in the consolidation of the court, above all the monarch, as the true political center, which also facilitated the king's growing resemblance to a "chief," "architect," or "father" (as contemporary sources

4 P. Cardim, *Portugal unido y separado. Felipe II, la unión de territorios y el debate sobre la condición política del Reino de Portugal* (Valladolid: Ediciones Universidad de Valladolid, 2014); P. Fernández Albaladejo, *La crisis de la monarquía* (Madrid: Marcial Pons-Crítica, 2009).

described him) who oversaw a complex monarchy. The changed image of the king led theorists to debate whether politics should be considered the exclusive concern of the king and his government. The advocates of the affirmative position, such as Pascoal José de Melo in Portugal and Clemente Peñalosa in Spain, did not, however, renounce the benefits of modernity such as, above all, long-distance, high-intensity, and high-volume trade. Rather, they argued that political power exclusively controlled by the court was necessary to compete on the increasingly complicated European imperial stage.[5]

There were, however, also voices warning that the tendency to reinforce the king's *domestic* power actually constituted a threat to the monarchy. They made the case for reinstating the power of political bodies to assist the king, as the *Cortes* in Portugal had done after the restoration of the country's monarchy in the seventeenth century. Most such voices came from political counselors who regarded the concentration of political power within a small circle around the monarch, particularly the possibility of courtiers using the idea of the king-father to govern the monarchy without political mediation, as a dangerous political experiment incompatible with tradition.[6]

As shown in the sections devoted to colonial law (Sections 3.1–3.3), the Portuguese and Spanish monarchies were not based on a conception of law as the pure expression of monarchical will. Customs, natural law, religion, privileges, and specific statutes and constitutions imposed limits on monarchical governments and their production of norms. Understanding these characteristics of the legal and political system allows us to better evaluate the debates that took place in the eighteenth century. The supporters of a personal and arbitrary government were in fact promoting a less *constitutional* idea of the monarchy than those who advocated for reinforcing the intermediate powers and traditional counseling institutions such as the *Cortes*.

One sign of the elites' desire to assist in the governing of the realm was the proliferation of the so-called *Sociedades de Amigos del País* ("Societies of Friends of the Country") or *Sociedades Económicas* ("Economic Societies") from the 1760s onwards. The main aim of these associations of local notables was the promotion of commerce, industry, and agriculture in their own community and area. They perceived their activities as very different from politics, which was the sphere of the king alone; instead, these *Sociedades* reflected the educated classes' commitment to the management of the spaces where most

5 J. L. Gómez Urdáñez, *Víctimas del absolutismo. Paradojas del poder en la España del siglo XVIII* (Madrid: Punto de Vista, 2020).

6 G. Paquette, *Enlightenment, Governance, and Reform in Spain and Its Empire, 1759–1808* (New York: Palgrave Macmillan, 2008), 56–93.

of their social life unfolded: families and cities (and, in the later period, also provinces). The pioneering *Real Sociedad Bascongada de Amigos del País* (1765) sought to prepare the male members of the local elites to be good fathers and local "public figures," capable of the efficient running of municipal governments, on occasion advocating for the extension of the system of provincial governments typical of the Basque region (*diputaciones*) to the rest of the monarchy. Such *Sociedades* also emerged in the American dominions of the Spanish monarchy.[7]

In line with this growing interest of the elites to play a role in government, various Spanish Enlightenment thinkers proposed plans for the creation of institutions or mechanisms for the participation of local elites in local or even "national" governments during the final decades of the eighteenth century. In the 1790s, Victorián de Villava, a former law professor at the Universidad Sertoriana de Huesca and subsequently public prosecutor at the *Audiencia de Charcas* (now Bolivia), proposed the creation of a series of territorial councils (which in America would replace the *audiencias*) that would send representatives to a "Council of the Nation" advising the monarch. Villava was among those who had introduced the new science of political economy to Spain through his translations of the works of Antonio Genovesi, Gaetano Filangieri, and Gian Rinaldo Carli. Other late eighteenth-century thinkers, such as Melchor Gaspar de Jovellanos or León de Arroyal, also saw in political economy a way of introducing some of the essential principles of European Enlightenment moral philosophy into the Catholic monarchy. Valentín de Foronda, a Basque intellectual who was one of the first Spanish *liberales*, wrote a text in which he advised Charles IV on the occasion of his coronation in 1788 – coinciding with the early stages of the constitutional revolution in France – to rule at all times guided by the notion of the rights of his subjects, such as freedom, property, and equality. These rights were thus already replacing religion, privileges, and natural law as the recognized limits on government, even monarchic government.[8]

By the final decades of the eighteenth century, therefore, the language of modern constitutionalism was already circulating in the Spanish and Portuguese monarchies, coexisting with the more traditional language of statutes and

7 J. Astigarraga, *The Spanish Enlightenment Revisited* (Oxford: Voltaire Foundation, 2015).

8 V. de Foronda, "Carta sobre lo que debe hacer un Príncipe que tenga colonias a gran distancia (1800)," in I. Fernández Sarasola (ed.), *Valentín de Foronda. Escritos políticos y constitucionales* (Bilbao: Universidad del País Vasco, [1813] 2002), 245–60. Villava's discourse on the reform of the monarchy can be found in J. M. Portillo Valdés, *La vida atlántica de Victorián de Villava* (Madrid: Doce Calles-Mapfre, 2009); L. de Arroyal, *Cartas político-económicas al conde de Lerena (1789–1795)* (Oviedo: Instituto Feijoo, 1971).

privileges. Spanish and Portuguese political thinkers also adopted some of the arguments of modern moral philosophy based on the idea of commercial society or on the ideal of the legal rationality of codification. They included the Brazilian José da Silva Lisboa, author of the *Principios de economía política*. Like Clemente de Peñalosa in Spain, Silva Lisboa never supposed that the reforms he promoted would also entail political rights, but other authors did, such as Manuel de Aguirre in Spain, and Antonio Nariño in Nueva Granada. They argued that the commercial freedoms that promoted the wealth of nations should be accompanied by some form of political empowerment of the nation, that is, some kind of political representation.[9]

Simultaneous to the appearance of a constitutional language, a certain proximity between Catholic culture and the principles of what was known as "modern philosophy" can be observed. Some of the principles addressed by eighteenth-century European moral philosophy, such as the significance of individual interest and self-esteem for the progress of societies, allude to it. As part of these attempts to integrate Enlightenment philosophy and Catholic culture, authors criticized fanaticism as a manifestation of a vacuous and exaggerated piety and recommended new readings of the Gospels in search of messages assimilable to modernity, such as the essentiality of rights.[10]

As the *Sociedades de Amigos del País* exemplified, the – originally medieval – idea that local political issues were the concern of local elites and corporations remained alive. Certain areas, however, continued to lie outside the realms of popular involvement and public debate: Religious questions were the sole domain of the Catholic Church authorities, and discussions of the government of the monarchy the exclusive sphere of the king and his councils.

These principles can be detected in many publications from the late eighteenth century onwards, for example, in the brochure announcing the publication of the *Diario Literario de México* (1768), written by José de Alzate. It is also possible to see how several intellectuals started to defy them by promoting debates that undoubtedly affected the government of the monarchy. This was the case, for example, of Isidoro de Antillon's *Discurso sobre el origen de la esclavitud de los negros* ("A Discourse Concerning the Origins of the Slavery of the

9 J. da Silva Lisboa, *Principios de economia politica para servir de introducção a tentativa econômica do author dos principios do direito mercantil* (Lisbon: Impressão Regia, 1804); Manuel de Aguirre, *Cartas y discursos del militar ingenuo al Correo de los Ciegos de Madrid* (San Sebastián: Real Sociedad Bascongada de Amigos del País, 1978 [1785]). In 1794, Antonio Nariño translated the French revolutionary *Déclaration des Droits de l'Homme et du Citoyen* as *Declaración de Derechos del Hombre y del Ciudadano* and printed clandestine copies of it, for which he was arrested.

10 J. Viejo, "El caso Climent. ¿Ilustración católica o catolicismo ilustrado?," *Hispania* 269 (2021), 651–81.

Blacks"), initially delivered at the Academy of Jurisprudence in Madrid in 1802 and subsequently published in print in 1811. "Its content is of no less interest to religion than to humanity," Antillón noted upon publication of his text. For him, "individual freedom," the right to "self-sufficiency," to the fruits "of one's work," and to "exist politically," were tantamount to "dogmas" and "sacrosanct rights." His terminology shows the degree of maturity that the language of constitutionalism had attained on the eve of the Iberian monarchies' Atlantic crises.[11]

Early Hispanic liberalism also called for a new reading of classical Spanish political, juridical, and theological theories, such as those of the School of Salamanca (see Section 3.2). Given this interest, identifying rights with dogmas and assigning them a "sacrosanct" value was hardly coincidental. Distancing themselves from the French revolutionary thinkers' secularization of political theory, most of the early liberals in the Iberian world were convinced that the Holy Scriptures (and a correct interpretation of them) constituted the most reliable source of political philosophy.

Already in the years before the crises that shook the Portuguese and Spanish monarchies from 1807/8 onwards, various authors had begun to question the status of the American territories. The *Carta dirigida a los españoles americanos* (1799) by Juan Pablo Viscardo, one of the Jesuits expelled from the Spanish dominions in 1767, and Francisco Miranda's expeditions to free *Tierra Firme* from Spanish rule (1804–1806) are the most radical manifestations in this respect. However, while both Viscardo and Miranda already advocated for independence from Spain, most American elites still regarded this as undesirable. These same elites, however, were very interested in a reconsideration of their situation within the monarchy's system of honors and offices and evinced a growing desire to assume control of the administration of the complex Latin American societies themselves.[12]

The most significant questioning of the colonial order in America, however, came from the ranks of the commoners. The decades preceding the imperial crises of 1808–1810 witnessed numerous popular uprisings – both indigenous and *mestizo* – in Mexico, Guatemala, Nueva Granada, and Peru. Between 1780 and 1783, the rebellion led by Gabriel Tupac Amaru posed the most serious threat to the Spanish colonial order established in the former Incan territories. Like the majority of popular uprisings during this period, it was the consequence of oppressive taxation and forms of forced labor like

11 I. de Antillón, *Disertación sobre el origen de la esclavitud de los negros* (Valencia: Domingo y Mompié, 1820 [1811]), 11.

12 J. P. Viscardo, *Carta dirigida a los Españoles Americanos* (Mexico City: Fondo de Cultura Económica, 2004).

the *mita*. It was, however, also a political revolution, and prefigured some of the political arguments used during the Creoles' revolutions of independence some decades later. Tupac Amaru and his followers sought to reformulate the relationship between the ruling Inca (who, following an Andean tradition, could perfectly well be the king of Spain) and his subjects in America, seeking more political autonomy, control over local resources, and to prevent the over-exploitation of local laborers.[13]

Imperial Crises, Constitutional Crises

As David Armitage has convincingly explained, the origin of constitutionalism in the West is closely linked to the crises of the European Atlantic empires.[14] The constitutional revolutions in the British and French empires had obvious consequences for their respective imperial orders. In the case of the British world, constitutional change both originated in, and was restricted to, its North American colonial dominions, whereas in France, the revolution began in the metropole but soon transcended it, leading to a complete revolution of the colonial order in Haiti that culminated in the creation of the first republic under Afro-American rule in 1804.

As explained in Chapter 4, the imperial crises of the Iberian monarchies at the start of the nineteenth century, though also forming part of the process initiated in North America in the 1770s, exhibited interesting unique features. Napoleon Bonaparte's taking control of Portugal forced the Portuguese court to adopt the unprecedented decision to transfer to the colonies. Its move to Rio de Janeiro in October 1807 proved decisive in facilitating Brazil's later monarchic transfer to independence (1822) and a new constitutional order (1824), as will be discussed in the following section. The Spanish crisis, meanwhile, was considerably more complex. Since the signing of the Peace of Basel with the French Republic in 1795, the Spanish monarchy had shown increasing dependence upon France. The Treaty of Subsidies (1803), according to which Carlos IV agreed to a monthly payment of a substantial sum (six million Spanish *reales*) in return for not getting involved in the war against England, did not prevent a confrontation with England, and finally led to the defeat of the Spanish Armada, under French command, at Trafalgar in 1805.

13 S. Serulnikov, *Conflictos sociales e insurrección en el mundo colonial andino. El norte de Potosí en el siglo XVIII* (Buenos Aires: Fondo de Cultura Económica, 2006); E. Tandéter, *Coacción y mercado. La minería de la plata en el Potosí colonial 1692–1826* (Buenos Aires: Siglo XXI, 2002); C. Walker, *The Tupac Amaru Rebellion* (Cambridge: Harvard University Press, 2014).

14 D. Armitage, "The First Atlantic Crisis: The American Revolution," in P. D. Morgan and M. A. Warsh (eds.), *Early North America in Global Perspective* (London: Routledge, 2014), 309–36.

The Spanish empire's defenselessness, with its silver and ships in the service of another empire, resulted in English attempts to take control of Montevideo and Buenos Aires, and encouraged Francisco de Miranda to undertake his failed endeavor to gain independence for Venezuela. This imperial crisis coincided with the culmination of a power struggle in the royal court involving Carlos IV, Queen María Luisa de Parma, her favorite, Manuel de Godoy, and a faction formed around Crown Prince Fernando. An initial conspiracy in 1807 failed, but in March 1808, the crown prince's party finally achieved its objective of forcing Carlos IV to abdicate in favor of the prince. The person who ultimately took advantage of this internal instability, however, was Napoleon Bonaparte, to whom Carlos IV illegally transferred all his dynastic rights in order to escape from his son's supporters, settling in France under the French emperor's protection. In April 1808, Crown Prince Fernando also gave in to French pressure and left Spain, ceding control of the Spanish monarchy to Napoleon. Just over a month later, the latter had approved a constitution for Spain and transferred the dynastic rights to his brother Joseph, until then king of Naples, who became José I of Spain.

If the transfer of the Portuguese Court to its colonial domains had enabled it to overcome the crisis, the Spanish royal family's move to France added a dynastic crisis to the imperial one. This led to the gathering of the first congresses and the drafting of the first constitutional projects in the Spanish monarchy's territories. Indeed, it was the rejection of Napoleon's dynastic interference in the Spanish monarchy that produced the first reflections about the nature of the crisis that transcended its imperial and dynastic characteristics and explored its repercussions in terms of sovereignty and governance.

Both in the Peninsula and in the overseas territories, the first reaction to the transfer of the dynastic rights to Napoleon, considered illegal by the majority of Spanish local and territorial elites, consisted in the formation of extraordinary institutions to maintain government in the absence of a legitimate monarch. Municipal actors formed local committees, known as *juntas*, which acted as sovereign entities. However, even though the *juntas*, as emergency representative institutions of the *pueblos*, exercised all the attributes of sovereignty and led the resistance to the French during the first phase of the Peninsular war, their aims were not revolutionary; on the contrary, they were created to safeguard monarchic sovereignty, not to disrupt it, by acting as temporary guardians of the state entrusted to them.[15]

15 M. Chust (ed.), 1808. *La eclosión juntera en el mundo hispano* (Mexico City: Fondo de Cultura Económica, 2007).

The need to coordinate the different *juntas* soon became apparent, and various forms of federation were created, both in the Peninsula and in America. The *Junta Suprema Central Gubernativa del Reino*, initially formed in September 1808 in Aranjuez, near Madrid, and later transferred to Seville and then Cádiz, sought to govern the entire Spanish empire.[16] While the legitimacy of the *juntas* formed in America was never recognized by Peninsular authorities, in 1809 the *Junta Central* decided to invite American representatives to join it. This invitation, however, differed from that sent to the European provinces of the monarchy. American dominions were granted representation by only one deputy for each colonial viceroyalty and general captaincy and not, like in Peninsular Spain, two for each provincial *junta*. American Creole elites immediately noted and denounced this unequal treatment.

The intensification of the crisis, caused by the royal family's transfer to France, the almost complete occupation of European Spain by the Napoleonic troops, and the chaotic nature of the *Junta Central*'s government, led public opinion to conclude that the crisis should be interpreted as a constitutional crisis, and that it was necessary to act accordingly. In April 1809, the *Junta Central* therefore decided to convene a truly singular session of the *Cortes*, in which the entire empire was called to participate. Again, however, colonial representation was to be significantly inferior in both quality and quantity to that of the European provinces, as the American Spaniards once again observed. In this *Cortes*, Peninsular representation was of various types, and included the local election of provincial representatives. The representatives of the American territories, by contrast, were to be nominated by the municipal councils of provincial capitals and subsequently determined by drawing of lots.[17]

By the time this extraordinary imperial congress assembled in Cádiz in September 1810, other representative assemblies were already in operation in America. The most active was in Caracas, which not only declared the independence of Venezuela (July 5, 1811) but also drafted the first federal constitution for the "Provinces of Venezuela" (December 21, 1811). Although the objectives of the constitutional congresses of Cádiz and Caracas were obviously very different (Venezuela's constitution considering it independent,

16 A brief summary of events in English can be found in J. E. Rodríguez, "The Process of Spanish American Independence," in T. H. Holloway (ed.), *A Companion to Latin American History* (Malden and Oxford: Blackwell Publishing, 2008), 195–214, at 196–200.

17 American representatives to the Spanish *Cortes* were perfectly aware of the differences between Peninsular and American representations and denounced these repeatedly: B. Rojas, *Documentos para el estudio de la cultura política de la transición. Juras, poderes e instrucciones. Nueva España y Capitanía General de Guatemala 1808–1820* (Mexico City: Instituto Mora, 2005).

while the Cádiz text still included Venezuela as part of the Spanish nation), they were both premised on the view, prevalent among the governing elites all across the Spanish empire, that the *juntas* were no longer suitable instruments of governance. The issue was no longer the need to safeguard sovereignty in the absence of a rightful king, but to control it in order to design a new political order. The legitimacy to proceed to debate and approve a constitution was based on the Cortes' assumption of national sovereignty.[18]

A New Political Order: The First Constitutions

1. From *Pueblos* to *Pueblo*: Sovereignty and Emancipation

The bourgeoning of Spanish constitutionalism during the imperial crises was striking. It contrasted with the Portuguese-Brazilian situation, where the establishment of the royal court in Rio de Janeiro and the British protectorate in the European part of the empire blocked similar experiments. This difference was partly also a consequence of the aforementioned differentiated colonial structure of Portuguese America, where provincial elites, even if they argued for autonomy, mostly accepted that the whole territory of the Portuguese dominion should become a single independent entity.[19] From that comparative perspective, the singularity of the Spanish crisis was the result of the unique coincidence of a monarchic-dynastic with an imperial crisis, which resulted in the *pueblos* taking the initiative from 1808 onwards.[20] With the gathering of the *Cortes* in 1810 and its decision to assume national sovereignty, the crisis turned constitutional, centering on the question of which political bodies were entitled to exercise sovereignty. On the basis of traditional Spanish political thought, the *pueblos* assumed that it was they who were entitled to do so, but soon new political actors claiming this capacity appeared on the scene: *la Nacion Española* (considered as comprising the inhabitants of both the Peninsula and the overseas territories), and the *pueblo* in the singular, a term denoting a new political community made up of all the *pueblos*.

Considered from the point of view of traditional jurisprudence, it was not surprising that the *pueblos* had assumed that it was they who were entitled to hold sovereignty in the event of major constitutional crisis. Already Jerónimo

18 R. Breña (ed.), *En el umbral de las revoluciones hispánicas 1810–1812* (Mexico City: El Colegio de México, 2010).

19 L. M. Bastos Pereira das Neves, "Estado e polítíca na independência," in K. Grinberg and R. Salles (eds.), *O Brasil Imperial (1808–1831)*, vol. I (Rio de Janeiro: Civilização Brasileira, 2009), 95–136.

20 The Spanish word *pueblo* refers not only to the settlement (village, town) but also, and above all, to the locally organized and incorporated political community.

Castillo de Bobadilla in the sixteenth century and Lorenzo Santayana y Bustillo in the eighteenth had argued that the core part of the "constitution" of the Spanish monarchy were the organized local communities called *pueblos*. Alongside the king, they were the only "essential" part of the monarchy (see Chapter 4). Despite their utmost relevance for the practical government of the monarchy, judicial and administrative institutions like councils, *audiencias*, *chancillerías*, and *corregimientos* were not conceptualized as fundamental building blocks of the empire. The *pueblos* were entitled to self-government and, above all, to have their own treasury and the tutelage of their own communities. Despite the fact that, during the eighteenth century, the tendency to represent the king as a "general father" of his subjects had eroded the idea of the *pueblos* as having governmental responsibility for themselves and their members, the consciousness of their essential constitutional role was very present in 1808, when the crisis of the monarchy demanded extraordinary – though still legal – responses. This is clear from the arguments for setting up *juntas* put forward by Spanish *pueblos* in 1808, and also in the debates during the meetings called by Viceroy José de Iturrigaray in Mexico City in 1810, in which the principal communities and institutions of Mexico City – the city council, royal *audiencia*, military, Church, and Indian *pueblos* – were attempting to formulate solutions to the monarchic crisis for New Spain.[21]

Let us now consider how political actors at the time concluded that sovereignty could reside in the nation and not in the king. As in the earlier constitutional debates in the United States and in Haiti, the attribution of sovereignty in the early nineteenth-century Iberian world stemmed from a reinterpretation of an old civil law concept known as "emancipation." This was an instrument that modern law had already reformulated in relation to its Roman original, but it continued to describe an act that accorded with the term's etymology: *ex manu capere*, the release of a person's hand from that of their tutor, typically the *pater familias* (see Section 3.3). In early modern European law, emancipation took place only in the family context. In 1783, the dictionary of the *Real Academia de la Lengua* defined it as the act of "the father releasing his children from his control, no longer holding their hands, and setting them free, so they might act alone, direct, and govern their affairs."[22]

21 For the idea of self-government of the *pueblos*, see B. Clavero, "Tutela administrativa o diálogos con Tocqueville," *Quaderni fiorentini per la Storia del Pensiero Giuridico Moderno* 24 (1995), 419–68. A contemporary formulation of this principle can be seen in the first chapter of Lorenzo Santayana Bustillo, *Gobierno político de los pueblos de España, y el corregidor, alcalde, y juez en ellos* (Zaragoza: Moreno, 1742).

22 Real Academia Española, *Diccionario de la lengua española* (Madrid: Ibarra, 1783).

An important role in the transformation of the concept of emancipation in the late eighteenth and early nineteenth centuries was played by the Swiss jurist Emmerich de Vattel's influential work on the law of nations – one of the books most frequently read by the delegates at the First Continental Congress in Philadelphia in 1774, when it began to consider the independence of the thirteen British colonies. De Vattel proposed transforming the concept of emancipation into an attribute not only of free and independent persons but also of nations. On both sides of the Atlantic, the phrase "free and independent" – formerly used by civil law to refer to familial emancipation, but now applying to new polities –appears in the first constitutional experiments.[23] This was the case both in the Spanish sphere and in Brazil from the 1820s onwards. The transition from *juntas* – intended to act as custodians of royal sovereignty – to *congresos* – which assumed national sovereignty – was marked by the adoption of the language of emancipation, now applied to a liberation from the power and sovereignty of the king, who, as we already have seen, was presented as the father of his *pueblos* by traditional juridical and political literature. Applied to the Spanish monarchy, Vattel's arguments implied that it should logically be the *pueblos,* as the natural authorities of their own communities, that carry out this self-emancipatory act.

2. The Appearance of the Nation as Body Politic

In contrast to the sovereignty of *pueblos* based on established political thought, the appearance of the nation as a political subject was an innovation. Previously, the term had been employed to refer to a particular community (the Spanish nation, but also the indian nation, for example), but never in a political sense that attributed political capacity or rights to that community. This key innovation in how the political community was conceptualized was usually expressed in the very first sentences of the new constitutions of the Ibero-American world. The nation already appeared in the earliest Spanish American constitutions, those of Caracas (1811) and Cádiz (1812). In 1824, when the first constitution of newly independent Brazil was drafted, its first article defined Brazil's empire as a political association of Brazilian citizens that "make up a free and independent nation, which

23 Emmerich de Vattel, *Le Droit de Gens ou Principes de la Loi Naturelle, Appliqués à la Conduite et aux Affaires des Nations et des Souveraines*, 2 vols. (London: s.n., 1758). The influence of Vattel's book on the American Congress is detailed in S. Pincus, *The Heart of the Declaration: The Founders' Case for an Activist Government* (New Haven: Yale University Press, 2016). I have explored the relevance of the idea of emancipation for the constitutional solution to the Spanish crisis in J. M. Portillo Valdés, *Una historia atlántica de los orígenes de la nación y el Estado. España y las Españas en el siglo XIX* (Madrid: Alianza Editorial, 2022).

does not maintain any kind of union or federation opposed to its independence with any other nation or federation." In the same year as the Brazilian constitution, Mexico's first federal constitution also stated in its first article: "The Mexican nation is forever free and independent of the Spanish government and of any other power."

The collective emancipation as *pueblo* (in the singular) or nation was not, however, a simple operation. As mentioned earlier, in the Spanish empire the *pueblos* had been the protagonists of the first reaction to the imperial crisis in 1808 and, unlike the nation, did have a past as political bodies. The concept of the political community as a free and independent nation was generally accepted by the first constituent congresses, who then faced the question of how to reconcile the sovereignty of the nation with that of the *pueblos*. The constitution most widely applied in Spanish America, that of Cádiz of 1812, implemented a system of provincial autonomy that generalized a form of territorial government modeled – as the commission that drafted the text explicitly stated – on the Basque-Navarran autonomous territories. It featured provincial councils whose members, like those of the representatives in the *Cortes*, were elected by the *vecinos*, that is, the emancipated residents (heads of families in the towns of the province). These provincial councils, presided over by a representative of the central government (*jefe político*) and a treasury supervisor (*intendente de hacienda*), were responsible for what was termed "interior administration," that is, the administration of provincial interests (markets, roads, the distribution of taxes, creation of new town councils, education, charity programs and, in America, "the conversion of the pagan indians").[24]

While this was the solution adopted at Cádiz, the first American constitutions tended to construct the relationship between nation and *pueblos* in terms of a federal structure. The earliest constitutional experiment produced in the Iberian American territories, that of Venezuela in 1811, followed the model of the (North American) Articles of the Confederation of 1781 by defining provinces as bodies endowed with "freedom and independence," but only "in the part of their sovereignty reserved to them" (art. 134). The same principle was established in 1824 upon the creation of the Central American Republic (which included Guatemala, Honduras, El Salvador, Costa Rica, Nicaragua, and eventually Chiapas, too): "Each of the states that form [the Central American Republic] is free and independent in its government and internal

24 For the category of *vecino* and its electoral relevance in a number of the earliest constitutions of the Hispanic world, see T. Herzog, *Vecinos y extranjeros. Hacerse español en la Edad Moderna* (Madrid: Alianza Editorial, 2006).

administration, and to [the states] appropriately belongs all the power that is not attributed by the constitution to the federal powers" (art. 10).

There were also territories in which the idea of the nation as a collective political body did not prosper, and where instead the *pueblos* became "free and independent" on their own (see Chapter 4). In 1821, after the failure of a general constitutional project for Río de la Plata, the province of Córdoba adopted a provisional constitution that stated that the province was "free and independent" so that "sovereignty resides essentially in it, and to it belongs the right to establish its fundamental laws by means of permanent constitutions" (art. 2).[25] Similar developments took place in Nueva Granada and Río de la Plata. *Villas* (autonomous villages), cities, or provinces proceeded to invoke the attribute of sovereignty to establish themselves as independent of both imperial and regional authorities. These free and independent *pueblos* formed temporary local unions and federations. An example of such a union were the Confederated Cities of the Valle del Cauca (1811–1815) in the former province of Popayán in Nueva Granada, which functioned according to the law of nations. Both this case and similar federations in the south of the continent should not be seen as examples of sovereignty having disintegrated, as these areas had never been united in a single nation or been considered to constitute a single *pueblo* in the first place. Instead, in these cases, sovereignty remained where traditionally it was meant to lie: with the *pueblos*.[26]

3. Citizenship

The first constitutions in the Iberian world also embraced the idea of the modern *ius gentium* that stated that free and independent nations were formed by equally free and independent – in other words, emancipated – citizens. This proved decisive in establishing an initial difference between *natural* and "citizen" (*ciudadano*). The former category could include "all," as established by most of the first Hispanic American constitutions (such as art. 8 of the 1824 Constitution of Central America Republic), or "all free men," as stated in the constitutions of Cádiz (1812) or of Peru (1823). Those "born in the territory" of a nation (a typical formulation), however, did not necessarily also fall into the category

25 Note that the word *provincia* in Río de la Plata had (and still has in Argentina today) the meaning of "state." In other parts of Spanish America, *estado* finally became the preferred term. See A. Agüero, "¿Provincias o Estados? El concepto de provincia y el primer constitucionalismo provincial rioplatense. Un enfoque ius-histórico," *Revista de Historia Americana y Argentina* 54(1) (2019), 137–75.

26 D. Gutiérrez Ardila, *Un nuevo Reino. Geografía política, pactismo y diplomacia durante el interregno en Nueva Granada (1808–1816)* (Bogotá: Universidad del Externado, 2010); Agüero, "¿Provincias o Estados?".

of citizen, because the latter required emancipation. "[B]eing married or older than twenty," "able to read and write," and "having some employment or trade, or professing some science or art, without subjection to any other person in the capacity of menial servant," were the attributes of citizens required by the first Bolivian Constitution of 1826 (art. 14). The key to accessing citizenship lay in independence – the essential condition, along with freedom, of the emancipated. This is why women and domestic employees, though *naturales*, could under no circumstances be citizens. The concept of a *ciudadana* (female citizen) was incompatible with early constitutional culture because, while women could be free, they were never independent of (emancipated from) their male family members. Citizenship in general terms was considered an attribute of a *vecino*, that is, the autonomous father and head of family. For example, the constitution of the Free State of Neiva (Nueva Granada) in 1815 listed as necessary qualities "being a free man, resident, father or head of family, or having a household and living of private income or working independently of others" (Tit. VII, art. 1).

The status of *vecino*, in turn, invoked a Catholic culture that was clearly reflected in the first Latin American constitutions.[27] The *vecino* was invariably a parishioner, that is, someone who participated in the rites and discipline of the Catholic Church. For this reason, the parish generally served as the basic electoral district, the census was taken from parish registers, and priests took part at the local electoral committees. In the earliest constitutional texts in the Hispanic world, Catholic rites were also present in other forms, particularly in the form of the oath as a mechanism of security and trust, as well as in the role of the Catholic mass and Te Deum in ceremonies of taking office. Furthermore, one element repeated in all the early constitutional texts in the Iberian world is the overlap between the body of the nation and the mystical body of the Church. Article 12 of the Constitution of Cádiz stated: "The religion of the Spanish nation is, and ever shall be, the Catholic Apostolic Roman and only true faith; the nation shall, by wise and just laws, protect it and prevent the exercise of any other." Similar formulations can be found in numerous other Ibero-American constitutions.[28]

27 The link between traditional culture and early constitutionalism is discussed by B. Clavero, *Constitucionalismo colonial. Oeconomía de Europa, Constitución de Cádiz y más acá* (Madrid: Universidad Autónoma de Madrid, 2016). A case study of the political relevance of *oeconomia* in early constitutionalism is R. Zamora, *Casa poblada y buen gobierno. Oeconomía católica y servicio personal en San Miguel de Tucumán, siglo XVIII* (Buenos Aires: Prometeo, 2017). See also Section 3.3 in this volume.

28 See, for example, the constitutions of Bolivia, 1826 art. 6 and of Peru, 1823 arts. 8 and 9. The Colombian constitution of 1821, though it contained no prescriptions regarding religion, nevertheless included a declaration of the Congress to the Colombian people stating that legislation should be always produced in accordance with Catholic dogma.

With respect to religion, Brazil was different. Its first constitution in 1824 adopted what in the 1820s was understood as the French model of the constitutional treatment of the religious question: establishing a state religion but permitting private worship of other faiths.[29] In the Spanish world, however, the norm was constitutional intolerance, which would subsequently become one of the most controversially debated issues on the continent.

4. The Judicial System and the Separation of Powers

It was also very common for the first constitutional texts to express the advisability of the existence of codes for civil and criminal litigations (on codification, see Section 5.2). In its article 179, guaranteeing the inviolability of the civil and political rights of citizens, the Brazilian empire's 1824 constitution instructed that "civil and criminal codes founded on the solid bases of justice and equity" were to be drawn up as soon as possible. However, though abolishing most privileges, the same article included an exception for cases that "by nature" required private trials. Hispanic constitutions, too, advocated the generalized implementation of a universal law, on the one hand, while continuing to recognize certain special *fueros* (charters) granted to particular groups or persons, on the other. The first constitution of the province of Córdoba in Río de la Plata established in 1821 that "in common causes, civil and criminal, there shall be but one form of trial, for all classes of persons." However, it also stated that "the clergy shall benefit from their state's charter in the terms provided for by law, and the military shall also enjoy theirs in the terms set out in the ordinance" (arts. 3 and 4).

The constitutions also attempted to create more organized and hierarchical judicial systems. A high court (*corte* or *tribunal supremo*) was usually established with both jurisdictional and disciplinary powers. It handled so-called state cases (involving senior dignitaries, ambassadors, or ministers), settled disputes between courts, and called upon the legislature to clarify the meaning of laws. It also acted as a kind of judicial council, since it had disciplinary authority over all lower courts. Usually, there were also appeal courts, like *tribunales superiores* or *audiencias* for more important cases, and, at a lower level, district or provincial courts.

Finally, many of these early constitutions maintained a form of community justice to provide arbitration and conciliation for the numerous minor local conflicts that occurred. Some constitutions, like Brazil's of 1824, established conciliation as an obligatory first step: "No suit whatever shall be begun without it being shown that a reconciliation has been attempted" (art. 161). It was

29 In the constitutional project aborted by the monarchical reaction in November 1823, freedom of religion was registered as one of the "Individual Rights of the Brazilians" (art. 7 III).

not necessary to have a law degree in order to act as a judge or participate in a jury in municipal courts (the formal judicial level closest to local communities that dealt with a large number of civil cases); common sense was deemed more important than juridical knowledge. However, as juries, though provided for in many of the first Latin American constitutions, were alien to the local cultures, a transitional period was included in most countries during which the institution was to be introduced and its use subsequently extended. For instance, article 175 of the Colombian constitution of 1821 stated: "One of Congress's first tasks will be to introduce trial by jury under certain circumstances, until, once the benefits of this institution are known to all, it is extended to all the criminal and civil cases in which it is habitually applied in other nations, with all the measures appropriate to this procedure."

The architects of the first Ibero-American constitutions created a distribution of powers that, as a rule, reflected a distrust of executive power. The latter was most closely associated with monarchic power – whether it actually took the form of a monarchy or not. The earlier constitutional texts thus placed special emphasis on limiting the executive power by transferring many of the competences that had previously been the monarch's to other powers and institutions. Significantly, this even included matters of state (foreign relations) that had previously clearly been the responsibility of the government. Matters such as declarations of war, or the conclusion of peace treaties or trade agreements, now passed through the filter of one of the parliamentary chambers. For example, article 101 of the 1811 Federal Constitution of Venezuela expressly prohibited the executive authority from waging war overseas without parliamentary consent. This provision, subsequently repeated in almost all the texts produced in the Hispano-American region, should be considered alongside other limitations of the executive power. These extended to issues relating to the security of citizens and their property, including fiscal matters, legal dispensations, the granting of privileges, and the cession of territory. Presidents, members of *directorios* (collective executives), or monarchs (where they existed) were charged with running the government and, above all, with the administration of the state and the implementation of laws, for which they could "issue decrees and orders," that is, use their regulatory powers. With the separation of powers, however, these took on a different meaning.

5. Education, Taxation, and National Defense

Early constitutions in the Iberian World also considered aspects of social life. The 1824 Central American constitution that federated Guatemala, Costa

Rica, Honduras, Nicaragua, and El Salvador declared education one of the competences of the federal Congress, and the Guatemalan state constitution, promulgated a year later, provided that "any citizen can establish private educational institutions" under the supervision of the government. Education was generally considered a national issue in early Latin American constitutions. In some texts, like the first Peruvian constitution of 1823 or the Chilean one of 1828, an entire title was devoted to "public education" as a citizen's right. Like legal codes or the tax system, education was considered to require some uniformity and to ideally encompass the whole of society. All three issues were closely linked to the idea of the equality of all citizens. The importance given to education as a distinctive marker of the citizen is visible in several constitutions' inclusion of literacy as a precondition for having the vote.

There was also an obvious link between equality, citizenship, and taxation. A shared principle of these early constitutions was summarized by the first Venezuelan constitution after the dissolution of Gran Colombia in 1830: "Taxes will be levied proportionally and will be effective without exemptions on the basis of *fuero* or privilege." Along with proportionality, many constitutions also stated that tax should be paid as a single contribution (*única contribución*). Enlightenment thinkers had repeatedly promoted this idea, which aimed at replacing the existing dense web of taxes with a single general tax assessed in proportion to the wealth of each citizen.

The principle of the equality of all citizens also underlay the constitutional provision for national defense as a citizen's obligation. Regular and standing armies were complemented by a national militia system in which citizens were locally organized for the defense of the republic and the constitution. In later years, however, conservatives tended to oppose these militias, considering them to pose a permanent risk of insurrection.[30]

A Second Constitutional Moment: Constitutions after Independence

After the representatives of New Spain left the *Cortes* of Madrid in 1821 for a Mexico that was being born as an independent nation, the presence of the Spanish monarchy in continental America faded rapidly. The *Cortes* of the "Liberal Triennium" (1820–1823) rejected the final attempt to maintain

30 R. Moreno Gutiérrez, *La trigarancia. Fuerzas armadas en la consumación de la independencia. Nueva España, 1820–1821* (Mexico City: Universidad Nacional Autónoma de México, 2016) showed how the conflicting ideas about citizenship, militias, and the regular army originated during the process of independence. The same was true in the area of fiscal ideas: E. Sánchez Santiró, *La imperiosa necesidad. Crisis y colapso del erario de la Nueva España (1808–1821)* (Mexico City: Instituto Mora, 2016).

a common body politic uniting Spain and Spanish America by means of a commonwealth. In Portugal, by contrast, one of the aims of the liberal revolution that began in Oporto in 1820 was to form a single nation in the "United Kingdom of Portugal, Brazil, and the Algarves." This vast kingdom, created in 1815 when the royal court resided first in Rio de Janeiro and then in Bahía, also incorporated the numerous Portuguese possessions in Africa and Asia. As was the case in Spain, the closer identification of the *Reino Unido* with a "Portuguese nation" in the constitution of 1822 marked the beginning of the separation of Brazil as an independent monarchy.

The American dominions of the two Iberian monarchies achieved independence as a result of very different developments (see also Chapter 4). The Portuguese court had been located in Brazil since 1807, and when João VI returned to Portugal in 1822 at the request of the revolutionary *Cortes*, he left his son Dom Pedro in charge of the government. Pedro subsequently declared Brazilian independence, and the new state came into being with barely any conflict with those who wanted to maintain unity with Portugal. In the territories of the Spanish monarchy, by contrast, the birth of the new republics occurred after more than a decade of both colonial and civil wars.[31] Even after independence, war did not disappear from the continent, but rather was transformed in the ensuing decades into internal conflicts within the different republics and, to a lesser extent, among them. In most of these civil conflicts, the constitution was the principal cause of dispute. From the mid-1820s onwards, both in Brazil and in Hispanic America (upon the termination of the conflict with the Spanish *madre patria*, the "motherland"), the essential question was how to shape and structure the new republics. It was one thing to achieve emancipation, but another, very different thing to decide how to use it, and the accompanying sovereignty, to create new political bodies.

The complex post-independence constitutional processes took place in contexts that had changed substantially in the fifteen years since the crises of the monarchy in 1808–1810. One effect of the long period of civil strife was what historiography has termed a "ruralization" of politics, consisting in the shift of the decision-making centers from important cities (capitals or major towns and cities) to smaller settlements, where a local leader and ruling group could launch a constitutional alternative to the government. This was very visible in the names of the different constitutional texts (*planes*) proposed

31 T. Pérez Vejo, *Elegía criolla. Una reinterpretación de las guerras de independencia hispanoamericanas* (Mexico City: Tusquets, 2010); J. P. Pimenta, *La independencia de Brasil y la experiencia hispanoamericana (1808–1822)* (Santiago de Chile: Dirección de Bibliotecas, Archivos y Museos, 2017).

by Mexican insurrectionists throughout the nineteenth century: the Plans of Casa Mata (1823), Ayutla (1854), Tacubaya (1857), and so forth. These developments involved a dispersion of constituent power that, to a degree, harked back to the idea that had re-emerged during the 1808–1810 crisis, namely, that each *pueblo* could be regarded as capable of assuming sovereignty. Unlike what happened then, however, in the decades after independence, the idea in various Spanish American territories was no longer to endow a *pueblo* with a constitution, but to locally initiate a process of constitutional change for the entire nation – which, in reality, often took the form of constitutions being replaced, as we shall see later.

In the following pages, I will discuss a number of key issues faced by those drafting – and subsequently revising – the independent polities' constitutions. Apart from the form of government (monarchy or republic) and of state structure (unitary or federal), they also had to decide questions that touched on the main ideological dividing lines between liberals and conservatives,[32] including, as Sol Serrano put it, the questions of what to do with God in the republic, and how to end *fueros* and privileges.[33]

The new republics inherited a complex internal social order. Whereas some features disappeared (such as distinctions of nobility), others, such as very clear ethnic dividing lines as well as distinctions awarded to specific sectors such as the clergy, the military, or merchants, were maintained. One of the disputes defining conflicting ideologies in the decades of republican consolidation centered on the government of society, with positions depending on whether society was conceptualized as a unitary whole or as formed by different bodies. This debate had considerable political importance in legitimizing the inclusion or exclusion of certain types of people from the political space.

It was also necessary to address the advisability of continuing to conflate – as the first constitutions had done – the political body of the nation with the mystical body of the Catholic Church. Whereas liberals saw this identification as limiting the process of civic emancipation and thought it should be revised, conservatives argued that it should be kept as a constitutive characteristic of Hispanic societies.

32 A note on the terminology: In nineteenth-century Latin America, the terms "liberals" and "conservatives" both denoted factions of liberalism, with the "liberals" adhering to progressive and the "conservatives" to moderate liberalism.

33 The "ruralization" of politics was first theorized by Antonio Annino in an essay now available as A. Annino, "Soberanías en lucha," in A. Annino, *Silencios y disputas en la historia de Hispanoamérica* (Bogotá: Universidad Externado-Taurus, 2014), 215–64. See also S. Serrano, *¿Qué hacer con Dios en la República? Política y secularización en Chile (1845–1885)* (Santiago de Chile: Fondo de Cultura Económica, 2008).

The Latin American constitutionalism of the 1820s–1860s also included a debate over the relative political weight of the various powers. As we saw earlier, the first texts were deeply suspicious of the executive power and leaned towards forms of government dependent upon parliament. In the 1830s, many actors – not only from the conservative wing, as one might expect, but also from the liberal side – began to voice criticism of this system.

Monarchy or Republic

Nearly all the new Latin American nations achieved their formal and actual independence after the enactment of the first constitutional texts. As in the United States or Haiti, declarations of independence were not directed at the former "motherland" but to "advise foreign powers of the determination to achieve independence" (Haiti, 1804). In the case Spain, its recognition of the new American republics was spread over a long period, lasting from 1836 (Mexico) to 1894 (Honduras). This contrasts significantly with Portugal, which by 1825 had already recognized Brazil's independence, and where the presence of the royal court and dynastic continuity had facilitated the transition towards an independent monarchy. Also implicit within declarations of independence was a complete separation (*independencia absoluta*) from the motherland, addressed to the new nations' own populations.

The declarations were issued surrounded by ceremonial that sought to transmit the solemnity of the announcement: a new nation was operative from then on in the context of the law of nations (*ius gentium*). These ceremonial acts were intended to demonstrate the different social bodies' support for independence. In 1904, the Peruvian artist Juan Lepiani recreated the ceremony held on July 28, 1821 in Lima's Plaza Mayor in a painting. Significantly, he depicted all the important corporations of the capital as having been present, as they would have been for royal proclamations or the entrances of viceroys: the town council and representatives of the clergy, university, commerce, army, and *pueblo*. We know that in advance of the ceremony, General San Martín had asked the city council, composed of local notables, to issue a statement about the advisability of independence. At no time was this statement expected to oppose independence; rather, it was meant to express the unity of the political body, as did the subsequent ceremony in the Plaza Mayor. In contrast to earlier proclamations of independence, the intention in Lima in 1821 was that the assembled political body would symbolize social continuity in the process of constituting the new republic: There was no social transformation, nor any territorial changes disrupting the continuity from viceroyalty to republic. Article 1 of the first Peruvian constitution of November 1823 proclaimed that united front: "All the provinces of Perú, assembled in one single body, form the Peruvian nation."[34]

Despite claims of continuity, however, the actual process of the formation of the new political bodies in Iberian America was very dynamic. In fact, today's Latin American political map could have ended up looking very different: When it declared independence, Mexico occupied a large area of what is now the United States of America and extended as far south as the former Chiapaneca region of the district of Guatemala; there was a Central American Republic (uniting present-day Guatemala, Honduras, El Salvador, Nicaragua, and Costa Rica); the entire island of Santo Domingo was under Haitian control until 1844; the United Provinces of Nueva Granada extended from Panamá to Ecuador (and included present-day Colombia and Venezuela); and Uruguay was a province of Brazil until 1830. Paraguay broke away from the former viceroyalty of Río de la Plata in 1811, followed in 1825 by Upper Peru, which was then renamed Bolivia. In the rest of the former domain of the viceroyalty, a system of provincial sovereignties was established to present a (precariously) united front to outsiders. Only Chile and Brazil became independent with borders largely similar to their current appearance, although they, too, underwent territorial changes throughout the nineteenth century.

The first urgent constitutional decisions that the new polities had to take concerned their form of government. Brazil was the only context favorable to a lasting monarchic solution, though even there, the monarchic option did not remain unchallenged. In fact, Brazil's first emperor, Dom Pedro I, was forced to abdicate in 1831, following an armed conflict with the Provinces of Río de la Plata that resulted in the loss of the province of Cisplatina (Uruguay). His handling of the conflict, combined with the dire consequences of the war, reopened a debate over the monarch's powers. These had been defined very broadly in the 1824 constitution, which Dom Pedro I had, in a demonstration of strength, imposed against those intending to delimit his scope of action more strictly in line with the Portuguese constitution of 1822. Uniquely, the 1824 constitution, following the theories of French political thinker Benjamin Constant, created a fourth state power in addition to the legislative, executive, and judiciary, called the "moderating power" (*poder moderador*). This was attributed to the king in order that he might "constantly assure the

34 For this process in Peru, see N. Sobrevilla Perea, "Entre proclamas, actas y una capitulación: la independencia peruana vista en sus actos de fundación," in A. Ávila, J. Dym and E. Pani (eds.), *Las declaraciones de independencia. Los textos fundamentales de las independencias americanas* (Mexico City: El Colegio de México, 2010), 241–74. This book also analyzes other cases of Latin American territories achieving independence.

independence, balance, and harmony of the other political powers" (art. 98), but in fact, translated into a broad royal prerogative to intervene in government and legislation. Along with this, the Council of State, appointed by the king at will for life, strengthened the executive pillar of the system, which as a whole centered on the monarch. Both the "moderating power" and the Council of State were suspended during the regency that governed on behalf of Dom Pedro II (in 1832 and 1834, respectively), in order to avoid the regents making use of powers solely belonging to the king. After Pedro had been elevated to the age of majority at the instigation of the liberals in 1841, when he was only fourteen years old, an ordinary law recreated the Council of State. However, since this was not a constitutional act, the emperor could exercise his "moderating power" freely, consulting the Council only when he deemed it necessary.[35] Upon the consolidation of the rule of Dom Pedro II, the conservative and liberal factions reached a common point of reference based upon the constitution of 1824. The revitalization of the essential instrument of the "moderating power" enabled the Brazilian empire and its successive governments during the second half of the nineteenth century to deal with some of the main political issues of the time. Among them were avoiding the separatist aspirations of some provinces and supporting the continuation of an economy linked to the maintenance of slavery in the face of the British blockade of the Atlantic slave trade. The consolidation of the system owed much to the agreement between the two main liberal factions for alternating in power without resorting to a coup d'état (as was the case in other Latin American countries).

Brazil was the only successful Latin American monarchy. The other attempt at establishing a monarchy right after independence, the Mexican first empire (1821–1823), failed, and the plans of Carlota Joaquina (the Portuguese queen consort and sister of Fernando VII of Spain) to create a great South American monarchy were never realized.[36]

Republic and Territory I: Federalism

One of the first objectives of the constitutions promulgated following independence was making the nation, as the new sovereign, and the republic, as

35 M. Duarte Dantas, "Constituição, poderes e cidadania na formação do Estado-Nacional brasileiro," in M. das Graças de Souza (ed.), *Rumos da cidadania. A crise da representação e a perda do espaço publico* (São Paulo: Instituto Prometheus, 2010), 19–58.

36 For monarchical attempts in Spanish America, see M. Ternavasio, *Candidata a la corona. La infanta Carlota Joaquina en el laberinto de las revoluciones hispanoamericanas* (Buenos Aires: Siglo XXI, 2015).

the new body politic, coincide. As already indicated in the previous section, this involved not only declaring independence from the former sovereign but also integrating a heterogeneous set of *pueblos*, which initially considered themselves perfectly entitled to exercise sovereignty. This was one of the causes for the changing political geography of many Latin American states in the first years following their independence. Boundaries, however, largely stabilized towards the middle of the nineteenth century, when the republics formed a map approximating the present one. For this to happen, Latin American constitutionalism had to impose a conception of "territory" that abandoned its identification with *iurisdictio* and instead assimilated it to *administratio*. Under Spanish rule, the political geography had not been conceived as a map of territories but of jurisdictional domains, but the new states needed to treat the territory as an administrative space, stripped of jurisdiction as an attribute of the territory.[37] It was only when this process was already consolidated that the representatives of the republics of Bolivia, Chile, Ecuador, Nueva Granada, and Peru at the American Congress of Lima (1847) proposed using *uti possidetis iuris* as a principle to determine the frontiers between republics. This principle consisted in a subrogation of the old colonial jurisdictions by the new nations. Identification of the "national" space with that of the preceding colonial territorial units was a notion that had appeared in early constitutions, such as that of Colombia in 1821, or those of Mexico and Central America in 1824. However, these texts established a double standard: On the one hand, they applied towards the exterior a principle of "national" territorial delimitation based on the old colonial jurisdictional districts. For example, the 1843 constitution of Ecuador stated: "The territory of the Republic of Ecuador … includes all the provinces of the ancient kingdom and presidency of Quito." On the other hand, they did not apply the same principle of replicating the former jurisdictions inside the republic, as can also be seen in the Colombian text of 1821 (art. 8): "The territory of the Republic shall be divided into Departments, the Departments into Provinces, the Provinces into *Cantones* [districts], and the *Cantones* into *Parroquias* [parishes]."

The new republics also faced another major dilemma when it came to connecting territory and state. It was one thing to make republic and nation

37 M. Llorente Sariñena, "Uti possidetis, ita domini eritis. International Law and the Historiography of the Territory," in M. Meccarelli and M. J. Solla Sastre (eds.), *Spatial and Temporal Dimensions for Legal History: Research Experiences and Itineraries* (Global Perspectives in Legal History 6) (Frankfurt am Main: Max-Planck-Institut für europäische Rechtsgeschichte, 2016), 131–72.

coincide, another to organize the state within that space once it had been delineated. Whether or not the new polities should be subdivided internally into territories with autonomous political powers was a question that until the final decades of the nineteenth century often divided the American republics to the point of civil conflict.

For reasons perhaps of spatial and temporal proximity, it is usually taken for granted that opting for a federal solution in Latin America was an imitation of the successful revolution in the Anglo-American North. Undoubtedly, a system like the United States' was of interest to the leaders of the post-independence Latin American republics. However, Latin American constitutional drafters also demonstrated a considerable capacity to innovate in this respect, and generated a different type of federalism that became very characteristic of this region. Unlike its North American counterpart, Latin American federalism blended national emancipation and sovereignty with the freedom and sovereignty of the individual federal states. When the drafters of the Mexican constitution opted for federalism in 1823 and 1824, they did so from a different premise to their northern neighbors: What was freeing itself from Spain was the "Mexican nation," whereas the term "nation" did not even appear in the constitution of the United States. The search for a similar expression in North American constitutionalism is fruitless because it was not "the United States" that emancipated themselves from the colonial power but the individual states, which subsequently formed the Union. By contrast, in Mexico, the emancipated nation was constituted first, and it then created the states, to the extent that they were specifically named in the Constitutive Act and in the 1824 constitution.[38] In other words, the states of the Mexican federation were born dependent upon the nation, and not, as in the United States, independent entities that subsequently formed the nation. This is why, as we have already seen, the Mexican nation was characterized in its constitution as a "free and independent" (i.e., emancipated) subject. According to article 6 of the 1824 *Acta Constitutiva* of Mexico, its federal states enjoyed the same status, but "exclusively in relation to their administration and internal government, as is detailed in this act and in the general constitution."

38 J. M. Portillo Valdés, "¿Un super omnia mexicano? Acerca de la soberanía nacional y el federalismo en la constitución de 1824," in B. Rojas (ed.), *Procesos constitucionales mexicanos. La constitución de 1824 y la antigua constitución* (Mexico City: Instituto Mora, 2017), 19–34. For the preception of equality among the federal states and the recognition of the superiority of the Mexican nation, see J. E. Rodríguez O., "'Ningún pueblo es superior a otro': Oaxaca and Mexican federalism," in J. E. Rodríguez O. (ed.), *The Divine Charter: Constitutionalism and Liberalism in Nineteenth-Century Mexico* (Lanham: Rowman and Littlefield, 2005), 65–108.

It was thus no coincidence that many federal states in Latin America included in their constitutions the expression "free and sovereign" rather than "free and independent" (which was the nation's particular condition), or specified, as in the case of the Central American Republic, that they were free and independent "in their internal government" (art. 10). The constitutions of the federal states were drafted immediately after the nation's federal constitution and in accordance with the latter. The Honduran constitution of 1825, adopted a year after the federal one of the Central American Republic (of which Honduras was part), reflected this logic when declaring the State of Honduras to be "free and independent in its internal administration and government" (art. 3). This internal administration and government involved the replication of national institutions (government, congress, and courts) at state level, and the states' autonomous capacity to produce their own civil, criminal, and commercial codes.

The distinction between the national and the "internal" government was fundamental to Latin American federalism, and in some cases did eventually lead to a federal system more similar to the United States of America. Between the 1850s and 1880s, one of the most radical federal experiments in Latin America took place in Colombia. The principle underlying the 1863 constitution that gave birth to the United States of Colombia was that an original sovereignty of the states was partly delegated to a "general government." It was the latter that the constitution sought to delimit, proceeding from the understanding that what was not general government remained a competence of the government of the states (art. 16). The Colombian text of 1863 contained provisions regarding the rights of states and of individuals, the separation of Church and state, and the relations between federal states and the institutions of central government. The individual states' constitutions were established on the basis of the federal constitution's principles, thus permitting the formation of a common republic.[39]

The 1850s also witnessed the creation of two other federal systems that, unlike the Colombian one, have endured to this day: in Argentina (1853–1860) and in Mexico (1857). For decades after the effective independence of Río de la Plata (1810), a constitutional union between Buenos Aires and the other

39 Federalism is not usually associated with Colombia, but its experience was significant in the nineteenth century, as described in D. Gutiérrez Ardila, "La nación federal," in M. Garrido, F. Hensel, and F. Ortega (eds.), *Historia de lo político* (Bogotá: Universidad Nacional-Universidad del Rosario, 2023), forthcoming; S. Kalmanovitz and E. López Rivera, "Las finanzas públicas de la Confederación Granadina y los Estados Unidos de Colombia (1850–1886)," in S. Kalmanovitz and E. López Rivera (eds.), *Las cuentas del federalismo colombiano* (Bogotá: Universidad Externado, 2022), 31–66.

provinces that had belonged to the viceroyalty had been prevented by a dispute over the former colonial capital's role within a new state. After the failure of Bernardino Rivadavia's centralist constitution of 1826, which precipitated a civil war, the various provinces remained effectively independent from each other. However, in 1853, following the proposals of the jurist Juan Bautista Alberdi, all provinces except Buenos Aires agreed to a common constitution. Buenos Aires joined the Argentine union in 1860 only after pushing through certain revisions to the original text. These reforms mainly concerned strengthening the provincial powers *vis-à-vis* the federal government, preventing, for example, control over the provincial constitutions by congress or the takeover of provincial institutions by central government. Buenos Aires also insisted on additional guarantees for individual liberties and claimed control over the customs office, which had been one of the main causes of dispute with the Argentine Confederation. The reformed constitution provided for a constitutional delay in relation to the status of Buenos Aires, initiating a long period of dispute over the government of the capital city between the national government and the province of Buenos Aires. In 1880, a law separated the province from the city of Buenos Aires, which was put under federal control, ending the long dispute over the place of the port city within the Argentine political body. Seventy years after the effective independence of Río de la Plata, federal and provincial powers found their respective ways of implementation and interaction leading to a versatile – rather than uniform – relationship between local and national.[40]

Republic and Territory II: Centralism

The previous section has shown that there was a strong tendency towards federalism in many of the constitutions of the independent Latin American republics, ultimately derived from the traditional concept of *pueblos* as communities governed autonomously by their councils. As we saw previously, the prominence of *pueblos* during the monarchic crisis of the early nineteenth century had catapulted them to the forefront of politics (see also Chapter 4). There was, however, also an opposing current in Latin American political thought which contributed to the design of constitutional systems described at the time as "centralist" and "unitary," in which the remnants of the political power of the *pueblos* were made to disappear. This tendency can already be perceived in the first constitutions of the Iberian world, but it was developed

40 See the works collected in P. Alonso and B. Bragoni (eds.), *El sistema federal argentino. Debates y coyunturas (1860–1910)* (Buenos Aires: Edhasa, 2015).

far more effectively in the middle decades of the nineteenth century. As discussed earlier, the first constitutions in Latin America projected towards the exterior a nation that coincided with previous colonial borders, while towards its interior that nation held regulatory control over what during the imperial period had been a multitude of territorial jurisdictions. This capacity of the national legislature to alter the internal territorial structure had already been expressed in article 11 of the Constitution of Cádiz: "A more convenient division of the Spanish territory shall be made as soon as the political circumstances of the nation permit."

This centralist tendency was reflected, for example, in the first constitution of the "State of Ecuador" in 1830, drawn up after the dissolution of the republic of Gran Colombia that had united Ecuador, Colombia, and Venezuela. The "State of Ecuador" was formed out of the merger of three provinces (Azuay, Guayas, and Quito) and, according to its constitution, occupied "the former Kingdom of Quito." In other words, it claimed for the new nation a territory that it attributed to a previous polity, which in this case was particularly confusing, as the Kingdom of Quito had been dependent on the viceroy of Peru.[41] Within the State of Ecuador, however, there was no recognition of the permanence of older jurisdictions or territorial structures. Instead, the entire space was considered at the disposal of the nation, which organized it as follows (art. 53): "The territory of the state is divided into departments, provinces, *cantones*, and *parroquias*. Political government of each department is vested in a Prefect, who is the direct agent of the Executive Power. Government of each province is vested in a Governor; each *canton* or group of *cantones*, if so decided by the government, shall be governed by a *corregidor* [local governor]; and the parishes by deputies."

A few years later, the 1833 Chilean constitution applied the principle laid down in Ecuador more successfully, as it remained in force until 1925. It defined the exterior borders of "the territory of Chile" using natural features (mountain ranges, deserts, oceans). Inside these borders, the country was subjected to a hierarchic administrative structure formed by provinces (headed by an *intendente*), departments (with a governor who reported to the *intendente*), sub-delegations (with sub-delegates subordinate to governors),

41 F. Morelli, *Territorio o nación. Reforma y disolución del espacio imperial en Ecuador, 1765–1830* (Madrid: Centro de Estudios Políticos y Constitucionales, 2005); M.-D. Demélas, *La invención de la política. Bolivia, Ecuador, Perú en el siglo XIX* (Lima: Instituto de Estudios Peruanos, 2003). More recently, A. I. Deidán de la Torre has reexamined the relationship between *pueblos* and sovereignty in Ecuador: A. I. Deidán de la Torre, *Pueblos y soberanía. Continuidades y rupturas conceptuales durante la insurgencia en el reino de Quito 1809–1813* (Quito: Instituto Ecuatoriano de Cultura Hispánica, 2016).

districts (with inspectors under the sub-delegates' command) and municipalities. Only on this last level was there citizen participation in the appointment of mayors and aldermen who, however, reported to the sub-delegates (or, in the case of a department's capital city, to the governor). The law that regulated local governments in 1854 (art. 25) defined municipalities as *cuerpos administrativos de los intereses locales*, administrative bodies that managed local interests.

The idea of the whole interior structure of a state being at the disposal of the central government to arrange as it saw fit was greatly influenced by conservative political thought. By mid-century, some of the principles of the so-called *Ciencia de la Administración* had reached the educated national elites in several Latin American countries. A number of legal treatises written around the middle of the century advocated for a more centralized state, as did the lectures delivered by Teodosio Lares in Mexico. Lares clearly positioned himself as following the Spanish scholars who had translated and disseminated the French theory of the administration as the "musculature" of the state, which should replace the nation as the main political subject. The ideal of the "administrative state" (see Section 6.1) imagined a system in which the "administrative power" (*poder administrativo*) regulated the government of society. According to Lares and other enthusiasts of the administrative state, it included a new kind of jurisdiction that put the judicial resolution of cases concerning administrative authorities (*contencioso administrativo*) under its control. Paulino Soares de Souza, viscount of Uruguai, promoted these ideas in Brazil, arguing for the extension of the central administration's competences and leaving to local governments only those aspects that were impossible for the central government to manage. Soares de Souza was the instigator of the law of December 3, 1841, which reinforced the executive power and restricted representative institutions both in the administrative and judicial systems.[42]

Latin American conservative political thought, then, tended to favor constitutional and legal systems in which the society's participation in political institutions was strictly limited. What we historians usually label as centralism was, in fact, a complex proposal based on the conception of society as an object of politics rather than as a political subject. Elective authorities at

42 T. Lares, *Lecciones de derecho administrativo dadas en el Ateneo mexicano* (Mexico City: Ignacio Cumplido, 1852); Visconde de Uruguai [P. Soares de Souza], *Ensaio sobre o direito administrativo* (Rio de Janeiro: Tipografia Nacional, 1862); M. Duarte Dantas, "O Codigo do Processo Criminal e a Reforma de 1841. Dois modelos de organização dos poderes," *História do Direito* 1(1) (2020), 96–121.

different administrative levels or the citizens' participation in the judiciary (by serving on juries) were seen as impediments to the effective deployment of state institutions over the entire territory of the republic.

Society, Economy, and Constitution

In the mid-nineteenth century, at the height of the final battle to establish a constitutional system of national scope in Río de la Plata (present-day Argentina), the political theorist and diplomat Juan Bautista Alberdi published an influential work with a view to guiding the efforts of the constitutional assembly. He argued that it was time to start a new phase of Spanish American constitutionalism. Up to his day, he argued, constitutionalism had been related to the struggle for independence, and constitutional texts thus solely concerned with establishing the new republics. This had led to the neglect of certain aspects of importance to modern societies: "During that period, in which democracy and independence were the sole ingredients of the constitutional proposal, wealth, material progress, commerce, the population, industry – in a nutshell, all economic interests – were accessories, secondary benefits, second-class interests, little known and little studied, and, needless to say, even less taken care of."[43]

Alberdi clearly intended to redirect constitutional thought towards aspects that had more to do with the relationship between society (and economy) and the state than with the nation. Once the latter was stabilized, it was time for Latin American liberalism to lay the constitutional foundations of the social order and to establish the principles that would allow for it to be governed and protected by the state. Once again, however, these were neither simple nor uncontroversial questions; on the contrary, they would continue to generate differing ideological positions that were frequently resolved only after civic hostilities that in many cases lasted into the first decades of the twentieth century.[44]

In the historiography, it is usual to refer to each nineteenth-century Latin American polity as having a single society (Mexican society, Argentine society, etc.). However, the existence of one national society was a controversial subject in the first Hispanic constitutions. On the one hand, these constitutions all aspired to generate the same law "for every type of person," as the Constitution

43 J. B. Alberdi, "Bases y Puntos de Partida para la Organización de la Confederación Argentina," in J. B. Alberdi, *Organización de la Confederación Argentina* (Bezanzon: José Joaquín, 1858), 3–4.

44 J. M. Portillo Valdés, *Historia mínima del constitucionalismo en América Latina* (Mexico City: El Colegio de México, 2015), 111–207.

of Cádiz had already declared in 1812. On the other hand, it, and other constitutions in the Iberian world, included significant exceptions for the clergy, the military, and public officials. Furthermore, the political geography of the republics that emerged from the monarchic collapse contained a plethora of political bodies created in towns and provinces. These bodies were no longer in possession of "their own law," that is, a charter per se, but many of them were conceived of as corporations endowed with their own political capacity. As can be more specifically explored in the section devoted to civil codification (Section 5.2), one of the explanations for the delay in effectively constituting civil society in the Latin American republics via the enactment of civil codes rested in the fact that the existence of a homogeneous civil society had not yet been effectively established. It was one thing to constitute the government (with a *constitución política*) and a different one to constitute society (with a *código civil*).

In the 1830s, post-independence political thinkers with such contrasting ideological beliefs as the conservative Mexican Lucas Alamán and the liberal José María Luis Mora arrived at similar conclusions when they identified *espíritu de cuerpo* or the "absolutism of corporations" as one of the republic's main shortcomings.[45] Andrés Bello, the influential Chilean intellectual who participated in various constitutional projects in the new South American republics, predicted in 1836 that these would eventually bring back together two elements whose connection had been severed in the first phase after independence: emancipation and the consolidation of a legal order as the basis of personal freedom. The first constitutions had concerned themselves with the former but, halfway into the century, the time had come to concentrate on the latter. To this end, Bello argued, it was necessary for constitutional drafting to take into account both political philosophy and social reality.[46]

Bello was also the main author of the Chilean Civil Code (1855), which exemplified his blend of philosophy and sociology (i.e., of theory and reality) and became very influential both in Spanish America and in Spain (see Section 5.2). Bello himself acknowledged that his approach resulted in legal products that could not reflect the liberal paradigm in all respects but argued that something similar was happening in the famous North American republic, too, where progress and slavery walked hand in hand. For Bello,

45 C. A. Hale, *El liberalismo mexicano en la época de Mora* (Madrid: Siglo XXI, 1985). *Espíritu de cuerpo* in Spanish had a negative connotation as related to selfishness and lack of the opposite, *espíritu público*.

46 A. Bello, "Las repúblicas Hispanoamericanas," in A. Bello, *Las repúblicas Hispano-Americanas. Autonomía cultural* (Cuadernos de Cultura Latinoamericana 11) (Mexico City: UNAM, 1978).

once national emancipation had been achieved, what really counted from a constitutional point of view was not the implementation of a philosophical ideal but the constitution's adaptation to social reality. Due to their ethnic and class differences, the Hispanic American societies had peculiarities that demanded special legal and constitutional treatment.

The type of constitutional thought demanded by Alberdi, Bello, and others thus had to include considerations of social order and economic development – in their words, the "progress" of the republics. The social order they envisioned required agreement that all inhabitants of the nation together constituted a single society and were subject to the same laws, thus these thinkers' insistence on suppressing any kind of particular law. However, Bello's, Alberdi's, and other mid-century authors' analysis of social reality convinced them that a homogenous society was more wishful thinking than fact. Slavery was, perhaps, the most obvious obstacle to imagining a society that was composed of different socio-economic classes but homogeneous according to the law.

The treatment of slavery provides an excellent vantage point for viewing the issue of how constitutions were able to accommodate the social and political order. Many of the first constitutions assumed a social order in which slavery continued to be commonplace and consequently established the condition of freedom as a prerequisite for forming part of the national community. The development of republican constitutionalism since the 1830s contained two potentially conflicting principles. On the one hand, many constitutions (as, e.g., the Uruguayan constitution of 1830, art. 131) established that everybody born in the republic was free and that human trafficking was forbidden within its borders. The policy of "free wombs" (i.e., that a child born of an enslaved woman is free) was part of this constitutional provision. These measures, implemented in most of the South American republics during the 1820s and 1830s, were understood as a correlate of the principle of equality, because they attempted to lay the foundations of a homogenous social sphere. On the other hand, however, the republics' liberal social order demanded scrupulous respect for property rights, which owners of enslaved people continued to enjoy. The Uruguayan example shows that the development of constitutional provisions was directed towards integrating the enslaved population into the nation via very similar mechanisms to the expropriation of land and other assets in the public interest, that is, by reimbursing owners the supposed "value" of the enslaved person from public funds.[47]

47 A. Borucki, *Abolicionismo y tráfico de esclavos en Montevideo tras la fundación republicana (1829–1853)* (Montevideo: Biblioteca Nacional, 2009).

There were also countries, such as Brazil or Cuba, where economic progress was based upon the intense use of the labor of enslaved persons. In these cases, the constitutions provided for the possibility of continuing this type of labor exploitation with different formulae, even beyond what was already contained in international agreements or in internal legislative or administrative provisions. The Spanish constitution of 1837 (which replaced the 1812 Cádiz constitution) introduced an additional provision that placed Cuba and Puerto Rico (as well as the Philippines) outside the constitutional space. The provision, which remained in force until 1869 and was repeated in the constitution of 1876, merely stated that "special laws" would be provided for the "overseas provinces." However, these never materialized, facilitating arbitrariness in the legal treatment of the trafficking and exploitation of enslaved persons in these areas until the prohibition of slavery in 1880.[48]

The Brazilian constitution of 1824, in force until the end of the reign of Dom Pedro II (1889), dealt with the tension between equality and the existence of enslaved persons in a singular fashion. It avoided the usual practice of establishing a distinction between nationality and citizenship. Instead, it defined the latter as the condition of "[t]hose who are born in Brazil and are *ingenuos* or freedmen" (art. 6, I). *Ingenuo* at the time had the legal meaning of having been born free and not having subsequently been enslaved. This definition of citizenship – which was the individual's sole form of constitutional existence – excluded enslaved persons, whose numbers were growing at the time. The mass production of coffee, which began during the reign of Dom Pedro II, was made possible by the large-scale trafficking of enslaved people from overseas, which continued until 1850. Subsequently, the trade of enslaved people became internal to Brazil, to be abolished only in the 1880s.

Another element of constitutional attempts to render the social space more uniform was the struggle to suppress local charters (*fueros*). While the intention to end these exceptions was already announced in the earliest constitutional texts, they persisted in accordance with special laws. These contradictions continued for decades after the formation of the independent republics. Article 13 of the Mexican constitution of 1857 is a good example of the legal suppression of *fueros*: "In the Mexican Republic, nobody can be judged according to exclusive laws, or by special courts. No person or corporation may have charters or enjoy emoluments that are not paid in compensation for a public service and fixed by law." Nevertheless, Tlaxcala, which

48 J. M. Fradera, *The Imperial Nation* (Princeton: Princeton University Press, 2018); J. A. Piqueras, *Negreros. Españoles en el tráfico y en los capitales escalvistas* (Madrid: Catarata, 2021).

had been upgraded from "territory" to "free and sovereign state" by the constituent assembly in 1856, had defended its "independence" with a call for the conservation of "its ancient *fueros*."[49]

The drafters of the 1857 Mexican constitution were expressly intent on abolishing the ecclesiastical *fuero* and whatever remained of the former status of indigenous *pueblos*. A series of complementary laws, known as the Reform Laws, were added to the constitution both before and after its promulgation. The first of these, called the Lerdo Law (after the minister who promoted it, Miguel Lerdo de Tejada), led to the dismantling of the corporatism of Mexican society by eliminating the patrimonial basis of peasant communities. Such measures were part of a more general abolition of any form of corporate ownership, which the Lerdo Law identified very precisely: "Under the name of corporations are included all religious communities of both sexes, fraternities and confraternities, congregations, brotherhoods, parishes, town halls, schools and, in general, any establishment or foundation of a perpetual or indefinite nature." Suppressing such long-standing forms of corporate social life was justified with reference to the idea that private property was a precondition for progress and social development.

The constitutionalism of the later nineteenth century intensified this imposition of the logic of private ownership. The Costa Rican constitution of 1871, among others, included an explicit ban on creating entailed estates: "The Republic does not recognize hereditary titles or *empleos venales* [bought offices that were often also inherited] or permit the creation of entailed estates" (art. 23). At stake was the reduction of all ownership to private ownership, and, therefore, bringing property under the owner's complete control. However, there were also constitutions that established the continuity of non-individual ownership of real estate, albeit subject to the logic of individual ownership: "The Church's real estate and the property belonging to educational or charitable establishments, to municipalities, or religious communities and corporations, will benefit from the same guarantees as those of individuals" (Bolivia, 1878 art. 17).

The prevailing liberal constitutional culture was thus based on (private) ownership. This radically conflicted with the indigenous communities' cultural values and concepts of property. Liberals saw this as evidence of the indigenous populations' inferior level of civilization which necessitated their

49 B. Hamnett, "El liberalismo en la Reforma mexicana, 1855–1876: Características y consecuencias," in R. Blancarte (ed.), *Las Leyes de Reforma y el Estado laico: importancia histórica y validez contemporánea* (Mexico City: El Colegio de México, 2013), 67–95. On Tlaxcala, see J. M. Portillo Valdés, *Fuero Indio. Tlaxcala y la identidad territorial entre la monarquía imperial y la república nacional 1787–1824* (Mexico City: El Colegio de México, 2014).

"cultural conversion" to progress and modern civic life. The most progressive Latin American constitution of the century, the Columbian Constitution of Rionegro (1863), expressed this idea very clearly (art. 173): "A special law shall govern sparsely populated Territories, or those occupied by indigenous tribes, which the State or States to which they belong agree to cede to the central government with the objective of fostering colonization and implementing material improvements." Note that "indigenous tribes" were not described as "populating" or "inhabiting" but merely "occupying" a territory, which the federal states and the general government should administer in order to civilize it. This was the same principle that Juan Bautista Alberdi formulated in an expression destined to become famous: "To govern is to populate" – but to populate with a very specific, supposedly more "civilized," type of human being.

The idea of a single, homogenous national society formed of just one legal kind of person raised the question of the breadth of suffrage. If originally the majority of the Latin American constitutions included an extensive franchise, considerably broader than what was usual at the time in the Western hemisphere, this was subsequently qualified in several ways.[50] It is important to bear in mind that the independent Latin American republics retained much of the colonial social order, modified only at the higher levels with the abolition of titled nobility.

The most effective constitutional mechanism in order to align the political with the social order was the definition of the citizen as an autonomous individual (free and independent, i.e., emancipated) discussed previously, which *de facto* excluded large sectors of society. Until the twentieth century, it prevented women's entry into the public space of representation. (Their presence in the public debate increased via other channels, such as through literature or by engaging in discussions of public affairs in private gatherings, but these were restricted, of course, to women from the upper echelons of society.) A supposed absence of autonomy also closed the doors to citizenship for the mainly *mestizo* or indigenous members of the lower social classes. Expressions like "domestic service," "lazy," or "lacking an honest way of living," employed by various constitutions as grounds for the suspension of citizenship, could result in interpretations that also excluded salaried workers

50 H. Sabato, *Republics of the New World: The Revolutionary Political Experiment in Nineteenth-Century Latin America* (Princeton: Princeton University Press, 2018); R. Warren, "Los tránsitos de la representación política en México, 1821–1857," in J. A. Aguilar Rivera (ed.), *Las elecciones y el gobierno representativo en México (1810–1910)* (Mexico City: Fondo de Cultura Económica, 2010), 55–94.

and others subject to different forms of supervision and control by employers, such as several kinds of *hacienda* workers (*gañanes, conchabados*). There were also complementary forms of excluding members of lower social and/ or economic status, such as requiring citizens to be literate or to fulfill certain moral criteria, derived from contemporary anthropological assumptions, that penalized practices such as transhumance or nudity.[51] Other circumstances that precluded citizenship also belonged to the sphere of moral values: Article 40 of the Peruvian constitution of 1860 stated that one could be excluded from citizenship "[f]or being flagrantly idle, a gambler, inebriate, or for being the culpable party in a divorce."

Nineteenth-century Latin American constitutions worked in concert with other equally effective instruments to ensure that the Creole elite would continue to dominate political representation. These included differentiated electoral systems with varying requirements for suffrage depending on whether elections were local, provincial, or national. Indirect electoral systems on various levels further restricted access to the higher strata of representation, which was limited, with very few exceptions, to those who already belonged to the economic and intellectual elites.

Progressive and conservative liberals argued at length over the relations between the social and the political order. The liberals, especially at the more radical end of the spectrum, aspired to the extension of citizenship to all married or even all adult males. The more moderate sectors preferred to keep eligibility for citizenship conditional on the fulfillment of certain cultural or moral criteria. What all agreed upon was that the social order should correspond to Creole cultural values and that this should be reflected in the constitution.[52]

By the 1870s, constitutions had established themselves in Latin America in the sense referred to by the Peruvian jurist José Silva Santisteban in the work quoted at the beginning of Section 5.1: They were the most important instrument of government. With the consolidation of the constitution as a basic political tenet, the political debate moved on to focus on the state's administration. To put it in metaphorical terms, the skeleton of the new political bodies – that is, the constitutions – that had emerged from the crisis of the

51 Exclusion from citizenship due to "moral or physical incapacity" could affect many indigenous communities categorized as "uncivilized": see Duarte Dantas, "Constituição, poderes e cidadania," 36.

52 The limits of this shared belief have been explored by J. E. Sanders, *The Vanguard of the Atlantic World: Creating Modernity, Nation, and Democracy in Nineteenth-Century Latin America* (Durham: Duke University Press, 2016); and T. H. Schaefer, *Liberalism as Utopia: The Rise and Fall of Legal Rule in PostColonial Mexico, 1820–1900* (Cambridge: Cambridge University Press, 2017).

Iberian empires was already consolidated by the 1870s. What Silva, Bello, or Alberdi deemed necessary then was to add musculature – that is, the administration – as Sections 5.2 and 6.1 will show.

. . .

5.2 Codifications

AGUSTÍN PARISE*

Codification was a global movement that aimed to shape the way in which the law was presented, studied, and applied. Though its origins lie in the eighteenth century, it developed significantly during the nineteenth century, mainly in the civil law world. Codifiers advocated for a new presentation and form of law that would replace the multitude of existing provisions. In its original conception, codification pursued the utopian goal of organizing all areas of the law in an organic, systematic, clear, accurate, and comprehensive way.[53] This global movement continued to evolve during the twentieth and twenty-first centuries, when it mainly experienced processes of revision,

* Part of the research and writing used for this chapter was previously presented in other forums: A. Parise, "The Place of the Louisiana Civil Code in the Hispanic Civil Codifications: Inclusion in the Comments to the Spanish Civil Code Project of 1851," *Louisiana Law Review* 68 (2008), 823–929; A. Parise, "Legal Transplants and Codification: Exploring the North American Sources of the Civil Code of Argentina (1871)," in J. A. Sánchez Cordero (ed.), *Legal Culture and Legal Transplants. La culture juridique et l'acculturation du droit* (Mexico City: UNAM, 2012), vol. I, 71–121; A. Parise, "Libraries of Civil Codes as Mirrors of Normative Transfers from Europe to the Americas: The Experiences of Lorimier in Quebec (1871–1890) and Varela in Argentina (1873–1875)," in T. Duve (ed), *Entanglements in Legal History: Conceptual Approaches, Global Perspectives on Legal History* (Frankfurt am Main: Max-Planck-Institut für europäische Rechtsgeschichte, 2015), 315–384; A. Parise, "Harmonization of Private Law in Latin America and the Emergence of Third-Generation Codes," in S. Vogenauer and R. Momberg (eds.), *The Future of Contract Law in Latin America: The Principles of Latin American Contract Law* (Oxford: Hart Publishing, 2017), 29–55; A. Parise, *Ownership Paradigms in American Civil Law Jurisdictions: Manifestations of the Shifts in the Legislation of Louisiana, Chile, and Argentina (16th–20th Centuries)* (Leiden: Brill Nijhof, 2017); A. Parise, "Sources of Law and Legal History," in U. Basset (ed.), *Introduction to the Law of Argentina* (Alphen aan den Rijn: Wolters Kluwer, 2018), 1–24; and A. Parise, "Using Metaphors to Explain the Construction of Societal *Buildings*: A look into the Codification of Civil Law in Latin America," in A. Parise and L. van Vliet (eds)., *Re- De- Co-dification? New Insights on the Codification of Private Law* (The Hague: Eleven International Publishing, 2018), 101–133.

53 L. Díez-Picazo and A. Gullón, *Sistema de Derecho Civil*, 4th ed. (Madrid: Tecnos, 1982), vol. I, 51; A. Alessandri Rodríguez and M. Somarriva Undurraga, *Curso de Derecho Civil, basado en las Explicaciones de los Profesores de la Universidad de Chile*, 2nd ed. (Santiago: Editorial Nascimento, 1945), vol. I, 49; and G. R. Carrió, "Judge Made Law under a Civil Code," *Louisiana Law Review* 41 (1981), 993–1005, at 993.

de-codification, and re-codification, but these lie outside the period covered in this section, which will focus on the nineteenth century.[54]

Constitutions and codes were seen as symbols of change and as constitutive elements of the different territories in nineteenth-century Latin America (on constitutions, see Section 5.1). At a time of prevailing liberalism, these *corpora* were part of a process that aimed to attain uniformity of laws while at the same time pursuing a juridical centralism that would help overcome the multiplicity of norms within a specific territory.[55] As tools for centralization[56] and symbols or juridical monuments of nation building, they ultimately helped to eliminate divisions and pluralism.[57] Despite these aims, drafters drew on an international, indeed global, pool of legal sources, as will be discussed in detail later. In the words of Thomas Duve, these constitutions and codes "have been part of a complex process of communication that, in some respects, possessed a global dimension. Constitutions and codes from different parts of the world circulated and were translated, literally and culturally, to a greater or lesser degree, into each nation's realities."[58] Looking at codes, it can be argued that there was a "contagion" of codification efforts across Latin America.[59] In addition, a number of local constitutions called for the adoption of codes (see Section 5.1).[60] This development offered proof of the "veneration" of these *corpora*, and it was accompanied by the emergence of specialized literature and the revision of the curricula at law schools, amongst other changes. That enthusiasm was succeeded by a conception that allowed the perception of the law "in action."[61] The decades that followed the enactments of the different codes however showed that the codes were not able to realize the utopian task they had been originally envisioned to achieve.[62]

This section will address the codification movement in nineteenth-century Latin America. It will focus on civil law codification as a means to narrow the scope of study, though it should be noted that at the time codification tended

54 See, amongst the copious literature, more recently: A. Parise and L. van Vliet (eds.), *Re- De- Co-dification? New Insights on the Codification of Private Law* (The Hague: Eleven International Publishing, 2018).

55 A. L. Fernández Álvarez, "Constitucionalismo y codificación civil. El proceso de centralización jurídica en el siglo diecinueve," *Direito em Movimento* 18(3) (2020), 39–76, at 41.

56 See Section 6.1 in this volume.

57 T. Duve, "What is Global Legal History?," *Comparative Legal History* 8(2) (2020), 73–115, at 92; and Fernández Álvarez, "Constitucionalismo y codificación civil," 65.

58 Duve, "What is Global Legal History?," 92.

59 See generally O. Moréteau and A. Parise, "Recodification in Louisiana and Latin America," *Tulane Law Review* 83 (2009), 1103–62.

60 See, for example, section 64, paragraph 11 of the Argentine Constitution of 1853.

61 M. R. Pugliese la Valle, "La 'idea de jurisprudencia' a través de los primeros años de la 'Revista de Jurisprudencia Argentina'," *Revista de Historia del Derecho* 22 (1994), 241–77, at 277.

62 R. Lesaffer, *European Legal History: A Cultural and Political Perspective* (Cambridge: Cambridge University Press, 2011), 510–11.

to cover five areas of law (civil, commercial, and criminal law, as well as civil and criminal procedure). Indeed, the different codification experiences – across areas of law and jurisdictions – merit attention beyond this section.

The late Carlos Ramos Núñez stated that codification as a legal paradigm had an impact in Latin America.[63] In order to understand this impact, it also needs to be placed within a pan-American context, and indeed understood as part of a global movement. This section will therefore look at codification within three dimensions, but always from a Latin American perspective. The first dimension introduces the codification movement by focusing on the endeavors in Europe. While codification soon spread across the globe, it also kept evolving in Europe throughout the period covered in this section, running parallel to the developments in the Americas.

The second dimension jumps across the Atlantic to focus exclusively on the development of codification in Latin America, discussing a selection of actors, events, and influences, and tracing some of the main codification efforts. The third dimension continues to focus on the Americas, but looks beyond Latin America to its northern neighbors, and explores two case studies, the civil codes of Louisiana (1825) and Quebec (1866), to trace the pan-American circulation of legal ideas. All three dimensions will also offer examples of failed codification endeavors, since the history of codification should not be written as a story of linear progress. A new paradigm does not become consensual overnight and can run along parallel paths in different parts of the globe. Accordingly, this section aims to offer insights into the traits that help explain the paradigmatic shift brought by codification in Latin America as part of a larger process around the globe.

Ramos Núñez, as already mentioned, argued that codification could be seen as a legal paradigm,[64] an overarching set of legal concepts, which was also combined with the prevailing ideologies in a certain society.[65] The late Peruvian jurist defined a "paradigm shift" as the generation of a new consensual model that changes the previous, long-established perspective of a certain scientific community.[66] A shift or scientific revolution will break

63 C. Ramos Núñez, *Codificación, Tecnología y Postmodernidad* (Lima: Ara Editores, 1996), 23.

64 Ramos Núñez, *Codificación*, 23.

65 E. P. Haba, "Ciencias del derecho, La controversia de paradigmas en la Teoría del Derecho contemporánea," in M. Ossorio y Florit et al. (eds.), *Enciclopedia Jurídica Omeba* (Buenos Aires: Driskill, 1996), vol. VII, 107–45, at 122.

66 Ramos Núñez, *Codificación*, 23; drawing on T. S. Kuhn, *The Structure of Scientific Revolutions*, 2nd ed. (Chicago: The University of Chicago Press, 1970). See also Haba, "Ciencias del derecho," 122. Some scholars have argued that the Kuhnian model should not be applied to the legal sciences; see, for example, U. de Vries, "Kuhn and Legal Research: A Reflexive Paradigmatic View on Legal Research," *Recht en Methode in onderzoek en onderwijs* 3(1) (2013), 7–25, at 11.

with a previous paradigm and set in place a new one that will be likewise accepted.[67]

The development of codification can be divided into four periods or stages from the time of its emergence until the present.[68] The first period is that of foundation. In this period, the enactment of a seminal code (or small number of codes) can be considered as sparking a codification movement in particular spaces, hence triggering a "contagion" of codes. Such a seminal text – like the Chilean civil code of 1857 – often served as a blueprint or model for future codification endeavors. The second period is that of expansion, which sees an accelerated growth in the number of codes enacted, many of which share common traits and build on existing models. The third period is that of differentiation. In this period, codifiers worked within societies that sought to distinguish their own national legal culture. They were able to use developments in their own court judgments, legislation, and doctrine as a means of differentiating their codes from previous products. The fourth period is that of globalization. In this period, drafters of codes sought to harmonize internal private law with that of other jurisdictions, trying to find an equilibrium between what is good for the individual and what is good for society, even beyond borders.[69] This section will only address the periods that took place during the nineteenth century – foundation and expansion – and will look at them within the global, Latin American, and pan-American dimensions. Periodization is an analytical tool; the various developmental stages described should not be understood as chronologically entirely distinct but could overlap.

Global Dimensions

The global spread of codification began on the European continent, where it can be traced back to the eighteenth century. Changes to the understanding of law had started with the Enlightenment and the humanist movement and continued in rationalistic natural law theorizing that led the way to codification.[70]

67 Ramos Núñez, *Codificación*, 23.

68 In previous studies, when looking at Latin America, the author of this chapter referred to "generations" of codes. For more information on generations of codes, see A. Parise, "Civil Law Codification in Latin America: Understanding First and Second Generation Codes," in J. M. Milo, J. H. A. Lokin, and J. M. Smits (eds.), *Tradition, Codification and Unification: Comparative-Historical Essays on Developments in Civil Law* (Cambridge: Intersentia, 2014), 183–93.

69 On this equilibrium, see A. A. Alterini, "Tendencias en la contratación moderna," in C. López Fernández, A. Caumont, and G. Caffera (eds.), *Estudios de Derecho Civil en Homenaje al Profesor Jorge Gamarra* (Montevideo: Fundación de Cultura Universitaria, 2001), 13–24.

70 A. Levaggi, *Manual de Historia del Derecho Argentino (Castellano-Indiano/Nacional)*, 2nd ed. (Buenos Aires: Depalma, 1996), vol. I, 185.

The new European political, intellectual, and legal environment offered a fertile ground for a movement that aimed to challenge previously uncontested dogmas.[71] Through the new European context, these ideas, including legal ideas, circulated around the globe and linked codification movements across and within continents. However, different political and social conditions provided different contexts for codification. Thus, while there were common legal bases and temporal parallels between different jurisdictions, each merits its own study.[72]

The enthusiasm for codification gained strength with the development of comparative legislation around the 1850s, for example, through concordances listing different jurisdictions' rules on various topics side-by-side.[73] Latin American legal thought was particularly influenced by the works of French and Spanish authors in this field.[74] One of these was Fortuné Anthoine de Saint-Joseph, who in 1840 produced the first edition of his concordance of civil codes that went on to circulate widely in Europe and the Americas.[75] The work provided a synoptic table that aided the comparison of the texts of the French civil code (1804) (later called *Code Napoléon*) with the texts of several other nineteenth-century codes.[76] In Spain, Florencio García Goyena directed readers through the text of the Spanish civil code project of 1851 and included a scholarly commentary on each of its articles.[77] Drafters of civil codes regarded these works as useful repositories of a multiplicity of provisions. Again in Spain, but at the start of the 1860s, Juan Antonio Seoane also published a work that provided formal sources, in this case, translations and transcriptions of both Spanish and foreign provisions

71 G. A. Weiss, "The Enchantment of Codification in the Common-Law World," *Yale Journal of International Law* 25 (2000), 435–532, at 453.

72 V. Tau Anzoátegui, *La Codificación en la Argentina (1810–1870). Mentalidad Social e Ideas Jurídicas*, 2nd rev. ed. (Buenos Aires: Librería Histórica – Emilio J. Perrot, 2008), 16.

73 V. Tau Anzoátegui, *Las Ideas Jurídicas en la Argentina (Siglos XIX–XX)* (Buenos Aires: Editorial Perrot, 1977), 79.

74 See generally A. Parise, "Las Concordancias Legislativas Decimonónicas: Instrumentos de Difusión del Derecho Continental Europeo en América," *Cuadernos de Historia del Derecho* 17 (2010), 171–206.

75 A. de Saint-Joseph, *Concordance entre les codes civils étrangers et le Code Napoléon* (Paris: Charles Hingray, 1840). The text was also translated into Italian and Japanese, further extending its readership. See G.-R. de Groot and A. Parise, "Anthoine de Saint-Joseph: A Nineteenth-Century Paladin for the Development of Comparative Legislation," in B. van Hofstraeten, J. van Rensch, T. Gehlen, G. de Groot, and C. H. van Rhee (eds.), *Ten definitieve recht doende … Louis Berkvens Amicorum* (Maastricht: Limburgs Geschied- en Oudheidkundig Genootschap, 2018), 70–93.

76 See generally de Saint-Joseph, *Concordance*.

77 F. García Goyena, *Concordancias, Motivos y Comentarios del Código Civil Español* (Madrid: Sociedad Tipográfico-Editorial, 1852), vols. I–IV.

that aimed to fill the *lacunae* that existed in the legislation of Spain and the Americas.[78]

In Europe, codification went through three of the four periods of its development during the nineteenth century: foundation, expansion, and differentiation. The foundation period was marked by the *Code Napoléon*,[79] and the French Exegetical School of jurists that developed following its adoption.[80] Apart from being in force in the French empire, its colonies, and the polities established in the wake of Napoleonic victories,[81] after the end of the Napoleonic Wars, the *Code Napoléon* was also adopted voluntarily in a number of territories, either by simply translating it or with considerable modifications.[82] It thus reached all continents. The Exegetical School occupied a paramount position in providing the intellectual context in which future codification projects developed. Its proponents, both scholars, and judges, interpreted the code's provisions by closely following their language (literal meaning) and by drawing on a body of prior works, such as those of Robert-Joseph Pothier and Jean Domat.[83] This exegesis was a way both of presenting and of teaching law,[84] and Charles Demolombe, the "prince of exegesis," advocated for the supremacy of written codified law, as did other representatives of the school.[85] The works of the

78 J. A. Seoane, *Jurisprudencia Civil vigente Española y Estranjera, según las sentencias del Tribunal Supremo desde el establecimiento de su jurisprudencia en 1838 hasta la fecha* (Madrid: Bailly-Bailliere, 1861), vii.

79 Foundation is not necessarily linked to the enactment of a first code, since earlier codes were enacted in Europe before the *Code Napoléon*.

80 The literature in English on the influence of that seminal French text is copious; see, for example, C. S. Lobingier, "Napoleon and His Code," *Harvard Law Review* 32 (1919), 114–34; J.-L. Halpérin, *The Civil Code*, trans. D. W. Gruning (Baton Rouge: Center of Civil Law Studies, 2000); and M. C. Mirow, "The Code Napoléon: Buried but Ruling in Latin America," *Denver Journal of International Law & Policy* 33 (2005), 179–94.

81 C. Seruzier, *Historical Summary of the French Codes with French and Foreign Bibliographical Annotations Concerning the General Principles of the Codes Followed by a Dissertation on Codification*, trans. D. A. Combe and M. S. Gruning (Littleton: Fred B. Rothman, 1979), 197; A. N. Yiannopoulos, *Louisiana Civil Law System: Course Outlines* (Baton Rouge: Claitor's Publishing Division, 1971), vol. I, 45.

82 Yiannopoulos, *Louisiana Civil Law*, vol. I, 45.

83 M. U. Salerno, "Un Retorno a las Fuentes del Código Civil Argentino: La Doctrina Francesa," in A. Levaggi (ed.), *Fuentes Ideológicas y Normativas de la Codificación Latinoamericana* (Buenos Aires: Universidad del Museo Social Argentino, 1992), 219–40, at 228; and A. N. Yiannopoulos, *Louisiana Civil Law System: Course Book* (Baton Rouge: Claitor's Publishing Division, 1977), part 1, 58.

84 C. Petit, "Lambert en la Tour Eiffel, o el derecho comparado de la Belle Époque," in A. Padoa-Schioppa (ed.), *La comparazione giuridica tra Otto e Novecento: In Memoria di Mario Rotondi* (Milan: Istituto Lombardo di scienze e lettere, 2001), 53–98, at 69.

85 A. Levaggi, "La Interpretación del Derecho en la Argentina en el Siglo XIX," *Revista de Historia del Derecho* 7 (1979), 23–121, at 29.

exponents of the Exegetical School were read together with the *Code Napoléon*, even leading to translations into other languages.[86]

At this point, a closer look into a specific provision can illustrate the impact of codes in substantive law. The *Code Napoléon*, especially in the area of property, was deemed a symbol of modernity and liberalism.[87] Property law occupied a central place in the French text.[88] Article 544 of the *Code Napoléon* was present in many codes that followed its model, sometimes taken over *verbatim*, in other cases substantively adapted. It read (in English translation): "[O]wnership is the right to enjoy and dispose of things in the most absolute manner, provided they are not used in a way prohibited by law or by regulations." This definition followed the proposals included in the drafts by Jean-Jacques-Régis de Cambacérès[89] of 1793, 1794, and 1796,[90] but also found a precedent in the *Projet de code civil* of 1800, and thus offers an example of how the "genetic" history of provisions can be traced.[91] The conceptualization provided by article 544 was the result of long-standing efforts to eradicate many of the feudalistic limitations on property.[92] This work reached its clearest expression in the writings of Pothier, who should perhaps be seen as the last of the "old" writers rather than the first of the "new."[93] Immediately after the enactment of the *Code Napoléon*, jurists claimed that the French article was related to parts of the *Corpus Iuris Civilis*.[94] This connection should not be overemphasized, however, as – even though many scholars claim that ownership was an absolute and indivisible right in Roman law – the

86 J. M. Díaz Couselo, "Francisco Gény en la Cultura Jurídica Argentina," *Revista de Historia del Derecho* 38 (2009), 1–18, at 17–18; and A. Aragoneses, *Un Jurista del Modernismo: Raymond Saleilles y los Orígenes del Derecho Comparado* (Madrid: Editorial Dykinson, 2009), 80.

87 J.-L. Halpérin, *Histoire du droit des biens* (Paris: Économica, 2008), 266.

88 Halpérin, *The Civil Code*, 37.

89 Halpérin, *Histoire du droit des biens*, 192.

90 See the wording of the different drafts in P. A. Fenet, *Recueil complet des travaux préparatoires du code civil, suivi d'une édition de ce code, [à] laquelle sont ajoutés les lois, décrets et ordonnances formant le complément de la législation civile de la France, et ou se trouvent indiqués, sous chaque article séparément, tous les passages du recueil qui s'y rattachent* (Paris: Au dépôt, rue Saint-André-des-Arcs, 1827), vol. I, nos. 51, 39, 116, and 243.

91 See the wording of the relevant article in *Projet de code civil, présenté par la commission nommée par le gouvernement* (Paris: De l'imprimerie de la République, 1801), 166.

92 P. Lira Urquieta, *El Código Civil y el Nuevo Derecho* (Santiago: Imprenta Nascimento, 1944), 166.

93 J.-L. Halpérin, *Histoire du droit privé français depuis 1804* (Paris: Presses Universitaires de France, 1996), 25; and C. Álvarez Alonso, *Lecciones de Historia del Constitucionalismo* (Madrid and Barcelona: Marcial Pons, 1999), 57–59.

94 For example, in 1805, Henri-Jean-Baptiste Dard stated the relevance of *Leg. 21, Cod. Mandate. Leg. I, § 4 et 13, ff. de aqua et aquae pluviae arcendae.* See H.-J.-B. Dard, *Code civil des Français, avec des notes indicatives des lois romaines, coutumes, ordonnances, édits et déclarations, qui ont rapport [à] chaque article; ou Conférence du Code civil avec les lois anciennes* (Paris: J.-A. Commaille, 1805), 104.

nineteenth-century ideas of liberalism were foreign to Roman law.[95] Article 544's definition did echo concepts of the French Revolution that related to ownership, however.[96] This might explain why Jean-Étienne-Marie Portalis wrote in the *exposé des motifs* that ownership was the fundamental right on which all social institutions rested.[97]

Bartolus of Sassoferrato deserves special attention due to his role in shaping the understanding of ownership, not only during the Middle Ages but also in the modern period, on both sides of the Atlantic. His celebrated understanding of ownership as *ius perfecte disponendi de re corporali nisi lege prohibeatur*[98] was highly regarded by future scholars, and influenced property law, ever since its conception in the fourteenth century.[99] For example, Gregorio López, when undertaking his seminal gloss of the *Siete Partidas*, likewise followed the criteria of commentators such as Bartolus, according to whom ownership meant the right to dispose of or to sell a corporeal thing when facing no prohibition by law.[100] That gloss showed the interaction of the text of the *Siete Partidas* with that of the renowned commentator.[101] Spanish Scholasticism (e.g., Luis de Molina) returned – with some nuances – to the definition of Bartolus.[102] That understanding of Bartolus was replicated almost *verbatim* by the architects of the *Code Napoléon*[103] and from there spread across the globe.

The expansion period of the codification paradigm was marked by the enactment of numerous codes across Europe within one century. Many of these built on the *Code Napoléon*, but some also benefited from local codes, pointing to a certain degree of cross-pollination. Examples of the expansion

95 F. Tomás y Valiente, "Manual de Historia del Derecho Español," in F. Tomás y Valiente, *Obras Completas* (Madrid: Centro de Estudios Políticos y Constitucionales, 1997), vol. II, 916–1577, at 1414; and T. Rüfner, "The Roman Concept of Ownership and the Medieval Doctrine of Dominium Utile," in J. W. Cairns and P. J. du Plessis (eds.), *The Creation of the Ius Commune: From Casus to Regula* (Edinburgh: Edinburgh University Press, 2010), 127–42, at 128.

96 A. Tunc, "The Grand Outlines of the Code Napoleon," *Tulane Law Review* 29 (1955), 431–52, at 448.

97 Fenet, *Recueil complet des travaux préparatoires du code civil*, vol. XI, 132.

98 This expression was coined in a comment of Bartolus to Digest 41, 2, 17, I, n. 4. See P. Grossi, "La proprietà nel sistema privatistico della Seconda Scolastica," in P. Grossi, *Il dominio e le cose: percezioni medievali e moderne dei diritti reali* (Milan: Giuffrè, 1992), 281–383, at 368.

99 See J. L. de los Mozos, *El Derecho de Propiedad: Crisis y Retorno a la Tradición Jurídica* (Madrid: Editorial Revista de Derecho Privado, 1993), 36; and Rüfner, "The Roman Concept of Ownership," 127.

100 I. Sánchez Bella, A. de la Hera, and C. Díaz Rementería, *Historia del Derecho Indiano* (Madrid: Editorial MAPFRE, 1992), 343.

101 A. Guzmán Brito, *La Codificación Civil en Iberoamérica. Siglos XIX y XX* (Santiago: Editorial Jurídica de Chile, 2000), 160.

102 De los Mozos, *El Derecho de Propiedad*, 36–38.

103 Rüfner, "The Roman Concept of Ownership," 127.

of codification are the civil codes of Austria (1811), the Netherlands (1838), and Italy (1865), to name but a few of the codes that also crossed continents and reached Latin America.[104] At the same time, the spread of codification was also fueled by the earlier-mentioned works of legislative concordances, in which drafters of codes could find "consolidated libraries" of previous examples.

The period of differentiation started at the end of the nineteenth century. It was marked by the drafting and adoption of the German civil code that took effect in 1900. The latter was a product of nineteenth-century German legal science and inspired the drafting of several twentieth-century codes, both in Europe and beyond.[105] This German product was able to distinguish itself, both in form and substance, from the antecedents that had been adopted across Europe. In Germany, the Historical School, and later Scientific Positivism, advocated for customs and traditions to be considered in potential codification efforts and for the objective interpretation of the law, respectively.[106]

Already during its European foundation period, the paradigm of codification began to spread across the globe. Jurists were interested in knowing the state of the art regarding civil law legislation in a succinct and comprehensive way, while examining ideas that existed in the codes of other states.[107] Another of the many existing examples of codification is found in Asia, when Japan promulgated a civil code in 1890, during the Meiji period.[108] Examples are also found in Africa, when David Santillana led the work on a draft civil and commercial code for Tunisia at the end of the nineteenth century.[109] The new century brought many new codification endeavors, such as the 1926 civil code in the Republic of Turkey, which aimed to modernize and secularize the law at the time of Mustafa Kemal Atatürk,[110] and the 1949 Egyptian civil code, led by Abd el-Razzâq el-Sanhourî, which shows an interplay of sources from Islamic law, local court decisions, and modern codes.[111] As Julio C. Rivera

104 See A. Parise, *Historia de la Codificación Civil del Estado de Luisiana y su Influencia en el Código Civil Argentino* (Buenos Aires: Eudeba, 2013), 184–354.

105 See generally M. Reimann, "Nineteenth Century German Legal Science," *Boston College Law Review* 31 (1990), 837–97.

106 C. Ramos Núñez, *El Código Napoleónico y su Recepción en América Latina* (Lima: Pontificia Universidad Católica del Perú, 1997), 237.

107 F. Stone, "A Primer on Codification," *Tulane Law Review* 29 (1955), 303–10, at 307.

108 A. Ortolani, "The Japanese Civil Code: Its First 120 Years," in Parise and van Vliet, *Re- De- Co-dification?*, 219–46, at 221.

109 See generally D. E. Stigall, *The Santillana Codes: The Civil Codes of Tunisia, Morocco, and Mauritania* (Lanham: Lexington Books, 2017).

110 See generally E. Özsunay, "The Scope and Structure of Civil Codes: The Turkish Experience," in J. C. Rivera (ed.), *The Scope and Structure of Civil Codes* (Dordrecht: Springer, 2013), 387–407.

111 See the brief note by G. M. Badr, "The New Egyptian Civil Code and the Unification of the Laws of Arab Countries," *Tulane Law Review* 30 (1956), 299–304.

stated, the nineteenth century was "the codification century of civil law,"[112] a time when private law tended to revolve around the new codes.

The Latin American Dimension

Ideas circulated across the Atlantic Ocean, and the paradigm of codification arrived in Latin America within the first decades after the adoption of the *Code Napoléon*. Codification occurred in a particular way in Latin America. It developed mainly during the second half of the nineteenth century and was shaped by the interaction of both European and local products. This comparatively late development allowed for the percolation of positivistic ideas, including those of the exegetical approach, and enabled the adaptation of models that had proven successful in other jurisdictions. The interaction of European and local products was specific to the region. The shared heritage (see Section 3.1) and language also facilitated the circulation and reception of local elaborations across the continent.

Codification in Latin America experienced two of the four periods during the nineteenth century: foundation and expansion. While a number of Latin American jurisdictions promulgated codes in the first half of the nineteenth century,[113] the foundation period can only be deemed to have properly started with the adoption of the civil code of Chile of 1857. This text, largely written by the Venezuelan Andrés Bello, had a massive impact in the region, and quickly led to other codification efforts. Bello had been working privately on his draft of a civil code for Chile for some years, and by 1835 had accomplished one-third of his project.[114] The years that followed were marked by Bello working together with special commissions.[115] From 1847, however, Bello once again undertook the drafting autonomously.[116] In 1853, the project was published, and subjected to review by a special commission.[117] Finally, it was sent to the Chilean National Congress, which approved the text in 1855.[118] In his work, Bello had taken inspiration from a multiplicity of sources. He

112 J. C. Rivera, "The Scope and Structure of Civil Codes: Relations with Commercial Law, Family Law, Consumer Law and Private International Law: A Comparative Approach," in J. C. Rivera (ed.), *The Scope and Structure of Civil Codes* (Dordrecht: Springer, 2013), 3–39, at 7.

113 Other codes followed in the region, before the enactment of the Chilean Code: Haiti (1826), Bolivia (1831), Peru (1836), Costa Rica (1841), and the Dominican Republic (1844).

114 Alessandri Rodríguez and Somarriva Undurraga, *Curso de Derecho Civil*, vol. I, 59.

115 A. Guzmán Brito, *Andrés Bello Codificador. Historia de la Fijación y Codificación del Derecho Civil en Chile* (Santiago: Ediciones de la Universidad de Chile, 1982), vol. I, 306–36.

116 Guzmán Brito, *Andrés Bello Codificador*, vol. I, 337–43.

117 Alessandri Rodríguez and Somarriva Undurraga, *Curso de Derecho Civil*, vol. I, 63. See the detailed study in Guzmán Brito, *Andrés Bello Codificador*, vol. I, 366–82.

118 Alessandri Rodríguez and Somarriva Undurraga, *Curso de Derecho Civil*, vol. I, 63.

benefited from, amongst others, the *Code Napoléon* and its commentators,[119] the works of Saint-Joseph and García Goyena,[120] the Louisiana Civil Code of 1825 (Louisiana Code),[121] as well as other nineteenth-century civil codes.[122] The work of Bello was grounded in the previous law, but this was restated according to modern codification techniques. It included the tenets of liberalism, while following the Roman and Spanish provisions. Bello, who was also known as a distinguished linguist, was able to maintain a perfect harmony between precision and succinctness for each article of his code, making his work not only an example of law drafting but also of linguistics.[123]

After the promulgation of the Chilean code, the expansion period of codification in Latin America was marked by the quick succession of enactments across the region. Codes were adopted in El Salvador (1860), Panama (1860), Ecuador (1861), Venezuela (1862), Uruguay (1868), Argentina (1871), Mexico (1871), Nicaragua (1871), Colombia (1873), Guatemala (1877), Paraguay (1877), Honduras (1880), Cuba (1889), and Puerto Rico (1889).[124] Enactments during that period were fueled by the already mentioned legislative concordances, particularly those of García Goyena and Saint-Joseph (which was also available in Spanish translation),[125] and by the model offered by the Chilean code. While these concordances mostly, though not exclusively, focused on European legislation,[126] the work of Bello became the Latin American blueprint for many codes.[127]

Latin American jurisdictions made use of the Chilean code in three different ways. A first group adopted it in its entirety with only minor changes to make it operational in their own jurisdictions. A second group created a new code, but one that was closely linked to and dependent on that of Chile.

119 For additional information regarding the use of the *Code Napoléon*, see M. C. Mirow, "Borrowing Private Law in Latin America: Andres Bello's Use of the Code Napoleon in Drafting the Chilean Civil Code," *Louisiana Law Review* 61 (2001), 291–329.

120 See also R. Knütel, "Influences of the Louisiana Civil Code in Latin America," *Tulane Law Review* 70 (1996), 1452–459.

121 Guzmán Brito, *Andrés Bello Codificador*, vol. I, 422.

122 V. Pescio Vargas, *Manual de Derecho Civil*, 2nd ed. (Santiago: Editorial Jurídica de Chile, 1978), vol. I, 115.

123 A. Guzmán Brito, *La Codificación Civil en Iberoamérica. Siglos XIX y XX* (Santiago: Editorial Jurídica de Chile, 2000), 373.

124 Codification took place in Brazil in 1917.

125 See generally Parise, *Historia de la Codificación*; A. Parise, "The Concordancias of Saint-Joseph: A Nineteenth-Century Spanish Translation of the Louisiana Civil Code," *Journal of Civil Law Studies* 9 (2016), 287–328.

126 For example, these works also examined the Louisiana Code of 1825 (discussed in the following section).

127 A. Guzmán Brito, *Vida y Obra de Andrés Bello especialmente considerado como Jurista* (Cizur Menor: Thomson-Aranzadi, 2008), 100; and M. C. Mirow, *Latin American Law: A History of Private Law and Institutions in Spanish America* (Austin: University of Texas Press, 2004), 137.

A third group used the Chilean code merely for inspiration, borrowing only isolated elements from it.[128] Three factors may explain the widespread influence of the Chilean code in Latin America: the shared historical background, the existing geographical similarities, and the uniformity of the Romance languages.[129] The specific Latin American interaction of works of concordances with the Chilean blueprint helps explain the speed with which codification spread across the region from the late 1850s onwards.

The dissemination of the Chilean code can be demonstrated by looking at one of its specific provisions. The law of property, once more, offers an example of the circulation of ideas. Bello adopted the liberal doctrine of the *Code Napoléon*, believing it to provide an essential building block for progress.[130] Article 582 of the Chilean code, therefore, read in its first paragraph: "[O]wnership (also called property) is the real right in a corporeal thing to enjoy and dispose thereof *as the owner wishes*, provided that it is not contrary to the law or the rights of a third party."[131] This article echoed the subjective right to enjoy and dispose arbitrarily of a thing as stated in article 544 of the *Code Napoléon*, discussed earlier.[132] The Chilean code's article 582, defining ownership as an absolute right, was in turn replicated throughout the continent. Several jurisdictions adopted the Chilean wording almost *verbatim* in their codes, such as El Salvador (1860), Panama (1860), Ecuador (1861), Venezuela (1862), Nicaragua (1871), Colombia (1873), and Honduras (1880).[133]

The development of codification in Latin America was not limited to enactments that closely replicated the Chilean text, however. The 1871 Argentine code by Dalmacio Vélez Sarsfield offers an illustration of an enactment that relied less on Bello's work and more on other sources. It also serves as proof that periods are not watertight compartments, since the Argentine text could also be placed within an early phase of the differentiation period. The Argentine code included notes for many of its articles, which were not part

128 B. Bravo Lira, "La difusión del código civil de Bello en los países de derecho castellano y portugués," *Revista de Estudios Histórico-Jurídicos* 7 (1982), 71–106, at 93–94.

129 Moréteau and Parise, "Recodification," 1123. The authors in that paper provided that understanding beyond the scope of the Chilean code.

130 P. Lira Urquieta, "Introducción al Código Civil de Andrés Bello," in R. Caldera (ed.), *Obras Completas de Andrés Bello*, 2nd ed. (Caracas: Fundación La Casa de Bello, 1981), vol. XIV, xiii–lxii, at xxxi.

131 As translated by J. Romanach, *Civil Code of Chile 2008: Translated into English with an Introduction and Index* (Baton Rouge: Lawrence Publishing, 2008), 94.

132 Guzmán Brito, *Andrés Bello Codificador*, vol. I, 455.

133 See article 608 of the code of El Salvador; article 732 of the code of Panama; article 571 of the code of Ecuador; article 1, law 1, Title 2, Book 2 of the code of Venezuela; article 582 of the code of Nicaragua; article 669 of the code of Colombia; and article 661 of the code of Honduras.

of the law but intended to inform the reader about Vélez Sarsfield's underlying reasoning.[134] Like a legislative history or *exposé des motifs*, they provided an additional element for the provisions' interpretation and served as guides when studying articles.[135] In 1865, Vélez Sarsfield wrote about the notes:

> I indicated the concordances between the articles of each title and the current laws and the codes of Europe and America, for an easier and more illustrated discussion of the draft.
>
> On occasion I had to include long notes in articles that solved archaic and serious matters which had been debated by jurists or when it was necessary to legislate in areas of law that needed to be moved from doctrine and turned into [positive] law.[136]

Having an eclectic approach to law,[137] Vélez Sarsfield incorporated into his work materials from many sources, including legislative acts, drafts of codes, codes, and doctrine.[138] As with other drafters, he used the ideas and codes that existed at the time.[139] Like Bello in Chile, he was especially interested in the jurists and works that theorized on modern law while building upon Roman law principles.[140] Finally, Vélez Sarsfield added local customs to these materials.[141] While the Argentinean codifier was well acquainted with Roman law and Castilian legislation, the archaic nature of those texts encouraged him to look for direct, modern models that reproduced those ideas: Augusto Teixeira de Freitas' draft of a civil code for Brazil, the *Code Napoléon*, the concordance of García Goyena, the Chilean code by Bello,[142] and the Louisiana Code. For example, Rolf Knütel has shown that Vélez Sarsfield used the Louisiana text because its regulations in the area of real rights were extracted mainly from the

134 L. Moisset de Espanés, "Reflexiones sobre las notas del código civil argentino," in *Studi sassaresi. V, Diritto romano, codificazioni e unità del sistema giuridico latinoamericano* (Milan: Giuffrè, 1981), 448–76, at 448.

135 A. Levaggi, *Dalmacio Vélez Sarsfield, Jurisconsulto* (Córdoba: Ciencia, Derecho y Sociedad, 2005), 209; M. O. Cobas and J. A. Zago, "La influencia de las 'notas' del código civil en la ciencia del derecho argentino y latinoamericano," in S. Schipani (ed.), *Dalmacio Vélez Sarsfield e il diritto latinoamericano* (Padua: CEDAM, 1991), 141–48, at 146–47; and R. Rivarola, *Instituciones del Derecho Civil Argentino: Programa de una Nueva Exposición del Derecho Civil* (Buenos Aires: Imprenta de Peuser, 1901), vol. I, 12.

136 D. Vélez Sarsfield, *Proyecto de Código Civil para la República Argentina, Libro Primero* (Buenos Aires: Imprenta de la Nación Argentina, 1865), v. See also Levaggi, *Dalmacio Vélez Sarsfield*, 204 and 310.

137 Guzmán Brito, *La Codificación Civil*, 453.

138 R. M. Salvat, "El Código Civil Argentino (Estudio General). Historia, Plan o Método y Fuentes," *Revista Argentina de Ciencias Políticas* 7 (1913), 420–37, at 436.

139 Levaggi, *Dalmacio Vélez Sarsfield*, 180.

140 Levaggi, *Dalmacio Vélez Sarsfield*, 180.

141 R. M. Salvat, *Tratado de Derecho Civil Argentino. Parte General*, 9th ed. (Buenos Aires: Tipográfica Ed. Argentina, 1950), vol. I, 132.

142 R. Zorraquín Becú, "La recepción de los derechos extranjeros en la Argentina durante el siglo XIX," *Revista de Historia del Derecho* 4 (1976), 325–59, at 350.

Projet of 1800, which followed the casuistry of Roman law. According to him, "the majority of the concepts which found their way into the Argentine civil code through the Louisiana codification are ideas developed in Roman law, ideas 'garbed in modern linguistic dresses.'"[143] Amongst many other sources, Vélez Sarsfield explicitly mentioned in his code the *Corpus Iuris Civilis*, the *Siete Partidas*, principles of canon law, the project of a civil code for the State of New York (1865), the codes of numerous jurisdictions (including Austria and Haiti), and many doctrinal works (such as William Blackstone, Domat, James Kent, Pothier, and Friedrich Carl von Savigny).[144] Even though French authors and the codes that followed the wording of the *Code Napoléon* predominated in his notes, Vélez Sarsfield did not limit himself to one particular school of thought, and his very diverse sources helped him to produce an eclectic code.

Not all Latin American jurisdictions adopted civil codes during the nineteenth century. Brazil, for example, waited until 1917,[145] although a criminal code was adopted as early as 1830.[146] Nevertheless, Brazil's Teixeira de Freitas deserves to be counted as one of the great Latin American civil law codifiers, the equal of Bello and Vélez Sarsfield. As early as 1824, the Imperial Constitution of Brazil recognized the need for criminal and civil codes.[147] In 1859, Teixeira de Freitas was appointed to draft a civil code; however, the result of his efforts was ultimately not adopted.[148] He had previously drafted his *Consolidação das Leis Civis*, which was intended to be an official work classifying and systematizing the laws of Brazil. In 1872, the Brazilian government terminated the contract

143 Knütel, "Influences of the Louisiana Civil Code," 1466–467.

144 See the notes to articles 2913 (*Corpus Iuris Civilis*), 455 (*Siete Partitas*), 14 (canon law), 2538 (New York), 19 (Austria), 325 (Haiti), 167 (Blackstone), 1198 (Domat), 3136 (Kent), 1650 (Pothier), and 3283 (Savigny).

145 For insights on the process towards the 1917 code, see S. Meira, "Gênese e elaboração do Código Civil brasileiro de 1917," in A. Levaggi (ed.), *Fuentes Ideológicas y Normativas de la Codificación Latinoamericana* (Buenos Aires: Universidad del Museo Social Argentino, 1992), 313–79; and M. Neves, "Ideas in Another Place? Liberal Constitution and the Codification of Private Law at the Turn of the 19th Century in Brazil," in M. R. Polotto, T. Keiser, and T. Duve (eds.), *Derecho Privado y Modernización. América Latina y Europa en la Primera Mitad del Siglo XX* (Frankfurt am Main: Max-Planck-Institut für Europäische Rechtsgeschichte, 2015), 47–81. On the codification of private law beyond the period covered in this chapter, and with special attention to the current state of slavery as a potential failure of codification, see B. Clavero, "Esclavitud y Codificación en Brasil, 1888–2017: Por una Historia Descolonizada del Derecho Latinoamericano," *Revista de Historia del Derecho* 55 (2018), 27–89.

146 See generally I. M. Poveda Velasco and E. Tomasevicius Filho, "The 1830 Criminal Code of the Brazilian Empire and Its Originality," in A. Masferrer (ed.), *The Western Codification of Criminal Law: A Revision of the Myth of its Predominant French Influence* (Cham: Springer, 2018), 341–68.

147 S. de Salvo Venosa, *Direito Civil* (São Paulo: Editora Atlas, 1987), vol. I, 107.

148 A. Wald, *Curso de Direito Civil Brasileiro*, 4th rev. ed. (São Paulo: Sugestões Literárias, 1975), 83.

with Teixeira de Freitas because he had changed his plan of work. However, he had already published part of it in the shape of a sketch (*Esboço*) from 1860 onwards, and this proved highly influential on the civil codification works of other countries, including in Argentina through the work of Vélez Sarsfield, as mentioned earlier.[149] Teixeira de Freitas' work offers a paramount example of the local circulation of ideas specific to Latin American codification.

There were a number of overarching motivations for governments and lawyers to undertake codification efforts in nineteenth-century Latin America. One was the intention to break with the past and with the Spanish, Portuguese, or French presence, respectively. The recently independent jurisdictions sought to end the normative subjugation that had existed during the previous period. A second motivation may be found in seeing the codes as constitutive elements of the new republics and states (see Chapter 4). As already mentioned, new territories included the need to promulgate codes within their legislative agendas, some even including references to codification in their constitutions (see also Section 5.1). Nineteenth-century codes in Latin America were part of projecting a sense of differentiation between Europe and the Americas, between former dependent territory and metropole.

A "culture" of the code developed in the Latin American jurisdictions soon after the enactment of these bodies of the law.[150] This development was similar to what had occurred at a global level, for example, in France after the adoption of the *Code Napoléon*. A look at Argentina offers an illustration. The Argentine code triggered positivistic, mainly exegetical approaches to the law, which were present in the works of scholars and judges during the second half of the nineteenth century and continued, though at a slower pace, well into the next century.[151] These scholars sought to identify the intention of the codifier and promoted the study of the letter of the law and of the code's sources.[152] Scholarly writings and judicial interpretations turned the code into a repository

149 Wald, *Curso de Direito*, 83.

150 On the "culture" of the code, see V. Tau Anzoátegui, "La 'Cultura del Código:' Un Debate Virtual entre Segovia y Sáez," *Revista de Historia del Derecho* 26 (1998), 539–64, at 543–44.

151 D. F. Esborraz, "La Individualización del Subsistema Jurídico Latinoamericano como Desarrollo Interno Propio del Sistema Jurídico Romanista: (II) La Contribución de la Ciencia Jurídica Argentina en la Primera Mitad del Siglo XX," *Roma e America Diritto Romano Comune* 24 (2007), 33–84, at 34–35; and Ramos Núñez, *El Código Napoleónico*, 200; and M. I. Seoane, *La Enseñanza del Derecho en la Argentina: Desde sus Orígenes hasta la Primera Década del Siglo XX* (Buenos Aires: Editorial Perrot, 1981), 68.

152 R. J. Vernengo, *La Interpretación Jurídica* (Mexico City: Universidad Nacional Autónoma de México, 1977), 77; and V. Tau Anzoátegui, "La Jurisprudencia Civil en la Cultura Jurídica Argentina (s. XIX–XX)," *Quaderni fiorentini per la storia del pensiero giuridico moderno* 40 (2011), 53–110, at 72.

of legal science with absolute value: The law was what the code stated.[153] The code was also the central focus of law teaching, together with the work of exegetical scholars.[154] Civil law teaching closely followed the structure of the code until 1910.[155] Scholars and judges looked for the legislator's intention in the notes, and turned to comparative legislation to trace the different sources used.[156] Other positivistic approaches, such as the ideas of Savigny and Scientific Positivism, were also popular in Argentine law schools, and these theories aided to the development of an eclectic legal thought.[157] The new century brought criticisms to extreme positivistic approaches,[158] and the social sciences liberated law from the narrow exegetical approach.[159] New approaches, presented in, for example, the seminal work of François Gény, still placed the code in the paramount position, but when interpreting its provisions also used doctrine, court decisions, comparative legislation, customs, and other social elements.[160] Codification as a paradigm was affected by this new context, which was not unique to Argentina, as the following section will show.

Pan-American Dimensions

The codification paradigm had a significant pan-American dimension during the nineteenth century. A look beyond Latin America to the North shows

153 V. Tau Anzoátegui, "Peculiaridad del Pensamiento Jurídico Argentino," in V. Tau Anzoátegui (ed.), *Antología del Pensamiento Jurídico Argentino (1901–1945)* (Buenos Aires: Instituto de Investigaciones de Historia del Derecho, 2007), vol. I, 11–35, at 19–20; and Tau Anzoátegui, "La 'Cultura del Código,'" 543–44.

154 E. Martínez Paz, *Dalmacio Vélez Sarsfield y el Código Civil Argentino* (Córdoba: Academia Nacional de Derecho y Ciencias Sociales de Córdoba, 2000 [1916]), 350; M. U. Salerno, "El Código de Vélez Sársfield," in J. H. Alterini et al. (eds.), *La Codificación: Raíces y Prospectiva II La Codificación en América* (Buenos Aires: EDUCA, 2004), 143–58, at 149; Tau Anzoátegui, *Las Ideas*, 113; M. U. Salerno, "Argentine," in Association Henri Capitant, *La Circulation du Modèle Juridique Français* (Paris: Litec, 1993), 121–24, at 123; and Tau Anzoátegui, "Peculiaridad del Pensamiento," 162.

155 M. U. Salerno, "Aporte de Héctor Lafaille a la Enseñanza del Derecho Civil," *Revista de Historia del Derecho* 2 (1974), 199–224, at 205; Tau Anzoátegui, "Peculiaridad del Pensamiento," 162; and A. Cháneton, *Historia de Vélez Sársfield* (Buenos Aires: Editorial "La Facultad", 1937), vol. II, 344.

156 Cháneton, *Historia de Vélez*, vol. II, 344; Levaggi, *Dalmacio Vélez Sarsfield*, 247; and Salerno, "Aporte de Héctor Lafaille," 207.

157 Levaggi, "La Interpretación," 78, 84–85; V. Tau Anzoátegui, "La Influencia Alemana en el Derecho Argentino: Un Programa para su Estudio Histórico," *Jahrbuch für Geschichte Lateinamerikas* 25 (1988), 607–34, at 623; and Tau Anzoátegui, *La Codificación*, 277–78 and 282; Tau Anzoátegui, *Las Ideas*, 114–15.

158 V. Tau Anzoátegui, "Los Juristas Argentinos de la Generación de 1910," *Revista de Historia del Derecho* 2 (1974), 225–83, at 241.

159 Tau Anzoátegui, "Peculiaridad del Pensamiento," 20; Tau Anzoátegui, *La Codificación*, 21; and Tau Anzoátegui, "La Jurisprudencia," 99.

160 Tau Anzoátegui, *Las Ideas*, 141; Levaggi, "La Interpretación," 120; Levaggi, *Dalmacio Vélez Sarsfield*, 249; and Díaz Couselo, "Francisco Gény," 1–2.

that codification was a global movement that invited dialogue across jurisdictions and legal systems, and that this was not limited to exchanges with Europe. Efforts towards the adoption of civil codes were undertaken in civil law and common law systems alike, as well as in mixed jurisdictions, such as the Canadian province of Quebec and the State of Louisiana. Codes produced in the Americas (also those produced beyond Latin America) were considered valuable sources by nineteenth-century drafters of civil codes across the globe.

The paradigm of codification in the Americas experienced two of the four periods during the nineteenth century: foundation and expansion. Louisiana offers a representative example of codification in the foundation period. In the early nineteenth century, the legal culture of Louisiana was an isolated "Civil Law island" surrounded by a "sea of Common Law," a status that had to be safeguarded to survive.[161] The French and Spanish occupation resulted in the introduction and subsequent preservation of the civil law system in that part of North America.[162] In 1769, the then governor of Louisiana, Alejandro O'Reilly, implemented the *Indiano* system[163] of government to replace the French laws (e.g., *Coutume de Paris*) in Louisiana.[164] The Spanish judicial records confirm that *Indiano* legal precepts applied in Louisiana.[165] Courts in that southern space continued to rely on Spanish legal sources even after the 1803 Louisiana Purchase, mainly during the first decades of the nineteenth century.[166]

In June 1806, James Brown and Louis Casimir Elisabeth Moreau-Lislet were appointed by the Legislature of the Territory of Orleans to draft a project of a civil code.[167] According to the resolution, the "two jurisconsults shall make the civil law by which this territory is now governed, the ground

161 A. Parise, "Non-Pecuniary Damages in the Louisiana Civil Code Article 1928: Originality in the Early Nineteenth Century and Its Projected Use in Further Codification Endeavors," unpublished LL.M. thesis, Louisiana State University (2006), 14.

162 See A. Parise, "Legal History," in A. A. Levasseur, J. R. Trahan, and D. Gruning (eds.), *The Legal System of Louisiana* (Durham: Carolina Academic Press, 2019), 1–8; and A. Parise, *Historia de la Codificación*, 29–55.

163 That is, the system of law that applied in American territories that belonged to the Spanish crown.

164 See the analysis in R. Batiza, "The Unity of Private Law in Louisiana under the Spanish Rule," *Inter-American Law Review* 4 (1962), 139–56, at 139.

165 J. W. Cairns, *Codification, Transplants and History: Law Reform in Louisiana (1808) and Quebec (1866)* (Clark: Talbot Publishing, 2015), 52. On the different special laws enacted for Louisiana, see K. Wallach, *Research in Louisiana Law*, 2nd ed. (Baton Rouge: Louisiana State University Press, 1960), 209–12.

166 See generally R. J. Rabalais, "The Influence of Spanish Laws and Treatises on the Jurisprudence of Louisiana: 1762–1828," *Louisiana Law Review* 42 (1982), 1485–1508, at 1485.

167 "A Resolution Relative to the Formation of a Civil Code," in *Acts Passed at the First Session of the First Legislature of the Territory of Orleans* (New Orleans: Bradford & Anderson, 1807), 214.

work of said code."[168] In March 1808, the Legislature promulgated Brown and Moreau-Lislet's work as the *Digest of the Civil Laws Now in Force in the Territory of Orleans* (Digest of 1808).[169] While it did not include an *exposé des motifs* explaining its sources,[170] a number of copies contain interleaves with manuscript notes dictated – or, in some cases, even written – by Moreau-Lislet.[171] One of these manuscripts, the de la Vergne volume, includes references to Roman and Spanish materials linked to the Digest's provisions,[172] as well as to French texts grounded in Roman law, such as the works of Pothier and Domat. In his analysis of the de la Vergne volume in 1971, Rodolfo Batiza identified the textual origins of 2,081 articles.[173] He concluded that approximately 85 percent of the articles' text had been extracted from French texts (such as the *Code Napoléon*, the *Projet* of 1800, and French commentators).[174] The following year, Robert A. Pascal published a reply claiming that French law, composed after elements of Roman, Romanized Frankish, Burgundian, and Visigothic origin, often resembled the Spanish law that derived from Roman or Roman-Visigothic origins.[175] He thus argued that, while the *Code Napoléon* provided a mine of texts written in French, the drafters had used French texts that in substance contained, or could be modified to contain, the Spanish-Roman law then in force in Louisiana.[176] Despite their disagreement, both Batiza's and Pascal's research made clear that the Digest's provisions were mainly taken from the civil law system, irrespective of whether their origins lay in French, Spanish, or Roman law. The Digest of 1808 was not a mere copy either of the *Code Napoléon* or of any other single text.[177]

There was a tendency in the Louisiana legal community to de-emphasize the importance of the Digest of 1808 after its enactment.[178] A remarkable and

168 "A Resolution," 214.

169 *A Digest of the Civil Laws Now in Force in the Territory of Orleans, With Alterations and Amendments Adapted to Its Present System of Government* (New Orleans: Bradford & Anderson, 1808).

170 J. Dainow, "Moreau Lislet's Notes On Sources of Louisiana Civil Code of 1808," *Louisiana Law Review* 19 (1958), 43–51, at 43.

171 J. W. Cairns, "The De la Vergne Volume and the Digest of 1808," *Tulane European and Civil Law Forum* 24 (2009), 31–81, at 74.

172 Cairns, "The De la Vergne Volume," 76–77.

173 R. Batiza, "The Louisiana Civil Code of 1808: Its Actual Sources and Present Relevance," *Tulane Law Review* 46 (1971), 4–165, at 11.

174 Batiza, "The Louisiana Civil Code," 12.

175 R. A. Pascal, "Sources of the Digest of 1808: A Reply to Professor Batiza," *Tulane Law Review* 46 (1972), 603–27, at 605.

176 Pascal, "Sources of the Digest," 605–6.

177 S. Herman, *The Louisiana Civil Code: A European Legacy for the United States* (New Orleans: Louisiana Bar Foundation, 1993), 32.

178 R. H. Kilbourne, *A History of the Louisiana Civil Code: The Formative Years, 1803–1839* (Baton Rouge: LSU Law Center Publications Institute, 1987), 62.

comprehensive codification movement started around the same time, with Edward Livingston as its central figure, a New York jurist who had moved to New Orleans in 1804. In March 1822, the Louisiana Legislature resolved that three jurists should be appointed to revise the Digest of 1808: Pierre Derbigny, Edward Livingston, and Moreau-Lislet.[179] The three submitted a preliminary report to the Louisiana Senate in February 1823, in which they stated that they would

> keep a reverent eye on those principles, which have received the sanction of time, and on the labors of the great Legislators, who have preceded us. The Laws of the *Partidas*, and other Statutes of Spain, the existing digest [of 1808] of our own Laws, the abundant stores of the English Jurisprudence, the comprehensive Codes of France, are so many rich mines from which we can draw treasures of Legislation.[180]

The Louisiana Legislature then ordered that the revision of the Digest of 1808 be printed and distributed, and ultimately the Louisiana Code took effect in 1825.[181] It went on to influence many codification endeavors across the globe due to its inclusion in the legislative concordances of Saint-Joseph and García Goyena and because copies were circulated to other jurisdictions.[182] The Louisiana Code offers an example of a codification endeavor that had an impact on the provisions of subsequent civil codes and linked the three dimensions: global, Latin American, and pan-American.

The expansion period of codification in North America was exemplified by the enactment of the 1866 civil code of Lower Canada (Quebec Code). Codification came as a natural and logical development in Quebec due to the latter's legal heritage and the success that the codification paradigm had had in France.[183] The ordered presentation of private law in the Quebec Code put an end to the "legal Babel"[184] that had previously existed, whilst aiming to

179 "Resolutions," in *Acts Passed at the Second Session of the Fifth Legislature of the State of Louisiana* (New Orleans: J. C. de St. Romes, 1822), 108.

180 E. Livingston, W. H. Byrnes, L. Moreau Lislet, P. Derbigny, and J. H. Tucker Jr., "Preliminary Report of the Code Commissioners: Dated February 13, 1823," in Louisiana Legal Archives, vol. I–II (New Orleans: Thos. J. Moran's Sons, 1937), lxxxv–xcv, at lxxxix.

181 "An Act Directing the Revision of the Civil Code and the Projected Codes of Commerce and of Procedure to Be Printed," in *Acts Passed at the First Session of the Sixth Legislature of the State of Louisiana* (s.l.: s.n., 1823), 68–71, at 68.

182 See generally Parise, *Historia de la Codificación*.

183 J. E. C. Brierley, "Reception of English Law in the Canadian Province of Quebec," in M. Doucet and J. Vanderlinden (eds.), *La réception des systèmes juridiques. Implantation et destin* (Brussels: Bruylant, 1994), 103–37, at 116.

184 D. Howes, "La domestication de la pensée juridique québécoise," *Anthropologie et Sociétés* 13(1) (1989), 103–25, at 109.

determine the private laws of Quebec.[185] It blended long-lasting civil law principles that could be traced back centuries with those shaped by rationalistic and liberal values derived from the Enlightenment,[186] and included elements of canon, English, French, and Roman laws as well as local provisions.[187] The codifying commission was composed of judges, who took leave during the drafting period. Chaired by René-Edouard Caron, it also included Augustin-Norbert Morin and Charles Dewey Day.[188] The commissioners undertook a critical examination of local and foreign laws, and they valued tradition, jurisprudential theory, and their own intuitive understanding of optimal provisions.[189] The sources of the Quebec Code were many, and the text reflected the law that had applied in the territory until its enactment.[190] The reports drafted by the commissioners referred to more than 350 different authorities and offer a convenient way of determining the sources of each provision.[191] Together with an internal memorandum by Caron, they show that the commissioners worked with an array of local and foreign sources (e.g., English law, Roman law, Scots law, US law), but drew above all on French materials.[192] The Louisiana Code played a prominent role, but as a model for form and language rather than substance.[193] The commissioners also looked into decisions adopted by local courts, and did not limit themselves to a single source for their normative transfers.[194] In their first report, they wrote

185 J. E. C. Brierley and R. A. Macdonald, *Quebec Civil Law: An Introduction to Quebec Private Law* (Toronto: Montgomery, 1993), 24; D. Howes, "La domestication," 109; and J. E. C. Brierley, "Quebec's Civil Law Codification: Viewed and Reviewed," *McGill Law Journal* 14 (1968), 521–89, at 542.

186 Brierley and Macdonald, *Quebec Civil Law*, 35.

187 E. Arroyo i Amayuelas, "From the Code Civil du Bas Canada (1866) to the Code Civil Quebecois (1991), or from the Consolidation to the Reform of the Law: A Reflection for Catalonia," in H. L. MacQueen, A. Vaquer, and S. Espiau Espiau (eds.), *Regional Private Laws and Codification in Europe* (Cambridge: Cambridge University Press, 2003), 267–87, at 272.

188 Brierley and Macdonald, *Quebec Civil Law*, 27.

189 J. W. Cairns, "Employment in the Civil Code of Lower Canada: Tradition and Political Economy in Legal Classification and Reform," *McGill Law Journal* 32 (1987), 673–710, at 709.

190 P. Mignault, "Le Code Civil de la Province de Quebec et son Interpretation," *The University of Toronto Law Journal* 1 (1935), 104–36, at 108; J. Richert and S. Richert, "The Impact of the Civil Code of Louisiana upon the Civil Code of Quebec of 1866," *Revue juridique Thémis de l'Université de Montréal* 8 (1973), 501–20, at 506.

191 Brierley, "Quebec's Civil Law," 552; and F. H. Lawson, *A Common Lawyer Looks at the Civil Law* (Ann Arbor: University of Michigan Law School, 1955), 50.

192 See the breakdown of sources in Brierley and Macdonald, *Quebec Civil Law*, 28, n. 96. See generally Cairns, *Codification, Transplants and History*. See also Brierley, "Quebec's Civil Law," 552.

193 Richert and Richert, "The Impact of the Civil Code," 518.

194 M. Karpacz, "La Cour d'appel et la rédaction du Code Civil," *Revue juridique Thémis de l'Université de Montréal* 6 (1971), 513–34, at 534. On the sources of the Quebec Code in general, see Cairns, *Codification, Transplants and History*.

> [we] have tried to avoid [acknowledged faults], and have sought for the means of doing so in the original sources of legislation on the subject, in the writings of the great jurists of France as well under the modern as the ancient system of her law, and in the careful comparison of these with the innovations which have been introduced by our local legislation and jurisprudence, or have silently grown up from the condition and circumstances of our population.[195]

The earlier statement of the commissioners reaffirms the broad approach they had to sources when writing their code for Quebec. In addition, it makes evident that commissioners were drafting a set of laws for a specific society at a specific time, hence they considered the particularities of their inhabitants and context.

Codification should not be deemed solely a success story, however, as already mentioned earlier. When focusing on the pan-American dimension, the efforts of David Dudley Field offer an example of codification endeavors that were not adopted in their place of conception. Field, influenced by the works of Jeremy Bentham, was the preeminent advocate for codification in the United States of America during the mid-nineteenth century.[196] After drafting a project of a civil code and four other code projects for the State of New York in the period 1847–1865, Field became one of the greatest proponents of codification in North America.[197] Many consider him the father of codification in the US and deem his *Project of a Civil Code for the State of New York* (the Project) of great importance for codification at that time.[198] The Project was presented by Field and Alex W. Bradford before the New York Legislature in February 1865. It had notes for two-thirds of its sections (articles), including references to, amongst others, related court decisions, revised statutes, the *Code Napoléon*, and the Louisiana Code.[199] Even though the Project never

195 *Civil Code of Lower Canada: First, Second and Third Reports* (Quebec: George E. Desbarats, 1865), 6.

196 S. Herman, "The Fate and the Future of Codification in America," *American Journal of Legal History* 40 (1996), 407–37, at 422. See generally R. Batiza, "Sources of the Field Civil Code: The Civil Law Influences on a Common Law Code," *Tulane Law Review* 60 (1986), 799–819.

197 Herman, "The Fate," 422; and C. M. Cook, *The American Codification Movement: A Study of Antebellum Legal Reform* (Westport: Greenwood Press, 1981), 187.

198 Cook, *The American Codification Movement*, 187.

199 See *The Civil Code of the State of New York. Reported Complete by the Commissioners of the Code* (Albany: Weed, Parsons & Co., 1865), ix. See also Batiza, "Sources of the Field Civil Code," 803. For example, the note to Chapter 2, Title 3, Part 4, Division 2 stated: "The provisions of this chapter, except § 455, are similar to those of the Code Napoleon and the Code of Louisiana." *The Civil Code of the State of New York*, 136. See also Herman, "The Fate," 423.

became law in New York (it was vetoed twice by the governor), its eight drafts and eighteen partial corrections were very influential.[200] For example, its provisions about the law of contracts were adopted by California, North Dakota, South Dakota, Georgia, Idaho, and Montana.[201] Moreover, during the early 1870s, the Californian code commissioners provided annotations in their work that significantly replicated the glosses by Field.[202] Field's Project also offers an example of the pan-American circulation of legal ideas: It served as a source for the codification works of, among others, Vélez Sarsfield, who had a copy of the Project in his private library.[203]

Closing Remarks

Codification as a legal paradigm developed during the nineteenth century in three dimensions: global, Latin American, and pan-American. It developed in different ways in different territories, combining with the prevailing ideologies in specific societies. Section 5.2 has shown that codification was shared by a legal community at a certain time and place but was also seen as part of scholarly debates that extended across continents and indeed around the globe. As pointed out by Ramos Núñez, codification triggered a scientific revolution that resulted in the generation of a consensual model that modified the historical perspective of the juridical community in Latin America and beyond. Accordingly, it can be claimed that codification broke with a previous consensual understanding in the law and as a result became a new paradigm.

The global dimension of codification was primarily traced to Europe in Section 5.2. There, an early and favorable environment existed for the development of this new legal paradigm. Codification experienced three periods in Europe during the nineteenth century. The first period, of foundation, was marked by the enactment of the French *Code* and the Exegetical School that emerged around that seminal corpus of private law. The impact of that code found very few barriers across the globe. The second period, of expansion, saw the proliferation of numerous codes, many building on the French

200 H. M. Field, *The Life of David Dudley Field* (New York: Charles Scribner's Sons, 1898), 88; and Anonymous, *Extracts from Notices of David Dudley Field* (New York: s.n., 1894), 39.

201 Herman, "The Fate," 425.

202 R. Parma, "The History of the Adoption of the Codes of California," *Law Library Journal* 22 (1929), 8–21, at 19.

203 See R. D. Rabinovich, "Alrededor del muy mencionado y poco conocido proyecto de código civil para el estado de Nueva York," *Revista de Historia del Derecho* 22 (1994), 279–87, at 279; Levaggi, *Dalmacio Vélez Sarsfield*, 196; and *Catálogo de la Donación de Vélez Sarsfield* (Córdoba: Biblioteca Mayor, 1980), 83.

antecedent. A "veneration" of codes had developed by that time and was likewise fueled by the studies on comparative legislation. The expansion period allowed for codes to be considered synonyms of state law. The third period, of differentiation, was closely related to the promulgation of the German Civil Code, which was able to distinguish itself, both in form and substance, from previous codes. It is worth noting that the global dimension of the codification paradigm extended beyond the nineteenth century. Future studies that extend their scope to the following centuries should look at the recurrent revision, de-codification, and re-codification experiences that took (and continue to take) place across the globe.

The Latin American dimension of codification showed the "veneration" of these *corpora* of private law during the nineteenth century. Two factors characterized the specific development of codification in the region: It developed mainly during the second half of the nineteenth century, and it was shaped by the interaction of European and local products. The history of codification in Latin America can be better understood by placing the enactments of codes within two periods. The first period, of foundation, started with the adoption of the Chilean code, even though previous codes had been enacted in the region. The influence of the Chilean text in Latin America can be compared only to that of the French code. In contrast to the latter, however, the Chilean code did not need to travel by means of translations. It, therefore, became a blueprint that facilitated the rapid expansion of codification in Latin America during the second half of the century.

For the second period, of expansion, Section 5.2 looked at the Argentine code, which showed once more that codes in the region benefited from both European and American sources. Abortive efforts are also part of the story of codification. A Latin American example of this was the codification work by Teixeira de Freitas for Brazil. However, even though it failed in its country of conception, his work was of paramount importance for other codification efforts that were able to benefit from its provisions. There was an overarching motivation for codes in Latin America with the intention to project a sense of differentiation between Europe and the Americas, between former dependent territory and metropole. Finally, this dimension engaged with the "culture" of the code that developed in Latin American jurisdictions. By that time, codes had come to be considered repositories of legal science and had gained a place of preeminence in, amongst other forums, the writings of scholars and the curricula of law schools.

Exploring the pan-American dimension showed that codification as a legal paradigm was not restricted to a specific space, to specific actors, or to specific legal systems. Concerning the latter, two codification case studies in mixed jurisdictions were explored. A key enactment during the foundation period was the civil code of Louisiana. Though it was initially conceived as a means to preserve that state's distinctive legal heritage, it also had a pan-American impact. The Louisiana Code reached Latin America not only due to the common Spanish past but also as a consequence of its inclusion in Saint-Joseph's and García Goyena's legislative concordances. The 1866 code of Quebec, another mixed jurisdiction, served as an exemplary case study for the expansion period. The use of sources was eclectic there, too, hence replicating the entanglements that were observed in Section 5.2 both for the Latin American and the global dimensions.

Codification, too, should not be considered a fairy tale moving toward a happy ending. The efforts of Field, one of the paramount champions of codification in the US, failed in his home state of New York. Like the drafts of Teixeira de Freitas, however, they proved to be successful in other states, both in the US and beyond, demonstrating once more that the shared paradigm of codification encouraged the circulation of legal ideas across continents. A look at the personal papers and private libraries of individual codifiers can help trace the circulation of legal ideas and the development of the codification paradigm during the nineteenth century.[204]

It is tempting to speak of an "enchantment" of nineteenth-century codification.[205] Section 5.2 pointed to a "veneration," to a "contagion," and to a "culture" of the codes. All these expressions aim to characterize a period in which the codification paradigm extended across Latin America, while at the same time being part of a global movement nurtured by the circulation of legal ideas. There were indeed three dimensions for codification, and they were all interconnected. This section also pointed to the fact that paradigmatic shifts do not occur overnight, and events that shape a paradigm can run in parallel in different parts of the globe. The insights presented in this section showed some of the traits that explain the paradigmatic shift brought by codification in Latin America and beyond. It was part of a larger process: a process that took place across the globe, building on ideas that were deemed universal at that time, and enabling the adaptation of the law to the needs of specific societies at specific periods.

. . .

204 See, for example, A. Parise, "A Translator's Toolbox: The Law, Moreau-Lislet's Library, and the Presence of Multilingual Dictionaries in Nineteenth-Century Louisiana," *Louisiana Law Review* 76 (2016), 1163–184.

205 See, for example, Weiss, "The Enchantment of Codification."

5.3 Contestations and Exclusions

MONICA DANTAS AND ROBERTO SABA

By the mid-1820s, all continental Spanish and Portuguese American colonies had achieved independence. Most had to endure long and bloody wars, and none got there without a fight. A few decades later, seventeen countries occupied the former colonial territories of Spain and Portugal, only two with frontiers similar to those they had at the beginning of the century, Chile and Brazil. Even in these two cases, the outcome of the independence process cannot be taken as the culminating point of state formation, not least because one must consider that constructing a state meant asserting its sovereignty over people as well as territory. No longer *los pueblos* or *os povos* (the peoples, in plural form) of colonial times, members of natural sovereign communities and corporations, but an abstract people, a nation composed of autonomous – and hopefully self-reliant – individuals. These new polities would ideally be composed of individuals equal before a man-made law who consented to being governed by nationally chosen authorities, which in turn were elected by all men qualified to vote. They would form a homogeneous nation made up of equal and free citizens (see also Chapter 4 and Sections 5.1 and 6.1).

For several reasons, all the above was easier said than done in Latin America. To begin with, unlike their European counterparts, all new Latin American states had to assert their sovereignty over pluri-ethnic populations. In some areas, indigenous people comprised over half of the population. Elsewhere, indigenous groups for all purposes ruled their own communities. Additionally, if theoretically freedom and equality were at the heart of these new nation-states, many countries still held large, enslaved populations, African-born or of African descent. Their "masters" thought they could do as they wished with their (human) property, states tried to regulate such relations, and enslaved persons constantly fought back, asserting their humanity at every turn. To further complicate things for nation builders, centuries of colonialism created an enormous population of free but for the most part destitute people. These were men and women who were neither enslaved nor indigenous but very often had African and Amerindian ancestry. They were variously called *mestizos*, *cholos*, *zambos*, *mulatos*, or *pardos*. Often landless and unskilled, they were for the most part not attached to any corporate body that had previously shaped Latin America. Even those who inhabited the cities and towns of Latin America and sometimes enjoyed corporate privileges suffered major setbacks when governments implemented new policies devised to develop a market economy and build a national society of (so-called) equals.

The fledgling nation-states of nineteenth-century Latin America were caught between the principles of equality and freedom, on the one hand, and the necessity to maintain order, on the other. Political elites forged laws and institutions designed to be homogeneously applied to all free persons, regardless of race or class, but they very often failed to do so. Different sectors experienced laws and institutions differently. And, in general, this new top-down order ended up harming indigenous, enslaved, and free poor communities. Homogenizing and individualizing forces threatened community values and survival strategies, they upended family and kinship ties, and often detached disadvantaged people from their homes and their lands. Therefore, nineteenth-century Latin America witnessed the outbreak of a myriad of contestations – more or less organized (and more or less violent) popular movements that pushed back against liberal ideals and policies.

Attempts to homogenize the nation and create a polity of individuals often backfired as disadvantaged communities recovered older (colonial) customs and manipulated newer (national) laws to assert their own agendas. Throughout the nineteenth century forces from below unsettled elite projects of state-building. They organized, petitioned, sued, marched, conspired, and (not infrequently) rioted. Sometimes these fierce struggles to protect their ways of life or create alternative ones lasted for decades. Yet towards the end of the century, they were defeated. Modernizing political elites coalesced with the transnational forces of industrial capitalism. Overwhelmed by the productive and destructive machinery at the service of the state, the poor and people of color were transformed into second-class citizens, excluded from the body politic, and made available for exploitation by capital and manipulation by political elites.

Indigenous America and the National Order

After the demographic collapse of the early colonial period, the indigenous population of Latin America grew during the eighteenth century and continued to do so in the nineteenth century, reaching over thirty million by the 1850s. In some countries, like Bolivia and Guatemala, indigenous people made up over 50 percent of the population, whereas in others they were less than 10 percent. Indigenous ways of life varied greatly according to political, social, cultural, economic, and environmental factors. Some were part of small groups who mixed agriculture with foraging and tried to steer clear from outsiders. A great number lived in settled peasant communities.

Although they cherished self-sufficiency, they could – and did – engage in exchanges with *criollos* and *mestizos*. Yet other indigenous peoples formed horse-riding and cattle-raising communities with expansive trading networks that controlled vast territories.

A renewed process of imperial expansion took place in the nineteenth century. Eager to acquire territories and markets and afraid of falling behind in the imperial race, European powers brutalized indigenous peoples in Africa, Asia, and Oceania. Although Latin America was freeing itself from European colonialism, indigenous people bore the brunt of the process of nation building there. No matter how and where indigenous communities lived, they posed a problem for the political elites who were trying to build nation-states in Latin America: How to integrate them into the new polities that professed equality before the law and sought to create a homogenous body of citizens? In colonial times, indigenous communities had inhabited a distinct political space, which the Spanish called *república de indios*. Imbued with liberal ideas, postcolonial leaders sought to unify the *res publica*. But for decades they saw most of their efforts frustrated. Indigenous people manipulated the new laws to maintain cohesive and independent communities. Not until the last quarter of the nineteenth century, when global economic forces reconfigured social and political arrangements in Latin America, did political elites succeed in breaking the back of resistant indigenous communities.

Land and Power

The revolutionary leaders of nineteenth-century Latin America envisioned nations in which all adult males (except enslaved persons), regardless of ethnicity, would be equal before the law. Indigenous men should be able to work and save money as individuals, become property owners, and exercise their rights as citizens. The new countries abolished the caste system and the special courts which had dealt separately with indigenous issues in colonial times. As the historian David J. Weber explains, these measures "represented the momentary triumph of classical liberalism, an ideology that sought to limit the power of the state and promote the liberty of the individual." As abusive as it had been, however, colonial rule had provided indigenous communities with a certain degree of stability and autonomy, exempting them from conscription, the Inquisition, and tithes. By revoking corporate institutions, the new nation-states created new forms of inequality and oppression. "In practice, these liberal measures left Indian communities vulnerable to rapacious non-Indian neighbors," Weber clarifies. "Stripped of their special legal status, Indians gradually lost control of their communal governments and communal resources, including mission lands."[206]

While some political leaders proposed – and sometimes carried out – the extermination of whole indigenous communities, most adopted an assimilationist approach. In their reformist drive, however, politicians of the independence era sought to erase indigenous cultures, absorbing these populations into the body of a homogeneous nation.[207] An exponent of Latin American liberalism, the Brazilian statesman José Bonifácio de Andrada, wrote in 1823 that the Brazilian government should work on introducing in indigenous villages "whites and mulattos already adapted in order to mix the races, connect reciprocal interests with our people, and make them all into one single body with the nation, stronger, instructed, and entrepreneurial."[208]

Although property requirements existed in most countries, many indigenous men could now vote for their representatives, and some were eligible to hold office. Following through with their liberal project, the new governments simultaneously removed restrictions preventing *mestizos* and *criollos* from inhabiting indigenous villages and participating in local politics. Progressively, outsiders came to dominate municipal governments. In the former Spanish colonies, the new *ayuntamientos* (town council) absorbed the colonial *pueblos de indios* – which had provided indigenous communities with autonomy to manage resources and decide collective matters. In Brazil, until 1875 the *câmaras municipais* (municipal councils) had no jurisdiction over indigenous territories (the *aldeamentos* created by the Portuguese Crown); yet they often disregarded the boundaries of such lands and distributed them to settlers in *emphyteusis*.[209]

Concomitantly, the constitutional governments abolished the tribute which the metropoles had extracted from indigenous communities in the colonial period. This was the fundamental step, they calculated, towards making former vassals of European monarchs into members of the new nations. Analyzing the actions of José de San Martín in Peru, the historian

206 D. J. Weber, *Bárbaros: Spaniards and Their Savages in the Age of Enlightenment* (New Haven: Yale University Press, 2005), 264.

207 A. Escobar Ohmstede, "Del dualismo étnico colonial a los intentos de homogeneidad en los primeros años del siglo XIX latinoamericano," *Alteridades* 28 (2004) 21–36.

208 J. B. de Andrada e Silva, "Apontamentos para a civilização dos índios bravos do Império do Brasil," in M. Dolhnikoff (ed.), *Projetos para o Brasil* (São Paulo: Companhia das Letras, 1998). Unless otherwise mentioned, all translations are by the authors.

209 For recent comparative approaches to the political history of indigenous communities in Latin America, see I. de Jong and A. Escobar Ohmstede (eds.), *Las Poblaciones Indígenas en la Conformación de las Naciones y los Estados en la América Latina Decimonónica* (Mexico City: El Colegio de México, 2016).

Nils Jacobsen notes: "If the state relinquished interest in the community as a source of revenue, then in the future it would have no reason to protect and guarantee its internal social and agrarian order. Abolition of tribute was thus a prerequisite for disestablishing common usufruct of land in the *ayllus*."[210] Simón Bolívar, Vicente Guerrero, and other revolutionary leaders thought the same way.

The emergence of industrial capitalism in the North Atlantic region and the consequent expansion of market relations triggered relentless pressures to privatize land and other natural resources in the nineteenth century. Latin American political elites, who actively participated in this global movement, came to see communal lands held by indigenous peoples as unproductive wastelands, bastions of backwardness in a rapidly developing global commercial order. Consequently, they sought to break these lands up into individual plots. Some imagined that indigenous men would become smallholders, owning land in fee simple, cultivating their plots with the help of family members (and perhaps some hired hands), and paying property taxes. Others were interested in the full commodification of land and the emergence of a free (and cheap) labor market, which would give birth to dynamic export economies. Communal lands would be auctioned off to the highest bidders – anyone who had the capital to improve them. The reformers reckoned that land privatization would not only foster commercial agriculture throughout Latin America but also make indigenous men into self-reliant and independent citizens, free from the tutelage of tribal or religious leaders.[211]

In the nineteenth century, a myriad of grassroots movements took shape in response to the expansion of imperialism and capitalism. From Australia to China, from South Africa to the American West, indigenous peoples resisted new laws that threatened their ways of life. Such movements were not pre-political uprisings of ignorant folk guided by messianic leaders. On the contrary, they were strategic actions carried out by people who had been trying to shape the modern world in the best way they could, using any tools available to them. In Latin America, when confronted with the expansion

210 N. Jacobsen, "Liberalism and Indian Communities in Peru, 1821–1920," in R. H. Jackson (ed.), *Liberals, the Church, and Indian Peasants: Corporate Lands and the Challenge of Reform in Nineteenth-Century Spanish America* (Albuquerque: University of New Mexico Press, 1997), 128.

211 M. T. Ducey, "Liberal Theory and Peasant Practice: Land and Power in Northern Veracruz, Mexico, 1826–1900," in R. H. Jackson (ed.), *Liberals, the Church, and Indian Peasants: Corporate Lands and the Challenge of Reform in Nineteenth-Century Spanish America* (Albuquerque: University of New Mexico Press, 1997); D. Marino, "Reformas estatales y estructuras indígenas. Los derechos de propiedad en México Central, norte de Argentina y sur de Bolivia, 1810–1910," *Boletín Americanista* 79 (2019), 151–72.

of liberal, modernizing nation-states, indigenous groups neither rejected the new legislations outright nor embraced them blindly. They acted according to local circumstances and adjusted their responses to the political reality of the fledgling Latin American countries. When facing encroachment by *criollos* or *mestizos*, indigenous communities could either manipulate the discourse of equal rights that the new regimes promoted or reframe the corporate privileges that colonial governments had granted them. Usually, the two approaches went hand in hand. Throughout the continent, indigenous people employed an array of strategies to preserve their way of life, from sabotage to petitioning, from judicial battles to armed rebellion. Although the law put state authorities in charge of communal resources, for decades indigenous communities resisted takeover – fiercely when necessary – retaining traditional forms of land management and resource distribution.[212]

In places where they made up a large section of the population, indigenous people relied on local authorities such as *prefectos*, *jueces auxiliaries*, and *jefes políticos* to advance their interests. Some indigenous men – usually those who held traditional posts of authority within their community – got elected to *ayuntamientos*. Historians have also found evidence of parallel indigenous councils that emerged alongside the *ayuntamientos* and performed a dual function: taking care of the internal affairs of the community and mediating the relations between indigenous people and government officials.[213] In many parts of Latin America, indigenous communities could elect *apoderados* to represent their interests in court and before the government. These legal representatives, usually well-articulated and well-connected indigenous men, oversaw issues that affected their communities, such as land leases and debts. Many *apoderados* soon transcended their legal roles and became political leaders capable of establishing alliances with other – indigenous, *mestizo*, or *criollo* – leaders.[214]

212 See, among others, T. Schaefer, *Liberalism as Utopia: The Rise and Fall of Legal Rule in PostColonial Mexico, 1820–1900* (New York: Cambridge University Press, 2017); B. Larson, *Trials of Nation Making: Liberalism, Race, and Ethnicity in the Andes, 1810–1910* (Cambridge: Cambridge University Press, 2004).

213 J. A. Fernández Molina, "De tenues lazos a pesadas cadenas. Los cabildos coloniales de El Salvador como arena de conflicto politico," in S. Herrera Gómez and M. Gómez (eds.), *Mestizaje, poder y Sociedad: Ensayos de historia colonial de las provincias de San Salvador y Sonsonate* (San Salvador: Flacso, 2003), 73–96.

214 P. Mendieta Parada, "Caminantes entre dos mundos: los apoderados indígenas en Bolivia (siglo XIX)," *Revista de Indias* 46(28) (2006), 761–82; L. B. Rodríguez, "El sistema de representación de indígenas en la transición a la república: los apoderados de la comunidad de Colalao y Tolombón en perspectiva comparative," in I. de Jong and A. Escobar Ohmstede (eds.), *Las Poblaciones Indígenas en la Conformación de las Naciones y los Estados en la América Latina Decimonónica* (Mexico City: El Colegio de México, 2016); A. Guerrero, "La coutume et l'État: Curagas et lieutenants politiques à Otavalo (Équateur) au XIXe siècle," *Annales: Économies, Sociétés, Civilisations* 47(2) (1992).

Holding on to their communal values, indigenous communities often manipulated the very laws that had been designed to privatize their lands. Community leaders or organized groups pulled resources to buy land. In theory, these landholdings became private property, but in practice, they continued to belong to the community. Indigenous people continued to treat rivers, lakes, swamps, and forests as inalienable commons. Further complicating things for reform-minded elites for decades after independence, in many parts of Latin America local authorities lacked the resources (such as police forces, census data, and land surveys) to enforce laws privatizing communal lands.[215]

Indigenous leaders were also able to establish alliances with *caudillos*, powerful political and military leaders who ruled much of Latin America during the nineteenth century. They favored *criollos* who would not interfere with their customs and offered them gifts (like cattle and manufactured goods), which indigenous communities considered tributes that the settlers owed them. Many fought side by side with their *caudillo* allies, helping them expand their power and territory. The Argentine liberal reformer Domingo Faustino Sarmiento was horrified to see the rancher Juan Manuel de Rosas ally himself with indigenous warriors to expand his power over the South American grasslands. "To intimidate the countryside," Sarmiento claimed, Rosas had "brought into the southern forts some savage tribes whose caciques were under his command."[216] Leaders like Rosa thrived in the first half of the nineteenth century because they managed to preserve the corporate logic of colonial times. As Sarmiento's bitter testimony made clear, this world was very distant from the national order that reform-minded leaders had devised at the time of independence.[217] Yet, contrary to what liberals like Sarmiento sought to argue, Latin America was no exception in the nineteenth century. The process of state building was not a straightforward process. Armed groups like the samurai in Tokugawa Japan, the Cossacks in Tsarist Russia, and the frontiersmen in the western United States challenged attempts of political centralization. Attempts to subject these groups to a national or an imperial order extended for decades.

War and Peace

In their struggle to establish legitimacy and pacify their (claimed) territories, the national governments shaped and bent and sometimes ignored or

215 J. Gutiérrez Ramos, "Comunidades indígenas, liberalismo y estados nacionales en los andes en el siglo XIX," *Anuario de Historia Regional y de las Fronteras* 4(1) (1998), 295–317.

216 D. F. Sarmiento, *Facundo: Civilization and Barbarism* (Berkeley: University of California Press, 2003 [1845]), 223.

217 On Rosas's policies, see J. Lynch, *Argentine Dictator: Juan Manuel de Rosas, 1829–1852* (Oxford: Clarendon, 1981).

even annulled their own laws in response to the actions of indigenous people. Often it was in the best interest of the nation-state to preserve the independence of indigenous communities. In some areas, like the dense forests of the Amazon Valley, the indigenous population lived too far away from any settler community to trouble the powers that be. In the Andes, where indigenous communities were the majority and elites faced devastating and costly wars, *criollo* and indigenous leaders struck a bargain. Driven by their need for funds, national authorities re-established the tribute that had been abolished by the founders. In exchange, tribute-paying indigenous communities received guarantees that secured their autonomy. To collect any tributes, Latin American states often had to rely on indigenous leaders themselves. Short on options, local authorities reached agreements with indigenous communities that resembled the privileges and exemptions of colonial times.[218]

In other regions, for example, the arid lands of northern Mexico or southern Chile and Argentina, indigenous groups such as the Comanches and the Mapuches had been expanding their territory, and in general behaving like land-based empires, since colonial times. In addition to indigenous weapons and military strategies, they relied on tools introduced by European colonizers and their descendants – like the horse and firearms – to mount formidable armies and defend their sovereignty. Especially in frontier areas, independent groups conducted raids on farms, ranches, and villages, and denied state officials access to their territories.[219] Indigenous peoples such as the Tobas and Wichí, who lived in the Chaco region between Bolivia and Argentina, manipulated state borders to their own advantage.[220] In some instances, indigenous groups took advantage of the presence of other (stronger) powers in order to resist struggling Latin American nation-states. Relying on trade and diplomatic relations with British Honduras, the Mayas of lowland Yucatán ruled the republic of Chan Santa Cruz from the 1840s to the 1890s and waged outright war against Mexico.[221] Latin America was not the only region to experience the phenomenon of indigenous peoples forming their own states and keeping intruders under control: the Sokoto Califate in West Africa and the

218 E. D. Langer, "Indigenous Independence in Spanish South America," in J. Tutino (ed.), *New Countries: Capitalism, Revolutions, and Nations in the Americas, 1750–1870* (Durham: Duke University Press, 2017), 361.

219 J. Bengoa, *Historia del Pueblo Mapuche. Siglos XIX y XX* (Santiago: Lom, 2000); P. Hämäläinen, *The Comanche Empire* (New Haven: Yale University Press, 2008).

220 E. D. Langer, "The Eastern Andean Frontier (Bolivia and Argentina) and Latin American Frontiers: Comparative Contexts (19th and 20th Centuries)," *The Americas* 59(1) (2002), 33–63.

221 N. A. Reed, *The Caste War of Yucatán*, rev. ed. (Stanford: Stanford University Press, 2001).

Kingdom of Hawaii in the Pacific are two among many examples. In time, colonizers would employ brutal tactics alongside outright fraud to dispossess indigenous communities. Yet the process was not foreordained, and for decades indigenous powers demonstrated that they were able to take control of their own political destinies.

At a loss on how to pacify independent indigenous groups, some Latin American political leaders resorted to treaties, which amounted to recognizing that the indigenous peoples formed their own autonomous nations within the territories claimed by constitutional governments. Carrying on a tradition from colonial times, the political elites of the Pampas and Araucanía engaged in *parlamentos* with indigenous powers, which culminated in peace treaties and the recognition of indigenous sovereignty over sprawling territories. Following legal principles common to both parties, indigenous and *criollo* leaders promised to *honrar la palabra dada* (honor the given word). Indigenous powers maintained embassies in the capital cities of Chilean and Argentine provinces. Indigenous leaders such as Juan Calfucurá – a Huilliche *cacique* who led his people to migrate from Araucanía to the Pampas – rose to prominent positions, being recognized by Chilean and Argentine authorities alike.[222]

Mexican authorities also did what they could to negotiate with, rather than fight against, independent indigenous groups. In 1822, the Comanche Capitán Guonique attended the coronation of Agustín de Iturbe in Mexico City and signed the *Tratado entre el Imperio Mexicano y la Nación Comanche*. In this treaty, Mexico granted the Comanches duty-free trade, recognized their right to capture wild horses near Mexican settlements, invited Comanche youths to study in Mexico City, and asked Comanche leaders to return Mexican prisoners (excepting those who wished to stay – whatever this meant). Article 4 in particular elucidated Mexico's (fragile) reliance on Comanche power on the northern borderlands: the Comanche Nation "will not allow any nation" – indigenous, American, or European – "to penetrate Mexico through its territory, resisting it with arms and warning the [Mexican] Emperor." National as well as local republican leaders who assumed control after the fall of Emperor Iturbide continued to negotiate with the Comanches.[223]

Diplomatic arrangements, however, only brought temporary truce. For decades indigenous powers demanded the continuation of the Spanish policy of gift-giving. Bolivia's federal government paid yearly duties to Chiriguano

222 On Mapuche diplomacy, see P. M. Herr, *Contested Nation: The Mapuche, Bandits, and State Formation in Nineteenth-Century Chile* (Albuquerque: University of New Mexico Press, 2019).

223 Hämäläinen, *Comanche Empire*, 191.

leaders from the 1830s through the 1860s. In certain areas, ranchers paid grazing fees known as *yerbaje* to indigenous groups.[224] Yet more often than not the new republics lacked the means to satisfy indigenous demands. Indigenous sovereigns switched alliances when governments failed to pay and did not hesitate to attack former allies. Mexico, which was struggling to keep internal conflicts under control in the 1830s, had no funds to spend on pacifying its vast northern territories. Comanche and Lipan Apache bands attacked *criollos*, *mestizos*, and sedentary indigenous communities. US Democrats led by President James K. Polk pointed to the Mexican inability to curb indigenous raids to justify the annexation of Texas and wage war on Mexico in the 1840s.[225]

At a loss on how to control the borderlands, leaders of the still young republics looked to the recent past, emulating the Spanish colonizer they had fought only recently. Aware that the central government did not have enough resources to impose its will on the Llanos of Venezuela and eastern Colombia, Simón Bolívar encouraged the establishment of Catholic missions there.[226] Similarly, President Antonio López de Santa Anna invited Jesuits (who had been expelled in 1767) to return to Mexico in 1843 and establish missions among Comanches and Apaches.[227] However, these efforts failed to pacify independent indigenous nations. As they had done in colonial borderlands, indigenous peoples took whatever advantages missionaries had to offer and used them to carry on with their resistance against settler encroachment.

Not all indigenous groups, however, had the power to protect themselves the way the Mapuches did against Chile and the Comanches against Mexico. And whenever settlers and state officials could bypass (their own) national laws in order to brutalize indigenous peoples, they did so without hesitation. Given the opportunity, military leaders such as José Gaspar Rodríguez de Francia of Paraguay would readily wage genocidal assaults against indigenous villages. Two Swiss naturalists who visited the Río de la Plata basin in the 1820s were astonished by what they saw: "These savages are now treated as ferocious beasts: war without quarter is made on them: they are relentlessly killed, whether they appear as friends or enemies."[228] In Brazil, a law passed in 1831 banned the colonial practice of abducting and enslaving

224 E. D. Langer, *Expecting Pears from an Elm Tree: Franciscan Missions on the Chiriguano Frontier in the Heart of South America, 1830–1949* (Durham: Duke University Press, 2009), 33.

225 B. DeLay, "Independent Indians and the U.S.-Mexican War," *American Historical Review* 112 (2007), 35–36.

226 Weber, *Bárbaros*, 268.

227 D. J. Weber, *The Mexican Frontier, 1821–1846: The American Southwest Under Mexico* (Albuquerque: University of New Mexico Press, 1982), 50.

228 J. R. Rengger and M. Longchamps, *The Reign of Doctor Joseph Gaspard Roderick de Francia in Paraguay* (London: T. Hurst, E. Chance, 1827), 52–53.

"hostile Indians". Yet indigenous slavery endured for decades thereafter, even close to the capital city. In the late 1840s, a British traveler noted that "Indians appear to be enslaved as much almost as negroes, and are bought and sold like them. In Rio a large number are made merchandise of."[229] The enslavement of indigenous people extended beyond Latin America. As the historian Andrés Reséndez demonstrates, Anglo-American settlers enslaved thousands of indigenous North Americans in the Trans-Mississippi West before the Civil War. The California Gold Rush brought this kind of exploitation to its cruelest.[230]

Violence against indigenous communities intensified by the middle of the nineteenth century, when Latin American nation-states tried once again to implement the anti-corporate vision of the independence period and passed a series of laws designed to convert communal tenancy into private property and transform indigenous peasants into a mobile workforce for commercial agriculture and mining. Some reformers thought that such a process of privatization would attract European immigrants to Latin American countries, advancing a process of *blanqueamiento* (whitening). Again, indigenous people resisted through legal and extra-legal means, and in any case, local officials rarely had the means to implement such legislation. Reformers and legislators in the national capitals felt frustrated with the lack effectiveness of such measures. Yet the new laws set the stage for a profound transformation that would soon materialize.[231]

The Second Conquest

In the last third of the nineteenth century, Latin America went through what historians call a "second conquest." Fueled by transformations in the centers of industrial capitalism, exports boomed. Commodity production expanded and intensified in Latin America as countries like Great Britain, the United States, and Germany demanded coffee, sugar, cacao, henequen, banana, wheat, beef, rubber, guano, nitrate, copper, tin, and other raw materials.

229 T. Ewbank, *Life in Brazil: Or, a Journal of a Visit to the Land of the Cocoa and the Palm* (New York: Harper & Brothers, 1856), 323. See also, Y. Miki, *Frontiers of Citizenship: A Black and Indigenous History of Postcolonial Brazil* (Cambridge: Cambridge University Press, 2019).

230 A. Reséndez, *The Other Slavery: The Uncovered Story of Indian Enslavement in America* (Boston: Houghton Mifflin Harcourt, 2016).

231 I. Figueroa, "Legislación marginal, desposesión indígena, civilización en proceso: Ecuador y Colombia," *Nómadas* 45 (2016), 43–57; C. A. Murgueitio Manrique, "El proceso de desamortización de las tierras indígenas durante las repúblicas liberales de México y Colombia, 1853–1876," *Anuario de Historia Regional y de las Fronteras* 20 (2015), 73–95.

Investments flowed from urban centers (within and without the continent) into rural areas. Railroads and steam navigation expanded rapidly from the coastal regions to the interior. The process of land privatization sped up and the demand for labor exploded. Local and foreign entrepreneurs found it unacceptable that indigenous communities continued to dedicate themselves to their own subsistence lifestyle rather than commercial activities. In response, legislators passed laws, codes, and regulations coercing indigenous peoples to provide workers for private enterprises.[232]

Albeit reliant on wage labor in the most developed economies, the global hegemony of industrial capitalism created a boom in unfree labor relations in peripheral economies. In El Salvador until the late 1870s, indigenous communities owned over one quarter of all lands, much of which was ideal for coffee cultivation. Under the modernizing reign of President Rafael Zaldívar, anybody could take over uncultivated lands provided that he planted at least one-quarter of it with coffee. Subsequently, new laws abolished *ejidos* (communal lands) and forced indigenous peasants into serving as *colonos*, or resident laborers, on the lands now appropriated by major planters.[233] A similar process took place in Guatemala. The *jefes políticos* came to play a central role, mediating between the coffee planters, who informed them of their labor needs, and the indigenous communities. Often, these state authorities were staffed by members of planter families who thus profited greatly from this system of exploitation. Debt peonage and the infamous *enganche* – a form of debt bondage – re-emerged in Guatemala and other parts of Latin America. Vagrancy laws and convict labor also became a means to force indigenous people to work for agricultural, construction, and mining entrepreneurs.[234] Similar to El Salvador and Guatemala, other parts of the Global South experienced a resurgence of indentured labor in the last decades of the nineteenth century. The kidnapping and enslavement practice of "blackbirding" in the South Pacific, for example, brutalized South Sea Islanders and helped develop sugar plantations in British Australia.

232 S. Topik and A. Wells (eds.), *The Second Conquest of Latin America: Coffee, Henequen, and Oil during the Export Boom, 1850–1930* (Austin: University of Texas Press, 1998).

233 A. Lauria-Santiago, *An Agrarian Republic: Commercial Agriculture and the Politics of Peasant Communities in El Salvador, 1823–1914* (Pittsburgh: University of Pittsburgh Press, 1999).

234 R. Falcón, "'No tenemos voluntad de ir al trabajo forzado…': una comparación de los nexos entre indígenas y jefaturas políticas en México y Guatemala (segunda mitad del siglo XIX)," in I. de Jong and A. Escobar Ohmstede (eds.), *Las Poblaciones Indígenas en la Conformación de las Naciones y los Estados en la América Latina Decimonónica* (Mexico City: El Colegio de México, 2016).

Wars of extermination, which had been devastating indigenous peoples the world over since the early modern era, came to a head in the second half of the nineteenth century. The Lakotas in the United States, the Zulus in South Africa, and the Boxers in China are just a few examples of local groups that were annihilated by the new industrial weapons of western powers. Armed intervention brought longstanding indigenous struggles to bloody endings in Latin America as well. In 1878, President Nicolás Avellaneda spoke to the Argentine Congress promising "the conquest, sooner rather than later, by reason or by force, of a handful of savages that destroy our principal wealth and impede us from definitively occupying, in the name of the law, of progress, and of our own security, the richest and most fertile territories of the Republic."[235] Between 1879 and 1884 the Argentine army waged total war against the Mapuches and other indigenous groups in the so-called Conquest of the Desert. The few survivors were subjected to programs of "regeneration," which consisted in dissolving their tribal governments, prohibiting them from speaking their native languages, and forcing them to perform hard labor. Following the model of the US Homestead Act of 1862, the Argentine government took indigenous lands and distributed them to ranchers and farmers.

Chile followed a similar path beginning in the mid-1880s, as soon as the War of the Pacific ended. Reduced to living in reservations, the descendants of the indigenous groups who had ruled southern Chile for centuries became an oppressed caste in the 1900s. Meanwhile, *criollo* settlers – reinforced by a large immigration wave from Europe – increased their domains and promoted the idea of an all-white Chile.[236] Although Bolivia had lost the War of the Pacific and faced a major political crisis, the Bolivian government also waged war against independent indigenous communities. The army established forts and colonies all over the Chaco region in the 1880s, whence soldiers hunted down Chiriguanos, Tobas, and Wichí, who were allegedly stealing cattle. In 1892 an uprising led by Apiaguaiki Tumpa broke out among the Chiriguanos and faced brutal retaliation. Thousands of Chiriguano men were murdered and thousands of Chiriguano women and children were sold into slavery in Sucre and Santa Cruz.[237]

235 N. Avellaneda cited in C. R. Larson, "The Conquest of the Desert: The Official Story," in C. R. Larson (ed.), *The Conquest of the Desert: Argentina's Indigenous Peoples and the Battle for History* (Albuquerque: University of New Mexico Press, 2020), 21.

236 J. Bengoa, "Chile Mestizo; Chile Indígena," in D. Maybury-Lewis, T. Macdonald, B. Maybury-Lewis, (eds.), *Manifest Destinies and Indigenous Peoples* (Cambridge: Harvard University Press, 2009), 133.

237 Langer, "Eastern Andean Frontier," 51.

By the turn of the century, industrial capitalism spread its destructive tentacles even into the heart of the Amazon. Fueled by the demands of manufacturers of shoes and tires, the rubber economy took over the Brazilian, Ecuadoran, Bolivian, and Peruvian Amazon. Traveling these regions in 1904–1905, the Brazilian journalist Euclides da Cunha described the violent campaigns to capture indigenous workers for rubber extraction: "This wilderness has seen an incalculable number of small battles in which tiny but well-armed groups have overthrown entire tribes, abruptly sacrificed because of the primitiveness of their arms and by their own valor in mounting head-on attacks against the repeating fire of carbines."[238] Terrorized into working in rubber extraction, indigenous laborers lived in abject conditions. They were forced to acquire overpriced food and supplies from the extractive companies and consequently soon fell into debt. And debt transformed them into peons. Ravaged by famine, disease, and torture, whole Amazonian indigenous communities succumbed. Rubber extraction also wreaked havoc elsewhere around the turn of the century. The indigenous inhabitants of the Congo Basin suffered similar forms of enslavement, torture, and genocide under the rule of the Belgian king as did the indigenous peoples of the Amazon Valley.

Perhaps more than any of his contemporaries, the modernizing dictator of Mexico Porfirio Díaz succeeded in defeating independent indigenous groups and attracting foreign investment. Beginning in 1882, Mexican authorities collaborated with US agencies to attack the Apaches and Comanches, seeking to restrict them to reservations. Long neglected, the northern Mexican states opened their doors for North American corporations interested in investing in railroads, agriculture, ranching, and mining.[239] The modernizing policies of the Porfiriato also brought suffering to indigenous people in the southern regions. After decades of war against the Mayas, Mexico was able to crush the Chan Santa Cruz movement, and Mexican settlers established profitable plantations in Yucatán. Two visitors to the state described the slave-like condition of the Mayas who labored in henequen fields: "Yucatan is governed by a group of millionaire monopolists whose interests are identical, banded together to deny all justice to the Indians, who, if need be, are treated in a way an Englishman would blush to treat his dog."[240]

238 E. da Cunha, "The Caucheros," in L. Sá, *The Amazon: Land without History* (New York: Oxford University Press, 2006), 56–57.

239 S. Truett, *Fugitive Landscapes: The Forgotten History of the U.S.–Mexico Borderlands* (New Haven: Yale University Press, 2006).

240 C. Arnold and F. J. T. Frost, *The American Egypt: A Record of Travel in Yucatan* (New York: Doubleday, Page & Company, 1909), 329.

Autonomous indigenous communities lost access to resources all over Latin America during the second conquest. The combined forces of the nation-state and (transnational) capital broke the back of communities that had long resisted the intrusion of alien interests in their territories. Often subjected to violence and assaulted by exploitative economic practices, they lost the capacity to rule their own destinies. While a few groups were able to retreat to isolated or unwelcoming regions, most became people without a country in their own ancestral lands.

Slavery in the Age of Freedom

By the middle of the nineteenth century, some four million enslaved Africans and enslaved people of African descent lived in Latin America. Most of them worked on sugar and coffee plantations, but enslaved workers were also essential for many other economic activities, including mining, ranching, logging, domestic work, construction, transportation, and all sorts of urban trades. The influx of enslaved Africans persisted in Latin America – especially in Brazil and Cuba – until the 1850s. Moreover, throughout the nineteenth century, enslaved men and women were transported from declining economic regions to new economic frontiers in Latin America.

Slavery presented a blatant contradiction to the claims of political elites that they were building nations based on ideals of freedom and equality. Enslaved persons' political actions made the contradiction all the more evident. Authorities encountered difficulties in regulating the master-slave relationship; slaveholders clearly showed their dissatisfaction at attempts by the state to improve the situation for the enslaved persons. Furthermore, European powers – with Great Britain at the forefront – were growing hostile to the institution and using the abolitionist cause to intervene in other countries' affairs. As enslaved men and women continued to fight against bondage, economic transformations and the emergence of new classes with new sensibilities spread an attitude of antislavery to different sectors of Latin American societies. Antislavery forces used legal and extra-legal means to confront the institution. It was a long struggle, but by the end of the nineteenth century, slavery had vanished in the hemisphere.

Gradualism and Regulation

As the wars of independence dragged on, "El Libertador" Simón Bolívar freed his enslaved workers and lamented the attitude of some of his fellow-revolutionaries: "It seems to me madness that a revolution for freedom expects to maintain slavery."[241] Slaveholding interests notwithstanding, war needs would shake the foundations of slavery in Latin America. Military commanders, lacking manpower and resources to pay free men, resorted to recruiting enslaved men. Often these recruits had no choice, being press-ganged by revolutionary armies. Yet the wars presented positive incentives as well. The perspective of attaining freedom lured enslaved men to join the revolutionary forces. Moreover, the independence struggle provided them opportunities to retaliate for past abuses, demonstrate loyalty to a leader or a homeland, assert their humanity and masculinity, make money, attain social influence, and even establish a career in the military.[242]

Yet despite the vital contribution of enslaved men to the cause of Latin American independence, only Chile, Mexico, and the United Provinces of Central America abolished slavery in the first years of independence. The Haitian occupying forces liberated enslaved persons in the Dominican Republic in 1822. Under Bolívar's rule, Gran Colombia passed a free womb law liberating all children of enslaved mothers born from July 1821 onward, but only after they reached the age of eighteen. The government also set up a manumission fund based on an inheritance tax. In the 1830s, however, the successor states of Colombia, Ecuador, and Venezuela slowed down the process of emancipation. Among other things, they imposed apprenticeship periods on the children of enslaved persons, which could extend until the age of twenty-six. A similar pattern emerged in Peru and Bolivia. Slaveholders often circumvented the laws, manumission funds dried up, and slavery thrived in plantation and mining areas. Only in the 1850s would these countries end slavery. Slavery persisted in Paraguay and Puerto Rico until the 1870s and in Cuba and Brazil until the 1880s.[243]

While Latin American masters insisted on their right to do as they wished with enslaved men and women, torturing them at will, the nineteenth-century Latin American state – imbued with enlightened ideas – sought to regulate these relations. More so than in the antebellum United States, where the doctrine of states' rights guaranteed that proslavery interests would avoid regulation from the central government, in Latin America the nation-state would directly intervene in master-slave relations. Brazil's 1830 Criminal Code sought to place the state in charge of punishing crimes committed by enslaved

241 S. Bolívar in P. Blanchard, "The Language of Liberation: Slave Voices in the Wars of Independence," *Hispanic American Historical Review* 82(3) (2002), 514.

242 P. Blanchard, "The Slave Soldiers of Spanish South America: From Independence to Abolition," in C. L. Brown and P. D. Morgan (eds.), *Arming Slaves: From Classical Times to the Modern Age* (New Haven: Yale University Press, 2006), 257–58.

243 H. S. Klein and B. Vinson III, *African Slavery in Latin America and the Caribbean* (Oxford: Oxford University Press, 2007).

persons, for example, by making judges responsible for determining the number of lashes – not exceeding fifty per day – that could be dealt. The state nonetheless made clear that its interventions were designed to protect public order and the lives of free persons. The same code determined the punishment for enslaved persons involved in insurrections: "Penalties – to the leaders – of death for the maximum degree; of perpetual *galés* [forced labor] for the medium; and of fifteen years for the minimum; – to all others – flogging."[244]

Brazilian masters also had the option of sending their enslaved workers to be punished in state-funded prisons. James Cooley Fletcher, an American missionary who lived in Brazil in the 1850s, observed that "[o]ne department of the *Casa da Correcao* is appropriated to the flogging of slaves, who are sent thither to be chastised for disobedience or for common misdemeanors." No matter how much the state tried to provide the means of controlling the enslaved population, however, Brazilian – and other Latin American – slaveholders did not give up their private punishments. "There are private floggings; and some of the most common expiations are the tin mask, the iron collar, and the log and chain," Fletcher continued.[245]

Although slavery persisted, all former Spanish colonies moved to abolish the transatlantic slave trade. Political elites saw in this act a means to gain British favor and recognition. The countries that remained under Spanish rule adopted a different path. In 1817, Spain had signed a treaty with Great Britain abolishing the slave trade to the colonies. The treaty was supposed to take effect in 1820, but the number of enslaved Africans entering Cuba and Puerto Rico only increased thereafter. In 1835, recognizing that the first treaty was ineffectual, the two empires signed a new one. Nevertheless, the slave trade continued to increase. Anglo-Americans – from the northern as well as the southern states – played a central role in this illegal trade. US authorities not only behaved leniently towards US nationals trafficking human beings to Cuba but got directly involved in the slave business. US consuls in Havana made lots of money providing sea letters (a kind of license for vessels and cargo) to traffickers, and the senator for Rhode Island James DeWolf made a fortune through the trade.[246]

244 V. Chieregati Costa, "A punição pela morte no Código Criminal do Império do Brasil: debates parlamentares e concepções jurídico-políticas na positivação das leis penais" in M. Duarte Dantas (ed.), *Da Corte ao Confronto. Capítulos de História do Brasil Oitocentista* (Belo Horizonte: Fino Traço, 2020).

245 D. P. Kidder and J. C. Fletcher, *Brazil and the Brazilians, Portrayed in Historical and Descriptive Sketches* (Philadelphia: Childs & Peterson, 1857), 131.

246 A. F. Corwin, *Spain and the Abolition of Slavery in Cuba, 1817–1886* (Austin: University of Texas Press, 1968); Leonardo Marques, *The United States and the Transatlantic Slave Trade to the Americas, 1776–1867* (New Haven: Yale University Press, 2016).

Despite the Law of November 7, 1831, stating that "all the slaves who enter the territory or ports of Brazil, coming from abroad, are free," Brazil imported over one million enslaved Africans from the time of independence to the early 1850s. The 1831 law became known as the *lei para inglês ver* (law for the British to see) – both a cruel joke and an act of defiance. Henry A. Wise, a major slaveholder from Virginia who served as the US Minister to Brazil in the 1840s, was appalled to see how powerful the traffickers had become in Rio de Janeiro. "It is not to be disguised nor palliated," he wrote to the US Secretary of State in 1845, "that this Court as well as this whole country is deeply inculpated in that trade.... Thus, the Govt itself is in fact a slave trading Govt against its own laws and treaties."[247] Only in 1850, after several diplomatic tensions unsettled Anglo-Brazilian relations, did Brazil terminate the transatlantic slave trade.[248]

Resistance and Rebellion

The British were not the only ones fighting slavery in Latin America. Enslaved persons themselves were the fiercest enemies of the institution. Wherever slavery persisted, enslaved men and women continued to use tactics inherited from colonial times in order to resist: slowing down work, appropriating goods, forming family and kinship ties, preserving and reinventing religious practices, absconding, building and protecting so-called maroon communities of formerly enslaved Africans and their descendants, accumulating resources to buy their freedom, organizing strikes and other demonstrations, and using violence against masters, overseers, or other abusers. As national and provincial capitals grew, enslaved persons found more opportunities to escape farms and plantations and hide among the anonymous masses. Moreover, as the judicial apparatus developed in postcolonial Latin America, numerous enslaved men and women went to court to sue their masters for negligence or brutalization. They incorporated the new language of national interests and citizenship rights into their pleas. Although an uprising like the Haitian Revolution never materialized in Latin America, generations of enslaved persons built a culture of resistance that undermined the system.

Enslaved persons and their allies insisted on using the laws that Latin American slaveholders tried to circumvent. Colombia, for example, established

247 H. A. Wise to J. Buchanan, Rio de Janeiro, December 9, 1846, in W. R. Manning (ed.), *Diplomatic Correspondence of the United States, Inter-American Affairs, 1831–1860* (Washington: Carnegie Endowment for International Peace, 1932), vol. II, 370.

248 L. Bethell, *The Abolition of the Brazilian Slave Trade: Britain, Brazil and the Slave Trade Question, 1807–1869* (Cambridge: Cambridge University Press, 1970).

manumission *juntas* in charge of liberating "honorable and industrious" slaves. Yet, as the historian Yesenia Barragan demonstrates for the northern parts of the Pacific lowlands of Colombia, publicly funded manumissions were scarce. Between 1821 and 1846, the *juntas* freed only seventeen persons in the region. In response to this poor outcome, enslaved persons pulled resources together and negotiated with masters and government officials to purchase their own freedom. "The acquisition of freedom papers was a public act," Barragan explains. "Enslaved lowlanders faced the notary, their master or masters, any family member or individual who paid for their freedom, two or three witnesses, and, in more contentious cases, the *procurador municipal* (municipal attorney)."[249]

Similarly, after seceding from Gran Colombia, Ecuadoran legislators cut the taxes that contributed to the manumission fund and made the process of self-purchase more difficult. But enslaved persons fought back. Soon the port city of Guayaquil, the key location of the Ecuadoran cacao trade, became a hub of antislavery activism. Runaways from the countryside as well as from the city found hiding places among friends, family, and others allies. Flight was dangerous, however, often leading to persecution and other unpredictable harm. Many enslaved Ecuadorans therefore used legal means to liberate themselves. They petitioned the *junta*, manipulating the language of citizenship rights to request more effective action from the authorities. They further protested that the manumission funds were depleted, and the manumission *junta* was nonoperational.[250]

If, on the one hand, enslaved persons made use of the law when they saw it could help them, on the other, they chose to flaunt regulations that hurt their interests. Slave mobility in Puerto Rico is a case in point. A legal instrument designed to protect slaveholding interests, the 1826 Slave Code comprised provisions ordering the arrest and jailing of any enslaved person who left the plantation without their master's permission. The code nonetheless legalized the customary right of enslaved persons engaging in productive activities in their free time and accumulating *peculio* (any amount of money), which could eventually be used for *coartación* (buying their freedom). Enslaved Puerto Ricans tended to their gardens and livestock, marketing their surplus outside their master's plantations. Others engaged in odd jobs for employers other than their masters. Enslaved men and women in Puerto Rico took

249 Y. Barragan, *Freedom's Captives: Slavery and Gradual Emancipation on the Colombian Black Pacific* (Cambridge: Cambridge University Press, 2021), 207.

250 C. Townsend, "In Search of Liberty: The Efforts of the Enslaved to Attain Abolition in Ecuador, 1822–1852," in D. J. Davis (ed.), *Beyond Slavery: The Multilayered Legacy of Africans in Latin America and the Caribbean* (Lanham: Rowan & Littlefield, 2007), 56.

advantage of the 1826 code when it came to their right to save money but often disregarded it when moving around to make such money.[251]

In some instances, enslaved persons strove to make unwritten customs into rights, and at times they succeeded. In Cuba, the uncodified practices of *coartación* and *pedir papel* (request paper to seek a new owner) endured in the nineteenth century. Enslaved men and women used such customary rights in cases the slaveholders failed to provide for their well-being or abused them. Yet, since these practices were only customary, their effectiveness depended on the views and whims of the slaveholders, who usually considered them an attack on their interests. Enslaved persons were not afraid to litigate, however, and judges were forced to consider what entitlements masters and their enslaved workers had under Spanish legal customs (see Section 1.4). In 1842, largely thanks to enslaved persons' persistence, the new Spanish *Reglamento de Esclavos* made these customary rights into law. Hence, the state acquired the power to decide whether enslaved people could purchase their freedom or find new masters.[252]

Enslaved persons also acted in ways reminiscent of indigenous groups, manipulating national borders to their own advantage. In southern Brazil, they took advantage of political tensions that were brewing in the neighboring country. The *Guerra Grande* in Uruguay (1839–1851) brought about military incursions, raiding campaigns, and intensive military recruitment – including that of enslaved men. The Colorado government of Montevideo, in desperate need for troops, abolished slavery in 1842. Four years later the Colorados' enemies, the Blancos, also proclaimed abolition to attract new recruits. Brazilian authorities calculated that some 900 runaways were living across the border in 1850. Soon slave catchers from Rio Grande do Sul began crossing the border and recapturing fugitives on Uruguayan soil. Some of these returnees, however, went to court to reclaim their freedom, arguing that the law of 1831 had made it illegal to introduce enslaved persons in Brazil.[253]

The court was just one of the arenas in which enslaved men and women fought for freedom. Inspired by a mass social movement in the English metropole and the activism of enslaved persons in the West Indian colonies, the British Empire abolished slavery in 1833. Soon abolitionism spread to other countries, and the United States – the largest and richest slave society in the

251 L. A. Figueroa, *Sugar, Slavery, and Freedom in Nineteenth-Century Puerto Rico* (Durham: University of North Carolina Press, 2005).

252 A. de la Fuente and A. J. Gross, *Becoming Free, Becoming Black: Race, Freedom, and Law in Cuba, Virginia, and Louisiana* (New York: Cambridge University Press, 2020), 173.

253 K. Grinberg, "Slavery, Manumission and the Law in Nineteenth-Century Brazil: Reflections on the Law of 1831 and the 'Principle of Liberty' on the Southern Frontier of the Brazilian Empire," *European Review of History* 16(3) (2009), 402.

world – found itself engulfed in a divisive debate over the expansion of slavery. Inspired by these major fissures in the Atlantic slave system, some enslaved communities in Latin America moved to overthrow the governments that kept them in chains. One of the most radical antislavery movements of the era took shape in northeastern Brazil. Enslaved Muslims in Salvador, Bahia, embraced the Islamic concept of Jihad (struggle or effort) to try to free themselves. In January 1835, during the Ramadan, some 600 Hausas and Yorubas organized an armed rebellion. They planned to establish an Islamic Califate and impose Sharia law in South American territory. The National Guard crushed the uprising and dozens of rebels were executed. Masters and other sectors of the free population panicked, and authorities redoubled their vigilance. In June 1835, parliament passed a law determining that enslaved persons who killed their masters, overseers, or their families would receive the death penalty. Article 2 clarified that insurrection would also be punished by death.[254]

The fear of a possible slave rebellion also rocked Cuba. After small and large uprisings took place in Matanzas and Cárdenas in 1843, authorities found out about a conspiracy planned for Christmas day. In blatant disregard of legal procedures, authorities tortured thousands of men and women who might have taken part in or known about the conspiracy. Writing for the *Knickerbocker* magazine in 1845, an American observer explained how the conspiracy got its name, "La Escalera": The rebels were taken to a room in which "stood a bloody ladder, where the accused were tied, with their heads downward, and whether free or slave, if they would not avow what the fiscal officer insinuated, were whipped to death by two stout mulattoes selected for this purpose."[255] State terror spread, affecting free as well as enslaved persons of color. Some three thousand persons were executed or died due to mistreatment. Slaveholders blamed the 1842 *Reglamento de Esclavos*, arguing that it had subverted the institution of slavery by making customs into laws and interfering in private master-slave relations.[256]

254 J. J. Reis, *Slave Rebellion in Brazil: The Muslim Uprising of 1835 in Bahia* (Baltimore: Johns Hopkins University Press, 1993); M. Barcia, "An Islamic Atlantic Revolution: Dan Fodio's Jihād and Slave Rebellion in Bahia and Cuba, 1804–1844," *Journal of African Diaspora Archaeology and Heritage* 2(1) (2013). Although Yorubas were responsible for one of the most dramatic slave insurrections in Brazil, many other smaller – but by no means less radical – movements drew on Bantu religious practices. See, for example, F. dos Santos Gomes, *Histórias de quilombolas. Mocambos e comunidades de senzalas no Rio de Janeiro, século XIX* (São Paulo: Companhia das Letras, 2006) and R. Figueiredo Pirola, *Senzala insurgente. Malungos, parentes e rebeldes nas fazendas de Campinas, 1832* (Campinas: UNICAMP, 2011).

255 "Letters from Cuba," *The Knickerbocker: Or, New-York Monthly Magazine*, July 1845.

256 A. Ferrer, *Cuba: An American History* (New York: Simon & Schuster, 2021), 104.

Many other conspiracies took place in Latin America. Although most ended up like La Escalera, crushed before even begun, they pushed authorities into regulating slavery more closely. And, as scholars have recently shown, the enactment of new codes, laws, and regulations created political opportunities for enslaved persons and other antislavery forces to organize.[257] Afraid of "other Haitis" and willing to do anything to preserve their wealth and power, slaveholders and authorities ramped up punitive measures. Yet in the second half of the nineteenth century, a liberal wave originating in the 1848 European movements for democracy and the Union triumph in the American Civil War swept Latin America. Enslaved persons increasingly gained support from sectors of the working and middle classes, and the agitation to end slavery could no longer be contained.

Abolition

By the 1850s, emancipation laws and enslaved persons' own efforts had gradually chipped away at the institution of slavery in most countries of Latin America. Whereas in Colombia, there had been some 54,000 unfree people at the end of the colonial period, that number shrank to 16,000 in 1851. Venezuela's enslaved population had dropped to almost half, from 64,000 in 1810 to 33,000 in 1854. Peru, where 89,000 human beings were held in chains in 1821, counted some 25,000 enslaved persons in 1854. The debate became not whether slavery should be ended but how to bring this about. Not surprisingly since they were champions of private property rights, the reformist governments of mid-century promised to compensate slaveholders but rarely had the means to do so.[258]

In the 1860s, a destructive civil war shattered the institution of slavery in the United States. War, a major force for legal changes throughout history, would also set the stage for the end of slavery in Latin America. When Brazil declared war on Paraguay, the government began to pay masters for slave recruits. Some enslaved men seized the opportunity, requesting that masters "sell" them to the government. Nearly 7,000 enslaved men served in the Brazilian Army during the Paraguayan War.[259] Dependent on the support of slaveholders, however, the Brazilian government did not pass any comprehensive act of emancipation during the war.[260]

257 A. Alonso, *The Last Abolition: The Brazilian Antislavery Movement, 1868–1888* (Cambridge: Cambridge University Press, 2021).

258 Klein and Vinson, *African Slavery*, 232.

259 H. Kraay, "Arming Slaves in Brazil from the Seventeenth Century to the Nineteenth Century," in C. L. Brown and P. D. Morgan (eds.), *Arming Slaves: From Classical Times to the Modern Age* (New Haven: Yale University Press, 2006), 169.

260 W. Peres Costa, *A Espada de Dâmocles: O Exército, a Guerra do Paraguai e a Crise do Império* (São Paulo: Hucitec, 1996).

However, the frustrating campaign against the Paraguayan dictator Francisco Solano López, which lasted much longer and was much bloodier than Brazilian elites had expected, rekindled political discussions about slavery and its effects on Brazilian society. When, scarcely one year after the end of the war, Prime Minister José Maria da Silva Paranhos, the Viscount of Rio Branco, proposed a free womb law to parliament, he stated that "I found myself [in Paraguay] ... amongst no less than 50,000 Brazilians, who were in touch with neighboring peoples, and I know for myself and through the confession of the most intelligent of them how many times the permanence of this odious institution in Brazil shamed and humiliated us before the foreigners."[261] On September 28, 1871, the so-called Rio Branco Law was ratified. It did not differ much from other free womb laws that had been implemented earlier in Latin America.

Spain's free womb law of 1870 was also a response to military conflict. As the Ten Year's War (1868–1878) unfolded across Cuba, enslaved persons in the eastern parts of the country – a region distant from the major plantation centers – ran away from their masters to join the rebel forces. Desperate for manpower, rebel leaders – some of whom were slaveholders – decided to end slavery in the regions they controlled. Soon the anticolonial cause and the antislavery causes became intertwined in Cuba.[262] Two years into the war, Segismundo Moret y Prendergast, Spain's minister of overseas provinces, reckoned that gradual emancipation legislation would show that the reform process could be controlled from above. However, this approach backfired. The Spanish Abolitionist Society and many rebellious Cubans thought the so-called Moret Law did not go far enough and asked for more.[263] Moreover, enslaved men and especially women proved themselves eager to use the law to seek freedom through the courts for themselves and their family and kin.[264]

Taking advantage of the conflict in the Spanish Antilles, Puerto Rican captives escaped en masse, and Spanish abolitionists concentrated their attacks on the island's labor system. In 1873, Spain ended slavery in Puerto Rico but stipulated that freedpeople would work for their former masters for an

261 J. M. da Silva Paranhos, speech at the Chamber of Deputies, July 14, 1871, in *Annaes do Parlamento Brazileiro. Câmara dos Srs. Deputados, Terceiro Anno da Décima Quarta Legislatura, Sessão de 1871*, (Rio de Janeiro: Typographia Imperial e Constitucional de J. Villeneuve, 1871), vol. III, 146.

262 A. Ferrer, "Armed Slaves and Anticolonial Insurgency in Late Nineteenth-Century Cuba," 310.

263 C. Schmidt-Nowara, *Slavery, Freedom, and Abolition in Latin America and the Atlantic World* (Albuquerque: University of New Mexico Press, 2011), 148.

264 C. Cowling, *Conceiving Freedom: Women of Color, Gender, and the Abolition of Slavery in Havana and Rio de Janeiro* (Chapel Hill: University of North Carolina Press, 2013), 61.

additional three years as compensation. Five years later, the Ten Years' War came to an end in Cuba. During the peace negotiations, Spanish commanders recognized that enslaved men who had joined the rebels in eastern Cuba were now free. Still, slavery remained entrenched in the sugar-producing western and central regions of the island.[265]

In 1880, pressured by the abolitionists' success in Puerto Rico and afraid of new rebellions in Cuba, Spain passed a law that made slaveholders into *patronos* and enslaved workers into *patrocinados*. Although labor relations changed little, the law established oversight *juntas*, gave *patrocinados* over the age of eighteen the right to receive "stipends" for their labor, protected enslaved families from separation, facilitated self-purchase, and – most significantly – established 1888 as the definitive date for total emancipation. But the abolitionists kept asking for more, and those workers that were still unfree took action. Some 11 percent of the *patrocinados* bought their own freedom, and about 7 percent were able to prove to the *juntas* that their *patronos* had disregarded the law and so attained their freedom. Two years before the date it had set, the government in Madrid yielded to the pressure and abolished slavery in Cuba.[266]

Brazil also faced great popular unrest around the question of slavery after the free womb law passed. Enslaved persons could now sue their masters for failure of registering them in a nationwide inventory or refusing to accept the registered value. The historian Celso Thomas Castilho observes that as the legal battles multiplied, they fundamentally undermined the authority of the slaveholders: "These lawsuits publicly exposed their owner's illegal maneuvers to evade the law; they injured their honor before their peers, and damaged their credibility before other slaves."[267] Enslaved persons' public actions made it into newspapers, inspired manumission ceremonies, strengthened abolitionist associations, and encouraged even more freedom suits.

In response to the general agitation, in 1884, Prime Minister Manoel Pinto de Souza Dantas of the Liberal Party presented a bill that would, among other things, free all captives who reached the age of sixty without compensation for their masters, fix slave prices, and expand the manumission fund. Accused of pandering to agitators, Dantas fell. The pragmatic Liberal Senator José Antonio Saraiva took his place to revise the bill. The new project made enslaved persons who reached the age of sixty work three more years to

265 Schmidt-Nowara, *Slavery, Freedom, and Abolition*, 149.
266 Schmidt-Nowara, *Slavery, Freedom, and Abolition*, 149–50.
267 C. T. Castilho, *Slave Emancipation and Transformations in Brazilian Political Citizenship* (Pittsburgh: University of Pittsburgh Press, 2016), 57.

compensate their masters and set slave prices above market values. Seeking to re-establish order, the revised bill determined that those who aided fugitives would be subjected to imprisonment.[268] The infamous "Law of the Sexagenarians," passed in September 1885, led the abolitionists to radicalize even further and adopt extra-legal means. Enslaved men and women took their destinies into their own hands. Violent clashes took place on plantations and in towns large and small. On May 13, 1888, Princess Isabel signed the so-called "Golden Law." Slavery was dead in the Americas.[269]

The struggle against slavery had been more than a fight against human bondage: it had also been a struggle for land, community, and the right to keep the fruits of one's labor. Like in Jamaica, where freedpeople sought to turn sugar plantations into food-producing farms controlled by the workers themselves, and in the United States, where they asked for "forty acres and a mule" during the Reconstruction period that followed the Civil War, freedpeople in Latin America envisioned a post-emancipation order in which they would enjoy community autonomy and personal safety. Yet as soon as they achieved formal freedom, the formerly enslaved suffered from the heavy hand of a state that sought to make them into a cheap source of labor. The black engineer and abolitionist André Rebouças related some dramatic events that took place in southeastern Brazil one year after emancipation. In Boituva, a town near the coffee-producing region of São Paulo, freedpeople settled on an abandoned farm, where they built shelter and began producing food for their subsistence. Coffee planters complained, and the police immediately attacked with utmost brutality. Two freedmen died and three were badly injured. The policemen burned their shacks, destroyed provisions, and evicted the survivors. Five days later, the police killed eight freedpeople twenty miles from there, in the town Tatuí. Rebouças was outraged: "It has been reported that on arrival they killed a couple of blacks and shot many others who, later, were found dead. Among the victims, there are two children who were burned inside a barn!!!"[270]

As slavery unraveled, Latin American elites – with varying degrees of success – sought to attract European immigrants. The newcomers not only expanded the workforce in rural areas but also were manipulated by Latin American governments seeking to whiten the population. Influenced by pseudo-scientific ideas about human races, Latin American political elites

268 R. E. Conrad, *The Destruction of Brazilian Slavery, 1850–1888* (Berkeley: University of California Press, 1972).
269 Alonso, *Last Abolition*.
270 A. Pinto Rebouças, "Imposto Territorial," *Revista de Engenharia* (1889).

were invested in diluting African blood. In addition to subjecting freedpeople and their descendants to eugenicist projects, Latin American elites would use racial ideas to deny them equality before the law. Even when legislation pretended to be colorblind, all over the hemisphere freedpeople and their descendants came to be treated as second-class citizens.

The Free Poor

In the aftermath of independence, Latin America was home to an extremely heterogeneous population. In some countries, indigenous peoples made up half of the population. In others, they had been decimated. In some, slavery had been abolished. In others, enslaved men and women amounted to one third of the population. But, in spite of these differences, all countries shared one feature: They contained an ever-growing number of free persons of various and mixed descents. And, in most parts, the vast majority of this free population was destitute.

For free men and women in Latin America, the post-independence reality promised a better future as national elites championed the establishment of constitutional governments supposed to rule over a body of citizens equal before the law. The process of state-building, however, left many promises and expectations unfulfilled. Not only was the rhetoric of equality and rights meant only for those considered capable of integrating the body politic – men of means, education, and preferably of European descent – but, as the majority painstakingly discovered, that same rhetoric eventually jeopardized their autonomy and livelihood.

As countries strove to ascertain control over boundaries and territories, and competing factions battled each other, the burdens of war fell harshly on the free poor. As governments and elites tried to make the most of expanding international markets, men and women were not only ousted from their lands but also forced into working for others under the most abhorrent conditions. Discourses of equality and elites' interests in profiting from a world market economy went hand in hand, and consequently, artisans and the urban free poor confronted a new reality in which former corporate privileges and many colonial policies that had guaranteed a moral economy no longer had a place. All over Latin America, the free poor tried to resist such changes, sometimes taking up arms. But even while they fiercely resisted change, governments fought back with even harsher laws in a process that eventually led to the criminalization of poverty.

Soldiers, Militiamen, and Guardsmen

In most of the Spanish American colonies, independence was achieved only after long wars, as is shown in Chapter 4. And even in Brazil, political separation came alongside violence. In most countries, independence did not put an end to armed conflicts – quite the contrary. For decades, men kept on fighting as different groups tried to seize control of the newly established states. Territorial disputes, not only among Latin American countries, but also against invading European or Anglo-American armies, also called for armed mobilization. And fighting wars – internal or external – meant gathering troops, more often than not engaging thousands of men. Such long-lasting belligerence had unforeseen consequences, not only for governments in the making but especially for those called to bear arms.

Professional armies recruited thousands of men, but citizen's guards (usually called civic or national guards or citizen's militias) also absorbed vast numbers of recruits. In Latin America, this type of militia only became a reality in the nineteenth century, but in parts of continental Europe – above all France – they dated back to the last decade of the previous century, when they were praised as the most appropriate force for free and equal men. In the 1780s, the Marquis of Condorcet did not mince his words with regard to standing armies. Such regular troops, he claimed, were incompatible with a "popular constitution." Praising the experience of the United States, he advocated that the citizens themselves should be the ones to bear arms, not professional soldiers. On the one hand, standing armies presented a threat to the sovereignty of the people and, on the other, having the citizens themselves fight for their homeland had the advantage of both "elevating the people's souls" and fostering their fondness for their country.[271] Condorcet did not live long enough to bear witness to such an experiment in his homeland. As for the United States, he was either unaware of or unwilling to acknowledge George Washington's troubles leading the so-called Continental Army.

In nineteenth-century Latin America, as previously in the United States and Revolutionary France, citizen's militias were supposed to include those with citizenship rights or, better, those who had the right to vote. All other men who did not fit the criteria were potential recruits for the professional army. Most were press-ganged and forced to serve for long periods of time. While these soldiers could and would be sent to different parts of a country, sometimes hundreds of miles away from their families, militiamen tended to be restricted to a relatively limited geographical area. Supposedly, this

271 Jean-Antoine-Nicolas de Condorcet, *Lettres d'un bourgeois de New-Haven à un citoyen de Virginie* (Paris: A. Condorcet O'Connor et M. F. Arago, 1847 [1787]), 72; Jean-Antoine-Nicolas de Condorcet, *Essai sur la Constitution et les fonctions des Assemblées provinciales, où l'on trouve un Plan pour la Constitution & l'Administration de la France* (1788), vol. I, 249–50.

restriction should make it possible for them to maintain their day-to-day activities. Furthermore, professional soldiers were subjected to corporal punishments, while militiamen should not be subject to such abuses. Chains of command also differed, as soldiers had to obey a clear hierarchical military structure imposed from the top, but militias generally could elect their officers – at least the lower ranks. Finally, whereas political rights were a necessary condition for becoming a militiaman, soldiers (unless granted a patent) were usually not allowed to vote.[272]

However, although in theory – and depending on place and time – these differences were clear-cut, in practice they tended to be blurred, and this was not a Latin American exception. According to the historian Hilda Sabato, "under special circumstances" militias could be "moved to more distant locations and assume extra duties that were not too different from those of the standing army."[273] Usually, that happened whenever the numbers in the professional armies were too low, or when governments were fighting a larger enemy contingent. But shortage of army personnel also led to the unlawful conscription of men not usually obligated to serve in the army, be it because they fulfilled the criteria for participating in the militia or because they were exempted due to their responsibility as upstanding breadwinners.

Some (often cruel) realities were shared by all who were called to serve. First, the threat of death, maiming, or permanent disability was always present. As stressed by the historian Juan-Carlos Garavaglia, from a handful of deceased in the so-called Battle of Ochomogo, in Costa Rica, to the hundreds of thousands who died during the Paraguayan War, "Hispanic-American wars left a trail of corpses."[274] However, serving presented yet other challenges beyond the bloody battles. Soldiers (and militiamen when fighting alongside the army) were supposed to receive pay for their services, even if a meager one. But financial constraints on governments, a widespread occurrence after the wars of independence and subsequent internal and external battles, led to continuous and long delays in payment. Furthermore, uniforms, guns, and ammunition were more often than not provided irregularly. As Chilean guardsmen in 1850 complained, this paucity of resources left them between a rock and a hard place. Failing to show up properly dressed was cause for punishment, but paying for their own uniforms could seriously harm their ability

272 H. Sabato, *Republics of the New World. The Revolutionary Political Experiment in 19th-Century Latin America* (Princeton & Oxford: Princeton University Press 2018), 92–97.

273 H. Sabato, *Republics of the New World*, 103.

274 J. C. Garavaglia, "Prólogo," in J. C. Garavaglia, J. Pro Ruiz, and E. Zimmermann (eds.), *Las Fuerzas de la Guerra en la construcción del Estado. América Latina, siglo XIX* (Rosário: Prósitoria Ediciones, 2012), 11.

to provide for their families.[275] To make things worse, even food provisions fell short. Recognizing this chaotic situation, a Mexican law from 1838 stipulated that whenever a soldier deserted because he had not been provided payment, barracks, food, or clothes, he should receive only mild punishment.[276]

Families were also deeply impacted by military service. Although breadwinners were not supposed to be drafted, many were. When that happened, petitions flooded the authorities, be they in charge of local, provincial, or central posts. Poor and often illiterate wives, mothers, and children – with the help of someone able to write – begged for their loved ones to be released, arguing that otherwise starvation and even death would be the family's fate. As families faced hardship, and authorities were usually deaf to their cries, many women and children chose to follow men to the battlefield. According to Garavaglia, some regiments in the pampa frontier in the mid-nineteenth century had as many soldiers as women and children.[277] In 1871, Alfredo d'Escragnolle Taunay, a Brazilian engineer who had served in the Paraguayan War, published an account of the 1867 Battle of Laguna in which he registered the impressive presence of soldiers' wives and widows. They marched behind the troops, on foot, carrying babies and toddlers, all marked by the "stigma of suffering and ultimate misery."[278] And although many states provided pensions, they were usually granted only to officers' families, despite the fact that foot soldiers and unpatented militiamen made up the vast majority of casualties.

Desertion plagued armed forces all over the western world. This was a lesson that Washington had already learned during the War of Independence, especially regarding the militias. It was a lesson that another Anglo-American general – Andrew Jackson – had to learn over and over again some decades later. French authorities were also plagued by this problem, beginning in the seventeenth century and extending into the next two centuries.[279] Latin America was no exception. The historian Claudia Ceja Andrade, writing

275 J. A. Wood, "Building a Society of Equals: the Popular Republican Movement in Santiago de Chile, 1818–1851," Ph.D. thesis, University of North Carolina (2000), 346.

276 A. Cacho Torres, "Entre la utilidad y la coerción. Los desertores: una compleja realidad del México independiente (1820–1842)," *Estudios de Historia Moderna y Contemporanea de México* 45 (2013), 48.

277 Garavaglia, "Prologo," 10.

278 A. d'Escragnolle Taunay, *A Retirada de Laguna*, trans. B. T. Ramiz Galvão, 3rd ed. (Brasília: Edições do Senado Federal, 2011 [1871]), vol. 149, 115.

279 C. E. Skeen, *Citizen Soldiers in the War of 1812* (Lexington: University Press of Kentucky, 1999); A. Forrest, *Conscripts and Deserters: The Army and French Society During the Revolution and Empire* (New York and Oxford: Oxford University Press, 1989); T. Hippler, *Citizens, Soldiers, and National Armies: Military Service in France and Germany, 1789–1830* (London and New York: Routledge, 2006).

about Mexico City from 1824 to 1859, points out that desertion was a pervasive reality for both the army and the militias. If most simply ran away, not once or twice but many times over the years, others, faced with future perils and the certainty of condemning their families to hopeless poverty, resorted to extreme measures. In order to be considered unfit for service – and being unable to present a doctor's affidavit stating a previous, debilitating condition (as those with better means were able to produce) – some of the poor chose to deliberately maim themselves. In 1842, a recruit used a machete to cut off four fingers on his right hand, an injury that led to his death after twenty days. Forty years later, a medical doctor registered that, among conscripted men, one common practice was to put a hand over a rifle and pull the trigger.[280]

As the historian Marisa Davio remarks in an article about Tucuman in the first half of the nineteenth century, the recurring legislation on desertion – common not only in Latin America but also in North America and Europe – must be understood as definitive proof of men's resistance to serving, whether in the army, militias, or guards. Depending on time and place, such regulations prescribed an array of different punishments, from corporal ones – such as lashes or even death – to property expropriation, further menacing the subsistence of one's family.[281]

Resistance to conscription sometimes led to full-fledged rebellion. On May 13, 1846, Juan Galán, commander of the "volunteers" of Tamaulipeco, Mexico, wrote a letter to Cirineo Monjarás of Sierra Gorda. Galán warned Monjarás that the Mexican government was trying to rally troops to fight the Texans. Among his reasons to advocate for general desertion, he referred to the slaughtering of Mexican troops in battle, specifically mentioning how officers behaved in such occasions: "As we bleed they [high-ranking officers] will be sleeping on their mattresses, and while they drink chocolate we'll be gunned down, dying in order for them to live."[282] The rebels of Sierra Gorda fought the government for over three years. Two decades later, in Argentina, when the national government declared war on Paraguay and ordered the provinces to recruit men to be sent to battle, an obscure peon of La Rioja,

280 C. Ceja Andrade, "Amanecer Paisano y dormir soldado … Resistencias frente al reclutamiento y el servicio militar em la ciudad de México (1824–1858)," *Estudios de Historia Moderna e Contemporánea de México* 55 (2018), 57–58.

281 M. Davio, "Vagos, traidores o desmotivados? Deserciones militares de sectores populares em Tucumán durante la primeira metade del siglo XIX," *Dimensión Antropológica*, 54 (2012), 29–49.

282 U. Ramírez Casas, "'Mientras los generales duermen.' Desobediencia militar y rebelión en Sierra Gorda durante el conflicto bélico entre México y los Estados Unidos, 1846–1849," *Estudios de Historia Moderna e Contemporánea de México* 60 (2020), 23.

in the words of the historian Ariel de La Fuente, "attacked the contingent destined for the Paraguayan front, liberated the draftees, and gathered a *montonera* [a paramilitary group] of around 500 gauchos."[283] Although not necessarily always involving that many people, attacks on those responsible for conscription were quite common in Latin America. Time and again, for most of the nineteenth century, local Brazilian authorities justified their inability to send recruits to war with the fact that local men – usually helped by family members and acquaintances – escaped local prisons or were forcefully taken from the custody of the armed forces.

The constant need for recruits – the "blood tribute" or "blood contingent," as it has been described in different countries on both sides of the Atlantic – not only threatened the daily lives of those who could be drafted but also the general economy. As early as 1824, the Buenos Aires press began publishing letters complaining of the disastrous impacts of a generalized state of war. One *labrador* (farmer) held the government responsible for the fact that crop yields were shrinking year after year. As more and more armed men were needed, and the best time for recruiters to find them was during the workday, many realized that regular occupations posed a threat to their well-being. Whenever workers heard rumors about conscription, they fled, hiding for days or weeks.[284] Such a practice extended across national borders and over decades. Yet brutal forms of recruitment persisted as wealthier men – planters, farmers, and cattle ranchers – had much to benefit from this ever-recurring menace to the poor.

Land and Labor

Amidst major social and political transformations, independence brought direct access to world markets for the young Latin American countries. The newly achieved commercial freedom impacted all new polities, although the timing and profitability differed from one region to another. Those less troubled by continuous warfare benefited earlier from the northern hemisphere's hunger for Latin American commodities. Yet even countries that faced, for decades, the negative impacts of war – which halted or severely diminished production, made investments more difficult, and often blocked access to fertile land – eventually found a place in the world market economy.

283 A. de la Fuente, *Children of Facundo: Caudillo and Gaucho Insurgency during the Argentine State-Formation Process (La Rioja, 1853–1870)* (Durham & London: Duke University Press, 2000), 12.

284 J. C. Garavaglia, "Ejército y milícia: los campesinos bonaerenses y el peso de las exigencias militares, 1810–1860," *Anuário IEHS* 18 (2003), 170.

As far as access to land was concerned, elite Latin Americans came up with effective strategies, from laws devised to abolish corporate communal property to outright expulsion (or even extermination) of indigenous peoples or the expulsion of squatters unable to produce proof of their landholdings. Although privatization (*desamortización*) of communal indigenous property had different impacts from region to region (as mentioned earlier), for the free poor in general privatization of Church or municipal property along with policies devised to sell public lands – the *baldios*, as they were called in Spanish America, or *terras devolutas* in Brazil – had dreadful consequences.

The privatization of Church property impacted different groups in different ways. First, as many poor tenants lived and labored on lands owned by secular clergy and, especially, regular orders, the process of privatization forced vast numbers of people out of their homes and from the land they tilled. Those who decided (or were forced) to stay faced harsher conditions imposed by the new, profit-driven proprietors. Despite the rhetoric of state responsibility for the welfare of its citizens, after these privatizations, the poor had to go without the many services and assistance once provided by the Church, such as hospitals, charitable facilities, and even schools. For a number of reasons, from lack of funds to lack of interest, governments failed to provide these. No wonder, then, that time and again the free poor in Latin America sided with the Church against the various government modernization efforts.[285]

The privatization of municipal communal property, on the other hand, not only impacted men and women who depended on this property to make a living, but also those who envisioned new municipalities as a means to be free from private landowners' control over their lives. According to the historian Maria Fernanda Barcos, in the province of Buenos Aires, legislation aimed at fostering the privatization of *ejidos* (municipal property) ultimately led many older occupants, mostly poor, to lose their right over the land.[286] In Mexico, the 1856 Lerdo Law and the privatization measures of the 1857 Constitution also took their toll on those who were not yet *vecinos* of a municipality (see Sections 3.3 and 5.1).[287] The historian Juan Carlos Sanchez Montiel points out

285 R. H. Jackson (ed.), *Liberals, the Church and Indian Peasants. Corporate Lands and the Challenge of Reform in Nineteenth-Century Spanish America* (Albuquerque: University of New Mexico, 1997).

286 M. F. Barcos, "Los ejidos de los pueblos a la luz del proceso de construcción del Estado, Guardia de Luján (Mercedes), 1810–1870," in J. C. Garavaglia and P. Gateau (eds.), *Mensurar la tierra, controlar el territorio. América Latina, siglos XVIII–XIX* (Rosario: Prohistoria Ediciones, 2011).

287 On *vecino* and *vecinidad*, T. Herzog, *Defining Nations: Immigrants and Citizens in Early Modern Spain and Spanish America* (New Haven: Yale University Press, 2003).

that many poor families who lived in *pueblos de hacienda* (small communities established on private lands) expected to be granted municipal status in order to escape the demands of private patrons while being guaranteed access to corporate lands that they could use as they saw fit (see Chapter 4). Privatization policies, though, meant that *pueblos de hacienda* converted into municipalities could no longer rely on corporate lands either to finance their new jurisdictional duties or provide for the livelihood of their inhabitants. The poor, unable to make ends meet, were forced to return to the status quo, despite their constant pleas to government authorities to be granted *ejidos*. In the end, their dependence on the landowners only got worse.[288]

In Brazil, prior to independence, most forests were deemed crown property. This custom remained in place after 1822. Since these woods could only be cut down by governmental order, usually to fulfill the demands of the naval industry, sugar planters, and other private entrepreneurs were kept at bay. The seventeenth-century introduction of Cayenne cane, whose bagasse could be used as fuel, mitigated the planters' problem. The free poor, on the other hand, relied heavily on crown forests. They not only foraged for food and fuel but also cleared small patches to grow manioc and other foodstuffs without attracting the authorities' prying eyes. But by the 1830s, when the liberals gained power and were able to further policies that weakened crown and corporate property, crown forests lost government protection and (as any other *terra devoluta*) could now be privatized. Forests located in land coveted for sugarcane expansion were the first to go. From 1832 to 1835, however, a major popular rebellion – which gathered together the free poor, indigenous peoples, and enslaved persons – shook the provinces of Alagoas and Pernambuco. One major grievance on the rebels' list was the slate of new liberal policies interfering with protected forests.[289]

Decades earlier, English authorities had faced similar widespread protests against policies regulating rights to the commons. Rural and urban folk fought for their customary rights to water, passages, grazing, gleaning, hunting small game, wood-gathering, and so on. Such rights, which had already been questioned in the previous century, came to the fore forcefully in the seventeenth century, both as targets of parliamentary enclosure acts and of new ideas regarding ownership. According to the influential historian E. P. Thompson,

288 J. C. Sanchez Montiel, "De poblados de hacienda a municípios en el Altiplano de San Luis Potosí," *Estudios de Historia Moderna e Contemporánea de México* 31 (2006), 57–81.

289 M. J. Maciel de Carvalho, "Um exército de índios, quilombolas e senhores de engenho contra os 'jacubinos': a Cabanada, 1832–1835," in M. Duarte Dantas (ed.), *Revoltas, motins, revoluções. Homens livres pobres e libertos no Brasil do século XIX*, 2nd ed. (São Paulo: Editora Alameda, 2018), 193.

from the time of Edward Coke to that of William Blackstone, England experienced "a hardening and concretion of the notion of property in land, and a reification of usages into properties which could be rented, sold or willed." In time such process would spread to other parts of the British Empire and beyond, much to the joy of the likes of Adam Smith, for whom "property was either 'perfect' and absolute or it was meaningless."[290] In order for perfect property to be ascertained, communal or corporate ownership had to cease to exist. In France, common rights were dealt a huge blow shortly after the Revolution; however, its death sentence came a few years later, when the 1804 Civil Code was approved (see Section 5.2).

But elites needed more than just land to profit from the international market. Without labor, land meant nothing. As stated earlier, wars – external and internal – had deep impacts on the labor market, as many were forced to abandon their daily activities in order to serve, and not only the free poor but also enslaved men were conscripted. In parts of Latin America, the process of independence disrupted slavery permanently, eventually leading to its demise. Other polities, either independent states or colonies, were able to stall antislavery forces. But even in these countries the end of the transatlantic slave trade and, afterward, policies such as free womb laws posed a threat to planters' ability to maintain and expand production. Whether they depended on an enslaved workforce or not, most Latin America elites approached labor shortage with a similar tool: the adoption of policies devised to criminalize poverty.

In 1878, sugar planters from five Brazilian provinces gathered in Recife to discuss and demand new policies to foster economic development. Besides the lack of credit, labor was their main concern. According to one of these planters, legislation reform was paramount as "existing laws only guarantee vagabondage and laziness under the pompous name of citizen's liberties." Those who attended or sent filled-out surveys agreed that a large portion of the country population was made of idle people whose habits of "indolence, dissipation, immorality, and anarchy" not only aggravated economic conditions but also threatened public safety, as they drove the masses to a life of crime. To face such a menace – especially troublesome due to the rising prices of enslaved workers – the government should criminalize any behavior that remotely resembled idleness. In other words, free people's resistance to work long hours for meager pay, if any pay at all, should be punished by the state. The planters gathered in Recife reminisced of years gone by, when war forced

290 E. P. Thompson, "Custom, Law and Common Right," in E. P. Thompson, *Customs in Common: Studies in Traditional Popular Culture* (New York: The New Press, 1993), 122 and 143.

the free poor to work in the fields in order to escape conscription, and migrants starving from year-long droughts accepted jobs in exchange for food only.[291]

Brazilian planters would have been thrilled at the prospect of adopting regulations like the ones that had been enforced in Argentina two decades earlier. In 1855, in Rosario, a new rural regulation determined that men who had a "known profession, trade, or occupation" should carry an official paper proving such employment, being obligated to present it upon request to those responsible for safeguarding public order. In addition to the police and other state authorities, Rosario landowners had the right to oversee the enforcement of this regulation. People who could not provide such papers could be forced to serve in the National Guard or toil in public works. Whereas some questioned the lawfulness of such measures (as they might infringe individual rights), most considered that "miserable families who have absolutely nothing, who do not work, do not farm, and do not even bother to keep straw on the roofs of theirs shacks," who surely abused the properties of others, had either to submit to work discipline, leave the province, or face punishment. Constitutions and rights should not get in the way of "improving the primitive conditions of these forgotten people, providing them with work, prosperity, education, well-being, that is, happiness…"[292]

Such processes of criminalization of poverty were also effective in the Spanish colony of Puerto Rico. In 1849, Governor Juan de la Pazuela passed a law regarding *jornaleros* (wage laborers). Henceforth all landless people had to carry a *libreta* (a paper booklet) containing information about their place of work along with any observations their employers deemed important. Authorities would review the *libretas*, searching for inconsistencies regarding current employment and any negative comments from employers. And the law had further implications. It also forbade the continuance of labor by *agregados* or *moradores* (tenants and dwellers). From then on, all people were forced to be either wage laborers or renters. Those unable to guarantee one or the other type of employment had to move to cities or face prison sentences. Most of the former tenants chose to become renters in order to avoid wage labor and maintain a somewhat independent lifestyle. But soon enough they found out that, despite some similarities with tenancy, becoming a renter

291 M. Duarte Dantas and V. Chieregati Costa, "O 'pomposo nome de liberdade do cidadão': tentativas de arregimentação e coerção da mão-de-obra livre no Império do Brasil," *Estudos Avançados* 87 (2016), 29–48.

292 M. Bonaudo, E. Sonzogni, and A. Klatt, "To Populate and to Discipline: Labor Market Construction in the Province of Santa Fe, Argentina, 1850–1890," *Latin American Perspectives* 26(1) (1999), 65–91.

put them in harm's way. Besides preventing renters from working on other farms, the new contracts had provisions compelling them to be employed on "land improvement, fence construction, and labor at harvest time" for their landlords. Falling short of one's contract obligations – or trying to evade them – entailed a set of punishments, from fines to imprisonment. No wonder such regulations resulted in an armed rebellion in 1868.[293]

Latin American governments and landed elites were, for the most part, following a trend already in place in many European countries. Back in 1797, Jeremy Bentham had written an essay proposing radical changes to England's Poor Laws. Basically, he championed the establishment of "industry houses" where "all persons, able-bodied or otherwise, having neither visible or assignable property, nor honest and sufficient means of livelihood" were to be forcefully committed.[294] Two years after his death, Bentham's ideas came to life as an 1834 law provided for the creation of workhouses in every parish of the country: Jail-like establishments where workmates – either men, women, or children – lived under extremely harsh conditions (as Charles Dickens famously portrayed in *Oliver Twist*) designed to curb their supposed laziness and encourage them to accept whatever job they could find. Similarly, in France of the 1840s, the unemployed poor were considered dangerous enemies of society and therefore had to be dealt with accordingly.[295]

By the end of the nineteenth century, most Latin American countries had passed laws criminalizing poverty. At the same time, responding to expanding international markets and nurturing hopes of peopling the new countries with men and women of "better habits and cultural backgrounds," landowners and government authorities turned to foreign immigrants. Reality, though, did not always live up to expectations for either those who arrived or the ones in need of laborers. Many immigrants who dared resist the abuse from Latin American elites, were subjected to similar criminalization as the local poor. Uncountable immigrants either organized to contest labor conditions, eventually setting up rebellions, or fled rural estates to pursue a better future in urban areas. But, just like rural inhabitants paid a dear price in the

293 F. Picó, *Historia general de Puerto Rico*, 4th ed. (San Juan: Ediciones Huracán, 2008), 190–91; L. Bergard, "Coffee and Rural Proletarization in Puerto Rico, 1840–1898," *Journal of Latin American Studies* 15(1) (1983), 83–100; L. Bergard, "Toward Puerto Rico's Grito de Lares: Coffee, Social Stratification, and Class Conflicts, 1828–1868," *The Hispanic American Historical Review* 60(4) (1980), 617–42.

294 J. Bentham, "Outline of a Work Entitled Pauper Management Improved," in J. Bowring (ed.), *The Works of Jeremy Bentham, Published under the Superintendence of his Executor, John Bowring* (Edinburgh: William Tait, 1843), vol. VIII, 370.

295 H.-A. Frégier, *Des classes dangereuses de la population dans les grandes villes, et des moyens de les rendre meilleures* (Paris: Chez J. B. Baillière, 1840).

process of state formation and commercial expansion, the urban poor were not much better off.

Deregulation and the Urban Poor

Like in Europe, in Latin America, the battle for equal rights meant dissolving corporate rights typical of *Ancien régime* societies, such as the privileges granted to artisan guilds and similar *corporae*. In England guilds had already lost importance by the eighteenth century; across the channel in France, where they had been abolished in 1791, Restoration provided a brief comeback for the guilds in the 1830s. In other parts of Europe, for example, in some Italian and German states, such corporate bodies were able to resist a while longer. Nonetheless, considering the continent as a whole, the nineteenth century came to be the era of their demise.[296] Even if such bodies were never as widespread and strong in the New World as they had been in the Old World, they undeniably played an important role in many Latin American cities. And in both Spanish and Portuguese America corporate privileges had been under scrutiny since the Bourbonic and Pombaline reforms.

Workers affiliated with guilds and similar bodies came to face major challenges in the aftermath of the wars for Independence. Reformers attacked the guilds' control over pricing as an impediment to the development of urban economies in Latin America. They also demonized the labor regulations imposed by the guilds. According to new liberal creeds, such privileged bodies should perish so that the doctrine of equal rights (incompatible with corporate privileges) could thrive, and local economies could more easily integrate a free world market. If a country were to benefit from growing international connections, they preached, its manufactured goods and food staples should be produced and exchanged according to market constraints – and not artisans' whims.

In colonial Latin America (as in some European countries), artisans had traditionally organized themselves in guilds or other institutions that played a similar role. In Brazil, for instance, artisans' brotherhoods (*irmandades* as they were called in Portuguese, or *cofradias* in Spanish) enjoyed many privileges granted to lay artisans' corporations.[297] In guilds, labor was usually organized according to craft. There were corporations of carpenters, masons, blacksmiths, goldsmiths, tailors, cobblers, millers, and bakers, among many others.

296 I. Katznelson and A. Zolberg, *Working-Class Formation: Nineteenth-Century Patterns in Western Europe and the United States* (Princeton: Princeton University Press, 1986); E. Hobsbawm, *The Age of Revolution, 1789–1848* (New York: Vintage Books, 1996).

297 Regarding confraternities in colonial Latin America, see Section 3.2.

A young man interested in working on a specific craft had to become apprentice in a master's workshop. If accepted, the apprentice would work in exchange for food, shelter, and training. After a number of years – depending on the master's evaluation – the apprentice would undergo an examination. If he passed, he would become an officer and be entitled to payment, even though he would continue to work in someone else's workshop. Later on, the officer could take another test to become a master. Only then he would be authorized to establish a workshop for himself and have others working for him. Municipal regulations guaranteed that no one could work as an artisan unless he was endorsed by such corporations. Hence, the guilds controlled learning and training in their crafts while tightly managing the labor market. Furthermore, they were entitled to verify the quality of the manufactured products.

Even before Latin American colonies became independent nations, some cities had been adopting legislation to ban guilds or similar bodies. Such was the case of Buenos Aires, where the municipality outlawed artisans' corporations in 1799. In other Spanish American cities, guilds faced challenges as provisions from the Cádiz constitution were adopted. Elsewhere they were dissolved by the early national constitutions, as occurred in Brazil in 1824. In other places, though, as was the case in Peru, guilds were not abolished until the second half of the nineteenth century.[298] In Mexico, although the first law suppressing guilds was passed in 1814, they remained active for decades thereafter. In 1834, the *Tribunal de Vagos* established that "masters are responsible for their apprentices' and officers' behavior, as they work in their shops." In 1843, Mexican authorities approved the establishment of the *Junta de Fomento de Artesanos*, determining that guilds' funds would now be transferred to this newly created institution. According to the historian Sonia Pérez Toledo, such regulations amounted to official recognition that such corporate bodies not only still existed but also continued to exert control over the artisans' labor and promote their interests.[299]

The artisans' ability to resist the laws that national elites devised to weaken or abolish their corporate privileges varied greatly. First, resistance was stronger

298 G. Di Meglio, T. Guzman, and M. Katz, "Artesanos hispano-americanos del siglo XIX: identidades, organizaciones y acción política," *Almanack* 23 (2019), 288–89; R. Bezerra de Freitas Barbosa, "O processo de extinção das corporações de ofício no Brasil: organização e resistência de um grupo de trabalhadores do recife (1787–1824)," in M. Duarte Dantas (ed.), *Da corte ao confronto. Capítulos de história do Brasil oitocentista* (Belo Horizonte: Editora Fino Traço, 2020), 89; I. García-Bryce Weinstein, *República con ciudadanos: los artesanos de Lima, 1821–1879* (Lima: IEP, 2008), 109.

299 S. Pérez Toledo, *Los hijos del trabajo. Los artesanos de la ciudad de México, 1780–1853* (Mexico City: El Colégio de México, Universidad Autónoma Metropolitana Iztapalapa, 1996), 150 and 198.

wherever artisans lived in large numbers. Since guilds and brotherhoods usually organized themselves by craft, some were more capable to resist than others. Second, economic constraints played a major role. In Peru, for instance, the country's tardiness in fully entering the world market economy – this only happened once guano became a major export commodity – largely accounts for the endurance of the guilds. Finally, political circumstances were usually a significant factor. According to the historian James Wood, the strength of a "popular republican movement" in Santiago, Chile, in the decades following independence, turned artisans into strong political players: They were entitled to vote and competing elite factions turned to them for support.[300] Artisans in Latin America were able to hold on to some of their privileges when facing challenges such as declining numbers or local price fluctuations. But when they encountered major disruptions – such as weakening political representation, the inexorable forces of the world market, and elite indifference or distrust – they either took up arms or tried to reinvent themselves, or both.

Artisans were behind many of the so-called protectionist rebellions occurring in urban areas of Latin America. Depending on each individual policy adopted by various governments, different craftsmen took up arms. Most revolted against the lowering or lifting of tariffs on imported goods that competed with the products they manufactured, claiming that cheap imports would drive them into poverty. Others demanded that raw materials be imported at the lowest cost possible in order to keep the price of their manufactured goods competitive. Yet others, facing inflation and depressed production due to wars and other contingencies, demanded food imports be free of taxes. Regardless of the reason, and despite political interests in promoting such movements to favor certain factions, armed protest meant a desperate effort on the part of artisans to maintain their livelihoods. And such rebellions shook many Latin American countries for decades.

Some craftsmen chose more peaceful strategies to counter elite distrust, liberal reforms, and everyday challenges. Creating mutual aid societies was one of them. Guilds and brotherhoods, in addition to all their activities mentioned earlier, collected funds to provide for those who fell ill, pay for funerals, and help widows and orphans when the head of the household was gone. As the nineteenth century progressed, however, there was not much else they could

300 Di Meglio, Guzman, and Katz, "Artesanos hispano-americanos del siglo XIX"; P. Gootenberg, "The Social Origins of Protectionism and Free Trade in Nineteenth-Century Lima," *Journal of Latin American Studies* 14(2) (1982), 329–58; P. Gootenberg, *Imagining Development: Economic Ideas in Peru's "Fictitious Prosperity" of Guano, 1840–1880* (Berkeley, Los Angeles, and Oxford: University of California Press, 1993); J. A. Wood, "Building a Society of Equals."

do. In contrast to colonial-era guilds and brotherhoods, they lost their ability to exert control over workforce training, labor regulations, and the quality and price of manufactured goods.

Not long after the Brazilian constitution of 1824 strictly forbade guilds and similar corporations, a group of carpenters, masons, and coopers created a mutual aid society in Recife. Gathering most of those who belonged to their artisans' brotherhood, the new society provided for their members in need and managed to ensure government support for night classes. For years, masters offered lessons for those interested in learning one of the crafts. But despite the services provided, they no longer had any say on who could or could not perform the different trades in Recife. And this loss had dire consequences. Barely any member of the society was now able to enter into contracts with the city. As earlier, the masters valued their workmanship, employing men trained in their craft and using quality materials. Recife authorities, however, were mainly interested in cutting costs. And manufacturers with money and no regard to the trade, who cut costs both in supplies and labor, employing unskilled hands, offered better prices.[301]

If deregulation of labor affected artisans' ability to earn a living, it also had other effects, which were perhaps less visible but surely as critical. Although since colonial times manual labor had been devalued as unbecoming for those with means in Latin America, craftsmen considered themselves – and were thus generally viewed by others – as situated above unskilled workers. Artisanal occupations enjoyed a special status as they entailed honor, knowledge, and independence. Craftsmen (at least the masters) were their own bosses, had years-long training, and were proud of their workmanship. Guilds and brotherhoods, besides controlling the labor market, assured their members a special place in local society – which was clearly reflected in their positions in religious processions and other public festivities.[302] Their demise, hence, had pernicious impacts. Artisans were to become just like any other worker. This would seem bad enough in an era of new clock-time work discipline and of laws criminalizing poverty, but it was worse yet in places where work was identified with slavery and other forms of bondage.[303]

301 M. Mac Cord, *Artífices da Cidadania. Mutualismo, educação e trabalho no Recife oitocentista* (Campinas: Editora UNICAMP, 2012), 304–7.

302 R. Di Stefano, H. Sabato, L. A. Romero, and J. L. Moreno, *De las cofradías a las organizaciones de la sociedad civil. Historia de la iniciativa associativa en Argentina, 1776–1990* (Buenos Aires: Edilab Editora, 2002).

303 E. P. Thompson, *The Making of the English Working Class* (London and New York: Penguin Books, 1968); T. C. Holt, *The Problem of Freedom: Race, Labor, and Politics in Jamaica and Britain, 1833–1938* (Baltimore and London: The Johns Hopkins University

Policies against both corporate privileges and protectionist policies ended up also affecting urban dwellers other than the artisans themselves. In colonial times, many regions in Latin America enjoyed some type of policy regulating the price of food staples. Although not all cities and towns had public granaries or grain exchange facilities, municipal authorities often found ways to lower food prices.[304] They did so because, as stated in 1747 by the crown attorney of the *Audiencia* (or royal court) of Guadalajara, "although anyone may do as he likes with his own property, in the things necessary for the sustenance of life, sellers should not be at liberty to set and raise prices freely."[305]

From the eighteenth century onward, however, even before Adam Smith published his *Wealth of Nations*, governments and other interested parties started questioning the validity of such regulations. Slowly but surely a moral economy, as defined by E. P. Thompson, gave way to free markets and free trade policies. A new economic model championing that a market "was never better regulated than when it was left to regulate itself" came to prevail. State interference and "popular prejudice" were set aside in favor of impersonal market rules.[306] As the historian Thomas C. Wright explains, after independence Latin America came under the banner of economic liberalism, witnessing a "radical change in the philosophy and institutions of urban provisioning" and awarding the urban poor "full responsibility for their own well-being."[307]

But, as it occurred in England and continental Europe, some authorities and especially the urban masses – born and raised under the sign of a moral economy – proved unwilling to bow down before the new economic credo. In 1858, residents of São Salvador da Bahia, in Brazil, protested the provincial president's autocratic resolution to close the city's public granary. Municipal councilors, who were almost all in favor of maintaining the facility, claimed that the provincial authority, under the spell of Adam Smith, had failed to

Press, 1992); H. M. Mattos, *Das cores do silêncio: os significados da liberdade no Sudeste escravista (Brasil, século XIX)*, 3rd rev. ed. (Campinas: Ed. UNICAMP, 2013).

304 J. C. Garavaglia and J. D. Gelman, "Rural History of the Rio de la Plata, 1600–1850: Results of a Historiographical Renaissance," *Latin American Research Review* 30(3) (1995), 84.

305 E. Van Young, *Hacienda and Market in Eighteenth-Century Mexico: The Rural Economy of the Guadalajara Region, 1675–1820* (Berkeley: University of California Press, 1981), 43.

306 E. P. Thompson, "The Moral Economy of the English Crowd in the Eighteenth Century," in E. P. Thompson, *Customs in Common: Studies in Traditional Popular Culture* (New York: The New Press, 1993), 182–83.

307 T. C. Wright, "The Politics of Urban Provisioning in Latin American History," in J. C. Super and T. C. Wright (eds.), *Food, Politics and Society in Latin America* (Lincoln: University of Nebraska Press, 1985), 26.

acknowledge that the people did not live off theories.[308] That same year, urban workers in Lima, Peru, protested against food policies – or the lack thereof – that threatened their well-being. They did so again for years to come. In 1867, for instance, they threw stones at shops and closed bakeries.[309] Similarly, bakers in Mexico City had been enduring decades of protest as prices rose far beyond what was considered fair, at least according to old customs and expectations.[310] Throughout Latin America, urban dwellers protested through peaceful as well as violent means, always favoring protectionist measures regulating food prices, making clear that such measures had a direct impact on their ability to survive. Oftentimes, when their demands converged with other interests, especially those of more influential groups, they were able to secure favorable conditions. As the years went by, however, the people's demands increasingly fell on deaf ears and the cold logic of the free market prevailed.

By the end of the nineteenth century, guilds were altogether extinct and the old moral economy policies were completely abandoned in Latin America. Adding insult to injury, the ever-growing production of export commodities brought about encroachment on lands previously devoted to food cultivation, thus contributing to high prices and frequent food shortages in urban areas. Such problems were made all the more devastating by the privatization of urban commons. As the urban poor lost their battles in Latin America, as market constraints spread to all areas of the economy, as specialized crafts were replaced by unskilled labor, the criminalization of poverty became the law of the land, terrorizing the poor in urban areas as well as the countryside.

Conclusion

In 1897, a group of soldiers returned to their hometown of Rio de Janeiro after months in the battlefield. Poor, unemployed, and lacking any kind of government assistance, they settled in one of the city's poorest areas, then called "Morro da Providência" (Providence Hill). Not long after, due to the overwhelming presence of those destitute soldiers who fought for the Republican

308 J. J. Reis and M. G. de Aguiar, "'Carne sem osso e farinha sem caroço': o motim de 1858 contra a carestia na Bahia," *Revista de História* 135 (1996); R. Graham, *Alimentar a cidade. Das vendedoras de rua à reforma liberal (Salvador, 1780–1860)* (São Paulo: Companhia das Letras, 2013).

309 V. C. Peloso, "Succulence and Sustenance: Region, Class, and Diet in Nineteenth-Century Peru," in J. C. Super and T. C. Wright (eds.), *Food, Politics and Society in Latin America* (Lincoln: University of Nebraska Press, 1985), 57–58.

310 R. Weis, *Bakers and Basques: A Social History of Bread in Mexico* (Albuquerque: University of New Mexico Press, 2012), 46–49.

Army, the area lost this name and earned a new epithet. Years later its name became a worldwide synonym for disenfranchised urban communities, which it retains until today: Morro da Favela (Favela Hill).[311] *Favela* or *faveleira* is a plant common to Brazil's semiarid regions. Its existence became nationally known as thousands of army personnel – together with cannons, machine guns, and other industrial weaponry – were sent to fight and destroy a backland town in Bahia between 1896 and 1897. Surrounded by these *favela* plants, the town of Canudos was the stage for one of the bloodiest episodes in Latin American history, which historians reckon left some thirty thousand dead.[312]

At the end of the war, newspapers celebrated the progressive forces of the Republic for ridding the country of an unwelcome community of thousands of backland free poor, indigenous people, and the so-called "May 13th" (a derogatory term for formerly enslaved persons who had become free when Brazil passed the emancipation law on May 13, 1888). However, unable to explain how the rebels were able to put up a formidable fight against the country's official army, many – from contemporaries such as the journalist Euclides da Cunha to twentieth-century academic historians – chose to explain the rebels' endurance and brave resistance as the effect of a messianic movement. Ignorant and gullible – so the story goes – the poor inhabitants of Bahia's backlands had become blind followers of a charismatic leader, Antonio Conselheiro, who supposedly had promised them heaven on earth.[313] Such a simplistic explanation, though, not only fails to account for the hazardous impacts of decades-long liberal policies – from land encroachment to criminalizing laws – but also for poor peoples' ability to understand and resist them. Unwilling to conform, the Canudos rebels were labeled as fanatics and denied a place in modern society. Exclusion in this case, as in many others throughout Latin American history, literally meant demise.[314]

The violence of the War of Canudos extended beyond the slaughtering of Bahia's rebel poor. The very soldiers who committed this massacre returned home to encounter nothing but poverty and exclusion: They became the inhabitants of the Morro da Favela. As it happened so many times in

311 L. do Prado Valladares, *A invenção da favela. Do mito de origem à favela.com* (Rio de Janeiro: Editora UFGV, 2005).

312 R. M. Levine, *Vale of Tears: Revisiting the Canudos Massacre in Northeastern Brazil, 1893–1897* (Berkeley: University of California Press, 1992).

313 For an interpretation of popular resistance as messianic or millenarian movements, which places religious fanaticism as the only possible avenue for the poor to speak out, see M. I. Pereira de Queiroz, O *Messianismo. No Brasil e no mundo* (São Paulo: Dominus, EDUSP, 1965).

314 M. Duarte Dantas, *Fronteiras movediças. A comarca de Itapicuru e a formação do arraial de Canudos (relações sociais na Bahia do século XIX)* (São Paulo: Hucitec, 2007).

nineteenth-century Latin America, the poor killed one another to further the projects of visionaries who could not care less about the welfare of ordinary men and women. Those who survived the wars the elite had created encountered poverty and exclusion at every turn. But the elites were more than satisfied: Another obstacle – another alternative way of life – had been removed from the path to political and economic "progress."

The story of Canudos and the Morro da Favela is one among many examples of how the combined forces of the state and capital oppressed the masses in nineteenth-century Latin America. Anti-corporate legislation began to be implemented during the process of independence and continued to be pushed by modernizing elites throughout the century. Resistance came primarily from those living at the margins of the new order, from indigenous and enslaved persons to the rural and urban impoverished workers. Resistance proved effective at times, but ultimately the new order envisioned by liberal elites triumphed. In the name of freedom and equality, the rulers of the new Latin American nations effectively destroyed institutions based on a corporate logic. Their efforts undeniably emancipated people who had lived under the yoke of slaveholders, priests, tribal rulers, and master craftsmen, among others, since colonial times. Yet such emancipation was accompanied by a brutal process of expropriation. Reformers made sure that the Latin American masses were to have no means to live outside nation-states and a capitalist system connected to global – overwhelming – forces.

Internal and external wars, land privatization, the extinction of corporate privileges, the expansion of production for export, and the imposition of wage-labor relations – to name some of the most important processes spreading throughout Latin America in the nineteenth century – combined to turn indigenous people, freedpeople and their descendants, and the rural and urban poor into a formally free but materially destitute workforce. As Section 5.3 has sought to show, these processes were protracted and contested, the victims were not passive observers but put up a brave resistance, and the perpetrators were not all-powerful or all-seeing. Yet as competing visions of society clashed in Latin America, alternatives to a national and capitalist order were brutally crushed. Relying on global networks and industrial tools, modernizing liberal elites managed to impose their interests – their ideals of order and progress – onto a whole continent.

6
The Omnipresence of the State? The Twentieth Century

6.1 Toward the Administrative State

EDUARDO ZIMMERMANN

Described recently as an ineffectual "Paper Leviathan,"[1] the nineteenth-century Latin American state was hardly an omnipresent figure. As we shall see, two distinctive features of the region's historical development appeared as obstacles to the construction of an efficient state administrative machinery. First, despite the alleged centralist colonial heritage,[2] many observers lamented the structural weakness of the Latin American states that obstructed minimum acceptable levels of administrative control. Second, the new disciplines of public administration and administrative law, two bodies of knowledge born in European monarchical settings, and its institutions, such as a separate administrative jurisdiction, seemed to be incompatible with the fervent republican and democratic spirit that ran through the new nations, notwithstanding the Brazilian empire.

Despite numerous difficulties, however, by the early twentieth century, the Latin American states had gone through considerable transformations. Traveling through South America at the time, James Bryce, author of the renowned *American Commonwealth*, stated that "the growth of property and the development of industrial habits" brought about by economic modernization in the region had a stabilizing effect and served as a motor of progress. His conclusion was positive, "taking the eleven South American states as a whole, their condition is better than it was sixty years ago," and comparisons with European ideal types of state development appeared unfair:

1 M. A. Centeno and A. E. Ferraro (eds.), *State and Nation Making in Latin America and Spain: Republics of the Possible* (Cambridge: Cambridge University Press, 2013), 399.
2 Cf. C. Véliz, *The Centralist Tradition of Latin America* (Princeton: Princeton University Press, 1980).

> Every sensible man feels that the problems of government are far more difficult than our grandfathers had perceived, and that men have still much to learn from a fuller experience. These things being so, ought not the judgment passed on the Spanish Americans to be more lenient? Their difficulties were greater than any European people had to face, and there is no need to be despondent for their future.[3]

By the mid-twentieth century, the outlook was decidedly more positive: Latin American states were providers of a wide array of public goods, the sheer size of the administrative machinery had grown dramatically, and political and administrative centralization was the dominant model. "Between 1930 and the early 1980s," observed Lawrence Whitehead, "the ambitions, resources, and capabilities of virtually all the region's public authorities were incommensurably greater than they had been a half century before."[4] Similarly, during the same period, administrative law and the new science of public administration had replaced many of the tenets of liberal constitutionalism that had hitherto delineated the relationships of state and society.

Despite particularities in the different countries in terms of economic development, geographic and climatic determinants, and socio-political evolution, the whole region had gone through a similar process of transformation on the way toward the modernization of state structures. Economic growth via integration into the expansion of Atlantic capitalism facilitated the process of state building by the gradual improvement of state capacities. At the same time, new global currents of legal thought offered a reconceptualization of the normative frameworks in which the states operated. Section 6.1 traces these changes in the structure of the Latin American states and its conceptual bases in legal thought. This process led to a gradual displacement of the classic liberal constitutional models that had framed the independent

3 J. Bryce, *South America: Observations and Impressions* (London: MacMillan, 1912), 546–49, at 551. See, in a similar vein, W. Knöbl, "State Building in Western Europe and the Americas in the Long Nineteenth Century: Some Preliminary Observations," in M. A. Centeno and A. E. Ferraro (eds.), *State and Nation Making in Latin America and Spain: Republics of the Possible* (Cambridge: Cambridge University Press, 2013), 75: "The early history of the state in the Americas, especially in Latin America, should be judged very cautiously. At least one should not fall into the trap to measure state's 'failures' against the yardstick of a state model that even in Europe did not exist...." Therefore, "it is not possible any longer to classify every missing or 'odd' feature of state building in Latin America as a decisive hindrance for a full breakthrough to political modernity."

4 L. Whitehead, "State Organization in Latin America Since 1930," in L. Bethell (ed.), *The Cambridge History of Latin America, vol. VI: 1930 to the Present, Part 2: Politics and Society* (Cambridge: Cambridge University Press, 1994), 12.

new nations in favor of innovative principles organizing ever-expanding state activities.

This does not imply that what took place was a passive reception of European and North American legal doctrine by local jurists or a recreation of a "myth of origin" about Latin American Law (see Section 1.4). Rather, as has been pointed out in the introduction to this volume, it reveals "that many other regions of the globe had to deal with similar questions and that debates taking place in Latin America were often linked to discussions elsewhere, to which they both contributed as well as received." There are two shared features of these new currents worth mentioning here. The first was a corpus of knowledge circulating mostly within the universe of "the law of jurists," and it was "state-centered and legalistic," set apart from other forms of understanding the origins of norms.[5] Second, this corpus offered a new perspective on the strong links between the process of institutionalization of certain academic disciplines or forms of social knowledge and modern state building in Latin America, and in particular the role of the global and the local in such processes.[6]

Section 6.1 comprises four sections. The first two sections deal with precedents involving the tradition of police power in the region and the debates about centralization of authority in mid-nineteenth-century Latin America. The final two sections address the two primary forces behind the growth of the administrative state in the region: First, the process of modernization and economic structural change in the new nations, and second, the impact of new global currents of legal thought that helped to consolidate in the region the new disciplines of public administration and administrative law.

Police Power and Administrative Jurisdiction

One of the most important contributions of the new legal history has been the re-evaluation of the "state-centered paradigm" and its place in the evolution of normativity throughout history. The idea that in a "well-ordered society" the government should be concerned with the general welfare of the

5 Cf. Duve & Herzog, Introduction; and Dias Paes Section 1.4 in this volume; T. Herzog, "Latin American Legal Pluralism: The Old and the New," *Quaderni fiorentini per la storia del pensiero giuridico moderno* 50(2) (2021), 705–36.

6 On this last point, see T. Duve, "What Is Global Legal History?," *Comparative Legal History* 8(2) (2020), 73–115; M. Plotkin and E. Zimmermann, "Introducción. Saberes de Estado en la Argentina, siglos XIX y XX," in M. Plotkin and E. Zimmermann (eds.), *Los saberes del Estado* (Buenos Aires: Edhasa, 2012), 9–28.

population, both in a spiritual and material sense, enjoys a long history with medieval roots – a tradition based on a very different rationale than that of the modern administrative state.[7]

The concept of "police" represents the starting point of our understanding of the functions of administration within the "jurisdictional paradigm": the regulation of conduct at the local level of matters pertaining to security, public health, morality and public order, as well as the development of commerce and economic transactions. In particular, as this literature emphasizes, these functions were seen as an extension of the patriarchal role within the household economy to the municipal environment (see also Section 3.3). As Castillo de Bovadilla stated in his *Política para corregidores* (1597): "The fair government of the household is the true model for the government of the Republic … because the household is like a small city, and the city is a large house…."[8] By the eighteenth century, the idea that the roots of state regulatory power laid in this notion of the police could be found in many different European sources. "By the public police and oeconomy I mean the due regulation and domestic order of the kingdom," is how Blackstone expressed it in his *Commentaries on the Laws of England*. The individuals of the state, "*like members of a well-governed family*, are bound to conform their general behavior to the rules of propriety, good neighborhood, and good manners, and to be decent, industrious, and inoffensive in their respective stations." Adam Smith's *Lectures on Justice, Police, Revenue and Arms* (1762–1763), Johann Justi's *Polizeiwissenschaft* (1756), Nicolas De La Mare's *Traité de la Police* (1722), and the Spaniard Tomás Valeriola's *Idea General de la Policía* (1808) offered similar interpretations of "police."[9]

7 Cf. A. Agüero (ed.), "Justicia y Administración entre el antiguo régimen y el orden liberal: lecturas ius-históricas," dossier no. 125, *Programa Interuniversitario de Historia Política*, http://historiapolitica.com/dossiers/dossier-justicia-y-administracion-entre-antiguo-regimen-y-orden-liberal-lecturas-ius-historicas/.

8 Cited in Spanish in A. Agüero, "Herramientas conceptuales de los juristas del derecho común en el dominio de la Administración," in M. Lorente (ed.), *La jurisdicción contencioso-administrativa en España. Una historia de sus orígenes* (Madrid: Consejo General del Poder Judicial, 2009), 32; see also R. Zamora, *Casa poblada y buen gobierno. Oeconomia católica y servicio personal en San Miguel de Tucumán, siglo XVIII* (Buenos Aires: Prometeo Libros, 2017), 117. All translations from Spanish and Portuguese are my own.

9 Cf. M. D. Dubber, *The Police Power: Patriarchy and the Foundations of American Government* (New York: Columbia University Press, 2005), 49; W. J. Novak, *The People's Welfare: Law & Regulation in Nineteenth-Century America* (Chapel Hill: The University of North Carolina Press, 1996), 12–14; M. Raeff, "The Well-Ordered Police State and the Development of Modernity in Seventeenth- and Eighteenth-Century Europe: An Attempt at a Comparative Approach," *The American Historical Review* 80(5) (1975), 1221–43; J. Vallejo, "Concepción de la policía," in Agüero (ed.), "Justicia y Administración," 1–23.

Police power thus understood was part of a process of "localization of the law" in the Hispanic colonial cities, a process that can be overlooked when we focus exclusively on the independent centralized national state as a source of the law (also see Sections 1.3, 1.4, 3.1, and 3.2).[10] Based on this considerable degree of normative autonomy, a large number of regulations on security, health, and public morality were sanctioned at the municipal level, gradually widening the scope of intervention of public authorities, and producing, as Jesús Vallejo put it, "state-generating" mechanisms ("*generaron Estado*").[11] The prevalence of local power to regulate such matters was a concept many of the Latin American constitutional orders of the independent era inherited. To illustrate this point, we can cite a number of decisions of the Argentine Supreme Court from the second half of the nineteenth century recognizing the legitimacy of police power developed by local authorities in Buenos Aires to regulate issues such as the location of markets and fairs, bull fighting rings, or slaughterhouses and tanneries in the city.[12] The political and administrative need of the many local normative orders in the region to exert greater degrees of control lent force to the arguments calling for further centralization as one of the elements the new administrative order would bring about, as we will see in the next section (see also Chapter 4).[13]

Hand in hand with the arguments about centralization, a second question was crucial to all the debates about the origins of administrative law in the region and its relation to the constitutional order. One of the legacies of the French Revolution and the First French Empire had been the creation of an

10 A. Agüero, "Ciudad y poder político en el Antiguo Régimen. La tradición castellana," *Cuadernos de Historia* 15 (2005), 127–30; A. Agüero, "Local Law and Localization of Law: Hispanic Legal Tradition and Colonial Culture (16th–18th Centuries)," in M. Meccarelli and M. J. Solla Sastre (eds.), *Spatial and Temporal Dimensions for Legal History: Research Experiences and Itineraries, Global Perspectives on Legal History* (Frankfurt am Main: Max-Planck-Institut für europäische Rechtsgeschichte, 2016), 101–29; A. Exbalin and F. Godicheau (eds.), *Los arrabales del imperio. Administrar los suburbios de las urbes en la Monarquía católica (Siglos XVI–XIX)* (Rosario: Prohistoria Ediciones, 2021), 11.

11 Vallejo, "Concepción de la policía," 12.

12 See Supreme Court of Argentina, "Varios puesteros próximos al Mercado del Centro c. Empresario del mismo Mercado," in *Fallos de la Corte Suprema de Justicia* 3:468 (1866); "Plaza de Toros," in *Fallos de la Corte Suprema de Justicia* 7:152 (1870); "Saladeristas Santiago, José y Jerónimo Podestá y otros c. Provincia de Buenos Aires," in *Fallos de la Corte Suprema de Justicia* 51:274 (1887).

13 Paradoxically, from the late nineteenth-century demands for centralization at the national level, administrative law now seems to be moving in the direction of de-nationalization, through the emergence of "global administrative law." See S. Cassese, "Administrative Law Without the State? The Challenge of Global Regulation," *New York University Journal of International Law and Politics* 37(4) (2005), 663–94; B. Kingsbury, N. Krisch, and R. B. Stewart, "The Emergence of Global Administrative Law," *Law and Contemporary Problems* 68(3) (2005), 15–61.

independent administrative jurisdiction that exempted public agents from being judged by ordinary courts of law for their acts as public functionaries. This institution was, on the one hand, "unthinkable" within the "anti-statist legal-political universe of the Ancien Regime,"[14] and, on the other, its conciliation with the principle of the separation of powers of liberal constitutionalism was problematic, to say the least; hence, the resistance it encountered in Latin American republics. This separate administrative jurisdiction ("*contencioso-administrativo*") was adopted in Latin America only twice over the course of the "long nineteenth century" (though it became much more common in the second half of the twentieth century). The first instance of its adoption took place in Mexico under the dictatorship of General Santa Anna, and was promoted by Teodosio Lares.[15] The second instance occurred in Colombia in conjunction with the 1913 *Ley 130*, which organized the administrative jurisdiction based on the 1886 constitutional clause granting the National Congress this power.[16]

As we shall see, the gradual separation of the new discipline of administrative law from the received wisdom of the liberal constitutionalism, which had inspired much of the organization of the new nations (also see Section 5.1), rapidly grew from the second half of the nineteenth century to the first decades of the twentieth century. Prior to this, constitutional debates of the mid-nineteenth century focused on the crucial issue of centralization – both for and against – as the key to understanding the success or failure of the new institutional orders.

14 *"No podía siquiera concebirse en el universo jurídico-político anti-estatal del antiguo régimen."* C. Garriga, "Gobierno y Justicia: El gobierno de la justicia," in M. Lorente (ed.), *La jurisdicción contencioso-administrativa en España. Una historia de sus orígenes* (Madrid: Consejo General del Poder Judicial, 2009), 47–50; L. Mannori, "Justicia y Administración entre Antiguo y Nuevo Régimen," *Revista Jurídica de la Universidad Autónoma de Madrid* 15 (2007), 125–46.

15 For more on Teodosio Lares' role in the development of the administrative jurisdiction in nineteenth-century Mexico, see A. Lira González, "El contencioso administrativo y el poder judicial en México a mediados del siglo XIX. Notas sobre la obra de Teodosio Lares," *Memoria del II Congreso de Historia del Derecho Mexicano* (Mexico City: Universidad Nacional Autónoma de México, 1981), 621–34; A. Lira González, "Lo contencioso administrativo, ejemplo difícil para el constitucionalismo mexicano," in E. Ferrer Mac-Gregor and A. Zaldívar Lelo de Larrea (eds.), *La ciencia del derecho procesal constitucional. Estudios en homenaje a Héctor Fix-Zamudio* (Mexico City: Universidad Nacional Autónoma de México, 2008), 289–319; A. Lempérière, "El liberalismo hispanoamericano en el espejo del derecho," *Revista de Historia del Derecho* 57 (2019).

16 A more detailed analysis of the Colombian case can be found in M. Malagón Pinzón, *Vivir en policía. Una contralectura de los orígenes del derecho administrativo colombiano* (Bogotá: Universidad Externado de Colombia, 2007), 120–23; and M. Malagón Pinzón, *El pensamiento administrativo sobre el Ministerio Público en Colombia e Hispanoamérica* (Bogotá: Universidad Externado de Colombia, Universidad de Los Andes, 2017).

Centralization and the Constitutional Organization of Latin American States

In 1870, the Panamanian jurist Justo Arosemena offered an explanation for the decades of institutional disruptions and economic stagnation that had afflicted the new nations –one often repeated by others over the years[17]. There was a clash between formal principles established in constitutional models taught by "the abstract science of politics" and the realities revealed by "an applied political science." It was the divergence between these adopted abstract models and the concrete legacy of societies marked by "colonialism and revolution" that explained the instability of constitutional principles in Hispanic America (see also Section 5.3).[18] Even if many other Latin American jurists and statesmen accepted such a diagnosis, it was very difficult to reach a consensus about the best remedy to cure the affliction. Did the problem reside in the election of an unsuitable institutional model or in the incapacity of Latin American elites to adapt any such model to the particular realities of the region?

Two decades earlier, in one of the first texts to be published on the science of public administration in the region, Colombian jurist Florentino González discussed similar problems. "Reading Bonnin" (one of the French forerunners of the discipline), González stated, "I found a preference for a type of centralization that neglects all local interest, and, unfortunately, I have realized that our laws have been based on such pernicious doctrines." However, it was in the work of Tocqueville that he found "a torch guiding me to a new field of research: setting Bonnin aside, I began to think about the ways in which Great Britain and the United States organized social interests, and understood that the root of our evils was in the spirit of centralization that lives in our laws."[19]

17 On the centrality of constitutional debates and the idea of modernity in the region, see Section 5.1 by Portillo Valdés in this volume.

18 J. Arosemena, *Constituciones políticas de la América meridional reunidas y comentadas por Justo Arosemena. Abogado de Colombia y de Chile* (Havre: Imprenta A. Lemale Ainé, 1870), vol. I, xxvi.

19 F. González, *Elementos de Ciencia Administrativa* (Quito: Imprenta de la Enseñanza, 1847), vol. I, iv–vi. Another early introduction to the discipline, in a shorter text, published that same year in Bogotá, was C. Pinzón, *Principios sobre Administración Pública* (Bogotá: Imprenta de J. A. Cualla, 1847). The classic text by C.-J. Bonnin, *Principes d'Administration Publique* (Paris: Clament, 1809) had been summarized in two Spanish translations a few years prior: *Compendio de los Principios de Administración. Escrito en francés por C. J. Bonnin,* trans. J. M. Saavedra (Madrid: Imprenta de don José Palacios, 1834), and *Ciencia Administrativa: Principios de Administración Pública. Estractados de la obra francesa de Carlos Juan Bonnin,* trans. E. Febres Cordero (Panamá: Imprenta de José Ángel Santos, 1838). See Malagón Pinzón, *El pensamiento administrativo.*

In 1869, now appointed as the first Chair of Constitutional Law at the University of Buenos Aires, González expanded these views in his textbook *Lecciones de Derecho Constitucional*. His support for a radical version of democratic republicanism was based on a distinction between what he identified as "the European system," an "artificial" tradition of centralizing monarchies, and the "American system" of federal representative republics, based on the model provided by the 1787 Philadelphia Constitution.[20] José Manuel Estrada, who succeeded González as Chair of Constitutional Law in Buenos Aires, was also a harsh critic of the principles of centralization espoused by European administrativism. Addressing the graduates of the law school in 1881, Estrada concluded that the new discipline was "an unhealthy phase of modern legislation," the scientific expression of the process of centralization whereby modern societies were "subjected by the state."[21]

On the opposite side were those who defended centralization as one of the pillars of political stability and efficient public administration the region was lacking. When studying the collection of mid-nineteenth-century Hispanic American constitutional texts, the Spaniard Manuel Colmeiro did not hesitate in proclaiming that the imitation of the US constitutional model had been a tragic error. For instance, he attributed the costly Mexican defeat against the United States in their recent war to the weak political structure created by the Mexican Federal Constitution of 1824.[22] A few years earlier, Colmeiro had published another very influential text on the origins of public administration in Latin America: his two-volume *Derecho Administrativo Español*. In this work, he explains the basic principles of the discipline, drawing the crucial distinction between political and administrative centralization. If administrative centralization posed the risk of an excessive absorption of functions by the central government, "disregarding the provincial and municipal realities," Colmeiro was much more sanguine about the importance of political centralization. A logical consequence arising from the reaction against medieval dislocation of territories and governments, centralization meant "the triumph of a common body of law over privilege, of order over anarchy, of the authority

20 F. González, *Lecciones de Derecho Constitucional*, 5th ed. (París: Librería de la Vda. de Ch. Bouret, 1909 [1869]), ix–xiv.

21 J. M. Estrada, "A los nuevos doctores. Discurso de Colación de Grados de la Facultad de Derecho y Ciencias Sociales, 1881," in J. M. Estrada, *Obras completas* (Buenos Aires: Compañía Sudamericana de Billetes de Banco, 1905), vol. XII, 260.

22 M. Colmeiro, *Derecho Constitucional de las repúblicas hispano-americanas* (Madrid, Valparaíso, and Lima: Librerías de Don Ángel Calleja, 1858), xiii–xiv and 383–84.

incarnated in the monarchy over the dispersion of social forces that had characterized feudalism."[23]

Latin American political elites, constantly battling the threat of provincial uprisings and territorial fragmentation, probably favored this energetic defense of a central state and its unitary conception of the law, one found in the first administrative law textbooks produced in the region that departed from Florentino González's position. The Mexican jurist Teodosio Lares, for instance, stated very forcefully that centralization went hand in hand with the new science of administration. In Spain, he added – grounding his views in a long-term historical interpretation – the efforts made by the Catholic monarchs in order to systematize and standardize legislation were the first signals of the advantages of administrative unification. He concluded, however, that administrative uniformity had grown stronger as a result of Napoleon's aspirations for more control in Revolutionary France, as well as the work of the *Conseil d'État*.[24]

Other nineteenth-century Latin American authors explicitly adapted and/or literally copied Colmeiro's work. The Chilean Santiago Pardo made clear that he had taken much of his 1859 textbook directly from the pages of the Spaniard's work, as did the Argentinean Ramón Ferreyra when writing his 1866 treatise. Both agreed that the principle of centralization was, as Pardo expressed it, "a condition inherent to a good administration." Ferreyra went even further:

> I believe that in countries where a natural propensity derived from race, mores, and precedents have always led to a centralized, unitary form of life ..., it is essential to set up a centralized administration in every activity. Without it, neither the rule by constitution nor any conception of responsibility would be possible.[25]

In a very different context, Paulino José Soares de Sousa, the Viscount of Uruguai, reflected along similar lines in his study of administrative law in the Brazilian empire. It was not the legacy of a monarchical tradition but instead the diversity of local conditions that seemed to inspire his analysis. Without centralization, he wondered, "how could we possibly unite the North and South of the

23 M. Colmeiro, *Derecho Administrativo Español*, 4th ed. (Madrid: Imprenta y Librería de Eduardo Martínez, 1876 [1850]), vol. I, cap. VI, "De la centralización," 19–32.

24 T. Lares, *Lecciones de Derecho Administrativo* (Mexico City: Imprenta de Ignacio Cumplido, 1852), 5–6.

25 R. Ferreyra, *Derecho administrativo general y argentino* (Buenos Aires: Imprenta de Pablo Coni, 1866), 167; S. Prado, *Principios Elementales de Derecho Administrativo Chileno* (Santiago: Imprenta Nacional, 1859), 14–15.

Empire, given so many dissimilarities in climate, territory, spirit, commercial interests, and social development? How could we promote the development of so many localities marked by indolence and inertia?"[26] The proposals introduced by the 1834 Additional Act of the Empire, conceding greater autonomy to the provinces through the establishment of provincial legislatures, were the main target of his criticism of liberal political decentralization. These were based, Soares de Sousa claimed, on "hatred of the central power" and would lead to "an anarchic and disorderly decentralization out of an exaggerated democratic opinion, … subversive and chaotic that would deliver a disarmed central executive power to provincial factions." He also condemned the idea of transplanting Anglo-American institutional models to Latin countries; those countries where this occurred fell into a political "barbarism."[27]

Juan Bautista Alberdi, one of the fathers of the 1853 Argentine Constitution, stated a different position based on two principles. The first one was that a republican order could and should defend the principles of *political* centralization. The problem faced by new nations was the excess of *administrative* centralized regulations imposed by colonial legislation:

> Amidst our proud independent republicanism, we maintained until recently a corpus of administrative and private laws that organized our economic serfdom in the *Leyes de Partida*, and even worse, in the *Leyes de Indias*, the *Novísima Recopilación*, and the *Reales Cédulas* dictated by absolutist monarchs…. The *Fuero Juzgo, Fuero Real, Leyes del Estilo, Siete Partidas, Ordenamiento de Alcalá, Ordenamiento Real, Nueva Recopilación, Recopilación de Indias, Reales Cédulas, Ordenanza de Minas, Ordenanzas de Bilbao, Ordenanza de Intendentes* show we are not lacking organizing principles. Maybe our disgrace lies in the excess of organization.[28]

As for the study of the new discipline, he advised a young student that France was not a suitable place to learn about administrative law, since it was not yet clear whether legislation in France would be "monarchical or republican."[29]

26 V. do Uruguai (P. J. Soares de Sousa), *Ensaio sobre o Direito Administrativo* (Rio de Janeiro: Typographia Nacional, 1862), vol. II, 177–78.

27 Do Uruguai, *Ensaio*, vol. II, 201 and 215–16. See also M. de Moraes Silveira, "'Referência ao Estado e instituições peculiares ao Brasil': Uma leitura do *Ensaio sobre o Direito Administrativo*," in C. Araújo Cabral, R. Amaro de Oliveira Lanari, T. L. T. Tolentino, and V. da Silva Cunha (eds.), *Cultura Intelectual em Perspectiva. Linguagens, Instituições e Trajetórias (Belo Horizonte: Letramento*, 2020), 187–207.

28 J. B. Alberdi, "Sistema económico y rentístico de la Confederación Argentina según su Constitución de 1853," in J. B. Alberdi, *Obras Completas de Juan Bautista Alberdi* (Buenos Aires: Imp., Lit. y Enc. de "La Tribuna Nacional", 1886), vol. IV, 208–9 and 244.

29 J. B. Alberdi, "Carta sobre los estudios convenientes para formar un abogado con arreglo a las necesidades de la sociedad actual en Sudamérica. Escrita por el abogado

Alberdi's second guiding principle pointed toward a renewal of public and private law that would serve as a suitable framework for the economic and social transformation of the new nations – one guided by the principles of classical political economy. The whole of South American public law during the initial decades after independence now seemed archaic and inadequate because its goals were now outdated:

> During that period – when democracy and independence were the only goal of our constitutions – wealth, material progress, commerce, population, industry, economic interests in general were considered secondary matters, accessories of a secondary order, badly studied and obviously not attended to.

The development of "free immigration, liberty of commerce, railways and unfettered industry" were the objectives that had to guide the new constitutionalism.[30]

Whether coming from a more conservative outlook aimed at preserving some of the features of the colonial past or within a liberal discourse looking for a dramatic transformation of the material reality, the law was now predominantly seen as a product emanating from a politically centralized national state. Other possible sources of norms and regulations of social life, such as provincial legislatures or the Church, were gradually subjected to this process of subordination (also see Section 5.2).

The centrifugal effects of strong regionalist movements and economic structural imbalances helped to consolidate a *caudillista* tradition of strong personalization of power in provincial leaders. This in turn led to the concentration of all functions of administration, legislation, and judicial power in one person, rendering the functional differentiation necessary for the process of rationalization of the law that liberal nation-builders saw as indispensable impossible.[31] During the period in which the federal regimes in many countries in the region were first organizing, those provinces that had up to this point considered themselves autonomous political spaces strongly resisted

Alberdi a un joven compatriota suyo, Estudiante de Derecho en la Universidad de Turín, en Italia (16 Apr. 1850)," in J. B. Alberdi, *Obras Completas de Juan Bautista Alberdi* (Buenos Aires: Imp., Lit. y Enc. de "La Tribuna Nacional", 1886), vol. III, 343–53.

30 J. B. Alberdi, "Bases y puntos de partida para la organización política de la República Argentina," in J. B. Alberdi, *Obras Completas de Juan Bautista Alberdi* (Buenos Aires: Imp., Lit. y Enc. de "La Tribuna Nacional", 1886), vol. III, cap. X, "Cuál debe ser el espíritu del nuevo derecho constitucional en Sud América," 388.

31 On *caudillismo*, see F. Safford, "The Problem of Political Order in Early Republican Spanish America," *Journal of Latin American Studies* 24 (1992), 83–97; J. C. Chasteen, "Making Sense of Caudillos and 'Revolutions' in Nineteenth-Century Latin America," in J. C. Chasteen and J. S. Tulchin (eds.), *Problems in Modern Latin American History: A Reader* (Wilmington: S.R. Books, 1994).

these centralizing tendencies, leading to bitter political conflicts and even civil wars. By the mid-nineteenth century, during the "heyday of liberal reform," the balance was tilted in favor of centralized national powers, for example, in Argentina and Mexico; on other occasions, for example, in Colombia, the provinces set very tight restrictions to the scope of the national government.[32]

Just as the provinces – as autonomous political entities – were seen as an obstacle to centralization, the Catholic Church was also a potential countervailing power that liberal nation-builders had to overcome in order to consolidate their rule. This was a thorny issue, given the age-old interplay between religion, morality, and the law in the Iberian world (see Section 3.2). Depending on several factors, such as the relative wealth and power of each of the national Churches, the different trajectories of the state-building processes, and the character and ideological leanings of the ruling elites, church-state relations varied among the different countries in the region. Despite the difference circumstances, the process of secularization, generally speaking, advanced hand in hand with the consolidation of state authority.[33]

Nineteenth-century Latin American elites embraced liberalism as an antidote to what they saw as the backwardness inherent in the legacy of these colonial institutions and values. Legal and judicial centralization played an important part in such a project. This juridical bent of Latin American liberal nation-building was expressed in the enthusiastic efforts made by those elites in favor of constitutionalism, codification, and the setting up of new judicial institutions at the local and national level. Along with the new constitutions (see Section 5.2), national codification was seen by defenders and opponents alike as an important political tool for the consolidation of a unified nation in Europe and Latin America (see Section 5.3). In this sense, codification operated

32 D. Bushnell and N. Macaulay, *The Emergence of Latin America in the Nineteenth Century* (Oxford: Oxford University Press), 193 and 221; T. E. Anna, "Inventing Mexico: Provincehood and Nationhood after Independence," *Bulletin of Latin American Research* 15(1) (1996), 7–17; J. C. Chiaramonte, "La formación de los estados nacionales en Iberoamérica," *Boletín del Instiuto Ravignani* 15 (1997), 143–65; A. Agüero, "Autonomía por soberanía provincial. Historia de un desplazamiento conceptual en el federalismo argentino (1860–1930)," *Quaderni fiorentini per la storia del pensiero giuridico moderno* 43(1) (2014), 341–92; M. Carmagnani (ed.), *Federalismos latinoamericanos: México/Brasil/Argentina* (Mexico City: Fondo de Cultura Económica, 1993); D. Bushnell, *The Making of Modern Colombia. A Nation in Spite of Itself* (Berkeley: University of California Press, 1993). See also Chapter 4 in this volume.

33 V. Tau Anzoátegui, *El jurista en el Nuevo Mundo. Pensamiento. Doctrina. Mentalidad* (Frankfurt am Main: Max-Planck-Institut für europäische Rechtsgeschichte, 2016), 26; J. Lynch, "The Catholic Church in Latin America, 1830–1930," in L. Bethell (ed.), *The Cambridge History of Latin America, vol. IV: c.1870 to 1930* (Cambridge: Cambridge University Press, 1986), 529–30, 546–47, and 563. See also chapters 3.2 and 5.3 in this volume.

on two different levels. On the one hand, the new codes offered the possibility of achieving a certain legal homogeneity in territories where fragmentation and plurality of normative orders was more the rule than the exception. On the other hand, it operated as a powerful symbol of nationhood, since each of the new nations, despite similarities in historical trajectories and shared colonial legacies, could present its own codes as an expression of its own particular legal system.[34] Just as those defending the legacy of Hispanic or Portuguese colonial institutions could criticize the blind following of the US constitutional model, others pointed in the opposite direction. One of the most serious flaws of the 1869 Argentine Civil Code, according to its opponents, was that the drafter of the Argentine text, Dalmacio Vélez Sarsfield, had reproduced the antidemocratic and monarchical spirit that pervaded its main sources: the Napoleonic Code and the Brazilian *Esboço da consolidacao das leis*.[35]

Given the increase in state capacities resulting from the integration of the region to the Atlantic economy, which translated into larger fiscal revenues, these centralizing tendencies accelerated from the 1870s onwards. This, in turn, allowed for increased state control over the territories and material resources, the development of a "cognitive capacity" within an administrative infrastructure to manage those resources, and the symbolic capital that sustained its legitimation.[36] The ascendancy of positivism and different versions of "scientific politics" provided a new ideological framework: Notions of "order and progress" and the civilizing role of commerce would gradually displace the more exalted versions of liberal republicanism of previous decades.[37]

34 For the role of codification in the processes of national unification in Europe, see M. John, *Politics and the Law in Late Nineteenth-Century Germany: The Origins of the Civil Code* (Oxford: Clarendon Press, 1989), 6–7 and 18–20; J. A. Davis, *Conflict and Control: Law and Order in Nineteenth-Century Italy* (London: MacMillan, 1988), 122–25. See also, V. Tau Anzoátegui, *La codificación en la Argentina (1810–1870). Mentalidad social e ideas jurídicas* (Buenos Aires: Imprenta de la Universidad, 1977), 30–31.

35 J. B. Alberdi, "El proyecto de Código Civil para la República Argentina (1868)," in J. B. Alberdi, *Obras Completas de J. B. Alberdi* (Buenos Aires: Imp. de "La Tribuna Nacional", 1886), vol. VII, 80–135; V. Fidel López, "Crítica Jurídica," *Revista de Buenos Aires* XX (1869), 106–39.

36 Lawrence Whitehead defines the "cognitive capacity" of the administration as "the sustained organization to collect, process, analyse and deliver the types of information about society needed for a modern state to monitor and interpret the impact of its measures." Cf. Whitehead, "State Organization," 46–47. See also M. A. Centeno and A. E. Ferraro, "Republics of the Possible: State Building in Latin America and Spain," in M. A. Centeno and A. E. Ferraro (eds.), *State and Nation Making in Latin America and Spain: Republics of the Possible* (Cambridge: Cambridge University Press, 2013), 10–12.

37 C. A. Hale, "Political and Social Ideas in Latin America, 1870–1930," in L. Bethell, ed., *The Cambridge History of Latin America, vol. IV: c.1870 to 1930* (Cambridge: Cambridge University Press, 1986), 367–441; J. E. Sanders, *The Vanguard of the Atlantic World: Creating Modernity, Nation, and Democracy in Nineteenth-Century Latin America* (Durham and

Economic and social transformations, in turn, generated new pressures on the states. The emergence of urban middle sectors created new demands for a more generous provision of public goods such as internal security, communication and transportation infrastructure, better labor conditions, public education and health, all of which culminated in a more general transformation of the idea of citizenship and social rights. Each of these steps produced changes in the legal framework within which the states operated, and they favored the replacement of a traditional conception of local rule by the new centralized administrative techniques.

Economic Growth and the Expansion of State Capacities

Latin American economies during the second half of the nineteenth century participated in Atlantic capitalism mostly through the exports of primary commodities and the reception of European capital investments and credit. Relative institutional stability and attenuation of military conflicts opened up new opportunities for economic growth, which, in turn, facilitated the consolidation and expansion of state capacities in the region. Larger fiscal revenues allowed governments to channel increased resources to their military and police forces, thus helping to maintain internal security and face international threats. In addition, provision of basic public goods (education, justice, communication and transportation infrastructure, public health, and housing) conferred greater presence and visibility to state institutions in the different territories and frequently ensured a stronger sense of loyalty to the ruling political groups. Lastly, inflows of capital investments and credit facilitated the financing of such provisions and thus enabled governments to avoid imposing a higher tax burden on social actors who might otherwise become alienated.[38]

Wars, Public Finance, and State Building

Did internal military clashes and international wars play a role in the consolidation and expansion of Latin American states? Charles Tilly's influential historical sociology established a link between wars, the organization of

London: Duke University Press, 2014), 176–224; H. Sabato, *Republics of the New World: The Revolutionary Political Experiment in Nineteenth-Century Latin America* (Princeton: Princeton University Press, 2018), 197–202.

38 For general overviews of Latin American economic history during this period, see W. Glade, "Latin America and the International Economy, 1870–1914", in L. Bethell (ed.), *The Cambridge History of Latin America, vol. IV: c.1870 to 1930* (Cambridge: Cambridge University Press, 1989), 1–56; and R. Thorp, "Latin America and the International Economy from the First World War to the World Depression," in L. Bethell (ed.), *The Cambridge History of Latin America, vol. IV: c.1870 to 1930* (Cambridge: Cambridge University Press, 1989), 57–82.

fiscal procedures for the extraction of economic resources, and the origins of modern European states. States made wars and wars made states, Tilly concluded.[39] In Latin America, however, the almost constant presence of military conflicts in the history of the new nations imposed an excessive burden on the rather modest nineteenth-century states, and its incipient fiscal structures.[40] Unlike what Tilly's observations suggested for the European case, Latin American wars, Miguel Centeno stated, only left a trail of "blood and debt."[41]

The increased capacities of Latin American states, including the financing of military forces, was not due to wars or more efficient internal taxation systems; instead, it was the steady inflow of income generated by the customs, given the growth of international trade, and the availability of credit. Steven Topik observed that Brazil's integration into the international economy was crucial to the formation of the Brazilian state, and his analysis could just as easily be applied to much of the region. On the whole, the "foreign umbilical cord" nurtured the local regimes. Whereas in Europe, according to Topik, "war made the state and the state made war, in Brazil trade made the state and allowed the state to avoid internal wars." Similarly, Juan Carlos Garavaglia said of nineteenth-century Argentina: "[A]ll the mystery of political struggle and the civil wars of the period ... can be summarized in the formula that linked for a long time the custom with the army."[42] Miguel Centeno compared custom revenues as a percentage of the total fiscal income between the UK and France, on the one hand, and Chile and Brazil, on the other. He showed the disproportionate presence of custom revenue (more

39 C. Tilly, "Reflections on the History of European State-Making," in C. Tilly (ed.), *The Formation of National States in Western Europe* (Princeton: Princeton University Press, 1975), 73–76; C. Tilly, "War Making and State Making as Organized Crime," in P. B. Evans, D. Rueschmeyer, and T. Skocpol (eds.), *Bringing the State Back In* (Cambridge: Cambridge University Press, 1985), 169–91.

40 J. C. Garavaglia, J. Pro Ruiz, and E. Zimmermann (eds.), *Las fuerzas de guerra en la construcción del Estado. América Latina, siglo XIX* (Rosario: Prohistoria, 2012); M. Deas, "The Fiscal Problems of Nineteenth-Century Colombia," *Journal of Latin American Studies* 14(2) (1982), 287–328.

41 M. Centeno, *Blood and Debt: War and the Nation-State in Latin America* (University Park: The Pennsylvania University Press, 2002). For other arguments about war and state-making in Latin America, see F. López-Alves, *State Formation and Democracy in Latin America, 1810–1900* (Durham: Duke University Press, 2000); M. J. Kurtz, *Latin American State Building in Comparative Perspective: Social Foundations of Institutional Order* (Cambridge: Cambridge University Press, 2013).

42 S. Topik, "The Hollow State: The Effect of the World Market on State-Building in Brazil in the Nineteenth Century," in J. Dunkerley (ed.), *Studies in the Formation of the Nation State in Latin America* (London: Institute of Latin American Studies, 2002), 112–32; J. C. Garavaglia, "La apoteosis del Leviathan: El estado en Buenos Aires durante la primera mitad del siglo XIX," *Latin American Research Review* 38(1) (2003), 135–68.

than two-thirds of the total) in the Latin American cases.[43] This dependency of fiscal revenue on foreign trade and international credit, therefore, was a crucial element in the history of state-building in the region, leaving a long-term legacy of weakness in the capacity to extract resources through taxation for much of the period.

Territoriality and State Capacities

Integration into the international economy also unevenly shaped the geographic distribution of economic activities within the new nations. Certain key products served as the primary engine of economic growth in specific regions: wool, hides, beef, and cereals in Argentina; copper and nitrates in Chile, coffee in Brazil and Colombia, guano and nitrates in Peru – to cite just a few examples. External demand coupled with a revolution in transportation and internal communication capable of satisfying this demand gave birth to a new economic geography that frequently generated a structural disequilibrium between regions. This imbalance resulted in political conflicts involving the national state and provincial governments or even clashes between different provinces. Therefore, debates about the relative merits of greater centralization or greater provincial autonomy involved not only doctrinal differences about constitutional theory but also a reflection on the different possibilities of economic development and political ascendancy of internal regions *vis-à-vis* the national states.

Railways and telegraphs became two of the most important means of development of the "infrastructural capacities" of the new states. They led to greater control of territoriality and facilitated centralization. Telegraphed communication about disturbances in any given province, for instance, made it possible for national governments to mobilize troops (by rail) and quickly pacify the situation and/or support friendly provincial authorities through federal intervention. The cases of Mexico, Argentina, and Brazil in the second half of the nineteenth century all illustrate the powerful role played by the railway – both with regard to its economic impact and how the effects of this impact were used as a tool to facilitate greater control over the territories by the national governments.[44] Similarly, centralized control of the territory

43 Centeno, *Blood and Debt*, 101–66.

44 See the cases analyzed in Carmagnani, *Federalismos Latinoamericanos*, 180–223; J. Coatsworth, *Growth Against Development: The Economic Impact of Railroads in Porfirian Mexico* (DeKalb: Northern Illinois University Press, 1981); C. M. Lewis, "The Political Economy of State-Making: The Argentine, 1852–1955," in J. Dunkerley (ed.), *Studies in the Formation of the Nation State in Latin America* (London: Institute of Latin American Studies, 2002), 161–88; S. Topik, *The Political Economy of the Brazilian State, 1889–1930* (Austin: University of Texas Press, 1987).

demanded and gradually produced the development of new "cognitive capacities" (see earlier footnote 36). Exploration and cartography, surveying the territories, establishing land registries and cadasters (both urban and rural), census taking, and compiling official statistics became crucial to the production of the "legibility" of society by state bureaucracies.[45] Postal services, established by private companies and "*mensajerías*," were eventually taken over by national governments.[46] Lastly, the development of national educational systems and federal judicial institutions also contributed to enhance the presence of the national government – both substantively and symbolically – along the territories, thus contributing to the consolidation of its authority.[47]

Two consequences emerged from these processes of expanding state capacities relevant to the gradual emergence of the administrative state in the region: the sanction of regulatory frameworks for these new public endeavors and the growth of new state bureaucracies. Regarding the first point, the law established a state monopoly for certain activities in some cases, while it regulated the private provision of certain services or utilities in others. In the case of Argentina, for instance, state ownership and management of postal services (public monopoly established by the 1876 *Ley 816*) and of water supply and drainage, the *Obras Sanitarias de la Nación* (the 1912 *Ley 8889*) were rare

45 J. C. Garavaglia and P. Gautreau (eds.), *Mensurar la tierra, controlar el territorio. América Latina, siglos XVIII–XIX* (Rosario: Prohistoria, State Building in Latin America, 2011); M. Loveman, "Census Taking and Nation Making in Nineteenth-Century Latin America," in Centeno and Ferraro, *State and Nation Making*, 329–355; Hernán Otero, *Estadística y Nación. Una historia conceptual del pensamiento censal de la Argentina moderna (1869–1914)* (Buenos Aires: Prometeo Libros, 2007); Nancy P. Appelbaum, "Envisioning the Nation: The Mid-Nineteenth-Century Colombian Chorographic Commission," in M. A. Centeno and A. E. Ferraro (eds.), *State and Nation Making in Latin America and Spain: Republics of the Possible* (Cambridge: Cambridge University Press, 2013), 375–95; J. C. Scott, *Seeing Like a State* (New Haven: Yale University Press, 1998), for a critical discussion of the consequences of the development of these state capacities for modern societies.

46 L. Caimari, "La carta y el paquete. Travesías de la palabra escrita entre Argentina y Chile a fines del siglo xix," *Anuario Colombiano de Historia Social y de la Cultura* 48(2) (2021), 177–208.

47 H. D. Soifer, "The Sources of Infrastructural Power: Evidence from Nineteenth-Century Chilean Education," *Latin American Research Review* 44(2) (2009), 158–80; H. D. Soifer, "Elite Preferences, Administrative Institutions, and Educational Development during Peru's Aristocratic Republic (1895–1919)," in M. A. Centeno and A. E. Ferraro (eds.), *State and Nation Making in Latin America and Spain: Republics of the Possible* (Cambridge: Cambridge University Press, 2013), 247–67; R. Salvatore, "Between *Empleomanía* and the Common Good: Expert Bureaucracies in Argentina (1870–1930)," in M. A. Centeno and A. E. Ferraro (eds.), *State and Nation Making in Latin America and Spain: Republics of the Possible* (Cambridge: Cambridge University Press, 2013), 225–46; E. Zimmermann (ed.), *Judicial Institutions in Nineteenth-Century Latin America* (London: Institute of Latin American Studies, 1999).

cases. On the other hand, private provision by concession was granted in the case of railways and electricity, with legislation regulating tariffs and conditions of service. A little later, licenses were granted for the provision of telephone services and the use of radio frequencies. It was only after the Second World War, in conjunction with the Perón administration, that Argentina underwent the large-scale nationalization of public services and utilities. This took place within the context of the expansion of the doctrine of "public service" (see next section), and it served as the foundation for a new conception of the state.[48] Mexico, in contrast, decided to nationalize the country's railway much earlier. Between 1903 and 1908, the Mexican government consolidated the different lines into one public national company, *Ferrocarriles Nacionales de México*, and granted a degree of managing autonomy to a semi-independent body consisting of executives from the merged companies.[49]

The number of people employed by the railway, postal service, schools, courts, and public institutions grew rapidly, and the regulatory bodies overseeing these activities, originally rather small and initially focused on national accounting, public finance (*hacienda*), and the organization of the armed forces and internal security, went on to become large bureaucracies.[50] By the end of the nineteenth century, public employment and its regulation had become a salient issue in the debates about the future of public administration in the different countries. The need to form a body of state bureaucrats with a shared sense of identity and purpose – one conducive to carrying out their functions efficiently, consistently, and competently – became a prime objective of the reformers. Only later did fears about the effects of electoral democratization on the administration of the state materialize, which served to reinforce the belief in the need to isolate state bureaucracies from the pressures exerted by party politics. This revealed the extent to which the perception of technical "experts" in the management of public affairs as an alternative to "ideology,"

48 H. A. Mairal, "La ideología del servicio público," *Revista de Derecho Administrativo* 5(14) (1993), 359–437.

49 P. Riguzzi, "Inversión extranjera e interés nacional en los ferrocarriles mexicanos, 1880–1914," in C. Marichal (ed.), *Las inversiones extranjeras en América Latina 1850–1930. Nuevos debates y problemas en historia económica comparada (Sección de obras de historia. Serie Ensayos)* (Mexico City: Fondo de Cultura Económica, El Colegio de México, Fideicomiso Historia de las Américas, 1995); Mairal, "La ideología," 359–437.

50 Detailed studies on various Latin American cases are compiled in J. C. Garavaglia and J. Pro Ruiz (eds.), *Latin American Bureaucracy and the State Building Process (1780–1860)* (Newcastle upon Tyne: Cambridge Scholars Publishing, 2013). See also D. Barría, "An Honourable Profession: Public Employees and Identity Construction in Chile, 1880–1920," *Bulletin of Latin American Research* 38(2) (2019), 179–91; E. López, "El proceso de formación de la burocracia estatal chilena, 1810–1930," in F. Rengifo (ed.), *Historia política de Chile, 1810–2010* (Santiago: Fondo de Cultura Económica, 2017), vol. II, 55–85.

corruption, demagogy, and the interests of political parties had progressed. This was part of a movement for the purification of public administration, allegedly corrupted by the "spoils system" advanced by political parties and advocated by specialists in public law.[51] In 1920s Argentina, Rafael Bielsa denounced *"empleomanía"* (the manic expansion of public employment) as a corruption of both the electoral institutions and of a healthy public administration. He contended that Argentine political life and the state financial situation could only be healed if the local *"política criolla"* were replaced by new scientific principles of public administration.

Technical Elites and Social Policies

By the early twentieth century, new social problems and new demands stemming from an expanded conception of citizenship in the region forced the Latin American state elites to elaborate and enforce more complex and sophisticated forms of public policy. This, as Lawrence Whitehead pointed out, "has provided the single most powerful impulse toward the construction of 'modern states' throughout Latin America."[52] Academics and university professors were summoned to contribute a new type of "social knowledge" that would serve as the foundation for the new state policies needed to address these economic, social, cultural, and political challenges. The global circulation of experts, ideas, and models for social policies (the "Atlantic Crossings" examined by Daniel Rodgers[53]) were a key part of state responses in Latin America to the "social question," and transfers and adaptations of "social technologies" abounded. As had been the case elsewhere, the "expert" became a key factor in the development of new techniques of governmentality in state-building in nineteenth-century Latin America. The march toward the administrative state made visible the ways in which "the symbols of knowledge – its acquisition, analysis and privileged possession – have come to occupy the cornerstone of authority."[54]

51 D. Kennedy, "Three Globalizations of Law and Legal Thought: 1850–2000," in D. Trubek and A. Santos (eds.), *The New Law and Economic Development: A Critical Appraisal* (Cambridge: Cambridge University Press, 2006), 19–73, sees the rise and isolation of administrative "experts" as one of the features of the second globalization of legal thought.

52 Whitehead, "State Organization," 14.

53 D. Rodgers, *Atlantic Crossings: Social Politics in a Progressive Age* (Cambridge: Harvard University Press, 1998).

54 R. MacLeod (ed.), *Government and Expertise: Specialists, Administrators and Professionals, 1860–1919* (Cambridge: Cambridge University Press, 1988), xiv and 1; J. Leonhard, "The Rise of the Modern Leviathan: State Functions and State Features," in S. Berger (ed.), *A Companion to Nineteenth Century Europe, 1789–1914* (Oxford: Blackwell, 2006), 144–45.

Public hygiene and the control of epidemics were the first fields in which the demand for expert knowledge went hand in hand with claims for increased centralization of authority in the national governments.[55] The coupling of social welfare concerns with the defense of "national interests" helped legitimize the more centralized authority of the new institutions and mechanisms of intervention. This joint claim was frequently used to overrule objections arising from the defense of individual rights, voluntary associations, or the autonomy of local governments. In 1892, for instance, a report of the Argentine National Department of Hygiene summarized this philosophy as follows: "Hygiene does not admit the principle that an individual is the master of his person or property to the point of causing harm to public health, nor that local powers proceed in sanitary matters independently of the central power."[56] Similar concerns were expressed by some of the most prominent names in the development of hygiene and public medicine in the region, such as Oswaldo Cruz in Brazil, Eduardo Liceaga in Mexico, as well as Eduardo Wilde and José María Ramos Mejía in Argentina. Their efforts often tended to strengthen an already highly centralized form of government, displacing local authorities or voluntary associations.[57]

Other aspects of the Latin American "social question" exhibited similar patterns. The gradual development of social policies and labor regulations was shaped by this convergence of new state technical elites and centralized decision-making processes at the national level as a response to both the social demands and the consequent change in the idea of the limits of the law as an instrument for state action. Lawyers were at the center of the development of new labor regulations, for instance. As the Spanish reformer Adolfo Posada formulated it in his 1890 essay "Law and the Social Question": "The

On "governmentality," see M. Foucault, *Security, Territory, Population: Lectures at the Collège de France, 1977–78* (London: Palgrave Macmillan, 2007). For a brief review of the literature on these processes in Latin America, see M. B. Plotkin and E. Zimmermann (eds.), *Los saberes del Estado* (Buenos Aires: Edhasa, 2012), 9–28.

55 Cf. M. Cueto (ed.), *Salud, cultura y sociedad en América Latina* (Lima: Instituto de Estudios Peruanos, 1996).

56 Departamento Nacional de Higiene, "Higiene administrativa. Deberes y derechos de las autoridades sanitarias", *Anales del Departamento Nacional de Higiene* 2 (1892), 18–27.

57 N. Stepan, *Beginnings of Brazilian Science: Oswaldo Cruz, Medical Research and Policy, 1890–1920* (New York: Science History Publications, 1976); T. Meade, "'Civilizing Rio de Janeiro': The Public Health Campaign and the Riot of 1904," *Journal of Social History* 20(2) (1986), 301–22; J. Needell, "The *Revolta Contra Vacina* of 1904: The Revolt Against 'Modernization' in *Belle-Époque* Rio de Janeiro," *Hispanic American Historical Review* 67(2) (1987), 233–69; M. Cueto, "Sanitation from Above: Yellow Fever and Foreign Intervention in Peru, 1919–1922," *The Hispanic American Historical Review* 72(1) (1992), 1–22.

law is something that inevitably has to be encountered every time one wants to transform and improve the condition of men."[58]

The countries in this region each followed their own developmental path to what has been referred to as the "welfare-regulatory" state, or the "mediatory state" in instances in which the provision of welfare services and the regulation of labor disputes took place. Nevertheless, they shared a similar chronology in which two moments stand out. The first involves the "social question" of the early twentieth century, when the early consequences of economic modernization – incipient industrialization, urbanization, migrations – shaped liberal reform policies. The second occurred following the Great Depression of the 1930s, when many Latin American governments, within the framework of a more generalized critique of liberal constitutionalism and capitalism, began experimenting with corporatist models.[59]

Faced with the new economic and social reality, Uruguay underwent the most significant state transformation in Latin America. José Batlle y Ordoñez, who served two separate presidencies (1903–1907 and 1911–1915), laid the foundation for what could be called the first welfare state in the region. Batlle launched an ambitious program of social reforms that included an expansion of public education; the enactment of legislation regarding the maximum working day, minimum wage, the right to strike; the establishment of a national pension system; and compensation for industrial accidents. In this case, the process of advancing social legislation seems to have been the result of government initiatives rather than a response to pressure from organized groups. In the decades that followed, however, the expansion of the welfare state in Uruguay responded to the pressures and influences of an organized and mobilized labor movement.[60]

Developments in Chile, Argentina, Brazil, and Mexico combined the previously mentioned pattern of a first phase of "a paternalistic approach to

58 A. Posada, "El derecho y la cuestión social," in A. Menger, *El derecho civil y los pobres* (Madrid: Librería General de Victoriano Suárez, 1898), 8. The essay was the preliminary study of Posada's translation of A. Menger's *Das Bürgerliche Recht und die besitzlosen Volksklassen (Civil Law and the Poor)* (Tübingen: Laupp, 1890). On the role of legal culture in the origins of the "welfare-regulatory" state, L. M. Friedman, "Legal Culture and the Welfare State," in G. Teubner (ed.), *Dilemmas of Law in the Welfare State* (Berlin and New York: Walter de Gruyter & Co., 1988), 13–27.

59 L. Fink and J. M. Palacio (eds.), *Labor Justice across the Americas* (Urbana: University of Illinois Press, 2017), 47 and 260; E. Zimmermann, "The Welfare State in Latin America," in M. Mirow and V. Uribe-Urán (eds.), *A Companion to the Legal History of Latin America* (Leiden: Brill, forthcoming).

60 F. López-Alves, "State Reform and Welfare in Uruguay, 1890–1930," J. Dunkerley (ed.), *Studies in the Formation of the Nation State in Latin America* (London: Institute of Latin American Studies, 2002), 94–111.

social reform" within the framework of liberal institutions, and later corporatist experiments.[61] As we shall see in the next section, the 1930s and 1940s witnessed more profound transformations, in part driven by the crisis and replacement of the model of economic development that had prevailed in the previous period. The governments of Getúlio Vargas in Brazil and Perón in Argentina followed in the footsteps of the military governments of Ibáñez in Chile and Uriburu in Argentina. They combined the development of import substitution industrialization (ISI) with political authoritarianism, the expansion of social policies, and higher degrees of state intervention in the regulation of the economy.[62] This transformation included a corporate strategy of co-optation of the labor movement and the development of social legislation through direct interaction between executive and social actors that occasionally weakened parliamentary institutions.

In conjunction with the structural transformations that shaped anew the Latin American states, local jurists and legal scholars discussed and promoted new global currents of legal thought reconceptualizing the state and its functions. One of the elements contributing to the progress of the region in the early twentieth century, to cite James Bryce once more, was an openness to "the currents of world opinion ... the principles and precedents in the art of government."[63] The circulation and adaptation of some of these "currents of opinion" – in this case, legal theories about the state – is the subject of the next section.

The "Administrative International"

Starting in the early twentieth century, different strands of legal and political thought circulating in the region offered new perspectives of the state and its regulatory powers[64]. Against the background of these welcomed ideas, the prior reservations regarding the administrative tradition, mentioned in the introduction to Section 6.1, gradually faded away. Crucial to this

61 A. Segura-Ubiergo, *The Political Economy of the Welfare State in Latin America: Globalization, Democracy, and Development* (Cambridge: Cambridge University Press, 2007); F. Rengifo, "Desigualdad e inclusión. La ruta del Estado de seguridad social chileno, 1920–1970," *Hispanic American Historical Review* 97(3) (2017), 485–522; J. M. Malloy, *The Politics of Social Security in Brazil* (Pittsburgh: University of Pittsburgh Press, 1979); T. Murai, "The Foundation of the Mexican Welfare State and Social Security Reform in the 1990s," *The Developing Economies* 42(2) (2004), 262–87.

62 Cf. P. Drinot and A. Knight (eds.), *The Great Depression in Latin America* (Durham and London: Duke University Press, 2014).

63 Bryce, *South America*, 549.

64 I thank José María Portillo Valdés for his observation about the rise of an "administrative international" in the period.

development was the way in which what was previously perceived in Latin America as opposing schools of thought on government and public administration – French versus Anglo-Americans – were gradually reconciled and fused into a new formula for approaching the development of the modern state. In the interwar period, new currents of European corporativist thought were added to the range of possible formulas for structuring state institutions and activities.

The impact of these currents of thought was shaped by the particular social mechanisms of the global circulation of knowledge operating differently in each nation. Book translations, lecture tours by European jurists, professional networking, specialized journals, parliamentary speeches, and the press were important channels for the dissemination of the new doctrines among the legal communities and the general public. In terms of content, all these currents shared a common thread: how to transcend the limited radius of action that liberal constitutionalism granted the state in modern society.

The political discourse of the French Third Republic, aided by the growing corpus of jurisprudence produced by the *Conseil d'État*, developed new doctrines about the relation of individuals and the state. If, on the one hand, judicial institutions should not block the action of administrative agents, then on the other, individuals needed to be protected from possible arbitrary actions by the state. The challenge was to transform a legacy of the *Ancien régime* into an effective system of protection of individual rights, while at the same time providing the state with new tools to efficiently face the challenges posed by economic and social modernization. These were the problems occupying some of the most distinguished French jurists of the period, such as Maurice Hauriou, Gastón Jèze, and Léon Duguit, all of whom exerted a great deal of influence within the Latin American legal academy.[65] The independent administrative jurisdiction so central to this tradition was, as we have seen, difficult to reconcile with the liberal constitutional framework inherited by many Latin American nations. A.V. Dicey's 1885 classic *Introduction to the Study of the Law of the Constitution* dedicated an entire chapter to the comparison of the rule of law with the French *"Droit Administratif."* Having analyzed

65 H. S. Jones, *The French State in Question: Public Law and Political Argument in the Third Republic* (Cambridge: Cambridge University Press, 1993), 45–54. On French administrative law, see also J. Donzelot, *L'invention du social. Essai sur le déclin des passions politiques* (Paris: Fayard, 1984); P. Rosanvallon, *L'État en France de 1789 à nos jours* (Paris: Seuil, 1990); and J.-M. Blanquer and M. Milet, *L'invention de l'État. Léon Duguit, Maurice Hauriou et la naissance du droit public moderne* (Paris: Odile Jacob, 2015).

many of the French authors' works, Dicey concluded that this tradition was completely alien to the British political tradition of the rule of law.[66]

This discrepancy was reinforced by the different traditions of thinking about the state and political development in continental Europe and the Anglo-American tradition. The latter, sometimes defined as a "stateless political culture," characterized by a fragmented or centrifugal understanding of public authority, represented the polar opposite of a more "state-centered" continental political culture, with its tendency to conceive public authority in unitary terms.[67]

By the late nineteenth century, however, that opposition was beginning to wane in the United States. In 1887, Woodrow Wilson claimed that:

> The English race ... has long and successfully studied the art of curbing executive power to the constant neglect of the art of perfecting executive methods. It has exercised itself much more in controlling than in energizing government. It has been more concerned to render government just and moderate than to make it facile, well ordered, and effective. English and American political history has been a history, not of administrative development, but of legislative oversight, – not of progress in governmental organization, but of advance in law-making and political criticism.

Wilson concluded by stating: "The weightier debates of constitutional principle are even yet by no means concluded; but they are no longer of more immediate practical moment than questions of administration. It is getting to be harder to run a constitution than to frame one."[68] Ernest Freund,

66 A. V. Dicey, ch. XII "Rule of Law Compared with *Droit Administratif*," in A. V. Dicey, *Introduction to the Study of the Law of the Constitution*, ed. R. E. Michener (Indianapolis: Liberty Classics, 1982 [1915]), 213–67. This strict opposition between the two systems established by Dicey was later discredited. See M. J. Horwitz, "Legal Realism, the Bureaucratic State, and the Rule of Law," in M. J. Horwitz, *The Transformation of American Law: 1870–1960. The Crisis of Legal Orthodoxy* (Oxford: Oxford University Press, 1992), 213–30. For recent re-evaluations of that relationship, see R. A. Epstein, "Why the Modern Administrative State Is Inconsistent with the Rule of Law," *New York University Journal of Law and Liberty* 3 (2008), 491–515; P. Hamburger, *Is Administrative Law Unlawful?* (Chicago: The University of Chicago Press, 2014).

67 Jones, *The French State in Question*, 12. See also S. Skowronek, *Building a New American State: The Expansion of National Administrative Capacities. 1877–1920* (Cambridge: Cambridge University Press, 1982), 3–18, on the sense of "statelessness" inherited in the American political tradition; and W. J. Novak, "The Myth of the 'Weak' American State," *American Historical Review* 113(3) (2008), 752–72, for a critical discussion.

68 W. Wilson, "The Study of Administration," *Political Science Quarterly* 2(2) (1887), 206. A few years later, Wilson expanded on this point: "We printed the *SELF* large and the *government* small in almost every administrative arrangement we made; and that is still our attitude and preference. We have found that even among ourselves such arrangements are not universally convenient or serviceable. They give us untrained officials,

another prominent American jurist, agreed with this assessment. In 1894, he stated that it was remarkable how little attention the branch of public law dealing with the organization and action of the government had received from English and American jurists. Comparing the administrative systems of Europe and America, he concluded that the systems of the former exhibited a clear technical superiority over the latter.[69]

Far from having established some sort of rivalry between jurists on both sides of the Atlantic, considerable advancement toward a fusion of the two systems was made just a few years later. In 1905, Frank Goodnow published his *Principles of the Administrative Law of the United States*, drawing on continental ideas to advance a non-court-centered theory of administrative law. Two years later, French administrativist Gaston Jèze – who soon thereafter visited Latin America and was instrumental in establishing fluid contacts with local specialists in administrative law and public finance – translated Goodnow's book into French. In his introduction, Jèze pointed out that Goodnow made clear just how false the idea was that the Anglo Americans did not have a tradition of administrative law.[70] Similarly, in 1906, Maurice Hauriou claimed, echoing the statements made earlier by Wilson in the United States, that the development of administrative law aimed at providing a complete theory of the state, and rightly so. The modern state had been concerned with constitutional forms and civic liberties in its early stages of development, Hauriou contended, but now, at a more mature stage of development, had passed from political idealism to economic realism, "that is, to an administrative regime."[71]

From the Latin American standpoint, this rapprochement of American and European sources was of great importance. Latin American jurists could now perceive that the old antagonism between the defenders of the liberal constitutionalism – associated with the "American Model" – and the tradition

and an expert civil service is almost unknown amongst us." W. Wilson, "Democracy and Efficiency," *The Atlantic Monthly* 87(521) (1901), 289–99.

69 E. Freund, "The Law of the Administration in America," *Political Science Quarterly* 9(3) (1894), 404 and 423.

70 F. Goodnow, *Les principes du droit administratif des États-Unis* (Paris: V. Giard & E. Brière, 1907), i–ii. See also Horwitz, *The Transformation of American Law*, 224–25.

71 M. Hauriou, *Préface sur le droit public* (Paris: Imprimerie Contant-Laguerre, 1906), iii: "L'État moderne a été peu administratif pendant les premiers siècles de son existence … en un mot, on était dans la période d'idéalisme politique qui marque la jeunesse des peuples. Mais l'évolution s'est poursuivie, l'État moderne a pris de la maturité, il est passé de l'idéalisme politique au réalisme économique, c'est-à-dire au régime administratif." See also J.-L. Mestre, "France. The Vicissitudes of a Tradition" in P. Cane, H. Hofmann, E. Ip, and P. Lindseth (eds.), *The Oxford Handbook of Comparative Administrative Law* (Oxford: Oxford University Press, 2021), 23–51.

of administrative law – in the past linked to the "Latin tradition" of monarchical absolutism – was beginning to fade away. A novel fusion of European and American doctrines was giving birth to a new way of conceptualizing the modern state, which coincided with the needs of Latin American governments facing profound structural changes in their societies. Lecture tours in Latin America by some of the most prestigious authors associated with the administrative law tradition, not to mention the circulation of new Spanish translations of their works, facilitated the discussion of these new currents in the region. Three names in particular need to be mentioned in this context: the French jurists Léon Duguit and Gaston Jèze, and the Spaniard Adolfo Posada.

To celebrate the centennial festivities of the independence movements in Spanish America, the Spanish jurist Adolfo Posada embarked on a lecture tour in 1910 to Argentina, Chile, Uruguay, and Paraguay. Lecturing in Buenos Aires on "The Modern Idea of the State," Posada revealed the influence of Léon Duguit's ideas on his own thought.[72] Posada had already translated Duguit's book *Le droit social et le droit individuel et la transformation de l'État* (1908) into Spanish. Published in Madrid as *La transformación del Estado*, Posada included both an introductory study reviewing Duguit's ideas and a survey of the recent American and European developments in the theory of the state.[73]

Duguit himself visited Argentina and Chile the following year. Although his 1911 Buenos Aires lectures were dedicated to the analysis of recent changes in civil law doctrine, Duguit was by that time an established figure in public law. He had already published a number of works in which he put forward a new way of conceptualizing the state. Based on his Buenos Aires lectures, he published *Les transformations de droit public* (1913), an influential book summarizing the new doctrines about the state.[74] In this work, he targeted the concept of national sovereignty, which he considered an insufficient conceptual

72 A. Posada, "La idea moderna del Estado," *Revista Argentina de Ciencias Políticas* 1 (1910), 64–75. On Posada's South American tours, E. Zimmermann, "La proyección de los viajes de Adolfo Posada y Rafael Altamira en el reformismo liberal argentino," in J. Uría (ed.), *Institucionismo y reforma social en España. El Grupo de Oviedo* (Madrid: Editorial Talasa, 2000); E. Morales Raya, "La experiencia americana de Adolfo Posada en Paraguay (1910)," *Temas Americanistas* 32 (2014), 111–26.

73 L. Duguit, *La transformación del Estado*, trans. A. Posada, 2nd ed. (Madrid: F. Beltrán, 1922). On Posada and Duguit, see J. L. Monereo Pérez, *La reforma social en España: Adolfo Posada* (Madrid: MTAS, 2003); J. L. Monereo Pérez and J. Calvo González, "Léon Duguit (1859–1928): Jurista de una sociedad en transformación," *Revista de Derecho Constitucional Europeo* 4 (2005), 483–547.

74 During the interwar years, the influence of Duguit's new perspective on the state was such that Harold Laski described him in 1932 as a new Montesquieu, who had authored a new legal science for a new world. H. Laski, "La conception de l'État de Léon Duguit," *Archives de Philosophie du droit et de sociologie juridique* 1–2 (1932), 121–34.

foundation for the state. "Public service" became the cornerstone of the new theoretical foundation of state authority. Rather than focusing on its power to rule, the state was a national cooperative that guaranteed the ordered functioning of public services and its regulation. "Governments," Duguit concluded in the preface to the 1921 edition translated by Posada, "are no more than the managers of the public services."[75]

In 1921, Adolfo Posada visited Buenos Aires for a second time, and the lectures he gave were later published in book form as *Teoría social y jurídica del Estado*. The following year, Posada published in Madrid new editions of his Duguit translation and of Woodrow Wilson's *The State*. Both Posada's translations and his own texts were instrumental in making new ideas about the state available to legal scholars in Latin America. This represented a fusion of European public law, renewed by the administrative law tradition of Duguit and Hauriou, and the authors behind the latest innovations of American political science, whom Posada also analyzed in his texts (Frank Goodnow, Charles Merriam, Woodrow Wilson, and W. Willoughby). This fusion, as Posada stated, oriented the state to "a positive mission of promoting collective material and spiritual progress, considering the community as a whole," an idea already embraced by Latin American jurists.[76] Two years prior, in 1919, the Chilean Alejandro Álvarez, one of the most prestigious Latin American jurists of the twentieth century, had already highlighted the convergence of these new trends and suggested an inevitable result: "[T]he new idea of the state and its attributes will sketch the new conception of the law and its future orientation. This new conception is inspired by *solidarity*, by virtue of which legal relations must be regulated with collective, not individual, interests in mind." Álvarez remarked that administrative law – via its regulation of public services, police, and hygiene – was progressively delimiting private property for the benefit of the common good.[77]

75 L. Duguit, *Les transformations de droit public* (Paris: Librairie Armand Colin, 1913), xvi and 12; Duguit, *Transformación del Estado*, 8. See also Mairal, "La ideología," 361–65, arguing that the notion of "public service" became the central concept of the Administrative law tradition. On the Duguit lectures in Buenos Aires, see E. Zimmermann, "'Un espíritu nuevo': la cuestión social y el Derecho en la Argentina, 1890–1930," *Revista de Indias* 73(257) (2013), 81–106; J. A. Herrera, "Léon Duguit en Buenos Aires: sociabilidad y política en la recepción de una teoría jurídica," *Anuario de Filosofía y Teoría del Derecho* 8 (2014), 147–77.

76 A. Posada, "La nueva orientación del derecho político," in L. Duguit, *La transformación del Estado*, trans. A. Posada, 2nd ed. (Madrid: F. Beltrán, 1922), 207–17. Para la relevancia de esos autores en el desarrollo de la ciencia política de los Estados Unidos y en la reelaboración de la teoría del estado, véase.

77 A. Álvarez, *De la necesidad de una nueva concepción del Derecho. Memoria de incorporación del Miembro Académico de la Facultad de Leyes* (Santiago de Chile: Universidad de Chile, 1919), 189–94.

In 1923, Gaston Jèze – who, together with Duguit and Maurice Hauriou, represented the vanguard in the development of administrative law in France – toured Argentina and Chile, lecturing on his area of expertise, namely, public finance. Jèze was at the time director of both the *Revue de droit public* and the *Revue de science et de législation financière*. At this point, the reform of public finance and taxation was an issue closely linked to the idea of a healthy public administration in the region, a view energetically pushed by US diplomacy and testified to by the "Kemmerer missions" in Colombia, Chile, Ecuador, Perú, Bolivia, Mexico, and Guatemala.[78] In Buenos Aires, Jèze lectured at the School of Economics of the University of Buenos Aires, and his audience included a number of cabinet ministers and even the president, Marcelo T. de Alvear. His lectures were published the following year in Buenos Aires under the title *Finanzas públicas de la República Argentina*.[79] A few years later, Jèze expressed a rather pessimistic view of the ways in which Argentine society had naturalized the running of budget deficits, both in private and public life.[80]

As president of the prestigious *Institut International de Droit Public*, Jèze was also instrumental in forging a network of personal relations with Latin American jurists. In 1930, the Chilean Alejandro Álvarez became a "*Membre Titulaire*" of the institute – a distinction he shared with some of the most famous names in European and American public law and political science, such as Berthélemy, Carré de Malberg, Hans Kelsen, Adolfo Posada, Roscoe Pound, Ernest Freund, and Frank Goodnow. Among the "*membres associés*" were the Argentineans Rafael Bielsa ("*doyen de la Faculté de Droit de Rosario*") and Juan Antonio González Calderón ("*professeur a l'Université de Buenos Aires*").[81]

78 Cf. P. W. Drake, *The Money Doctor in the Andes: The Kemmerer Missions, 1923–1933* (Durham: Duke University Press, 1989); E. S. Rosenberg, *Financial Missionaries to the World: The Politics and Culture of Dollar Diplomacy* (Cambridge: Harvard University Press, 1999), 155–66.

79 G. Jèze, *Las finanzas públicas de la República Argentina* (Buenos Aires: Le Courier de la Plata, 1924). On Jèze in Argentina see N. Bacolla, "La visita de Gaston Jèze a la Argentina en 1923. Circulación de ideas y claves de recepción: entre las experiencias de la Tercera República y la reforma política argentina," *Cuadernos del Ciesal* 10(12) (2013), 51–72; A. V. Persello, "Administración Pública y política: las transformaciones en el sistema tributario en los años '30'," *Seminario Problemas de la Historia Argentina Contemporánea* (Buenos Aires: Universidad Nacional de San Martín, 2010); J. A. Sánchez Román, *Los argentinos y los impuestos. Lazos frágiles entre sociedad y fisco en el siglo XX* (Buenos Aires: Siglo XXI Editores, 2013).

80 "Le déficit budgétaire est la plaie des finances argentines. Mais il n'a jamais beaucoup effrayé les Argentins, qui sont habitués à dépenser au delá de leurs revenus. C'est la coutume chez les particuliers. Quoi d'étonnant à constater les mêmes errements dans la gestion des deniers publics?" G. Jèze, "La situation des finances publiques," in T. A. Le Bretón, R. Gache, G. Jèze, L. Diffloth, M. Daireaux, P. Janet, F. Legueu, and F. Georges-Picot, *Initiation à la vie en Argentine (Choses d'Amérique)* (Paris: A. Colin, 1935), 54.

81 Institut de Droit International, *Annuaire de l'Institut International de Droit Public* (Paris: Les Presses universitaires de France, 1930), 20–24. In the following years (1932–1934)

As part of his South American tour, Jèze also lectured in the Argentine city of Rosario, where the dean of the law school, Rafael Bielsa, welcomed him.[82] In his 1923 Rosario lectures, Jèze touched on two other central topics in the development of the modern conception of the administrative state. One was the role of "public service" in a democratic state, and the other focused on the protection of individual rights through the development of legal actions against the arbitrary actions of public officials. When it comes to the topic of the "public service school," Jèze can be seen as a disciple of Duguit, who was a pioneer in this field. Public service, he reiterated, had replaced the idea of sovereignty as the foundation of the state and become "the fundamental notion of modern public law." Governments were the managers of these cooperatives of public services, and their actions as such were considered acts of public power. Administrative law was, largely, the body of norms regulating the working of public services.[83] In Rosario, he expanded these ideas, discussing the "democratic organization" of public services and its administrative regime.[84] As for the second theme, Hauriou had already claimed that the jurisprudence of the *Conseil d'État* had shown an evolution from its foundations on the prerogative of the administration to a jurisdiction of "equity."[85] In "*La defensa del ciudadano ante el avance del poder público*," another Rosario lecture that was expanded on in a French version and later published in *Institut's Annuaire*, Jèze claimed that the remedies developed by French administrative jurisprudence represented not only the single most important legal creation by French jurists but also the best possible protection of individual liberties known to the world.[86]

Bielsa published several contributions in the *Annuaire* on topics such as federal intervention in the provinces, the development of administrative regulations, and legal remedies and actions in Argentina.

82 M. Á. De Marco, "Rafael Bielsa y la conformación de un nuevo modelo de formación científica universitaria", *Revista de Historia del Derecho* 35 (2007), 83–171; M. Á. De Marco, "Estado, Universidad y política en la modernización argentina, 1927–1930. El aporte de lo regional al proceso nacional," *Temas de historia argentina y americana* 6 (2007), 49–80.

83 V. Kondylis, "La conception de la fonction publique dans l'œuvre de Gaston Jèze," *Revue d'histoire des facultés de droit et de la culture juridique, du monde des juristes et du livre juridique* 12 (1991), 43–54.

84 De Marco, "Rafael Bielsa," 99.

85 M. Hauriou, "Le dévelopment de la jurisprudence administrative depuis 1870," in Société de législation comparée, *Les transformations du droit dans les principaux pays depuis cinquante ans (1869–1919). Livre du cinquantenaire de la Société de législation comparée* (Paris: Librairie Générale de Droit et de Jurisprudence, 1923), vol II, 7.

86 G. Jèze, "Les libertés individuelles," in Institut de Droit International, *Annuaire de l'institut international de droit public* (Paris: Les Presses universitaires de France, 1929), 180: the *recours en excès de pouvoir*, «la plus merveilleuse création des juristes» was "l'arme la plus efficace, la plus économique et la plus pratique qui existe au monde pour défendre

The 1930s: Economic Crisis, Ideological Realignments, and Corporativism

It is widely acknowledged that the Great Depression of the 1930s brought about a number of far-reaching changes in Latin America. In the economic sphere, for example, there was the shift from export-led growth to ISI; in the political arena, there were numerous military coups replacing democratic regimes; and ideologically speaking, the simultaneous process of critique of capitalism and liberal democracy. As we have already discussed, the move toward centralization on the part of the national states had already started years earlier. But this global economic crisis served as a catalyst that accelerated this process and eventually set the stage for an even greater level of intervention in social and economic matters.[87] Moreover, the crisis revealed the circulation of similar models of state intervention. As Patel has pointed out, "the Great Depression did not just unmake and reestablish global links; it sometimes also synchronized debates, and even the political and societal answers given to them."[88]

The two most popular types of response regarding the organization of the state circulating in the West were the American New Deal, which quickly became a global icon for reformers everywhere, and the new experiments in corporativism launched by fascist regimes in Europe. Despite the very different ideological basis underpinning these two approaches, the "strange legal culture of the 1930s" and commonalities in terms of policy meant that a combination of the two was even possible.[89]

In the United States, the growth of administrative state action in the social and economic spheres resulted in the creation of multiple boards, commissions, and authorities that carried out functions traditionally assigned to the legislative and judicial branches. As one observer pointed out at the time, the increasing complexity of social phenomena had rendered the old theories and

les libertés." See also Jones, *The French State in Question*, 207–8: "The rejuvenators of the tradition of juristic reflection about the state … recognized that administrative justice had a vital role to play in giving substance to the concept of a state subject to law…. The separate administrative jurisdiction established … in French public life … has proved to be in some respects a much more effective protector of the rights and liberties of the citizen than the English legal tradition championed by Dicey."

87 Cf. Drinot and Knight, *The Great Depression*, 1–6.

88 K. K. Patel, *The New Deal: A Global History* (Princeton: Princeton University Press, 2016), 43.

89 On the New Deal as a "global icon," Patel, 298–300; on the "strange legal culture of the 1930s" and the presence of non-fascist corporativism in the New Deal, see J. Q. Whitman, "Of Corporatism, Fascism, and the First New Deal," *The American Journal of Comparative Law* 39(4) (1991), 747–78.

doctrines concerning the separation of powers obsolete. As a consequence of this situation:

> The most significant fact connected with this development has been the tendency to place final and conclusive authority in the hands of administrative officers, and thereby to exclude from the control of the judiciary a continually widening field of governmental authority.... Contrary to the insistence of many legal writers and judges that the principles of Anglo-American law were opposed to the growth of administrative law, it has found a secure place in these systems.[90]

The New Deal presented another feature relevant to the development of the administrative state: the demand for a more efficient administrative management of the executive branch. In 1937, President Roosevelt formed the Brownlow Committee to study the issue. When presenting the committee's results, he insisted that this was a long-standing problem, and that "the republican form of government" now demanded devotion to the task of "making that Government efficient."[91]

The other engine of state transformations was the adoption of models of corporativism that combined economic elements of labor and capital organization with a political project of transforming the models of representation of classical liberal democracy. In Brazil, after initial resistance during the First Republic (1889–1930) to the advancement of state intervention in economic and social matters, the demands posed by issues such as public health, urban planning, and the "social question" eased the transition toward an expanded administrative action. After the pioneering work of the Viscount of Uruguai, cited previously, it was Augusto Olympio Viveiros de Castro, with his early twentieth-century treatise *Tratado de sciencia da administração e direito administrativo*, who led the development of administrative law in the country.[92]

90 C. Grove Haines, "Effects of the Growth of Administrative Law upon Traditional Anglo-American Legal Theories and Practices," *The American Political Science Review* 26(5) (1932), 875–94.

91 "We know good management in the home, on the farm, and in business, big and little. If any nation can find the way to effective government, it should be the American people through their own democratic institutions," concluded Roosevelt. The President's Committee on Administrative Management, *Administrative Management in the Government of the United States* (Washington: United States Government Printing Office, 1937), iii.

92 A. O. Viveiros de Castro, *Tratado de sciencia da administração e direito administrativo*, 3rd ed. (Rio de Janeiro: Jacintho Ribeiro dos Santos Livreiro-Editor, 1914). See also A. Cerqueira-Leite Seelander, "O Direito Administrativo e a expansão do Estado na Primeira República: Notas preliminares a uma história da doutrina administrativa no Brasil," *Revista do Instituto Histórico e Geográfico Brasileiro* 485 (2021), 165–202.

In the 1930s, the works by Oliveira Vianna pointed to a more aggressive line of change, aiming at a substitution of liberal forms of political and economic organization with a corporativist framework. In his *Problemas de política objetiva* (1930), Vianna claimed that parliaments were "an expensive luxury" to be "cultivated only to a certain extent." Technical councils and the administrative organization of social classes were going to replace them (parliaments) as the true representative of mass opinion and the organs for the elaboration of the law. A few years later, in *Problemas de Direito Corporativo* (1938), he argued in favor of "functional and corporative autarchies" to replace "territorial autarchies (federalism and political decentralization)" and the expansion of "administrative tribunals."[93]

Similar developments were taking place in Argentina in the late 1920s, anticipating some of the initiatives of the 1930 military coup. A bill presented to the Chamber of Deputies in 1927 proposed a change in parliamentary representation in order to incorporate "industrial and economic interests" (*"las fuerzas vivas industriales y económicas"*). The following year, another bill directly proposed the adoption of a "National Corporative Organization," patterned after the models developed in Italy and Spain, creating technical councils and a more representative parliament than the one formed by "an amorphous universal suffrage."[94] Nevertheless, opposition by all of the political parties doomed the military government to reform the 1853 constitution in order to incorporate "functional representation" as a means of "perfecting democracy."[95]

It was clear at this point that the traditional conceptualization of the liberal state was in crisis. There was now a search for new foundations, and these could take one of three forms: the principles of public service or social solidarity developed mainly in France, the consolidation of the American school of public administration that received an important boost with Roosevelt's New Deal, or the principles of corporativism. In 1936, the Argentinean jurist

93 O. Vianna, *Problemas de política objetiva*, 2nd ed. (Sao Paulo: Companhia Editora Nacional, 1947 [1930]), 179; O. Vianna, *Problemas de Direito Corporativo* (Rio de Janeiro: J. Olympio, 1938), 49–50. See also F. R. Madeira Pinto, "A administrativização do direito constitucional: Oliveira Vianna e a absorção dos poderes legislativos e judiciário pelas corporações administrativas," *História do Direito* 2(3) (2021), 210–23; and W. Guandalini Jr. and A. Codato, "O Código Administrativo do Estado Novo: A distribuição jurídica do poder politico na ditadura," *Estudos Históricos* 29(58) (2016), 481–504.

94 *Diario de Sesiones de la Cámara de Diputados*, 14 Sept. 1927, 613–14; 21 Sept. 1928, 678–82.

95 On the military government's attempts to reform the constitution in Argentina, see J. L. Romero, *Las ideas políticas en Argentina* (Buenos Aires: Fondo de Cultura Económica, 1975); C. Ibarguren, *La historia que he vivido* (Buenos Aires: Ediciones Dictio, 1977). On the debates about state organization and public administration, see Persello, "Administración Pública y política."

Rafael Bielsa summarized how much this process of abandoning the liberal legal thinking, inherited from the nineteenth century, had spread throughout the region in favor of a legal philosophy that expanded the range of state activities. The mission of the jurist, Bielsa said, was:

> … to collaborate in the work of integration of public law, abandoning somewhat the overly broad formulas of that liberal political philosophy that has dominated the last century, formulas that served for the great proclamations stamped on constitutions, but which have not proved very efficient in the domain of the *concrete activity of the state.*[96]

A few years later, another Argentinean jurist, Arturo Sampay, followed a similar path in his book *The Crisis of the Liberal-Bourgeois Rule of Law* (1942). Sampay, who became one of the leading jurists of the *Peronista* regime, analyzed contemporary varieties of state organization: the fascist state, the Russian Soviet state, the national-socialist state, and the corporative state of Portugal. Sampay, citing the Romanian theoretician of corporativism Mihail Manoilesco, concluded: "[T]he twentieth century will be the century of corporatism, as the nineteenth century has been the century of liberalism."[97] This preference for corporatist formulas at the time of thinking up new constitutions was most fully manifested in the regimes of Getúlio Vargas in Brazil and Juan Domingo Perón in Argentina. The 1934 and 1937 Brazilian constitutions as well as the 1949 Argentine Constitution all exhibited this strong tendency toward the corporatist structuring of social interests accompanied by a pronounced concentration of authority in the national executive.[98]

The second half of the twentieth century brought with it new waves of military coups, with tragic consequences for human rights (see Sections 6.2 and 6.3). After a new wave of democratization, constitutional reforms tended to follow a similar pattern of concentration of authority in the "engine room of

96 R. Bielsa, "El desarrollo institucional del derecho administrativo y la jurisdicción contenciosa. Discurso de incorporación a la Academia Nacional de Derecho y Ciencias Sociales, 20 de agosto de 1936," in R. Bielsa (ed.), *Estudios de Derecho Público. Derecho Administrativo* (Buenos Aires: Editorial Depalma, 1950).

97 A. Sampay, *La crisis del estado de derecho liberal-burgués* (Buenos Aires: Losada, 1942), 353. See also, S. T. Ramella, "Arturo Enrique Sampay (Argentina, 1911–77)," in M. C. Mirow and R. Domingo (eds.), *Law and Christianity in Latin America: The Work of Great Jurists* (London: Routledge, 2021), 470–82.

98 G. L. Negretto, "El populismo constitucional en América Latina. Análisis crítico de la Constitución Argentina de 1949," in A. Luna-Fabritius, P. Mijangos y González, and R. Rojas Gutiérrez (eds.), *De Cádiz al Siglo XXI. Doscientos años de constitucionalismo en México e Hispanoamérica (1812–2012)* (Mexico City: Taurus, CIDE, 2012); L. Vita, "Weimar in Argentina: A Transnational Analysis of the 1949 Constitutional Reform," *Rechtsgeschichte – Legal History* 27 (2019), 176–83.

the constitution," as Roberto Gargarella put it, "without taking into account the impact that the organization of power tends to have upon those very rights."[99] The ascendance of the administrative state did little to improve the "weak culture of rights"[100] that had developed in the region during the early phases of independent life.

. . .

6.2 Dictatorships

CRISTIANO PAIXÃO

Dictatorships dominate the historical landscape of Latin America in the second half of the twentieth century. Authoritarian regimes established between the late 1950s and the mid-1970s developed and multiplied tools of repression and formed internal networks of collaboration. These authoritarian experiences had a significant impact on legal and judicial institutions, freedoms, and guarantees for citizens, groups, and political associations. There are multiple perspectives from which to observe the operation and language of law in these settings and understand the numerous influences, exchanges, and interrelations with other legal concepts and ideas developed or applied in countries outside the American continent.

In the following, I suggest to analyze these issues by looking at several aspects. First, I discuss the problematic relations between the authoritarian regimes and the constitutions that were in force when the dictatorships were established. I then turn to the role played by the judiciary and several other institutions in the development and consolidation of Latin American authoritarian regimes and describe the complex web of transnational repression by and resistance to Latin American dictatorships. This web of repression included the so-called Operation Condor, an initiative launched by the Chilean regime, in which several other countries participated (see also Section 5.3). The web of resistance is exemplified by the activities of the Second Russell Tribunal, which gave expression to various forms of resistance and solidarity with Latin America throughout the world. Finally, I will emphasize the impact of the repressive experience on the construction of

99 R. Gargarella, *Latin American Constitutionalism, 1810–2010. The Engine Room of the Constitution* (Oxford: Oxford University Press, 2013), 185.

100 C. Garriga (ed.), *Historia y Constitución. Trayectos del constitucionalismo hispano* (Mexico City: Instituto de Investigaciones Dr. José María Luis Mora, 2010), 19.

memorial sites around Latin America and will describe the biographic itineraries of three members of the Brazilian resistance. The analysis will focus on the historical developments that took place in the 1960s, 1970s, and 1980s, when ruptures, coups d'état, internal conflicts, and regime changes occurred more frequently.

Institutional Breaks: Constitutionalism, Coups d'État and the Role of the Judicial Power

There is no such thing as a "particular type" of Latin American dictatorship. Throughout the twentieth century, the region had many authoritarian regimes, and it is impossible to identify a "dominant form" that would allow for generalization. As will be highlighted here, there were common elements to several of these dictatorships, but it is also important to remember that there were many differences.

Establishing a dictatorship usually required the breakdown of the existing order. More often than not, such a breakdown involved a coup d'état – which in many countries had the military as protagonists, along with varying degrees of civilian participation. From a legal historical perspective, this kind of collapse implied a change in the foundations of legality. Establishing a dictatorship also involved redefining the legal order. This was one of the initial challenges of all attempts to seize power – and retain it – by force: overcoming barriers and constraints to the exercise of political power (which usually requires rotating governments, periodic elections, and the regular functioning of legal institutions run by civilians). However, the removal of the existing legal order usually implied not only a negative element, the obliterating of the already-existent legal bases. It also required presenting an alternative model to the existing legal framework.

In his study of the authoritarian regimes implemented in Chile and Argentina in the 1970s, Robert Barros expressly refers to the challenge of trying to destroy the legal foundation that existed in the period prior to the coups d'état that occurred in 1973 and 1976, respectively. According to Barros, the Chilean and Argentine dictatorships needed to bring about an abrupt transformation of the existing constitutional frameworks, and this occurred in two distinct thematic areas.[101] The first included an attack on the constitution as a higher law and the subversion of the classical separation of powers. In

101 R. Barros, "Courts Out of Context: Authoritarian Sources of Judicial Failure in Chile (1973–1990) and Argentina (1976–1983)," in T. Ginsburg, T. Moustafa (ed.), *Rule by Law: The Politics of Courts in Authoritarian Regimes* (Cambridge: Cambridge University Press, 2008), 156–79.

order to be successful, authoritarian governments must concentrate powers, intervene in parliamentary houses, and curtail the autonomy of the judiciary. For this to happen and result in a legal norm, the barriers set by constitutions of a liberal nature and informed by modern constitutionalism have to be removed. The second obstacle to the establishment of a dictatorship are the limits imposed by the very concept of the rule of law. If a political regime engages in acts such as imposing arbitrary arrests, declaring a state of siege or emergency, and persecuting or punishing its people, it becomes impossible to fulfill individual and collective guarantees, including the right to due legal process and to a full defense, for instance.

The incompatibility of the measures implemented by the Chilean and Argentine dictatorships with the standards of modern constitutionalism is thus evident. In both cases, existing governments were overthrown, parliaments were closed, the military openly assumed power, and emergency measures were adopted swiftly, including punishments, persecutions, state violence, and executions.[102] The same dynamic had already been displayed in the civil-military coup that occurred in Brazil in 1964, but with one key distinction: In the case of Brazil, the periods of parliamentary closure were relatively brief. However, many members of parliament – no less than 173 congressmen, according to the official figures from the House of Representatives – were expelled, which evidently affected the composition of Congress.[103] As a result, the legislative branch maintained a pro-regime majority for twenty-one years. Apart from this, the Brazilian dictatorship comprised all the features mentioned earlier.[104]

102 On the dictatorships in Argentina and Chile, see L. Bethell (ed.), *The Cambridge History of Latin America, vol. VIII: Latin America Since 1930: Spanish South America* (Cambridge: Cambridge University Press, 1999); J. Dávila, *Dictatorship in South America* (Chichester: Wiley-Blackwell, 2013); J. Grigera and L. Zorzoli (eds.), *The Argentinian Dictatorship and Its Legacy: Rethinking the Proceso* (Cham: Palgrave Macmillan, 2020); G. Águila, S. Garaño, and P. Scatizza (eds.), *Represión estatal y violencia paraestatal en la historia reciente argentina: Nuevos abordajes a 40 años del golpe de Estado* (La Plata: Universidad Nacional de La Plata. Facultad de Humanidades y Ciencias de la Educación, 2016); F. Finchelstein, *The Ideological Origins of the Dirty War: Fascism, Populism, and Dictatorship in Twentieth Century Argentina* (New-York: Oxford University Press, 2014); W.F. Sater and S. Collier, *Historia de Chile, 1808–2017* (Madrid: Akal, 2019); G. Salazar and J. Pinto, *Historia contemporánea de Chile I: Estado, legitimidad, ciudadanía* (Santiago de Chile: LOM, 1999).

103 D.B. Azevedo, M.N. Rabat, *Parlamento mutilado – deputados federais cassados pela ditadura de 1964* (Brasília: Edições Câmara dos Deputados, 2012), 19–23.

104 For an overview on the Brazilian military dictatorship, see A. Alonso and M. Dolhnikoff (eds.), *1964: do golpe à democracia* (São Paulo: Hedra, 2005); C.M. Santos, E. Teles, and J.A. Teles (eds.), *Desarquivando a ditadura: memória e justiça no Brasil* (São Paulo: Hucitec, 2009), vol. I/II; J. Ferreira and L.A.N. Delgado (eds.), *O Brasil*

From a legal history perspective, the Latin American dictatorships engaged in "de-constitutionalization" operations. These activities – in particular during the time immediately after the institutional and political break with the previous regime – took the shape of assaults on the established constitutional order. These operations were of a "de-constitutive" nature, in order to enable the implementation of extraordinary measures.[105]

These regimes then proceeded to issue unilateral norms, enforced by military commanders, which granted special powers to the newly installed government and had an element of self-protection – these acts could not be reviewed by the judiciary or any other branch of government. In Brazil, as of April 9, 1964, the so-called "institutional acts" selectively amended the pre-existing constitutional order and allowed the practice of "complementary acts" by government authorities.[106] In Chile, the so-called *bandos* were issued, signed by the military *junta* that assumed power on September 11, 1973; these acts were military documents declaring a state of war (in this case, an internal conflict) and emphasizing, among other aspects, patriotism, order, respect, discipline, and hierarchy as the values to be observed by the Chilean society from that moment onwards. In a second step, several decrees were issued which gradually modified the text of the 1925 Constitution, while a jurists' committee drafted a bill for a new constitution.[107] In Argentina, the military *junta* that took power on March 24, 1976, elaborated *actas institucionales*,

Republicano: o tempo do regime autoritário – ditadura militar e redemocratização, Quarta República (1964–1985) (Rio de Janeiro: Civilização Brasileira, 2019); R.P.S. Motta, *Passados presentes: o golpe de 1964 e a ditadura militar* (Rio de Janeiro: Zahar, 2021); C. Fico, "Ditadura militar brasileira: aproximações teóricas e historiográficas," *Tempo & Argumento*, 9(20) (2017), 5–74, and C. Fico, *Além do golpe: versões e controvérsias sobre 1964 e a Ditadura Militar* (Rio de Janeiro: Record, 2004).

105 On the topic of de-constitutionalization, see G. Pisarello, *Procesos constituyentes: caminos para la ruptura democrática* (Madrid: Trotta, 2014), 79–105; B. de S. Santos, *Construindo as Epistemologias do Sul: Antologia essencial – vol. II: Para um pensamento alternativo de alternativas* (Ciudad Autónoma de Buenos Aires: CLACSO, 2018), 245–46; M. Meccarelli and C. Paixão, "Costituzione e democrazia in emergenza: il problema delle categorie analitiche," in G. De Cosimo (ed.), *Curare la democrazia. Una riflessione multidisciplinare* (Padova: Wolters Kluwer/CEDAM, 2022).

106 C. Paixão, "Entre regra e exceção: normas constitucionais e atos institucionais na ditadura militar brasileira (1964–1985)," *História do Direito: RHD*, vol. I (1) (2020), 227–41; L.A.A. Barbosa, *História constitucional brasileira: mudança constitucional, autoritarismo e democracia no Brasil pós-1964* (Brasília: Edições Câmara, 2018), 49–141.

107 R. Barros, *Constitutionalism and Dictatorship: Pinochet, the Junta, and the 1980 Constitution* (Cambridge: Cambridge University Press, 2004), 36–116; E. P. González and F. Z. Urbina, "La doctrina del gobierno de facto y las actas constitucionales de 1976: juristas chilenos avalando decretos leyes," *História do Direito: RHD* 2(3) (2021), 244–71; D. G. M. Araneda, "Legitimación e institucionalización. El poder militar disciplinario en Chile: bandos y decretos ley (1973–74)," *Estudios – Revista del Centro de Estudios Avanzados* 44 (2020), 185–206.

secret documents that suppressed guarantees set forth in the national constitution, decreed a state of emergency, and allowed the adoption of repressive measures against political opponents.[108]

Addressing these questions implies two different political developments. The first and most evident one was the Cold War. Latin America found itself in the zone of influence of the United States, which had become concerned about the growing number of left wing movements made up of peasants, workers, students, and liberal professionals, who increasingly occupied prominent positions and exerted a controlling influence within political parties. As a result, a close collaboration between the Latin American business sector and military and representatives of the US government developed, which included the training of the security forces of Latin American military governments on US soil. These concerns of the United States were amplified in 1959 with the unfolding of the Cuban Revolution.[109]

Another political conflict, which occurred between the late 1950s and early 1960s and was pivotal to the setup of Latin American dictatorships, was the Algerian War of Independence, which engaged the armed forces and political leaders of France. As is well known, one of the consequences of this war was the emergence of a clandestine force, the Secret Army Organization, within the French military. This organization expressed a radical opposition to Algeria's demands for independence and proceeded to act through the systematic use of torture, the infiltration of the independence movements by agents, and violence against civilians. The rationale for these actions was the idea that the "enemy" was not a conventional army, but a group that engaged in guerrilla warfare and had to be fought with more effective methods of repression. This clandestine organization engaged in what it described as a "revolutionary war."[110]

108 J. P. Bohoslavsky, "Introducción – entre complicidad militante, complacencia banal y valiente independencia," in J. P. Bohoslavsky (ed.), *¿Usted también, doctor? Complicidad de jueces, fiscales y abogados durante la dictadura* (Buenos Aires: Siglo Veintiuno, 2015), 15–27. The institutional acts from the whole dictatorship period are accessible at: www.argentina.gob.ar/defensa/archivos-abiertos/centro-de-documentos-digitalizados/Fondo-Junta-Militar (last accessed July 20, 2022).

109 S. Mainwaring and A. Pérez-Liñán, *Democracies and Dictatorships in Latin America: Emergence, Survival, and Fall* (Cambridge: Cambridge University Press, 2013), 63–92; C. Fico, *O Grande Irmão: da Operação Brother Sam aos anos de chumbo – O Governo dos Estados Unidos e a ditadura militar brasileira* (Rio de Janeiro: Civilização Brasileira, 2008).

110 M. Evans, *Algeria: France's Undeclared War* (Oxford: Oxford University Press, 2012); D. Leroux, "Promouvoir une armée révolutionnaire pendant la guerre d'Algérie: Le Centre d'instruction pacification et contre-guérilla d'Arzew (1957–1959)," *Vingtième Siècle. Revue d'Histoire.* 120 (2013), 101–12; J. R. Martins Filho, "Tortura e ideologia: os militares brasileiros e a doutrina da *guerre révolutionnaire* (1959–1974)," in Santos, Teles, and Teles, *Desarquivando a ditadura*, vol. I, 179–202.

The national security doctrine developed in South American countries to justify the coups d'état was directly inspired by this concept of revolutionary war. Four French lieutenant-colonels were sent to the Argentine War College in 1957 to train Argentine military personnel. In 1959, a Brazilian colonel, who had participated in the training sessions in Argentina, brought the basics of the revolutionary war to the Brazilian War College. This exchange remained active until the early 1960s; Argentinian and Brazilian documents on national security clearly show the impact of the concept of revolutionary war on Latin American actors.[111]

After successive coups d'état had taken place in Latin America, the dictatorial regimes began to search for consolidating formulas. These included procedures for rotation in the occupation of executive positions (many dictatorships had collegiate military *juntas*), agreements with segments of the political class, and responses to external pressure calling for a reduction of repressive actions. In this context, the ruling military, with greater or lesser support from civilians, moved to propose, at various levels of organization, solutions that would allow for the institutionalization of the regime – which, in many cases, involved the establishment of a new constitutional order. According to Alain Rouquié, the question that then followed was whether the rulers had *constituent capacity*, that is, whether they would succeed in re-constitutionalizing their authoritarian regimes, giving them new bases.[112]

The results were quite different in each country. In 1980, the regime in Chile succeeded in enacting a constitution that contained several self-protection mechanisms, that is, devices for blocking possible democratization efforts.[113] In Uruguay, a different scenario played out: The military government eventually proposed a draft for a new constitution, but this was rejected in a plebiscite, and negotiations began for the restoration of power to civilians.[114] In Brazil, the military regime imposed a constitution in 1967 and then took two years to elaborate another, but it did not have sufficient power to ensure that these norms (or any further constitution) would endure after the end of the

111 Martins Filho, "Tortura e ideologia" 180–82.

112 A. Rouquié, *À l'Ombre des Dictatures. La Démocratie en Amérique Latine* (Paris: Albin Michel, 2010), 136–48.

113 On the 1980 Chilean Constitution, see C. Paixão, "Past and Future of Authoritarian Regimes: Constitution, Transition to Democracy and Amnesty in Brazil and Chile," *Giornale di Storia Costituzionale* 30(2) (2015), 89–105; Barros, *Constitutionalism and Dictatorship*, 167–254; Dávila, *Dictatorship in South America*, 156–78.

114 A. Marchesi and P. Winn, "Uruguay: los tiempos de la memoria," in P. Winn, A. Marchesi, F. Lorenz, and S.J. Stern (eds.), *No hay mañana sin ayer – Uruguay y las batallas por la memoria histórica en el Cono Sur* (Santiago: LOM, 2014), 121–204, at 127–30.

military government. The twilight of the Brazilian dictatorship came about through a process of re-democratization through a constituent assembly.[115] The outcomes were numerous and diverse, but the analysis of the strategies employed to institutionalize regimes (whether successful or not) – and, therefore, to leave binding rules for the future – can be a good starting point from which to observe the various authoritarian regimes installed in Latin America in the second half of the twentieth century.[116]

Recent studies of Latin American dictatorships integrate dimensions that were not widely covered in the years immediately following the demise of these authoritarian regimes. At that early stage, the research had still focused on the strategies and forms of transition from authoritarianism to democracy, or the repressive structures and modes of resistance. However, more recently, other aspects have received greater attention, such as the role of certain institutions, the connection between the exercise of political power and economic agents,[117] or even themes related to morality and culture.[118]

115 C. Paixão, "Autonomia, democracia e poder constituinte no Brasil: disputas conceituais na experiência constitucional brasileira (1964–2014)," *Quaderni fiorentini per la Storia del Pensiero Giuridico Moderno* 43(1) (2014), 415–58; Barbosa, *História constitucional brasileira*, 143–247.

116 We will not deal directly with Central American dictatorships, due to the region's specific context, with its experiences of rural guerrilla warfare and armed conflicts involving paramilitary groups. For a general overview see L. Bethell (ed.), *The Cambridge History of Latin America, vol. VII: Latin America Since 1930: Mexico, Central America and the Caribbean* (Cambridge: Cambridge University Press, 1996), 161–599; J.J. Moore Jr, "Problems with Forgiveness: Granting Amnesty under the Arias Plan in Nicaragua and El Salvador," *Stanford Law Review*. 43(3) (1991), 733–77; L.E.A.F. Bastos, "A anistia brasileira em comparação com as da América Latina: uma análise na perspectiva do direito internacional," in Santos, Teles, and Teles, *Desarquivando a ditadura*, vol. II, 386–405.

117 Regarding the involvement of companies (multinationals or not) and economic agents in general in the emergence and consolidation of authoritarian regimes in Latin America, see the following references: H. Verbitsky and J. P. Bohoslavsky (eds.), *Cuentas pendientes: Los cómplices económicos de la dictadura* (Buenos Aires: Siglo Veintiuno, 2019); L.A. Payne and G. Pereira, "Corporate Complicity in International Human Rights Violations," *Annual Review of Law and Social Science* 12 (2016), 63–84; J. P. Bohoslavsky and M. Torelly, "Cumplicidade financeira na ditadura brasileira: implicações atuais," *Revista de Anistia Política e Justiça de Transição* 6 (2011), 70–116; P.H.P. Campos, R.V.M. Brandão, and R.L.C.N. Lemos (eds.), *Empresariado e ditadura no Brasil* (Rio de Janeiro: Consequência, 2020); P.E. Ghigliani (ed.), *Procesos represivos, empresas, trabajadores/as y sindicatos en América Latina: Actas del II Encuentro Internacional de la RIProR, La Plata, marzo 2019* (La Plata: Universidade Nacional de La Plata – Facultad de Humanidades y Ciencias de la Educación, 2021).

118 There is a wide range of literature on these topics. I mention, for illustrative purposes, works by D. D'Antonio, "State, Filmmaking, and Sexuality during the Military Dictatorship in Argentina (1976–1983)," in Grigera and Zorzoli, *The Argentinian Dictatorship and Its Legacy*, 123–46; M. Napolitano, "'Vencer Satã só com orações': políticas culturais e cultura de oposição no Brasil dos anos 1970," in D. Rollemberg

From a legal history point of view, one topic that deserves emphasis is the role played by judges and courts (and the justice system in general) in the establishment of Latin American dictatorships. This includes, of course, attempts undertaken by these regimes to legitimize breaking the rule of law and to normalize the emergency measures which they inevitably used for repressive purposes.

A common trait in the Argentine, Chilean, and Brazilian dictatorships was that the vast majority of courts and judges supported them. Obviously, there were isolated cases of resistance and confrontation by members of the judiciary, but those were the exception. As a rule, there was collaboration, support, and peaceful coexistence between the judiciary and the dictatorships. There are many explanations for this: the connection between those holding judicial positions and the political and economic elites, the significant power of co-optation held by the military governments with respect to staffing the courts (especially those at the highest levels), a strong sense of hierarchy and obedience in the ranks of the judiciary, and the fact that the countries analyzed here (particularly Brazil and Argentina) had experienced authoritarian regimes prior to the ones inaugurated in the 1960s and 1970s, regimes that required modes of collaboration and dialogue between the military and the judicial authorities.

Of course, the situations varied to certain degrees. In a pioneering study, Anthony Pereira indicates three trends in the countries mentioned here.[119] In Brazil, the regime achieved a high degree of judicialization, that is, the Brazilian dictatorship managed to establish links with the judiciary and thereby succeeded in conferring some measure of formality to its acts. Chile's approach was similar yet different in that the Pinochet regime made extensive use of military – not civilian – legal institutes and procedures, such as martial law and the publication of *bandos*. In Argentina, the military dictatorship resorted less to the judiciary because of the experience immediately prior to the 1976 coup.

and S. Quadrat (eds.), *A construção social dos regimes autoritários: legitimidade, consenso e consentimento no século XX – Brasil e América Latina* (Rio de Janeiro: Civilização Brasileira, 2010), 145–74; I.J. Hinojosa, "Discurso cultural da ditadura chilena: entre a pátria e o mercado," in R.P.S. Motta (ed.), *Ditaduras militares: Brasil, Argentina, Chile e Uruguai* (Belo Horizonte: Ed. UFMG, 2015), 313–33; A. Marchesi, "'Una parte del pueblo uruguayo feliz, contento, alegre': los caminos culturales del consenso autoritario durante la dictadura," in C. Demasi et. al., *La dictadura Cívico-Militar: Uruguay 1973–1985* (Montevideo: Ediciones de la Banda Oriental, 2013), 323–98.

119 A.W. Pereira, *Political (In)Justice: Authoritarianism and the Rule of Law in Brazil, Chile, and Argentina* (Pittsburgh: University of Pittsburgh Press, 2005); A.W. Pereira, "Sistemas judiciais e repressão política no Brasil, Chile e Argentina," in Santos, Teles, and Teles, *Desarquivando a ditadura*, vol. I, 203–24.

Juan Pablo Bohoslavsky describes how the military regime that lasted until 1973 sought to repress opponents by means of trials in a special court called "Camarón." When the Peronists reassumed power, the court was disbanded, and those that had been convicted received amnesty. This experience might have been a decisive factor why the agents of the Argentinian dictatorship unleashed a fierce policy of clandestine elimination of opponents outside the judicial proceedings, through executions and disappearances.[120]

These differences between the various countries, however, do not conceal the common element their regimes shared: the judiciary in these countries continued to carry out its activities during the dictatorships. More importantly, in the vast majority of cases, it acquiesced to the emergency procedures in place, which ended up weakening the use of legal procedures aimed at defending liberty, such as *habeas corpus*. In the overview offered by Bohoslavsky, this complicity is presented as a feature of several authoritarian regimes during the twentieth century (not only on the American continent):

> Authoritarian governments are usually interested, to a greater or lesser extent, in using the judiciary to promote and implement their own political agendas. From Russia under Stalin, Germany under Hitler, Spain under Franco, to Brazil during the dictatorship, South Africa during apartheid or Chile under Pinochet, repressive regimes generally have used the judiciary for their criminal purposes.[121]

These common features might have been the result of two different levels of judicial activity which consolidated during the dictatorships. On one level, there was the provision of ordinary jurisdiction, that is, the regular (and public) exercise of judicial power to adjudicate cases in compliance with the laws, codes, and procedural guarantees. On a second, less transparent level, more malleable types of jurisdictions were frequently created for emergency measures, such as for example, military tribunals. At this second level, there were fewer procedural guarantees, equality between the parties was not ensured, and political persecution was permitted.

The coexistence of two levels of judicial activity was nothing new. As Mario Sbriccoli and Massimo Meccarelli point out, this binary division originated in nineteenth-century Europe. There, the first level consisted of the codes and ordinary laws concerning criminal prosecution. On the second level were the so-called "special laws," which were present in dictatorial contexts: "national

120 Bohoslavsky, "Introducción," 18 and 36.

121 Bohoslavsky, "Introducción," 20 (unless otherwise indicated, all translations are by the author).

security" laws, extraordinary procedural norms for special courts, and military regulations. According to these two authors, the reason for this division was the necessity for European governments (in particular Italy and France) to control certain political movements that challenged the established order (such as anarchism, for example). The ordinary criminal jurisdiction proved insufficient to organize state repression: special rules and procedures were thus created[122] and a double level of legality established.[123]

Latin American dictatorial regimes shared common legal objectives, which they pursued in different ways. However, the transitional justice that developed in these countries after the dictatorships ended varied in form, intensity, and duration (see Section 6.3). Argentina was where the greatest resort to the judiciary took place, to prosecute those responsible for human rights violations during the dictatorship (which lasted from 1976 to 1983). According to an estimate by Human Rights Watch, based on data compiled through September 2019, in Argentina 3,329 persons were investigated for crimes against humanity, 997 persons were convicted, and 162 acquitted.[124]

In one of these lawsuits, the Argentine public prosecutor's office filed a criminal action to hold a number of judges, prosecutors, defenders, and judicial officials responsible for crimes against humanity in the province of Mendoza. The verdict handed down by the Oral Court in Criminal Court No. 1 of Mendoza, following extensive evidence gathered from four different criminal cases, led to the sentencing to life imprisonment of two former federal judges, a former federal prosecutor, and a public defender as well as other members of the justice system.[125] The ruling in this case, which became known as *"juicio a los jueces,"* was affirmed, concerning the four cited

122 Here a fitting account is provided by Robert Barros: "Under the imperative of the emergency situation, constitutionally anticipated emergency powers allowed the abeyance of regular legal forms. The chief instrument that effected and typified this type of displacement of law was the provision for administrative arrest and detention without legal cause or due process under powers given by a state of siege." (Barros, "Courts Out of Context," 165).

123 M. Sbriccoli, "Caratteri originari e tratti permanenti del sistema penale italiano (1860–1990)," in L. Violante (ed.), *Storia d'Italia: legge, diritto, giustizia – Annali 14* (Torino, Einaudi, 1998), 487–551; M. Meccarelli, "Paradigmi dell'eccezione nella parabola della modernità penale," *Quaderni Storici* 131(2) (2009), 493–521.

124 See the Human Rights Watch report for Argentina at www.hrw.org/es/world-report/2021/country-chapters/377399#438aba (last accessed July 8, 2022).

125 The verdicts are described by the Argentine public prosecutor's office as follows: "Chamber IV of the Federal Criminal Cassation Division upheld the life sentences imposed on former magistrates Luis Miret (who died in September 2017), Guillermo Max Petra Recabarren, Rolando Evaristo Carrizo and Otilio Romano, convicted in July 2017 by the Federal Oral Federal Court No. 1 of Mendoza for their responsibility in crimes against humanity that consisted, according to the case, the crimes of abusive

convictions, by Chamber IV of the Federal Criminal Cassation Division, in a ruling released on September 6, 2019.

In Chile, where charges of human rights violations have been analyzed, especially since the imprisonment of former dictator Augusto Pinochet in London in 1998 following an order issued by the judge Baltasar Garzón,[126] there has been a significant movement by judges to examine the complicity of the judiciary with the dictatorship. On September 5, 2013 (just as the fortieth anniversary of the coup d'état was approaching) the National Association of Judicial Magistrates of Chile released a statement with an explicit appeal to be forgiven by the victims of the dictatorship (and their families) and Chilean society itself "for having failed, at this crucial moment in history, to guide, challenge and motivate our professional association and its members not to give up the fulfillment of their most basic and essential duties."[127]

Institutions and Social Movements: The Catholic Church, Students, and Workers

A central element in the analysis of the dictatorial regimes that emerged in Latin America in the post-war context is the complex role (or rather roles) played by the Catholic Church, both by its leadership and by lower-ranking priests. In Brazil, Chile and Argentina, the Catholic Church lent support to the coups d'état of 1964, 1973, and 1976. This was vital, because these coups cannot be understood only in their institutional perspective. Instead, the deposition of civilian governments in Latin America involved some degree of engagement in questions of morality and culture by the conservative forces in society. In Argentina, the regime assigned itself the task of carrying out a "process of national reorganization."[128] In Brazil, the coup of 1964 was preceded by a series of demonstrations summoned by Catholic groups – these were presented as marches "with God for the family and for freedom."[129]

deprivation of liberty, torture, aggravated homicide, breach of duty and illicit association, which the court considered as crimes against humanity perpetrated in the context of the international crime of genocide." www.fiscales.gob.ar/lesa-humanidad/juicio-a-los-jueces-casacion-confirmo-la-condena-a-prision-perpetua-de-cuatro-magistrados-por-crimenes-de-lesa-humanidad-en-mendoza/ (last accessed July 2022).

126 The main sources for the case that culminated in Pinochet's arrest are available in R. Brody and M. Ratner (eds.), *The Pinochet Papers: The Case of Augusto Pinochet in Spain and Britain* (The Hague: Kluwer Law International, 2000).

127 See https://elpais.com/internacional/2013/09/05/actualidad/1378356025_053445.html (last accessed June 30, 2022).

128 Finchelstein, *Ideological Origins*, 122–25.

129 A. Presot, "Celebrando a 'Revolução': as Marchas da Família com Deus pela Liberdade e o Golpe de 1964," in Rollemberg and Quadrat, *A construção social*, 71–96.

Engagement with morals and culture, however, was also evident on the other side of the spectrum. Before the coups d'état, there were organized, active student movements (which later would become central in the resistance to the dictatorships). The 1960s witnessed waves of demands for new patterns of socializing, freedom, and artistic expression.[130] In several countries around the world, students' revolts took place, and Latin America was part of this process, which also involved brutal repression by the state, as was the case in Mexico in 1968. In that country, which was about to host the Olympic Games, the university students movement grew throughout 1968. This was accompanied by an increasing number of demands made by health professionals, railway workers, peasants, and others. The goal of these movements was the improvement of living conditions and the full application of the 1917 Constitution, and one of the key instruments of these protests was strike.

The Mexican student movement participated in these struggles, with which it shared both the agenda and the methods. Student strikes were common, especially at the Universidad Nacional Autónoma de México (UNAM) and the Instituto Politécnico Nacional (IPN). The actions taken by the military and police forces (which included paramilitary groups) to quash these protests were usually violent and excessive. On October 2, 1968, the so-called "Massacre of Tlatelolco" took place in the *Plaza de las Tres Culturas*. Hundreds of students were killed by repressive forces, and the military subsequently occupied the university.[131]

In 1971, there was a new crackdown on student activity in Mexico. Similarly to the mobilization of 1968, the students advanced demands related to access to education, to university autonomy, and, above all, to internal democracy in the universities. Teachers and workers stood in solidarity with the students. However, on June 10 a group of paramilitaries known as "los halcones" violently crushed a student march, which resulted in approximately 120 students being killed. The episode, as traumatic as the Tlatelolco massacre, became known as "El Halconazo."[132]

130 R. P. S. Motta, "As políticas universitárias das ditaduras militares do Brasil, da Argentina e do Chile," in Motta, *Ditaduras militares*, 37–60; M. P. Araujo, "Esquerdas, juventude e radicalidade na América Latina nos anos 1960 e 1970," in C. Fico, M. M. Ferreira, M. P. Araujo, and S. Quadrat (eds.), *Ditadura e Democracia na América Latina: balanço histórico e perspectivas* (Rio de Janeiro: FGV, 2008), 247–73.

131 On the historical background leading up to the massacre, see P. H. Smith, "Mexico Since 1946," in Bethell, *The Cambridge History of Latin America, vol. VII*, 120–24.

132 C. V. Ovalle et al. (eds.), *A 50 Años del Halconazo – 10 de junio de 1971 – antología documental* (Mexico City: Instituto Nacional de Estudios Históricos de las Revoluciones de México, 2021); Smith, "Mexico Since 1946," 127–28.

Such brutal repression responded to a broader context of demands by students that were also voiced in other places, most famously in France and the United States, as part of the opposition against the Vietnam War. Gilberto Guevara Niebla, a student at UNAM and a student leader, said that "through television we knew what was happening in the United States and with the young people in France."[133]

Student movements were also very active in South American countries. In Argentina and Uruguay, they were integral elements of clandestine organizations such as the *Montoneros* and the *Tupamaros*, which began to carry out armed actions against political and military targets even before the 1973 and 1976 coups d'état. In Chile, the student movement was largely connected to the *Unidad Popular* throughout the turbulent presidency of Salvador Allende.[134] In Brazil, the National Union of Students was deeply involved in social causes and was part of movements fighting for better education, increased state participation in the economy, and improved living conditions for the low-income population. In all these countries, the student movements were among the main targets of the military regimes when those seized power.[135]

One of the outstanding features of these movements was the complex web of relationships and influences of which they formed part. They modeled themselves after the Chinese and Cuban revolutions and the orthodox orientation of Soviet communism; however, as is usual in such movements, there was much internal tension among the various currents.

This revolutionary, transgressive element of nonconformity adopted by the student movements was unacceptable to Catholic orthodoxy, Catholicism

133 A. Nájar, "La matanza de Tlatelolco: qué pasó el 2 de octubre de 1968, cuando un brutal golpe contra estudiantes cambió a México para siempre," BBC News Mundo, Mexico, Oct 2, 2018, updated Oct 2, 2020, www.bbc.com/mundo/noticias-america-latina-45714908 (last accessed June 13, 2022).

134 The *Unidad Popular* was a political and electoral coalition of parties, movements and social organizations of the center and the left led by Salvador Allende, who won the 1970 presidential election. A. Aggio, "O Chile de Allende: entre a derrota e o fracasso," in Fico et al., *Ditadura e Democracia na América Latina*, 77–93; A. Faure, "Las Batallas Cronopolíticas durante la Unidad Popular en Chile (1970–1973): Un esbozo de análisis," *Res Publica – Revista de Historia de las Ideas Políticas*, 24(3) (2021), 495–504. For the 1970 election, R. Simon, *O Brasil contra a democracia: a ditadura, o golpe no Chile e a Guerra Fria na América do Sul* (São Paulo: Companhia das Letras, 2021), 27–55.

135 H. Merele, "El proceso represivo en los años setenta constitucionales. De la 'depuración' interna del peronismo al accionar de las organizaciones paraestatales," in Águila, Garaño, and Scatizza, *Represión estatal*, 99–123; C. Aldrighi, *La Izquierda Armada: Ideología, ética e identidad en el MLN-Tupamaros* (Montevideo: Trilce, 2001); M.P.N. Araújo, "Memória e debate sobre a luta armada no Brasil e na Argentina," in S. Quadrat and D. Rollemberg (eds.), *História e memória das ditaduras do século XX* (Rio de Janeiro: FGV, 2015), vol. II, 245–64.

still being the vastly dominant religion in Latin America in the 1950s and 1960s. Furthermore, members of the ecclesiastical leadership had personal connections with the military and political elite. It was thus natural that the higher echelons of the Church would have a positive view of the institutional breakdown fostered by the military coups. The proposal of the dictatorial regimes encompassed a return to traditional values and social practices, especially in relation to the concept of family. In Brazil, the National Conference of Bishops of Brazil (CNBB) declared support for the coup of 1964, in Chile, the Episcopal Conference (CECH) offered to promote "national reconciliation" after the coup of September 11, 1973, and in the case of Argentina, the close ties between bishops and other segments of the Church and the military is documented in many historical sources.[136]

However, this was not the end of the story. While much of the Church hierarchy supported the coups, it is important to remember the role played by some segments of the Catholic Church in criticizing, resisting, and combating dictatorial regimes. Thus, if some members and organs of the Church were partners in repression, others were victims (often fatal) of these same dictatorships. How was this possible?

In a text from his youth, the controversial author and polemist Carl Schmitt (himself a practicing Catholic) summed up a central characteristic of the Roman Church: It can be classified as a "*complexio oppositorum*," that is, as a political body that houses in its ranks prelates with opposing orientations on Christian doctrine and on the role of the Church.[137] This insight fits the situation during the Latin American dictatorships, where the Church exhibited this kind of duality towards the regimes. Maria Angélica Cruz, in her analysis of the behavior of the Catholic Church during the Chilean regime, uses the expression "double game" – on the one hand, the Church conferred legitimacy to the military coup, on the other, it was concerned about the victims of the repression and tried to support them.[138] According to the author, over the course of the regime, the Church's dominant stance became more critical of the repression.

One of the main reasons for this ambivalent attitude of the Church was the orientation that emerged after the Second Vatican Council, concluded

136 C. Fico, *O golpe de 1964 – momentos decisivos* (Rio de Janeiro: FGV, 2014), 7–8; Finchelstein, *Ideological Origins*, 122–53; M.A. Cruz, "A Igreja católica, a ditadura e os dilemas da memória no Chile," in Quadrat and Rollemberg, *História e memória*, vol. I, 369–93.

137 C. Schmitt, *Roman Catholicism and Political Form* (Westport: Greenwood Publishing Group, 1996), 5–10.

138 Cruz, "A Igreja católica," 373–75.

in 1965. The renewal of the pastoral constitution envisaged by the Council would require increasing the number of organs and entities within the Church dedicated to the "social question," as well as to the question of how to bring the clergy and the low-income populations, especially peasants and workers, closer to one another. In Chile, the *Vicaría de la Solidariedad* was created, and in Brazil, there were the *Comunidades Eclesiais de Base*. Across the poorest communities in Latin America, the Church employed large numbers of priests – many from outside the Americas – not only for traditional evangelization efforts, but also to offer incentives for self-organization, to support the fight for social rights, and to mobilize people to demand agrarian reforms and political emancipation.[139]

As was to be expected, these activities were suppressed immediately by the military regimes, resulting in tensions on two different levels. Within the Church, differences increased between parts of the ecclesiastical leadership (who tended to support or collaborate with the dictatorial regimes) and priests dedicated to implementing the social doctrine established in the Second Vatican Council (who maintained a critical stance and resisted repressive measures). Rifts appeared between the Church and the military, and specific reprisals were carried out against religious orders and priests who had a leading role in public life and civil society.

It has been reported that under the Argentine dictatorship, at least twenty Catholic priests were murdered or disappeared, a hundred were kidnapped and taken to clandestine detention centers, and nine seminarians were murdered or disappeared. Two French nuns, Alice Domon, and Léonie Duquet, went missing in December 1977.[140] In the Brazilian countryside, especially in the north-eastern states, the presence of Italian and French priests was very common. At the end of the Brazilian dictatorship, an Italian priest, Vito Miracapillo, refused to celebrate a mass in commemoration of Brazil's independence, claiming that the country could not be considered an independent nation, given the precarious living conditions of a large part of its population. This made national news, and the minister of justice decided to expel the

139 For an account of this shift in Catholic Church, see L. A. N. Delgado and M. Passos, "Catolicismo: direitos sociais e direitos humanos (1960–1970)," in Ferreira and Delgado, *O Brasil Republicano*, 93–131.

140 For the estimation of the number of dead and missing, see *El Clarín*, March 20, 2006, updated February 24, 2017. The source for the newspaper is the *Movimiento Ecuménico por los Derechos Humanos*. For victims' names and facts about the crimes, see www.desaparecidos.org/arg/iglesia/des.html and www.desaparecidos.org/arg/iglesia/muertos.html (last accessed July 21, 2022). On the case of the French nuns, see M. S. Catoggio, "Las desaparecidas de la Iglesia: desentramando historias y memorias de mujeres en Argentina," in Águila, Garaño, and Scatizza, *Represión estatal*, 99–123.

priest from Brazil. This case is often mentioned as an example of the complicity of the judiciary with the policies of the military regime. Four *habeas corpus* proceedings brought before the Supreme Court, which sought the nullification of the expulsion decree, were unsuccessful.[141]

Finally, a crucial episode for the downfall of the Brazilian dictatorship was the murder of Vladimir Herzog and the reaction it triggered. Vladimir Herzog was born into a Jewish family in the city of Osijek, in the former Yugoslavia (now Croatia). His family moved to the Bosnian town of Banja Luka, and, with Nazi troops approaching, the family sought refuge in Italy. They lived in small towns in Veneto and the Marche until they managed to migrate to Brazil. A naturalized Brazilian, Vladimir graduated in philosophy at the University of São Paulo and became a very active journalist in the 1960s and 1970s. He covered the inauguration of Brasília in 1960, worked in the main newsrooms, was a correspondent for the BBC in London for three years, and then joined the staff of TV Cultura in São Paulo, where he took the post of director of journalism. He had ties to the Brazilian Communist Party (PCB), as did many other journalists at that time. Upon responding to a summons to give a statement in a police facility in São Paulo, he was arrested on the spot, tortured, and killed by the dictatorship's security forces on October 25, 1975.[142]

On October 31, 1975, an ecumenical service was held in the Cathedral of São Paulo in memory of Vladimir Herzog. At that time, the archdiocese of São Paulo was led by Cardinal Dom Paulo Evaristo Arns, an active defender of human rights who had publicly exposed the violations committed by the military regime. It is estimated that about eight thousand people attended the ceremony, which was celebrated by Dom Paulo, Rabbi Henry Sobel, and the Presbyterian Reverend Jaime Wright in defiance of the regime's express orders. This celebration signaled the resumption of protagonism by civil society in the struggle against the dictatorship, and Herzog gained the status of

141 The ruling from the *Supremo Tribunal Federal* (Brazilian Supreme Court) was issued in Habeas Corpus No. 58.409-8, *Diário da Justiça* from 28 Nov 1980. On this topic, see M. P. S. L. G. Dalledone, *O padre e a pátria: direito, transição politica e o Supremo Tribunal Federal na expulsão de Vito Miracapillo (1980)* (Brasília: PhD Dissertation, University of Brasília Law School, 2016).

142 N. Miranda and C. Tibúrcio, *Dos filhos deste solo – mortos e desaparecidos políticos durante a ditadura militar: a responsabilidade do Estado* (São Paulo: Perseu Abramo/Boitempo, 2008), 423–24; M. H. M. Alves, *Estado e Oposição no Brasil (1964–1984)* (Petrópolis: Vozes, 1984), 201–8; M. V. M. Benevides, *Fé na luta: a Comissão Justiça e Paz de São Paulo, da ditadura à democratização* (São Paulo: Lettera.doc, 2009), 65–109; P. Montero, A. Brum, and R. Quintanilha, "Ritos católicos e ritos civis: a configuração da fala pública da Igreja Católica em dois atos em memória de Vladimir Herzog (1975/2015)," *Mana – Estudos de Antropologia Social* 22(3) (2016), 705–35.

a martyr. In 1978 (still under the authoritarian regime), a federal judge recognized the responsibility of the Brazilian state in Herzog's death, yet the proceedings continued for many years without any official recognition. Finally, on March 15, 2018, the Inter-American Court of Human Rights condemned the Brazilian state, explicitly pointing out "the failure to investigate, and also prosecute and punish those responsible for the torture and murder of Vladimir Herzog committed in a widespread and systematic context of attacks on the civilian population."[143]

Operation Condor, Its Origins and Aftermath: Collaborative Networks and Crimes on a Global Scale

One of the most discussed and researched feature of mid-twentieth century South American military dictatorships is the so-called Operation Condor, a program to carry out repressive operations. Created in the late 1970s by the Chilean dictatorship, it also involved the participation of Argentina, Uruguay, Bolivia, Paraguay, and Brazil. The structure and activities of Operation Condor are important, but it is also essential to point out that this operation was only part of a much more extensive and complex web of relations between Latin American countries as well as between them and other centers of power, such as the United States, European nations, and the former Soviet Union. The study of these links reveals the global character of the political struggles waged on the American continent during the period of the dictatorships.

Between the end of the 1960s and the beginning of the 1970s, the range of political options in Latin America was broad, particularly in the southern part of the continent. Brazil and Paraguay already had conservative military regimes due to the influence of the United States; however, in other countries the situation was different. In 1970, the *Unidad Popular*, which included left wing political associations, came to power in Chile with a pro-state platform to fight social inequality. In Bolivia, there were several coups d'état, but some of the generals who then held the presidency were supported by social movements.[144] These generals took a nationalist stance, moved away from the US sphere of influence, and nationalized industries. As noted earlier, in Argentina and Uruguay, students and workers actively mobilized against the

143 Inter-American Court of Human Rights, *Herzog et. al. v. Brazil*, judgment of March 15, 2018, www.corteidh.or.cr/docs/casos/articulos/seriec_353_ing.pdf (last accessed July 31, 2022).

144 For an overview, see L. Whitehead, "Bolivia since 1930," in Bethell, *The Cambridge History of Latin America, vol. VIII*, 509–83.

central governments, and guerrilla groups began to operate (*Montoneros* and *Tupamaros*).

As is well known, the Cuban Revolution, which concluded in 1959, exerted immense influence on political and social movements throughout the American continent. Ernesto Che Guevara, Argentinean by birth and one of the leaders of the Cuban Revolution, continued to engage in political activities outside Cuba and was murdered in Bolivia in 1967. With the rapprochement between Cuba and the Soviet regime, and given the strong influence of the United States in the region, the Cold War gained an additional dimension. Predictably, the US security apparatus began to operate in Latin America, always aiming to prevent the emergence of new regimes such as the one in Cuba.

Several documents recently declassified by the US government reveal the intense diplomatic and espionage activities carried out in order to contain possible leftist regimes. For this to succeed, forming alliances with dictatorships was crucial. A recently revealed memo documents a conversation between President Richard Nixon, Secretary of State Henry Kissinger, and British Prime Minister Edward Heath at a meeting in Bermuda on December 20, 1971. Nixon and Heath discuss Cuba and its possible influence in South America, with Nixon saying that in Chile "the left is in trouble, and there are forces at work which we are not discouraging," referring to the moves by US authorities to destabilize the Allende government. The conversation also reflected concerns with what was transpiring in Uruguay, where left and center-left parties created the *Frente Amplio*, and it seemed possible that it could win the elections (which it did not). According to Nixon, "Brazilians helped rig the Uruguayan election."[145] Whether this was true or not, we know that, given Brazil's interest in monitoring (and persecuting) Brazilian exiles on the other side of the border, there was intense participation by the Brazilian military regime in the repression of Uruguayan guerrilla forces.

The results of this coordination were clear. During the 1970s, dictatorships prevailed in South America. In Bolivia, General Hugo Banzer led a coup d'état. His predecessor, General Juan José Torres, was one of the first victims of Operation Condor. He was killed by a Bolivian military command (with the participation of Chilean agents linked to the CIA) in Buenos Aires, in July 1976.[146] In Uruguay, the President of the Republic Juan María Bordaberry led

145 White House Memorandum, Dec. 20, 1971, page 2, https://nsarchive2.gwu.edu/NSAEBB/NSAEBB71/doc15.pdf (last accessed July 31, 2022).

146 J. P. McSherry, "Cross-Border Terrorism: Operation Condor," *NACLA Report on the Americas* 32(6) (1999), 34–35.

a self-coup, closed the Congress, and began acting as a dictator until he was deposed by a military *junta* that assumed *de facto* power in the country.[147] In Chile, the September 11, 1973 coup took place, and in Argentina, the "national reorganization process" started in March 1976. Most of the South American countries were now military dictatorships aligned with the United States at the international level.

Cooperation between the different military forces was also evident. Many Brazilian political exiles lived in Chile; a number of them were arrested and held at the National Stadium in Santiago and report having been tortured by Brazilian military personnel.[148] Argentine commandos were looking for exiles in Brazil, and on some occasions, groups composed of Brazilian and Argentinean soldiers tortured the exiles they tracked down. However, while collaboration throughout the 1970s was random, in 1976 Chile proposed a broader initiative, the earlier-mentioned Operation Condor.

This new type of collaboration was discussed between members of the armed forces and intelligence communities of the South American countries in a meeting that took place in Chile from November 25 to December 1, 1975, attended by delegations from Brazil, Argentina, Paraguay, Uruguay, and Bolivia. As previously stated, the military and security forces of the various dictatorships had already pursued joint activities and conducted operations in more than one country. At this November meeting, however, Chile sought to establish a more systematical approach to these operations.[149] Its immediate goal was to intensify efforts to detain opponents of the military regimes who were exiled in other countries.[150]

The plan did not end there. While collaboration between dictatorships and their security and intelligence bodies continued (both inside and outside Condor), another cooperative plan emerged from an initiative by the

147 F. Lessa, *Justicia o impunidad? Cuentas pendientes en el Uruguay post-dictadura* (Montevideo: Debate, 2014), 55–72.

148 R. Simon, *O Brasil contra a democracia*, 236–52.

149 Despite being present at the meeting, Brazil did not sign the official document that established Operation Condor; formal adhesion only took place in June 1976. Simon, *O Brasil contra a democracia*, 332. In 1978 Ecuador and Peru joined the group, F. Lessa, "Justice Entrepreneurs and the Struggle for Accountability in South America: Comparative Reflections on Transitional Justice and Operation Condor," in C. Paixão and M. Meccarelli (eds.), *Comparing Transitions to Democracy: Law and Justice in South America and Europe* (Cham: Springer, 2021), 111–36, at 123.

150 For a more general overview of Operation Condor, for example, F. Lessa, "Justice beyond Borders: The Operation Condor Trial and Accountability for Transnational Crimes in South America," *International Journal of m* 9 (2015), 494–506; Simon, *O Brasil contra a democracia*, 329–38; J. Dinges, *The Condor Years: How Pinochet and His Allies Brought Terrorism to Three Continents* (New York: The New Press, 2004), and

Chilean, Argentine, and Uruguayan regimes: Operation Teseo. Its purpose was to expand activities beyond the boundaries of the Americas. As various coups d'état occurred in South America, many exiles who initially went to Uruguay, Chile, and Argentina sought new places of refuge, particularly in Europe. Paris and Lisbon concentrated the largest number of regime opponents. Operation Teseo was a plot intended to enable the assassination of exiles living in Europe.

The Chilean regime already had some experience in operating outside its own borders. Dina (*Dirección de Inteligencia Nacional*), Chile's political police, had been active on European territory. In Rome, on October 5, 1975, Chilean agents, with the backing of militants from an Italian extreme right-wing group, shot Bernardo Leighton, a Christian Democrat politician and former interior minister of Chile, and his wife Anita Fresno. Both survived the attack, albeit with serious injuries. In addition to Dina agents, Stefano Delle Chiaie, a known member of the radical right-wing group *Avanguarda Nazionale*, also participated in the assassination. Delle Chiaie, who had met with Pinochet in Madrid a month earlier, was assisted by Michael Townley, a US citizen who was a Dina agent.[151] Townley had also been involved in the murder of the Chilean general Carlos Prats and his wife in Buenos Aires on September 30, 1974.[152]

An equally well-known case was an operation executed outside of Condor's channels that resulted in the killing of Orlando Letelier, who had served as minister in Allende's government. Letelier was murdered in Washington DC on September 19, 1976; the assassination was organized and executed by Dina, again with the participation of Michael Townley, among many other agents. Armando Fernández Larios, one of these agents, was present at the attack on September 11, 1973, on the Palacio de la Moneda, the seat of the Chilean government, occupied at the time by Salvador Allende. Fernández Larios had also taken part in several repressive actions by a group that became known in Chile as the "Caravans of Death," and he traveled throughout Brazil in 1976 before heading to Washington to be part of the Letelier killing.[153]

S. V. Quadrat, "Violência política e justiça sem fronteiras," in Santos, Teles, and Teles, *Desarquivando a ditadura*, vol. I, 250–66.

151 US intelligence report on Dina's activities, Jan. 21, 1982, pages 3–6. https://nsarchive2.gwu.edu/NSAEBB/NSAEBB8/ch02-01.htm (last accessed July 31, 2022).

152 US intelligence report, pages 5–6.

153 Simon, *O Brasil contra a democracia*, 319. Larios would confess in the 1980s to his participation in Letelier's murder. He agreed to enter into a plea bargain with the United States Department of Justice in which he obtained a reduced sentence and provided information about the operation that resulted in Letelier's death. Criminal Case No. 78-0367. The plea agreement is available at https://cja.org/wp-content/uploads/downloads/lariosPleabargain.pdf (last accessed July 31, 2022).

Although there were transnational collaborative networks involving Chilean, Argentine, and Uruguayan agencies (with most operations originating in Chile), some of these networks were fragile. The US government was visibly upset with the operation against Letelier, which resulted in the death of a US citizen, Ronni Moffit, who had been working with Allende's former minister. In addition, after a group consisting of Argentine and Uruguayan military was sent to Paris with the purpose of assassinating Uruguayan opponents living there, the French intelligence services became aware of their presence (as part of Operation Teseo), alerted the possible targets, and protested the situation to the Chilean Embassy in Paris.[154]

The extension of collaboration between South American dictatorships, which ranged from persecuting opponents on the American continent to collaborating in their elimination even on European territory, was made possible through the participation of European extreme right-wing groups. Pinochet, while in Spain for Franco's funerals, contacted extremist groups in order to obtain support for killings across Europe.[155] As Branch and Propper rightly point out, the timing was symbolic, as Pinochet sought to be identified with the legacy of Francoism and considered himself "the historical re-creation of Franco."[156]

In the early 1980s, in the context of intensified Cold War clashes, and driven by the election of Ronald Reagan as president of the United States, Argentina became the leading country in transnational political repression. How this complex and intricate situation came about illustrates the impressive ability of the United States (and its allies in Latin America) to interfere in the political struggles fought in countries located in the US sphere of influence.

When Reagan took office, there were several areas of tension with the Soviet Union. The Cold War theater of operations was about to shift into a higher gear after a period of relative stability. One of Reagan's main targets was the new Sandinista regime in Nicaragua, which was established following a civil war that culminated in the removal from power of the then-dictator Anastasio Somoza. Members of the US government planned to provide training to the so-called *contras*, who opposed the Sandinista regime. The US Congress, with the Democratic Party holding the majority, vetoed the sale

154 Simon, *O Brasil contra a democracia*, 333–34.

155 See R. Vilaro, "Pinochet mantuvo conversaciones secretas en Madrid durante los funerales de Franco para actuar contra la oposición chilena," El Pais, April 13, 1982, https://elpais.com/diario/1982/04/13/internacional/387496804_850215.html (last accessed July 31, 2022).

156 T. Branch and E. Propper, *Labyrinth* (New York: Viking Press, 1982), 314.

of arms to the Nicaraguan opposition. To tackle this situation, the solution chosen was to activate sectors of the repressive apparatus in Latin America. Argentine military offered training to paramilitary groups in Guatemala and sold weapons to the *contras* with the support of the US government. Sectors of the collaborative network that had already been activated in the 1970s in Europe were once again put into action. Stefano Delle Chiaie, the Italian far-right militant who, as we have already seen, assisted the Chilean dictatorship in actions in Europe, traveled to Bolivia and Argentina where he collaborated directly with members of the Argentine government in their joint efforts with the United States to supply weapons and training to the Nicaraguan *contras*. The partnership between Argentina and sectors of the US government came to an end in 1982, when the Falklands (also known as Malvinas) War broke out and the United States supported Britain.[157]

According to the data collected by Francesca Lessa in the database on South America's Transnational Human Rights Violations, between August 1969 and February 1981, 805 people fell victim to this transnational repression (which, as we have seen, was broader than Operation Condor). Among these were 382 cases of illegal detention with torture, 367 deaths or disappearances, and 25 kidnappings of babies. The victims' nationalities were distributed as follows: 384 Uruguayans, 191 Argentineans, 115 Chileans, 40 Paraguayans, 33 Brazilians, 13 Peruvians, 17 Bolivians, and 12 others (the United States, Italy, France, Cuba, Great Britain, and Spain).[158]

Operation Condor, given its scope and the countless human rights violations it inflicted, was the subject of important lawsuits in several countries that sought to establish the responsibility of the perpetrators. These cases – which have the potential to raise new questions because of the emergence and disclosure of previously unknown sources – are central to understanding different features of the operation, but they are also an important source for legal history. It is well established that authoritarian regimes tend to lack transparency and publicity in their actions. Secrecy becomes the rule, and there is no public control over governmental actions. Hence, lawsuits concerning the criminal accountability of agents who have perpetrated human rights violations play a central role, also in the writing of legal history. With instruments

157 For an elaborate description of the complex web of connections between multiple countries and regimes established in the context of US influence in Central America, which also involved, among others, Israel, Taiwan, El Salvador, and Guatemala, see P. D. Scott, "Contragate: Reagan, Foreign Money, and the Contra Deal," *Crime and Social Justice* 27/28 (1987), 110–48.

158 Database available at: https://sites.google.com/view/operationcondorjustice/database (last accessed July 31, 2022). Also Lessa, "Justice Entrepreneurs," 124.

such as universal jurisdiction and doctrines such as the imprescriptibility of crimes against humanity, the judicial authorities are able – when the political circumstances of each nation permit this openness – to carry out an impartial investigation and examination of the authoritarian past.[159]

Lawsuits can recreate factual contexts, draw attention to collected documentation and testimonies, and bypass restrictions, for example, in crimes against humanity, where statutory limitations don't apply. Criminal judges have broad powers to collect evidence – they can summon witnesses, request documents, carry out inspections, and ask that technical evidence be produced. In this way, judicial institutions play multiple roles. They hold agents accountable for rights violations, they contribute to the knowledge of history, and they can also provide reparation, as survivors, as well as descendants of victims, are eligible to receive restitution for past events.

With respect to Operation Condor, at least two cases are of particular historical interest. The first one is a trial held by the Argentine judiciary – Oral Court in Federal Criminal Court No. 1 – which concluded on May 27, 2016. This was a major criminal lawsuit, which was initiated in 1999 and encompassed a variety of related cases. Of the seventeen defendants who were tried, fifteen were sentenced to terms ranging from 8 to 25 years in prison. The victims were of many nationalities: There were Argentineans, Bolivians, Chileans, Paraguayans, Peruvians, and Uruguayans.[160] The second significant criminal case regarding the accountability of agents involved in Operation Condor was brought before Italian courts, since some of the victims held Italian nationality and the Italian Penal Code allows the persecution of crimes committed outside Italy. In a first trial, the *III Corte di Assise di Roma* condemned several of the defendants to sentences up to life imprisonment. However, in the judgment released on January 17, 2017, most of the accused (nineteen out of twenty-seven) were acquitted. An appeal was filed, and the first-instance decision was reversed by the *Corte di Assise di Appello di Roma, Sezione 1 bis*. The grounds of the decision were published on December 27, 2019. In addition to the eight life sentences already handed down by the lower

159 On the importance of court records, see C. Ginzburg, *Il Giudice e lo Storico – Considerazioni in margine al processo Sofri* (Milano: Feltrinelli, 2006); J-C. Passeron and J. Revel, "Penser par cas. Raisonner à partir de singularités," in J-C. Passeron and J. Revel (eds.), *Penser par cas* (Paris: Éditions de l'EHESS, 2005), 9–44, and A. Farge, *Le goût de l'archive* (Paris: Seuil, 1997).

160 The ruling can be found, in its complete form, on the official web page of the Attorney General's Office of the Argentine public prosecutor's office: www.mpf.gob.ar/plan-condor/files/2019/04/Sentencia-Plan-C%C3%B3ndor.pdf (last accessed July 31, 2022).

court – including life imprisonment for Luis Garcia Meza, former president of Bolivia – the appellate court ordered the conviction of sixteen further defendants, leaving only one acquitted. The defendants – of Uruguayan, Chilean, Bolivian, and Peruvian nationalities – were held accountable for the murder of forty-three people. After this ruling, an appeal was filed with the *Corte Suprema di Cassazione*, which, through the *I Sezione Penale*, upheld the convictions imposed (with the exception of one defendant who had died during the trial) and modified only part of the civil reparations.[161]

As Francesca Lessa pointed out, these trials revealed the depth and complexity of the transnational network of repression, torture, killings, and disappearances that was built up in the 1970s. Moreover, these cases prompted national judicial authorities to carry out new investigations into human rights violations committed against victims from various countries.[162]

Transnational Legal Mobilization: The Second Russell Tribunal for Latin America

As explained previously, the thinking of regimes in Latin America was influenced by the decolonization process in Africa and Asia; the Cold War – and even more so the Cuban Revolution – pushed the region into a position of global prominence. The strategic importance of what transpired across the continent became clear in the 1970s, when a transnational mobilization of solidarity with Latin American peoples emerged, initially as a byproduct of the so-called Russell Tribunal. This extra-judicial "International War Crimes Tribunal," held between 1966 and 1967 and charged with investigating the US-American intervention in Vietnam, was an initiative of the philosopher Bertrand Russell, who invited Jean-Paul Sartre and Simone de Beauvoir to head the tribunal's formation. Several other political and cultural figures, mostly from western Europe, joined the tribunal, which held two sessions in Sweden and Denmark in 1967.[163]

161 The first-instance judgment, the ruling of the *Corte di Appello* and the verdict of the *Corte Suprema di Cassazione* are available on the webpage 24 marzo Onlus (an Italian NGO). Cf. www.24marzo.it/ (last accessed July 31, 2022). For an in-depth discussion on the importance of the Italian case, see F. Lessa, "Operation Condor: the Responsibility of the Middle Rank," *Justiceinfo.net*, January 21, (2020), available at: www.justiceinfo.net/en/43584-operation-condor-responsibility-middle-rank.html (last accessed July 31, 2022).

162 Lessa, "Justice Entrepreneurs," 133–34.

163 For the setting up and unfolding of the first Russell Tribunal, see the account by U. Tulli, "Wielding the Human Rights Weapon against the American Empire: The Second Russell Tribunal and Human Rights in Transatlantic Relations," *Journal of Transatlantic Studies* 19 (2021), 215–37, esp. 218–24.

One of the participants of this first Russell Tribunal, the Italian politician Lelio Basso, was a member of the Italian resistance, acted as a representative on the Constituent Assembly formed in the post-war period, and served as a deputy and senator. During a visit to Chile in 1971, Basso instigated contact with Brazilian exiles who opposed the dictatorship, such as Theotonio dos Santos, Almino Affonso (who had been a minister in the João Goulart government, overthrown in 1964 by the military), Herbert de Souza, and José Serra (a former student leader). This group of exiles asked Basso to set up a new tribunal, similar to the one created to investigate the American intervention in Vietnam, but with the purpose of inquiring into and prosecuting the military dictatorship in Brazil.[164]

Basso returned to Italy convinced of the need to set up a second Russell Tribunal. Initially, this was intended to hear only the Brazilian case. However, with the coup d'état staged by Pinochet and the Chilean armed forces on September 11, 1973, it became clear that the military spread of dictatorships in Latin America had reached a point that required an expansion of the tribunal's scope. Accordingly, the cases of the dictatorial regimes in Chile and, subsequently, Uruguay and Bolivia were included. One of the tribunal's main lines of investigation was US intervention in local political affairs and the role of transnational companies in supporting the military and civilian sectors willing to break away from democratic regimes (particularly those of Brazil and Chile, which had a statist orientation and engaged in the nationalization of foreign companies).

CIA-produced documents indicate that the move to establish the second Russell Tribunal was closely monitored by the United States. Three reports, written between November 1973 and March 1974, outlined the minutiae of the tribunal's formation. In November 1973, a communiqué from the American Embassy in Brussels noted: "Although the tribunal had been conceived originally to investigate allegations of torture and political repression in Brazil, it was the unanimous decision of the participants in the Brussels meeting that the tribunal should extend its investigations to Chile and other Latin American countries."[165] Another US intelligence report, written in the last days of March 1974, disclosed that the tribunal had designated a session to "hear testimony

164 Regarding Basso's first contacts with the Brazilian exiles and the steps necessary to establish the Tribunal, see S. Fraudatario, "Le Reti di solidarietà per il Tribunale Russell II negli archive dela Fondazione Lelio e Lisli Basso," in G. Monina (ed.), *Memorie di repressione, resistenza e solidarietà in Brasile e in America Latina* (Rome: Ediesse, 2013), 315–60.

165 Report from the American Embassy in Brussels, dated 3 November 1973, www.cia.gov/readingroom/docs/DOC_0005431000.pdf (last accessed July 31, 2022).

and accept documentation and reports assembled by various commissions on violation of human rights in Brazil, Chile, Uruguay, Paraguay, Bolivia, and Guatemala." The document then went on to list some of the participants, among them Lelio Basso, Vladimir Dedijer, Gabriel Garcia Marquez, Herbert Marcuse, Albert Soboul, Pierre Vidal-Naquet, and François Rigaux. Later, the report added that "Simone de Beauvoir and Jean-Paul Sartre would be unable to continue their tribunal activities because of ill health."[166]

After considerable efforts by Lelio Basso, Linda Bimbi (an Italian nun who had lived in Brazil for many years), and other collaborators, the financial means to convene the second Russell Tribunal were secured. The tribunal held three sessions: in Rome from March 30 to April 6, 1974, in Brussels from January 11 to 18, 1975, and again in Rome from January 10 to 18, 1976.[167] The proceedings produced abundant evidence regarding the dictatorial regimes in Latin America. This evidence enables an understanding of the global dimension of the political struggles that were waged in the region. The tribunal's conclusions had considerable repercussions in the international sphere, but curiously enough, until now, there is no significant literature describing and analyzing its activities. As Umberto Tulli points out, "the 'second' Russell is a neglected and overlooked field of research," especially when compared with the Vietnam War Tribunal.[168] Yet, as Tulli himself makes clear, there were substantial differences between the two iterations, even if many of the members were the same. The first Russell Tribunal scrutinized the United States' behavior as a country that had initiated an armed conflict with another nation, which led to the perpetration of war crimes. The second tribunal, however, depicted another form of US-American intervention, which included economic influence and the role of large multinational corporations. What was

166 CIA report dated late March 1974, www.cia.gov/readingroom/docs/DOC_0005430997.pdf (last accessed July 31, 2022).

167 Fraudatario, "Le Reti di solidarietà," 318.

168 Tulli, "Wielding the Human Rights Weapon," 216. There are nevertheless important publishing initiatives of the proceedings of the second Russell Tribunal, notably the effort made by Giuseppe Tosi and Lúcia de Fátima Guerra Ferreira, professors at the Federal University of Paraíba, Brazil, who organized, with the support of the Amnesty Commission of the Brazilian Ministry of Justice, the full publication of the proceedings in four different volumes. G. Tosi and L.F.G. Ferreira (eds.), *Brasil, violação dos direitos humanos – Tribunal Russell II* (João Pessoa: Ed. UFPB, 2014). There is considerable literature in Italy related to the trajectory of human rights activists such as Lelio Basso, Linda Bimbi, Salvatore Senese and others. S. Rodotà, "Prefazione," in L. Basso, *Il principe senza scettro* (Milano: Feltrinelli, 1998), 7–13; G. Tognoni, "Prefazione," in Monina, *Memorie di repressione*, 9–16; A. Mulas, "Lelio Basso e l'America Latina (1961–1978): Un percorso politico, intellettuale e umano," in G. Monina (ed.), *Novecento contemporaneo. Studi su Lelio Basso* (Rome: Ediesse, 2009), 157–82.

under discussion here was the economic model itself, as well as the emergence of networks of solidarity and resistance. Thus, Tulli concludes, "the first Russell Tribunal was a specific expression of a global movement against the Vietnam War, whereas the second drew inspiration from transnational activism for human rights."[169]

Transnational mobilization of solidarity was evident not only in the activities of the tribunal, but also in the efforts to establish it. Simona Fraudatario reports a proliferation of international committees that supported the creation of the tribunal: following Lelio Basso and Linda Bimbi's trips to several European countries, committees were formed in the Netherlands, Belgium, West Germany, and France. The mobilization spread to other countries and continents: In the United States, student groups in Chicago and Philadelphia came up with supporting manifestos. In Toronto, a Bertrand Russell Tribunal Canadian Support Committee was created, and similar bodies were established in Panama, Puerto Rico, and Argentina – the latter in 1975, before the military coup that would drag the country into a new dictatorship took place.[170]

The verdict issued by the second Russell Tribunal was published at the closing of the first session, which took place in Rome between March 30 and April 5, 1974. In the concluding part of the ruling, the tribunal "declares guilty of serious, repeated and systematic violations of human rights, the authorities who in fact exercise power in Brazil, Chile, Uruguay and Bolivia."[171] Lelio Basso, the jury's president, produced the closing passage, in which he paid tribute to the victims of the dictatorships and their families. Basso stated that "tragic faces" had been present in the tribunal, bearing witness to the atrocities committed by the authoritarian regimes. However, the text ended in an uplifting tone:

> The men and women who today, in most Latin American countries, suffer hidden and locked away in their cells, in the darkness imposed by the hood,

169 Tulli, "Wielding the Human Rights Weapon," 216. On the discussion around the economic models in dispute, see the careful analysis by D. Conti, "La repression politico-sociale in Brasile nelle carte del Tribunal Russell II," in Monina, *Memorie di repressione*, 91–130.

170 Fraudatario, "Le Reti di solidarietà," 347–51. The author mentions a manifesto "to men of good will" released in early 1972, when the tribunal was still being designed with emphasis on the Brazilian case. According to Fraudatario, "the manifesto was signed by numerous Latin American and European personalities representative of the political, scientific, Catholic, Protestant world and the world of music, cinema, theater, arts, and literature … [such as] poet Pablo Neruda, singer Mercedes Sosa, actress Inda Ledesma, writer Gilles Martinet, painter Renato Guttuso, film director Ettore Scola, philosopher Noam Chomsky" ("Le Reti di solidarietà," 353).

171 For the full text of the verdict, see G. Tosi and L. F. G. Ferreira (eds.), *Chile, Bolívia e Uruguai: Atas da Primeira Sessão do Tribunal Russell II* (João Pessoa: Ed. UFPB, 2014), 361–74. The excerpt quoted is on page 371.

in forced isolation, or else, who lead an uncertain and tragic life in secrecy, threatened at every moment, are living witnesses that alert us that it is not necessary to wait for the sun to rise in order to believe in the light. This light that today shines in their indomitable hearts, tomorrow will illuminate the new paths of humanity.[172]

Urban Interventions in the Post-Dictatorship Period: Memory Sites

The dictatorships' brutal actions created a topography of repression. As Francesca Lessa remarked regarding Operation Condor, "[o]ne major location of crimes was Buenos Aires, due to the large number of political exiles living there since the 1960s," but other cities also accommodated locations (usually secret) for the practice of human rights violations. In 1976 Argentina, a clandestine detention center called *Automotores Orletti* was the site for activities related to Operation Condor. Other secret locations were *Pozo de Banfield* and *Pozo de Quilmes*. In Chile, there were the *Villa Grimaldi* and *Londres 38*; in Uruguay, the *Punta Gorda* house, a site called *300 Carlos*, and the Intelligence and Defense Service (SID) building; and in Paraguay, the Department of Police Investigations in Asunción. All these places fulfilled the same role.[173]

South American dictatorships were overcome, and processes of re-democratization began in the 1980s. In some countries, politicians linked to the dictatorships accumulated sufficient political capital during the re-democratization process to remain influential even after the dictatorships ceased to exist. The most striking examples are Brazil and Chile. But even where this kind of continuity was possible, spaces of memory connected to the time of repression emerged. Torture centers, clandestine detention camps, secret places for the interrogation, torture, and execution of opponents had become part of the landscape of South American cities; now questions were raised as to what should be done with these repressive structures, which epitomized the state terror inflicted by the dictatorial regimes.

The subsequent fate of these places varied greatly. In many countries, a number of military and police facilities involved in the repression continue to fulfill their original functions. Others, however, carried greater symbolism and stood as reminders of the oppression, and consequently underwent a re-dedication of their purpose. In Chile, two sites were converted into memory sites: *Londres 38* (a house located in central Santiago) and *Villa Grimaldi* (a property located on the outskirts of the Chilean capital) had served as

172 Basso in Tosi and Guerra, *Chile, Bolívia e Uruguai*, 377–78.
173 Lessa, "Justice Entrepreneurs," 125.

clandestine sites for the detention, torture, execution, and disappearance of hundreds of opponents of various nationalities. After the dictatorship, and mainly at the initiative of former president Michelle Bachelet, these places have become memory museums that seek to reconstruct the resistance to the Chilean dictatorship and bear witness to the trajectories of the victims. They are joined by the "Museum of Memory and Human Rights," also located in Santiago, which is renowned for its innovative use of transparent materials and the various shades of light inside and outside, creating an architectural and museological ensemble that focuses on remembering the victims of the Chilean regime.[174]

In Argentina, the *Parque de la Memoria* or "Memorial Park," which is located in the Belgrano neighborhood of Buenos Aires and includes the *Monumento a las Victimas del Terrorismo de Estado* or "Monument to the Victims" fulfills the same task. The park is situated near the estuary of the *Río de la Plata*, into which the bodies of opponents who have disappeared have been thrown; it is also in close proximity to one of the most notorious detention, torture, and execution centers of the Argentine regime, the *ESMA – Escuela de Mecánica de la Armada*, which has also been transformed into a memory museum (*Espacio Memoria y Derechos Humanos*). By providing these kinds of memory sites, urban interventions can shift the memory of oppression, reconnect the city to the river that is one of its main symbols, and enable a public display of recollection and remembering.[175]

In a seminal text, Andreas Huyssen highlights the layers of historicity that are revealed in the uncovering and processing of memories of these periods of arbitrary rule, and its unfolding in relation to the global context of human rights violations in the twentieth century. Huyssen connects the architectural and political choices featured in the design of the Memorial Park with two other major memorial sites conceived in a post-traumatic context: the Jewish Museum in Berlin and the Vietnam Veterans Memorial in Washington DC. While Huyssen refuses to draw a direct analogy between the Argentine dictatorship with its state terrorism and the Third Reich or the American invasion of Vietnam, he nonetheless mentions evidently common features between these monuments: for instance, asymmetrical lines that punctuate

174 For the site Londres 38, see www.londres38.cl/1937/w3-channel.html; for Villa Grimaldi, http://villagrimaldi.cl/; for the Museum of Memory and Human Rights, https://web.museodelamemoria.cl/ (all websites last accessed July 21, 2022).

175 For the Parque de la Memoria, see https://parquedelamemoria.org.ar/; for Espacio Memoria y Derechos Humanos, www.espaciomemoria.ar/ (both websites last accessed July 21, 2022).

the tortuous path of the political history of the twentieth century, expressing a fragmentation, an interruption of projects (with the persistence of empty spaces inside the building, a clear option in the Jewish Museum in Berlin); walls with inscriptions of the victims' names; and the use of underground spaces. With regard to the victims of the Argentine dictatorship (students and workers honored on the walls of the Monument to the Victims), Huyssen notes that the Buenos Aires Park "is also part of the global legacy of 1968, together with the mass shooting of students in Mexico City and the Soviet invasion of Czechoslovakia."[176]

Another urban intervention related to repression by authoritarian regimes is the transformation of the *Punta Carretas* prison in Montevideo. Inaugurated as a regular prison in 1915, it gradually also became a political prison where several members of guerrilla groups were detained before and after the coup d'état of 1973. This penitentiary, which eventually became a maximum-security prison, was abandoned in the late 1980s and then, between 1991 and 1994, converted into a luxury shopping mall.[177] In a suggestive analysis, Susana Draper connects the opening of the mall to the failure to recall the crimes of the Uruguayan military regime. She explains that, after the restoration of democracy in Uruguay, the 1986 *Ley de Caducidad de la Pretensión Punitiva del Estado* granted amnesty for crimes committed during the dictatorship, including those committed by agents of the regime. The law was submitted to a referendum, followed by a plebiscite, in March 1989, with the majority of votes cast in favor of the project. According to Draper, the conversion of the prison into a shopping mall must be understood within this broader historical process, which involved a new vision of the future and a "metaphor for a peculiar form of transition from the carceral past to the consumerist present." This became clear, according to the author: "After the decision voted in the plebiscite, the new prison-mall became both the paradoxical monument to forgetting and the prized example of the new regime's discourse, transactions, and measures."[178]

176 A. Huyssen, *Present Pasts: Urban Palimpsests and the Politics of Memory* (Stanford: Stanford University Press, 2003), 105.

177 See https://montevideoantiguo.net/index.php/ausentes/penal-de-punta-carretas.html. It is worth noting that the mall's website, when referring to the building's history, only mentions the opening, in 1915, of a penitentiary, emphasizing that the prison was a "building of truly impressive intensity." See www.puntacarretas.com.uy/nosotros/ (both websites mentioned in this footnote were last accessed July 21, 2022).

178 Both excerpts quoted in this paragraph are from S. Draper, *Afterlives of Confinement: Spatial Transitions in Postdictatorship Latin America* (Pittsburgh: University of Pittsburgh Press, 2012), 23. For reflections on memory sites, among many others, J. Winter, "Sites of Memory," in S. Radstone and B. Schwarz (eds.), *Memory: Histories, Theories, Debates*

Transnational Journeys: Paths of Resistance

The opponents of Latin American dictatorships included peasants, workers, students, dissenting members of the military, and several other social segments. Between the 1960s and 1970s, they reflected an enormous range of ideological tendencies, groups preaching political change, and texts that could inspire acts of resistance. There were various options for action: The opposition could engage exclusively in the "institutional way," that is, attempt to defeat the dictatorship in a peaceful manner, through the procedures established in the legal system then in force – or follow the path of open defiance, using armed struggle and guerrilla warfare.

This diversity is manifested in the trajectories of three opponents to the Brazilian military dictatorship. As will be demonstrated, each biographical path featured a selection of choices, contact with many different sources of influences, and journeys around the world before and during the Brazilian dictatorship (which began with the coup d'état of March/April 1964). These individual experiences exemplify many of the dilemmas faced by groups that opposed the Latin American authoritarian regimes, as well as many of the possible strategies for combating them.

1 Davi Capistrano da Costa (1913–1974)

Capistrano's biographical journey is connected to some of the main political conflicts of the twentieth century. Born in a small town in the Brazilian Northeast region, Davi Capistrano joined the ranks of the PCB and became involved in a military uprising against the government of President Getúlio Vargas in 1935. Sentenced to prison, he managed to escape into exile in Uruguay. He then joined a group of Latin Americans who volunteered to fight on the Republican side in the Spanish Civil War – the International Brigades, more specifically the Garibaldi Brigade, commanded by Italian communist leader Luigi Longo. He participated in several battles, including the famous Ebro campaign.

When the Spanish conflict ended (with the victory of the Francoist forces), Capistrano moved to France. There he was recruited by André Marty, a communist leader, and participated in the French Resistance at the beginning of World War II. Early in the conflict, he was taken prisoner and detained in

(New York: Fordham University Press, 2010), 312–24; P. Connerton, *How Modernity Forgets* (Cambridge: Cambridge University Press, 2009), 7–39 and 132–47; A. Assmann, *Cultural Memory and Western Civilization: Functions, Media, Archives* (Cambridge: Cambridge University Press, 2013), 312–24.

the Gurs detention camp in the Pyrenees (run by the Vichy Regime). After several years of detention, Capistrano was released and returned to Uruguay. In 1944, after Brazil entered World War II, he returned to his home country and enlisted in the Brazilian army. However, because his conviction for participating in the 1935 uprising was still in force, Capistrano remained in prison in the state of Rio de Janeiro until April 1945, when he was granted amnesty.

Following the end of the Vargas regime, Capistrano performed various political functions in the Communist Party, and was elected a state deputy in Pernambuco (a north-eastern Brazilian state). When the communist party was outlawed in 1947, Capistrano nevertheless remained politically active in secret and continued to hold party positions. In the 1950s, he was sent to a leadership training school of the Communist Party of the Soviet Union in Moscow for two years. Upon his return to Brazil, he continued being politically active, always within the structures of the Communist Party.

Soon after the 1964 coup d'état, Capistrano came under persecution by the military regime. He nonetheless managed to remain active in the resistance movement, even editing an underground newspaper. His party sent him to Czechoslovakia in 1972, and he spent two years in Prague. When, upon returning to Brazil in March 1974, Capistrano crossed the Uruguayan border, he was intercepted by agents of the military government; it is presumed that he was taken to a clandestine torture and detention center in the city of Petrópolis and executed there. His remains have never been located, and he is recognized by statute as a politically disappeared person.

Davi Capistrano remained attached to the PCB throughout his political life and followed the party's orientation in the struggle against the dictatorship. The party had opted for a "peaceful way" of fighting the Brazilian military regime, that is, it rejected the armed struggle as an instrument of resistance. After the other organizations that opposed the regime were annihilated or neutralized by the military, an operation to eliminate the main leaders of the PCB was also unleashed. It was in this operation that Capistrano was captured, detained, and murdered.[179]

179 The information related to Capistrano's itinerary was taken from several sources, the main ones being: Centro de Pesquisa e Documentação de História Contemporânea do Brasil; "Davi Capistrano da Costa," in *Dicionário Histórico-Biográfico Brasileiro*; www.fgv.br/cpdoc/acervo/dicionarios/verbete-biografico/davi-capistrano-da-costa (last accessed July 25, 2022); N. Miranda and C. Tibúrcio, *Dos filhos deste solo*, 406–8; Report of the Brazilian National Truth Commission (2015, vol. III, 1616–621), http://cnv.memoriasreveladas.gov.br/images/pdf/relatorio/volume_3_digital.pdf (last accessed July 31, 2022). On the involvement of Brazilians in the Spanish Civil War, see P. R. Almeida, "Brasileiros na Guerra Civil Espanhola: combatentes na luta contra o

2 Carlos Marighella (1911–1969)

Of the three opponents to the Brazilian dictatorship portrayed here, only Carlos Marighella, born in Salvador (Bahia), was not a politically disappeared person. One of the most prominent leaders of the resistance, his trajectory is unique and remarkable. In his youth, he joined the Communist Party and moved to Rio de Janeiro, where he frequently clashed with the political police of Getúlio Vargas, president of the Republic between 1930 and 1945. He was arrested and tortured several times. At the end of Vargas' regime, he was released, returned to political activity, and was elected to the National Constituent Assembly. He played an active role in drafting the Brazilian Constitution of 1946.

In 1952, Marighella traveled to China to study its revolution. He continued to be active in the PCB until 1964, when the coup d'état took place in Brazil. From then on, he distanced himself from the party's choice of how to resist the dictatorship. As mentioned earlier, the PCB opted for peaceful resistance and refused to engage in an armed struggle or to build guerrilla units, but Marighella pursued a different option. In 1967 he traveled to Cuba for the First Conference of the Latin American Solidarity Organization. There, he came into contact with members of communist groups from across Latin America, including Ernesto Che Guevara. He was expelled from the PCB for his defense of the armed struggle as a method to combat the Brazilian military dictatorship.

Back in Brazil, in February 1968 Marighella founded the *Ação Libertadora Nacional* (ALN, National Liberation Action), which was organized in small autonomous units with the purpose of executing direct actions to fight the regime, such as bank robberies, attacks on military institutions, and participation in the kidnapping of diplomats and foreign representatives. This line of action was innovative, as it combined the "guerrilla focus," widely used in the Cuban Revolution, with urban guerrilla tactics. It was the creation of this particular form of action that brought a global attention to Marighella.

In 1969 Marighella wrote the "Minimanual of the Urban Guerrilla," a small book (fifty-one typewritten pages) that had a significant impact on revolutionary struggles beyond the American continent. Marighella became known to the European public through an interview given to the Belgian journalist Conrad Detrez, published in *Front* magazine in November 1969. That same

fascismo," *Revista de Sociologia e Política* 12 (1999), 35–66. On the Gurs detention camp, see A. Rutkowski, "Le camp d'internement de Gurs," *Le Monde Juif* 16(4) (1980), 128–47.

year, texts authored by Marighella were published in *Les Temps Modernes* on the initiative of Jean-Paul Sartre (who had received them in Rome in a French translation by an ALN member, Ana Corbisier). The Minimanual was published in France by Éditions du Seuil in March 1970. The French Ministry of the Interior decided to prohibit the book's sale, which generated an immediate reaction from twenty-four publishers who re-released it and, by doing so, rendered the ban ineffective. In 1971 the Minimanual was published in English, and its readership grew quickly in the context of student revolts and the political struggles in Europe and Latin America.

Contemporary interpretations of the Minimanual as well as Marighella's own proposals for how to combat dictatorship hold that he was mainly influenced by the actions of the French resistance during the German occupation in World War II, the initiatives of the Algerian guerrillas in the War for Independence, and the fight against British colonial domination in Palestine in the 1940s. Marighella himself, when interviewed by Conrad Detrez, named the Vietnamese struggle against US invasion and the military actions undertaken by the Cuban revolutionaries as significant.

Marighella was killed in an ambush by Brazilian forces in São Paulo on November 4, 1969. After the end of the military regime, he was recognized by two state commissions as a victim of the dictatorship. His remains were transported to his hometown Salvador, where they rest in a tomb designed by the architect Oscar Niemeyer. The writer Jorge Amado and the abbot of the São Bento Monastery, Dom Timóteo Anastácio, delivered the eulogy at the funeral ceremony held on December 10, 1979.[180]

3 Osvaldo Orlando da Costa (1938–1974)

One of the most remarkable characters of the Brazilian resistance to the dictatorship was Osvaldo Orlando da Costa. Born in the countryside of Minas Gerais (southeastern Brazil), the grandson of slaves, Osvaldo da Costa

180 All information regarding Carlos Marighella and the Minimanual of the Urban Guerrilla was taken from the following sources, among several others: M. Magalhães, *Marighella: o guerrilheiro que incendiou o mundo* (São Paulo: Companhia das Letras, 2012), 499–512; M. Malin, "Carlos Marighella," in *Dicionário Histórico-Biográfico Brasileiro*, Centro de Pesquisa e Documentação de História Contemporânea do Brasil; www.fgv.br/cpdoc/acervo/dicionarios/verbete-biografico/marighella-carlos (last accessed July 25, 2022); J. Gorender, *Combate nas trevas – a esquerda brasileira: das ilusões perdidas à luta armada* (São Paulo: Ática, 1987), 153–78; Miranda and Tibúrcio, *Dos filhos deste solo*, 96–103; Report of the Brazilian National Truth Commission (2015, vol. III, 361–73), available at: http://cnv.memoriasreveladas.gov.br/images/pdf/relatorio/volume_3_digital.pdf (last accessed July 31, 2022). The English edition of the Minimanual: C. Marighella, *Mini-Manual of the Urban Guerrilla* (Montreal: Abraham Guillen Press, 2002).

moved to Rio de Janeiro where he took a technical course on mechanics and engineering. He was a boxer, competing and winning tournaments in the state of Rio de Janeiro, and also served in the army, graduating with the rank of officer.

The year 1961 represented the beginning of a unique period in Brazil's social and political history. Pressure from workers and unions for reforms increased, as did the protest against economic inequality. At the same time, the international situation after the Cuban Revolution was tense and full of uncertainties. North American pressure against the government of João Goulart was growing, and internal initiatives for political destabilization were taking shape. In that same year, 1961, Osvaldo da Costa had his first international experience: He was awarded a scholarship and went to Czechoslovakia to study mining engineering at the Technical University of Prague. It was during his time in Europe that his political militancy was consolidated. He joined the Communist Party of Brazil (PCdoB), a party that split off from the PCB and its orthodox Soviet orientation. In April 1964, right after the coup d'état in Brazil, Osvaldo da Costa left for military training in China, where he stayed for six months, in Beijing and Nanking.

The PCdoB chose to adopt the Chinese and Albanian political line of action. This model was of a "pure" guerrilla focus, that is, warfare that was entirely connected to the life of the peasants. The idea, mirrored in the experiences of the Chinese revolution, was to stimulate a revolution by establishing a rural guerrilla war, in places that were difficult to access for the repressive forces. For the strategy conceived by the PCdoB, "the revolutionary struggle would have its most important stage in the Brazilian rural area, through a war sustained, from its beginning, by strong popular contingents, especially peasants."[181]

The leadership of the PCdoB decided to establish the base for its guerilla activities in a remote area in northern Brazil, on the banks of the Araguaia River. Osvaldo Orlando da Costa was the first party leader to arrive there and established solid ties with the region's population. Several accounts testify to his popularity among the peasants. After several unsuccessful attempts to disband the fighters of the PCdoB, the Brazilian army decided to annihilate the guerrillas. The vast majority of guerrilla members were summarily executed, and many are still missing. In 1995, during the period of Brazilian re-democratization, a federal law recognized the killing and disappearance of persons by the state for political reasons. Of the 136 cases known at that time,

181 Miranda and Tibúrcio, *Dos filhos deste solo*, 231.

fifty-eight are PCdoB guerrilla fighters from Araguaia. Osvaldo da Costa was one of the last to be executed, according to sources, in February 1974. His body was never found.[182]

Concluding Remarks

Latin American dictatorships made extensive use of various legal mechanisms. Parliaments and courts suffered intervention in their institutional operations or were simply closed down. In addition, the legal system was used as a tool for repression, investigation, and the punishment of opponents. This leading role of legal institutions can be explained by two factors, both addressed throughout Section 6.2: the attempt to legitimize the regimes (which sought to consolidate themselves in institutional terms) and the wish to persecute and punish opponents (through the activation of courts and prosecuting agencies).

It is important, however, to place many of the reasons used by political actors (military and civilian) to justify the institutional break with the preexisting regimes within the context of the Cold War and contemporary geopolitical conflicts, which greatly affected the continent but were nonetheless external to Latin America. These conditions influenced the political and legal practice of the dictatorships and triggered the creation of networks of collaboration and resistance, which then also spread beyond Latin America. In other words, the global element was a central feature of the dictatorships and worked as an active and intense factor for mobilizing both repressive forces and resistance movements. The pivotal role of the Cold War and its aftermath, for example, was crucial to the building and consolidation of dictatorships, as exemplified by Operation Condor, which was one of the modalities employed for expanding repressive activities. At the same time, resistance to authoritarian regimes also relied on an intense transnational mobilization through political actors, organizations, and institutions that reached a global sphere of action on behalf of freedom and human rights.

As we reach the final stage of our historical reconstruction, one question remains to be asked: How did the dictatorships come to an end?

182 Information about Osvaldo Orlando da Costa comes from the following sources: R.L. Petta, *A memória dos moradores do Araguaia sobre "Osvaldão": liderança, luta e resistência!* (São Paulo: Masters Dissertation, School of Arts, Sciences and Humanities, 2017), 31–43; R. Vecchi, "O passado subtraído da desaparição forçada: Araguaia como palimpsesto," *Estudos de literatura brasileira contemporânea* 43 (2014), 133–49; Gorender, *Combate nas trevas*, 207–41; Miranda and Tibúrcio, *Dos filhos deste solo*, 230–72; Report of the Brazilian National Truth Commission (2015, vol. III, 1590–594), available at: http://cnv.memoriasreveladas.gov.br/images/pdf/relatorio/volume_3_digital.pdf (last accessed July 31, 2022).

The decline of authoritarian regimes was shaped by a mix of different elements. Foreign policies, economic issues, and actions by opponents all contributed to this demise. Nevertheless, the patterns, speed, and outcomes of this demise were different in each case. As noted earlier, Latin American dictatorships, notably the ones in Chile, Brazil, and Argentina, shared a foundational element: the search for a legal justification. Institutional acts, *bandos*, decree-laws, secret acts, in short, a series of rules established by military *juntas* all sought to translate into legal terms the violent break with the rule of law. These disruptive measures were followed by attempts at institutionalization of varying intensity, form, and time, as observed earlier.

This authoritarian legacy had to be confronted. Persecution, torture, executions, and disappearances presented a huge challenge for transitional justice policies (see, in this regard, Section 6.3). Moreover, these practices cast a shadow over the institutionalization of the post-dictatorship legal order. Doubts have arisen as to how to deal with the remaining elements of the authoritarian legal order. What to do with the constitutional documents produced by the dictatorships? What type of continuity or disruption must be established between the practices of legal professionals in the authoritarian and the democratic periods?

Naturally, the answers will be diverse. Consider, briefly, as a mode of example, the challenges involved in the constitution-making process. At first glance, Brazil and Chile seem to have followed similar paths. In both cases, intense negotiations took place between the military occupants of power and civilian politicians interested in re-democratization. In both countries, the military retained a considerable share of the political power even at the end of the authoritarian regime. The similarities end there, however, as the chronology was very different. In Brazil, a constitution was enacted immediately after the end of the dictatorship, with significant democratizing elements. In Chile, the 1980 constitution, drafted by a commission directly controlled by the military *junta* and led by jurists loyal to the regime, was upheld.[183] Evidently, factors other than a constitution are also involved in defining the continuity or rupture of the legal system, such as the efficacy of amnesties

183 On September 4, 2022, a referendum was held on the draft constitution proposed by a Constitutional Convention elected in 2020 with the specific purpose of preparing a new constitution for Chile. The text was rejected by the majority of voters (about 62 percent voted for rejection, 38 percent for approval). The 1980 Constitution remains in full force. For a general overview, see www.bbc.com/mundo/noticias-america-latina-62790788 (last accessed Feb. 20, 2023). For a discussion, from various perspectives, of the factors that led to the text's rejection, see the symposium organized by I-CONnect (blog of the International Journal of Constitutional Law): www.iconnectblog.com/tag/chilean-constitution/ (last accessed Feb. 20, 2023).

granted during the dictatorship, the permanence of authoritarian practices in democratic periods, and many others.

In all these cases, a time-driven operation came into play. First, the most essential question was how to overcome mechanisms granting exceptions, which were typical of authoritarian regimes. But the new democratic regimes also faced another risk – which, to a certain extent, persisted throughout the post-dictatorial period in Latin America – namely the normalization of the authoritarian rule, that is, incorporating legal practices developed during the dictatorships into democratic regimes.

The literature on the demise of dictatorships tended not to center on this risk of normalization. Instead, a persistent topic in the historical literature related to authoritarian regimes, especially in Latin America, included narratives of transition. For a long time, the end of dictatorships was associated with the form, duration, and characteristics of political processes labeled "transitions." An extensive literature has built up on the subject, including a discrete field of political science, the so-called "transitology."[184] Nevertheless, narratives of transition have their pitfalls; they grant a special status to the supposed "time of transition," which should enable societies that lived under dictatorships to prepare for a transition to democratic rule. But what constituted this time of transition? Historical observation indicates that Latin American nations that faced dictatorships in the context of the Cold War were affected (and still are) by the political struggles waged between the regime (and its civilian and military supporters) and the various forms of resistance (articulated both internally and through transnational mobilization). As a result, there are no qualitative differences between the "time of dictatorships" and the "time of transitions." Instead, there are different phases of political dispute, with the "transition" being merely a stage in this struggle, in which the political actors seek to maintain a certain amount of power and influence.[185] Naming

184 See, among many other references, G. O'Donnell, P. C. Schmitter, and L. Whitehead (eds.), *Transitions from Authoritarian Rule: Latin America* (Baltimore and London: Johns Hopkins University Press, 1993); J. J. Linz and A. Stepan, *Problems of Democratic Transition and Consolidation: Southern Europe, South America, and Post-Communist Europe* (Baltimore and London: Johns Hopkins University Press, 1996); K. Stoner and M. McFaul (eds.), *Transitions to Democracy: A Comparative Perspective* (Baltimore: Johns Hopkins University Press, 2013).

185 For a critical approach on the idea of transition, see the pioneering works of W. Thayer, *La crisis no moderna de la Universidad moderna (epílogo de El Conflicto de las Facultades)* (Santiago de Chile: Editorial Cuarto Propio, 1996); Thayer, "La firma Pinochet," *Re-Presentaciones – Investigación en Comunicación* 15 (2021), 122–43. See also C. Paixão and C. P. Carvalho, "Mudança constitucional, luta política e o caminho para a democracia: uma análise do "emendão" de 1982," *História do Direito: RHD* 2(3) (2021), 300–19.

a particular time "transition" may confer greater density to this period, but it tends to overemphasize the willingness to negotiate by those occupying power. Suffice it to consider the cases of Chile and Brazil, where the military retained political capital even after the end of the dictatorships. In these cases, the transition concealed strategies by the exiting regime to exert influence in the ensuing political arena. The time of transition lingered after the dictatorial regime and projected its effects into the immediate future.[186] This issue, transition, illustrates the complexity of the debate surrounding dictatorships, their frequent use of legal institutions and emergency measures, and their impact on the democratic regimes that were established thereafter, often bringing to the forefront their particular features, setbacks, and uncertainties.

. . .

6.3 Transitional Justice and Human Rights

RUTI TEITEL AND VALERIA VEGH WEIS

This section examines the relations between human rights, transitional justice, and the global legal framework. While most narratives that examine this issue tend to focus on how European powers contributed to the development of these fields, we wish to offer a different perspective, that of the Latin American contribution. In this section, we will show that the development of human rights law and transitional justice during the late twentieth and early twenty-first centuries were the consequence of crucial struggles that, in periods of political transition, sought to respond to mass atrocities and demanded different forms of accountability. As a result, since the 1980s, the most significant advancements in human rights and the most remarkable transitional processes worldwide happened in the Global South (mainly in Latin America but also in South Africa and Rwanda, among many others).[187]

186 This concept of transition time has been called, by Massimo Meccarelli, a kind of "ascriptive time." Cf., in this regard, M. Meccarelli, "Time of innovation and time of transition shaping the legal dimension: A methodological approach from legal history," in M. Meccarelli, C. Paixão, and C. Roesler (eds.), *Innovation and Transition in Law: Experiences and Theoretical Settings* (Madrid: Dykinson, 2020), 23–44; on the historical significance of transitions, also C. Paixão and M. Meccarelli, "Constituent power and constitution-making process in Brazil: concepts, themes, problems," *Giornale di Storia Costituzionale* 4(2) (2020), 29–54.

187 D. A. Zysman Quirós, "Punishment, Democracy and Transitional Justice in Argentina (1983–2015)," *International Journal for Crime, Justice and Social Democracy* 6(1) (2017), 88–102.

Our aim therefore is to break with a narrative that understands normative transfers as unidirectional processes that begin with empires and imperial legal projects, and insists that the Global South can (must?) learn from the experience of the Global North. This account has been so pervasive that it has led, in the words of Santos, to an "epistemicide" that "either silenced or made invisible, irrelevant, or non-existent" the expertise of populations traditionally subjected to colonial or neocolonial sociability. Santos concludes that "in the last 500 years, the colonized world has not just been a source of raw materials for the industries of the metropolis, it has also been a source of raw materials for metropolitan sciences."[188]

Breaking with the mainstream logic that centered on the European contribution or that, in the exceptional instances when it did pay attention to the South, tended to look at it from a Northern perspective and was largely expressed by Northern scholars and practitioners, this section aims to clarify the role of Latin American actors as vital participants in, and not just recipients of, European and international law.[189] Moreover, the section will pay attention to the crucial role of Latin American civil society in initiating legal innovations, particularly in Argentina.[190] In this regard, it will demonstrate how norms transfer from and to the Americas, and from and to the European and international spheres, operate not only in terms of the relevant legal regimes and related jurisprudence but also by affecting social practices and politics.

To elaborate this argument, this section focuses on the normative development of a distinctive human rights violation: the crime of "enforced disappearances." This account illuminates the role of Latin America and its strong civil society as the leading normative protagonists within a network of global interactions that function through a dialogic process in which Latin America both *draws from* and *informs* law and legal practices elsewhere

188 See B. de Sousa Santos and M. P. Meneses (eds.), *Knowledges Born in the Struggle: Constructing the Epistemologies of the Global South* (New York: Routledge, 2020), xvii–xliii, Chapters 3 and 4.

189 J. Braithwaite, "Criminology, Peacebuilding and Transitional Justice: Lessons from the Global South," in K. Carrington, R. Hogg, J. Scott, and M. Sozzo (eds.), *The Palgrave Handbook of Criminology and the Global South* (New York: Palgrave Macmillan, 2018), 971–90; V. Vegh Weis, "Towards a Critical Green Southern Criminology: An Analysis of Criminal Selectivity, Indigenous Peoples and Green Harms in Argentina," *International Journal for Crime, Justice and Social Democracy* 8(3) (2019), 38–55; K. Härter and V. Vegh Weis, "Transnational Criminal Law in Transatlantic Perspective (1870–1945): Introductory Notes, Initial Results," *Rechtsgeschichte – Legal History* 30 (2022), 84–94. On the term Latin America and its multiple dimensions, see Duve and Herzog's introduction to this volume.

190 K. Sikkink, "From Pariah State to Global Protagonist: Argentina and the Struggle for International Human Rights," *Latin American Politics and Society* 50(1) (2008), 1–29.

around the globe. Specifically, it will highlight the contributions of the Inter-American Human Rights System and engaged Southern civil society actors such as NGOs or lawyers for victims' families, who have developed and brought to court claims after successive administrations failed to respond to wrongdoings, giving birth to a creative jurisprudence that has also influenced European and international law.[191]

The Southern Perspective

Global agreements on civil and political rights can work as valuable tools to prevent violations of human rights through early denunciation or, when these violations have already taken place, to bring awareness both locally and internationally to these breaches. Most particularly, international human rights and humanitarian law can be used by engaged social actors to push forward democratic transformations after periods of political violence, to bring perpetrators to justice before either domestic or international courts, to secure reparations for victims, and even to help develop public policies aimed at avoiding the repetition of such crimes.

Given these characteristics of modern geopolitical history (colonization, neocolonization) and the experiences with massive violence, resistance, and transition to democracy, it is not surprising that the South has been a true laboratory of transitional justice, especially in the 1980s and early 1990s. Yet as Carozza points out:

> [E]ven among human rights enthusiasts and activists, Latin America has long been regarded as the object of human rights concerns more than a contributor to human rights thinking. Or rather, its "contributions" have been perceived almost exclusively in negative terms. For example, the creativity of its repressive regimes in fashioning new forms of abuse, like the "disappearance," provoked the governments and human rights organizations of Europe and North America to come up with new norms and institutions to address the problems.... But the affirmative dimensions of human rights in Latin America, instead, have much more often been seen to be tarnished and inferior copies of grand, rich European ideas.[192]

Identifying the problematic logic behind this structural silencing or systemic diminishment of Southern contributions, the field of Southern/Decolonial

191 For a comprehensive discussion of these petitions, see P. Palacios Zuloaga, "Judging Human Rights in Latin America: The Riddle of Compliance in Inter-American Human Rights Law," unpublished J.S.D. dissertation, New York University (2013).

192 P. Carozza, "From Conquest to Constitutions: Retrieving a Latin American Tradition of the Idea of Human Rights," *Human Rights Quarterly* 25 (2003), 281–313, at 283.

Studies seeks to shed light on how such views hinder the democratization of knowledge and limit the story that can be told. Because research has generally excluded the experiences and perspectives of the Global South, we still lack a deeper analysis of fundamental issues that would enrich our understanding of violations in the Global North and, potentially, worldwide.[193] Among other things, this is the case because neither human rights instruments nor the jurisprudence emanating from regional and global tribunals can be understood as politically neutral or informed solely by legal and / or constitutional principles. Instead, it is inevitably shaped by struggles and interests based on criteria of class, gender, race, and ethnicity, among others.

A Marxist critique to the first universal normative instrument, the Declaration of the Rights of Man and the Citizen passed by the French revolutionary National Assembly in 1789, argued that reality was ignored in the text.[194] According to this critique, while the "citizen" (the abstract figure) was conceived as a rights holder who represents the ideal version of the law, the "man" (the concrete person) was the real person, conditioned by the socio-economic context that may well inhibit the enforcement of the proclaimed rights.[195] For example, the Declaration established the formal freedom to work, but the market imposes limits that may leave many unemployed; the Declaration recognized freedom of speech and association, but exercising it requires the appropriate means, which are often not readily available, hence resulting in the silencing of many views.[196] Similarly, international law also generally assumes the formal equality of all actors, requiring states and individuals to comply with the same globalizing normative order despite the radically varying situations and the consequently different efforts demanded of each member state to achieve the stipulated aims.[197] In other

193 B. de Sousa Santos, *Epistemologies of the South: Justice against Epistemicide* (Epistemologies of the South) (New York: Routledge, 2014).

194 For a related contemporary critique, see S. Moyn, *The Last Utopia: Human Rights in History* (Cambridge: Harvard University Press, 2010); L. Obregón, "Peripheral Histories of International Law," *Annual Review of Law and Social Science* 15 (2019), 437–51.

195 V. Vegh Weis, *Marxism and Criminology: A History of Criminal Selectivity* (Studies in Critical Social Sciences 104) (Leiden: Brill, 2017); and V. Vegh Weis, "A Marxist Analysis of International Criminal Law and Its Potential as a Counter-Hegemonic Project," in F. Jeßberger, L. Steinl, and K. Mehta (eds.), *International Criminal Law – A Counter-Hegemonic Project?* (International Criminal Justice Series 31) (The Hague: T.M.C. Asser Press 2022), 63–84.

196 K. Marx, "On *The Jewish Question*" (1843), *Marxists Internet Archive*, www.marxists.org/archive/marx/works/1844/jewish-question/ (last accessed Feb. 17, 2023).

197 Vegh Weis, "A Marxist Analysis."

words, international law speaks to the global, but it tends to overlook structural differences and diversity in local contexts.

This Northern conception of human rights has been characterized in the following way:

> [R]ights are universally valid irrespective of the social, political and cultural context in which different human rights regimes operate in the diverse regions of the world; they start from a conception of human nature that is individual, self-sustaining and qualitatively different from non-human nature; universal declarations, multilateral institutions (courts and commissions) and non-governmental organizations (predominantly based in the North) define what is a human rights violation; the recurrent phenomenon of double standards in assessing human rights compliance in no way compromises the universal validity of human rights; respect for human rights is much more problematic in the global South than in the global North.[198]

Yet, from a Southern viewpoint, rights are often understood to be contextualized, with civil and political rights conceptualized as indivisibly attached to socio-economic ones. In the South, rights are often considered a collective, not an individual enterprise. It is often the case that fundamental rights for the South (e.g., debt relief as a human right) are ignored by Northern member states. Often ignored phenomena in the North can be incorporated as fundamental rights in the South, including a stand for debt relief, historical justice for the colonial past, and global equality.[199] The expansion of human rights to include collective and historical claims is a result of the crucial particularities regarding normative knowledge in the South, where it is not conceived in abstract academic settings and detached from social suffering, but, on the contrary, is generally "born in struggles against capitalism, colonialism, and patriarchy, produced by the social groups and classes that have suffered most from the injustices caused by such domination," and where expertise is entwined with social processes on the ground.[200]

Drawing attention to Southern contributions to human rights thinking and transitional justice does not seek to displace or negate but rather aims

198 B. de Sousa Santos, *If God Were a Human Rights Activist* (Stanford: Stanford University Press, 2015).

199 R. Teitel, *Transitional Justice* (New York: Oxford University Press, 2000); and W. Kaleck, "On Double Standards and Emerging European Custom on Accountability for Colonial Crimes," in M. Bergsmo, W. Kaleck, and K. Yin Hlaing (eds.), *Colonial Wrongs and Access to International Law* (Brussels: Torkel Opsahl Academic EPublisher, 2020), 1–40.

200 Sousa Santos and Meneses, *Knowledges Born in the Struggle*; B. de Sousa Santos and B. Sena Martins, *El pluriverso de los derechos humanos. La diversidad de las luchas por la dignidad* (Epistemologías del Sur) (Mexico City: Ediciones AKAL, 2020).

to *complement* prevailing knowledge of Northern legal developments. Santos conceptualized this view as an "ecology of knowledge."[201] Contrary to "knowledge transfers," a term often used to describe how knowledge evolves and spreads, stressing disequilibrium, tensions, contradictions, and conflict, Santos uses the expression "ecology of knowledge" to highlight stability and equilibrium. The phrase also expresses an aspiration to redress the balance in our knowledge cosmovision, as it views Northern or Southern "bits" of knowledge in and of themselves as partial or incomplete, and acknowledges this reciprocal incompleteness as a necessary condition for summing up in order to build comprehensive knowledge.[202]

When applied at the jurisprudential level, "ecology of knowledge" can be framed as "cross judging," that is, the regular reference to jurisprudence of courts and tribunals from other legal systems, often outside hierarchic or other conventions relating to uses of precedent or sources of law.[203] In the context of international law, cross-judging describes the transfer of legal knowledge to and from the different regional courts and international bodies. It takes place even when the various courts do not explicitly cite each other, and reveals how approaches taken by different tribunals can strengthen each other's arguments. Thus, while international law is often characterized as decentralized, fragmented, and lacking in legal integration *vis-a-vis* domestic law, cross-judging provides a counter-narrative,[204] emphasizing the existence of a network of global interactions through a dialogic process in which Latin America both *draws from* and *informs* law and legal practices elsewhere around the globe.

Human Rights and Transitional Justice in Latin America: The Crime of Enforced Disappearance and the Centrality of Grassroots Organizations

Human rights are strongly entangled with the contemporary history of Latin America. Of particular importance are Latin American contributions to the development of transitional justice in the 1970s and 1980s. Though transitional

201 Sousa Santos, *Epistemologies of the South.*

202 Sousa Santos and Meneses, *Knowledges Born in the Struggle.*

203 R. Teitel and R. Howse, "Cross-Judging: Tribunalization in a Fragmented but Interconnected Global Order. Symposium – The Normalizing of Adjudication in Complex International Governance Regimes: Patterns, Possibilities, and Problems," *New York University Journal of International Law and Politics* 41 (2009), 959–90.

204 M. Koskenniemi and the Study Group of the UN International Law Commission, "Fragmentation of International Law: Difficulties Arising From the Diversification and Expansion of International Law," A/CN.4/L.702 (Geneva: United Nations, 2006), https://legal.un.org/ilc/documentation/english/a_cn4_l682.pdf (last accessed Jan. 19, 2022).

justice as an area of study only emerged around twenty years ago, it has rapidly acquired recognition as an independent field.[205] This recognition is based on the observation that similar experiences in dealing with the aftermath of periods of state repression and atrocities "travel" from one country and region to another and very often use the language and the instruments of the law in general and human rights in particular. In other words, norms, legal practices, and networks from one region are replicated, transformed, and vernacularized in others under new and local premises. Transitional justice seeks to capture these entanglements as well as to adopt a forward-looking emphasis that wishes to transform cross-knowledge into mechanisms that would guarantee non-recurrence through prevention.

The term "transitional justice" was coined by Ruti Teitel, who defined it as "a distinctive conception of law and justice in the context of political transformation."[206] The leading Global North NGO working on the topic, the International Center for Transitional Justice (ICTJ), refers to transitional justice as "a branch of justice that states a different approach to the conventional, assumed by societies to address the legacy of widespread and systematic violations of human rights."[207] Another key definition relates to the forms of justice. The UN Secretary-General's report *The rule of law and transitional justice in conflict and post conflict societies* defined transitional justice as comprising "the full range of processes and mechanisms associated with a society's attempts to come to terms with a legacy of large-scale past abuses,"[208] Stanley Cohen described it as "how societies going through democratic changes should deal with atrocities committed by the previous regime,"[209] and, according to Jon Elster, it is "made up of the processes of trials, purges, and reparations that take place after the transition from one political regime to another."[210] Overall,

205 K. McEvoy, "Travel, Dilemmas and Nonrecurrence: Observations on the 'Respectabilisation' of Transitional Justice," *International Journal of Transitional Justice* 12(2) (2018), 185–93; R. Teitel, *Globalizing Transitional Justice: Contemporary Essays* (New York: Oxford University Press, 2014).

206 Teitel, *Transitional Justice*, 4; R. Teitel, "Transitional Jurisprudence: The Role of Law in Political Transformation," *The Yale Law Journal* 106(7) (1997), 2009–80.

207 International Center for Transitional Justice (ICTJ), "What is Transitional Justice?," *International Center for Transitional Justice* (2020), www.ictj.org/about/transitional-justice (last accessed Mar. 27, 2023).

208 UN Secretary-General, *The Rule of Law and Transitional Justice in Conflict and Post Conflict Societies*, S/2004/616 (Aug. 23, 2004), 4.

209 S. Cohen, "Unspeakable Memories and Commensurable Laws," in S. Karstedt (ed.), *Legal Institutions and Collective Memories, Unspeakable Memories* (Oxford: Hart Publishing, 2009), 27–39, at 29.

210 J. Elster, *Closing the Books: Transitional Justice in Historical Perspective* (Cambridge: Cambridge University Press, 2004), 1.

transitional justice encompasses the broad range of mechanisms and practices that make it possible to transition from a period of massive persecution or related abuses to a more human rights-protective aftermath.

Latin American contributions to transitional justice are tied to the political situation in the 1970s and 1980s. During this period and amid the geopolitics of the Cold War, the so-called "Operation Condor," a network of collaborations between dictatorships in the region orchestrated with the support of the United States, aimed at eliminating left wing movements. Argentina, Bolivia, Brazil, Chile, Paraguay, Uruguay, and, to a lesser extent, Colombia, Peru, and Venezuela were involved in this continental program of military terror. Meanwhile, Panama was under the dictatorship of Manuel Antonio Noriega; Colombia was struggling with a long-lasting armed conflict, and Guatemala and the Dominican Republic were amid civil war.[211] The regional policy of terror was predicated on extrajudicial killings and torture, but also on a novel method later labeled "enforced disappearances": a pattern of abductions of civilians followed by governmental cover-up and a blackout of information about the victims.

In these cases, the state was the perpetrator, and therefore would not be the one pushing for accountability, nor could the criminal justice system be employed to stop these violations. Instead, a bottom-up movement emerged, even amid the state terror, which sought justice abroad by appealing to organizations and public opinion on the international level. In an important legal strategy of resistance, civil society organizations promoted and defended the notion of "disappearance" as a specific legal category of atrocity, describing those subjected to this unlawful practice as the "disappeared" or *desaparecidos*. Particularly active were the "Mothers and Grandmothers of Plaza de Mayo" in Argentina, who realized early on the political potential of the term.[212] Accepting the lack of information as proof of the death of their children, they argued, would be to absolve the state from the responsibility of accounting for their lives. Sticking to the category of "disappeared," therefore, became an act of resistance and a tool for sustaining claims before the state.[213] Through systematic claims-making and denunciation of the kidnappings, relatives of

211 J. Agüero García, "América Latina Durante La Guerra Fría (1947–1989): Una Introducción," *InterSedes* 17(35) (2016), 2–34.

212 V. Vegh Weis "The Relevance of Victims' Organizations in Transitional Justice Processes: The Case of the Grandmothers of Plaza de Mayo in Argentina," *Intercultural Human Rights Law Review* 12 (2017), 1–70.

213 E. Schindel, "Under-Researched, Transnational, Silent: Disappearances in Transit to Europe," www.law.ox.ac.uk/research-subject-groups/centre-criminology/centreborder-criminologies/blog/2020/10/under-researched (last accessed Jan. 20, 2022).

the victims helped give a new name to state terror by creating a new legal category that established the concept of "enforced disappearance." In other words,

> rather than being passive spectators of the international theatre, Latin Americans became writers, directors, producers, and actors of the international response to enforced disappearances. In addition, their strategic advocacy promoted the transformation of the international legal system to respond to the needs and reality present in Latin America.[214]

Latin American human rights activism also led to additional developments. Relatives of the forced disappeared in Latin America gathered in a continental network, FEDEFAM (*Federación Latinoamericana de Familiares de Detenidos-Desaparecidos*), and gave the definitive impulse to the creation of a UN Working Group on Forced and Involuntary Disappearances in the 1980s, the first thematic mechanism on this crime with a universal mandate.[215] This working group, in turn, fostered the approval of a treaty specifically focused on this crime. In 2006, the UN General Assembly issued the International Convention for the Protection of All Persons from Enforced Disappearance, which in article 2 defines the crime as "the arrest, detention, abduction or any other form of deprivation of liberty by agents of the State or by persons or groups of persons acting with the authorization, support or acquiescence of the State, followed by a refusal to acknowledge the deprivation of liberty or by concealment of the fate or whereabouts of the disappeared person, which place such a person outside the protection of the law." The implementation is monitored by the Committee on Enforced Disappearances.

Latin American activism has also been crucial in promoting the development of other practices, such as forensic examinations, to prove enforced disappearances. In more philosophical terms, this activism also made it possible to distinguish death, even murder, from disappearance, by illuminating the consequences of the ongoing denial or cover-up, which impedes closure and the possibility of mourning.[216]

214 A. E. Dulitzky, "The Latin-American Flavor of Enforced Disappearances," *Chicago Journal of International Law* 19(2) (2019), 423–89.

215 Federación Latinoamericana de Asociaciones de Familiares de Detenidos-Desaparecidos (FEDEFAM), "Fighting against Forced Disappearances in Latin America," www.desaparecidos.org/fedefam/eng.html.

216 G. Gatti, "Las narrativas del detenido-desaparecido (o de los problemas de la representación ante las catástrofes sociales)," *CONfines. Revista de Relaciones Internationales y Cienca Política* 4(2) (2006), 27–38, www.redalyc.org/pdf/633/63320403.pdf (last accessed Jan. 25, 2022).

Born out of grassroots usage as part of civil struggle against Latin American dictatorships, denunciations of forced disappearances ultimately gave way to the transitional justice processes of the 1980s.[217] When the transitions to democracy took place, these grassroots actors also occupied a central role in fostering transitional justice remedies that would seek justice for victims of enforced disappearances – as well as of other crimes, including extrajudicial killings and torture – in a particular manner that would set new paths worldwide. It is generally agreed that the modern history of human rights began with the Nuremberg Trials in the aftermath of the Second World War along with associated developments, such as the United Nations Charter, the Universal Declaration of Human Rights, and subsequent covenants.[218] Notwithstanding the horrors of the Holocaust, the focus at Nuremberg and related war crimes trials was on the perpetrators rather than the victims. By contrast, transitional justice as it evolved in Latin America, and to some extent South Africa in the 1990s, was distinct because it explicitly referred to the needs of victims and these actors were involved in the deliberations. The aim was to express "an awareness of the centrality of victims/survivors and their needs throughout the process."[219]

A crucial means of meeting victims' needs for information and recognition are truth commissions, which have evolved into mechanisms for victims to bear witness. The first modern commission was the 1983 Argentine truth commission, also known as the National Commission on the Disappearance of Persons (*Comisión Nacional sobre la Desaparición de Personas*, CONADEP). Since the creation of this commission, over forty others have been established worldwide to investigate massive human rights violations, with more than a third taking place in Latin America.[220] CONADEP's success, which paved the way for similar commissions elsewhere around the globe, was tied to the commitment of civil society organizations.[221] Grassroots activism not only helped raise awareness of the centrality of the crime of enforced disappearance, it also supported CONADEP's work while pushing the scope of its

217 See Section 6.2 in this volume.

218 R. Teitel, "Human Rights Genealogy," *Fordham Law Review* 66(2) (1997), 301–18.

219 S. Robins "Towards Victim-Centered Transitional Justice: Understanding the Needs of Families of the Disappeared in Postconflict Nepal," *International Journal of Transitional Justice* 5(1) (2011), 75–98.

220 E. Skaar, E. Wiebelhaus-Brahm, and J. García-Godos, *Exploring Truth Commission Recommendations in a Comparative Perspective: Beyond Words* (Series on Transitional Justice 27) (Cambridge: Intersentia, 2022), vol. I.

221 E. Crenzel, "Argentina's National Commission on the Disappearance of Persons: Contributions to Transitional Justice," *International Journal of Transitional Justice* 2(2) (2008), 173–91.

mandate. For example, during the commission's investigative period, the victims' organizations pushed it to search for the disappeared in different locations. Later on, they also pressed the commission to issue more ambitious recommendations. Once the final CONADEP report, entitled *Nunca Más*, was released, the victims' networks helped disseminate the commission's findings and established them as the authoritative record. Subsequently, these findings led to further accountability by providing the basis for the initiation of criminal cases.[222] Subsequent truth commissions have followed the example of CONADEP by moving away from expert and forensic-led truth-gathering processes to emphasizing survivor testimony, civil society participation, and grassroots projects.[223] In fact, CONADEP's findings led to the Junta Trial (1985), the first criminal process carried out by domestic judges and deploying domestic law that judged the Argentinean perpetrators of massive human rights violations. This process was made possible by the testimonies of courageous survivors and relatives of victims who dared to testify – despite the ongoing risks, given that there was still military opposition, which later led to limiting the prosecutions.[224]

Chile supplies another pathbreaking example of influential transitional justice practices involving strong grassroots organizations and two truth commissions that elaborated detailed recommendations and produced broad memorialization. Indeed, even during Pinochet's dictatorship, human rights groups and relatives of the victims documented and called international attention to the pervasiveness of enforced disappearances and demanded these be recognized as human rights violations.[225] After the transition to democracy in 1990, a first truth commission was convened. However, civil society organizations, particularly the *Cómisión Etica contra la Tortura y la Organización de Defensa Popular*, demanded that the government go beyond the institution of a

222 V. Vegh Weis, "Exploring the World's First Successful Truth Commission: Argentina's CONADEP and the Role of Victims in Truth-Seeking," *Journal of Human Rights Practice* (2023), https://doi.org/10.1093/jhuman/huac060 (last accessed Mar. 27, 2023); P. Lundy and M. McGovern, "The Role of Community in Participatory Transitional Justice," in K. McEvoy and L. McGregor (eds.), *Transitional Justice from Below: Grassroots Activism and the Struggle for Change* (Human Rights Law in Perspective 14) (Oxford and Portland: Hart Publishing, 2008), 99–120.

223 R. Teitel, "Transitional Justice Genealogy," *Harvard Human Rights Journal* 16 (2003), 69–94.

224 V. Vegh Weis, "Argentine Truth Commission," in S. Parmentier (ed.), *Romero: Memory Papers* (Leuven: Leuven University Press, forthcoming).

225 J. Zalaquett, "The Emergence of 'Disappearances' as a Normative Issue Presentation," in C. Booth Walling and S. Waltz (eds.), *Human Rights: From Practice to Policy. Proceedings of a Research Workshop Gerald R. Ford School of Public Policy* (Ann Arbor: University of Michigan, 2010).

simple truth commission and instead create a new mechanism with a broader scope. The result was the Investigative Commission on Truth, Justice and Reparation (*Comisión Investigadora de Verdad, Justicia y Reparación*), which was instituted a decade later.

Later on, the truth commissions in Peru and Guatemala marked another milestone by including – though not without shortcomings[226] – the voices of indigenous peoples and rural communities, who had been systematically marginalized from the political discussion despite the fact that they had been targeted by massive violence during the civil conflicts:[227] For example, 75 percent of the 69,000 people forcibly disappeared and murdered in the Peruvian conflict had Quechua or other indigenous languages as their mother tongue.[228]

An even more recent example of how Latin American grassroots involvement produced legal innovations regarding the crime of enforced disappearances comes from Colombia, where it is estimated that there were between 80,000 and 120,000 victims of such crimes. There, in light of the indifference of the state, relatives of the victims and entire communities developed their own legal and fact-finding methods to seek out the disappeared. Among their many successes was their ability to push the government to legally recognize this crime in 2000 and to create a special unit aimed at tracing those whose whereabouts are unknown, the *Unidad de Búsqueda de Personas dadas por Desaparecidas* (UBPD).[229]

This normative creativity and legal innovation persists in Latin America, drawing from its immediate political past and giving birth to what some have termed a "justice cascade" in human rights, that is, a sustained imperative for accountability and human rights enforcement in the region and globally.[230] The use of human rights discourse helped ensure that these local developments transcended their place of origin and shaped the understandings both

226 P. E. Andriessen, "La Comisión de la Verdad y Reconciliación peruana como una plataforma para la sanación comunal. Un análisis psicosocial," *Xipe Totek* 2(118) (2020), 132–49.

227 S. Rodríguez Maeso, "Política del testimonio y reconocimiento en las comisiones de la verdad guatemalteca y peruana: En torno a la figura del 'indio subversivo'," *Revista Crítica de Ciências Sociais* 88 (2010), 23–55.

228 "El Perú, 10 años después de la Comisión de la Verdad," *ICTJ*, www.ictj.org/es/news/peru-10-anos-despues-de-la-comision-de-la-verdad (last accessed Mar. 27, 2023).

229 Comisión de la Verdad, "Reconocemos su búsqueda incansable: la búsqueda de familiares desaparecidos en Colombia," Aug. 23, 2019, https://web.comisiondelaverdad.co/actualidad/noticias/reconocemos-su-busqueda-incansable-busqueda-familiares-desaparecidos-colombia (last accessed Mar. 27, 2023).

230 K. Sikkink, *The Justice Cascade: How Human Rights Prosecutors Are Changing World Politics* (New York: W. W. Norton & Co, 2011).

of repression and of responses to it globally, leading to the creation of unprecedented legal mechanisms.[231]

The Inter-American Human Rights System

Particularly significant within the Latin American grassroots legal innovations has been the deployment of the Inter-American Human Rights System. Even before the transition to democracy, civil society organizations throughout Latin America valued the role of regional legal bodies, most particularly the Inter-American rights system, which they identified as an important resource that would enable them to amplify their demands in the international arena and to redress the lack of sufficient support from local legal institutions. Members of civil society organizations demanded justice but also wished to generate awareness of extrajudicial killings, gender-based and other crimes by looking for specific legal solutions. Within a few decades, these demands generated jurisprudence, which in turn inspired change worldwide.[232]

The Inter-American Human Rights System was born in 1948, when the Ninth International Conference of American States approved the American Declaration of the Rights and Duties of Man as well as the Charter of the Organization of the American States (OAS), which were both aimed at ensuring full respect for human rights on the American continent. The Charter created the Inter-American Commission on Human Rights (IACHR), which was established a decade later in 1959. The Commission, headquartered in Costa Rica since its foundation, has three functions: It receives individual complaints on human rights violations, monitors the situation of human rights in member states by issuing an annual report, and has developed "priority" thematic areas. In 2019, transitional justice became one of these priority areas through the establishment of the Rapporteurship on Memory, Truth, and Justice, which supports "contributions to the fight against impunity and the promotion of comprehensive reparation, truth, and memory in the continent, evidencing the structural links between the past and the present."[233]

In 1979, the OAS also established the Inter-American Court of Human Rights as a regional body with jurisdiction to interpret and apply the American Convention of Human Rights in cases presented by individuals or groups from the member states. The Court, also located in Costa Rica, is composed of seven judges and has jurisdiction within twenty-five of the thirty-five

231 Vegh Weis, "Relevance of Victims' Organizations," 1–70.

232 Sikkink, *The Justice Cascade*.

233 For more on the rapporteurship, see the IACHR website: www.oas.org/en/IACHR/jsform/?File=/en/IACHR/r/MVJ/default.asp (last accessed Mar. 27, 2023).

member states of the OAS. The judges meet in at least seven sessions per year, during which they host hearings and issue resolutions. The cases they hear can involve adjudication, in which the Court determines if a state has incurred in international responsibility for violating a right included in the American Convention or other human rights treaties that form part of the Inter-American System. The Court's decisions can include provisional measures when there is a serious, urgent risk that irreparable harm will occur; can consist of advisory opinions, answering questions posted by member states on the interpretation of the American Convention; and can assess compliance with the issued judgments. The Court's judgments are binding and not subject to appeal.[234] From its very early days, the Inter-American Court of Human Rights has been adjudicating cases involving transitional justice. Its first contentious case, *Velasquez Rodriguez v. Honduras,* decided in 1988, remains a landmark in jurisprudence, establishing rights for the disappeared and their kin to truth and other reparatory measures.[235]

The Inter-American Human Rights System was informed by, benefited from, and developed because of the engagement by Latin American civil society. From relatively humble beginnings as a fledgling entity for rights-related adjudication, over time, the IACHR and the Inter-American Court of Human Rights became solidly established bodies on equal footing with their counterparts in other world regions (the European Court of Human Rights and the African Court of Justice and Human Rights), initiating and engaging in continuous dialogue with these other bodies.

The importance of civil society activism in the promotion of the Inter-American Human Rights System can be demonstrated, for example, by the outcomes of Report 28/92, written by the IACHR.[236] The report concluded that two Argentine impunity-related laws – the Full Stop Law (Law no. 23,492 of December 12, 1986) and the Due Obedience Law (Law no. 23,521 of June 4, 1987) – as well as the pardon decrees that followed at the end of the 1980s and beginning of the 1990s, were incompatible with the American Declaration of the Rights and Duties of Man and the American Convention on Human

234 "What is the IACHR?," *IACHR*, www.oas.org/en/IACHR/jsForm/?File=/en/iachr/mandate/what.asp (last accessed Mar. 27, 2023).

235 *Velasquez-Rodriguez v. Honduras*, judgment (merits), IACtHR (ser. C) no. 4 (July 29, 1988), para. 153. The Inter-American Court's judgments are cited using the official English translations available on the Court's website, https://corteidh.or.cr/casos_sentencias.cfm?lang=en (last accessed Apr. 3, 2023).

236 Inter-American Commission of Human Rights, *Annual Report of the Inter-American Commission on Human Rights 1992–1993*, Report no. 28/92 (Oct. 2, 1992), www.cidh.oas.org/annualrep/92eng/argentina10.147.htm (last accessed Mar. 27, 2023).

Rights. The document recommended that the Argentine government award compensation to the victims of the dictatorship and that it "adopt the necessary measures to clarify the facts and identify those responsible for the Human Rights violations." The report was used by civil society organizations to fight impunity and sustain the struggle for truth, justice, reparations, and guarantees of non-repetition, thus becoming a milestone in the transitional justice process. When in 1995, an army official, Captain Adolfo Scilingo, confessed on a radio broadcast that he had thrown people out of government jets into the sea, the Center for Legal and Social Studies (CELS) – a leading human rights organization in the country – invoked the Commission's Report 28/92 to pressure the Argentine justice system to prosecute in order to obtain information about what had transpired.[237] While the case would ultimately necessitate transnational action in the form of Spanish intervention, it was enormously consequential in Argentina in reopening the question of accountability and another phase of trials. Although the IACHR issued similar reports in reference to other Latin American countries, the victims' organizations there did not use these to pressure for accountability.[238]

The judges of the Inter-American Court have demonstrated a strong commitment to the protection of human rights. In 2006, they ruled that human rights provide a significant basis for normative interpretation and that international human rights law also includes the judgments of the Court, including both the judicial opinions as well as their rationale.[239] The Inter-American Court has continuously asserted that international law can operate as a normative constraint on positive law.[240] Judge Cançado Trindade, for example, offered in 2001:

> The very emergence and consolidation of the *corpus juris* of the International Law of Human Rights are due to the reaction of the *universal juridical conscience* to the recurrent abuses committed against human beings, often warranted by positive law: with that, the Law (*el Derecho*) came to the encounter of the human being, the ultimate addressee of its norms of protection.... With the demystification of the postulates of voluntarist positivism, it became evident one can only find an answer to the problem of the foundations and validity of

237 Inter-American Commission on Human Rights, *Annual Report of the Inter-American Commission on Human Rights 1992–1993*, OEA/Ser.L/V/II.83 Doc. 14 (1993).

238 H. Verbitsky, "La sombra de la memoria," *Pagina/12* (Dec. 14, 2014), www.pagina12.com.ar/diario/autores/horacio_verbitsky/index-2014-12-14.html (last accessed Mar. 27, 2023).

239 *Almonacid-Arellano v. Chile*, judgment (preliminary objections, merits, reparations and costs), IACtHR (ser. C) no. 154 (Sept. 26, 2006); and *La Cantuta v. Peru*, judgment (merits, reparations and costs), IACtHR (ser. C) no. 162 (Nov. 29, 2006), para. 80.

240 C. Hesse and R. Post (eds.), *Human Rights in Political Transitions: Gettysburg to Bosnia* (New York: Zone Books, 1999).

> general international law in the universal juridical conscience, starting with the assertion of the idea of an objective justice. As a manifestation of this latter, the rights of the human being have been affirmed, emanating directly from international law, and not subjected, thereby, to the vicissitudes of domestic law.[241]

This understanding embodies an approach to legal interpretation that considers the effective transformation of deeply entrenched structures toward a more egalitarian or democratic society one of the paramount goals of interpretative practice, which has been conceptualized by some as "Latin American transformative constitutionalism."[242]

The Inter-American Court of Human Rights has also systematically recognized the centrality of grassroots actors, particularly of victims, in promoting these rights-related changes. Judge Cançado Trindade stated that "it is the International Law of Human Rights that, clearly and decidedly, comes to rescue the central position of the victims, as it is oriented towards their protection and the satisfaction of their needs."[243] Similarly, in other cases, the Inter-American Court pointed out that the state's obligation to provide reparations to victims constitutes the cornerstone of the system of international human rights protection.

The Transmission of Knowledge: Latin American Usage and Innovation and European Jurisprudence

The jurisprudence of the Inter-American Court of Human Rights, most particularly regarding the crime of enforced disappearance, relied on the American Convention on Human Rights. It has drawn extensively on an innovative continental legal framework that puts human rights and victims at the center, and has also engaged with global and regional legal developments, an array of international conventions, and the use of comparative law across judicial systems.[244] The Court adopted the judicial practice of interpretation

241 *The Right to Information on Consular Assistance in the Framework of the Guarantees of the Due Process of Law*, advisory opinion OC 16/99 (concurring opinion of Judge A. A. Cançado Trindade), IACtHR (ser. A) no. 16 (Oct. 1, 1999), paras. 4 and 14 (emphases in the original).

242 A. von Bogdandy and R. Urueña, "International Transformative Constitutionalism in Latin America," *American Journal of International Law* 114(3) (2020), 403–42, at 405. On Latin American constitutionalism before the twentieth century, see Section 5.1 in this volume.

243 *"Street Children" (Villagran-Morales et al.) v. Guatemala*, judgment (reparation and costs) (separate opinion of Judge A. A. Cançado Trindade), IACtHR (ser. C) no. 77 (May 26, 2001), para. 15.

244 See for example, *Heliodoro Portugal v. Panama*, judgment (preliminary objections, merits, reparations and costs), IACtHR (ser. C) no. 186 (Aug. 12, 2008), para. 31 n. 15 and para. 111 n. 70.

across jurisdictions,[245] relying in part on the case law of the European Court of Human Rights (ECHR).[246] For example, it referred to the ECHR's verdict in *Kurt v. Turkey*, which emphasized "the fundamental importance of the guarantees contained in Article 5 [of the European Convention of Human Rights] for securing the right of individuals in a democracy to be free from arbitrary detention at the hands of the authorities" or the obligation to interpret narrowly any exception to "a most basic guarantee of individual freedom."[247]

Drawing on these European precedents, the Inter-American Court of Human Rights developed distinctive doctrines regarding the legal dimensions of enforced disappearance, most particularly, concerning the responsibility of the state for crimes committed by individuals who complied with its orders. In one of its seminal decisions, *La Cantuta v. Peru* in 2006, the Court distinguished its novel analysis from the prevailing understanding of state responsibility whether under international law, international criminal law, or domestic law:

> *International liability of the States arises automatically with an international wrong attributable to the State* and, unlike under domestic criminal law, in order to establish that there has been a violation of the rights enshrined in the American Convention, it is not necessary to determine the responsibility of its author or their intention, nor is it necessary to identify individually the agents who are attributed with the violations. In this context, the Court ascertains the international liability of the State in this case, which may not be made modeled after structures that belong exclusively to domestic or international criminal law, which in turn defines responsibility or individual criminal liability; nor is it necessary to define the scope of action and rank of each state officials involved in the events.[248]

In another seminal decision (*Goiburú et al.*), the Court turned to highlight the relevance of the context of the crime for its impact on the "increase in State's international responsibility."[249] In this case, the relevant context was "Operation Condor" and the regional collaboration between dictatorships in 1970s Latin America, when "the intelligence services of several countries of the Southern Cone ... established a criminal inter-State organization with a

245 Teitel and Howse, "Cross-Judging."

246 See for example, *Gomes Lund et al. v. Brazil*, judgment (preliminary objections, merits, reparations and costs), IACtHR (ser. C) no. 219 (Nov. 24, 2010), para. 145.

247 *Kurt v. Turkey*, no. 15/1997/799/1002, ECHR 1998-III, para. 122.

248 *La Cantuta v. Peru*, judgment (merits, reparations and costs), para. 156 (emphasis added.)

249 *Goiburú et al. v. Paraguay*, judgment (merits, reparations and costs), IACtHR (ser. C) no. 153 (Sept. 22, 2006), paras. 86–94.

complex assemblage, the scope of which is still being revealed today; in other words, there was a systematic practice of 'State terrorism' at an inter-State level." This transnational practice was understood by the court as being in "absolute contradiction to the principal objects and purposes of the organization of the international community in both international bodies and the American Convention itself."[250] The Court also stated that it had verified that a "general situation of impunity" had existed at the time, which had "conditioned the protection of the rights in question."[251] Even after the fall of the dictatorial regime in 1989, the practice of enforced disappearance had "reproduce[d] the conditions of impunity."[252] The Court's recognition of this context became the basis for shedding light on the transnational dimension of the crimes of enforced disappearance, conceived as violations towards all (*erga omnes*), and therefore triggering also the responsibility of other states, and the international community.[253]

In its interpretation of the American Convention, and in drawing yet also innovating on what the ECHR had established, the Inter-American Court of Human Rights also concluded as early as 1988 that enforced disappearance constituted a complex offense because it involves multiple ongoing offenses, including systemic denials and failure to prevent, investigate, and punish.[254] Thus, as explicitly stated in the case of *Gomes Lund*, it can be defined as "the unlawful detention by agents or governmental agencies or organized groups of private individuals acting in the name of the State or counting on its support, authorization or consent,"[255] but also as "the refusal to acknowledge the detention and to reveal the situation or the whereabouts of the interested person."[256] On this basis, the Court concluded that the state's refusal "to acknowledge the detention and to reveal the situation or the whereabouts of the interested person" constitutes the crime of enforced disappearance regardless of whether the original act can be attributed to the state or not.[257] This was a significant shift in the understanding of accountability: Even where states may not be the direct perpetrators of the crimes, they can still be found accountable in terms of their ongoing

250 *Goiburú et al. v. Paraguay*, judgment (merits, reparations and costs), para. 72.

251 Ibid., para. 88. 252 Ibid., para. 89. 253 Ibid., paras. 93, 128 and 129.

254 *Velásquez-Rodriguez v. Honduras*, judgment (merits), IACtHR (ser. C) no. 4 (July 29, 1988), para. 147.

255 *Gomes Lund et al. v. Brazil*, judgment (preliminary objections, merits, reparations and costs), para. 102.

256 Ibid., para. 104.

257 *Gomes Lund et al. v. Brazil*, judgment (preliminary objections, merits, reparations and costs).

obligation to investigate the offenses and to search for the whereabouts of those who had disappeared, among other duties.

An added distinctive dimension of the Inter-American Court of Human Rights' characterization of the complex character of the crime of enforced disappearance was the judicial determination that this violation could be conceived as a continuous offense: an "autonomous offense of a continuing or permanent nature with its multiple elements";[258] a "permanent and ongoing" crime.[259] The crime of disappearance, the Court ruled, begins with the "deprivation of liberty ..., followed by the lack of information regarding the whereabouts, and continues until the whereabouts of the disappeared person are found and the true identity is revealed with certainty."[260] Here too, the Court elaborated its jurisprudence based on precedents in the ECHR, most particularly, in *Varnava and Others v. Turkey*, where the ECHR found that Turkey was obliged to provide an account of the fate of disappeared people and that this obligation was of a continuing nature regardless of the passage of time.[261]

In line with this comprehensive definition, the Inter-American Court of Human Rights offered what would become a jurisprudential landmark in terms of the characterization and timing of the remedy requested, solving some of the difficulties entailed in questions of retroactivity and impact on the pursuit of remedies in cases after the passage of time. Once the Court introduced its interpretation of enforced disappearances as both a complex and continuous crime, it cleared the way for a ruling that human rights litigation was possible for kidnappings that had occurred decades (in some cases half a century) before. For example, in the milestone case of *Heliodoro Portugal*, the Court evaluated whether it had jurisdiction to hear a case involving an abduction that occurred at the hands of state officials in 1970, long before Panama had accepted the jurisdiction of the regional human rights court. Notwithstanding the arguable jurisdictional issues as well as the passage of time, the Court concluded that the offense at stake should not be considered as merely involving detention or loss of life, but rather that "the deprivation

258 *Heliodoro Portugal v. Panama*, judgment (preliminary objections, merits, reparations and costs), para. 112.

259 *Goiburú et al. v. Paraguay*, judgment (merits, reparations and costs).

260 *Gomes Lund et al. v. Brazil*, judgment (preliminary objections, merits, reparations and costs), para. 103.

261 *Varnava and Others v. Turkey* [GC], nos. 16064/90, 16065/90, 16066/90, 16068/90, 16069/90, 16070/90, 16071/90, 16072/90 and 16073/90, ECHR 2009-V. Incidentally, in its decision, the ECHR itself drew heavily on jurisprudence of the Inter-American Court, as will be discussed later.

of liberty of the individual must be understood merely as the beginning of the constitution of a complex violation that is prolonged over time until the fate and whereabouts of the alleged victim are established."[262] For the Court, the violation, in this case, was considered to be ongoing until the victim's remains were identified in 2000, even though this was three decades after the abduction.[263] The Court further observed that "the general obligation to ensure the human rights embodied in the [American] Convention [on Human Rights], contained in article 1(1), gives rise to the obligation to investigate violations of the substantive rights that should be protected, ensured or guaranteed...."[264] It also established that the extended passage of time in and of itself demonstrated the need for accountability, and ultimately set the basis for supranational judicial intervention of the sort provided by the regional rights court, as it pointed to the political failure and/or deeply rooted pathology of impunity that justifies judicial review as both plausible and legitimate.[265]

The Transmission of Knowledge: European and International Law Usage and Innovation on Latin American Jurisprudence

The earlier discussion has demonstrated how the Inter-American Court of Human Rights has both used European jurisprudence to inform its decisions and subsequently introduced important innovations that developed it further. To what extent have international law and regional bodies, such as the ECHR, in turn, learned from the jurisprudence generated in Latin America?

There are numerous illustrations of such cross-judging taking place. For example, in *Margus v. Croatia*, the ECHR, reviewing atrocities that had been committed in 1991 during the Balkan conflicts/Croatian war, relied on an amnesty doctrine that originated in the Inter-American Court of Human Rights.[266] Following the logic of the Inter-American Court in *Barrios Altos v. Peru*, the ECHR found that the Croatian amnesty law constituted an illegal exercise of impunity, because a blanket amnesty aimed at shielding perpetrators from

262 *Heliodoro Portugal v. Panama*, judgment (preliminary objections, merits, reparations and costs), para. 112.

263 *Heliodoro Portugal v. Panama*, judgment (preliminary objections, merits, reparations and costs), para. 113, referring to the violation of article 7 of the American Convention on Human Rights.

264 *Heliodoro Portugal v. Panama*, judgment (preliminary objections, merits, reparations and costs), para. 115.

265 L. E. Fletcher, J. Rowen, and H. M. Weinstein, "Context, Timing and the Dynamics of Transitional Justice: A Historical Perspective," *Human Rights Quarterly* 31(1) (2009), 163–220.

266 *Margus v. Croatia*, [GC], no. 4455/10, ECHR 2014-III.

prosecution would be in contravention of multiple provisions of conventions of human rights, including the rights to investigation, truth, and justice:[267]

> The Court also notes the jurisprudence of the Inter-American Court of Human Rights, notably the above-cited cases of *Barrios Altos*, *Gomes Lund et al.*, *Gelman* and *The Massacres of El Mozote and Nearby Places*, where that court took a firmer stance and, relying on its previous findings, as well as those of the Inter-American Commission on Human Rights, the organs of the United Nations and other universal and regional organs for the protection of human rights, found that no amnesties were acceptable in connection with grave breaches of fundamental human rights since any such amnesty would seriously undermine the States' duty to investigate and punish the perpetrators of such acts (see *Gelman*, § 195, and *Gomes Lund et al.*, § 171…). It emphasised that such amnesties contravene irrevocable rights recognised by international human rights law (see *Gomes Lund et al.*, § 171).[268]

The European Court seemed to have followed the logic of the IACHR, which had ruled:

> Amnesty laws and provisions designed to prevent investigation and punishment for Human Rights abuses violate non-derogable human rights by obstructing victims' access to justice, preventing victims from knowing the truth, and blocking victims' access to adequate reparations…. By adopting the amnesty laws, the State prevented the deceased victims' next of kin and surviving victims from being able to be heard by a judge, in violation of Article 8(1) (Right to a Hearing Within Reasonable Time by a Competent and Independent Tribunal)…. Similarly, the amnesty laws prevented the State from investigating, capturing, prosecuting, and convicting the individuals responsible for the Barrios Altos massacre, thus violating the right to judicial protection for the victims and victims' next of kin in violation of Article 25…. By violating these articles through the implementation of its amnesty laws, the State necessarily violated its general obligation of Article 1(1) (Obligation to Respect Rights), as well as its obligation to adopt internal legislation in support of these rights encompassed by Article 2.[269]

Relying on these decisions and recommendations, as well as on a vast array of international law materials, the ECHR thus concluded that a significant

267 *Barrios Altos v. Peru*, judgment (merits), IACtHR (ser. C) no.75 (Mar. 14, 2001). In this case, the court interpreted the American Convention of Human Rights. See *Margus v. Croatia*, para. 19.

268 *Margus v. Croatia*, para. 138.

269 K. Benson, "Barrios Altos v. Peru," *Loyola of Los Angeles International and Comparative Law Review* 37(4) (2015), 1145–174, at 1157 (internal citations removed), https://iachr.lls.edu/sites/default/files/iachr/Cases/Barrios_Altos_v_Peru/benson_barrios_altos_v._peru.pdf (last accessed Mar. 27, 2023).

doctrine had developed against such amnesties being applicable to violations of human rights of the sort at issue in the case it was reviewing.

With regards to the crime of enforced disappearance, there are various examples of norm transfer from Latin America to Europe and international law relating to the passage of time and issues of retroactivity. In several cases that shared characteristics with Latin American disappearances, the ECHR explicitly invoked the Inter-American Court of Human Rights and the UN Human Rights Committee. For example, in *Varnava and others*, a case involving the disappearance of Greek Cypriots during the 1970s where adjudication occurred after a considerable passage of time (as discussed earlier), the European Court noted the relevance of dealing with the allegations of denial of justice or judicial protection "even where the disappearance occurred before recognition of its jurisdiction."[270] To make its point, the European Court relied on instances from the Inter-American Court as well as the Inter-American Commission of Human Rights dealing with the international law on enforced disappearances. It declared enforced disappearance as a continuing act[271] and stated that the state had a procedural obligation to investigate.[272] As we saw earlier, this declaration was later taken up by the Inter-American Court, which used it to coin a new doctrine regarding the particular character of the crime of enforced disappearance that entails that "[t]he State still has an obligation to investigate until it can determine by presumption the fate or whereabouts of the person."[273]

Somewhat similarly – though without explicitly mentioning the Inter-American Court – the European Court ruled in *Timurtaş* that Turkey's investigation of disappearances had been "inadequate and therefore in breach of the State's procedural obligations to protect the right to life."[274] It also found, as the Inter-American Court had done before, that the delay involved in the investigation of the case should be considered part of the basis for judicial intervention:

> [T]he lethargy displayed by the investigating authorities poignantly bears out the importance of the prompt judicial intervention required by Articles 5, 3

270 *Varnava and Others v. Turkey*, para. 147.

271 *Blake v. Guatemala*, judgment (preliminary objections), IACtHR (ser. C) no. 27 (July 2, 1996). See factsheet at www.corteidh.or.cr/cf/jurisprudencia2/ficha_tecnica.cfm?lang=es&nId_Ficha=317 (last accessed Mar. 27, 2023).

272 *Valle Jaramillo et al. v. Colombia*, judgment (merits, reparations and costs), IACtHR (ser. C) no. 192 (Nov. 27, 2008).

273 United Nations Human Rights Council, *Report of the Working Group on Enforced or Involuntary Disappearances*, UN Doc. A/HRC/16/48 (Jan. 26, 2011).

274 *Timurtaş v. Turkey*, no. 23531/94, ECHR 2000-VI, para. 90.

> and 4 of the [European] Convention [of Human Rights] which … may lead to the detection and prevention of life-threatening measures in violation of the fundamental guarantees contained in Article 2.[275]

The European Court was equally inspired by the Inter-American Court and the Latin American Human Rights System when it began insisting on the relevance of context, for example, to justify European jurisdiction over the so-called "war on terror."[276] Among other things, the Inter-American Court has helped elaborate new duties of prevention and accountability, investigation, repair, punishment, and other remedies, such as the erection of monuments or establishing museums.[277] What is still unclear, however, is whether the Inter-American precedents, which have already impacted the international law of state responsibility, would also recognize the duties of the state not only as deriving from the initial offense but also as arising because of the state's subsequent failure to act.[278]

Thus we can see that there is an evident connection between the jurisprudence of the Inter-American Court and the ECHR, with both sharing an understanding of the central features of the crime of enforced disappearance, as well as of a range of other related issues regarding state responsibility and the existence of a "right of accountability" that can override doctrinal obstacles regarding important questions such as standing, state attribution, evidence, or exhaustion of local remedies. The result is the continuous expansion of state responsibilities deriving from the protection of the core human right to life.

Furthermore, the influence of doctrines and practices originating in Latin America is felt beyond the regional human rights bodies, such as the ECHR, as it penetrates international organs as well. For example, there is an emerging consensus in the UN Human Rights Committee regarding state responsibility and duty of accountability for human rights violations.[279] Relatedly, the International Court of Justice and the International Criminal Court have been conceptualizing state responsibility for past human rights abuses,

275 *Timurtaş v. Turkey*, para. 89.

276 *El-Masri v. The Former Yugoslav Republic of Macedonia* [GC], no. 39630/09, ECHR 2012-VI.

277 *Goiburú et al. v. Paraguay*, judgment (merits, reparations and costs), para. 254.

278 R. Teitel, "Transitional Justice and Judicial Activism – A Right to Accountability," *Cornell International Law Journal* 48(2) (2015), 385–422.

279 UN Human Rights Committee, *Concluding Observations on the Second Periodic Report on Bosnia and Herzegovina* (Geneva: UN, 2012); see *Report of the Special Rapporteur on the Promotion of Truth, Justice, Reparation and Guarantees of Non-Recurrence, Pablo de Greiff*, UN Doc. A/HRC/21/46 (Aug. 9, 2012).

including enforced disappearances, equally in terms of the duties to investigate, prosecute, and remedy.[280] The text of the International Convention for the Protection of All Persons from Enforced Disappearance (2010) builds on the Inter-American Convention on Enforced Disappearance of Persons (dated 1994),[281] defining the offense as "the arrest, detention, abduction or any other form of deprivation of liberty that is perpetrated by agents of the State or by persons or groups of persons acting with the authorization, support or acquiescence of the State, followed by a refusal to acknowledge the deprivation of liberty."[282]

Norm transfer, however, is not only operative on the jurisprudential and institutional level. The inputs from the Inter-American System and the normative, activist, and jurisprudential work regarding enforced disappearances have proved pivotal to the exploration of international crimes perpetrated in the Mediterranean in relation to asylum seekers. The UN Working Group on Enforced and Involuntary Disappearances, originally promoted by FEDEFAM, currently focuses on the crimes in the Mediterranean Sea and characterizes disappearances in the context of migration as "an involuntary but direct consequence of the actions of the State."[283] Genuinely global cross-knowledge enables the drawing of these connections, and many more.

Conclusions

Section 6.3 has drawn attention to the role of the Global South, specifically Latin America, in the development of international human rights and transitional justice, most particularly, the legal emergence of a core international crime that has been at the crux of the story of human rights violations both in the region and globally: enforced disappearances. This grievous offense offers a remarkable landmark for the construction of a truly global history of human rights and transitional justice and introduces "an alternative account

280 *Application of Convention on Prevention and Punishment of Crime of Genocide (Bosnia and Herzegovina v. Serbia and Montenegro)*, judgment, ICJ Reports (Feb. 26, 2007); and Rome Statute of the International Criminal Court, July 17, 1998, 2187 UNTS. 91, preamble (referring to jurisdiction along with complementarity basis); Teitel, "Transitional Justice and Judicial Activism."

281 E. Schindel, "Deaths and Disappearances in Migration to Europe: Exploring the Uses of a Transnationalized Category," *American Behavioral Scientist* 64 (2020), 389–407.

282 Office of the High Commissioner for Human Rights, "International Convention for the Protection of All Persons from Enforced Disappearance" (Dec. 23, 2010), art. 2.

283 Working Group on Enforced or Involuntary Disappearances, *Report of the Working Group on Enforced or Involuntary Disappearances on Enforced Disappearances in the Context of Migration*, Note by the Secretariat, UN Doc. A/HRC/36/39/Add.2 (July 28, 2017), para. 82.

to the prevailing narrative of the evolution of the human rights idea and movement, one which restores Latin America to its rightful place having a central and leading role in developing a proper framework, which has then been diffused throughout the world."[284]

Employing the concept of "ecology of knowledge" and observing "cross-judging," Section 6.3 demonstrated that retrieving Southern knowledges does not necessarily involve disregarding or displacing the contributions of the North, but rather fosters fruitful dialogue in order to elaborate a comprehensive epistemic understanding. In this regard, the section explored how the Inter-American Court of Human Rights learned and incorporated inputs from the ECHR and international law, innovated on them, and in turn influenced European and international norms.

Finally, the section also sheds light on the role of civil society actors and grassroots organizations in pushing forward normative developments, which in turn have been put into force through practices in both the domestic and the international arena. The study of the example of enforced disappearance – a crime against humanity – revealed that the development of this offense, and the related jurisprudence, was largely impelled/driven by the work of NGOs as petitioners, or by lawyers for victims' families, after successive administrations failed to respond to wrongdoing. Further research is needed to explore the uneven knowledge distribution and silenced contributions in the normative transfers *from* the regional bodies *to* each individual state and *from* these states *to* the regional bodies.

284 Dulitzky, "Latin-American Flavor."

7

Beyond the State: Can State Law Survive in the Twenty-First Century?

DANIEL BONILLA MALDONADO*

The classic nation-state was the legal and political structure that shaped Latin American political communities since their independence from the Spanish and Portuguese empires in the nineteenth century and until the end of the twentieth century (see also Sections 5.1–5.3).[1] This model of state intended to create a culturally homogeneous, legally monist, and politically sovereign polity structured around the grammar of modern constitutionalism.[2] However, this form of state was a normative project which was historically at odds with the social realities of Latin America and that was only partially materialized in the region (see also Section 5.3).[3] On one hand, there was tension between the monocultural nature of the model and the cultural diversity that has characterized Latin American political communities since the days of colonization.[4] Indigenous and African-American peoples, among other non-dominant cultures, were ignored by a legal, political, and cultural project that aimed to create a white, Catholic, and Spanish- or Portuguese-speaking nation in each of the region's countries.[5] Policies of assimilation, integration, or violent elimination implemented by the Latin American nation-states in order to achieve monoculturalism were not able

* I would like to thank Luis Enrique Penagos for his excellent work as a research assistant for this chapter.

1 H. J. König, "Discursos de identidad, Estado-nación y ciudadanía en América Latina: viejos problemas, nuevos enfoques y dimensiones," *Historia y Sociedad* 11 (2005), 18–19.

2 P. Hirst and G. Thompson, "Globalization and the Future of the Nation State," *Economy and Society* 24 (1995), 408–42.

3 König, "Discursos de identidad," 19.

4 G. Kirkpatrick, "Spanish American Narrative, 1810–1920," in J. King (ed.), *The Cambridge Companion to Modern Latin American Culture* (Cambridge: Cambridge University Press, 2004), 62.

5 König, "Discursos de identidad," 15; Kirkpatrick, "Spanish American Narrative," 63.

to eliminate minority cultures and therefore failed to configure culturally homogeneous nations.[6]

On the other hand, the states' legal systems were not always applied throughout the territory or to all citizens. The idea that each state would have a single legal system that should be universally applied was not fully realized (see Section 6.1). The state's official law and administrative apparatus were not always able to operate throughout the respective national territory or to obligate all citizens. Likewise, state law competed with other normative orders, such as indigenous legal systems, informal normative orders of the peripheral neighborhoods in some cities of the region, and rural justice systems for the control of individuals' consciences and behaviors (see also Chapters 2 and 4 and Sections 3.1 and 5.3).[7] Finally, the project of creating a legal and political unit that was (internally) autonomous and (externally) independent was not fully materialized either. The theoretical absolute sovereignty of states clashed with the constellation of sovereignties that existed in their territories in practice. Latin American states didn't always monopolize the political power or the capacity to create law, nor did they have the monopoly of force within their societies.[8] Internally and externally, the state competed with other sources of legal creation and political action, and with other agents, such as indigenous authorities and criminal organizations, that established coercive apparatuses in some segments of their territory.

The sovereign, monocultural, and monist model of state dominant in Latin America underwent important transformations at the end of the 1980s and the beginning of the 1990s.[9] During these years, a wave of constitutional reforms that aimed to confront the legitimacy deficits of the prevailing state model, its inefficacy, and the separation between social reality and its political and legal structures, as well as to eliminate the discursive and practical questioning of

6 K. von Benda-Beckmann and B. Turner, "Legal Pluralism, Social Theory, and the State," *The Journal of Legal Pluralism and Unofficial Law* 50(3) (2018), 256; F. López-Álves, "Nation-states and National States: Latin America in Comparative Perspective," in M. Hanagan and C. Tilly (eds.), *Contention and Trust in Cities and States* (New York: Springer, 2011), 118–19.

7 R. Sieder, "Legal Pluralism and Fragmented Sovereignties: Legality and Illegality in Latin America," in R. Sieder, K. Ansolabehere, and T. Alfonso (eds.), *Routledge Handbook of Law and Society in Latin America* (New York: Routledge, 2019), 60.

8 J. Lemaitre, "Law and Violence in Latin America," in R. Sieder, K. Ansolabehere, and T. Alfonso (eds.), *Routledge Handbook of Law and Society in Latin America* (New York: Routledge, 2019), 90.

9 R. Z. Yrigoyen, "El horizonte del constitucionalismo pluralista: del multiculturalismo a la descolonización," in C. Rodríguez (ed.), *El derecho en América Latina. Un mapa para el pensamiento jurídico del siglo XXI* (Buenos Aires: Siglo XXI Editores, 2011), 139–42.

the state monopoly of force, was set in motion.[10] The constitutional reforms in Brazil (1988), Colombia (1991), Peru (1993), Bolivia (1994), Paraguay (1992), and Ecuador (1994), among other countries, sought to construct legally plural, multicultural states that would have an effective presence throughout the territory. More precisely, the multicultural constitutions that were drafted at the end of the twentieth century in Latin America acknowledge the cultural diversity that shapes the societies of the region, redistribute the political power and the capacity to create law among the various cultural communities that form them, and recognize a broad spectrum of rights.[11] These and other measures also aimed to apply the state's administrative apparatus and plural official law throughout the territory and to all citizens. In this way, the classic nation-state's project of creating a culturally homogeneous nation was replaced by one that recognizes, protects, and promotes cultural heterogeneity. Likewise, the legal monism that structured the nineteenth-century state project was substituted by a weak legal pluralism that complexifies processes of legal creation, although it continues to revolve around the vocabulary and grammar of modern constitutionalism.[12] The multicultural liberal model currently in place in numerous Latin American countries recognizes the existence of the cultural minorities' legal systems, primarily indigenous and occasionally Afro-Latin American ones, and it establishes a set of cultural rights that seek to protect and promote their cultural traditions.

However, in the first decade of the twenty-first century, the multicultural liberal model was itself replaced in some Latin American countries, such as Ecuador (2007) and Bolivia (2009), by a radical intercultural model that offers a new form of imagining states in the region. This model is structured around the principles of plurinationality and interculturality, and it deepens the weak legal pluralism that had already been recognized in the multicultural legal model.[13] This new normative project seeks to reconceptualize how the constitutive discourses and practices of a culturally diverse state are conceived, while simultaneously delving into some of the multicultural processes that had been initiated with its predecessor. However, both models, the multicultural liberal as well as the radical intercultural one, remain normatively

10 R. Uprimny, "Las transformaciones constitucionales recientes en América Latina: tendencias y desafíos," in C. Rodríguez (ed.), *El derecho en América Latina. Un mapa para el pensamiento jurídico del siglo XXI* (Buenos Aires: Siglo XXI Editores, 2011), 111–21.

11 Uprimny, "Las transformaciones," 122–25; Yrigoyen, "El horizonte," 139–43.

12 Yrigoyen, "El horizonte," 142.

13 D. Bonilla, "El constitucionalismo radical ambiental y la diversidad cultural en América Latina. Los derechos de la naturaleza y el buen vivir en Ecuador y Bolivia," *Revista Derecho del Estado* 42 (2018), 9.

committed to the idea that the states of the region must be absolutely sovereign. The state is the basic unit around which cultural groups as well as the international community, should be structured. In addition, the state must be completely autonomous and independent; it must be the supreme source of political and legal power within its territory, and it must not depend on any external entity, politically or legally. Nonetheless, both models formally open the national legal system to international law, through mechanisms such as the constitutional bloc, which will be described in greater detail below, and the increasingly copious incorporation of international treaties into the national system. The remarkable number of bilateral or multilateral treaties that were incorporated into the national legal orders over the last thirty-six years, or the systematic and continuous application of treaties like those of the Inter-American Human Rights System, further enrich the weak legal pluralism that is at the heart of both these models (see Section 6.3). These bilateral and multilateral treaties also exert external pressure on the traditional concept of sovereignty, demonstrating its porous discursive and practical nature.

Despite these attempts, the normative projects promoted by the multicultural liberal and radical intercultural states also failed to fully apply the internally plural legal systems that were constitutionally recognized throughout the territories under their jurisdiction. During the last three-and-a-half decades, to varying degrees and as occurred during the reign of the monocultural-monist state, Latin American states featured a constellation of sovereignties; they were not formed by a single central star, the state star, from which all the legal and political power within the state emanates. This way, official weak legal pluralism has coexisted with strong legal pluralism, as the official sources of law – which primarily include congress, regional legislatures, national and regional governments, and cultural minorities' authorities – compete, interact, are transformed, and overlap with other sources of legal creation and with illegal or extralegal political powers, such as paramilitary and guerrilla groups, drug-trafficking cartels, and community organizations.

In this constellation of sovereignties, the state legal system does not recognize other sources of legal creation. Rather, it tries to eliminate them. In like manner, alternative normative systems don't recognize state law, or they ignore it. Sometimes they try to suppress state law (subversive groups); at other times they violate it or apply it only selectively (community organizations); or they partially replace it, but without attempting to subvert state lawfully (drug-trafficking organizations). In all of these cases, the official and unofficial normative systems interact with and modify each other. For example, the extralegal property systems that regulate the neighborhoods on the periphery of many Latin American cities use categories that are central in the official legal system, like "sale," "promise of sale," and "property," but they give them different meanings. Present-day Latin American legal systems are therefore structured around the conceptual opposition of legal / illegal and legal / extralegal.

This chapter describes and examines the ways in which the sovereign, monocultural, and monist state that was dominant in Latin America starting in the nineteenth century mutated over the last thirty-six years and analyzes the legal and political elements that remained stable despite these formal transformations. It also demonstrates that, despite numerous predictions that the state would weaken or disappear altogether, it remains the political and legal unit around which twenty-first-century Latin American political communities are structured. For these purposes, the chapter is divided into two parts. The first includes three sections. In the first of these, I briefly examine the elements constituting the sovereign, monocultural, and monist state, as we can only understand the transformations experienced by Latin American states in recent history if we also understand the model which is undergoing this transformation, if we also get a grasp of the discursive and practical adversary being replaced. In the second section, I study the structural components of the multicultural liberal and radical intercultural models that replaced the classic nation-state model. In the third section, I explore the discursive and practical challenges generated by illegal or extralegal normative systems coexisting with the internally diverse state law recognized by the multicultural liberal and radical intercultural models. Consequently, in this section, I examine the strong legal pluralism that characterizes contemporary Latin American states. Thus, this first part studies the mutations or challenges generated primarily by internal pressures of three basic features of the classic Latin American nation-state: a homogeneous culture, a sole and universal state legal system, and absolute sovereignty.

The second part of this chapter explores the transformations or challenges experienced by the multicultural liberal and radical intercultural state primarily as a consequence of external variables and is divided into two sections. In the first, I analyze the concept of constitutional bloc and examine the Inter-American Human Rights System to illustrate how this concept operates. In the second section, I study the bilateral or multilateral treaties signed by Latin American States in the course of the last three-and-a-half decades, primarily. I argue that these external factors further pluralize the sources for creating law in contemporary Latin American states and make them more complex, weaken the concept of absolute sovereignty they are committed to, and contribute to either questioning or protecting the cultural diversity recognized by the state models currently dominant in the region. The analysis of the external weak legal pluralism that characterizes Latin American states carried out in this second part of the chapter thus complements the analysis of internal weak legal pluralism undertaken in the first part.[14] It closes with an examination of how the discourses and practices under study are connected with global processes. The transformations and challenges that Latin American states have experienced in the last thirty-six years are not unique. Rather, they are part of discursive and practical patterns that are also reproduced and reinterpreted, to varying degrees and with significant nuances, elsewhere.

The Sovereign, Monocultural, and Monist State

Latin American societies chose the nation-state model to organize themselves politically and legally after achieving independence from the Spanish and Portuguese empires in the nineteenth century (see also Chapter 4).[15] Mimicking developments elsewhere, the Latin American elites who led these developments structured their political communities around the model of the nation-state, which drew on the Treaty of Westphalia as well as the revolutions in the United States and France as central conceptual and historical sources.[16] These processes of creation therefore partially reproduced those leading to the creation of nation-states in Europe during the eighteenth and nineteenth centuries and, as of the second half of the twentieth century, also entered into dialogue with processes of decolonization in Asia and Africa.[17]

14 The constitutionality bloc and multilateral and bilateral treaties are not the only discourses and practices that constitute Latin American external legal pluralism. Other issues such as the interactions between private international law and national legal systems, the arrival and consolidation of large multinationals to the region, canon law, or the discourse of global legal pluralism are also part of or have impacted on this dimension of Latin American law and politics. I do not examine these last four issues for the following reasons: first, because, arguably, the constitutionality bloc and multilateral and bilateral treaties have played a central role in the construction of Latin American law in the last three and a half decades. These issues have structured or influenced constitutional issues in ways that private international law, the economic activities of large multinationals, or the discourse of global legal pluralism have not; second, for reasons of space, I cannot analyze all the issues that I would like to explore regarding Latin America's external legal pluralism.

15 König, "Discursos de identidad," 18–19.

16 Hirst and Thompson, "Globalization," 409–11.

17 D. Bonilla and M. Riegner, "Decolonization," in R. Grote, F. Lachenmann and R. Wolfrum (eds.), *Max Planck Encyclopedia of Comparative Constitutional Law* (Oxford: Oxford University Press, 2020).

The state model they adopted revolved around the following six elements: (i) for each nation there should be a state; (ii) the nation exists prior to the state. The nation creates the state to give itself a political and legal form that protects, promotes, and allows it to flourish; (iii) each nation has a cultural *ethos*, an identity that distinguishes it from other nations. The nation is therefore culturally homogeneous; (iv) the state must be sovereign: internally it must be autonomous and externally it must be independent; (v) the state's law must reflect the nation's *ethos*. Law must be an epiphenomenon of culture. It is an instrument that the state has in order to protect and reproduce the nation's identity, not an instrument to transform it; and (vi) the legal system that reflects the nation's *ethos* must be applied throughout the state's territory; there should not be any other normative order that competes with it (see Sections 5.1 and 5.2).

The mimetic process of constructing postcolonial political communities in Latin America, which was conjugated with rich and complex creative processes within the chosen canon, was structured around three categories that shaped, interpreted, and concretized the elements that constitute the nation-state model: time, space, and subject. First, the moment of independence, which was achieved through violence, marks both a break with the empire and the emergence of a new political community.[18] The existence of this new legal and political structure is both crystallized and formalized with the issuance of a constitution. After violence, law arises; the constitution signals the emergence of a new political community.[19] It also formalizes victories achieved on the battlefield. Latin American postcolonial societies of the nineteenth century therefore decided on the structures required to shape the new political communities by means of legal and political processes that ended with the issuance of a constitution.[20] To do so, they decided how to interpret the colonial past[21] and its links with both the post-revolutionary present and the future of the new political community.[22] Constitutions therefore emerge as autobiographical texts; documents that determine who the new political communities were, who they are, and what they want to be (see Section 5.1).

18 T. Halperin-Donghi, *Historia contemporánea de América Latina* (Madrid: Alianza Editorial, 2005), 135–36.

19 H. G. Espiell, "El constitucionalismo latinoamericano y la codificación en el siglo XIX," *Anuario Iberoamericano de Justicia Constitucional* 6 (2002), 147–49.

20 R. Gargarella, *Latin American Constitutionalism, 1810–2010* (Oxford: Oxford University Press, 2013), 1–5.

21 Gargarella, *Latin American Constitutionalism*, 62–63.

22 Ibid., 84–85.

To articulate their legal and political identities, Latin American postcolonial societies called upon the vocabulary and grammar of modern constitutionalism. The new constitutions were structured around categories like "state," "nation," "rights," "citizen," "separation of powers," "president," "congress" and "judges," as well as the rules for applying and interpreting these categories.[23] Revolutionary violence led to the generation of a new political reality, a reality that consciously broke with the imperial and colonial past. Paradoxically, however, as the mimetic process around which the new political communities in Latin America were structured revolved around the concept of nation-state, it maintained political and conceptual ties with the imperial Europe that these communities wanted to break with.[24] Contrary to the independence of the United States, however, the Latin American revolutions did not end with the issuance of constitutions that then remained stable for a long period of time.[25] In the twentieth century, no fewer than 103 constitutions were enacted in the region.[26] Nevertheless, those that were promulgated between 1850 and 1900, the foundational period of Latin American constitutionalism, are the ones that consolidated the process of nation-state creation in the region.[27] Constitutions like those issued in Argentina in 1853, Colombia in 1886, Peru in 1860, Ecuador in 1869, and Brazil in 1891 form the bases for the Latin American nation-states – the states which, through multiple transformations, shaped the region's political and legal life during the twentieth century.

Second, the post-revolutionary Latin American constitutions (centralist or federalist; liberal, conservative, or republican) constructed the new political communities around a particular conceptual geography: the sovereign state. This space is shaped around the three classic categories modern constitutionalism associates with the concept of state: territory, population, and administrative apparatus.[28] The post-revolutionary constitutions also characterize this conceptual geography as autonomous and independent. Internally, the state is an entity with the capacity to create the legal norms that govern it and to regulate the behaviors of its citizens.[29] Externally, it does not depend

23 Espiell, "El constitucionalismo," 150.

24 T. Halperin-Donghi, *Historia contemporánea*, 135–36.

25 Gargarella, *Latin American Constitutionalism*, 1.

26 Ibid., 1. 27 Ibid., 20–43.

28 R. Michaels, "Globalisation and Law: Law Beyond the State," in R. Banakar and M. Travers (eds.), *Law and Society Theory* (Oxford: Hart Publishing, 2013), 294.

29 H. Kelsen, *General Theory of Law and State* (Cambridge: Harvard University Press, 1949), 189.

on any other political organization, institution, or entity.[30] The heteronomy of the colonial period, with the imposition of Spanish or Portuguese law in the colonies as well as the political subordination to imperial institutions, was thus abandoned. The foundational Latin American constitutions indicated that the obligations of the new postcolonial legal and political spaces would always be self-imposed.

Postcolonial constitutions in Latin America therefore extrapolated the characteristics of the autonomous and rational subject (sovereign) from the liberal interpretation of the grammar of modern constitutionalism to the conceptual geographies they constructed to shape their political communities. The norms that govern the state should only be created within this legal and political space, just as the norms that regulate the individual's good life project should only be constructed within the individual's conscience. Consequently, no external entity has the power to impose norms on the state. Borders delimit the jurisdictions where the legal structures each state autonomously creates can be applied. Likewise, borders partially determine the state's identity; borders, like the bodies of individuals, define the contours that differentiate the political and legal "self" from the "other."[31] The conceptual geography created by the Latin American constitutions is therefore understood as absolutely sovereign; according to it, a porous sovereignty would involve ceding the state's autonomy[32].

In addition, within the state's borders, there should be only one legal order, which must be applied universally. The new political communities in Latin America would break with the colonial stratified society; they would distance themselves from a legal system formed by sets of norms that were only applied to particular social groups, such as the nobility, the clergy, the peasantry, and indigenous groups.[33] The state legal system would be applied throughout the territory and to all citizens. Consequently, the monist nature of the legal system that governed across Latin American postcolonial states was founded on central categories of modern constitutionalism like equality, autonomy, and legal security.[34] In addition, the monist legal system included a set of civil and political rights held by all citizens, in order to protect the autonomy and basic equality of

30 Michaels, "Globalisation," 297. 31 Michaels, "Globalisation," 294.

32 V. Das and D. Poole, "State and its Margins: Comparative Ethnographies," in V. Das and D. Poole (eds.), *Anthropology in the Margins of the State* (Oxford: Oxford University Press, 2004), 7.

33 López-Álves, "Nation-states," 120.

34 D. Bonilla, "Extralegal Property, Legal Monism, and Pluralism," *Inter-American Law Review* 40 (2009), 204–14.

all.[35] Based on a liberal interpretation of the grammar of modern constitutionalism, these rights also protect the particular forms and turns citizens give their national culture.[36] However, the particular culture that citizens autonomously commit to is assigned to the private sphere, privatized, and protected by means of individual rights, such as freedom of expression, freedom of conscience, and freedom of association.[37] Culture is important for the nation-state model. The societal culture that welds the nation together and gives it identity, as well as the cultures that citizens can generate within this common cultural framework, are constitutive elements of the nation-state model.

Third, the nineteenth-century postcolonial Latin American constitutions also constructed the transtemporal collective subject that both creates the state and exercises sovereignty within its borders: the nation. The nation imagined is a culturally homogeneous subject; a subject that is white, Catholic, and Spanish- or Portuguese-speaking. The mimetic construction of the new political communities makes another appearance. The Latin American nation that is thus forged is identical to the imagined nation of the old Spanish and Portuguese empires. It is a nation radically dissociated from the culturally diverse societies that actually existed in nineteenth-century Latin America (see also Section 5.3).[38] In this nation, indigenous peoples, Afro-Latin Americans, and mixed-race individuals, who together form the demographic majorities, are not included.[39] The nation constructed by the post-revolutionary constitutions is therefore in reality a normative project, not the reflection of a social reality.[40] Contrary to the legal and political model, the nation in Latin America, like the nation in Europe, does not exist prior to the state; the state constructs it, or intends to do so.[41] In addition, the nation imagined in Europe and Latin America concentrates political power and the capacity to create law within the state; it is the transtemporal collective subject which inhabits the conceptual and material geography that is the state. The nation is also the collective subject that determines the purposes of the state by the direct or indirect creation of the law that is applied within its borders – a law that should reflect the *ethos* that supposedly characterizes it.

35 R. Gargarella, "Sobre el 'nuevo constitucionalismo latinoamericano'," *Revista Uruguaya de Ciencia Política* 27 (2018), 114.

36 T. Modood, *Multiculturalism* (Cambridge: Polity, 2013), 20–23 and 29–30.

37 L. Stroubouli-Lanefelt, *Multiculturalism, Liberalism and the Burden of Assimilation* (Stockholm: Stockholm University, 2012), 25–26 and 59–60.

38 F. López-Álves, "Visions of the National: Natural Endowments, Futures, and the Evils of Men," in M. A. Centeno and A. E. Ferraro (eds.), *State and Nation Making in Latin America and Spain* (Cambridge: Cambridge University Press, 2013), 256.

39 Espiell, "El constitucionalismo," 158–60.

40 Ibid., 156.

41 López-Álves, "Nation-states," 114.

In France, for example, the paradigmatic nation-state, no culturally homogeneous group existed before the creation of the French state; the French culture that has historically been associated with, among other things, rationalism, Catholicism, and the French language, did not exist. Rather, there was a set of heterogeneous cultural groups: the Bretons, the Gauls, and the Celts, to name some, who spoke their own languages and adhered to various religions including Catholicism, animism, and paganism. With the revolution of 1787, the process of constructing the French nation-state, which had been initiated by the absolute monarchies of Louis XIV and Louis XV, intersected with liberalism. As a result, the constitution of 1791 declared the French state to be a constitutional monarchy structured around individual rights.[42] The Colombian constitution of 1886 and the Argentine constitution of 1853, paradigmatically reproducing the sovereign, monist, and monocultural state model that prevailed in the Latin American region until the end of the twentieth century, also partially mimicked processes similar to the ones that constructed the French nation and justified the constitution of 1791.[43] Eventually, other communities in other geographies would have to face similar challenges, for example in Asia and Africa with what has been called the move from Westminster to Eastminster in the postcolonial constitutions of India, Sri Lanka, Malaysia, and Ghana,[44] among others, and the construction of the independent states of French-speaking Africa such as Algeria.[45]

The Liberal Multicultural State and Weak Legal Pluralism

At the end of the 1980s and beginning of the 1990s, Latin America experienced a wave of constitutional changes. These constituent processes had the primary objectives of addressing the states' deficit of legitimacy[46];

42 W. Safran, "State, Nation, National Identity, and Citizenship: France as a Test Case," *International Political Science Review* 12(3) (1991), 219–38.

43 I do not elaborate on these examples as Chapter 5 of this book examines them in detail. Other examples can be found in the Chilean constitution of 1833, articles 1, 2, 3, 4; Political Constitution of the Mexican Republic of 1857, articles 39, 40, 41, Third Title; Political Constitution of the Peruvian Republic of 1856, articles 1, 2, 3, 4.

44 H. Kumarasingham, "Eastminster: Decolonisation and State-Building in British Asia," in H. Kumarasingham (ed.), *Constitution-Making in Asia: Decolonisation and State-Building in the Aftermath of the British Empire* (New York: Routledge, 2016), 1.

45 J. Go, "A Globalizing Costitutionalism?: Views from the Postcolony, 1945–2000," *International Sociology* 18(1) (2003), 71.

46 R. Viciano and R. Martínez, "Los procesos constituyentes latinomericanos y el nuevo paradigma constitucional," *Revista del Instituto de Ciencias Jurídicas de Puebla, Instituto de Investigaciones Jurídicas de la UNAM* 25 (2010), 10–21.

increasing their levels of efficacy; eliminating the gap between social reality and the legal, political, and cultural structures promoted by the old constitutions; and neutralizing entities such as guerrilla organizations, paramilitary groups, and organized crime (primarily associated with drug trafficking) – all of which undermine state legal and political systems by means of violence.[47]

The new Latin American constitutions explicitly called into question the monist nation-state model. First, late twentieth-century Latin American societies faced – as the postcolonial societies of the region had done in the nineteenth century – the challenge of how to interpret their past in order to construct their present and announce their future.[48] This temporal axis became central for the reconstruction of their political, legal, and cultural identities. By the end of the 1980s and beginning of the 1990s, Latin American societies rejected the monocultural and monist project promoted by the foundational constitutions; a project that, with modifications, had dominated the greater part of the Latin American twentieth century. Instead, they sought to adopt new constitutions designed to reflect the social realities that had been ignored and devalued by previous ones.[49] Law and society should mirror each other. The legal and political present of Latin American societies should reflect the social present, which on matters of cultural diversity was not very different than the one that shaped the nineteenth-century societies in the region. Because Latin America had been (and remains) a culturally diverse region, constituted by the intersection of European, indigenous, and African cultures, the monocultural and monist constitutional past of the region's states should no longer form part of the present legal and political identities. In addition, the future was to be constructed by recognizing and including all citizens, not only those that the nation-state's normative project had considered valuable: white, Catholic, and Spanish- or Portuguese-speaking. Consequently, the new Latin American multicultural constitutions were both a descriptive undertaking and a normative project of multicultural state.[50]

Second, Latin American multicultural constitutions replaced the culturally homogeneous transtemporal collective subject promoted by the

47 Uprimny, "Las transformaciones," 112.

48 J. Couso, "Radical Democracy and the 'New Latin American Constitutionalism'," *Seminario de Teoría Política y Constitucional en Latinoamérica* (2014), https://law.yale.edu/sites/default/files/documents/pdf/sela/SELA13_Couso_CV_Eng_20130516.pdf (last accessed Sep. 22, 2021).

49 Yrigoyen, "El horizonte," 139–43.

50 Uprimny, "Las transformaciones," 112; Gargarella, "Sobre el 'nuevo constitucionalismo'," 115.

nation-state model with a culturally heterogeneous transtemporal collective subject. The nations of Brazil, Colombia, Peru, Paraguay, and Ecuador, among others, recognized and accommodated the indigenous peoples in their constitutions.[51] Occasionally, as happened in Brazil and Colombia, these nations also recognized and accommodated the Afro-Latin American cultural minorities.[52] The new multicultural nation-state was thus structured around a regime of cultural majorities/cultural minorities. The white/creole, Catholic, and Spanish- or Portuguese-speaking majority remained at the center of the nation. Indigenous and African minorities, now fully legally recognized and protected, revolved around it like satellites. In addition, the multicultural constitutions recognized a set of cultural principles and rights that acknowledged minority cultures as a constitutive part of the nation and allowed for protecting and reproducing their cultural traditions, among others, the rights of self-government and representation.[53] Though in these constitutions, the multicultural Latin American nation is now an internally complex subject, a multiple subjects, it continues to be imagined as a collective subject that existed in the past, exists in the present, and will exist in the future. The multicultural nation preexists the state; it creates the state, although, in the new Latin American constitutions, sovereignty does not reside in the nation anymore, but in the people who constitute it.[54] The people are envisaged as a transtemporal collective subject consisting of all the members of the political community. The nation is imagined as the transtemporal collective subject that is defined by the category "culture" and that overlaps with "the people."

51 Constitución de la República Federativa de Brasil de 1988, article 231; Constitución Política de Colombia de 1991, article 7; Constitución Política del Perú de 1993, article 89; Constitución de la República del Paraguay de 1992, article 62; Constitución de la República del Ecuador, article 56; D. L. Van Cott, "Latin America: Constitutional Reform and Ethnic Right," *Parliamentary Affairs* 53 (2000), 42; R. Gargarella, "Latin America's Contribution to Constitutionalism," in R. Sieder, K. Ansolabehere, and T. Alfonso (eds.), *Routledge Handbook of Law and Society in Latin America* (New York: Routledge, 2019), 31.

52 Constitución de la República Federativa de Brasil de 1988, article 215, 1; Constitución Política de Colombia de 1991, article 7, Transitory article 55.

53 Constitución Política de Colombia of 1991, articles 7, 10, 19, 246, 329, 330; Constitución Política de los Estados Mexicanos de 1917, article 2; Constitución Política del Perú of 1993, articles 89 and 149; Constitución Política de la República Federativa del Brasil of 1988, articles 210, 215, 231, 232; Constitución de la República del Ecuador de 2008, articles 242 and 257.

54 Constitución de la República Federativa de Brasil of 1988, Preamble; Constitución Política de Colombia of 1991, Preamble; Constitución Política del Perú of 1993, Preamble; Constitución de la República del Paraguay of 1992, Preamble; Constitución de la República del Ecuador, Preamble.

Third, the Latin American multicultural constitutions replace the legal monism of the nation-state model with a weak legal pluralism.[55] Nevertheless, they remain committed to the concept of absolute sovereignty that structures the classic model of the foundational constitutions of Latin America. Latin American legal monism imagines the legal system as a hierarchical structure that concentrates the power to create law in the democratically elected federal or central institutions which represent the citizens.[56] National or federal congresses are the primary source of state law, and departmental, state, or municipal institutions (e.g., state assemblies or municipal councils) only have the power to create legal norms that develop the normative frameworks created by congresses. In monism, national institutions are formed by public officials democratically elected by the members of the political community, the normative systems of cultural minorities are not recognized, and the authorities of indigenous or Afro-Latin American peoples are not considered to be entities that can create law.[57]

In contrast, the multicultural constitutions of the late 1980s and early 1990s recognize the existence of indigenous minorities' legal systems, occasionally also those of culturally diverse Afro-Latin American minorities, and include them within the state's legal system. The new constitutions also acknowledge that the authorities of cultural minorities have the capacity to create law. However, they remain committed to the concept of absolute sovereignty and do not accord equal footing to these laws and bodies. According to the model they propose, the power of the authorities of cultural minorities to create law is subordinated to the constitution and statutes, in particular, to legal norms related to fundamental rights.[58] The criteria utilized by citizens, and in particular by public officials, to identify the norms that can be validly considered as legal norms,[59] are multiplied. However, the multicultural liberal model embraced by the new Latin American constitutions only promotes one rule of recognition.[60] State law must be multiple in a cultural key, but it must be applied throughout the state's territory and throughout the territory of cultural minorities. This is achieved via the recognition of self-government rights and indigenous or Afro-Latin American jurisdictions, from which other more

55 Uprimny, "Las transformaciones," 114. 56 Yrigoyen, "El horizonte," 139.

57 Yrigoyen, "El horizonte," 140.

58 Constitución Política de Colombia of 1991, article 246; Constitución Política del Perú of 1993, article 89; Constitución de la República del Ecuador of 2008, article 171; Constitución Política de Paraguay of 1991, article 62.

59 H. L. A. Hart, *The Concept of Law* (New York: Oxford University Press, 1994), 100.

60 Hart, *Concept of Law*, 100–10.

specific cultural rights are derived, for example, the right to collective ownership of their ancestral territories, the right to life of the cultural community, and the right to use their languages publicly.[61] This way, the new constitutions allow cultural minorities to create legal norms for regulating both the public life of their collectivities and the private life of their members. Nevertheless, the individuals who constitute cultural minorities are also holders of the fundamental rights that are recognized in the constitutions. Indigenous and culturally diverse Afro-Latin American peoples therefore have a dual citizenship, a multicultural one.[62]

The multicultural Latin American constitutions of the late 1980s and early 1990s are therefore cut across structurally by the tension between two principles, that of cultural unity and that of cultural diversity.[63] Latin American political communities are imagined as united in their diversity; as a single entity consisting of multiple cultures with some common traditions. This general tension is constituted by two sub-tensions that generate significant conceptual and practical challenges. The first of these is the tension between individual rights and indigenous self-government rights, which can sometimes lead to the creation and application of illiberal principles and rules.[64] This manifests daily in issues like gender inequality, the physical punishments some indigenous communities impose on those who violate their legal norms (e.g., whippings or the stocks), and the procedures these communities employ to judge and condemn their members for violating the law (e.g., the presence of a lawyer for the accused is not required, only of his family). In addition, the presuppositions on which liberal individual rights are based are not always recognized or shared by the normative systems of cultural minorities. The idea that subjects are autonomous and rational, that they are holders of rights that protect them from the undue intervention of the state in their good life projects, the separation between the public and private spheres, and the political equality of all individuals, to name a few, are not always part of the legal systems of Latin American cultural minorities. The tension is therefore simultaneously conceptual and practical; it replicates the tension that exists in international treaties that, like ILO Convention 169 on Indigenous

61 Constitución de la República Federativa de Brasil of 1988, articles 210, 215, 231; Constitución Política de Colombia of 1991, articles 10, 286, 329; Constitución Política del Perú of 1993, article 89; Constitución de la República del Paraguay of 1992, article 64; Constitución de la República de Nicaragua of 1987, article 180.

62 Modood, *Multiculturalism*, 108–9.

63 Van Cott, "Latin America," 42–43; Yrigoyen, "El horizonte," 141.

64 D. Bonilla, *La constitución multicultural* (Bogotá: Siglo del Hombre Editores, 2006), 148–97.

and Tribal Peoples, influenced the construction of the multicultural Latin American constitutions.[65]

This type of legal pluralism, which can be identified as "weak" and centers around cultural principles and rights, is based on two core principles of the liberal canon: autonomy and equality.[66] The multicultural liberal state model is structured around new interpretations or turns of the vocabulary and grammar of modern constitutionalism. The model argues that individual autonomy is never exercised in a vacuum but only ever in particular cultural contexts.[67] The subject constructs and modifies its good life projects within the options, always limited, never infinite, offered by the cultural context it is immersed in. Individual identity is therefore always shaped on particular horizons of meaning.[68] Cultural rights have the objective of protecting cultures that give meaning to the lives of individuals who at the same time construct these cultures and are constructed by them. For the multicultural liberal model, defending culture thus involves defending autonomy. Subjects can change culture, of course. However, these transformations usually generate very high costs for subjects, such as the loss of meaning of vital projects, individual and collective self-esteem issues, and moral and political tensions with members of the cultures they arrive in.[69] The multicultural liberal model affirms that the state cannot impose these costs on its citizens.[70]

The multicultural liberal model is also based on the idea that all the cultures which constitute a state should have the same opportunities to reproduce their traditions.[71] The majority culture has an advantage over the minority cultures in achieving this objective. The economic, human, and political resources at the disposal of the majority, in part, because it controls the administrative apparatus of the state as well as its budget, allows it to protect and promote its culture. Likewise, this inequality between the majority and the minorities allows the former to exert undue influence on the culture of the latter. The majority culture, and the state that protects it, can implement policies of assimilation or integration intended to eliminate

65 Gargarella, "Latin America's Contribution," 31–32.

66 W. Kymlicka, *Multicultural Citizenship: A Liberal Theory of Minority Rights* (Oxford: Oxford University Press, 1995), 34.

67 J. Tully, *Strange Multiplicity: Constitutionalism in an Age of Diversity* (Cambridge: Cambridge University Press, 1997), 189.

68 C. Joppke and S. Lukes, "Introduction: Multicultural Questions," in C. Joppke and S. Lukes (eds.), *Multicultural Questions* (Oxford: Oxford University Press, 2002), 9–10.

69 Kymlicka, *Multicultural*, 85.

70 Kymlicka, *Multicultural*, 86.

71 S. Benhabib, "'Nous' et 'les Autres' The Politics of Complex Cultural Dialogue in a Global Civilization," in C. Joppke and S. Lukes (eds.), *Multicultural Questions* (Oxford: Oxford University Press, 2002), 54.

cultural minorities.[72] Consequently, cultural rights emerge as legal and political instruments that allow for leveling the playing field of cultural reproduction within the state and that enable cultural minorities to defend themselves against the homogenizing impulses of the majorities.[73] They also allow cultural minorities to use their traditions to effectively regulate the public and private life of their communities.

These justifications for the multicultural liberal state model were articulated paradigmatically by the liberal political philosophy responsible for the cultural shift that took place in the 1990s. The arguments, presented by authors like Charles Taylor and Will Kymlicka, had a global impact. They influenced the discussions on how to recognize and include cultural minorities in both the Global North and South. Similarly, they influenced the establishment of international treaties that regulate matters related to cultural minorities, like ILO Convention 169. These international instruments were a relevant variable for constructing the Latin American multicultural constitutions, along with the work of cultural minority organizations, liberal and progressive political parties, national and international human rights NGOs, and pressure from engaged citizens such as students and workers.

The second of the abovementioned sub-tensions is generated by the conflict between the principle of political unity, which imagines the *polis* as a single entity cohering around a legal and political order,[74] and the rights of self-government, concretized in rights like the collective ownership of land, the right to determine who can travel across or settle on ancestral territories, and the right to prior consultation. Self-government rights serve as foundation for the creation of jurisdictions over which indigenous communities, and occasionally Afro-Latin American communities, have legal and political authority. This tension between rights and principles generates conceptual and practical problems of magnitude, such as conflicts over the authorities that are competent to judge the crimes committed by individuals of the majority culture in indigenous territory;[75] conflicts of jurisdiction

72 Modood, *Multiculturalism*, 44.

73 M. Bachvarova, "Multicultural Accommodation and the Ideal of Non-Domination," *Critical Review of International Social and Political Philosophy* 17 (2013), 652–73.

74 C. L. Carr, *Liberalism and Pluralism: The Politics of E pluribus unum* (New York: Palgrave Macmillan, 2010), 87–92.

75 R. Ariza, "Teoría y práctica en el ejercicio de la jurisdicción especial indígena en Colombia," in R. Huber, J. C. Martínez, C. Lachenal, and R. Ariza (eds.), *Hacia sistemas jurídicos plurales. Reflexiones y experiencias de coordinación entre el derecho estatal y el derecho indígena* (Bogotá: Konrad-Adenauer-Stiftung, 2008), 261–81.

connected to the presence of military forces within indigenous territories to confront subversive activities or activities related to drug trafficking;[76] and conflicts over the exploitation of non-renewable natural resources situated within indigenous lands.[77] Attempts to understand these conceptual and practical problems must bear in mind that Latin American multicultural constitutions recognize the rights of due process and freedom of movement, acknowledge that military and police forces must maintain public order throughout the territory, and declare that the state or the nation is the owner of the subsoil.

The multicultural liberal state model, thus far discussed in abstract, takes shape paradigmatically in the Colombian constitution of 1991 and the Brazilian constitution of 1988.[78] Among Latin American states, the Colombian multicultural liberal constitution perhaps embodies the model best and most completely. The Colombian multicultural state, via the jurisprudence of the Constitutional Court, has also attempted most directly and extensively to resolve the tensions that cut across the model and to develop the content of each of the cultural principles and rights that form it. The multicultural narrative constructed by the constitution of 1991 consists of the following three sets of elements: cultural principles, self-government rights, and special representation rights. The cultural principles declare that the "Colombian Social State of Law" (*Estado Social de Derecho*) is pluralist;[79] that the state must recognize and protect the nation's ethnic and cultural diversity;[80] and that the state must protect the nation's cultural richness.[81] Furthermore, article 1 declares that Colombia is a unitary republic.[82]

The rights of self-government recognize that the indigenous and culturally diverse Afro-Colombian communities can govern themselves autonomously "in conformity with the constitution and the laws."[83] Self-government rights open the space to indigenous and Afro-Colombian jurisdictions;[84] they recognize collective ownership of indigenous reservations (*resguardos*) and

76 C. A. Osorio, "Autonomía indígena y democracia en Colombia," *El Ágora USB* 17 (2017), 111.

77 N. Zúñiga, "Conflictos por recursos naturales y pueblos indígenas," *Pensamiento Propio* 22 (2006), 3–4.

78 This model of state is also embodied in the Constitución Política de los Estados Unidos Mexicanos of 1914, article 2; Constitución Política del Perú of 1993, article 2–19, article 17, 89; Constitución Política de Paraguay of 1992, articles 1, 62, 63, 140; Constitución del Ecuador of 2006, articles 1, 2, 11–12, 56, 57, 58, 59, 60, 377.

79 Constitución Política de la República de Colombia of 1991, article 1.

80 Ibid., article 7.

81 Ibid., article 8.

82 Ibid., article 1.

83 Ibid., articles 287, 330, Transitory article 55; Law 70 of 1993.

84 Ibid., article 246, Transitory article 55; Law 70 of 1993.

Afro-Colombian territories;[85] they allow for declaring indigenous lands as territorial entities of the state;[86] they establish the right to prior consultation;[87] and they allow indigenous languages to be declared official in their territories. Special representation rights are granted to indigenous and Afro-Colombian communities in special electoral districts.[88] Finally, the 1991 constitution promulgates a broad bill of rights that applies to all citizens, includes the individual rights defended by political liberalism[89], and declares that sovereignty resides in the people, who exercise it directly or by means of their representatives.[90]

The structure of the multicultural constitution of 1991 directly contradicts the legal and cultural monism of the classic nation-state and is a pristine reproduction of the multicultural liberal state model. The culturally homogeneous nation of the 1886 constitution is replaced by a culturally heterogeneous nation. The indigenous and Afro-Colombian individuals, who made up the nation from its beginning, are now being formally recognized by the legal and political system, the constitution breaks with the identification between the state and the Catholic religion, and indigenous languages are recognized as official within their territories. Likewise, legal monism is replaced by a weak legal pluralism that includes the authorities of cultural minorities as a source of legal creation. The indigenous and culturally diverse Afro-Colombian authorities are part of the bureaucratic structure of the Colombian state and are empowered to create legal norms to govern their communities. Nevertheless, these culturally diverse public officials and legal norms are subordinated to the constitution and to the laws promulgated by the national congress. Finally, the constitution makes explicit the conflict between cultural unity and cultural diversity that cuts across multicultural Latin American constitutions: Self-government rights collide with the unitary nature of the state and with the individual rights that give shape to its bill of rights. The classic nation-state's ideal of absolute sovereignty, which now resides in the people, remains firm.

The Brazilian constitution of 1988 is less ambitious than the Colombian one of 1991 with respect to the recognition and inclusion of cultural minorities. It recognizes fewer cultural principles and rights, and some of their content is more general. The heart of the multicultural constitution of 1988

85 Ibid., article 329, Transitory article 55; Law 70 of 1993. 86 Ibid., article 286.
87 Ibid., article 330, paragraph. 88 Ibid., articles 171, 176; Law 70 of 1993.
89 Ibid., Title II, Chapter 1. 90 Ibid., article 3.

is contained in the preamble and in title VIII, chapter VIII, which regulates matters related to indigenous communities.[91] First, the constitution stipulates that the state should have the objective of promoting a pluralist society.[92] It recognizes indigenous communities' self-government rights;[93] the original and permanent possession of their ancestral territories; the usufruct of natural resources that are on the surface of their lands,[94] lands which are declared inalienable and imprescriptible;[95] and the right to be heard regarding the exploitation of mineral or water resources situated within their territories.[96] Similarly, the constitution recognizes that indigenous individuals, communities, and organizations have the capacity to defend their rights in court.[97] The constitution of 1988 also recognizes a set of rights that aim to protect the cultural identities of indigenous and Afro-Brazilian communities, such as the right of indigenous communities to use their languages and methods of learning in public education;[98] the recognition that the state must protect indigenous and Afro-Brazilian cultural forms of expression;[99] and the recognition of the historic value of *quilombos* (settlements founded by people of African origin).[100] Finally, the constitution of 1988 declares that all power emanates from the people;[101] it recognizes a broad spectrum of individual, social, and collective rights;[102] and it indicates that all citizens can gather peacefully (but without weapons) in public spaces and prohibits associations of a paramilitary nature.[103]

The constitution of 1988 is structured around the multicultural liberal model in a clear and precise manner. It locates the majority culture – imagined as white, Portuguese speaking, and Catholic – at the center of the

91 The 1988 constitution includes other articles that regulate matters related to cultural minorities. However, these articles typically refer to the powers that the federal government has over matters of interest to indigenous communities, among others, art. 20–XI, which declares that the lands traditionally occupied by indigenous groups are property of the Union; art. 22–XIV, which states that the Union is solely responsible for legislating on indigenous populations' issues; art. 49–XVI, which recognizes the exclusive competence of the national congress to authorize, in indigenous lands, the exploitation and use of hydrological resources and the search and extraction of mineral wealth as well as art. 176–1, which indicates that the exploitation of mineral resources in indigenous territories may be authorized for reasons of national interest; art. 109, which grants jurisdiction to federal judges to process and judge conflicts over indigenous rights; and art. 129–V, which gives the public prosecutor the function of judicially defending the rights of indigenous people.

92 Constitución de la República Federativa de Brasil of 1988, Preamble.

93 Ibid., article 231. 94 Ibid., article 231. 95 Ibid., article 31–4.

96 Ibid., article 231–3. 97 Ibid., article 232. 98 Ibid., article 210–2.

99 Ibid., article 15–1. 100 Ibid., article 15–V–5. 101 Ibid., article 1, paragraph.

102 Ibid., Title II, ch. I, II, IV. 103 Ibid., article 5–XVI and XVII.

state, and it places cultural minorities, primarily indigenous communities, spinning around it, with culturally diverse Afro-Brazilian communities in the margins. In order to protect cultural minorities from the undue interference by the state and the majority culture, the constitution bestows on them a series of cultural rights. Finally, it recognizes all individual rights protected by political liberalism, declares that sovereignty is rooted in the people, and grants the state the monopoly of force. Nevertheless, the narrative constructed by the Brazilian constitution of 1988, Latin America's first multicultural constitution drafted before the promulgation of ILO Convention 169, has fewer dimensions and is less complex on cultural matters than others in Latin America. Contrary to, for example, the Colombian constitution of 1991, it does not recognize the collective ownership of indigenous territories (only the possession – ownership resides in the federal state). It does not explicitly recognize an indigenous jurisdiction or the right to prior consultation – although it could be inferred that these are derived from the general rights of self-government, which are in effect recognized – and it does not grant any special representation rights. Finally, the culturally diverse Afro-Brazilian communities are awarded only marginal recognition in the constitution of 1988.

As mentioned above, the Colombian constitution of 1991 and the Brazilian constitution of 1988 paradigmatically reflect the multicultural liberal and pluralist model in Latin America. However, the model is also reproduced, with nuances and variations, in other countries of the Global North and South. The multicultural liberal and pluralist model has been configured as a global discursive and practical pattern since the end of the 1980s. For example, the tensions between individual and self-government rights or between the principle of political unity and rights of self-government that cut across the constitutions of Colombia and Brazil also structure central legal or political matters for states as dissimilar as South Africa, India, Spain, Great Britain, and the Netherlands. In South Africa, the Constitutional Court has engaged widely with the relationship between customs and individual rights, discussing matters such as the differences between static customs and live customs, the authorities that can determine what the customs of a particular cultural minority are, or the limits of customs in light of the right to gender equality.[104] In India, the Supreme

104 C. Albertyn, "Cultural Diversity, 'Living Law,' and Women's Rights in South Africa," in D. Bonilla (ed.), *Constitutionalism of the Global South: The Activist Tribunals of India, South Africa, and Colombia* (Cambridge: Cambridge University Press, 2013), 163–210.

Court has ruled extensively on the tensions between individual rights and minority religions, the conflicts between the rights of majority religions and those of minority religions, and on how to weigh the territorial rights of indigenous peoples against the rights of the state or private companies interested in exploiting the natural resources situated in such territories.[105] Finally, the challenges of integrating non-Christian cultural minorities in the Netherlands are an iteration of the tensions between individual rights and cultural rights which are common in the Latin American multicultural liberal states. Likewise, the political and legal conflicts between the Spanish state and Catalonia or between Scotland and the British state powerfully reproduce the tensions between the principle of political unity and the rights of self-government of cultural minorities that shape the multicultural liberal and pluralist state.[106]

The Radical Intercultural State

In the first decade of the twenty-first century, Ecuador and Bolivia initiated a new process of constitutional reforms.[107] The Ecuadorian constitution of 2008 and the Bolivian constitution of 2009 question parts of the multicultural liberal model that impelled the previous constitutional transformations in the region.[108] They represent a new, radically intercultural model, which looks to the recent constitutional past to challenge its descriptive and normative limits.[109] It proposes that the constitutional present must reflect the society more precisely and construct a type of state that protects and promotes this reality. The type of cultural diversity that constitutes countries like Ecuador and Bolivia does not fit within the cultural majority / minorities approach that is at the center of the multicultural liberal model.[110] In Bolivia, indigenous peoples have historically been a demographic majority (around

105 G. Mahajan, "Keeping the Faith: Legitimizing Democracy through Judicial Practices in India," in D. Bonilla (ed.), *Constitutionalism of the Global South: The Activist Tribunals of India, South Africa, and Colombia* (Cambridge: Cambridge University Press, 2013), 211–42.

106 E. Dalle Mulle and I. Serrano, "Between a Principled and a Consequentialist Logic: Theory and Practice of Secession in Catalonia and Scotland," *Nations and Nationalism* 25(2) (2019), 630–51.

107 C. Gregor, "Nuevas narrativas constitucionales en Bolivia y Ecuador: el buen vivir y los derechos de la naturaleza," *Latinoamérica* 59 (2014), 10.

108 Bonilla, "El constitucionalismo," 6.

109 J. Lazarte, "Plurinacionalismo y multiculturalismo en la Asamblea Constituyente de Bolivia," *Revista Internacional de Filosofía Política* 33 (2009).

110 Bonilla, "El constitucionalismo," 9.

60 percent of the population), although they have been a minority in terms of the relative power they have had at their disposal.[111] In Ecuador, indigenous peoples have historically constituted around 40 percent of the population.[112] These cultural minorities understand themselves as nations that have not been granted participation, or representation of their legitimate interests in the multicultural liberal state. The legal and political past is once again understood as a set of structures that cannot contribute to creating a collective identity that truly embraces the complexity of the cultural diversity of the political communities it regulates.

Consequently, the radical intercultural model is structured around the principles of plurinationality and interculturality.[113] The concept of an "internally diverse nation" is replaced by that of "nations." The state is no longer imagined as formed by an internally multiple transtemporal collective subject, but by a set of transtemporal collective subjects. In the radical intercultural state, the central noun of the multicultural liberal state narrative – "nation" – is pluralized. The previous structure of a majority culture in the center and minorities cultures surrounding it like satellites is replaced by one in which all nations that form the state occupy the center of the political community. All nations are imagined as equal parts of the whole, as pieces that have equal relations with the unit. However, the radical intercultural model remains committed to the cultural rights that are the core component of the multicultural liberal model. Radical interculturalism considers cultural rights to be a useful instrument for confronting the imbalance of power that has historically existed between the nations that form the Ecuadorian and Bolivian political communities. The constitutions of both countries recognize that indigenous nations have the right, among others, to self-government, cultural identity, prior consultation, collective ownership of their lands, and to use their languages in public life (the indigenous languages are declared official).[114]

111 Economic Commission for Latin America and the Caribbean (ECLAC), *Guaranteeing Indigenous People's Rights in Latin America: Progress in the Past Decade and Remaining Challenges* (Santiago: ECLAC, 2014), 37.

112 M. Becker, "Correa, Indigenous Movements, and the Writing of a New Constitution in Ecuador," *Latin American Perspectives* 38 (2011), 48.

113 Constitución Política de la República de Ecuador of 2008, article 1; Constitución Política del Estado Plurinacional de Bolivia of 2009, article 1; Bonilla, "El constitucionalismo," 9.

114 Constitución Política del Estado Plurinacional de Bolivia of 2009, articles 2, 5, 30–2, 289, 394–3, 403; Constitución Política de la República de Ecuador of 2008, articles 2, 57, 58, 59, 60, 171.

The relations between nations and the way in which they contribute to the construction of the state also changes. While the multicultural liberal model does not explicitly commit to a political principle that regulates interactions between the majority and the minorities, the radical intercultural model is committed to the principle of interculturality.[115] In the multicultural liberal model, the political inertia that comes from the classic nation-state model, as well as the power differentials that characterize the relationship between the cultural majority and cultural minorities, tend to convert cultural minorities into political and cultural monads in order to protect them from interference by the majority. In contrast to this, the radical intercultural model envisions the dialogue between nations as the principle that guides the joint construction of the state.[116] The transtemporal collective subjects that form the state do not exist as isolated and autonomous units which share a territory and only interact when there is a conflict of jurisdictions. Rather, the guiding normative principle for nations is the interaction between one another, and therefore their mutual influence and transformation.[117] In the radical intercultural model, the state is constructed by the dialogue among nations. Its structure, contours, and macro discursive and practical dynamics are defined and redefined by processes of communication among these collective subjects.[118]

Finally, the radical intercultural state maintains the weak legal pluralism that characterizes the multicultural liberal model, although it deepens it. The system of sources for legal creation includes indigenous nations' institutions in addition to the institutions that commonly have the capacity to promulgate legal rules and principles in a liberal democracy (the legislative and executive branches of government).[119] However, the model also includes principles and rules that allow for equal participation in the state's institutions, such as the multicultural formation of the Bolivian constitutional court[120] and the provincial assemblies and municipal councils in Ecuador and Bolivia, as well as the creation of indigenous jurisdictions that have a horizontal relation with the state's jurisdiction.[121] Nevertheless, the deepest changes in the legal pluralism that shapes the radical intercultural state result from the inclusion of

115 Bonilla, "El constitucionalismo," 10–11. 116 Ibid., 10–11.
117 Ibid., 10. 118 Ibid., 10.
119 Constitución Política del Estado Plurinacional de Bolivia of 2009, articles 146, 190, 192; Constitución Política de la República de Ecuador of 2008, article 171.
120 Constitución Política del Estado Plurinacional de Bolivia of 2009, article 197.
121 Ibid., articles 179–2, 192–3; Constitución Política de la República de Ecuador of 2008, article 171.

the rights of nature and the principle of good living in the Ecuadorian and Bolivian legal orders.[122] These two innovations generated by Andean constitutionalism originate in indigenous epistemologies and worldviews, which historically had been marginalized in the political life of Ecuador and Bolivia. Indigenous cultures provide some of the structural elements of the constitutions that govern all the nations which configure the Ecuadorian and Bolivian states. The rights of nature and the principle of good living question the dominant geopolitics of legal knowledge that considers indigenous cultures to be poor contexts for the creation of original legal products.[123]

The rights of nature regard *pachamama* ("Mother Earth") as a subject of rights. Consequently, they call into question the idea, central in modern constitutionalism, that only autonomous and rational individuals, subjects with agency, can be considered holders of rights and obligations. In the Ecuadorian and Bolivian legal orders, nature, a nonhuman entity, has rights such as the right to life and to the recovery of its vital cycles.[124] The rights of nature recognized by the Bolivian and Ecuadorian constitutions question the anthropocentrism that has traditionally sustained the relations between human beings and nature in modernity and forms the basis for one of the central components of modern liberal democracies: the market economy.[125] From this point of view, nature is not a thing created for human beings; it is not a means to satisfy their aims. Nature is not a resource that human beings can exploit indefinitely to satisfy their needs and desires. In this perspective, nature and human beings do not have a vertical relationship. In the radical intercultural model, biocentrism, which understands human beings as only another element of nature – an element that has rights as well as obligations toward other components of the unit – replaces anthropocentrism.[126] The rights of nature are thus a hybrid that mixes elements of the vocabulary and grammar

122 Constitución Política de la República de Ecuador, Title II, Chapter 7; Title VII; Constitución Política del Estado Plurinacional de Bolivia, articles 8 and 9; Law 300 of 2012 of the Estado Plurinacional de Bolivia.

123 Bonilla, "El constitucionalismo," 11.

124 Constitución Política de la República de Ecuador of 2008, articles 71, 72; Law 300 of 2012 of the Estado Plurinacional de Bolivia.

125 R. Lalander, "Entre el ecocentrismo y el pragmatismo ambiental: Consideraciones inductivas sobre desarrollo, extractivismo y los derechos de la naturaleza en Bolivia y Ecuador," *Revista Chilena de Derecho y Ciencia Política* 6 (2015), 118–19; E. Gudynas, "La ecología política del giro biocéntrico en la nueva Constitución de Ecuador," *Revista de Estudios Sociales* (2009), 37–39; S. Radcliffe, "Development for a Postneoliberal Era? Sumak kawsay, Living Well and the Limits to Decolonisation in Ecuador," *Geoforum* 43 (2012), 241.

126 Gudynas, "La ecología," 37–39.

of modern constitutionalism, like "rights," "subject of rights," "obligations," "agency" and "autonomy" with elements of the cultures of indigenous peoples, for example, the concept of nature as a living being.

The principle of good living defends a holistic view of the universe that calls into question the atomism that has dominated a part of the liberal tradition.[127] The subject is no longer understood as a fundamentally closed and isolated unit seeking to construct its good life projects autonomously and rationally. From this perspective, the subject is always interpreted in relation to its environment. The individual is always constructed and developed in networks of relationships that include both the human "other" and other organic and inorganic components of the universe. The backbone of the holism of *sumak kawsay*, the Quechua term for "good living," is formed by the following four principles: (i) relationality (individuals are parts of a whole, not isolated subjects, who share the same space and construct society by the aggregation of their decisions); (ii) complementarity (the parts complement each other; they are not *a priori* in conflict and should not compete among themselves); (iii) balance (the aim of the interaction should be to achieve an equilibrium between the parts that is always contingent and always in transformation); and (iv) reciprocity (the parts should be disposed to a constant giving and receiving in order to achieve the desired balance).[128] The principle of good living is perhaps the only contribution to the radical intercultural state model that does not originate or represent a turn in the grammar of modern constitutionalism. It is a principle that emerges and is nurtured on the cosmogonies of the Andean indigenous communities.

The legal innovations articulated by the Latin American intercultural model are in dialogue with the discursive patterns around which some legal creations in other countries of the Global North and South have been structured in the twenty-first century. The recognition of rights to the Whanganui river in New Zealand, the Yarra river in Australia, and the Ganges and Yamuna rivers in India, as well as the recognition of rights to ecosystems in some small US towns like Toledo and Grant Township, enter into implicit or explicit dialogue with the recognition of rights to nature and the principle of good living in Ecuador and Bolivia. In New Zealand, Australia, India, and the United States, as happens in the Andean countries, the recognition of the

127 R. Llasag Fernández, "El sumak kawsay y sus restricciones constitucionales," *Revista de Derecho UASB* 12 (2009), 113–25.

128 C. Silva Portero, "¿Qué es el buen vivir en la Constitución?," in R. Ávila (ed.), *La Constitución del 2008 en el contexto andino. Análisis desde la doctrina y el derecho comparado* (Quito: Ministerio de Justicia y Derechos Humanos, 2008), 112–19.

rights to certain ecosystems intersects with notable epistemological and ethical changes. On one hand, a vindication of indigenous cultures (New Zealand and Australia) or religious traditions (India) provides rich spaces for the production of legal knowledge. On the other hand, there is an explicit defense of biocentric perspectives that question the anthropocentrism that has been the focal point in modern law and culture.[129]

Constellation of Sovereignties and Strong Legal Pluralism

In Latin America, the discontinuities between the classic nation-state model, the multicultural liberal state model, and the radical intercultural state model are notable. The Latin American multicultural liberal state reacts to the monocultural and monist nature of the nation-state model by recognizing and including cultural minorities, primarily by means of cultural principles and rights and the articulation of a weak legal pluralism in its system of legal sources. The radical intercultural model reacts to the notion of a culturally diverse nation that structures the model it replaces (the multicultural liberal state), as well as to the conceptual regime that situates the majority culture at the state's center and cultural minorities as satellites that revolve around it. Likewise, the intercultural model breaks with the notion that cultures are monads which repel or try to conquer each other. The radical intercultural model replaces these discourses and practices with the principles of plurinationality, interculturality, and good living, as well as with the rights of nature. The radical intercultural model therefore breaks with the political economy of legal knowledge dominant in both the classic nation-state model and in the multicultural liberal model. The epistemologies and worldviews of historically marginalized nations come to form central dimensions of the constitutional model that is now applied to all citizens.

However, the continuities between the models are equally notable. In all three models, there is a commitment to the vocabulary and grammar of modern constitutionalism, and they all are structured around individual rights and the principle of absolute sovereignty of the state, which includes the state's monopoly of force. In the multicultural liberal model and the intercultural model, there is a commitment to cultural rights as instruments for protecting and promoting the cultures of minorities. Both models configure their

129 M. Tănăsescu, "Rights of Nature, Legal Personality, and Indigenous Philosophies," *Transnational Environmental Law* 9(3) (2020), 429–53.

legal systems around a weak legal pluralism that usually corresponds to an internally complex rule of recognition constructed in a cultural key. The rule of recognition is not a rule on paper. Rather, it is a practice by which public officials, primarily, identify which norms belong to the legal system by using criteria that recognize both the typical institutions of a contemporary liberal democracy and the institutions of cultural minorities as sources of law.

Extralegality and Illegality: Strong Legal Pluralism

The normative project of the Latin American multicultural and intercultural states that seek to construct a single legal and political system with multiple hierarchized sources, applied throughout the state's territory, and backed by a single official coercive apparatus, has not yet fully materialized. Since the late eighties, as before, in various degrees and forms, the sovereignty of Latin American states and official law have constantly competed with illegal or extralegal normative systems that control sections of the state territory.[130] These alternative normative systems do not, or only partially, recognize the sovereignty of the state. Nevertheless, in practice, the state legal system and the alternative normative systems interact, overlap, and transform each other.[131] Some of these normative systems are illegal; others, extralegal.[132] The former, the normative systems of some guerrilla or paramilitary groups, for example, not only ignore and violate state law but intend to replace it.[133] Other illegal normative systems, like those of the transnational Central American gangs or the large Mexican drug trafficking organizations, do not seek to replace official law entirely, although they violate it and want to neutralize its operation in the areas they control.[134] The extralegal normative systems differ from this in that they ignore official law but do not necessarily violate it. Examples are the alternative systems to state-regulated private property that operate in a significant part of the peripheral neighborhoods of Latin American cities.[135]

130 M. Goodale, "Legalities and Illegalities," in D. Poole (ed.), *A Companion to Latin American Anthropology* (Hoboken: Blackwell, 2008), 214–29.

131 Bonilla, "Extralegal Property," 219–26; B. de Sousa Santos, "Two Democracies, Two Legalities: Participatory Budgeting in Porto Alegre, Brazil," in B. de Sousa Santos and C. A. Rodríguez-Garavito (eds.), *Law and Globalization from Below: Towards A Cosmopolitan Legality* (Cambridge: Cambridge University Press, 2005), 311.

132 Sieder, "Legal Pluralism," 56–57.

133 T. P. Wickham-Crowley, "The Rise (and Sometimes Fall) of Guerilla Governments in Latin America," *Sociological Forum* 2 (1987), 478.

134 Sieder, "Legal Pluralism," 59. 135 Bonilla, "Extralegal Property," 215–19.

Thus, it emerges that the multicultural liberal and radical intercultural states in Latin America are constituted by a constellation of sovereignties. The principle of absolute sovereignty that dominates the modern legal/political consciousness imagines the state as a galaxy formed by a single star where political power and the capacity to create law are concentrated. In contrast, the Latin American constellation of sovereignties is made up of a varied set of stars that have diverse forms and concentrate varying levels of legal and political power – dwarf stars, giant stars, red and white stars, for example. As in any constellation, these sovereign stars attract, repel, crash into, nurture, and sometimes destroy each other. Consequently, the constellation of sovereignties that exists within the Latin American states operates around two conceptual oppositions: legal/illegal and legal/extralegal. State law, which usually concentrates greater power than the alternative normative systems, categorizes as illegal all those rules and principles that are outside of its limits and violate its norms.[136] State law also seeks to destroy any normative system that calls into question the sources from which it emanates, even if these alternative normative systems do not violate its rules and principles.[137] Official modern law always has imperial aspirations; it wants to dominate the entire space that exists within state borders.[138] Ideally, state territory and official law should correspond one to one, should overlap perfectly, should dovetail fully. Typically, the sovereign should be one and only one, the nation and the people.

The constellation of sovereignties that exists within Latin American states shows that the sovereign people or nations that are represented by the institutions of indirect liberal democracies compete with other imagined sovereigns, like the "true people" or part of the "true people" who are represented by another type of institution, such as the guerrilla commander, the central command, the drug lord, the gang boss, the community organization. The normative systems created by guerrilla groups like the "Shining Path" (*Sendero Luminoso*) in Peru, the Zapatista National Liberation Army (*Ejercito Zapatista de Liberación Nacional*, EZLN) in Mexico, the Revolutionary Armed Forces (*Fuerzas Armadas Revolucionarias*, FARC) and the National Liberation

136 Sieder, "Legal Pluralism," 56–57.

137 J. Lemaitre, "¿Constitución o barbarie? Cómo repensar el derecho en las 'zonas sin ley'" in C. Rodríguez (ed.), *El derecho en América Latina. Un mapa para el pensamiento jurídico del siglo XXI* (Buenos Aires: Siglo XXI Editores, 2011), 51–52.

138 M. García, "Estado, territorio y ciudadanía en Colombia," in M. García (ed.), *Jueces sin Estado: La justicia colombiana en zonas de conflicto armado* (Bogotá: Siglo del Hombre Editores, 2008), 19.

Army (*Ejército de Liberación Nacional*, ELN) in Colombia are good examples of a first type of strong pluralism that has developed in Latin America.

In these cases, the illegal normative systems not only do not recognize the state legal system, but they also seek to replace it by means of violence.[139] These alternative normative systems call upon political reasons to justify their existence. Generally, these reasons revolve around arguments of class or redistribution, as in the case of *Sendero Luminoso*, FARC, and the ELN.[140] These arguments sometimes intersect with ethnic or recognition arguments, as in the case of EZLN.[141] The state legal system is therefore seen as illegitimate or unjust, as a consequence of the triumph of a social class (the bourgeoisie) over the people, or as the triumph of a majority culture over minority cultures.[142] The guerrilla normative system is seen as the correct vehicle of the true interests of the people or indigenous minorities, and therefore also as just and legitimate.[143] Nevertheless, none of these guerrilla normative systems has managed to replace the state legal system completely. Guerrilla groups have not managed to defeat the state by military means, and it does not seem that those still in existence after the peace process between FARC and the Colombian state and the near total defeat of *Sendero Luminoso* could do so.

However, although they may not succeed in controlling the state, these illegal normative systems have been applied systematically and continuously in areas of state territory that have been (or were) historically controlled by guerrilla movements. In areas like Ayacucho in Peru, Chiapas in Mexico, and the Colombian Orinoco and Amazon basins, the conduct of citizens is (or, historically, was) regulated, and conflicts arising between them are or were solved, by the guerrilla normative systems and their institutions such as revolutionary courts or the revolutionary "tax" collection units. In these areas, guerrilla legal systems usually coexist with state legal systems. For example, revolutionary judges coexist with judges assigned by the state to the farthest municipalities of national geographies, as well as the police, military forces, and some executive branch authorities like mayors and municipal councils.

139 Lemaitre, "¿Constitución o barbarie?," 58.

140 G. H. McCormick, "The Shining Path and Peruvian Terrorism," *Journal of Strategic Studies* 10 (1987), 113; R. Gott, *Guerilla Movements in Latin America* (Garden City: Doubleday, 1971), 230–68.

141 C. Cortéz-Ruiz, "The Struggle Towards Rights and Communitarian Citizenship: The Zapatista Movement in Mexico," in L. Thompson and C. Tapscott (eds.), *Citizenship and Social Movements: Perspectives from the Global South* (London: Zed Books, 2010), 160–61.

142 Wickham-Crowley, "The Rise," 477.

143 Ibid., 478–85.

In these spaces, typically distant from the centers of state legal and political power, the two normative systems, the guerrilla and the official, compete for control of citizens' consciences and actions. However, in these areas, the normative systems of the subversive groups are the ones imposed *de facto* and the ones that effectively regulate the territory and its inhabitants. In Chiapas, Ayacucho, or Arauca, for example, guerrilla rules and principles control (or controlled) issues as varied as land disputes, romantic infidelities, robberies, homicides, or the effective use of state resources managed by municipalities.[144] In these areas, state law generally only exists on paper; the state institutions are isolated and ineffective and cannot act without the authorization of guerrilla institutions, such as front commanders, the central command, or revolutionary councils. In these areas of Mexico, Ayacucho, and Arauca, guerrilla law is the law in action, the law that is effectively applied to individuals.

The guerilla does not recognize state law but, of course, the state legal order does not recognize guerrilla normative systems either. Rather, it categorizes them as illegal and tries to eliminate them by using the coercive apparatus at its disposal. However, states like Peru, Mexico, and Colombia have not managed to achieve this objective, due to their historical weakness in political, economic, and military matters. These states therefore accept the existence of the normative systems that seek to subvert the established legal and political order as a fact, albeit an undesirable one. Nevertheless, they simultaneously assert the legitimacy of the state legal system and the illegitimacy of the guerrilla normative order. The official legal order is presented as a consequence of the social contract upon which the state is founded, and as created by institutions where these three liberal democracies concentrate the power to make law. In contrast, in the eyes of the state, the normative systems of the subversive groups are artifacts created by politically illegitimate minority factions, imposed only by means of violence.

The coexistence of the state legal system and the guerrilla normative systems in countries like Peru, Mexico, and Colombia is powerful evidence of Latin America's strong legal pluralism. In the territories of these countries, at least two sovereigns and two rules of recognition compete. The sovereign people who are recognized in the constitutions and represented, primarily, by congresses and presidents, compete with the "true people" who are recognized in the statutes of the guerrilla movements and represented by central commands, revolutionary councils, or front commanders. Consequently, the

144 G. Trejo, "Redefining the Territorial Bases of Power: Peasants, Indians and Guerrilla Warfare in Chiapas, Mexico," *International Journal of Multicultural Societies* 4 (2002), 7.

criteria employed by both public officials and guerrilla authorities to identify the norms that form each system, the rules of recognition of each normative order, are mutually exclusive. Of course, this does not mean that the two normative systems are isolated from each other. On the contrary, these systems continuously interact and modify each other. Interlegality is one of the principles regulating not only the weak state pluralism that is a consequence of the constitutional recognition of cultural diversity, but also the strong legal pluralism that arises as a consequence of the incomplete materialization of the monocultural, multicultural, or intercultural nation-state models in some parts of Latin America.[145] State law not only enters into dialogue, but it intersects with, transforms, and collides with the law of Latin American indigenous and black minorities. State law also reluctantly enters into dialogue with, intersects, transforms, and collides with the guerrilla normative orders that partially dominate some regions of the state's territory.[146]

For example, judges who work in areas of the Colombian departments of Norte de Santander and Santander, which are controlled by ELN, do not initiate proceedings related to certain types of severe crimes like homicides. They open them formally but do not take any action to find the guilty parties, or they act to fulfill this objective only when the front commander allows them to do so. Likewise, in Peru, the activities of the peasant patrols (*rondas campesinas*), the Peruvian state judges, and *Sendero Luminoso* judges intersect (or rather, they used to) for resolving matters related to cattle theft in rural areas of the Cajamarca region.[147] Similar arrangements can be found with the police units stationed in small towns of the department of Cauca in Colombia or the state of Chiapas in Mexico. In these towns, the police, one of the state agencies in charge of enforcing the state's legal system, only has the capacity for operating in the areas surrounding the station where their agents live and work. In the rest of the town, as well as in the rural areas of the municipality, the guerrilla fronts are the ones who control the territory and its inhabitants.[148] In addition, citizens recognize the guerrilla authorities as sources for the creation of norms actually applicable within the municipality, the norms that effectively determine until what time bars are open, the type of compensation that must be paid if you harm another individual's

145 B. de Sousa Santos, *Toward a New Common Sense: Law, Science and Politics in the Paradigmatic Transition* (London and New York: Routledge, 1995), 473.
146 Goodale, "Legalities and Illegalities," 216.
147 E. Picolli, "El pluralismo jurídico y político en Perú: el caso de las Rondas Campesinas de Cajamarca," *Íconos. Revista de Ciencias Sociales* 31 (2008), 28–31.
148 Trejo, "Redefining the Territorial," 7.

interests, or the punishment you must submit to if you commit a robbery or a homicide, for example.

The constellation of sovereignties that constitutes Latin American states is also formed by the normative systems created by transnational criminal structures like the Mexican drug-trafficking cartels, the *Comando Vermelho* (Red Command) and the *Primeiro Comando da Capital* (First Capital Command) in Brazil, and the *Mara Salvatrucha* and *Barrio 18* (Neighborhood 18) gangs in El Salvador and Guatemala. However, the normative systems created by these illegal organizations do not seek to subvert the established political order and replace the entire state legal system. Rather, these organizations aim to neutralize the application of those norms of the official legal system that create obstacles to their illicit activities and to promulgate norms that allow for maintaining order and safety in the areas they control.[149] In the municipalities of Chihuahua State controlled by the Juárez cartel, in the *favelas* of Rio de Janeiro dominated by *Comando Vermelho*, and in the marginal neighborhoods of San Salvador occupied by *Mara Salvatrucha*, for example, the daily life of the population is controlled in part by the norms created by the drug lords and gang bosses that lead these criminal organizations.[150] Access to these rural or urban spaces, interactions between the criminal organizations and the "civilians" that inhabit these spaces, the payment of "taxes" to guarantee the safety of businesses, and silence with respect to any illicit activity in the area, for example, are all matters regulated by the normative systems created by these illegal organizations.[151] Furthermore, in the areas dominated by these criminal structures, the state has no – or only a nominal or fragmentary – presence, and the official legal system becomes a set of norms on paper when its mandates collide with the interests of the cartels or transnational gangs. Of course, the state legal system does not recognize these illegal normative systems and periodically tries to eliminate or weaken them. The state legal system, as well as the institutions that enforce it, maintain a sporadic or partial presence by means of police or military operations, providing some social services, or demanding payment of property taxes, among other measures.

149 E. Desmond, *Drugs and Democracy in Rio de Janeiro: Trafficking, Social Networks, and Public Security* (Chapel Hill: The University of North Carolina Press, 2006), 202–4.

150 R. Duarte, C. de Macedo, and M. Ferreira, "Violent Nonstate Actors and the Emergence of Hybrid Governance in South America," *Latin American Research Review* 56 (2021), 40–42; E. Ellis, "Las drogas, las pandillas, el crimen organizado transnacional y los 'espacios mal gobernados' en las Américas," *Air & Space Power Journal* (2014), 19–27.

151 Trejo, "Redefining the Territorial," 7.

In these areas of Mexico, Brazil, El Salvador, and Guatemala, at least two sovereigns and two rules of recognition thus compete. The people and congress compete with the drug lord and the gang boss; the state legal system competes with the normative system of the cartel or gang; the criteria utilized by citizens and members of criminal organizations to identify the valid norms partially exclude the criteria utilized by public officials to fulfill this same goal. Strong legal pluralism describes these phenomena well. However, as in the case of the guerrilla normative systems and the state legal system, in this situation (the coexistence of gangs, cartels, and the state), the normative systems in competition constantly interact and transform each other.[152] In this set up, the state legal system transforms and re-accommodates itself as a consequence of its interaction with the illegal normative systems created by cartels and transnational gangs. This takes the shape of state policies of non-intervention in certain neighborhoods, municipalities, or illegal economic activities, or policies to reduce prison sentences. Further examples, as articulated in Mexico by former president Enrique Peña Nieto in Mexico, or by the Salvadorian president Nayib Bukele, are policies that seek to improve gang members' conditions of imprisonment in exchange for a reduction in the violence exercised by drug-trafficking organizations or multinational gangs.[153]

These discursive and practical patterns that are common in Latin America are only one species of the genus "strong legal pluralism" that is materialized globally. In Asia and Africa, for example, strong legal pluralism is present paradigmatically in two central phenomena in the continents' recent legal and political history: the coexistence of traditional indigenous legal systems, postcolonial state legal systems, and colonial legal norms after decolonization began at the end of the Second World War and ended in the late 1970s;[154] and the coexistence of several legal orders during the post-conflict processes that ended with internal armed conflicts.[155]

The constellation of sovereignties in Latin American states is constituted by two conceptual oppositions. First, that of legal/illegal, which cuts across the relations between state law and the normative systems of guerrillas,

152 Goodale, "Legalities and Illegalities," 216.

153 J. García, "Una investigación arroja nuevas pruebas de la negociación de Bukele con las pandillas de El Salvador," *El País* (2021), https://elpais.com/internacional/2021-08-24/se-publican-nuevas-pruebas-sobre-la-negociacion-de-bukele-con-las-pandillas-de-el-salvador.html (last accessed Oct. 1, 2021).

154 B. Tamanaha, "Understanding Legal Pluralism: Past to Present, Local to Global," *Sydney Law Review* 30(3) (2008).

155 L. Grenfell, *Promoting the Rule of Law in Post-Conflict States* (Cambridge: Cambridge University Press, 2013), 59–90.

cartels, and transnational gangs. Second, that of legal/extralegal, which influences relations in many ways. It cuts across the relations between the official legal system and the community normative systems governing questions like property and possession of real estate in the peripheral neighborhoods of large Latin American cities;[156] labor relations in remote rural areas; resolution of conflicts between members of some peasant communities[157] and the ways small businesses are organized without forming corporations.[158]

In all these cases, the non-state normative systems do not have the objective of subverting the official legal system, partially replacing it, or violating the norms that form it, although this does happen sometimes. Rather, the aim of these unofficial normative systems is to regulate activities that are not controlled effectively by the state legal system and that are developed on the margins of the parts of society that the state formally controls.[159] The state legal systems have a set of norms at their disposal which discursively regulate these activities throughout national territory. Nevertheless, as a consequence of the political or economic weaknesses of the region's states, these legal norms are not applied or are only partially applied in the margins of Latin American societies. Here, the extralegal normative systems not only coexist with the state legal system, but both interact with and transform each other. Again, as in the case of the illegal normative systems, interlegality is the principle that regulates this encounter, and two mutually exclusive sovereigns and sets of rules exist side by side. On one hand, there are the people represented by the legislative and executive branches of government, as well as the laws and decrees they promulgate to regulate particular matters of the national reality. On the other, there are the people who, given the absence of the state and the ineffectiveness of its legal system, use the institutions established to represent their interests, like communal action councils or peasant

156 B. de Sousa Santos, "The Law of The Oppressed: The Construction of and Reproduction of Legality in Pasargada," *Law and Society Review* 12 (1977), 89.

157 D. Goldstein, "'In Our Own Hands': Lynching, Justice, and the Law in Bolivia," *American Ethnologist* 30 (2003), 24–25.

158 Instituto Libertad y Democracia, *Evaluación preliminar de la economía extralegal en 12 países de América Latina y el Caribe* (Lima: ILD, 2007).

159 R. S. Meinzen-Dick and R. Pradhan, *Legal Pluralism and Dynamic Property Rights* (CGIAR Systemwide Program on Collective Action and Property Rights, CAPRi Working Paper No. 22) (Washington: IFPRI, 2002), 1–2 and 26, available at http://ideas.repecorg/p/fpr/worpps/22.html (last accessed Jan. 2, 2023); F. von Benda-Beckmann, K. von Benda-Beckmann, and J. Eckert, "Rules of Law and Laws of Ruling: Law and Governance Between Past and Future," in F. von Benda-Beckmann, K. von Benda-Beckmann, and J. Eckert (eds.), *Rules of Law and Laws of Ruling: On The Governance of Law* (Farnham: Ashgate Publishing, 2009), 3–5; Goldstein, "In Our Own," 24–25.

organizations, to create a set of norms parallel to state norms to regulate matters that are necessary for the proper functioning of social life.

A paradigmatic and very widespread example of this type of strong pluralism in Latin America is that of the extralegal property systems in coexistence with the rules and principles of the state legal systems for regulating "official" property.[160] In the legal systems of Latin American liberal democracies, the concept of property is designed, justified, and then regulated based on liberal political philosophy.[161] In the great majority of Latin American constitutions or civil codes, the individual right to property is seen as either absolute or limited by its social and ecological functions. Latin American liberal legal orders regulate this right in great detail, in categories such as title, mode, and registration procedures in public institutions, like the office for registration of public instruments, or private persons and institutions with public functions, for example, notaries. Consequently, individuals have the right to use, abuse, and collect profits from the things that they own. However, in some cases, these rights are limited by duties imposed on owners by statutes or the constitution to use real estate productively or to protect the environment. Finally, owners can transfer their rights by means of instruments such as public deeds, donation contracts, or inheritances, which are formalized through processes before state institutions.

Nevertheless, approximately 50 percent of the Latin American population lives in peripheral neighborhoods, where real estate is not regulated by the state legal system.[162] These neighborhoods were constructed on public or private lands that were occupied by individuals with few socioeconomic resources or by illegal builders. Given their illegal origin, the state cannot recognize any property rights over the lots and the houses built on these lands. However, neighborhood organizations or communal action boards in cities like São Paulo, Lima, La Paz, Quito, and Bogotá have created extralegal normative systems that regulate ownership of real estate in the areas under their jurisdiction.[163] Generally, as happens in the Jerusalén neighborhood of

160 K. A. Gould, D. R. Carter, and R. K. Shrestha, "Extra-legal Land Market Dynamics on a Guatemalan Agricultural Frontier: Implications for Neoliberal Land Policies," *Land Use Policy* 23 (2006), 408; G. Barnes, "Lessons Learned: An Evaluation of Land Administration Initiatives in Latin America Over the Past Two Decades," *Land Use Policy* 20 (2003), 367.

161 J. Locke, *Segundo Tratado sobre el gobierno civil: un ensayo acerca del verdadero origen, alcance y fin del gobierno civil* (Madrid: Alianza, 1990), ch. 5.

162 Bonilla, "Extralegal Property," 209.

163 C. Hinchey Trujillo, "La Puesta en Práctica de la Campaña de Seguridad en la Tenencia de la Vivienda en América Latina y el Caribe," in *Las campañas mundiales de seguridad en la tenencia de la vivienda y por una mejor gobernabilidad urbana en América Latina y el Caribe* (SERIE seminarios y conferencias 12) (Santiago de Chile: CEPAL, 2001), 25.

the Ciudad Bolívar district in Bogotá, this extralegal system is constituted by a set of rules and principles that use categories of state law, resignifying them. In Jerusalén, to continue with the example, the communal action board (*Junta de Acción Comunal*, JAC) determined that the owner of a piece of land is the person who works on it, in particular, the person who builds on it. Likewise, the JAC created a book to register owners, as well as changes in the ownership of real estate. Finally, this extralegal property system in Jerusalén recognizes the validity of private documents that the neighborhood's inhabitants call "contract of sale" or "promise of sale." These documents use categories of the state legal system but do not meet the formal requirements that this system demands to recognize them as valid. Nevertheless, within the neighborhood, these documents are the accepted means of transferring property.

In Jerusalén, therefore, as in many other peripheral neighborhoods of Latin American cities, the extralegal legal system is in constant interaction with the state legal system.[164] For example, the official legal system has in many cases had to give formal recognition to the existence of these neighborhoods, even though it cannot recognize property rights over the real estate inside them. As such, the state has been able to construct or improve streets in these peripheral neighborhoods and provide essential public services like water, sewer systems, and electricity, and to charge "property" taxes. Likewise, the extralegal legal system constantly makes use of the state legal system to achieve aims it considers valuable, such as authenticating the extralegal documents of property transfer before public notaries and formalizing sworn statements where the neighborhood's inhabitants recognize that they are the owners of real estate.

Community organizations do not create these extralegal property systems because they are in discord with the aims or contents of the state property system. Rather, they create them because it is impossible to apply official property rules and principles in the neighborhood. This, in turn, is due to the fact that much of the land occupation was illegal and that the state is generally absent as well as indifferent to their interests – and yet a matter as important, and one that could potentially generate many conflicts, as property must be regulated. The state constantly articulates policies to "legalize" these neighborhoods, and, as such, to eliminate the sovereigns, rules, and principles that compete with their property law. However, these policies are not always effective, for reasons that range from citizens' lack of confidence

164 Bonilla, "Extralegal Property," 224–25.

in the state to the economic costs for the neighborhoods' inhabitants and the bureaucratic obstacles that must be overcome to materialize them.

The coexistence of the state and extralegal systems of property in many cities of Latin America offers particularly strong evidence of some of the arguments that justify legal monism and explain extralegal strong legal pluralism. Arguably, a single statewide legal property system is based on a series of values that are central for liberal modernity and generate a series of practical advantages for citizens of a liberal democracy. On one hand, the concept of a single state system of property is founded on the principles of equality, universality, legal security, and autonomy.[165] The state property system starts from the basis that all citizens are equal and therefore all legal norms should be applied to them equally. The rights and duties generated by the recognition of individual property by the state must be applied to all members of the political community without distinction. This also guarantees that citizens know what the legal consequences of their actions are, and that they can therefore decide autonomously and in an informed manner what courses of action they wish to take with respect to their properties and the properties of others. Likewise, a monist state property system reduces the cognitive costs related to determining the norms applicable to conflicts over property that arise between citizens;[166] it contributes to the proper functioning of the market economy, which needs a common concept of property and some common rules on property to guarantee the unimpeded exchange of goods and services;[167] and it legitimizes the legal norms that aim to solve the problems arising around matters as complex and difficult as property.[168]

Nevertheless, legal monism in the realm of property is only a normative project in Latin America. In the region, six of every eight buildings are constructed outside the state market economy's limits, and around 80 percent of the real estate is not controlled by the state legal property system.[169] Extralegal strong legal pluralism is therefore the rule rather than the exception. This legal pluralism regarding property is also generally constructed in bottom-up processes as a consequence of the state's absence or the state legal system's indifference to the social reality of the most socioeconomically vulnerable individuals in the political community.[170]

165 Bonilla, "Extralegal Property," 204–7.
166 J. Waldron, *The Right to Private Property* (Oxford: Oxford University Press, 1990), 43.
167 H. Soto, *The Mystery of Capital* (London: Black Swan, 2001), 7 and 10.
168 Waldron, *The Right*, 162. 169 Soto, *The Mystery*, 85.
170 Bonilla, "Extralegal Property."

As happens with other forms of pluralism, this extralegal strong legal pluralism as it exists in Latin America is an iteration of a pattern that cuts across the reality of a good part of the globe. In countries like Egypt, the Philippines, and Vietnam, the strong pluralism of property is also the rule rather than the exception.[171] Extralegal strong legal pluralism in Latin America is a species of a genus that is present in a good part of the globe: In Africa and Asia, it is also manifest in areas other than urban real estate, for example, in issues like the use of water and rural land[172] and fishing rights.[173]

Sovereignty, International Law, and Weak Legal Pluralism

The monist, monocultural sovereign state, as argued earlier, was a normative project that ignored the legal and cultural reality of Latin American societies. The societies of Latin America were (and are) culturally diverse and legally plural. The normative projects of the sovereign states, legally pluralist and multicultural or intercultural, sought to close the gap between the official legal and political structure and the social reality. Consequently, these projects recognized and accommodated the legal and cultural diversity that existed in Latin American societies. The primary discursive and practical instrument these models of state used to achieve this objective was weak legal pluralism. Using this legal tool, the multicultural and intercultural state models made their rule of recognition more complex and included indigenous and Afro-Latin American institutions among those generating law. This internal weak legal pluralism was primarily an achievement of the actions taken by indigenous and Afro-Latin American peoples, non-governmental organizations that defend the interests of these communities, some liberal or progressive parties, and the constitutional reform processes which opened spaces for a politically engaged citizenry that questioned the weaknesses of the hegemonic monocultural and monist model in Latin America at the end of the 1980s. The weak legal pluralism is therefore a consequence primarily of

171 Soto, *The Mystery*, 254; Bonilla, "Extralegal Property," 209.

172 R. Meinzen-Dick and L. Nkonya, "Understanding Legal Pluralism in Water and Land Rights: Lessons from Africa and Asia," in B. van Koppen, M. Giordano, and J. Butterworth (eds.), *Community-Based Water Law and Water Resource Management Reform in Developing Countries* (Cambridge: Ebrary, 2007).

173 M. Bavinck, M. Sowman, and A. Menon, "Theorizing Participatory Governance in Contexts of Legal Pluralism – A Conceptual Reconnaissance of Fishing Conflicts and Their Resolution," in M. Bavinck, L. Pellegrini, and E. Mostert (eds.), *Conflict over Natural Resources in the Global South: Conceptual Approaches* (Leiden: CRC Press, 2014).

domestic variables, of internal factors that acted in a coordinated or separate manner to transform the legal and political systems of the region. The move from the monist and monocultural state to the legally plural states that recognize cultural diversity thus generates a discontinuity in Latin American legal and political history with respect to the categories culture and law.

However, with respect to the third category that shapes the Latin American state models analyzed in this chapter, sovereignty, interpreted as an absolute concept, there is a profound continuity in Latin American legal and political history. The monist and monocultural model as well as the multicultural and intercultural pluralist models are all committed to the concept of absolute sovereignty. At the same time, this concept is questioned from within by a strong legal pluralism that is also the consequence of internal discursive and practical patterns: illegal or extralegal normative orders created by guerrilla groups, transnational criminal structures, or peripheral communities in which the state law only operates marginally. Like the weak legal pluralism established by the constitutions, Latin American strong legal pluralism is also a consequence, primarily, of internal variables that act jointly or in a coordinated manner to question or challenge the sovereign state.

However, all these processes of internal legal and political change are not isolated from international discursive or practical patterns. The legal pluralism that recognizes Latin American cultural diversity, as well as the strong legal pluralism of the region, are influenced by variables such as the international law on cultural minorities, primarily ILO Convention 169; international law that promotes and regulates the war on drugs, especially the Single Convention on Narcotic Drugs of 1961 (modified in 1972), the Convention on Psychotropic Substances of 1971, and the United Nations Convention Against Illicit Traffic in Narcotic Drugs and Psychotropic Substances of 1988; the international law on migrations; the globalization of classic liberalism and its concept of individual property; and the political, economic, cultural, and military influence of the United States in the region. These international factors are not the primary source of the strong and weak legal pluralisms that characterize Latin American states; rather, they interact with the internal variables that constitute the center from which these diverse legal forms emerge.

However, over the last thirty-six years, the sovereign and legally plural Latin American state model has become even more complex as a consequence of its interaction with international law.[174] The dialogue between

174 A. Serbín, "Regionalismo y soberanía nacional en América Latina: los nuevos desafíos," *Documentos CRIES* 15 (2010), 5–6.

and mutual influence of the national legal systems and the international legal orders has generated an external weak legal pluralism that coexists with the internal strong and weak legal pluralisms that I examined above. The rules of recognition in the region's countries are further complicated by the inclusion of criteria that incorporate international law into the internal system of sources of law.[175] This process of interaction and mutual influence of national and international law has primarily occurred through the following two legal mechanisms: that of the constitutional bloc, which has energized the relationship between the internal legal systems and international human rights law (including the Inter-American system), and the multiplication of multilateral and bilateral trade and integration treaties signed by the region's countries. These instruments have led to an increased questioning of the concept of absolute sovereignty that the monist and monocultural model of state is committed to, as are the Latin American multicultural and intercultural state models. The constitutional bloc as well as multilateral and bilateral trade and integration treaties have thrown the porous nature of the Latin American states' sovereignty into sharp relief, and they have deepened the weak legal pluralism of the region's legal system from the outside.

The constitutional bloc and the notable increase in multilateralism and bilateralism in Latin America also echo, nurture, or dialogue with global discursive and practical patterns. For example, the human rights systems in both Europe and Africa confront challenges analogous to those of Latin American countries with respect to the relationship that regional human rights law, and the courts that interpret it, should have with national laws and courts. Questions like the margin of member countries' discretionality, the weakening of the classic concept of sovereignty, the efficacy of regional court rulings, and the political tensions between authoritarian governments and human rights tribunals cut across the African and European human rights systems.[176] Finally, Latin American multilateralism and bilateralism reflect, echo, or dialogue with the large number of multilateral and bilateral treaties signed in Asia, Africa, and Europe that create regional blocs around political or economic values, such as the European Union, the African Union of Nations, the Community of East Africa, the South African Development Community, the

175 H. Nogueira, "Las constituciones y los tratados en materia de derechos humanos: América Latina y Chile," *Ius et Praxis* 6 (2000), 237–41; M. G. Monroy, "El derecho internacional como fuente del derecho constitucional," *Anuario Colombiano de Derecho Internacional* 1 (2008), 108–9.

176 A. von Bogdandy, H. Fix-Fierro, and M. Morales (eds.), *Ius constitutionale commune en América Latina: Rasgos, potencialidades y desafíos* (Mexico City: Universidad Nacional Autónoma de México, 2014).

West African Economic and Monetary Union, the Association of Southeast Asian Nations, the South Asian Association for Regional Cooperation, the Bay of Bengal Initiative, the South Asian Free Trade Area, the Eurasian Economic Community, and the [Asian] Economic Cooperation Organization.

The Constitutional Bloc

The constitutional bloc is a legal mechanism that expands the concept of the supreme norm of the legal system.[177] The supreme norm of a national legal order is generally identified with its constitution and this, in turn, is identified with its text. The political charter is nothing other than the set of articles collected in the document that we name "constitution." Constitutional bloc, instead, allows for imagining the supreme norm as including not only the constitution but also other legal norms, such as international human rights treaties and organic and statutory laws. The constitutional bloc can fulfill a variety of functions, such as expanding the rights that are recognized in the internal legal order, serving as a tool for interpreting the legal system, or being used as a parameter of constitutionality,[178] that is, as a standard for evaluating the processes by which the subordinate norms of the system are created, as well as their contents. As will be shown below, this mechanism has been incorporated into legal systems of various Latin American countries by means of constitutional reforms or via constitutional jurisprudence.

The concept of the constitutional bloc has some common roots in Latin America.[179] It is originally a legal transplant from the French legal system.[180] In 1971, the Constitutional Council of France decided that it would include not only the constitution then in force (that of 1958), but also the Universal Declaration of Human Rights and the principles of the constitution of 1946 within the parameters of constitutionality.[181] This decision sought to solve

177 R. Uprimny, "El bloque de constitucionalidad en Colombia. Un análisis jurisprudencial y un ensayo de sistematización doctrinal," in D. O'Donnell, I. M. Uprimny, and A. Villa (comp.), *Compilación de Jurisprudencia y doctrina nacional e internacional* (Bogotá: Oficina Alto Comisionado de Naciones Unidas para los Derechos Humanos, 2001), 2–5.

178 Uprimny, "El bloque," 3; Nogueira, "Las constituciones," 243–45.

179 M. E. Góngora, "La difusión del bloque de constitucionalidad en la jurisprudencia Latinoamericana y su potencial en la construcción del ius constitutionale commune latinoamericano," in A. von Bogdandy, H. Fix-Fierro, and M. Morales (eds.), *Ius constitutionale commune en América Latina: Rasgos, potencialidades y desafíos* (Mexico City: Universidad Nacional Autónoma de México, 2014), 305–6.

180 A. A. Zeballos, "Supremacía constitucional y bloque de constitucionalidad: el ejercicio de armonización de dos sistemas de derecho en Colombia," *Pensamiento Jurídico* 47 (2018), 26.

181 Uprimny, "El bloque," 6–8.

the problem generated by the absence of a bill of rights in the constitution of 1958. This transplant arrived in Latin America, in part directly from France and in part through the Spanish legal system, which had also imported it from the French legal order and used it as a tool to solve problems of competencies between the national state and autonomous communities. In addition to the constitution of 1978, the Spanish constitutional bloc includes the autonomic statutes and the organic laws that distribute competencies between the state and autonomous communities.[182] The Spanish concept of constitutional bloc does not include international law or grant constitutional hierarchy to the statutes that form it, although the Spanish constitution does contain a reference to international human rights law as a hermeneutic instrument for interpreting the legal system. This transplant traveled to Latin America as a consequence of the constitutional reforms made in the region over the last thirty-six years in Argentina, Colombia, Peru, Ecuador, and Bolivia, for example, or it migrated through the jurisprudence of several Constitutional Courts like that of Costa Rica and the Supreme Court of Justice of Panamá.[183]

However, this imported legal product hasn't remained stable in Latin America, but has undergone a series of adaptations as a consequence of local interpretations and cross-fertilization generated by the dialogue between Latin American legal systems, primarily their constitutional courts and their legal scholars. In Latin America, the constitutional bloc has the following general characteristics: It is formed (i) by a set of constitutional norms that refer to international human rights law and incorporate it into internal law; (ii) and/or by a set of rulings issued by constitutional courts that interpret these clauses or import directly the institution; (iii) and, sometimes, by a set of statutes, like the statutory or organic laws, that have a higher status than ordinary laws. Likewise, (iv) the constitutional referral clauses or the jurisprudence that typically interprets them recognize international human rights law treaties as having constitutional or supralegal status; and (v) these referral clauses or judicial opinions allow these treaties to be applied internally by means of constitutional or legal procedures or actions like concrete and diffuse judicial review (*amparo* or *tutela*) or abstract judicial review (*actio popularis*). So, while the European constitutional bloc incorporates national legal norms as a parameter of constitutionality, Latin American constitutional bloc

182 V. Suelt-Cock, "El bloque de constitucionalidad como mecanismo de interpretación constitucional. Aproximación a los contenidos del bloque en derechos en Colombia," *Vniversitas* 133 (2016), 317–19.

183 Góngora, "La difusión," 302–5.

includes international legal norms.[184] Likewise, while the constitutional bloc in Europe does not always grant constitutional hierarchy to the internal legal norms that are part of the parameters of constitutionality, the Latin American constitutional bloc, in the great majority of countries, grants constitutional hierarchy to international human rights treaties.[185]

The constitutional clauses that remit to international law in Latin America are primarily of two types: interpretative and constitutive. The former seeks to have internal law, particularly constitutions and their bills of rights, to be filled with content by means of international human rights law.[186] The latter grants international human rights law constitutional status, enabling it to serve, with some statutes like statutory or organic ones, as a standard for evaluating the constitutionality of inferior legal norms, like ordinary laws or decrees.[187] In some countries, the constitutional bloc also includes clauses that recognize rights accepted in international human rights law or which are considered as "inherently" part of what it means to be human, as fundamental rights even though they are not specified in the constitution.[188] Finally, the constitutional bloc in Latin America sometimes also includes clauses that regulate particular legal procedures, such as the approval of and withdrawal from human rights treaties.[189]

The precise contents and interpretations of these clauses vary from country to country. For example, Colombia has emphasized the difference between constitutional bloc in the broad sense and in the strict sense,[190] Peru has used the mechanism primarily to resolve issues of competency between the central state and the provinces,[191] and yet others like Argentina have concentrated part of the discussion on the different uses of the institution: either as a hermeneutic tool that should permeate the entire legal system or as an instrument

184 Góngora, "La difusión," 308.

185 C. León and V. Wong, "Cláusulas de apertura al derecho internacional de los Derechos Humanos: Constituciones iberoamericanas," *Foro, Nueva Época* 18(2) (2015), 102–23.

186 Constitución Política de Colombia of 1991, article 93; Constitución Política del Estado Plurinacional de Bolivia of 2009, articles 13, 256; Constitución Política del Perú of 1993, fourth final and transitory provision.

187 Constitución Política de Colombia of 1991, articles 151, 152, 153.

188 Constitución Política de la República del Ecuador of 2008, articles 17, 18, 19; Constitución Política de Colombia of 1991, article 44; Constitución Política de la Nación Argentina of 1853 (amended in 1994), article 33; Constitución Política del Perú of 1993, article 3.

189 Constitución Política de la Nación Argentina of 1853 (amended in 1994), article 75.

190 Constitutional Court of Colombia, judgment C-191/98 (May 6, 1998).

191 A. D. Meza, "El denominado bloque de constitucionalidad como parámetro de interpretación constitucional, ¿es necesario en el Perú?," *Revista Oficial del Poder Judicial* 7 (2012), 158–59.

for the courts to apply their powers of judicial review.[192] This way, while the concept "constitutional bloc" makes the will of the states in the region explicit by integrating international human rights law into internal law, and it has some common general characteristics, no uniform understanding of the mechanism "constitutional bloc" exists in the region. In addition, the constitutional bloc has been used to discuss an enormous diversity of issues. For example, it served to declare unconstitutional the General Forestry Law in Colombia,[193] section 2 of article 459 of the Criminal Code in Argentina,[194] and article 240 of the Organic Judicial Branch Law in Costa Rica.[195]

The transplant of the constitutional bloc and its adaptations, as well as its continuous use in the region by the courts and civil society, can be explained by the following intersecting elements: (i) states have historically used internal law to violate human rights, not to protect them, or they have interpreted bills of rights as norms on paper or aspirational norms rather than norms in action or for direct and immediate application; (ii) the incorporation of international human rights law (IHRL) into internal law allows for confronting rooted patterns of human rights violations in the region. The mechanism has been widely used by social organizations, academia, and the judiciary to defend human rights;[196] (iii) the prestige that international law has in Latin America, as well as the internal and external political cost triggered by violations, allows for a more effective defense of human rights;[197] (iv) the implicit application of a functionalist perspective on comparative law, which assumes that Latin American societies importing legal knowledge have problems analogous to the European societies exporting it, that European societies have the most efficient tools for confronting these problems, and that both groups of legal orders are part of the same legal family, civil law, which facilitates the importation/exportation of

192 M. E. Góngora, "El Bloque de Constitucionalidad en Argentina y su relevancia en la lucha contra la impunidad," Centro de Derchos Humanos de Nuremberg (2007), 10.

193 Constitutional Court of Colombia, decision C-030/08-030 (Jan. 23, 2008); D. Bonilla, "Derecho internacional, diversidad cultural y resistencia social: el caso de la Ley general forestal en Colombia," *International Law, Revista Colombiana de Derecho Internacional* 27 (2015), 84–86.

194 Supreme Court of Argentina, *Giroldi, Horacio David y otro s/recurso de casación*, case no. 32/93 (Apr. 7, 1995), considerando 12; Góngora, "El bloque," 24.

195 Supreme Court of Costa Rica, Sala Constitucional, judgment no. 1147-90 (Sept. 21, 1990); V. Orozco, "El valor normativo de los Instrumentos Internacionales en materia de Derechos Humanos en el Sistema de Justicia Constitucional Costarricense: El caso particular de la jurisprudencia de la Corte Interamericana de Derechos Humanos," *Revista Judicial* 113 (2014), 16.

196 D. Bonilla (ed.), *Justicia colectiva, medio ambiente y democracia participativa* (Bogotá: Ediciones Uniandes, 2010).

197 Bonilla, "Derecho internacional," 43.

legal knowledge;[198] (v) the implementation of the dominant geopolitics of legal knowledge, which assumes that Latin America is a poor context for the creation of legal knowledge and therefore should import legal products from the Global North to confront the social problems afflicting it;[199] (vi) the low cognitive and economic costs of importing a legal product that is interpreted as legitimate and efficient;[200] (vii) the legitimation of the courts and social organizations that use international human rights law internally to defend fundamental rights; (viii) the possibility of creating internal and external alliances between dissimilar social and political groups for defending human rights around IHRL given its legitimacy and the multiplicity of rights it consecrates;[201] (ix) the fact that the processes of democratization which impelled the constitutional reforms at the end of 1980s and beginning of the 1990s sought to re-legitimize states, in part, by means of the effective protection of human rights; (x) the need to specify the place that international law should occupy in the national system of sources of law; and (xi) the ease with which human rights travel: They have historically been interpreted as rights which all human beings have from birth or rights that, while contingent (not natural), should be made universal to protect valuable principles like autonomy and equality.

In sum, the constitutional bloc is a legal mechanism that opens national legal systems to the international legal order, puts the two types of legal systems in dialogue, and enables their mutual transformation. The constitutional clauses remitting to international law and the jurisprudence that interprets them are therefore tools by which a weak external legal pluralism is created in the region. The constitutional bloc maintains the distinction between the national legal orders and the international legal order. However, it also functions like a lock and sluice gates: It allows international human rights law to enter the waters of national law, and it carries international human rights law towards the source of the system of internal laws, such that it comes to occupy the same place as the constitution in this hierarchy. The constitutional bloc expands the concept of supreme norm and incorporates international human rights law as one of its components.

The constitutional bloc therefore shows the porous nature of state sovereignty in contemporary Latin American states. International treaties are

198 A. Watson, *Society and Legal Change* (Philadelphia: Temple University Press, 2001); A. Watson, "Legal Transplants and European Private Law," *Electronic Journal of Comparative Law* 4 (2000).

199 D. Bonilla, "Introduction," in D. Bonilla (ed.), *Constitutionalism of the Global South* (Cambridge: Cambridge University Press, 2013), 1–39.

200 Bonilla, "Derecho internacional," 43–44.

201 Bonilla, "Derecho internacional," 45.

generally created between parties that do not have the same power; their contents are not the consequence of an agreement reached by abstract collective subjects of equal status. Rather, they are agreements where collective subjects with greater economic, political, military, and cultural power impose or influence the central contents of these treaties in a notable, sometimes disproportionate, manner.[202] Although international human rights treaties are incorporated into Latin American national legal systems by means of a decision of the primary constituent (referral clauses) or by a decision of the executive (negotiation and agreement) and the legislature (ratification), who represent the sovereign people, their contents depend at least partially on the will of other sovereign states and the international institutions in charge of applying them. Of course, the constitutional bloc does not eliminate the concept of state sovereignty. Nevertheless, it punctures it at various points on the surface, makes it porous. Sovereignty no longer resides absolutely in the people or the nation but slides towards the international community to some degree, particularly towards its most powerful members. The classic model of modern sovereignty is weakened. The sovereign state that acts as an instrument of the people or the nation, also sovereign, yields spaces to and intersects with international law and the multilateral or bilateral states and institutions that construct it.

The constitutionalization of international law and the internationalization of constitutional law in the region is not a unique Latin American process. Rather, is it nurtured by and interacts with other experiences like that of the European Union, where the interaction with and overlap of international human rights law, supranational human rights law, and the constitutional law of the member states is the rule rather than the exception.[203]

The Constitutional Bloc in Operation: The Inter-American Human Rights System

The Inter-American Human Rights System is structured around the American Declaration of the Rights and Duties of Man, the American Convention on Human Rights, the Inter-American Commission on Human Rights (IACHR),

202 C. F. Murphy, "Coacción económica y tratados desiguales," *Estudios Internacionales* 14 (1970), 82–86; United Nations Conference on the Law of Treaties, *Declaration on the Prohibition of Military, Political or Economic Coercion in the Conclusion of Treaties* (1969); M. W. Mutua, "What Is TWAIL?," *Proceedings of the ASIL Ann. Meeting* 94 (2000), 31.

203 S. Piattoni, "Multi-level Governance: A Historical and Conceptual Analysis," *European Integration* 31 (2009), 163–80.

and the Inter-American Court of Human Rights (IACourtHR) (see also Sections 6.2 and 6.3).[204] The Commission was created in 1959, and went into operation in 1960; the Court was created in 1969 and took up work only in 1979. Currently, twenty countries accept the jurisdiction of the IACourtHR: Argentina, Barbados, Bolivia, Brazil, Chile, Colombia, Costa Rica, Ecuador, El Salvador, Guatemala, Haiti, Honduras, Mexico, Nicaragua, Panama, Paraguay, Peru, Dominican Republic, Suriname, and Uruguay.[205] As the Inter-American system has been operating in the region for a little more than five decades, it predates the period that this chapter focuses on. Nevertheless, the constitutional bloc is an institution that has facilitated and energized the relationship between the Inter-American system and the national legal systems. In particular, it has enabled a dialogue, albeit one not free of tensions, between international human rights law and Latin American constitutional law.[206] Consequently, it is a good example of how the external weak legal pluralism consolidated by the constitutional bloc operates and how this pluralism has deepened the weakening of the modern, absolute concept of sovereignty in the region's states.

The primary interlocutor for the dialogue between international law and Latin American constitutional law has been the IACourtHR; this court has subsidiary competence with respect to the national legal systems and the constitutional courts in the region. The jurisdiction of the IACourtHR on contentious cases and its reception by the Latin American constitutional courts can be interpreted in two ways. On one hand, the American Convention on Human Rights can be viewed as an Inter-American bill of rights that is applied by the IACourtHR. Consequently, member states' constitutional courts would be among the instruments for the Inter-American system to apply the IACourtHR's rulings locally. This interpretation would then argue that international human rights law has primacy over national law, that the IACourtHR has a status above that of the national courts in the defense of Latin American human rights, and that the dialogue between the IACourtHR and national courts is vertical in nature. The external weak pluralism consolidated by the

204 M. Castañeda, *El Derecho Internacional de los Derechos Humanos y su recepción nacional* (Mexico City: Comisión Nacional de los Derechos Humanos, 2018), 135–60; F. Arias and J. Galindo, "El sistema interamericano de Derechos Humanos," in G. R. Bandeira, R. Urueña, and A. Torres (eds.), *Protección Multinivel de Derechos Humanos* (Barcelona: Red de Derechos Humanos y Educación Superior, 2013), 131–35.

205 Corte Interamericana de Derechos Humanos, *ABC de la Corte Interamericana de Derechos Humanos: El qué, cómo, cuándo, dónde y porqué de la Corte Interamericana. Preguntas frecuentes* (San José: Corte IDH, 2018), 6.

206 V. Abramovich, "Poderes regulatorios estatales en el pluralismo jurídico global," *Global Campus Human Rights Journal* 1 (2017), 146.

constitutional bloc would also give a normative basis to this interpretation. In many countries of Latin America, the constitutional bloc gives constitutional status to the American Convention on Human Rights, as part of international human rights law. This convention would therefore be one of the parameters of constitutionality employed to evaluate internal law, and the authorized interpreter of the convention is the IACourtHR. Consequently, the jurisprudence of the IACourtHR would be mandatory for national courts, who would contribute to implementing it. This argument is further supported by the so-called "control of conventionality" that all authorities of the convention's member states would be obligated to accept.[207] This interpretation would also guarantee that there is an Inter-American human rights law that is applied homogeneously throughout the region.[208] It would likewise create some common standards for containing those Latin American governments that violate human rights. The IACourtHR's rulings on whether nationally granted amnesties are admissible under the convention are a good example of how this interpretation operates and of its support by the IACourtHR.[209]

The weak pluralism created by this interpretation of the constitutional bloc and its relationship with the Inter-American Human Rights System would be vertical in nature and would significantly weaken the concept of absolute sovereignty which the states in the region are committed to. The will of the sovereign states would be limited by the decisions of an international tribunal formed by a set of judges, the great majority of which are foreigners, who are not democratically elected, and who may be citizens of countries that have not ratified the convention and have therefore not recognized the competency of the IACourtHR, although these states must belong to the OAS, the Organization of American States.[210] These same sovereign states would be limited by the convention that these judges interpret and apply, a convention that was created by a set of collective subjects with different degrees of political, economic, military, and cultural power a little more than four decades ago.

207 M. F. Quinche, "El control de convencionalidad y el sistema colombiano," *Revista Iberoamericana de Derecho Constitucional Procesal* 12 (2009), 167–68; Arias and Galindo, "El sistema interamericano," 131–35.

208 A. von Bogdandy, "Ius Constitutionale Communeen América Latina: una mirada a un constitucionalismo transformador," *Revista Derecho del Estado* 34 (2015), 10–13; R. Urueña, "Luchas locales, cortes internacionales. Una exploración de la protección multinivel de los derechos humanos en América Latina," *Revista Derecho del Estado* 30 (2013), 301–28.

209 *Masacres de El Mozote y lugares aledaños vs. El Salvador*, judgment (merits, reparations and costs), Inter-American Court of Human Rights (series C) no. 252 (Oct. 25, 2012), parag. 284.

210 Convención Americana de Derechos Humanos, article 52.

On the other hand, the relationship between the IACourtHR and the national courts can be interpreted as a form of horizontal external weak pluralism. This interpretation would argue that the Inter-American Human Rights System does not create a vertical relationship between the IACourtHR and national courts. The IACourtHR has subsidiary competency, which only operates when national courts have failed in the protection of human rights. The system does not include any principle or rule that locates the IACourtHR above national courts, and it does not include a mechanism to guarantee compliance with the rulings of the IACourtHR by national courts (or other branches of government in the member states). However, the IACourtHR has a generic competency in supervising compliance with its rulings, and the national authorities also have a generic obligation to comply with them and to apply control of conventionality to their legal systems. Rather, it is argued from this second perspective that the system has been structured, and so operates in practice, as a horizontal Inter-American legal space where the IACourtHR and the national courts are in constant interaction, to give content to the American Convention of Human Rights, to harmonize it with national law, and to apply it in member states.[211] This dialogue becomes evident, for example, in a notable number of rulings by the Colombian Constitutional Court,[212] the Argentine Supreme Court of Justice,[213] and the Peruvian Constitutional Tribunal.[214] In these rulings, the national courts apply the jurisprudence of the IACourtHR to solve cases related to abstract or concrete judicial review. Furthermore, the IACourtHR has used the jurisprudence of courts in Argentina, Costa Rica, and Colombia in some of its contentious cases.[215] This interpretation also allows for the understanding that all these courts have the same objective in the region: protecting human rights.

211 Urueña, "Luchas locales," 301–28.

212 Constitutional Court of Colombia, judgment C-578 (Dec. 4, 1995), decision C-358 (Aug. 5, 1997), judgment C-228 (Apr. 3, 2002), decision C-578/02 (July 30, 2002), judgment C-590/05 (June 8, 2005).

213 Supreme Court of Argentina, recurse de hecho, *Simón, Julio Héctor s/Privación de la libertad y otros*, case no. 17.768 (June 14, 2005); L. A. Franco, "Recepción de la jurisprudencia interamericana en el ordenamiento jurídico argentino," in S. García and M. Castañeda (eds.), *Recepción nacional del derecho internacional de los derechos humanos y admisión de la competencia contenciosa de la Corte Interamericana* (Mexico City: UNAM, 2009), 157–71.

214 Constitutional Court of Peru, *John McCarter*, file no. 0174-2006-PHC/TC (July 7, 2006); *César Alfonso Ausin de Irruarízaga*, file no. 8817-2005-PHC/TC (July 7, 2006); *Santiago Martín Rivas*, file no. 4587-2004-AA/TC (Nov. 29, 2005).

215 *Bedoya Lima et al. v. Colombia*, judgment (merits, reparations and costs), Inter-American Court of Human Rights (series C) no. 431 (Aug. 26, 2021).

This horizontal external weak pluralism creates a common Inter-American space for protecting human rights in both the international and the national context. It is argued from this second perspective that this type of dialogue-driven weak pluralism is facilitated and energized by the mechanism "constitutional bloc." This mechanism allows national courts to apply both the convention and the jurisprudence of its authorized interpreter, the IACourtHR, directly. The constitutional bloc, by incorporating international human rights into internal law, and by granting constitutional status to these types of treaties, creates a dynamic channel of communication between international law and national law that is mediated by national courts. This interlegality also generates a virtuous circle that allows for legitimizing both the IACourtHR and national courts. The former is perceived not as a foreign and faraway court that is imposed on national courts, but as a tribunal that acts jointly with national courts to defend human rights on the continent. The latter are legitimized by using international law – an instrument that, as I mentioned above, enjoys high prestige in the region. National courts are also legitimized by presenting themselves as institutions that use all the legal resources available nationally and internationally to protect citizens' human rights. However, as with the first interpretation, the second also calls into question the concept of absolute sovereignty that cuts across the political and legal history of the region, in part due to its ties with the principle of non-intervention, in part because of its connections with the Calvo and Drago doctrines.[216] Again, a set of foreign judges who are appointed, not elected, and who may be citizens of any country that belongs to the OAS, even though it may not be party to the convention, and who are interpreting an international treaty created by multiple states with different degrees of power in drafting it, have notable influence on national legal and political systems.

Multilateral and Bilateral Trade and Integration Treaties

The external weak pluralism created by the concept of constitutional bloc puts the Latin American state, law, and society into dialogue. These three categories interact and transform each other as a consequence of the interpretation and application of international human rights law in the national legal systems. The constitutionalization of international law and the internationalization of

216 F. Arias, "Dinámica del derecho a la no-intervención en América del Siglo XIX," *Pensamiento Jurídico* 36 (2013), 194–200.

constitutional law limit the actions of the region's states and protect the fundamental interests of civil society and the citizens that form it. This type of external weak legal pluralism creates a national/international public order that has the objective of protecting the human rights of all citizens in the region.[217] The external weak legal pluralism created by means of the dialogue and interaction between internal law as well as by the multilateral and bilateral trade and integration treaties that have multiplied notably in the last thirty-six years includes another category in the equation: the market. All these treaties include international trade as a central component of the dialogue between internal and international law.[218] In this second form of external weak legal pluralism, the state, law, and society interact to obtain economic benefits for all countries that are party to the treaties, though some of these treaties also include other objectives, such as the integration of political communities in the region. All these treaties, then, are transactional treaties where each party must provide capacities or goods, for example, the capacity to regulate matters of customs or international tariffs, in order to receive others, such as favorable access to other countries' markets.[219]

The notable number of international trade and integration treaties that have been signed in Latin America over the last three-and-a-half decades, including MERCOSUR, the Andean Community of Nations (CAN), the Union of South American Nations (UNASUR), the Bolivarian Alliance for the Peoples of Our America (ALBA), the World Trade Organization (WTO), and the trade treaties between the United States and Peru and the United States and Colombia, thus limit state sovereignty in order to obtain economic and political benefits that are considered particularly valuable for Latin American states.[220] These treaties also render Latin American external weak pluralism more complex; they include new criteria in the rules of recognition that structure the internal legal systems, as well as new institutions and normative orders that enter into dialogue with internal law such as the Andean Parliament, the Andean Tribunal, the Council of Heads of State and Government and the Secretariat General of UNASUR, the WTO Dispute Settlement Body, and the panels of

217 G. Aguilar, "La internacionalización del derecho constitucional," *Estudios Constitucionales* 5 (2007), 229.

218 F. Quispe-Remón, "Problemas y perspectivas de procesos de integración en América Latina," *International Law: Revista Colombiana de Derecho Internacional* 16 (2010), 280.

219 J. C. Fernández Rozas, "Los modelos de integración en América Latina y el Caribe y el Derecho internacional privado," *Iberoamérica ante los procesos de integración. Actas de las XVIII Jornadas de Profesores de Derecho Internacional y Relaciones Internacionales* (Madrid: Boletín Oficial del Estado, 2000), 22.

220 Quispe-Remón, "Problemas y perspectivas," 265–79.

arbitrators appointed to resolve the disputes resulting from the application of the free trade treaty between the United States and Colombia.

The international treaties that have been created in the region during the last three-and-a-half decades can be divided into two large groups: the classic liberal trade treaties and the post-liberal political integration treaties. The first, which sometimes include some political dimensions, have the primary objective of trade liberalization, the creation of economies of scale, the deregulation of the economy, the firm insertion of Latin American economies into the world economic system, and the limitation of the state's regulatory power.[221] CAN, MERCOSUR, the Community of Latin American and Caribbean States, the World Trade Organization, the bilateral trade treaties that countries such as Peru, Chile, and Colombia have signed with the United States, and the not-yet-concluded American Free Trade Area (AFTA) are paradigmatic examples of this type of treaty. The second group of treaties, which sometimes comprise some economic dimensions, have as primary aims the integration of the region (excluding the United States from the regional blocs), questioning the Washington Consensus that forms the basis for classic liberal trade treaties, the return of "developmentalist" policies, the strengthening of the state's capacities for regulation, the strengthening of the state's competencies for intervening in the economy, the consolidation of a state capitalism, and the consolidation of democracy in the region.[222] This second type of treaty is in turn divided into those led by Brazil, like UNASUR, and those led by Venezuela, like ALBA. This division has been generated by the geopolitical interests of each of these countries (each wants to position itself firmly as a leader in the region); by the acceptance (Brazil) or rejection (Venezuela) of globalization of markets; and by the relationship they want to promote with the United States (Brazil aims for a respectful distance and Venezuela wants confrontation and rejection).[223]

So it emerges that Latin American multilateralism is profoundly heterogeneous and fragmented. There are many competing trade or integration treaties developed in parallel fashion, though they pursue analogous aims, and treaties that try to materialize contradictory objectives, such as the promotion of an interventionist state or that of a minimal state. In addition, most treaties have a governmental origin without the continuous and systematic intervention by civil society, business people, unions, or non-governmental

221 A. Malamud, "Conceptos, teorías y debates sobre la integración regional," *Norteamérica* 6 (2011), 230–37; Huerta, "Los tratados," 13–15; Fernández Rozas, "Los modelos," 14–15.

222 Serbín, "Regionalismo y soberanía," 10.

223 Ibid., 13.

organizations. Similarly, most of these treaties have not created a dense multilateral institutionality or a supranational normativity that effectively allows for achieving the long-term aims they pursue.[224]

On an abstract level, all these treaties, as well as the external weak legal pluralism they generate, can be interpreted in light of the conceptual opposition fragmentation/unity.[225] On one hand, historically the countries of Latin America have been committed to the principle of absolute national sovereignty and to a series of related international law principles that complement and develop it, such as the principles of non-intervention and self-determination. Consequently, this discursive and practical dynamic promotes the separation and isolation of states from one another. On the other hand, the multilateralism or bilateralism that incentivizes these treaties drives the union of states and the creation of supranational entities and rules which limit state sovereignty, as well as the principles of self-determination and non-intervention.[226] The constellation of normative orders and institutions that create these treaties promotes the creation of blocs of countries that share a set of political or economic objectives. Nevertheless, to fulfill these aims, this legal and institutional constellation restricts the state's capacity to decide internal matters of enormous importance, such as regulation of the market, taxes imposed on citizens or companies, goods and services for import or export, subsidies that should be given to key sectors of the economy like agriculture, and subsidies that should be granted to public services.

In practice, however, the limitations placed on state sovereignty by these treaties is not always notable. Factors like the lack of resources, the asymmetries of power between countries, continuous noncompliance with agreed-upon rules, the lack of concrete and precise objectives and means, ideological differences among governments, and the intergovernmental and presidentialist nature of the creation and application of treaties have resulted in a significant part of multilateral or bilateral Latin American treaties not having been successfully implemented in the long term.[227] A few classic liberal multilateral or bilateral trade treaties are the exception to this rule. These treaties focus primarily on economic matters and present a notable imbalance of power between the member states. For example, within the WTO

224 Quispe-Remón, "Problemas y perspectivas," 286.

225 M. P. Ospina, "El proceso de toma de decisiones en el Mercosur y el TLCAN: la disyuntiva entre integración regional y soberanía nacional en América Latina," *Colombia Internacional* 100 (2019), 240–45.

226 Fernández Rozas, "Los modelos," 15–16; Ospina, "El proceso," 240–45.

227 Quispe-Remón, "Problemas y perspectivas," 282–87.

framework, the United States, Canada, and Western Europe interact with the states of Latin America, and in the bilateral free trade treaties the United States interacts with countries like Colombia, Chile, and Peru.

The unequal distribution of power among member states of these bilateral treaties, as well as the economic benefits they generate for the strongest parties, have led to the development of rules and institutions which significantly limit state sovereignty. The following three examples illustrate this argument paradigmatically. The first is that of the tribunals of arbitrators that should typically decide on how to resolve the controversies arising between member states.[228] These tribunals, which replace national legal systems, have historically been constituted primarily of jurists of the Global North, and have traditionally ruled continuously and systematically against the countries of the Global South, including those in Latin America.

The second example concerns the legal security or legal stability clauses that have been interpreted by the arbitrators or the institutions created by the treaties as stipulating that there cannot be any change in the expectations that international investors had when they entered national markets.[229] This interpretation has led to a radical limitation of the state's regulatory powers; any new national legal norm that negatively affects the business of international investors is understood as a violation of free trade treaties. For example, this interpretation has led to the understanding that the state doesn't have the competency to subsidize public services in times of crisis or to modify the rules related to taxes when there are significant changes in the national, regional, or global political and economic situation.[230]

The third example is the principle of not permitting distinctions between national products and international products, or between national industry and multinational industries.[231] This severely limits the capacity of Latin American states to intervene in the economy or to submit multinational companies to certain types of requirements. For example, these principles have prohibited states in the region from requiring that multinational companies produce goods or provide services only in certain economic sectors; from subsidizing certain sectors such as farming, which is central for political

228 T. Allee and P. Hardt, "Delegating Differences: Bilateral Investment Treaties and Bargaining Over Dispute Resolution Provisions," *International Studies Quarterly* 54 (2010), 3–5; Abramovich, "Poderes regulatorios," 148–89.

229 Abramovich, "Poderes regulatorios," 148–49.

230 J. Estay, "América Latina en las negociaciones comerciales multilaterales y hemisféricas," in J. Estay (ed.), *La economía mundial y América Latina. Tendencias, problemas y desafíos* (Buenos Aires: Consejo Latinoamericano de Ciencias Sociales, 2005), 199.

231 Acuerdo General sobre Aranceles Aduaneros y Comercio de 1994, article 3.

reasons or food security; or from requiring that the multinationals transfer technology or limiting the earnings that these companies can send to their headquarters, typically located in other countries.[232]

In summary, the trade and integration treaties that have been created in Latin America over the last thirty-six years make the external weak legal pluralism generated by the constitutional bloc more complex. All these treaties, with greater or lesser success, construct a set of international norms and institutions that interact and modify (and are modified by) national legal systems. Moreover, they make the rules of recognition of domestic legal orders more complex by including criteria for identifying the national system's valid norms that refer to multilateral or bilateral international norms that promote Latin American trade or integration.

Conclusions

The state remains the unit that shapes Latin American societies legally and politically. However, this unit has mutated significantly over the last thirty-six years. The monist and monocultural sovereign state that emerged with independence from Spain and Portugal in the nineteenth century and was dominant until the end of the 1980s was transfigured into multicultural states or legally plural intercultural states with porous or limited sovereignties. Consequently, the changes experienced by the states in the region during the last three-and-a-half decades have revolved around the following three axes: First, around political and legal recognition and inclusion of the cultural diversity that characterizes Latin American societies. Second, around the recognition of internal and external weak legal pluralism. The former opens the rule of recognition of the national legal systems to more complexity, so that the institutions of indigenous or Afro-Latin American peoples can be considered sources of legal creation. The latter makes the rule of recognition more complex in order to enable the inclusion of international human rights law and multilateral or bilateral trade or integration treaties in the national law system. In both cases, the state legal system enters into dialogue and interacts with other legal orders: those of cultural minorities and international law. And in both cases, the concept of absolute sovereignty that Latin American states have historically been committed to is weakened. Finally, the Latin American multicultural or intercultural state has tried to eliminate, with

232 A. Huerta, "Los tratados de libre comercio impulsados por Estados Unidos en América Latina y la profundización del subdesarrollo," *Contaduría y Administración* 221 (2007), 17.

partial success, the constellation of sovereignties that forms the strong legal pluralism which has historically cut across, and further decreased, its sovereignty. Multicultural and intercultural states in Latin America have tried to eliminate the normative systems created by, among others, guerrilla groups, transnational criminal organizations, and the marginalized communities of the region's large cities. However, all these transformations are not happening in isolation. Rather, they materialize in, and in turn modify, global discursive and practical patterns related to how states should recognize and include cultural diversity and human rights, how the market economy and regional integration should be promoted, and what strategies should be articulated and implemented to confront the illegal or extralegal normative orders that compete with official law.

Both the state and official law in Latin America have been challenged and transformed, by illegal and extralegal internal normative orders as well as by the international legal system over the last three-and-a-half decades. However, these alternative internal or external normative systems do not appear to have the potential to make the state or official law disappear in the region. The state is the political form through which Latin American political communities will continue to organize themselves in the foreseeable future. Likewise, state law will be one of the central normative structures for social control in Latin America in the decades to come. The solidity, legitimacy, and fairness of these political and legal structures, however, are another matter. Consolidating the rule of law and making it an instrument for material justice is a process that will also be part of the future of all Latin Americans.

Index

Printed by Integrated Books International,
United States of America